More praise for *American Law in the Twentieth Century*

"This lively and well-written book will assume a sig[nificant place] in legal and historical scholarship."—John R. Wun[z, *The] History: Reviews of New Books*

"In a work of ambitious scope and vision, the author offers a vivid, insightful overview of U.S. law and society in the twentieth century. . . . This substantial work covers both legal and historical developments and convincingly situates U.S. law in its broader social context."—*Library Journal*

"The book is a valuable reminder that legal history is intrinsically connected to American political and judicial behavior. Indeed, the high quality of the scholarship makes it very useful as a reference book across the disciplines, and professors teaching law and society, legal history, or even constitutional law courses can easily adopt it for classroom use since its anecdotal style is not only entertaining, but also quite accessible for students. On balance, *American Law* is a worthy addition to the literature and a fine addition to the library of anyone interested in being introduced to contemporary American law."—Christopher P. Banks, *Law and Politics Book Review*

"Lawrence Friedman already is widely recognized as our foremost legal historian. With this lively, cogent, and wise account of the broad sweep of the twentieth century, Friedman shows that he is not only master of the microscope and the telescope, but of the periscope and the kaleidoscope as well. *American Law in the Twentieth Century* is a wonderfully illuminating and substantial study, but it is also a great read."—Aviam Soifer, Boston College Law School

"This is a work of vast scope and ambition, nothing less than a history of the whole sweep of a huge and complex subject, a social history of American law in the twentieth century. It is a very impressive, thoroughly researched book, but the writing is clear and colloquial and lively, a pleasure to read."—Robert W. Gordon, Yale Law School.

"Friedman is the best writer of our generation about the American legal system. *American Law in the Twentieth Century* teaches us so much because the author combines real data with real insight into the nation's past and present. Friedman commands the theories and ideologies that so entertain legal scholars, but he is always skeptical of the latest fashion. He never bends history to serve the constantly shifting conventional wisdom. And, not the least, Friedman's metaphors, analogies and editorial asides make his work always a delight to read."—Stewart Macauley, University of Wisconsin-Madison Law School

American Law in the 20th Century

Lawrence M. Friedman

Yale University Press   New Haven and London

Designed by Sonia Shannon
Set in Bulmer type by Keystone Typesetting, Inc.
Printed in the United States of America by R.R. Donnelley & Sons,
Harrisonburg, Virginia.

The Library of Congress has cataloged the hardcover edition as follows:
Friedman, Lawrence Meir, 1930–
American law in the twentieth century / Lawrence M. Friedman.
p. cm.
Includes bibliographical references and index.
ISBN 0-300-09137-0 (cloth : alk. paper)
ISBN 0-300-10299-2 (pbk. : alk. paper)
1. Law—United States—History—20th century. I. Title.
KF385.A4 F7 2002
349.73—dc21   2001003332

A catalogue record for this book is available from
the British Library.

The paper in this book meets the guidelines for permanence and
durability of the Committee on Production Guidelines for Book
Longevity of the Council on Library Resources.

10 9 8 7 6 5 4 3

For Leah, Jane, Amy, Paul, Sarah, David, and Lucy

Contents

Part III The Way We Live Now: The Reagan and Post-Reagan Years

Preface

The end of the twentieth century is the occasion, or the excuse, for this book. In it, I have tried to tell at least the essence of the story of what happened to American law and the American legal system in the century just past; and why it happened as it did; how American society made and remade the law; and what the law, in turn, did to and for American society.

There are, of course, many ways to tell the story; and many different approaches. A lot depends on how one conceives of that amorphous, bulky entity we can call "the legal system." One central question concerns the autonomy of law: is this a kingdom of its own, ruled by lawyers and judges, which grows and decays in accordance with its own rules, its own inner program? Or is it, rather, an integral part of the larger society, so that changes in the world bring about, inevitably, corresponding changes in the law? I lean very heavily toward the second interpretation, for reasons that I hope will become clear as you turn these pages; and this approach, or attitude, colors the way I have written this book.

A book about law or the legal system of this sort inevitably runs up against the challenge of defining its subject. What, after all, *is* the law? What constitutes the legal system? There is no single definition that people agree on. Many people think of law and the legal system in rather narrow terms—courts, police, judges, juries, and lawyers. But law is a dominant, pervasive, massive presence in this society. Everything—absolutely everything—that is done by government (at all levels) is done by, through, under the color of, and occasionally in defiance of, law. A complete story of the role of law in society could include a complete economic history, for example, because the whole banking enterprise is governed by law, and the work of the Federal Reserve banks, to give just one example, is governed by rules and statutes. The complete story of the role of law could also include a complete political history, too: elections and parliamentary maneuvering are all part of "the legal system" in an expanded but certainly not far-fetched sense.

And this is only one rather formal view of law. In a broad sense, all rule-making and enforcement, all social control, in any organization, can be considered a kind of "law." So factories, hospitals, universities, and banks—not to mention gangs, clans, clubs, and big families—have a "legal system," a system for making rules and seeing that they are carried out; and no doubt these "legal systems" are eminently worth studying.

I am aware of these definitions, and these difficulties. But my goal is necessarily more modest. I have to deal with a more conventional idea of law—less conventional than the idea most law schools convey, but more conventional than the expanded images I have sketched in the last two paragraphs. This history will focus mostly on the main institutions and trends that people usually think of as "legal." But the exact boundaries of the legal realm will remain somewhat blurred and indistinct; and at all times there will be, in the background, an awareness that law *has* no firm, tight, visible boundaries, and that social context, and social meaning, are at the heart of the way it lives, breathes, and moves.

Even under the narrowest of definitions, the amount of material on the subject of twentieth-century law is immense—in essence, endless. The shelves of the law libraries are jammed with materials—hundreds of thousands of books, periodicals, reports of cases, statutes, municipal ordinances, and so on. In recent years, millions of bits and bytes of material have been stored in electronic memories that seem limitless and inexhaustible. The most difficult part of the job was picking and choosing among all the books and articles written about the subject, the oceans of primary material, the stacks of stuff that piled end to end could encircle the world. The results are, no doubt, somewhat idiosyncratic; they obviously reflect the things I know best or am most interested in; but that would be true for *anybody* who tried a book of this kind. The legal system has become a vast, ubiquitous presence in the twentieth century. Nobody can absorb it all, or master even a small fraction of it: not as it was in 2000, or for that matter, as it was in 1900, 1901, or 1902. Moreover, the twentieth century, and its law, were so full of chaos and incident, drama and development, stasis and change, that it is clearly impossible to capture the essence in a single modest volume.

A lot of choices must be made. Some are easy. Nobody could write a history of American law in the twentieth century and leave out the rise of the administrative state, especially under Roosevelt's New Deal; or ignore *Brown v.*

Board of Education, the civil rights movement, and the explosion of "rights" that followed it. But once you cross the frontier of the unavoidable and the obvious, there are problems of inclusion and exclusion. Most of what lawyers do is technical, humdrum, and obscure. In the aggregate, getting divorces for people or arranging for the sale of houses or filling out tax returns or organizing small corporations may mean more to society than most of the great Supreme Court dramas. But it is devilishly hard to chronicle the quiet underbelly of legal process. It will, I am sure, be easy to carp at my choices, at what was left out and what was put in. I make no apologies for the way I have chosen to tell the story.

It isn't, of course, exclusively *my* story. Many people helped me along the way. Most of all, there are the dozens of scholars whose work I rely on here. They populate the hundreds of footnotes. I have often tried to check what scholars say against the primary sources; but life is too short to do this consistently. Anybody who writes a general account of any subject is necessarily at the mercy of and indebted to the books and essays already written. In the bibliographical note at the end of this book, I have mentioned some of the best and most useful of the works I have dipped into, as suggestions for further reading, but also as a way of saying thanks. I wish also to give special thanks to Robert W. Gordon, who made encouraging, helpful, and amazingly erudite suggestions for improving this work. Thanks, too, to Dan Heaton at Yale University Press for his great job of editing.

I have also had real help from any number of students in the past few years. Some of them worked directly on this book, scurrying about checking sources, writing memos and the like. They include Paul Berks, Paul William Davies, Shannon Petersen, Iddo Porat, and Issi Rosenzvi. I want to thank them for their contribution. I have also profited from the papers that students have written in my courses over the years. I want to mention at least a few of them who made especially valuable contributions: Lesley Barnhorn, Ari Lefkovits, Cliff Liu, Frederick Sparks, and James Sweet. My assistant, Mary Tye, helped me in innumerable ways. I want also to thank those of my colleagues who have listened to this or that talk or read this or that draft and commented. Lastly, I owe a very special word of thanks to the staff of the Stanford Law Library—especially Paul Lomio, David Bridgman, Erica Wayne, and Andrew Gurthet. They went the extra mile in trying to help me out with sources, tracking down odd bits of information, borrowing books, and so on. There are bigger law libraries than Stanford's, but I doubt that there are better ones. I also want to thank my family, especially my wife, Leah. This help was deeper and subtler than that of my other benefactors. Despite all the perturbations in American family life—some of that story is in this book—the family remains (well, *my* family at least), as Christopher Lasch put it, a haven in a heartless world.

Introduction

The Way We Were, the Way We Were Going to Be

Just as on December 31, 1999, on December 31, 1899, there were celebrations, festivities, and discussions of what the past century had wrought, and what the new one might bring. The celebration in 1899 was a little less feverish, perhaps—after all, it was the start of a new century, not the start of what most people considered a whole new millennium; but Americans partied and drank and hailed the new year with gusto. The *New York Times* reported that one couple, William Witt and Ann Waddilove of Jersey City, got themselves married at Leiderkrantz Hall a minute after midnight—eager to be the first couple to tie the knot in the brand-new century. It was a cold winter; and snow fell on most of the country on New Year's Day. A fresh inch of snow, for example, coated the streets of Washington, D.C., where thousands of citizens came to pay their respects to President McKinley at his gala New Year's Day reception.[1]

Nobody, of course, had a crystal ball; nobody could know what the new century was going to bring. One thing, and one thing only, was certain: it would usher in enormous change. Certainly that had been the nineteenth-century experience. This was true for society in general, and for the legal system as well. The legal system of the United States had changed in the course of the nineteenth century, and in almost revolutionary ways. In 1800 independence was new—less than a generation old—and the country was, in a sense, still wet behind the ears. It had a new Constitution, and a new court system. It was still a common-law country (what else could it be?), but it had already, during the colonial period, created its own versions or dialects of the common law; and the process of making new law, free from British models, would only accelerate in the century to come.

Economically, the United States in 1800 was a nation of farmers. It was essentially a chain of settlements, strung out along the eastern seaboard. There was, to be sure, vigorous ocean trade, and trade with the West Indies. The interior was mostly terra incognita, "wilderness." Only a few pioneers had penetrated that wilderness. The forests and plains were, of course, the home of the native peoples. But they were for the most part beyond the reach of the coastal legal systems. The settlers in 1800 were overwhelmingly Protestant and overwhelmingly white; there was a black population, concentrated in the southern states, and the vast majority of them were slaves. There had been slaves in every northern colony as well, but slavery was never central to the economy of, say, Pennsylvania or Rhode Island; and in 1800 slavery in the North was moribund. The states were much more isolated than they would be later. Travel was slow and tortuous. Communication was just as slow.

The same Constitution was in force at the end of the century as in the beginning. It had been amended from time to time, and some of the amendments were quite significant; but the basic structure of the government had been preserved—the presidency, the Congress, federalism, the system of courts. The United States, however, was not the same country. It had grown enormously. It was a continental giant, and an industrial empire; it was becoming more and more urban, and its great cities—some of which, like Chicago, had not even existed in 1800—were filled with millions of immigrants deposited on these shores from Europe. They lived in crowded neighborhoods with their many, many children. New York City was a babel of languages, religions, and cultures. In 1800 nobody had even dreamed of the railroad, the telegraph, the typewriter, the telephone; electricity was something you teased out of lightning with a kite. At the end of the century, new inventions had transformed the lives of Americans. It was the dawn of the age of the automobile. Nobody could know what was coming, but people knew, or thought they knew, that the future would be the stuff of H. G. Wells and science fiction.

Legal change had been almost equally dramatic and revolutionary—and in every field of law.[2] Tort law, corporation law, divorce law—these were tiny bumps and dots on the legal map in 1800; in 1900 they were powerful areas of law. In 1900 slavery had gone; but a bitter kind of serfdom had replaced it in the South. In 1800 *Marbury v. Madison* had not yet been decided, nor *Dred Scott*, nor the Slaughterhouse cases, the civil rights cases, and the other great decisions of the century. Nobody in 1800 had heard of the fellow-servant rule; contract and corporation law were in their infancy. A Rip van Winkle of the law who went to sleep in 1800 and woke up as the bells clanged in 1900 would have found the table talk of lawyers about their trade almost totally incomprehensible—almost, but not quite, a foreign tongue.

The twentieth century, however, would outdo its predecessor in sheer velocity of change. Change went from a walk, to a run, to travel on a supersonic jet. Indeed, in a recent book on the rights revolution, Samuel Walker invokes the Rip van Winkle theme to describe how astonished a person would be who slept a mere forty years, from 1956 to 1996.[3] This book will tell the story of those massive changes—in brief. I say "in brief" because the law is immeasurably vast, and it shifts and writhes and turns and changes from year to year. Necessarily, this book is about highlights; or rather, as I said in the preface, about one person's idea of what the highlights are.

Some of the main themes are obvious. I will tick off a few of them here. First is the rise of the welfare-regulatory state. The role of government had been growing throughout the nineteenth century. Even in the so-called period of laissez-faire, the state meddled and monitored far more than most people believe.[4] But this role swelled to bursting in the twentieth century. Most of the boards, commissions, agencies and the like that play so powerful a role in governing the economy and polity—the Securities and Exchange Commission, the Social Security Administration, OSHA, the FDA, and so on—were children of the twentieth century. So was the federal income tax. So were zoning regulations. So were environmental protection laws. So was the war on drugs. Today, there is hardly any aspect of our lives that *some* regulatory agency does not touch: the food we eat, the money we earn and how we invest it, where we live, and how; how our houses are built or our apartments managed, and so on. And most of these regulations were devised in the twentieth century.

The same is true of welfare. Perhaps we are seeing the end of "welfare as we know it"; but what we know about welfare is strictly twentieth century—a product of the New Deal, and the Great Society. And even those who fulminate against the welfare state want to keep (or do not dare attack) Social Security and Medicare, at least in some form; and no one talks much about putting an end to workers' compensation, or unemployment insurance, or disaster relief. All of these, too, are products of the twentieth century—a century of the social safety net; and of a belief in "total justice."[5]

The United States, like all developed countries, is a welfare-regulatory state—a state that, on the one hand, regulates many businesses and activities; and, on the other hand, provides free education, pensions, and some forms of medical benefits. Such a state, necessarily, is also an administrative and legislative state. Bureaucracy is in control of the gears and levers of power. But if the courts have lost power, relatively speaking (and even that is debatable), they have gained tremendous power absolutely. For one thing, the United States is a common-law country; the common law is still alive and well; and in common-law countries judges wield great power. There are still areas of law where the courts make the rules—and remake them, too, as they please. And the common-law spirit is still extremely strong. The legislatures pass laws; but the courts interpret them; and although judges like to talk about how much they defer to legislatures, and how only the legislature can actually change the law, what they do contradicts their words. Indeed, they do protest too much. A determined court may turn even the most plain-spoken statute inside out and upside down. True, the legislature can almost always win this tug of war; can almost always force the courts to bend to its will, by passing new laws; but in the interim, the courts exert great power; and often it is the courts that prevail—it is their interpretation, their point of view, which ends up with more staying power.

The twentieth century was also the century of judicial review. The courts, in this country, claim the right and the power to decide whether laws passed by Congress or the states measure up to the Constitution. If these laws do not, the courts can declare them null and void. This power was asserted very rarely in the first half of the nineteenth century; more commonly, and at a growing pace, in the second half. In the twentieth century it more than came into its own. It was a century in which the Supreme Court could throw major New Deal programs into oblivion; or, later on, throw out every last state law on abortion, every last state law on segregation, every last state law about the penalty of death.

But judicial review is more than control over Congress and the state assemblies. It includes the power to review, and check, and monitor, all other branches and sub-branches of government, including the lower civil service. The courts ride herd—somewhat fitfully, to be sure—over the dozens and dozens of boards and agencies, federal, state, and local, that are so salient an aspect of twentieth-century government. This is a story that has its ups and down, but mostly (in this century) ups: the Food and Drug Administration, the local zoning board, the Social Security Agency—all of these have enormous power and discretion, but the courts are definitely there in the background, with authority to insist that the right procedures be followed, and the rules of the game obeyed.

A second theme is the shift of power and authority to Washington—to the national government. The United States began as a federation of states.

Throughout the nineteenth century, the guts of the working legal system was in the states, or perhaps even lower down the scale of authority. Washington was a swampy, drowsy village on the Potomac, snoring in its summer heat and mosquitoes. New York, Chicago, and other cities—Cincinnati, St. Louis, New Orleans—exploded with economic and cultural vitality; they were the real capitals, the capitals of money and commerce, of art and of life.

In 1900 this was still a profoundly decentralized country; but change was clearly on the way. Technology and social change had shifted the center of gravity. In 1800 it took months for news, mail, cargo, and people to travel from one end of the country to another. There were no railroads, no great canals, no turnpikes. Then came the railroad era. By 1900 the whole country was tied together with these muscular bands of iron. The telegraph and telephone made it possible to send messages from Alaska to the tip of Florida, from Maine to California. These devices seem primitive today, but they were light years beyond communication as it stood in 1800. By the year 2000, a voice and an image in one part of the country could be flashed to another part in nanoseconds. Or even less. This was the century of radio and television; then, toward the end, satellites, e-mail, and the internet. By the year 2000, by the new millennium, the whole world was linked, and words could move across continents, in basically no time at all.

If people could talk across the whole country, from one end to the other, it meant that they spoke, as it were, a common language; and shared a common culture. One country and one culture—and one economy—implied, or seemed to imply, for most of the century, one core, one central nervous system. That is, one capital; and one chief executive, the president. The process accelerated during the Great Depression. The economy collapsed and there was panic in the streets. Only the center held firm, under the charismatic leadership of Franklin D. Roosevelt. Washington, D.C., awoke from its long sleep and began to buzz with activity.

Roosevelt was a great leader, and a great *modern* leader. He made masterful use of the arts of public relations. His was a thrilling voice on radio. The presidency became, more than ever, the center of national attention. Later, there came television—and now the face, the voice, the movements of the president were everywhere. Television ensured the rise of the "imperial presidency." Not all the presidents since Roosevelt were natural-born emperors. Most of them were pygmies, intellectually and otherwise, but then so were most Roman emperors. There were many weak and insignificant presidents; but there could no longer be a weak and insignificant presidential office. After all, the United States was a great power—by 2000, the *only* superpower. This man, this president, was the man with his finger on the button, the voice on the hot line. This man could destroy the world. Congress also passed countless acts which vested vast, almost uncontrolled power in the president; and the president, in the latter half of the century, held in his hands almost exclusive powers of peace and of war.

Curiously, in the age of the imperial president, the *public* came to matter much more than it did in the days of, say, Lincoln or even Teddy Roosevelt. The imperial president was also the public-opinion president—more and more, in the late twentieth century, he was the president who shifted like a weather vane, who teetered this way and that as opinion polls, focus groups, and letters from the public dictated. It was also a presidency that practiced, in turn, all the dark arts of manipulation, spin control, and so on. Thus leader and public were locked in a kind of dance of reciprocity. The political elites led the public around by the nose; but they were in turn the prisoners of the public. What brought this about was the sheer immediacy of television and the media in general.

For most of the century, the forces of centralization swept everything before them. As the new century begins, are we now balanced on the brink of another turn of the wheel? Technology welded the country together; will technology now lead the way to some kind of fragmentation, or even disintegration? Is the smooth, unified surface about to be shattered into a thousand little pieces? In the "information era," nobody needs to be anyplace in particular; a woman in Detroit calls an airline, and somebody (or a machine) answers in Arizona or Florida; credit card companies route financial business through South Dakota; a few yuppie pioneers move to Montana and "access" their offices in Baltimore. Where these trends are going no one yet knows; nor how it will affect the political system, the family, the economy—and the law.

The twentieth century was the century of the "law explosion." The sheer size and scale of the legal system grew fantastically. In some ways, it is awfully hard to measure a legal system. Law is more than words on paper, it is an operating machine, a system; and its full meaning in society is too elusive to be easily captured. Still, there are some crude ways at least of getting an idea of the total dimensions; and wherever we look, we see signs of elephantiasis. Take, for example, the Federal Register. Since the 1930s, all federal notices, orders, proposed regulations, and the like have to be recorded in the dreary pages of this yearly book. The Federal Register is truly monstrous in size; it has sometimes run to as many as 75,000 pages a year. This is probably a greater quantity of sheer legal *stuff* than the combined statutes and regulations of all the states, and the federal government, in, say, 1880. Meanwhile, every state, city, and town, as well as the federal government, is busy churning out new laws, ordinances, and rules. The books of reported cases, federal and state, are also growing faster than ever before; there are thousands and thousands of volumes on the shelves of the law libraries, and millions of bits and bytes in cyberspace.

What brought all this about? Why is there so much "law" in the United States? Is there more "law" in this country than in other developed countries—Japan, for example? Possibly. But the growth in legal stuff is pan-Western, and probably global. Changes in legal culture account for a lot of the growth. The supply of law is bigger because the demand is bigger. We will explore this issue as we go along. Once again, we have to point a finger of blame at technology. Our fancy new machines help boost the demand for law. Take, for example, the automobile. At the beginning of the century, they were rare—toys for the rich. John D. Spreckels paid a $2 fee for registering his White steamer in 1905 in California—the first in the state. In 1914 there were 123,516 automobiles registered in California; in 1924, 1,125,381, plus nearly 200,000 trucks.[6] By the end of the century everybody had a car, except the very, very poor (and some city dwellers, particularly in Manhattan). The suburban family was, typically, a two-car or three-car family. And the streets were crowded with buses, vans, "sports utility vehicles," motorcycles, taxicabs—this was, no doubt, an automotive society.

What impact has all this had on the law? To begin with, there is traffic law: a tremendous presence in our lives, something we encounter every day—parking, speed limits, rules of the road. There were traffic rules in the horse-and-buggy days, but they hardly amounted to much. Today, in each state, there is a vast traffic code. There are driver's license laws, and laws about drunken driving. There are laws about registration and license plates. There are rules and regulations on safety in the manufacture of cars. More recently, we find seat belt laws (and helmet laws for motorcycles). The indirect influences are even more vast: what the automobile has meant to mobility, to suburban growth—and to American culture and aspirations.

Technology affects law in manifold obvious ways. First of all, there is overt regulation—control of the airwaves, the Civil Aeronautics Board, rules about cyberporn, and so on. But the impact is more subtle and pervasive. It is obvious that "the pill" and other ways of preventing babies has had an effect on the so-called sexual revolution. But in less obvious ways, so did the washing machine and the stall shower. They made nudity an everyday affair. Poor people, in the past, had rarely undressed or changed clothes. Above all, the affluence that technology helped bring about has had the greatest impact on society, and hence on the law. Affluence meant bigger homes, and more privacy. It fostered individualism. It made leisure available to everybody; because of this, fun industries—industries of leisure and entertainment—grew to be among the largest in the country. The media and the leisure industries also helped produce a celebrity culture. And this culture in turn helped create the imperial presidency.

In the last third of the twentieth century, there were constant complaints about a "litigation explosion." Rigorous scholarship was more cautious on this point; but no matter—the public was convinced of it.[7] And, to be honest, smoke means at least *some* sort of fire. *Some* kinds of litigation had indeed exploded (though other kinds had quietly, even stealthily, faded away). And these exploding types—like medical malpractice, or sex discrimination cases—were noisy and controversial, and socially significant to boot.

The liability explosion in the field of torts—mostly cases about personal injury—was real enough. The niggardly, narrow rules of the nineteenth century were dismantled in the twentieth, and replaced with more "liberal" rules. Products liability, which hardly existed in the nineteenth century, and medical malpractice, which was quite rare, now were common enough to induce real panic among businesspeople and insurance companies, and in the conclaves of the healers. The media were full of horror stories about frivolous lawsuits. Egged on by those who had a money stake in the matter, legislatures (and some courts) began to rein in liability. But despite this reaction, the *scale* of liability litigation was still enormous in 2000, measured by the standards of 1900.

One explosion was undeniable: the explosion in numbers in the legal profession. The crowd of lawyers grew steadily throughout American history; but in the period after the Second World War, it was runaway growth. It says something about our country that by now we have nearly a million lawyers—and that the ratio of lawyers to the population is twenty times or more that of Japan. There has been a kind of ballooning in the size of law firms, too. In 1950 a firm of one hundred was considered a giant. In the 1990s the largest firms had more than a thousand lawyers on their rolls. The profession *looks* different, too. It is no longer (since the 1960s) almost exclusively white, and almost exclusively male.

The Bill of Rights was added to the Constitution in the late eighteenth century. But the way courts and people *understand* the Bill of Rights is something that changes over time; and dramatically so. The Supreme Court did not decide a single important case on freedom of speech before the time of the First World War. The first key cases grew out of hysteria against leftists during the war (and as a response to the Russian Revolution). The power to censor dirty books was not seriously questioned in the Court until the 1950s.

In the early part of the century, civil rights cases, too, were rare. In 1896, in *Plessy v. Ferguson*, the Supreme Court, in one of its more dismal moments, put its stamp of approval on the doctrine of "separate but equal"; this meant full steam ahead for American apartheid.[8] White supremacy ruled the South, and the legal system, federal and state, hardly uttered a peep in opposition.

American law in the nineteenth century was inward-looking and domestic. America had grown into an empire; but it was strictly a domestic empire. Even the native peoples were defined as "domestic dependent nations." There were dreams of expansion into Nicaragua or Cuba, but nothing came of them. Hawaii was annexed and turned into a territory; it was not overtly colonized. The Spanish-American War changed this situation. Once the United States grabbed Puerto Rico and the Philippines, it became a true empire; for the first time, it held territories that it did not intend to groom for statehood. These regions were something truly new and different; they were not "territories" in the classical sense; they were colonial possessions.

This colonial legacy, and the masses of immigrants who poured into the United States in the late nineteenth and early twentieth century, brought on a kind of identity crisis; or perhaps a culture war, which left its mark all over the legal system—in criminal law, family law, and above all the law of immigration and citizenship. Nativism and isolationism had always been elements of the culture. Now the old-line Americans felt threatened. Many of them wanted to pull up the drawbridge and retreat into the castle. But how could they? The United States was part of the world, and became more and more so. It took part in the two world wars in the twentieth century. After the first one, the country did turn its back on the rest of the globe (or tried to); it also experienced one of its worst episodes of xenophobia—not to mention the revival of the Ku Klux Klan. Another triumph of nativism was the 1924 immigration act. In the nineteenth century, laws were passed to keep out the Chinese; the twentieth century added the quota system, shutting the gates as much as possible on riffraff from the south and east of Europe. What was wanted was solid, Protestant immigration from the north of Europe; and nothing else.

After the Second World War, isolation was finally completely impossible. The United States was so obviously a big power, so grown-up, so much a part of the world system that there was no way to crawl back into its shell. Some mental habits of fortress America did survive. Chauvinism was alive and well. There were even those who thought the United Nations—its headquarters was in New York City—was part of a communist plot. This was the era of McCarthyism, and cold-war paranoia. But while the storms of the cold war raged, the world was shrinking all around; distances melted into insignificance; the world was becoming a single entity, a single *system*.

The world system included people of all races and religions and cultures. The United States was diverse to begin with, and became more diverse. Isolation was doomed. The United States did not abandon the United Nations; instead, it dominated it, and tried to bend it to its own American will. The tight immigration laws had to give way. The system of national quotas ended in 1965; the laws that kept out Asians were repealed. In the last part of the century, the "teeming masses" of immigrants consisted not of Europeans but of millions of people from places like China, Korea, Vietnam, India, not to mention Samoa and the Philippines; and from Mexico, the Dominican Republic, Nicaragua, Haiti, and all over Latin America. *Illegal* immigration became, for the first time in American history, a major political and legal issue; it focused attention mostly on the porous southern border.

At the end of the century, there were signs of a new (or modified) form of culture war. What *was* America, as the door to the new millennium opened? What did it stand for? Who owned its soul? This was the age of what we might call *plural equality*. At one time, there was a single strong, well-defined majority: white Protestants. And, of course, within the ranks of white Protestants, it was the men who called the tune. This majority believed in a kind of freedom; it was much more permissive than the ruling classes of most European countries. Minority religions, for example, were tolerated. The word is important: tolerated. Tolerated means allowed—and not much more.

That was then. Then came now. Now the country no longer had that kind of majority. Now it was a country made up of minorities. The civil rights movement, from 1950 on, changed America in a deep and permanent way. The movement found an ally in the Supreme Court, under Earl Warren, and in (most of the) federal courts. White supremacy lost its foothold in the law. So did male supremacy, somewhat later. All sorts of groups that had been suppressed and ignored, the deviant or the silenced, came out of the closet or the basement and demanded rights, a share of power, and, above all, legitimacy. The parade of subordinated people seemed to have no end. It included Hispanics, Asians, the native peoples, students, gay people, old people, deaf people, illegitimate children, prisoners. There were more and more of these groups clamoring for a place in the sun; they became more and more assertive; they fought battle after battle, mostly of the legal sort. The final chapter is still to be written—of course. There were plenty of instances of resistance and backlash. But the net result was a different America, a more plural America, an America made up of a rainbow of cultures and colors and norms.

The phrase "plural equality" does not begin to capture the essence of what had happened in America. In the first days of the civil rights movement, one of the prime goals was integration—what black people wanted, in a way, was assimilation, or at least the right to assimilate. The cry was: take us into the mainstream. We want to eat in your restaurants, sleep in your hotels, work in your factories, play on your ball teams, sing in your operas. We want our share of America. This was the basic program; and the other minorities, of whatever stripe, wanted something analogous—whether it was the right of a woman to be a big-league umpire or to work in a coal mine, or the right of a guy in a wheelchair to ride in everybody else's bus.

Partly because of a sense of disillusionment, and partly because of other, more deep-seated causes, the goals shifted drastically over the years. Now the theme was no longer simply assimilation or political and economic equality: open the door and let us in. No longer were the "others" saying: we are like you, we are like everybody, treat us accordingly. Now the theme was: we are different; we are ourselves; we are a separate nation, a separate culture. Now one began to hear people say black is beautiful, and there was gay pride, and deaf pride, and women who said that women were better than men (more caring, more tolerant, more intelligent); and one was told, too, that old people do too have sex and maybe better sex than young people, and they are *not* doddering fools; and then, also, there was a kind of resurgence of native religions and customs and languages and ways of life. The word *nation* in "queer nation" or the "Woodstock nation" was not just a metaphor. There *was* a sense of nationhood, a sense of personal sovereignty, behind the metaphor; and the nationhood of these and other groups was, for many people who bound themselves to the group, all too real.

Many Americans, of course, were horrified to see their flag ripped into shreds, as it were; horrified to see the mirror of American unity shatter into splinters of glass. They longed for the days when there was unity and harmony. Of course, in many ways those days never really existed; but people overlooked that fact, or were simply unaware of it. The horrors (real or imagined) of the present blotted out the horrors of the past. Backlash translated itself into political action: the English-only movement, for example; the campaign against affirmative action; immigration controls; the revolt of the Christian Right. So far, all that has happened is a certain nibbling around the edges of pluralism. Affirmative action is definitely in bad odor, legally speaking. The courts are chipping away at prisoners' rights. Still, despite what some people say, there is never any end to the historical process; history is a river that never dries up; it always flows on, and its currents are full of swirling surprises. Where all the ins and outs, the reactions and counterreactions, will lead in the end is anybody's guess.

But whatever the path, one thing has been and continues to be a clear, obvious, and bedrock fact: the law, and the use of law, is here to stay. All conflicts, disputes, compromises, arrangements, movements—all aspects of society, high and low—express themselves and are expressed through law, at least to some degree and in some fashion. All modern societies, in fact, are law-ridden societies. Even countries like Japan, which claim they are not. Whatever their differences, all modern states govern by and through law: whether the materials are laws, court decisions, decrees, regulations, administrative guidelines—the informal gives way to the formal, custom is replaced by law; old understandings and consensuses melt away, and the result is what we see, today, and probably tomorrow, in the United States: a society of law and of laws.

I

The Old Order

1

Structure, Power, and Form

American Public Law, 1900–1932

In many ways, the American scheme of government has been a model of stability. The constitutional system, set up in the late eighteenth century, has turned out to be tough and durable. Not many countries can match the American record. In 1900 the scheme of government seemed, essentially, the same as it had always been. In Europe, upheavals and revolutions had rocked France, Germany, Italy, and Spain. There was no counterpart in the United States. There was, of course, the Civil War—a huge, bloody exception. Still, Jefferson or John Adams, if brought back to life in 1900, would have found the frame of government at least recognizable. The president was still the head of state and head of government; there was still a Senate and House of Representatives; there was still a Supreme Court. Many new states had joined the union; but they were formed on the pattern of the old ones. Even the White House would look pretty much the same.

Jefferson and Adams were extremely intelligent men; and after the shock of familiarity wore off, as they began to probe deeper into the nature of American government, they would find themselves puzzled and even (maybe) horrified; they would find themselves in a realm of mysteries and changes. The Constitution and its system were really *not* the same at all, except on paper. They were like an old building whose facade had been lovingly preserved; but the guts had been torn out, and plumbing, wiring, and the very shape of the rooms had been redone so often and so thoroughly that hardly a bit of the original was still actually there. America faced twentieth-century problems; and these problems reacted on the institutions that were called on to solve them. Nothing seemed different; but then nothing was really the same.

The Supreme Court That Said No

The highest court of the land was the United States Supreme Court, in 1900 as in 1800. It sits, in lonely splendor, at the top of the federal system of justice. This was, by 1900, a three-tiered system—trial courts (district courts), appeal courts (the circuit courts), and the Supreme Court above them all. The federal courts decided cases that arose under federal laws, and under the federal Constitution. They also decided "diversity" cases—cases between citizens of different states—if these cases were worth a certain amount and met certain threshold standards. All federal cases could crawl up the ladder of appeals and, if lucky or controversial enough, reach the Supreme Court. That court also, on occasion, heard appeals from the highest state courts, in cases which presented some sort of federal or constitutional question.

The system was, of course, still strongly federal; and though the United States Supreme Court had a kind of imperial authority, each state had its own constitution, its own laws, its own supreme court. The local high-court judges were the kings of local law; and in their sphere they were all-powerful. A decision of the Ohio Supreme Court, on a matter coming under the Ohio Constitution, was (99 percent of the time) absolutely final; there was no recourse to the federal courts at all.

For obvious reasons, the United States Supreme Court grabs most of the headlines and attention. From the very beginning of its history, it has made news—good news and bad news. The early twentieth century was no exception. The Supreme Court had always had its share of hot political cases; but the number of these grew steadily over the years, and there was something of a bulge in the late nineteenth century. Before 1870 the Supreme Court occasionally had to decide whether a statute of some state violated the federal Constitution; it did the same—but very, very rarely—for federal statutes. By 1900 the Court was deciding many more cases than before on constitutional issues; and it had developed some startling doctrines—doctrines of judicial review—which it used, from time to time, to slash and burn programs of federal and state legislation, which, in the Court's judgment, violated the Constitution.

The early twentieth century, in some ways, was the high-water mark of this new activism. Looking backward, we are apt to label this as *conservative* activism—an activism very different from the activism which, as we shall see, developed after the 1940s. In particular, *Lochner v. New York* (1905), famous or infamous, has come to stand as a symbol of the work of a court that said no, defiantly, to what many people at the time defined as progress.[1]

The background of *Lochner* was this: New York State had in 1897 passed a law which, among other things, regulated bakeries, and the conditions of work inside bakeries. Much of the statute had to do with sanitary conditions. Every bakery had to have a "proper wash-room and water-closet . . . apart from the bake-room"; bakeries had to be properly ventilated; nobody was to sleep in a bake-room; no domestic animals, except cats, were allowed in any room used to bake in, or where flour or meal products were stored. These provisions were not in serious dispute. But the act also provided that no employee of a bakery "shall be required or permitted to work in a . . . bakery . . . more than sixty hours in any one week, or more than ten hours in any one day."[2] This was the sticking point—the source of controversy.

Joseph Lochner, who owned a small bakery in Utica, New York, was accused of letting a worker work more than sixty hours in a week. He was convicted and fined $50. Lochner appealed all the way through the New York court system and up to the United States Supreme Court. A majority of the Court, in an opinion written by Justice Rufus Peckham, thought that the law was unconstitutional. How long bakers worked had nothing to do with public health, in Peckham's opinion; in fact, Peckham hinted darkly, the law had been passed "from other motives." These "motives" were not specified; but what Peckham meant was obvious, and he said so elsewhere in his opinion: this was a *labor* law, a law that took sides in the struggle between management and labor. And in so doing, in Peckham's view, it did a disservice to the public interest; moreover, it interfered with the freedom of workers and their bosses—their right to enter into whatever contract of labor they chose. This right was protected (he said) by the Constitution of the United States, specifically, by the Fourteenth Amendment to the Constitution. That amendment provided that no state could deprive its people of life, liberty, or property without "due process of law." The bakery law interfered with the "liberty" to enter into labor contracts, and the state could not infringe upon this right.

Not everyone on the Court agreed with Peckham. John Marshall Harlan dissented vigorously—bakers, he pointed out, lived short, dismal lives in an inferno of heat and flour dust. Their hours *were* a health issue, he insisted. This trenchant and relevant critique was overshadowed, however, by the dissent of Oliver Wendell Holmes, Jr., written in Holmes's best gnomic and pithy style. The Fourteenth Amendment, he said, "does not enact Mr. Herbert Spencer's Social Statics." The Constitution was "not intended to embody a particular economic theory"; and the word *liberty* in the Fourteenth Amendment is "perverted when it is held to prevent the natural outcome of a dominant opinion."

In a sense, Holmes and Peckham saw eye to eye. They agreed on the issue—though not on the outcome. The issue was the right of states to interfere in the workings of the economy. That right, Peckham thought, was severely limited—by the Constitution, in fact. A kind of laissez-faire ideology was implicit in the constitutional scheme. Not an extreme ideology; the states did have regulatory powers. They could act to protect public health, safety, and morals. But the courts had a duty to draw the line between regulation that was acceptable—regulation which fell within this protected zone—and regulation that was not. The bakers' statute went too far. To Holmes, however, the majority opinion was reading its own version of a free-market philosophy into the Constitution. Holmes was willing to defer much more to the elected legislature.

Lochner was not the only case to pose the issue of the limits of regulation. In *Adair v. United States* (1908), the Supreme Court confronted a common industrial practice.[3] Some employers demanded that workers sign so-called yellow dog contracts; that is, workers had to promise not to join a union. An act of Congress, passed in 1898, forbade railroad employers from discriminating "against any employee because of his membership in . . . a labor . . . organization."[4] Adair, an agent of the Louisville and Nashville Railroad, was accused of firing a locomotive fireman, Coppage, because he was a member of the Order of Locomotive Firemen. The Supreme Court, referring to the same notion of "liberty of contract" that they leaned on in *Lochner,* struck down the statute.[5]

Cases of this type were—not surprisingly—controversial. To organized labor, the courts were reactionary institutions that sided with the bosses. The Supreme Court acted, at least sometimes, as if the Constitution itself ruled out various types of social reform. If legislatures thought they could smooth out the sharp, jagged edges of capitalism, or mount an attack on the gross inequalities of income, power, and influence that capitalism dragged with it—well, they were wrong. Capitalism, in Europe and North America, has since become much tamer, subdued by the welfare-regulatory state. But this twist in the fortunes of capitalism still lay in the future. In *Coppage v. Kansas* (1914), the Supreme Court revisited the *Adair* case.[6] The earlier case had involved a federal statute; here it was the state of Kansas that had outlawed the yellow dog contract. The Court struck down the statute, citing *Adair*. Justice Mahlon Pitney delivered himself of the following:

> No doubt, wherever the right of private property exists, there must and will be inequalities of fortune. . . . Indeed a little reflection will show that wherever the right of private property and the right of free contract co-exist, each party when contracting is inevitably more or less influenced by . . . whether he has much property, or little, or none. . . . It is self-evident that, unless all things are held in common, some persons must have more property than others. [Thus] it is from the nature of things impossible to uphold freedom of contract and the right of private property without at the same time recognizing as legitimate those inequalities of fortune that are the necessary result of the exercise of those rights.[7]

The reader will note such phrases as "the nature of things." Pitney's Constitution was, as it were, designed to freeze the status quo—to sanctify if not the distribution of wealth and income itself, then at least the structures that led to that distribution.

Nowhere did the Supreme Court appear more stubborn, retrograde, and intransigent than in the struggle against child labor. Most of the industrial states had laws against child labor by 1900.[8] Children had always worked, helping families on the farm, or as apprentices; but in the industrial age, "child labor" now meant kids under sixteen slaving long hours in factories; they were a pool of cheap and expendable labor. Courts tended to uphold child-labor laws as valid; but enforcement was another question. The South constituted one gigantic, gaping loophole. In 1900 most of the spinners in southern cotton mills were under fourteen. The South, in general, had no child-labor laws on its books; and the business community in the South wanted to keep it that way. Muckraking exposés fed anger in the North and led to calls for action; more to the point, perhaps, New England textile mills and other industries were deathly afraid that the low-wage South would suck their businesses away. The South would not reform itself—that was clear. The only hope to stop the race to the bottom was to get legislation out of Washington—legislation on a national scale. After many years of agitation over the issue of child labor, Congress passed a law in 1916 to try to get children out of factories and mines. The act applied to any mine or quarry that hired children under sixteen, or factories that hired children under fourteen (or allowed children between fourteen and sixteen to work more than eight hours a day, or six days a week; or at night or in the early morning). These mines, quarries, and factories were not to ship their goods and products in interstate commerce.[9] Violaters were subject to fines for a first offense; fines and jail time for repeat offenses.

By that time it was part of the normal life cycle of a major labor or welfare statute to run the gamut of the federal courts. In a test case, Roland H. Dagenhart, who worked in a cotton mill in Charlotte, North Carolina, brought an action on behalf of himself and his two minor sons to enjoin enforcement of the child-labor law.[10] The Supreme Court, in a narrow 5–4 decision, struck down the law in 1918.[11] Congress could regulate "interstate commerce" under the Constitution; but this statute, according to Justice Day (speaking for the majority) went too far. It also exerted "a power as to a purely local matter to which Federal authority does not extend." If Congress could prohibit this kind of goods from moving in interstate commerce, it could prohibit anything at all from crossing state lines. This would destroy the authority of the states over "local matters," and unsettle the whole American system of government. (Four justices, speaking through Oliver Wendell Holmes, Jr., dissented.)

If we take the Court at face value, it was worried mostly about the federal system—the distribution of power between federal and state governments. In some ways, indeed, it *was* this system, this structure, that lay at the root of the problem. The United States was, by law and custom, a giant free-trade area. It was an economic but not a cultural or political unit—or, for that matter, a legal unit. This was the reason why child labor had to be dealt with on a national scale.

The Supreme Court had become, as we have seen, something of an activist court in the late nineteenth and early twentieth centuries; quite a few state statutes fell in the process. But here it was a federal statute, a solemn act of Congress, that the Court declared void. This was a much rarer event (at least until the New Deal era). It was also an event that Congress did not take lying down. After the Supreme Court said no to the child-labor law, Congress tried another tack. It passed a tax law in 1919 which put an "excise tax" of 10 percent on the net profits of any mine or factory hiring children.[12] The definition of "child labor" was exactly the same as it had been in the law that came to grief in *Hammer v. Dagenhart*. The power of Congress to tax, it was believed, was broader than its power to regulate commerce. But when the law was challenged, the Supreme Court said no again. This was no "tax" at all; it was simply another attempt to get rid of child labor, and that was beyond the power of Congress: "a court must be blind not to see that the so-called tax is imposed to stop the employment of children."[13]

The text of *Hammer v. Dagenhart* makes sense, if you read it in isolation. The justices who wrote the majority opinion were undoubtedly sincere in thinking that Congress had limited power; that the law went too far; that whether you liked the law or not, Congress had no power to pass it. But how could these justices reconcile this decision with *Hoke v. United States* (1913), in which the Court upheld the famous Mann Act?[14] Why was it that Congress could make it a crime to take a woman across state lines for "immoral" purposes; or could keep lottery tickets out of the stream of commerce; but had no power over shirts and pants made with the blood and sweat of small children?[15]

There are, of course, technical differences between the cases in which the Court said yes and the cases in which the Court said no. There were issues of legal doctrine, which were important (or at least the judges said they were—and perhaps even thought they were). There was the ideology of limited government. Neither the federal government nor the states had a free hand to do what they liked. Only businesses "affected with a public interest" could be regulated.[16] The states had the "police power"—that is, the power to make laws to protect or advance the public health or safety or welfare. But all these were vague, shifting, contested concepts.[17] They were incapable of actually deciding cases. They were technically significant, but they did not go to the heart of the matter.

Is there anything that really reconciles the flood of cases, the decisions flowing this way and that? Is there anything that can make them consistent? Perhaps not. But if there is, it is not to be found on the face of the laws, or in the text of the opinions; or in strictly legal logic.

Perhaps we can best explain these decisions by asking: who were these nine learned justices? What sort of men sat on this Court? And the answer is: middle-aged men, fairly conservative; churchgoing men who believed in traditional values and clean living; honorable men, according to their lights, men who worried about the fate of their country, and who were frightened of the tidal waves of social change that they saw washing over the United States. The Mann Act stood for decency and traditional values, against decay, vice, and prostitution. In *Muller v. Oregon* (1908) a law on the working hours of women was upheld; this was a labor law, to be sure; but it also stood for family values, domesticity, and motherhood.[18] Perhaps the justices could have looked at the child-labor laws in this light—as a law about families and children and the future of the country. But on the *federal* level, child-labor laws seemed to stand for something else, something frightening and novel: a more collective, centrally governed economy. And for this the justices were simply unprepared.

Still, it is important not to exaggerate what the conservative justices did. The cases where the Supreme Court said no were the cases that made headlines and became famous. But there were many more cases in which the court said yes—cases like *Muller v. Oregon* itself. Five years before *Hammer v. Dagenhart*, in 1913, the Supreme Court, in a unanimous opinion, told the states that they had the absolute right "to prohibit the employment of persons of tender years in dangerous occupations."[19] Twelve years after *Lochner*, in *Bunting v. Oregon* (1917), the Supreme Court, without so much as mentioning *Lochner*, upheld an Oregon statute which said that "No person shall be employed in any mill, factory or manufacturing establishment . . . more than ten hours in any one day."[20]

Cases like *Lochner* are famous (or infamous). But the states did a lot of regulating; and their laws, by and large, had an easy time with the court. The "yes" cases—the ones that upheld legislation—are, for the most part, much more obscure. In *Leonard & Leonard v. Earle* (1929), the Court confronted a Maryland law of 1927; the subject was oysters.[21] Maryland oyster packers, under this law, had to get a state license; and they had to turn over to the state 10 percent of the "shells of the oysters shucked" in the packer's establishment. These shells were not worth much, but the state intended to put them back in the sea, to furnish support and lime for the growth of spat. The Leonards did not want to give these shells to Maryland; the law, they claimed, violated their property rights and denied them the "equal protection of the laws" (the famous phrase from the Fourteenth Amendment). The Court turned them down. The (unanimous) opinion was written by McReynolds, perhaps the crustiest conservative on the Court. He thought the claims of the Leonards were "groundless"; that the law was neither "oppressive nor arbitrary," and that the Constitution provided no cover for "selfish" packers who were trying to "escape an entirely reasonable contribution and . . . to thwart a great conservation measure."

Most regulatory cases were more like the *Leonard* case than like *Lochner*. It is, in fact, too simple-minded to portray the justices as frightened, reactionary men, defending a dying social order. They were not cardboard conservatives. In their decisions, they seemed to wobble this way or that. What they feared the most, it seems, was excess. They had little or no understanding of what it was like to work in a factory or a sweatshop; and they were terrified of radical winds blowing in from across the Atlantic. But they did not shrink from moderate reform. They were perfectly willing to uphold *some* regulation of business, if they considered it necessary for this or that reason. Their instincts were not so much reactionary as soundly upper middle class.

Moreover, every generation has its own definition of "progressive." *Muller v. Oregon* was a great victory for people who considered themselves progressive in their day. It was applauded by most women's groups (though not all). Today, the opinion seems so utterly sexist that it is hard to read it without wincing. There is all that talk about "women's physical structure," the need to have "healthy mothers," the statement that "woman has always been dependent upon man," that she was in need of protection "from the greed as well as the passion of man," and so on.[22] The Supreme Court was crucified in its day because the justices refused to let the states, or state agencies, regulate railroad and utility rates, at least in some cases; but today, in an age of free markets, and a kind of capitalist triumphalism, rate regulation has gone completely out of fashion. Indeed, to many economists (and ordinary people) rate regulation seems like a bad historical joke.

The justices were surely not radical; they had what strikes some people today as an inordinate respect for the rights of property, and they seemed to lack empathy or understanding for factory workers and other people who worked with their hands and lived lives of poverty and insecurity. But even their respect for property rights was highly selective. The justices upheld quite a few restrictions on property rights. In *Welch v. Swasey* (1909), for example, Welch wanted to erect a building on his lot higher than the Boston building commissioners would allow.[23] The Supreme Court denied his claim. The same Rufus Peckham who wrote the majority opinion in *Lochner* now talked about his "reluctance" to second-guess the city of Boston, or the legislature of Massachusetts. In this case, Peckham did not see any "unreasonable interference with the rights of property." In *Hadacheck v. Sebastian, Chief of Police of Los Angeles* (1915), Hadacheck owned a brickyard outside the city limits; but Los Angeles, swelling and expanding even then, swallowed up the land and it became part of the city.[24] By ordinance, no brickyards were allowed in certain parts of the city. Hadacheck now owned, basically, a hole in the ground and an illegal brickworks. But the Court turned a deaf ear to his complaints: "There must be progress, and if in its march private interests are in the way they must yield to the good of the community."[25]

In short, the justices, and judges in general, were cautious and incremental. They did not consistently adhere to any economic philosophy. They simply reacted in the way that respectable, moderate conservatives of their day would naturally react. Hence it is perhaps a bit unfair to judge them by what history has come to call mistakes.[26] What is beyond question is that the judges exercised power. Even when they seemed not to—when they approved and upheld, instead of saying no—they must have been aware that their stamp of approval was vital, and had an awesome finality.

Whether a law was wise or good or not was no business of the justices: this was a mantra that they chanted, time and again. Still, one wonders. *Jay Burns Baking Company v. Bryan* (1924) was another case involving baking and bread—perhaps bread had some magical effect on the Supreme Court.[27] Nebraska in its wisdom passed a bread law in 1921. Every loaf of bread sold in the state had to be sold in half-pound, one-pound, one-and-a-half-pound loaves, or in "multiples of one pound." The statute had some rather peculiar features; nobody was supposed to sell bread that weighed *more* than the statutory figure, within certain tolerances. The majority of the justices thought this provision was "not necessary for the protection of purchasers against . . . fraud"; furthermore, that the law subjected bakers and bread sellers to "essentially unreasonable and arbitrary" restrictions; and that therefore the law was "repugnant to the Fourteenth Amendment." In form, this was just a case of "interpretation": what did the Constitution mean? The modern reader, though, cannot help feeling that the justices thought that the law was stupid, and acted accordingly.

There were so many decisions passing judgment on state (and federal) statutes that it is hard to sum them up in any simple formula. But as this case indicates, judges did, at times, seem to exercise a veto over legislation—as if they were something like super state governors. In *Chicago, Milwaukee and St. Paul Railroad Company v. Wisconsin* (1915), the statute in question was hardly earthshaking.[28] It had to do with railroad sleeping cars—a dying breed by the year 2000, but much more significant in 1915. Railroads sold various kinds of sleeping arrangements; compartments were the most expensive; somewhat cheaper were units where the sleepers were stacked one top of the other, in an upper and lower berth. Under the law (passed in 1911), whenever a person occupied a lower berth, and the upper berth was unsold, "the upper berth shall not be let down, but shall remain closed," giving the lower berth, of course, much more room. The Court found the statute unconstitutional: "The right of the State to regulate public carriers in the interest of the public is very great." But that does not "warrant an unreasonable interference with the right of management." Case closed.

State Courts

In legal education as of 2000 the spotlight shines most brightly on the United States Supreme Court; and legal scholarship in general busies itself interpreting, analyzing, and critiquing that Court's decisions. But the state Supreme Courts, and the state systems, are important institutions. And they were, of course, even more important at the turn of the century, before the vast expansion of federal power.

The *Lochner* case is famous; but there were important forerunners of *Lochner* on the state level. It was in the state supreme courts that some important doctrines of constitutional law first saw the light of day—doctrines of due process, or liberty of contract. Naturally, there were considerable differences among the states. Some were more attracted to a kind of legalized laissez-faire than others. Most regulatory statutes did pass the constitutional test. The exceptions, of course, made the most stir. Ernst Freund, writing in 1904, was surely right when he pointed to the "vast amount of police legislation"—that is, laws on public safety and health—and observed that, under modern conditions, the state "was readily conceded more incisive powers than despotic governments would have dared to claim in former times."[29]

A lot depended—this was true, too, at the level of the United States Supreme Court—on *what* was regulated. The more cogent the argument that the statute served some safety or health purpose, the easier a time the statute had. The courts were generally friendly, too, to occupational licensing laws.[30] These laws had mushroomed in the late nineteenth century—laws licensing doctors, nurses, pharmacists, indeed, all of the health professions, including osteopaths and veterinarians. There were also laws licensing undertakers, horseshoers, plumbers, and barbers. Almost always the rationale was expressed in terms of public health or safety. A New Hampshire statute, licensing "embalmers of dead human bodies," demanded practical experience, knowledge about infection and disinfection, and "intelligent comprehension of the rudiments of human anatomy."[31] The Texas barber-licensing law talked about the "skill" barbers needed—barbers had to be able to prepare the tools, shave, and cut hair, with "sufficient knowledge concerning the common diseases of the face and skin," and how to avoid spreading or aggravating these diseases.[32] A cynic or neoliberal would most likely stress something else: the desire to monopolize barbering or embalming, to close ranks against outsiders, to control output, recruitment, and, not least of all, prices. This would be just as true of doctors or veterinarians as of barbers and embalmers. Laws regulating the more elegant professions were invariably sustained. But the licensing of horseshoers got a rather sour reception in the courts; and there were mixed results on the licensing of plumbers. Barbers, on the other hand, did well: the barber, as a judge in Washington state pointed out in 1907, does his work "directly on the person."[33] On balance, courts were much more likely to sympathize with professional people, and skilled artisans, than with laborers and unskilled workers, and their unions.

Like the Supreme Court, the state courts were quite tolerant of restrictions on the use of land. They regularly approved of proto-zoning measures—again, usually justified on grounds of health or safety (for example, fire protection). There were limits, however. Could cities and states ban or regulate billboards? The results were mixed. Sometimes the billboards won. In a Massachusetts case (1905), Boston's park commissioners had the authority to make "reasonable" rules about "signs, posters or advertisements in or near to or visible from public parks." The commission had turned down a sign because it was too tall—it was seven and a half feet high, "with black letters on an orange ground," and advertised a "household utensil." The court felt that billboards were a "natural" and indeed "ordinary and remunerative" use of land; and the commission had no power to prohibit them, or restrict them unduly.[34]

One of the thorniest problems was the problem of rate regulation: setting prices for electric companies, telephone companies, railroads, waterworks, and other public utilities. There was a rich harvest of case law on the subject— dozens and dozens of cases. Behind virtually every one of these cases was an issue and a struggle. The general rules were clear enough. The courts, in general, admitted that the states had a right to control what these companies charged. The Maine public utilities statute, fairly typically, gave the Public Utility Commission authority over rates: these rates had to be "reasonable and just," taking into "due consideration" the "fair value" of the property the utility owned, "its rights and plant as a going concern," and also "business risk and depreciation."[35] Nobody doubted that the companies, in short, were entitled to a "fair return" on their investment.[36] But what was a fair return? Obviously, there was no single, simple answer. If the rates were set *too* low, however—if they did not "yield a reasonable return," as the Supreme Court put it, in a case out of West Virginia—then they were "unjust, unreasonable and confiscatory," and violated the Fourteenth Amendment; they took away the company's property, without "due process of law."[37] Of course, the public wanted rates as low as possible. These triangular struggles—public, companies, and administrative bodies—were all too often dumped on the courts. The courts then faced the unenviable job of trying to decide very technical questions, which had no obvious right answers. Page after page of numbers, arguments, estimates, and statistics fill the opinion of a federal judge, who, in 1908 had to determine whether the Spring Valley Water Company, which supplied San Francisco with its water, was entitled to more money than the city wanted to allow it. What was a fair return on the property of the water company? What was that property worth in the first place? One estimate was three times as high as another estimate. How much depreciation should be allowed? What was the fairest rate of return? A brute political and economic fact underlay the tangled mess: "The people must have water, and the company must continue to supply them. Having once enlisted in the public service, the company cannot withdraw."[38] The utilities, businesses "affected with a public interest," had both rights and duties; and the courts would monitor both.

At the state level, issues touching labor, particularly organized labor, were particularly touchy—wages, hours, conditions of work, and whether to join unions or not. Many states regulated hours and work conditions of women. Some state cases upheld this kind of regulation, both before *Muller v. Oregon* and after. A Nebraska case from 1902 upheld its statute (which fixed maximum hours for women in factories). Women, said the court, "are unable, by reason of their physical limitations, to endure the same hours of exhaustive labor as . . . adult males." Certain kinds of work, which men could do easily, would "wreck the constitutions and destroy the health of women"; this might render them "incapable of bearing their share of the burdens of the family and the home."[39] In *Ritchie & Co. v. Wayman* (1910), the Supreme Court of Illinois passed on a law which set a ten-hour limit for the workday of women in factories.[40] The court upheld the law; weak, sick women "cannot be the mothers of vigorous children."[41] What was unusual about this case was that it basically discarded a well-known Illinois case from the late nineteenth century, which had essentially gone the other way.[42] The earlier case had been vigorously attacked by progressives. The 1910 case suggests that in some sense the tide had turned: that the courts would become, as time went on, less and less likely to interpose themselves in favor of business, and against the legislative will.

2

The Legal Profession in the
Early Twentieth Century

At the turn of the century, according to the census, there were 108,000 lawyers and judges (almost all of them men) in the United States.[1] We have considerable information about who the lawyers were, how they were organized, and the like—much less about what lawyers actually did. We do know that the bar was, then as now, highly stratified. At the top were the "Wall Street lawyers," the good, gray, competent, conservative men who handled the affairs of big business. A few lawyers, also rich and powerful, worked for and represented the great corporations—especially the railroad giants. In the middle were ordinary lawyers, handling humdrum matters for small merchants, well-to-do citizens, and the like; these lawyers could be found in every city and town, and in every big-city neighborhood. At the bottom were marginal men, who eked out a living from scraps of work given out by courts, or bits of business from friends and neighbors. Socially if not economically at the lowest circle of the profession were the "ambulance chasers," personal-injury lawyers who raced to the scene of accidents, or to hospital rooms, to sign up victims of crashes, smashes, explosions, and fires. They needed to be fast, to get to the victim before the company's claims adjuster came with a sheaf of releases to sign. Among their clients, there were, of course, a large number of fakers—con artists who specialized in slipping on banana peels, or falling off trains, and the like; Irving Fuhr, who flourished in New York in the 1920s, was a "flopper," a "specialist in vault-light, manhole cover, and cellar-door flops."[2] Sometimes, the lawyers who represented these hungry crooks were themselves hungry and unscrupulous men.

The "ambulance chaser" was, for the most part, a lawyer operating on his own; he stood right on the brink of disreputability, or in fact went over the edge. The Wall Street lawyer, on the other hand, was a member of a bright and shining elite. Unlike the personal-injury lawyer, the Wall Street lawyer tended more to work in a team: to be a member of a *firm* of lawyers—a partnership. Firm lawyers were still a small minority of the profession. In Philadelphia in 1905, there were about 1,900 lawyers (only three of them were women); and most of these lawyers were solo practitioners. There were fifty-five two-man partnerships, ten firms with three partners, and one with four. A few firms had between six and ten lawyers in their offices, if you include juniors.[3] Over the years, the firms grew in size. Ropes and Gray in Boston listed fourteen lawyers in 1930.[4] In Houston, Vinson and Elkins, founded in 1917, had seventeen lawyers in 1929; thirteen of them were partners who shared in the profits.[5]

The biggest firms were in New York City. In 1931 Sullivan & Cromwell listed twenty-six "Partners and Principal Associates" in a firm that claimed to do business in New York, Paris, and Buenos Aires.[6] As the firms got larger, they faced the problem of how to organize themselves. The method they came up with has often been called the "Cravath system," after Paul Cravath, a partner in a Wall Street firm, who devised it and put it in place in his firm around the turn of the century. Before Cravath, law firms really had no organization; each partner worked more or less for himself, with the help of assistants or law students, who often got no money for their efforts. Cravath tightened the system. Firm lawyers were divided into two classes, partners and associates. The associates were hired fresh out of law school and worked on a salary basis. Cravath hired only those he considered the best. A man with less than a B average at Harvard, he felt, "either had a mind not adapted to the law or lacked purpose and ambition." It took plenty of purpose and ambition to make the grade at Cravath. Firm lawyers, like professors and army officers, operated on an up-or-out system. They either "made partner" after a period of years (five or six, as a rule), or had to go seek their fortune somewhere else.[7]

This system caught on; it became the norm. It obviously suited the needs of the growing law firms. It spread beyond New York. For example, the partnership of Miller, Mack, and Fairchild, formed in Milwaukee in 1906, almost immediately began to imitate the Cravath system and "recruit associates from the leaders of law-school classes." One of the first recruits was James B. Blake, a graduate of the University of Chicago Law School; he joined the firm in 1907 as an associate, and made partner in 1915.[8]

In the small towns, of course, lawyers worked on their own, or in little partnerships of two or three. Small-town lawyers were mostly in the general practice of law. In the directory listing for John N. Patterson, of Washington, Pennsylvania (1910), we read: "Land Titles Examined and Abstracts Furnished." Many lawyers in smaller towns, like Francis C. Wilson of Santa Fe, New Mexico (1919), claimed a "General Practice in all State and Federal Courts." They sometimes advertised that they had "notaries and stenographers in the office." A lawyer of Des Moines, Iowa, James C. Hume, was "engaged in the general practice. This means that my services are at the disposal of any one who wants them." Coffin & Rippey, also of Des Moines, boasted in the same year of an "efficient and well organized Commercial Department. Prompt, persistent, and personal attention given to collections." In fact, collection work—mopping up debts and claims—was a staple of many practices. J. B. Larimer, of Topeka, promised good service to the "interests of Non-residents, Mortgage Foreclosures . . . and the Settlement of Estates," all throughout Kansas. He had not only a stenographer and a typewriter but also "Long Distance Bell Telephone No. 1694."[9]

Wall Street lawyers shunned the limelight; their personalities were dim and gray; they moved and worked within sanctuaries of wealth and prominence. They gained clients through networks, in country clubs, and by means of personal contacts. They were almost exclusively white Protestants. In the powerful railroad industry, the many small railroads had consolidated by 1900 into a handful of big interstate nets. The railroad companies had their general counsel—often a major outside law firm—but they also had local counsel as well. In the South, for example, there was a "three-tiered" system. A big road like the Southern Railway had an in-house general counsel, who was in charge of the legal problems of the whole system. Under his command were "district attorneys" in each state, who tried big cases and did some lobbying work in state legislatures. They also hired (and fired) local lawyers who represented the railroad in every dusty town and county seat along the road—defending the railroad, for example, against the dozens and dozens of lawsuits for personal injuries.[10]

The ordinary lawyer, the lawyer with "one-shot" clients, could not rely on contacts, or country clubs, or retainers from big business to put money in his pocket. These lawyers needed ways to advertise, to get their name across to potential clients. Hence they tended to be flamboyant, outrageous; these were the lawyers who *did* want their names in the paper, who *did* want or need notoriety. Some of them became almost legendary courtroom lawyers: men like Max Steuer of New York, or Samuel Leibowitz. Steuer (1870?–1940), the "greatest trial lawyer" of his time, was said to earn $1 million a year in his prime—an astronomical sum in those days.[11] Leibowitz (1893–1978) defended the Scottsboro boys—black youths accused of rape in a notorious trial—and later served on the bench.

But probably the most famous trial lawyer was Clarence Darrow (1857–1938).[12] A radical, a free thinker, often in trouble, a spellbinding orator, Darrow was involved in some of the most notorious trials of the century. Darrow defended the "Wobblies"—the International Workers of the World—and other radicals, he took the case of the McNamara brothers, accused of dynamiting the plant of the *Los Angeles Times* in 1910, he argued against the death penalty for Loeb and Leopold in their sensational murder trial, and he battled with William Jennings Bryan in the famous Scopes "monkey trial."

Women and blacks continued to be rare beasts in the profession. By the end of the nineteenth century, women had been admitted to practice in the majority of the states. But never in any quantity. In Philadelphia, where, as we saw, there were three women lawyers in 1905, there were still only four women listed as practicing law in 1920. In that year Ada Lewis Sawyer became a member of the bar of Rhode Island—the first lawyer admitted to practice in that state.[13] Theron Strong of New York City, writing his reminiscences in 1914, claimed he had "never yet seen a woman plead a case of any kind in court," had only once even met a woman lawyer, and thought it was safe to say that "there is no prospect that woman will be seen except as a *rara avis* in the ranks of the legal fraternity." A few women did get admitted to practice in New York, but (according to Strong), "having gained this right, little use is made of it."[14] Black lawyers were also uncommon—there were, according to the census, only 798 in the country in 1910; in Philadelphia, in 1910, there were thirteen black lawyers in practice, out of more than two thousand lawyers in the city.[15]

Barriers against women and blacks were extremely high in the practice— the few who were admitted to the bar had virtually no hope of a job in a law firm. There were barriers, too, against Jews, at least in the larger firms. Felix

Frankfurter complained in the 1920s that none of the "so-called desirable firms will take a Jew," even with a Harvard degree.[16] But Jewish lawyers were hardly uncommon. In New York City in the 1920s, there were almost as many Cohens and Cohns practicing law as there were Smiths.[17] Jews flocked to the legal profession: they made up 26 percent of the freshly admitted lawyers in New York City between 1900 and 1910; and an amazing 80 percent between 1930 and 1934 (the percentage dropped somewhat in later years).[18] In the big cities, there were Jewish law firms—Chicago's Levinson, Becker, Schwartz, and Frank, for example, in the 1920s—just as there were Jewish clubs and Jewish fraternities; but mixing Jew and Gentile in one firm was fairly uncommon. It was an unusual event when Louis Weiss went into partnership in 1923 with a Protestant, John F. Wharton, to create a firm which was deliberately made up of Jews and non-Jews.[19] Jews were overrepresented among solo practitioners and lawyers with "one-shot" clients.

Bad as they were to women and minorities, the professions were a shade more open than the general business world; after all, a lawyer can always practice on her own. A case in point is Sadie Tabbler Massell Alexander (1898–1989). She earned a Ph.D. from the Wharton School of the University of Pennsylvania, in 1921—apparently the first black woman in the United States to earn this degree. In the big world, she had two great strikes against her; and nobody was willing to give her a decent job. She turned to law as an alternative. In 1927 she became the first black woman to graduate from the University of Pennsylvania Law School, and the first black woman admitted to the Pennsylvania bar. She worked for the city of Philadelphia, as an assistant city solicitor, and then entered private practice with her husband.[20]

Legal Education

When the nineteenth century began, the young man who wanted to work as a lawyer (a woman lawyer was then unthinkable) learned the ropes as an apprentice: clerking in the office of some established lawyer. There were a few law schools in the early nineteenth century, but they were not much better, or more rigorous, than apprenticeship. The law schools that were attached to universities—Harvard was the earliest—were hardly different from free-standing law schools in this regard. Harvard, however, began a revolution in legal education from 1870 on, under the leadership of a new dean, Christopher Columbus

Langdell.[21] Langdell considered law a science, which had to be taught in a scientific way. The students were supposed to extract the principles of law from reading appellate cases. The most startling of his innovations was in fact the case method—teaching law not by lecture but by Socratic questions and answers. The students would study appellate cases, selected and collected in "case-books"; the questions and answers would be based on these cases. Langdell also invented (one might say) the law professor. The Harvard faculty had always consisted of distinguished lawyers and judges—men who had made their mark in the legal world. Joseph Story, for example, a justice of the United States Supreme Court, once taught law at Harvard on the side. Langdell rejected this notion, and began to hire young, bright men—men who had done nothing much at the bar, but who were good (he thought) at the Langdell method of teaching.

By the turn of the century, the Harvard method had made enormous progress; it had spread far beyond its original mother church in Cambridge, Massachusetts. In the early twentieth century the Harvard method became totally triumphant, sweeping aside all opposition, and destroying (as it were) everything in its path. The case method, for example, was introduced at Yale in 1903. Arthur Corbin and John W. Edgerton were the young Turks who brought in this alien method, but it was only "grudgingly accepted"; and the whole faculty had to approve each particular adoption of a casebook. This lasted until 1912, when the faculty decided that any professor could use "the case system of instruction" without getting general approval.[22]

In many schools the conversion to the Harvard method came about when some Harvard-trained missionary arrived, either as a faculty member or as dean. This occurred, for example, at Tulane in 1906.[23] The brand-new University of Chicago Law School imported Joseph Henry Beale, Jr., from Harvard to help create a school "on the model of the Harvard Law School," a school which would impart "pure law" to students by means of the case method.[24]

The American Bar Association, from a relatively early date, took an interest in law schools, their standards, their organization. The "Association of American Law Schools" was formed in 1900. Twenty-five schools signed on, and within a year there were thirty-two members, out of just over one hundred law schools. The aim was "the improvement of legal education in America"; and each member school paid $10 as annual dues.[25] The AALS, too, was concerned with standards. For membership, a school had to meet the association's prerequisites—on size of faculty, admission policy, and even number of books in the library. The AALS had something of an elite flavor; a resolution, adopted in 1912, declared that night law courses "inevitably" tend to "lower educational standards," although the association later softened somewhat on this issue (and the night law schools, not surprisingly, refused to go quietly out of business).[26]

The triumph of the Harvard method was also the triumph of the Harvard Law School, which claimed a kind of leadership in American legal education. It supplied, as we have seen, missionaries who went into the hinterlands to preach the One True Method. In 1925–1926, out of 605 law teachers who taught at AALS-member law schools, no fewer than 143, or 24 percent, were graduates of the Harvard Law School. In 1948 Harvard provided the same percentage, 375 out of 1553.[27]

What made the ins and outs of the Harvard method and its clones all the more important was the fact that the apprenticeship method was traveling the long dusty road to extinction. The main road, and soon the only road, to the bar went through the law schools. Law firms now had telephones, typewriters, and stenographers (mainly women); they had little need for young male gofers and clerks who hung around the office and picked up the business by osmosis. Morever, the apprentice system depended on a cosy world of close, interpersonal ties and relationships. It assumed a uniformity of background, habits, ways of thought. In the big cities, full of immigrants, diverse, heterogeneous, with growing clusters of ethnic lawyers, formal apprenticeship had no real place in the system. Informally, of course, it survived. Students fresh out of law school had to learn the ropes on the job—in firms, or government offices.

Nonetheless, it is fair to say that the burden of training shifted dramatically to law schools. At the turn of the century, there were some thirteen thousand students studying law in law schools—the number had more than doubled in ten years. The largest law school in 1901–2, the University of Michigan Law School, had 854 students; Harvard, in third place, had 632.[28] In 1870 only one out of four of those admitted to the bar had gone to law school; by 1910, two-thirds were law school graduates.[29] In New York 18 percent of those who applied for the bar in 1900 had no law school training; in 1922, out of 643 who were taking the New York state bar examination for the first time, only nine lacked this training.[30]

Moreover, big business needed, and demanded, a corps of sophisticated lawyers. Law schools were considered a more efficient way of meeting the demand than clerkship. After all, a hundred students could be crammed into a classroom, fed the same material, put through the same process. Arguably, too, they got a better (if less practical) education. The Socratic method, as practiced in Harvard and its satellite schools, was supposed to produce a finely honed legal mind. Whether it did this or not is another question. Not everybody believed, as C. C. Langdell did, that law was a "science," and that learning the principles of law was training in the principles of legal science. The concept of "legal science" was complex and hard to pin down, and it came in various versions.[31] In any event, Langdell's formulation did not dominate legal thought very long. The faith in "legal science" ebbed in the twentieth century. But oddly enough, Langdell's methods, the pedagogical techniques, and the way the curriculum got organized, survived him—in fact, these got stronger and stronger, and spread from school to school. What happened was simply this: Langdell's system was repackaged as a superior kind of skills training; whether or not there was a science of law, the method taught the student how to "think like a lawyer." This meant mastering the law school brand of mental acrobatics, along with the fine art of argument—on both sides of an issue, if necessary.

Law schools continued to breed like rabbits. Many of the new schools were part-time and offered night classes. Day schools increased from fifty-one to seventy-nine between 1890 and 1910; night schools, however, grew faster in the same period, from ten to forty-five.[32] These schools were concentrated in the cities, and they produced a high proportion of the urban lawyers. There were also "mixed" law schools, which allowed students to choose day or night. Indeed, there were schools that had three options: Fordham, for example, had a morning, afternoon and evening division. In 1926 there were 388 morning students, 386 in the afternoon division, and 680 night students.[33] These evening and part-time schools supplied the ranks of Greek lawyers, Jewish lawyers, Irish and Italian lawyers, and other lawyers who took care of clients in immigrant communities; they turned out neighborhood lawyers, mostly generalists, along with lawyers who specialized in certain claims—personal injuries, for example. Ultimately, their graduates did well in local politics, and became judges, mayors, and aldermen. The alumni of these schools did not scale the heights of Wall Street. But they were important people of bench, bar, and city hall.

Bar organizations, and leading lights in the profession, distrusted the night schools and the lawyers they turned out. The upper-crust lawyers worried about the prestige of their profession—and they worried about money, too. They saw a profound threat in the rising numbers of lawyers. One solution to the problem was to raise standards: to require some college work before law school. John Henry Wigmore, dean of Northwestern, felt strongly on the subject: the bar, he wrote in 1915, was "overcrowded with incompetent, shiftless, ill-fitted lawyers, who degrade the methods of the law and cheapen the quality of services by unlimited competition." He thought their numbers "should be reduced by one-half." Wigmore wanted to require two years of college—this would help get rid of the "spawning mass of promiscuous semi-intelligence which now enters the bar."[34]

The night schools, of course, survived; they filled a need, and they had their defenders. One of the most vigorous was Edward T. Lee, of the John Marshall Law School in Chicago. John Marshall was an upstart, founded in 1899 and unconnected to a university. Lee, as dean, was outspoken in defense of his school—and in his opposition to the case method. In 1929 Lee lit into the ABA and the AALS, the legal education establishment; he called them "educational racketeers" because of their passion for the case method. Lee refused to hire anybody to teach at his school who had less than five years of experience in practice. He rejected those who came "fresh from a law school."[35] He also spoke out against the requirement of two years of college; this was "stacking the cards and loading the dice" against the "people who are not favored by wealth and opportunity."[36]

His night students, he admitted, were not, as a class, "as well prepared intellectually for the law as day students"; but they made up for this lack through "pluck, energy, perseverance, and enthusiasm." The night schools made sure that America was a land of "opportunity"; in the night schools there were "Christians and Jews, white and black, and yellow." Thus the night schools helped to "leaven the undigested classes"—they were part of the melting pot. But above all, Lee pointed out, they kept the doors open for "hundreds of worthy young men" who had to earn their daily bread, and thus could not be full-time students by day.[37]

In some ways, Lee took a patronizing attitude toward his own students—and his "humble" and "local" school. It was, he said, not in the business of training geniuses. It was training what he called "mechanics of the law." The man "who paints your house does not need to know anything about the paintings of Raphael and Michelangelo at all"; all he needs to do is a "good, artistic job on your house."[38]

In spite of Lee, standards of admission to law school, at least in the day schools, kept ratcheting upward. In 1896 Harvard had decided that only college graduates were to be admitted to its holy ground. In 1915 the University of Pennsylvania became the second law school to make college education a prerequisite; Pittsburgh followed at the beginning of the 1920s. The American Bar Association recommended that law schools require some college work. By 1920 many schools were following this advice—they required three years (University of Chicago), or (more commonly) two or one year of college.[39] Gradually, other schools fell into line. The University of Buffalo Law School, for example, decided to admit nobody after the entering class of 1925 who did not have a year of college; and after 1927, two years.[40] Eventually, all schools—including John Marshall and the other night and part-time schools—came to require a college education.

If it was harder to get into law school, and harder to get out, it was also harder to become a full-fledged member of the bar. The profession itself—certainly the top layer of it—was eager to tighten standards. Wigmore was not the only one who thought the bar was overcrowded. It was a common complaint—Herbert Harley, secretary of the American Judicature Society, wrote in 1914 that there "are too many lawyers by far." One of the problems, Harley said, was "easy admission." This made the profession "topsy-turvy. There is a survival of the fittest but the specifications of fitness are wrong." A crowded bar "puts a premium on sharp practices."[41] This lament was, of course, no different from the lament of many other professions and occupations; they all liked the idea of cutting down on numbers, in the interests of getting a good return on their investment in education and preparation. There was also the notion that certain good old days were gone, and the bar was filling up with immigrant riffraff.

In the nineteenth century, in many states, the "bar examination" was fairly perfunctory. The young lawyer-to-be hunted up a friendly judge and answered a few questions. In some cases—Indiana was a notorious example—there were no bar examinations at all. The Indiana Constitution provided, from 1851 on, that "every person of good moral character being a voter, shall be entitled to admission to practice law in all courts of justice" (Art. 7, §21). Toward the end of the century a few states began to set up central boards of examiners, and require written exams. By 1917 there were central boards of bar examiners in thirty-seven jurisdictions.[42] The lawyers of Indiana mounted a series of campaigns to repeal the obnoxious provision which seemed to give anybody at all the right to practice law. They succeeded (after several tries) in 1932. The bar examinations varied from state to state—some were more professional than others; some were tough, and some were easy. In Kansas, every single candidate (of fifty-three) passed the bar in 1904; 97 percent in 1922, 88 percent in 1933; but in some other states, particularly in the 1920s, half or fewer of the candidates passed. Industrial states with big immigrant populations were tougher than small, rural states. External events had an influence as well: in California in 1932, in the depths of the Depression, the pass rate dropped from just over half (for first-time takers), to about a third. This was obviously a kind of "quota," though bar examiners rarely admitted that this is what they were doing.[43]

The American Bar Association also launched an attack on the so-called diploma privilege. A school had the diploma privilege if its graduates were automatically members of the bar, without the further fuss of a bar exam. The legal elites were all in favor of stopping the flood of lawyers and law schools; and the diploma privilege encouraged the founding of new law schools. It would be most unfortunate, said Herbert Goodrich, dean of the University of Pennsylvania Law School and president of the Association of American Law Schools, speaking in 1931, if "any Tom, Dick or Harry . . . could start a law school and grind out graduates who would forthwith be admitted to the practice of law."[44] At one time, the diploma privilege was common—sixteen states granted it in 1890—but, because of opposition from elements in the bar, it had tougher going in the twentieth century. Michigan, for example, ended it in 1913, at the request of the faculty of the University of Michigan. Minnesota and California got rid of it in 1917; and by 1938, it was down to eleven states (though later it had something of a revival).[45]

Organization of the Bar

The bar association movement was born in the 1870s. Machine politics corrupted city government (in New York very notably); and dirty politics tarnished the good name of lawyers and judges (such as it was). The American Bar Association began as a kind of club of respectable lawyers—definitely not as a mass professional organization. It was concerned with the honor and prestige of the profession. In the early years of the new century, a committee of the Bar Association called for a code of ethics. The code was sorely needed, because the bar had departed from its "pristine glory." The code would "provide a beacon light on the mountain of high resolve."[46] The bar adopted the proposed code, the Canons of Professional Ethics, at a meeting in Seattle, Washington, in 1908.

The preamble to the canons recited that the "future of the Republic . . . depends upon our maintenance of Justice pure and unsullied." It would be hard to argue with many, or most, of the canons: lawyers should avoid conflicts of interest; they should represent their clients "with undivided fidelity" and keep the client's secrets; they should never "commingle" the client's money with their own; they should not overcharge; they should use their "best efforts to restrain and to prevent" clients "from doing those things which the lawyer himself ought not to do"; they should be "punctual" with regard to clients and act with "candor and fairness" to courts and lawyers.

But the canons also reflected the needs and desires of the top layer of lawyers. The code was couched in terms that suited that segment of the bar. For example, canon 27 forbade "circulars or advertisements"; or getting business "by indirection through touters of any kind"; it even banned indirect advertisement "by furnishing or inspiring newspaper comments concerning causes in which the lawyer has been or is engaged." Behavior that would "defy the traditions and lower the tone of our high calling" was "intolerable." A lawyer's "most worthy and effective advertisement" was his "reputation for professional capacity and fidelity to trust." Wall Street lawyers, of course, did not need to advertise. Young ethnic lawyers, with one-shot clients (victims, say, of streetcar accidents) had to scramble for a living; for them, advertising would have been useful—but the code of lawyerly ethics ruled it out.

The canons also tried to canonize monopoly control over all the activities where a nonlawyer *might* compete. The bar fought against "unauthorized practice"; it did not allow lawyers to enter into partnerships with nonlawyers; and, like monopolists everywhere, it engaged in a bit of genteel price-fixing through local fee schedules.[47] Lawyers, according to canon 12, were to "avoid charges which overestimate their advice and services," but also those which "undervalue" them. (They could lower fees for poor people, however, and "reasonable requests of brother lawyers, and of their widows and orphans without ample means," were to "receive special and kindly consideration.") The canons also cast a beady eye on the contingent fee. This practice was used mostly by personal injury lawyers. The lawyer agreed to take a cut of the winnings rather than charge an hourly fee. There was no other way a working-man, hit by a streetcar, or battered on the job, could afford a lawyer. Wall Street never used the contingent fee. The canons did not ban such fees, but insisted that they had to be "under the supervision of the Court," to protect clients from "unjust charges" (canon 13).[48]

The American Bar Association, after all, was an elite body. Only a minority of the bar joined (or were allowed to join); only 3 percent of American lawyers belonged to the ABA in 1910, 9 percent in 1920, 17 percent in 1930. There were state and local bars, but they were hardly more inclusive. For example, only about 10 percent of California's lawyers were members of the California Bar Association in 1917.[49]

The bar association movement had been, in origin, a reform movement. Now that it had retreated into a stubborn, insular elitism, some progressive lawyers advanced another idea: integrate the bar—that is, create a single state association, which all lawyers had to join. This "integrated" bar could police the profession, and lobby for reforms. A leading advocate was Herbert Harley, founder (in 1913) of the American Judicature Society. North Dakota (1921) was the first state to break the ice and integrate, followed by Alabama (1923), Idaho (1923), and New Mexico (1925). The big states, for the time being at least, said no.[50]

The American Bar Association was not only elite, it was also lily-white. In 1912 the executive committee of the American Bar Association admitted three black lawyers, not realizing what it had done. When it discovered that these three lawyers were in fact black, the executive committee, horrified, passed a resolution canceling their admission, and sent the matter to the whole associa-tion. There the question was vigorously debated, and in the end, a compromise was reached: these three could remain, but on future applications any prospec-tive member had to reveal his race. For decades to come, the ABA was racially "pure."[51] Black lawyers, meanwhile, organized on their own: a Cook County group was established as early as 1914. The National Bar Association, founded by twelve black lawyers, came into existence in 1925.

The ABA did not admit women, either, until 1918; and the Association of the Bar of the City of New York waited until 1937 before opening its doors.[52] In general, the ABCNY in the 1920s still kept its restrictive philosophy—it was a club of elites, not a big professional umbrella; its membership then and for years afterward consisted largely of Protestant, big-firm lawyers. Jews, the Irish, and the Italians were seriously underrepresented.[53] Elite lawyers as a group were probably no worse than the rest of the country in the various degrees and shades of prejudice; but they were certainly no better.

Court Structure and Jurisdiction

The Supreme Court is, and always has been, the most famous court of the country—supremely august. It is also, as of 2001, a very hard court to get to. Thousands of litigants try to scale these heights, but only a few each year succeed. The Court picks and chooses among all these potential cases; it only takes cases it wants to take—cases it considers of paramount importance, for whatever reason. A hundred years ago, the Supreme Court was already the apex of the judicial system. Yet someone who leafed through reports of its decisions would be surprised to see many rather ordinary, run-of-the-mill cases. In 1909, for example, the Court decided a case, out of the Territory of Oklahoma, about a boy who was injured at a railroad depot; a stockholders' suit against an insurance company; a case from the District of Columbia on a government contract to build a filtration plant; and a number of fairly routine bankruptcy cases.[54] These cases were "federal" because they involved citizens of different states, or came out of the territories or the District of Columbia. The Court in 2000 would not touch such cases with a ten-foot pole.

There were many attempts to reform the jurisdiction of the Supreme Court—to cut down its workload, in essence; and to allow it to control the size and the reach of its docket.[55] The situation was improved in 1916, when Congress passed a law which, among other things, gave the Court the power to refuse to hear employer liability cases.[56] But the major change came with passage of an act of Congress in 1925.[57] This law gave the Supreme Court far more wiggle-room than ever before, far more power to decide what it would and would not hear. The effect on the Court was dramatic. In 1924 the Supreme Court handled 271 cases which it had had to take, and 78 over which it had discretion.[58] By 1929 the Court was deciding fewer cases (219 for the 1929–30 term); and these were evenly split between the "obligatory" and the "discretionary."[59]

On the state level, structural reforms were also necessary. Each state, of course, had its own system of courts; probably no two were exactly the same. Typically, there was a court for petty matters—the basement of the system, as it were—a trial court for ordinary cases, and, at the top, a supreme court to hear appeals. In states with small populations, whoever lost at the trial court level could appeal directly to the state supreme court. The highest court of, say, Vermont or Idaho, could easily handle the traffic. But courts in states with growing populations began to find the situation almost intolerable: too many cases for the high court to dispose of. One solution was to add extra judges—to make the court bigger, and perhaps split it into separate panels. Another was to add "commissioners" (auxiliary judges) to help out with the caseload. Still a third was to develop a system which had three tiers above the petty court level— a system like that of the federal courts. That is, these states added a layer of intermediate courts, as a buffer between the trial courts and the state supreme court. This intermediate court would allow any litigant an appeal; but only special cases would go all the way up to the top.

All these solutions were already in use, in some states, in the nineteenth century. In the twentieth century, more states began to experiment with structural change, out of sheer necessity. Florida, for example, amended its constitution in 1902 to double the size of its court. Now there would be six justices, not three; and they could divide themselves into two groups of three.[60] The legislature of California in 1903 proposed a constitutional amendment (which succeeded), introducing a system of intermediate appellate courts. The booming economy and the growing population made the existing system "inadequate."[61] This reform gave the Supreme Court of California power to control most of its swollen docket; the appellate courts would be, for most litigants, the end of the line.

3

The Law of
Business and Commerce

According to that great president Calvin Coolidge, the chief business of America is business. That may or may not be true; but the chief business of *law* is certainly business. Murder, divorce, and race relations may be sexier subjects; from the media, the public gets infinite quantities of information or misinformation about criminal justice; but the workaday law is largely hidden from view. The lawyer's daily routine is basically about mundane things, and chiefly about doing business—about buying and selling; about real estate; about organizing and running partnerships and corporations; about stocks and bonds; in short, about commerce, money, trade, finance, corporations and partnerships—the economic bones and stays of business life.

This had been the case throughout the nineteenth century, and continued to be so throughout the twentieth as well. But the economy had been transformed in the nineteenth century. At the start of the century, most Americans lived on farms. At the end, they lived in cities; and they worked not on farms but in factories, mines, department stores, and shops. In 1900, out of some twenty-nine million people at work, less than a quarter were farmers; their numbers were dwarfed by those who made a living apart from the farm.[1] The trend would only continue and grow stronger.

The basic farm unit was the family farm; there were, of course, big farms and little farms. But certainly nobody in 1900 owned a chain of farms, or multistate farms, or a dominant share of the wheat, corn, or hog business. Industry was another matter. More and more, it was *big* business that dominated the economy. The scale of enterprise had been growing steadily. Mergers and consolidations were sweeping the country. In the 1880s and 1890s, in particular, there was a huge increase in these mergers—reaching a kind of climax just before the turn of the century. Big fish swallowed up little fish. Small, local railroads had become giant railroad nets. Monster combinations, like Standard Oil and United States Steel, spread their tentacles throughout the country. Bigness was a fact—and more and more, an issue—in economic life. By the beginning of the twentieth century, many of the country's great industries were dominated by a few huge firms: in food, tobacco, electrical machinery, and primary metals.[2]

In some ways, in the previous chapter, when we talked about high courts and big constitutional cases, we were putting the cart before the horse. The states enacted thousands of laws, the cities enacted thousands of ordinances, year in and year out. Many of these—most of these—were about business and doing business. Only a tiny percentage ever ended up before the Supreme Court—or any court. What the Supreme Court reacted to, in the great cases that made headlines, was only a tiny part of a vast mass of legal matter. This consisted, for the most part, of cases arising under laws that were controversial from the start. These were regulatory laws, laws to tame, control, or (sometimes) support how business did business, how labor labored, and the like. Business-related laws were the staples of legislative life. Moreover, business disputes and claims were the bread and butter of most American lawyers. Most claims and disputes never got past a lawyer's office—or the offices of two lawyers. A small fraction went to court.

This does not mean that court law was insignificant. Some was; some was not. Lawyers gave advice with "the law" in the background—encoded inside their heads. They negotiated with each other in the light of the way they expected courts to react. Court law, in other words, was often living law, in the sense that it affected (in the end) the way businessmen behaved. But often, too, it was irrelevant. How, and why, court law turns into living law—or becomes irrelevant—reflects a subtle process, and one we know very little about.

One Law Out of Many

"Business," of course, was not a monolith. There was big business and little business and in-between business; there were grocery stores and steel mills and coal mines and haberdasheries. The *scale* of business, however, was changing. Technology was turning a cluster of individual states into a single economic unit—a gigantic free-trade area. The national scale of business life was a fact of the twentieth century, a fact which, as the century went on, became more and more significant. Already, in the nineteenth century, the railroad, the telegraph, and the telephone were powerful forces unifying the economy. Now came the automobile, airplanes, radio, TV, and, toward the end of the century, the internet.

A lot of legal activity, in commercial law and in corporation law, reflected the way business was growing and spilling over borders. The United States had become one big economy; but it was not one big legal system. Each state was "sovereign," which meant that it had its own set of laws. There were as many different laws about the sale of goods, negotiable instruments (checks, promissory notes, bills of exchange), installment sales, and the like, as there were states (ultimately fifty versions, plus the District of Columbia, Guam, the Virgin Islands, and Puerto Rico). These laws were, on the whole, not *that* different. They certainly had a family resemblance. But a lawyer cannot give advice on the basis of approximations; she has to get things exactly right. And a company trying to sell its gadgets everywhere from Maine to California finds it awkward if method A and form B are legal here and illegal there; and method C and form D are valid here, invalid there.

The trouble was not just lack of uniformity. There was, often enough, a deeper lack. Judges were probably on the whole eager to do the right thing, and to encourage good business practices. But they were lawyers, not merchants; how could they have that kind of delicate intuition, that fingertip-sense, that leads to sensible results (sensible, that is, from the standpoint of business people)? Business was supple, inventive, and changing fast. Businesses looked for nooks and niches in the market; and also for clever new ways to do what it, and the market, wanted to do. The law was supple, too; but perhaps not supple enough for everybody's tastes. Some of its rules and technicalities seemed archaic—some had simply outlived their usefulness. Courts were likely to pull up these weeds; but perhaps not immediately, and, in the jumble of fifty states, there would always be a few states that marched to the wrong drummer or to the tune of an off-key trumpet. Statutes—well drafted, technically correct, non-legalistic—seemed the best way out.

The "uniform laws" movement was an attempt to impose some kind of order on a ragged and disorderly system. In 1889 the American Bar Association appointed a committee to produce some ideas about uniformity. The committee came up with a plan. Each state would appoint a commissioner; and the commissioners would meet, confer, discuss, and propose uniform laws. In 1892 the commissioners held their first annual conference. By 1912 every state had appointed a commissioner.

The first product of the Commissioners on Uniform State Laws was a Negotiable Instruments Law, drafted in 1896. It was based on a British model; and it was extremely successful: every state had adopted it by 1916. Next came a Uniform Sales Act. The commissioners asked Samuel Williston of the Harvard Law School to draft a sales act in 1902. He labored away and produced a draft; this was also roughly based on a British model, the Sale of Goods Act (1893); in 1906 the Uniform Sales Act was launched.[3] This too was extremely successful. Some states adopted it almost immediately, and more than thirty had it on their books by the 1940s.[4] It was followed by a Uniform Warehouse Receipts Act (1906), a Uniform Bill of Ladings Act (1909), a Uniform Conditional Sales Act (1918), and a Uniform Trust Receipts Act (1933). A federal Bill of Ladings Act was passed in 1916.[5] Some of these acts were more successful in getting themselves adopted than others; none of them covered the whole of the country, though the Warehouse Receipts Act had a total of forty-five adoptions by 1922. The Bill of Ladings Act had twenty-four adoptions, but only seven states saw fit to enact the Uniform Conditional Sales Act during this period. Whether uniform texts led to uniform interpretations is another question. Certainly, there was no way to force courts to read the statutes the same way. But these laws did smooth out some of the bumps and obstacles that stood in the way of a national law of commerce.

A case in point is the Uniform Trust Receipts Act (1933).[6] Banks used these documents ("trust receipts") to finance businesses which were importing goods from abroad. Then, in the automobile business, finance companies began to use them to help dealers pay for cars. One story has it that that "crotchety individualist" Henry Ford was at the root of the problem; he insisted "that all cars be paid for in full and in cash before they left the factory" for the dealer's showroom. Where would the dealers get the money? The trust receipt was the answer. The cars would move to the dealer, but the dealer would never actually own the cars—title would pass from the manufacturer to the finance company, which paid for the cars; and then, in the end, to the men and women who actually bought the car. The finance company would have a security interest, first in the car, then in the money which John or Jane paid over.

This seems straightforward enough. But there were all sorts of problems fitting this arrangement into the standard doctrines of commercial law— problems which the courts wrestled with, sometimes to the satisfaction of the finance companies, sometimes not. The trust receipts act was drafted to deal with the issues these cases raised; and, in short, to standardize and validate the trust receipt practices of the companies. Finance companies, banks, and commercial lawyers were the brains and the brawn behind this, of course, and behind the uniform laws in general. The average citizen, and even the average businessman, knew very little about these laws; and whatever squabbling went on was, as it were, within the family.

Belly-Up: The Law of Bankruptcy

Business floated on a sea of credit. Commercial law was, in large part, law about credit: about lending and borrowing, and about security, collateral, and safety for lenders. Sellers searched for ways to protect their interests in hard goods— cars, pianos, sewing machines, tractors—sold "on time," and for credit. They needed to find some legal ropes and bands to tie these goods down until all the money was paid. They looked for similar devices for goods that moved from factories to wholesalers to retailers to members of the public. Virtually all of the uniform laws addressed one aspect or another of this problem. The ropes had to be tight enough to protect the lender; but not so tight as to stifle sales or hurt the economy. Lenders and borrowers were locked together in a relationship that was supposed to be for their mutual benefit—something like the idea of a marriage. But not all marriages work, and neither do relationships of credit. Debtors sometimes cannot or will not pay. When this happens, they may (and often do) leave the normal world of business dealings, and enter into that circle of commercial hell called bankruptcy.

The federal Constitution gave Congress the power to enact a bankruptcy law. But for most of the nineteenth century, Congress did not take up the challenge. There was no long-term federal bankruptcy law; a few laws were passed, but they died quick deaths. Most of the action—partial, unsatisfactory, and very nonuniform—was in the states. In 1898, however, Congress finally passed a bankruptcy law which turned out to have staying power. It survives to this day (much amended, to be sure). At last, there was a national system, run by the federal courts, and (in theory) uniform throughout the country.

The 1898 act provided both for voluntary and involuntary bankruptcy. A debtor could jump into bankruptcy himself, or be dragged into it by his creditors. "Referees" had the main job of administering the law. A referee served for a two-year term. From the very outset, business was brisk: for the year ending September 30, 1904, the federal courts received 13,784 petitions in bankruptcy.[7]

The law of bankruptcy was, and is, arcane, highly technical—a specialty of its own. But the social meaning of bankruptcy changes over the years. At one time, of course, debtors could be sent to debtors' prison; and bankruptcy carried a heavy load of stigma. But a society that encourages risk-taking, and rewards entrepreneurs, must also give the risk taker a chance to fail honorably, and the right to start all over again. Second chances are essential to this kind of society; they are a kind of safety net for businesses (and wage earners, for that matter). They make risk-taking, as it were, less risky. If you put a net under a tightrope, you will get more people who are willing to try to walk it than if you take the net away.

This was one major job of bankruptcy laws: giving debtors a second chance. It had other jobs. One of the main ones was fairness to creditors. Bankruptcy law avoided, or tried to avoid, an unseemly rush by creditors to pick flesh from the dying bones of a business. The law established which debts had to be paid first, which ones next, which ones last; and tried to apportion the carcass among the creditors in as fair a way as possible.

Debt and bankruptcy are part of normal business life. But there are also abnormal times. Debt was of course a major issue during the Great Depression. As the economy spiraled downward, it carried with it hundreds of businesses, big, medium, and small. Banks failed by the dozens. This was hard on people who had trusted the bank with their money. Bankruptcy was a growth business in the 1930s.

Railroads were part of the financial disaster of the thirties. Still, it is one thing for a corner grocery to go out of business; it is another thing entirely for a railroad to fail. Since the mid-nineteenth century, railroads could be put into "receivership," a zombielike state of suspended animation, in which the corporation as such was neither dead nor alive. The trains kept running; meanwhile, the body of the old organization—the railroad corporation—was reorganized and reincarnated, often under new ownership. The federal courts, sitting as courts of equity, handled these receiverships. The Railroad Reorganization Act of 1933 was an attempt to streamline and modernize the ways and procedures for reorganizing railroads.[8] It did not do away with the old procedure, but it offered an alternative—reorganization under the aegis of the bankruptcy courts.[9]

The Law of Corporations

The age of big business is the age of the corporation. A bakery or a rooming house can organize as a "sole proprietorship"; a bunch of lawyers can form a partnership; but big business is typically a corporation, with shares of stock, a board of directors, and limited liability. The modern business corporation was, essentially, a product of the nineteenth century.[10] In the twentieth century, it was clearly the dominant form of business association. In 1916 there were no fewer than 341,000 corporations in the country; and they accounted for the vast bulk of the goods that the country produced.[11] Corporations were chartered state by state—there was no federal corporation law. Each state had a general law of corporations, which applied to every business; and special laws for special kinds of corporations. Thus Florida, as of 1920, had a separate code or separate provisions for banking corporations, building and loan associations, insurance companies, surety companies, express companies, railroad and canal companies, and telegraph and telephone companies. There were also provisions in Florida law for not-for-profit corporations.

The general corporation laws were of course the most important; but what impact they had on the actual operation of businesses is another question. In this country, with its federal system, a business can incorporate in one state and do business somewhere else (or everywhere else). Since the late nineteenth century, there had been a kind of race to the bottom, as states tried to lure companies to choose their state to be chartered in. They offered lower taxes, or lax and more lax laws. New Jersey was one of these luring states. In the last decade of the nineteenth century, New Jersey enacted laws which made its corporate climate flexible and inviting. New Jersey also permitted holding companies—any corporation could buy and hold the securities of any other corporation. Its merger laws were extremely permissive as well.[12]

New Jersey soon faced a formidable rival—little Delaware, which copied New Jersey's laws, and threw in lower fees and taxes as a sweetener, in 1899.

Ultimately, Delaware won the race. In 1913, under Governor Woodrow Wilson, the New Jersey legislature enacted a group of antitrust and regulatory laws that were known as the Seven Sisters. These laws did not last very long; but they seemed severe, and so they helped tip the scales toward Delaware. In any event, Delaware was a small state; it really needed the corporate fees. It was therefore more reliable than a bigger, more industrial, more heterogeneous state like New Jersey. In 1899 corporate revenues made up less than 10 percent of Delaware's pitiful state budget of half a million dollars. In 1920 Delaware earned a million and a half dollars from corporation fees and franchise taxes—almost a third of the state's budget of $4,700,000.[13]

The race to the bottom was not confined to these two states. Indeed, some important innovations started elsewhere. For example, New York in 1912 passed a law which allowed corporations to issue "no par" stock. Shares of stock typically had "par values," say, $100, which meant that the buyer was supposed to pay this amount for each share. "No par" stock lacked any par value. This gave the managers much more flexibility; they "now had discretion to raise or lower the sales price of corporate shares."[14] Stock could also be issued in exchange for property or services, which gave the managers and promoters ample opportunity to "water" the stock—that is, sell it to favored buyers at bargain prices.

But Delaware still managed to meet and beat the competition. It passed consistently permissive laws—laws which let corporations do, essentially, whatever they wanted. And it copied when it had to: it permitted no-par stock, for example, in 1917.[15] And Delaware made *its* statute more attractive to promoters and organizers.

All of this bottom-racing did not, of course, go unnoticed. There were critics who felt that Delaware was letting corporations get away with (rather vaguely defined) murder. What was the solution? One suggestion was to get rid of the state charter system and enact a federal incorporation law. Presidents Theodore Roosevelt and William Howard Taft proposed such a law, and between 1900 and the outbreak of the First World War many bills to this end were introduced into Congress. But the state charter system was too deeply entrenched, and had strong support from business; nothing came of these attempts at national legislation.[16] Corporations continued to fly state flags of convenience, and to shop around for the most convenient, hospitable forum. Increasingly, of course, that meant Delaware. Of some six hundred companies traded in 1932 on the New York Stock Exchange, 34 percent were incorporated in little Delaware.[17]

Corporation law, then, was practically speaking the law of a few flagship states—notably Delaware. But it is probably wrong to look on this development entirely as a pathology of a federal system. The corporation by 1900 was obviously here to stay; and the idea of restricting or regulating corporations as such had come to seem archaic or even ridiculous. In the twentieth century, as Willard Hurst put it, "both state and federal law . . . in effect accepted corporations in such sizes and shapes as businessmen could develop them."[18] The corporation was a business form that was thrown open to anybody who wanted to use it, without much fuss or red tape. So, for example, under the Illinois General Corporation Act of 1919, a corporation could be organized "for any lawful purpose"; and starting a corporation was simplicity itself: any three people could act as incorporators, filling out a rather cut-and-dried form and filing it with the secretary of state.[19]

Corporation law, then, turned its attention to the internal affairs of corporations. How should corporations be run? What were the rights of minority stockholders? What were the duties of directors, promoters, officers? The case law of corporations came out of litigation on these issues. Generally speaking, the courts cut a great deal of slack for the managers of companies; rarely did they interfere with the business judgment of directors and officers. On the other hand, directors and officers were "fiduciaries"; they had a duty to act on behalf of the corporation and its shareholders. They were not entitled to profit personally from the job (except for big salaries, of course), and, under the "corporate opportunity doctrine," if an "opportunity" came along that would have benefited the company, they would not be allowed to grab it for their own private gain. So in the famous case of *Guth v. Loft* (1939), Guth, who controlled Loft (basically a candy and syrup company), became angry with the Coca-Cola Company and decided to switch to Pepsi-Cola to fill Loft's needs for soft drinks.[20] Pepsi-Cola, as it happens, had gone bankrupt during the Depression. Guth essentially bought it out, made it a going concern, and got rich in the process. But the money, said the Delaware court, should have gone to Loft: corporate managers "are not permitted to use their position of trust and confidence to further their private interests."

State corporation laws, then, essentially let corporations alone, except for abuses of this type. The states, instead, regulated specific businesses—railroads, or insurance companies, or food manufacturers—rather than corporations in general. The railroads were a particularly rich field for legislation. Railroads were vital to the economy; they were also powerful, dangerous, sometimes spectacularly or wildly mismanaged, and, after the initial boom period, deeply controversial. Federal regulation took off in 1887, with the passage of the Interstate Commerce Act.[21] This major statute created an Interstate Commerce Commission. The point was to control the railroads, to force them to charge just and reasonable rates and treat all customers equally, without kickbacks and preferences to pet (or large) shippers.

The ICC and its act had a stormy history.[22] The act itself was a response to the anger and fear of farmers and small merchants, who felt themselves crushed by the octopus—the mighty railroad nets. But the octopus itself had considerable political muscle; and some of the commissioners, and some of the courts, were more pro-octopus than the smaller shippers would have liked. Railroad regulation was still a controversial subject in the early twentieth century. There were strong forces on both sides. The Elkins Act, passed by Congress in 1903, took its popular name from Senator Stephen Elkins, a close ally of the Pennsylvania Railroad.[23] The Elkins Act made it illegal to offer rebates to customers, and imposed fines on companies that offered rebates, and on customers who took the offers. It was generally felt that the act was hard to enforce, and that it made little difference in practice.[24]

More significant was the Hepburn Act (1906).[25] Theodore Roosevelt had asked Congress in 1904 to give the ICC the power to set maximum rates. In 1906 Congress gave him what he asked for, essentially. The statute also empowered the ICC to appoint examiners and agents, and to oversee the railroads' accounting practices. The ICC was also given jurisdiction over express companies, sleeping-car companies, and oil pipelines. There were now to be seven rather than five commissioners, and their pay was increased. The number of formal complaints raced upward: in 1905 only 65 were filed with the ICC, but in 1908 there were 554, then 1,097 in 1909; informal complaints (there were only 503 of these in 1905) rose to 4,435 in 1909.[26]

The Mann-Elkins Act (1910) was the third in this series of laws aimed at giving the ICC more muscle. It gave the ICC control of telegraph, telephone, and cable companies. The commission now also had authority to suspend proposed increases in rates, and to examine whether proposed rates were reasonable or not. As Bruce Wyman put it, writing in 1915, the railroads and other utilities were too strong for the country's good; they had natural monopolies; and in a monopoly situation regulation is absolutely necessary; otherwise, "we may drift into a position where we may be forced into public ownership and operation," a drastic step with "unknowable consequences." For this reason, advocates of state regulation "are really the conservatives."[27]

The Mann-Elkins Act also resurrected the so-called long- and short-haul clause of the ICC. That clause made it unlawful for a railroad to charge passengers or freight more "for a shorter than a longer distance over the same line, in the same direction, the shorter being included within the longer distance"—a practice very familiar to people at the beginning of the twenty-first century who fly anywhere on the airlines. Railroads running between New York and Chicago, say, were not supposed to charge more to ship goods from New York or Chicago to some small town in Ohio, halfway in between, than for the "long" haul, that is, New York to Chicago. But the courts had made a hash of this clause. They allowed this kind of discrimination, if necessary to meet competition. Because many railroads served Chicago, and only one probably served the little town in Ohio, the lower long-haul fares were easy to justify.

The railroads had insisted all along, and successfully, that it was wrong to think the fare to the small town in Ohio was high: rather, the fare from New York to Chicago was low, and this was because the railroads had to compete with each other, or with carriers who shipped by water. The whole thing was simply the magical market at work. But the losers—the merchants and shippers in the town in Ohio, for example, and others like them—were not willing to bow to the almighty market; and they had a good deal of political strength in the aggregate. Under Mann-Elkins, the discrimination at the heart of the long- and short-haul clause was allowed only "in special cases," and only if the ICC, after "investigation," approved.[28]

Antitrust Law and Policy

There was important legislation on the subject of the "trusts" (monopolies and restraints of trade) in the late nineteenth century. The Sherman Antitrust Act (1890) was a landmark law. The Sherman Act, which outlawed "monopolies," and "contracts in restraint of trade," was passed by Congress in an atmosphere of near hysteria.[29] What touched off the debate was the formation of giant businesses, like Rockefeller's Standard Oil, which gobbled up all rivals and were thus able to put a knife to the throat of consumers and small businesses.

The Sherman Act was directed at economic *power;* there was no clear economic theory behind it. Classical theory, like Darwin's theory of natural selection, exalted the market—competition would inevitably bring about lower prices and better products. Companies that were inefficient would simply die a natural death. But this comfortable theory did not fit one situation: that is, where a company became *so* efficient (or ruthless), that it drove everyone else out of the market. At that point, as Herbert Hovenkamp has pointed out, the "theory fell apart, and competitive evolution stopped dead."[30] Market theory, in other words, had been framed in an era in which most businesses were small, local, and intensely competitive. Now the top businesses were big—huge—gigantic; and their tentacles spread over the whole country. It was not just a question of economic efficiency, or higher prices for consumers; it was also the sense of threat, the danger to small business people, to the little shop on the corner. The trust crisis was a culture crisis as much as it was a crisis in prices and business.

Since the passage of the Sherman Act, antitrust law and policy had mostly been made in the courts. Unlike other major regulatory statutes, the Sherman Act was short, gnomic, terse—a page and a half of text. It never defined its key terms. It set up no administrative agency with power to issue rules and regulations. Its meaning, therefore, had to be hammered out in the course of enforcement. Interpretation (by federal courts) was all. Early cases seemed narrow, crabbed, designed to clip the wings of the Sherman Act. And federal enforcement was weak and vacillating.[31]

The Northern Securities case (1904) was an important decision, and a major turning point.[32] The case involved a holding company: that is, a corporation put together for the purpose of owning shares in other corporations. The Northern Securities Company was chartered in New Jersey, a state sometimes called the "mother of trusts." The company ran nothing, made nothing, employed almost nobody; its only role in life was to act as a vessel for J. P. Morgan, James J. Hill, and other railroad and finance moguls. Into the company they poured the shares of the Northern Pacific Railway and the Great Northern system; the result was a giant railroad combination, dominating traffic from Minnesota to the Pacific Northwest. It was this structure that the government aimed to destroy.

Whether the Sherman Act applied to holding companies at all was debatable, at least up to that point in time. The new president, Theodore Roosevelt, was committed to "trust-busting." He created a special division, inside the Department of Justice, to enforce the Sherman Act; and saw to it that the division had money enough to grease its wheels. Before Roosevelt's intervention, the government had brought at most one or two prosecutions a year. Now production stepped up drastically; and the government brought a number of large, significant cases.

The Northern Securities case was the first fruit of this activity. And the government won its case in the Supreme Court—though by the narrowest of margins (5–4). At issue was the very meaning and purpose of antitrust policy. Justice Harlan, for the majority, called the securities company a "powerful consolidated corporation" whose goal in life was to crush the competition. If it succeeded, then the "entire commerce of the immense territory in the northern part of the United States between the Great Lakes and the Pacific at Puget Sound" would be "at the mercy of a single holding corporation."[33]

It was a famous victory; and it bolstered Theodore Roosevelt's reputation as an enemy of the trusts. Yet four justices disagreed—one of them Oliver Wendell Holmes, Jr. Did the Sherman Act apply to railroads at all? No less an authority than Christopher Columbus Langdell, former dean of the Harvard Law School, was one of the doubters: the "only thing that a railway company can monopolize," he wrote, "is the carrying of goods and passengers for hire"; this was not "trade or commerce."[34] The dissenters made another point: the Sherman Act had no bearing on bigness as such; if a single rich person bought up all the shares of two railroads, that would not violate the act (they felt). Holmes conceded that some people felt the statute was "meant to strike at combinations great enough to cause . . . anxiety"; but he rejected the "popular" idea of what a monopoly was in favor of an "accurate and legal conception."[35] He looked for the meaning of the act in the common-law concept of "restraint of trade." The act outlawed only contracts and combinations which tried to exclude other people from competing, or tried to divvy up territory, or engaged in modes of market competition which went beyond an invisible line that divided good from evil. All this, of course, was extremely vague—and so was the Sherman Act itself.

It was still popular to try to break up monopolies; and the government won another victory, shortly after the Northern Securities case, when it smashed the so-called Beef Trust. The meatpackers were a tough lot, who indulged in price-fixing, blacklisting, and secret railroad rebates; they also chopped up the country into territories, and divided it among themselves.[36] This was classic anti-competitive behavior. The government won at the trial; and the court issued an injunction, forbidding the companies from violating the Sherman Act, and outlawing certain specific practices. The Supreme Court unanimously upheld this decision.[37]

Still, hysteria over trusts had subsided. The courts seemed to recognize that big business was here to stay; trust-busting was appropriate only for the worst offenders. In 1911 came two landmark Supreme Court decisions. One of them—the Standard Oil case—is famous for enunciating the so-called rule of reason.[38] The Sherman Act did not apply to bigness as such, or to power as such; but only to "unreasonable" bigness and power—restraints that were unfair or oppressive (a slippery concept, to be sure).[39] This was a break with one of the historical foundations on which antitrust policy rested: fear of huge, overwhelming conglomerates, whose power was an evil in itself, a threat to American values. The Court felt otherwise. There were good trusts and bad trusts. And it was a signal to the government, too: stay out of the market, except in emergency cases. In fact, the case itself, despite its rhetoric, gave no comfort to Standard Oil; the lower court ordered Standard to dissolve the oil trust, and break itself into pieces; the Supreme Court affirmed. In the American Tobacco case, the court restated its new "rule of reason"; but the giant tobacco combine also lost its case.[40]

Still, the "rule of reason" was a warning sign to those who, like Louis D. Brandeis, were opposed to "bigness" as such. In *United States v. U.S. Steel* (1920), the Court applied the rule of reason, and U.S. Steel, one of the largest corporations in the world, survived intact.[41] The steel company, the Court admitted, was very big; but it had resorted to "none of the brutalities and tyrannies" that the Court confronted in other cases (Rockefeller's Standard Oil, for example). Bigness without badness was not enough.

There was no question that the economy was changing, rapidly and dramatically—shifting from agriculture to manufacturing, and from small to large to very large business. From the standpoint of the beginning of the twenty-first century, business ethics often seemed to be on the level of the modern Russian mafia. The securities market was essentially unregulated. Big, strong robber barons welded together companies to form huge oligopolies. Workers, farmers, and small businessmen by the millions resented what they felt was the crushing power of the large corporations. Politically, if not economically, something had to be done.

The forces that prevailed, legally speaking, were the forces of moderate reform.[42] Socialism—strong government control of the economy, public ownership of big industry, banking, and the like—in many ways never left the starting post in the United States. To be sure, there was something of an exception for "natural" monopolies. As of 1927 more than 80 percent of the "central water supply systems" were "publicly owned"; and cities often owned their power and light companies—more than 2,500 of these city-owned companies existed, or more than 40 percent of the total.[43] Still, most major utilities remained in private hands—telephone and telegraph companies, and railroads. The trust-busting of the federal government, despite the occasional Standard Oil–type case, was directed mostly at small-scale cartels, not at big-business combines. Yet the idea of some form of federal control, some monitoring, some oversight over corporate America, had genuine appeal to millions of people. As early as 1903, Congress established a Bureau of Corporations, within the (new) Department of Commerce and Labor, headed by a commissioner of corporations. This commissioner would have power to make "diligent investigations" into the "organization, conduct, and management of any corporation."[44] More was needed than sporadic prosecutions and sporadic court cases. In 1914 Congress passed an act creating the Federal Trade Commission, made up of five members, and specifically transferred to the FTC the powers and duties of the Bureau of Corporations.[45]

The commission was (as is usually the case) something of a compromise. There were those who wanted to force all large corporations to register with the commission, and even to submit contracts, agreements, and the like for approval.[46] But this never came to pass. The commission had authority to take action against "unfair" methods of competition. It could investigate, it could hold hearings, it could issue orders to "cease and desist" if it found unfairness. But it was a striking fact that the act said nothing about the *meaning* of this word *unfair,* which is (to say the least) somewhat indefinite.

Less than a month later, Congress dropped the other shoe when it passed the Clayton Act, an act to "supplement existing laws against unlawful restraints and monopolies."[47] The Clayton Act put flesh on the bones of the FTC Act. It specified certain business methods as unfair—for example, no company was to sell or lease goods or machinery on condition that the buyer would not deal with a competitor, if the effect of such a deal would be to "lessen competition or tend to create a monopoly." A corporation that swallowed up another company also violated the act if the acquisition tended to lessen competition or create a monopoly.

These statutes were more detailed than the Sherman Act, and, what is even more significant, the law created an actual agency—an institution, a building, a staff, books and records, a bureaucracy, a budget. Power, expert knowledge, and experience could attach to all these over the years. Before the FTC Act, the Justice Department handled antitrust cases along with all its other duties. And these cases, as the attorney general reported in 1905, "taxed the resources of the Department to the utmost."[48] The big cases tended to wind up in court. This meant that issues of tremendous size and complexity—and *cases* of tremendous size and complexity—would fall into the lap of men trained in law, not economics, business, or any other relevant field.

This was a problem for the department; and it was also a problem for the courts. The Supreme Court noted, somewhat querulously, that the record in the Standard Oil case was "inordinately voluminous, consisting of twenty-three volumes of printed matter, aggregating about twelve thousand pages, containing a vast amount of confusing and conflicting testimony relating to innumerable, complex and varied business transactions extending over a period of nearly forty years."[49] And much, much worse was yet to come, in the far-off future, in cases involving IBM, or AT&T, or Microsoft. Somehow, stumbling and guessing, the courts would have to cope.

Regulation of Business

As these examples make clear, it would be a mistake to describe the first part of the twentieth century as a period in which big business won triumph after triumph, and in which the market was essentially unregulated. It was a free-market economy, but never a pure one. Workers, smallholders, farmers, and shopkeepers did have the vote; and a good deal of their political wants were enacted into law; all the conflicts in the case law that we have discussed came out of these laws. And business did not always adamantly refuse any attempt at regulation. Nor did business always speak with one voice. Businesses often preferred gentle, soothing regulation to the cutthroat competition of the market.

Better a captive, sweetheart agency (as the ICC sometimes was) than the competitive jungle.

On the whole, regulation that appealed to the middle class was much more likely to get enacted than programs pushed by the labor unions. One landmark was the passage of the first federal food and drug law (1906). This was the end point of a long struggle.[50] There were, of course, many state laws about food quality—for example, a Missouri law made it a crime to sell "the flesh of any animal" that died "otherwise than by slaughter" or which was diseased, or to sell "unwholesome bread or drink," or to "fraudulently adulterate, for the purpose of sale, anything intended for food or drink, or any drugs or medicines."[51] But, typically, there was not much follow-up; the states did not do much in the way of enforcement; and in a federal union, these laws had little power to control products sold all over the country. Dr. Harvey Wiley, within the federal government, had struggled for years to expose rotten and dangerous food products, and to get Congress to do something about it. Nothing much happened until Upton Sinclair published his novel *The Jungle* in 1906, and set off a firestorm of public indignation.

The Jungle is a powerful book, a searing indictment of the dark underside of the American dream. It tells the story of a Lithuanian immigrant, Jurgis Rudkus, his family, and his tragic fate in Chicago. There are vivid, horrifying descriptions of conditions in the meatpacking plants of the city Carl Sandburg called "hog butcher to the world," where Rudkus went to work. Moldy sausage would be "dosed with borax and glycerine," then "dumped into the hoppers," and later sold to the American public. The meat was stored in rat-infested rooms; the companies put out poisoned bread to kill the rats; but rats, bread, and meat would all end up as processed products. In one scene out of hell, Sinclair described how workmen in the "cooking rooms" sometimes fell into large vats, and were boiled until "all but the bones of them had gone out to the world as Durham's Pure Leaf Lard."

All of this shocked and nauseated the public, from low to high; the president himself, Theodore Roosevelt, was appalled when he read these accounts. He appointed investigators, who essentially confirmed what Sinclair had written. In the political tempest that followed, a meat inspection act, and the food act itself, sailed through Congress. The food companies and the meatpackers fought to prevent the laws from passing; but even they came to bow to the inevitable. Or even eagerly embrace it. As one executive admitted, "the sale of meat and meat products had been more than cut in two."[52] Under these conditions, a strong law might help the meatpackers and food companies by restoring public confidence. Then people would be willing to buy Chicago's meat products again.

The Food and Drug Act illustrates quite graphically how incidents and scandals shape the development of law. The forces people like to call special interests usually get their way, sometimes by sinister means, more often because they have the loudest voices and the most to offer politicians—campaign contributions, among other things. The public, by and large, is inert—busy with its own affairs or, after the dawn of the glorious age of television, sitting with a six-pack in front of the flickering screen.

Nevertheless, in a democratic society, the public has vast *potential* power; it is there, latent, submerged, like the deadly force inside a hand grenade, before the pin is pulled. A scandal or incident is an event that pulls the pin; it sets off an explosion of public indignation, rage—and power. The history of the food and drug law is one prominent example. There will be many others. In an age of mass media, and mass communication, the role of scandal and incident in lawmaking was bound to multiply.

The history of the Food and Drug Act also illustrates some of the limits of scandal and incident. Sinclair was committed to socialism. He had written his book to show the evils of a raw capitalist society. The reaction to the book was a grave disappointment to Sinclair. It had an impact, to be sure; but it did nothing much for the socialist cause. As Sinclair said, "I aimed at the public's heart, and by accident I hit it in the stomach."[53] But it was not an accident. Middle-class people learned from the scandal what they wanted to learn; they took what had meaning for *their* lives. And that meaning was in the food they ate, not in the miserable lives of the workmen whose body and blood had contaminated their middle-class food.

Not that government, federal and state, was completely callous about the working conditions of millions of wage earners. This was, after all, a large body of people; and most of them were voters. Work accidents were taking a terrible toll: more than 3,000 men died in coal mine accidents in 1907; and railroad accidents killed 4,500 employees in the same year.[54] And danger was present in other jobs as well—for steelworkers, laundry workers, construction workers.

This was the period in which workers' compensation laws were passed. And it was hard to argue against safety regulation, especially on the railroads. Nobody wanted trains to crash or derail. In coal mines, only the workers got killed; but in railroad accidents, passengers were also at risk. People had a selfish interest, too, in the health and welfare of railroad workers; after all, these were the people manning and driving the trains. President Roosevelt reminded Congress in 1907 that the safety of passengers depended on the "vigilance and alertness" of workers; in response, Congress passed an Hours of Service Act.[55] No railroad employee was to be on duty "for a longer period than sixteen consecutive hours" in any day; operators and train dispatchers had a general nine-hour limit, raised to thirteen in stations operated only during the day.

Even when public safety was not necessarily an issue, there were moves to improve the safety record of the railroads. A federal law of 1893 provided, among other things, that railroads had to be equipped with power brakes and automatic couplers.[56] An act of 1908 made it unlawful for a company "to use any locomotive . . . not equipped with an ash pan, which can be dumped or emptied and cleaned without the necessity of any employee going under such locomotive"; this was meant to eliminate one frightful source of accidents.[57] A law of 1910 strengthened the report requirements of the railroads; they had to inform the Interstate Commerce Commission each month about "all collisions, derailments, or other accidents," if there was any damage to equipment, or any injury to somebody's body; the ICC had broad powers, too, to investigate accidents.[58] Boiler explosions were another major source of injury and death on the roads. An act of 1911 made it unlawful to run a train with an unsafe boiler; the law gave federal inspectors power to inspect and repair locomotive boilers, and to notify railroads when their boilers were not in good condition.[59]

Federal regulation of coal mines lagged behind regulation of railroads. But 1907 was a crucial year: in December, 362 men died in Monongah, West Virginia, after a coal mine explosion; 703 men, all told, died that month from explosions, capping a year of disaster in the pits.[60] Western miners had long agitated for a federal department of mines; some companies and unions now added their voices, and in 1910 Congress did create a Bureau of Mines, within the Department of the Interior.[61] The bureau was told to make "diligent investigation" of methods of mining, with the goal of finding ways to prevent accidents. But the bureau had no power to do anything more. For the time being, at least, only state officials would police the dangerous tunnels of coal.

Off-Center: Regulation in the States

Legal history, like American history in general, tends to suffer from a kind of federal bias. It focuses on what Washington does, and tends to neglect the state and local governments. Of course, the growing power and importance of the federal government is one of the overarching themes of twentieth-century legal history. But federalism, and the commitment to state power—and fear and hatred of the central government—were still very strong themes, even dogmas, in American political and legal thought. "States' rights" was usually a cover or disguise for real, brutal, tough economic and social interests; but the slogan itself had considerable bite.

Thus in 1900, and for decades afterward (and still today), the states do very much matter. The same is true of the cities. An ordinance of New York City in 1910, say, affected far more people than any act passed by the legislature of Wyoming or New Hampshire. Moreover, what states and cities did, how much they spent, how much they regulated, grew greatly in the twentieth century. Not, to be sure, as much as the federal leviathan; but in absolute terms, very much indeed.

Almost all states had their own railroad laws, and laws about related institutions (grain warehouses, for example). Railroad regulation had, by 1900, a longish history in the states. In the 1870s, the Midwest had the so-called Granger laws, which created commissions to regulate the railroads (and control their rate-making power). These laws did not last; and they had, moreover, one massive defect: in a federal system, they were impotent to control the giant interstate nets. The natural solution was federal law, which came to pass in 1887, with the creation of the Interstate Commerce Commission, as we have seen.[62] The states, however, maintained their own elaborate regulatory schemes in the twentieth century—Minnesota, for example, had a Railroad and Warehouse Commission of its own, with power to determine whether rates were "unreasonable."[63] This was by no means exceptional. The state laws also concerned themselves with safety. So the railroad commissioners of Kentucky could demand "improvements" and changes in tracks, bridges, and tunnels for safety purposes.[64] And Massachusetts law contained page after page of rules on railroad safety, in excruciating detail; not only the usual stuff about couplers, brakes, and boilers, but even the specification that every train had to have, "in case of accident," "two jack screws, two crow bars, one pinch bar, one claw bar, one spike hammer, two sharp axes, and ropes or chains"; and a rule that no passenger car could be "lighted by naphtha, nor by an illuminating oil or fluid made in part of naphtha or which will ignite at a temperature of less than three hundred degrees Fahrenheit."[65]

Business and trade regulation in the states was heavy and significant. It reflected, naturally, the parochial concerns of the particular state. If we look at the laws of Nebraska for 1909, representing the harvest of one session of the legislature, we are not surprised to find laws about agricultural products. The very first law of the session provided that nobody should sell vinegar as "apple, orchard, or cider vinegar," unless it was the "legitimate product of pure apple juice." Other laws provided that stallions "kept for public service" (as studs, in other words) had to be "registered" in a recognized stud book; there were elaborate provisions dealing with unregistered stallions. Still another statute provided that owners of "swine" that died of disease had to burn the carcass "completely" within forty-eight hours. A statute also provided for the inspection of horses and cattle by "inspectors of stock shipments" before they could be sent out of a county.[66]

But Nebraska was not concerned only with its farm folks. The work of this session reflects business and other interests as well. Occupational licensing, for example, is represented: a statute made it illegal "to practice professional nursing as a Registered Nurse" without a "certificate of registration"; getting the certificate required, among other things, two or more years of training.[67] An amendment to the local food and drug law spelled out the meaning of *misbranded:* any "imitation" offered for sale under a false name, for example; food products containing "any alcohol, morphine, opium, cocaine, heroin, alpha or beta eucaine, chloroform, cannabis indica, chloral hydrate or acetanilide, phenacetin . . . belladonna," or any "derivatives" of these substances, had to be properly labeled.[68] Another statute regulated sanitary conditions inside food-processing plants, restaurants, groceries, meat markets, and bakeries, in mind-numbing detail. For example, windows "and other openings of every food producing or distributing establishment" had to have "screen doors and wire window screens of not coarser than 14 mesh wire gauze," during the "fly season." Cuspidors had to be provided, and emptied and washed out daily. Workers with a long list of diseases, from bubonic plague through mumps to chicken pox were to be excluded from workplaces used to make, pack, or sell foods. Power to enforce the act was handed over to the state's Food, Drug and Dairy Inspector.[69]

Of course, each state had its own economy, its own political brew, its own culture. Vermont in 1915 passed a statute setting the legal weight of a gallon of maple syrup—not something Nebraska was likely to care much about.[70] Arizona enacted in 1929 an elaborate Fruit and Vegetable Standardization Act, which created an "office of supervisor of inspection," and, in addition to general provisions, laid down special rules for cantaloupes (they had to be "well netted, well formed and mature . . . not . . . wilted, spongy or flabby," or bruised, sunburnt, or insect-ridden), what kind of crates they were to be packed in, and how each pack was to be marked.[71] Arizona was thinking of the export market. Food and product statutes were concerned either with upholding the quality of what the state produced and sold; or what its own citizens ate and consumed; or both. Weights and measures were typically regulated. In Texas in the 1920s the "standard folding onion crate" could not be "less than 19⅝ inches long, 11¾₆ wide and 9¹³⁄₁₆ inches deep." There were rigid standards of quality for peaches, tomatoes, oranges, onions, cabbages, Bartlett pears, snap beans, and Irish potatoes; each product was divided into grades of quality: Extra Fancy Bartlett pears were the best, next came Fancy (same as Extra Fancy, but allowed to contain "ten per cent slightly scarred fruit and slight blemishes"), Choice, and Culls. A long statute declared "Pectinophora gossypiella, Saunders, known as the pink bollworm," a "public nuisance and a menace to the cotton industry"; its "eradication" was a "public necessity."[72]

It is easy to be cynical about the health and safety motivations of some state laws—the majority of the justices in the *Lochner* case were perhaps right to be suspicious of the motives behind the law regulating bakeries. But there *was* in fact an increased interest in taking care of the health of the citizen. After all, in an urban, mass-production economy, what people ate and drank, the medicines they took, the machines they used were out of their immediate control; these goods and products were made by strangers, perhaps faraway strangers, under conditions the buyer could know nothing about. As society learned more about what caused disease, what spread disease, and what cured disease, pressure increased for collective action—no one person could guarantee clean water, or deal with an epidemic on her own. Texas, for example, created a state Board of Health in 1909, made up of "seven legally qualified physicians of good professional standing, graduates of reputable medical colleges," and at least ten years experience tending to the sick of Texas. Later (1917) the board was told to appoint a registrar of vital statistics, and to employ a "chemist and bacteriologist." The board was given power from the beginning to inspect any "public building, factory, slaughter house, packing house, abattoir, dairy, bakery, manufactory, hotel, restaurant and any other public place," to help in the "enforcement of the rules of the sanitary code for Texas and of any health law, sanitary law or quarantine regulation." The law also provided for county and city health officers. The sanitary code in question consisted, as of 1925, of eighty-six rules about contagious diseases, quarantine, health records, and the like; rules that, for example, laid down that nobody with "contagious catarrhal conjunctivitis" could go to school; rules about the disposing of dead bodies, and how death certificates were to be made out; a rule requiring cuspidors "in adequate numbers" in all depots and railroad stations; and rules about toilets and sanitary conditions on trains, in sleeping cars, and in stations (rule 70 prohibited spitting or brushing your teeth in "basins used for lavatory purposes"). The sanitary code was, like so many other aspects of southern life, tinged with race prejudice: rule 72 provided that "Negro porters shall not sleep in sleeping car berths nor use bedding intended for white passengers."[73]

Health and safety laws continued to proliferate in Texas. An act of 1918 required all doctors to report cases of "syphilis, gonorrhea, and chancroid," and to "instruct" their patients "in measures for preventing the spread" of the disease, and "the necessity for treatment until cured." The state also required (1921) all "doctors, midwives, nurses" to use "prophylactic drops" in the eyes of every newborn baby, consisting of a "one percent solution of silver nitrate," in order to "prevent opthalmia neonatorum"; the Board of Health was to make these drops available "free of cost to the poor of the State." Texas also had an elaborate food and drug law from 1911 on. There were many differences between the states in details, of course; but the efforts to promote public health were quite general.

The states also concerned themselves with safety—in schools, hotels, factories, and mines. An Illinois act of 1919 laid down the rule that all buildings four or more stories in height had to have "one or more metallic ladder or stairs or other approved fire escapes."[74] Many northern states had elaborate factory laws—Pennsylvania, for one. These statutes contained both general rules (employers had to provide a safe working place) and specific ones (for example, that elevator shafts had to be enclosed).[75] Many laws provided for a board, agency, or commission with power to inspect and report—the Industrial Commission of Ohio, for example, had this power; and within the commission, a "chief inspector of mines" had jurisdiction to enforce the elaborate regulation of coal mines.[76] Coal mines, as we have seen, were especially dangerous places; and almost every state had some sort of safety law even in the nineteenth century, though Texas passed its law only in 1907.[77]

Even more obscure than the state laws were the thousands of municipal ordinances that regulated economic life in the cities. In the aggregate, however, they were extremely important. They had a big impact on ordinary people, and ordinary businesses. Building permits are a perfect example. Thus in the small city of Fresno, California, in 1911, it was unlawful to "proceed with the erection, construction, alteration, repair, moving or demolition, of any business or other structure" costing more than $20 without a "written permit . . . from the City Engineer." An applicant had to provide the engineer with a "full and complete set of plans and specifications."[78] The ordinance was full and detailed: for buildings of two stories or less in height, "the studding for the outside walls and bearing partitions" were to be not less than "2×4 inches"; all "wood beams or joists shall be trimmed away at least one and one-half inches from all flues and chimneys," and so on. The ordinance was more than forty dense pages long. No doubt many of the provisions of many of the ordinances were dictated by concerns other than safety and health—union interests are an obvious example. But mixed motives in the regulatory fabric are not the exception but the rule.

Were these safety laws enforced? It is hard to tell. There are grounds for skepticism. It is one thing to pass a law calling for mine safety or ventilation in bakeries; it is quite another thing to enforce it. Enforcement is never automatic. It takes time, money, and people. Mine-safety laws, for example, were never adequately enforced. In Kentucky in 1905 there were 203 mines, with a huge output of coal, and only two inspectors. The coal mining states paid low salaries to state inspectors; and many of the inspectors did a poor job of inspecting.[79] It is likely that a similar story could be told about factory inspection, child-labor laws, and the other forms of regulation that needed a staff of enforcers.

Money, Banking, and Taxation

Everybody knows and cares about the dollar, the five-dollar bill, and the other green pieces of paper, as well as the coins that we get and spend. The American of the twenty-first century takes a stable currency for granted. But there was no national system of currency in the nineteenth century. Issues of money and banking perturbed the political and economic life of the country, perhaps as much as any other subject. The law of contracts, suretyship, debt collection, bankruptcy, and so many other fields reflected and responded to problems of money and banking.

The nineteenth century, too, was plagued with recurrent panics, crashes, and crises. In disaster times, which came roughly twenty years apart, banks failed, companies went belly up, jobs were lost, and hunger stalked the land. Part of the blame always fell on the money system, or the banks, or both. In 1864 the National Banking Act created a new kind of bank: national banks, holding national charters. A tax on state banknotes, enacted in 1865, forced most of the state-chartered banks to join the national system. But reform, and a truly centralized banking system, were products of the twentieth century. Banking continued, at first, to be mostly local and small-scale. Meanwhile, the states all tried their hand at bank regulation. Each state had a banking code; most had some sort of banking commissioner. Special rules applied to banks: typically, they were required to keep a reserve fund—in Connecticut, for example, in the early part of the century, the bank had to keep 12 percent of its demand deposits and 5 percent of its time deposits as a reserve; the Connecticut code also had special regulations for private banks, savings banks, and building and loan associations. Some states even went so far as to experiment with a system of guaranteeing deposits—Oklahoma was a pioneer, with its Depositors' Guaranty Fund, and a number of western and midwestern states followed suit.[80] But bank failures proved too much of a burden for the state systems to bear; the Oklahoma law was repealed in 1923.[81]

The Federal Reserve Act of 1913 was a milestone in economic history.[82] This massive law created a system of regional Federal Reserve banks. A Federal Reserve Board, sitting on top of the system, had supervisory power. But the district banks were the key to the system. The Federal Reserve system was not, in other words, a central bank but "a system of regional clearinghouses."[83] Ultimately, of course, it became a powerful weapon of fiscal and monetary control.

Banks were in the business of lending money, of course; but their loans were not for the ordinary citizen. The urban poor, and especially the immigrant poor, had to go to the loan shark for money. Historically, the states had passed usury laws, which put a ceiling on the rate of interest that a lender could legally charge. Anything higher was "usury" and illegal. In Georgia, for example, anything over 8 percent was illegal.[84] In the first decade of the century, some states tried other ways to get a grip on the business of small loans. One way was to insist that only people or companies with a state license could be in the business of making small loans.[85] The loan-shark business was not so easily gotten rid of, however. In Georgia, despite small-loan laws and usury laws, the loan shark continued to thrive, lending small sums at enormous rates of interest to poor blacks and whites; during the Depression, even more people felt compelled to resort to this dubious source.[86] The loan sharks constituted a kind of "underground federal reserve system"; the shark sold the "most expensive money in the world," and his collection procedures were, to put it gently, "out of the ordinary." Organized crime controlled much of this business; yet, on the other hand, the shark provided "liquidity" at a time "when all other sources of instant money have dried up."[87]

Insurance companies were among the most important financial institutions in 1900 (as indeed they were in 2000). The biggest insurance company at the time, Mutual, had assets of $326 million—more than twice the assets of the largest bank, National City Bank.[88] There was a long and continuing tradition of state regulation. In Wisconsin, for example, the legislature passed about eight hundred statutes dealing with insurance in the half-century between 1906 and 1959.[89] By the 1920s every state had a special official, usually called the "insurance commissioner" or the like, charged with overseeing the industry and the thick brew of regulatory laws.[90]

The insurance companies were rich and powerful; and their business ethics rose no higher than those of other rich and powerful institutions of the day. An important event in the history of regulation was the Armstrong Committee investigation in New York in 1905–1906. New York was the home of many insurance companies. Its influence on insurance law and practice was also great because it was the juiciest plum of a market. If a man bought a policy in New York, because he lived there, it was New York law that governed the transaction—never mind whether the company was, for example, a Delaware corporation. As is often the case, a scandal touched off the investigation. A young heir, beneficiary of a trust that controlled the Equitable Life Assurance Company (with more than $300 million in assets), threw a lavish party. The company footed the bills; the newspapers made a big deal of all this; they followed it up with reports of corruption and financial hanky-panky in the industry. The legislature responded by setting up what came to be called the Armstrong

Committee. Charles Evans Hughes was its counsel. The committee produced seven volumes of testimony, evidence, and exhibits documenting all sorts of chicanery and corruption. The result was a thick package of reforms, enacted in 1906.[91] The law aimed to reduce the political power of the companies. They were not to make political contributions, and their lobbyists were forced to register. The law also opened up the courts to lawsuits by policyholders. It prescribed standard policy terms. These laws then served as a model for tough regulation in other states as well.[92] In Wisconsin the state went so far as to offer its own public life insurance; the law went into effect in 1913, although not many citizens signed on.[93]

Taxation

Taxation today is a legal and social affair of vast importance. Few bodies of law are more important; and vast battalions of lawyers, accountants, and financial advisers batten off its complexities, its slippery slopes, its traps and opportunities. Government has, of course, always had to raise money to pay for its activities. But governments in the nineteenth century did so much less than they do today; from the modern standpoint, their tax bite was as soft as a kiss. The revenues of the federal government in the nineteenth century were on a scale so low that they seem ludicrous today. At the dawn of the twentieth century, the federal government had to make do with piddling returns from customs duties on imported goods, taxes on whiskey, playing cards, and the like, and returns from land sales. The total revenues of the federal government in 1902 were $653 million.[94] A hundred years later, the Pentagon could not survive a day on what the whole federal government took in then.

As government expanded, its hunger for money grew accordingly. Today the great money engine of the federal government is the income tax. It had its troubles getting started. Congress, after considerable wrangling, passed an income tax law in 1894. But in 1895, in *Pollock v. Farmers' Loan and Trust Company,* the Supreme Court declared this modest tax unconstitutional.[95] Because this was a constitutional decision, it could be undone only by amending the Constitution itself. A proposal to allow an income tax law passed both houses of Congress overwhelmingly in 1909 (the vote in the Senate was actually unanimous). The amendment (number 16) then went to the states for ratification; Wyoming, New Mexico, and Delaware put it over the top on February 3,

1913; and it became the law of the land.[96] In the same year, Congress duly enacted an income tax law.[97]

The income tax, so bitterly contested and denounced, looks positively toothless and benign from the vantage point of the year 2000. The original law had a top rate of 6 percent, for incomes over five hundred thousand dollars a year. The income tax was not of much concern to the ordinary worker; only about 2 percent of the labor force filed returns from 1913 to 1915.[98] Under the 1916 version, the first three thousand dollars of income was exempt—four thousand for a married couple. This left the average household definitely out. On incomes above three thousand dollars, the basic tax rate was a crushing 2 percent. There was, on top of this, an "additional tax," graduated and progressive; its highest rate was 13 percent, on incomes over $2 million—which meant that almost nobody but a Rockefeller would conceivably pay it.[99]

The tax was extremely unpopular (no surprise) with the rich, and with most business people. They saw it as the camel's nose under the tent, which indeed it was. Soon after the income tax came into being, however, the United States joined the Allies in the First World War. The president was Woodrow Wilson, a Democrat; and the Wilson administration decided to finance the war through the income tax, together with an excess-profits tax. The War Revenue Act of 1917 dramatically increased the rates. For the first time, the government found itself relying heavily on this law for its money. The income tax had accounted for about 16 percent of the government's revenues before 1917; this rose to more than 50 percent during the war years.[100]

When the Republicans returned to power, they got rid of the excess-profits tax; in the 1920s they passed laws which taxed capital gains at rates lower than ordinary income, and they threw a bone (or many bones) to business—for example, the oil and gas depletion allowance. Many businessmen, to be sure, wanted to get rid of the income tax altogether, and replace it with something suitably regressive, like a national sales tax. But Andrew Mellon, who was President Harding's secretary of the treasury, resisted; and he managed to persuade enough Republicans and businesspeople that *some* degree of progressive taxation was socially responsible (and would look that way to the public).[101]

In 1916 the federal government also adopted a tax on estates of the dead.[102] Again, the rates seem to us (looking backward) rather modest. The first fifty thousand dollars was exempt; the rates climbed to a maximum of 10 percent, on estates over $5 million. This was, then, a death tax that only the very rich would ever have to pay; and it was hardly confiscatory. But it had a certain amount of symbolic value: it expressed the policy of cutting the great dynastic fortunes down to size.

In some ways, the federal government was merely following in the footsteps of the states. Twenty-seven of forty-six states had by 1903 some form of death tax; ten years later, thirty-five of forty-eight states.[103] Death taxes in the states were mostly of a type different from the federal model. They were not estate taxes at all (that is, taxes on the whole estate), but inheritance taxes (taxes on inherited shares of a dead man's assets). Under an inheritance tax scheme, the amount of the tax can depend on who inherits—close kin are preferred to "strangers." In New Mexico, for example, as of the 1920s, the first ten thousand dollars left to a child was free of tax, and the child paid only 1 percent on the rest of his inheritance. Money left to a nonrelative, on the other hand, was taxed at 5 percent, and only five hundred dollars was exempt. Usually the death taxes did not bite very deeply—New Mexico's 5 percent top was hardly confiscatory. In New York the highest rate in the early 1920s was 3 percent. There were exceptions, however: the top rate in West Virginia (on gifts to nonrelatives of more than a half-million dollars) was 35 percent, a staggering rate for those days.

In general, the income tax did not loom that large in the states. For the most part, the states squeezed what money they could out of general property taxes. In practice, in many states, this meant taxes on land. Typically, the key job fell to county assessors, who had to compile lists of property and decide on their "actual cash value." The tax was then a certain percentage of this value. In Kentucky, as of 1922, the tax (on "all real and personal estate") was fixed at forty cents for each one hundred dollars of assessed property.[104] In some states, by custom, the "actual" value was a fiction; property was listed as some fraction of the real or market value. In states that tried to assess personal property as well as land, there were typically lists of exempt property. In Iowa, for example (as of 1919), farm produce was exempt, poultry, "ten stands of bees," all "swine and sheep under six months of age," and wool recently shorn; farm equipment was also free of taxation, along with the "team, wagon, and horses of the teamster or drayman," and the "tools of any mechanic," all these up to the value of three hundred dollars.[105] The property tax usually provided the states with the lion's share of revenue. In Kansas in 1913 the state got about two-thirds of its total income from property taxes; the counties got 88 percent of their revenue from this source, and cities received 58 percent.[106] States also often had various excise taxes, license fees, corporation fees, special taxes on utilities and banks, and a ragbag of other taxes, including automobile license fees. In Florida, for example, as of 1920, the state required licenses essentially from any business, occupation, or profession. The amounts varied: dealers in alligators were charged ten dollars a year "for each place of business"; opticians and operators of "Turkish, Russian, vapor or other baths" paid the same; but photographers paid only five dollars and bakeries three. In a few cases, the taxes seemed frankly confiscatory—less for revenue than for prohibition. "Clairvoyants, or spirit mediums" had to pay five hundred dollars, and the same was true for "astrologists."[107]

The bland and boring texts of state tax laws often concealed bitter political and economic battles. Taxation of mines and mining was an issue in Montana, for example, where Anaconda, true to its name, had much of the state squeezed between its muscular coils.[108] Taxation of railroad properties was a significant issue in many states—and also a significant source of ready money. California, collecting some $20 million in the fiscal year that ended June 30, 1917, got its biggest bite (nearly $7 million) from "railroads, including street railways." Light, heat, and power companies contributed another $2½ million. Inheritance taxes brought in about the same amount; the rest was small potatoes, including "fish and game licenses" ($26,500) and fees of the "Surveyor General and Register" of the State Land Office ($3,500).[109]

A person or a business in, say, 1920, could hardly foresee the stratospheric rates of the later years. Still, to contemporaries, the taxes seemed onerous enough; and the national game of tax evasion was well under way. John H. Sears, a Wall Street lawyer, published a book in 1922 with the engaging title *Minimizing Taxes*. His preface was nothing if not frank. The book, he said, was written "from the taxpayers' point of view." According to Sears, his book would not offer tricks or loopholes; but it would emphasize ways of "avoidance," rather than "evasion." For Sears tax avoidance amounted almost to a patriotic duty: "He who takes the way of lesser tax helps to guide taxation into a safer highway for all"; this noble soul also exposed "prominent evils in the system of taxation." For this reason, he claimed, his book would "perform a useful service."[110] The government, no doubt, felt differently. The battle between the revenue service and the taxpayers, a battle waged with audits, loopholes, and all manner of arcane weapons, had only just begun.

Labor and the Law

Labor unrest was not, of course, an invention of the twentieth century. When the nineteenth century began, this was a country of smallholders (at least in the North); in any event, basically a country of farmers. By the time the century ended, there were millions of landless urban workers—men and women who earned their bread by working in mines, factories, railroad yards, and sweatshops. Millions of these workers and their families lived from hand to mouth, from paycheck to paycheck, often in conditions of misery and squalor. It was a precarious world, a world with very little of what later came to be called the social safety net; and certainly no form of job security. If times got hard, companies simply laid off workers or cut their pay. The captains of industry, the rich owners and proprietors, sitting in their big houses on top of the hill, were on the whole exceedingly hostile toward organized labor. They could also be quite ruthless in defense of what they considered their God-given rights. Scab labor and Pinkerton detectives were artillery in the class war; and the local police or National Guard, all too often, acted as private armies for the suppression of labor.

Struggles between labor and management were at times extremely bitter, at times even bloody. This had been true since the late nineteenth century. President Cleveland used federal troops to help break the Pullman strike in the 1890s. Theodore Roosevelt, during the anthracite coal strike of 1902, tried to keep some sort of neutral balance between the United Mine Workers and the coal operators; he worked hard to settle the strike, and did not call in federal troops. But only a year later, he sent troops to Arizona Territory, where miners and mine owners were locked in bitter dispute. Roosevelt, as one scholar put it, was a "patrician paternalist," and certainly no fan of the unions. Still, this was an improvement, from labor's standpoint, over what had gone before.[111]

Labor-management struggles often spilled over from the streets into the courts. Here they might run up against a legal wall of steel: cold, formalistic, implacable. Many judges had a deep suspicion, even fear, of strikes. Strikes were never declared per se illegal. The principle of "the liberty of strikes" was so "firmly established through custom and public sentiment," Ernst Freund wrote in 1904, that "it is no longer questioned by any American court."[112] But as Freund went on to say, "actual violence or crime" was not to be condoned simply because it happened during a strike. And courts were often willing to use their legal weapons to counter "coercion," threats, and boycotts.

The most powerful weapon against the unions, and against strikes, was the labor injunction. An injunction is a court order, demanding that someone either do something, or stop doing something. It is powerful because it must be obeyed. If you disobey, you can be put in jail (for contempt of court)—essentially without trial.

The injunction was an ancient device, developed by the courts of equity. It was and is enormously useful in all sorts of contexts. But in the late nineteenth century, it began to appear in the courts as a strike-breaking tool.[113] If the court issued an injunction against, say, the leaders of a union, and the injunction was not obeyed, these leaders could be summarily thrown into prison. The courts in fact issued hundreds and hundreds of these injunctions. One scholar has estimated that 105 labor injunctions were issued in the 1880s; 410 in the 1890s; 850 in the 1900s; 835 in the 1910s; and 2,130 in the 1920s.[114] Labor feared and dreaded the injunction.

The Clayton Act (1914), which as we saw revamped and expanded the antitrust laws, specifically declared that "the labor of a human being is not a commodity or article of commerce"; nothing in the antitrust laws was to be construed as preventing workers from forming unions, and no union was to be declared an illegal combination or conspiracy. The Clayton Act also laid down the rule that "no restraining order or injunction" was to be granted "in any case between an employer and employees" arising out of a labor dispute, unless "necessary to prevent irreparable injury to property, or to a property right."[115] Yet as interpreted by the courts, the Clayton Act did nothing to stop the blizzard of injunctions. In 1917, for example, ladies' garment workers went on strike in Chicago. Employers ran to the federal court, and the courts quickly issued restraining orders. Police arrested one thousand pickets in two weeks; and five leaders of the strike were sent to jail for their roles at prostrike rallies or in encouraging picketing.[116]

The Supreme Court was equally cavalier about section 20 of the Clayton Act. In 1921, in a case involving a secondary boycott, the Court essentially reduced section 20 to empty words. The section, according to the Court, was not intended to change existing law.[117] Later cases bolstered this interpretation.

As Felix Frankfurter and Nathan Greene remarked, the Clayton Act "came as clay into the hands of the federal courts"; and they made the act into an *anti*union instrument—turning it, in a way, on its head: "The more things are legislatively changed, the more they remain the same judicially."[118]

But labor was not without political power; some states passed laws, in one form or another, against labor injunctions, or exempting unions from antitrust suits and the charge of restraint of trade. These laws, too, fared badly in the courts. Many of them were declared null and void. The Supreme Court took a similar attitude in *Truax v. Corrigan* (1921).[119] The statute here was Arizona's; and the case involved a restaurant called the English Kitchen in Bisbee. The workers had gone on strike, and were picketing the restaurant. The picketing was successful—business dropped off dramatically. A bare majority of the Supreme Court, speaking through Chief Justice Taft, invalidated the Arizona statute that allowed peaceful picketing and forbade injunctions. Business, said Taft, was "property," and the scurrilous, libelous acts of the picketers destroyed "property" in a way that the state could not condone.

Even statutes that survived judicial attack were, according to William E. Forbath, "vitiated by narrow construction."[120] Nonetheless, the days of the labor injunction were numbered. In 1930 President Hoover nominated Judge John J. Parker to be a justice of the Supreme Court. Parker, a southern Republican, had issued a labor injunction in 1927 against the United Mine Workers. The American Federation of Labor mounted a campaign against Parker; and on May 7, 1930, the Senate rejected him, by a vote of 41–39—a rare event indeed. By this time the labor injunction was doomed; it was too unpopular, politically. In 1932 President Hoover signed the Norris–La Guardia bill, which had passed both houses with huge majorities, and which was meant to put an end to the labor injunction, once and for all.[121]

The labor injunction had terrorized organized labor for some forty years. Some scholars think that the crushing impact of legal repression—the labor injunction was an important aspect of this repression—fundamentally altered the character of the American labor movement. Mossbacks on the bench not only inflicted "irreparable injury" on this or that union, strike, or item on labor's wish list; they seduced the movement (or coerced it) into a "negative and anti-statist" mode. British courts, of course, were just as reactionary, if not more so; but they did not have the power to strike down acts of Parliament—and this was a crucial difference. In the United States, organized labor faced an implacable and powerful bench. Hence, like a person condemned to die in the gas chamber, labor developed a one-track legal mind, an obsession which sucked all of its energies into the search for an end to the "judge-made regime" of repression, and drew it away from broader goals—such as the formation of a labor party, of the type which flourished in Europe.[122]

Whether this reasoning is right or wrong—and in what proportions—is not easy to say. It is true that some segments of the labor movement lost their radical edge, if they had ever had one. David Dubinsky, of the—ostensibly socialist—International Ladies Garment Workers Union remarked that "unions need capitalism like a fish needs water." Workers needed jobs; their livelihood depended on profits and economic growth. It was a matter of survival.[123]

Moreover, the states did pass a good deal of prounion legislation. Minnesota, for example, outlawed blacklists and yellow-dog contracts in the early years of the twentieth century.[124] A great many of these prolabor statutes either never got challenged in court or withstood challenges. Not all courts were antiunion; and, indeed, the legal climate for labor unions got distinctly better in the early years of the century; the New Deal, in the 1930s, was openly and blatantly prounion, and much of the union program got translated into law.

The *Lochner* case was, in form, a health law; Rufus Peckham saw right through it (he said). Still, even the most rabid fan of laissez-faire had to concede *some* power to the state, to make rules to protect the public health, or the public safety. Legislatures often used this power (the "police power") as a kind of cover, shield, or disguise. For example, Wisconsin passed a statute in 1907 which required small passenger trains (three or fewer cars) to carry at least "one engineer, one fireman, one conductor and one brakeman"; larger trains had to have two brakemen.[125] Surely one point of the law was to make more jobs for members of railroad brotherhoods; but the proponents could make a strong, persuasive claim that skimpy crews were a danger to the riding public. And the line between regulation of labor and regulation of public safety and health is not an easy one to draw. After all, better health and safety conditions were among the goals of the labor movement.

War and Peace

In 1917 the United States went to war again, throwing its weight on the side of France and England in World War I. As usual, war meant massive intervention in the economy. The federal government scrambled to produce a huge army and navy, and the equipment and material that went with these. Running a war called for massive infusions of money. Much of it was raised in the form of Liberty Bonds floated by the federal government. The War Finance Corporation was established in 1918, with an appropriation of half a billion dollars, to provide credits for war industries.[126]

Patriotism and conformity were also major needs of the war period, at least as the government saw it. The modern law of civil liberties, as we shall see, got a jump start from World War I—though this was in reaction to grim and repressive laws, including laws on "sedition." The war created, as war always does, a sense of emergency; and led to a vast expansion of the authority of the central government. The Lever Act of 1917 gave the president almost dictatorial power over food and fuel.[127] President Wilson (with rather dubious legal and constitutional authority) seized control of all the railroads and water transportation systems, everything except local streetcar lines—an extraordinary move. But Congress ratified the president's action, and passed a statute giving him almost uncontrolled discretion to deal with the roads, including the right to enter into agreements about their income, taxes, and the way they maintained themselves.[128] The government later seized control of telegraph and cable lines.[129]

The war also brought to a halt, by federal law, a lot of ordinary legal transactions. Nobody, during the war, could evict a soldier's family, or repossess a seaman's piano or car, without court approval.[130] The government built housing for shipyard workers, and tried to stop rent-gouging in the District of Columbia: Congress decreed that all leases in the capital were to continue as they were, and the tenants were to stay put as long as they paid rent "at the agreed rate."[131] Of course, many of these interventions were only temporary. They died along with the wartime emergency. When the government ran the railroads and the telegraph companies, there was some sentiment (in and out of government) to just keep on doing this—in other words, to nationalize these industries. But in the end everything returned to normal.

The war had a dramatic but mixed impact on labor relations. There was a major wave of strikes after the United States declared war; in 1917 more than a million workers went out on strike.[132] In the domains of western copper and lumber companies, federal troops intervened to end the strikes. The army never drew much of a line between the AFL and the radical IWW, and the net result was basically a strike-breaking, antiunion operation.

Yet in other regards, the war was a bonanza for the unions. War created an intense shortage of labor. The Wilson administration created a National War Labor Board in 1918; it had five representatives of management, and five of labor, chosen by the AFL. The NWLB had no real power to enforce its decisions; but it was at times surprisingly effective. It also "transformed labor-management relations from a basically private arena to a semipublic one"; and this changed the "historical balance of power between workers and bosses in many industries." Between 1917 and 1920 unions gained more than two million members, and reached a total membership of about five million.[133] Even greater days were to come.

4

Crime and Punishment in
the New Century

efore the twentieth century, Washington, D.C., and the federal
government did not have much to do with criminal justice; this
was mostly a job for the states. Not entirely, of course: the
District of Columbia was federal, and had a criminal justice
system; so did the territories, and such new prizes as Puerto
Rico and the Philippines. But outside of these federal domains,
plus army bases, ships at sea, and national parks, the national government was
not a major player in the business of labeling, catching, and punishing killers,
thieves, and other no-goods. There were, of course, federal crimes—smuggling, violations of tax laws, illegal immigration, counterfeiting, and the like;
also mail fraud, or shooting at a postman ("or his horse"); there were military
offenses, and maritime offenses (mutiny on the high seas, piracy, and similar
crimes).[1] Some of these were significant crimes, but none of them added up to
very much, quantitatively speaking. The attorney general reported that in the
fiscal year ending June 30, 1905, the federal courts terminated 18,163 criminal
cases, in the entire country.[2] Overwhelmingly, the action in criminal justice was
in the states. It was probably inevitable that the general push toward the center
in the twentieth century would increase the federal role in criminal justice.[3] The
regulatory state brought about the invention of a lot of new crimes, big and
small. Every new addition to the federal armory carried with it a kind of
criminal coda; each new statute made it a crime to violate, willfully or otherwise,
the rules laid down in the text, or created by the new federal agency. Thus,

under the Pure Food Act of 1906, anybody who shipped "adulterated or misbranded" food from one state to another was guilty of a misdemeanor. A law of 1925 (the Alaska Game Act) which set up an Alaska Game Commission provided for nonresident hunting licenses, and established rules (no poisoned bait, for example); any violation of any provision of the law was a misdemeanor, carrying fines or imprisonment up to six months.[4]

The federal government had been such small potatoes in the criminal-justice business in the late nineteenth century that it did not even have a proper prison of its own until 1891; federal prisoners (other than military ones) were lodged as paying guests in state jails and penitentiaries. The federal government, for example, paid forty cents a head per day to the sheriff of Alameda County, California, to take care of federal prisoners lodged in the county jail. (These prisoners at least ate three meals a day; the locals ate two—probably because for them the daily allowance was a mere twenty-five cents).[5] Fort Leavenworth, Kansas, was the first federal prison; another opened in Atlanta in 1902; by 1930 there were five. One of these was a women's prison, which opened in 1927 at Alderson, West Virginia.[6]

The numbers of federal prisoners were, at first, quite small: there were fewer than two thousand in 1890; and still only three thousand in 1915. Fort Leavenworth had the biggest share of these prisoners: more than one thousand prisoners by 1910, double that ten years later.[7] By 1930 there were thirteen thousand federal prisoners (plus an equal number of military prisoners).[8] In 1910 the Mann Act made it a crime to take a woman across state lines for "immoral purposes"; after 1919, under the National Motor Vehicle Theft Act, if you took a stolen car or truck across a state line, this was also a federal crime (and no need for a woman inside the car).[9] This law, in particular, helped fill the federal prisons. Finally, drug and Prohibition laws provided a steady stream of customers for federal cells in the 1920s. In any event, crime, like commerce, had gone interstate; it had become more mobile—not to mention the rise of so-called organized crime.

As the role of the federal government increased—with new crimes, new prisons, and new roles—it developed new institutions of enforcement. The federal government had no real detective force, at the beginning of the century, except for the Secret Service (Department of the Treasury)—a group formed mainly to fight counterfeiting. The Department of Justice often "borrowed" some of these men; but this was hardly a satisfactory arrangement. In 1908

Attorney General Charles I. Bonaparte (yes, he was a relative of Napoleon) set up a Bureau of Investigation, inside the Justice Department.[10] This eventually mutated into the Federal Bureau of Investigation (the FBI); in 1924 J. Edgar Hoover took over as director, and the rest, as the saying goes, is history.

Hoover, to give him his due, turned the FBI into a rather mighty tool of interstate crime fighting. He made the FBI more scientific and efficient; the FBI opened its own crime laboratory in 1932. Hoover's FBI also made a serious attempt to gather more accurate statistics on crime. The Uniform Crime Reports, issued from 1930 on, presented data on seven serious felonies (the so-called "index" crimes). The UCR had its flaws—it was dependent on data supplied by local law enforcement—but it was better than anything gathered previously.[11]

Hoover was also a master of publicity and public relations. He made himself (and the FBI) famous; he was a genius at getting credit for catching and killing "celebrity bandits"—John Dillinger or Bonnie and Clyde. In any event, its list of the "ten most wanted" and the like, and the exploits of the "G-men," became part of America's folklore during the 1920s and 1930s. This was the period of Prohibition, the heyday of "Scarface" Al Capone; of gangster movies with Jimmy Cagney and Edward G. Robinson, a period when Americans were at once fascinated and repelled by the larger-than-life figures of the tough guys, the gangsters who amassed enormous power—and the men who fought against them.[12]

Hoover was also, alas, a master of intrigue. During the McCarthy era, Hoover made the FBI almost synonymous with red-baiting and right-wing paranoia; during the cold-war era of the 1950s, Hoover was a powerful, untouchable figure, almost a law unto himself. Even presidents, it was said, were frightened of Hoover's files; the FBI infiltrated left-wing and civil rights organizations; it harassed Martin Luther King, Jr. Hoover was obsessed with communism, and the dangers to the polity from wild-eyed radicals, or those he defined as such. But as long as he lived, no one in high office dared challenge his regime.

The Criminal Trial

Most of the work of the legal system is dull, obscure, maddeningly technical—and, to be honest, boring for everybody but committed lawyers. The criminal trial is an exception. Trials are part of the national folklore. It would be hard to imagine popular culture—novels, magazines, movies, TV shows—if some insane, despotic law made it illegal to show criminal justice at work; made it illegal to make a movie about a trial, or to broadcast a cop show. Everybody has a kind of gut familiarity with the general rhythm of the criminal trial and its central images: the judge on his bench, with the American flag behind it; the lawyers battling each other, like knights jousting on horseback; the cross-examination of witnesses, and the cries of "objection!" from lawyers who bounce up and down to put in their protests; the twelve jurors sitting in their box, listening, nodding their heads; the tense wait for the verdict; the brief, gnomic announcement from the foreman of the jury; the reaction of the defendant, and the spectators, and so on. Millions of people have served on juries (millions more have wriggled out of the duty); and trial by jury is enshrined as a kind of sacred right in the state and federal constitutions.[13]

In the real world of criminal justice, trial by jury is the exception, not the rule. To begin with, most petty crimes do not go to a jury. At the base of the criminal justice system, in every state, are minor criminal courts. They go under various names: police courts, municipal courts, justice of the peace courts. Here thousands of cases get processed, the plankton of the criminal justice system: cases of drunkenness, petty theft, vagrancy. As one judge, William N. Gemmill of the Municipal Court of Chicago put it in 1914, the defendants in these courts constitute an "army of defeat," shiftless "derelicts," "driftwood cast upon a turbulent sea."[14] Indeed, the typical defendant in police court has been someone poor and desperate, someone on the margins of society, helpless and lawyerless. Many of them have been homeless people—"tramps" or hobos—or alcoholics, drug addicts, prostitutes. "Due process" is on a vacation in these petty courts. Justice, like man's life as Hobbes described it in a state of nature, was generally nasty, brutish, and short. Judges typically gave the defendants short shrift. Drunks and tramps got small fines, or (in the alternative) a short stay in the county jail. For many of these men (and women), justice was a revolving door. They would come to court, lose, serve a while, get out; and soon be back again. Eventually, the middle class entered these courts in larger numbers, thanks to the automobile and traffic laws. In Suffolk County, Massachusetts, there were 88,222 prosecutions in 1931–1934. No fewer than 39,614 of these were for drunkenness, and 26,433 for "violating motor vehicle and traffic laws."[15]

Even for felonies, for serious crimes, trial by jury has been on a steady downward spiral since the early nineteenth century. Fewer and fewer even of serious cases were going to the jury by 1900. Most men (and women) accused of big crimes were pleading guilty—sometimes or usually as part of a plea bargain. That is, they admitted to some level of guilt; in exchange, the prosecution charged them with fewer crimes, or less serious crimes, or dropped some of the charges; or hinted that the prosecution would get them a lighter sentence than they might otherwise expect. In Cleveland's Court of Common Pleas, around 1920, a little fewer than one of four felony cases went to trial; in almost half, the defendant pleaded guilty. In the rest, the case was dismissed.[16] In the federal courts, in the fiscal year ending June 30, 1940, only about 10 percent of the felony cases actually went to a jury: 4,941 out of 48,856.[17] In many places, all around the country, trial by jury was the exception, not the rule. Nobody, however, could beat the record of little Rhode Island: 632 defendants were accused of serious crimes in 1939. Seven of these cases were dismissed. All the others pleaded guilty. Not one single defendant faced a jury of his or her peers.[18]

Of course, not all defendants were willing to bargain; nor were all prosecutors. When the stakes were very high, as in murder cases, one or the other side, or both, might insist on trial by jury. But even in homicide cases, bargaining was common: a prosecutor could always dangle a lesser offense (manslaughter, for example) before a defendant as an inducement to give up the fight. In New Haven, Connecticut, in the 1920s, of seventeen defendants charged with murder, seven persisted in pleading not guilty; ten eventually pleaded guilty to a lesser charge.[19]

There were also defendants in the twentieth century who preferred not to go before a jury, even though they were pleading not guilty. Their cases were heard before a judge sitting alone. These were the so-called bench trials. Essentially, the bench trial was a product of the twentieth century. It had been the practice in Maryland in the nineteenth century; but Maryland, apparently, stood alone. It was even once a matter of some doubt whether a state could, constitutionally speaking, *allow* a defendant to waive his sacred right to trial by jury. In the 1920s the situation changed. Michigan, for example, passed a law in 1927 giving a defendant "the right to waive the determination of the facts by a jury" and, "if he so elect," to be tried "before the court without a jury."[20] In Maryland, where the practice was well established, it was praised as "beneficial" and efficient: a "judge sitting alone can readily dispose of three times

as many cases as when sitting with a jury." In Maryland nonjury cases far outnumbered jury cases in the 1920s; it was especially popular with "Charges of a
revolting nature." "Negroes," we are told, preferred bench trial, "in the justified
belief that the judge will be free from the racial prejudice so commonly exhibited by jurors."[21] In Ohio in the 1930s lawyers also urged clients to choose
bench trial for "cases in which community anger was aroused."[22] The Supreme
Court gave its approval to bench trials (in federal courts) in 1930.[23] Eventually,
almost all states came to allow bench trial; and in some states (Virginia, Mississippi) it became enormously popular for felony cases.[24]

What explains the decline of trial by jury, and in particular, the fantastic
career of "copping a plea"? One answer that immediately comes to mind is
speed and efficiency. Plea bargaining saves time and money; trials drag on, and
they are expensive to run. Plea bargaining is a great boon in congested urban
courts. All this is true enough, but plea bargaining flourishes also in places
where courts are neither crowded nor urban—Alaska, for example. In fact, plea
bargaining is everywhere; and it has been around for more than a century.[25] In
Alameda County, California, around the turn of the century, a fair number of
defendants (something over 10 percent), plea-bargained. They changed their
plea from not guilty to guilty of some lesser or fewer charges as part of a deal.
One William Carlin, for example, was charged with rape and abduction in 1910.
After making a deal with the deputy district attorney, he pleaded guilty to
abduction; and the rape charge was dropped.[26]

In essence, plea bargaining is a way to solve the problem of routine in
criminal justice. Why fire off the whole grand artillery of the modern criminal
trial in an open-and-shut case—a case, for example, of a man caught red-
handed robbing a drug store, who has, let us say, three prior convictions and no
reasonable defense? Before plea bargaining became routine, these people went
to trial—but the trials were quick, slapdash; they were typically lawyerless, and
many of them started and finished in half an hour or even less. It is this system
of mass-production "trials," not the full-blown trial that we see on TV, that plea
bargaining replaced. Plea bargaining was, in a way, more of the same; but it
shifted the burden of decision from a jury of amateurs to a corps of full-time
professionals. In the course of the twentieth century, plea bargaining became
more and more common, until (ultimately) it dominated felony proceedings
utterly.

On Stage

Trial by jury, then, was rapidly becoming less common; but this does not mean that trial by jury was unimportant. Trial meant something, first of all, to the people who were called for jury service. Many were called; fewer were chosen. Some were excused; others were dismissed when the attorney for this side or that challenged them. The percentages seemed to vary, state by state; in Illinois in the late 1920s, about half of those called were excused, but less than 10 percent a few years later in Massachusetts.[27] Trials, once they began, were longer than they had been in the nineteenth century, but the typical trial was not particularly long. In Illinois in 1927 the average juror served for seven days; only 2 percent of the jurors served longer than fifteen days.[28]

In the twentieth century, no less than the nineteenth, there was always a handful of big, splashy trials—cases which caught the public attention, sensational and dramatic events. These were the cases that filled column after column of newspaper print. Of course, only a few people could actually be present in the courtroom. The rest had to attend vicariously. But this was the age of the yellow press, the age of "sob sisters," the age of Hearst. The newspapers were only too happy to report these trials, and the more sensational, the more prurient, the better.

The sensation of 1907 was the trial of Harry K. Thaw for the murder of Stanford White.[29] White was one of America's most famous architects; his firm, McKim, Mead, and White, designed big, flashy, ornate buildings, often based on European models; the firm designed the New York *Herald* building, and the Colony Club of New York. Thaw, who killed him, also came from a distinguished family. He married Evelyn Nesbit, one of the famous "Floradora girls" of Broadway. She was a young woman of exquisite beauty. Thaw shot White to death in front of a horrified crowd in Madison Square Garden—a building White himself had designed. Thaw's technical defense was "temporary insanity." But the real defense was quite different. White, he claimed, was a rogue, a cad, a bounder—a man who had deflowered his wife when she was just a girl, first drugging her, and then accomplishing her "ruin." The trial was the "most spectacular criminal case . . . that ever sucked dry the descriptive reservoirs of the American press."[30] It had everything: sex, romance, show business, and the lifestyles of the rich and infamous.

The trial dragged on for months; and the jury could not agree; they wrangled endlessly over a decision. Thaw was tried again; this time, the jury found Thaw not guilty by reason of insanity. He was shipped off to the State Asylum for the Criminally Insane, at Mattewan, in New York State. He ran away, went to Canada, was extradited, and found himself back in the asylum. In 1915 he was declared sane, and finally released.

Every year there were sensational trials of this type—often involving jealousy, love triangles, and the like; trials filled with darkly sexual innuendo. They were lush dramas, embroidered with juicy details (some of them fake) in the daily press. These trials satisfied some deep-seated hunger of the bourgeoisie. The newspapers clucked and scolded and pretended to be appalled; but these sordid affairs gave off the rotting perfume of forbidden fruit. In the age of TV, worse was yet to come.

In any event, a criminal trial is almost inherently dramatic, certainly in the common-law system. Above all, it is the jury that makes them dramatic. As Leon Green put it in 1930, take the jury "out of the courthouse," and "the drama is gone. . . . There is no tenseness. . . . The attendants drop back into their humdrum ways. The crowd is made up of a few parties at interest and the habitual loungers."[31] The presence of the jury enhances—perhaps it even creates—the drama of the criminal trial. Bench trials are almost inevitably drier, less histrionic. The judge is a wise, even jaded, professional. Stirring speeches and dramatics mean nothing to him.

The jury deliberates in secret; and its verdict consists of one or two words; the jury never explains why it did what it did.[32] Juries are not supposed to be "lawless"; they are supposed to follow the judge's instructions on the law; a jury that tossed a coin, or reached an "irrational" or "prejudiced" decision would be doing something wrong—in theory.

But the secrecy of the jury room makes it impossible to tell whether the jury is following the rules. Secrecy allows the jury to bend and twist the official rules. The rules can be bright, clear, and brittle; giving them to a jury makes them (secretly) subtle, supple, and nuanced. The jury, much more than the judge, is the province of so-called "unwritten laws"—norms that are reflected in *patterns* of jury verdicts, but which the formal law is blind to. One irate commentator, writing in 1906, referred to a system of "jury-made lawlessness, or *juries' imprudence,* which recognizes rights that are forbidden by law and denies rights that are granted by law." Tongue in cheek, he set out a "decalogue" of the "jurisprudence of lawlessness"—for example: "Any man who seduces an innocent girl may, without a hearing, be shot, or stabbed to death by . . . any near relative"; or "In prosecutions for stealing horses, cattle or hogs, the presumption of innocence is shifted in favor of the live stock, and the accused is presumed to be guilty."[33]

This was satire; but it reflected a real situation. It was true that a man who shot his wife's lover was hard to convict, because of the "unwritten law." In one case from 1937, Paul Wright, in Glendale, California, shot his wife Evelyn, and a man named John Kimmel who had been his best friend. Wright had been asleep; he woke up to hear a single note, "repeated over and over on the piano." In the living room, he found his wife and his friend on the piano bench; John's fly was open. A kind of "white flame" exploded in Paul Wright's brain, he told the jury. The defense was the same as Harry Thaw's: temporary insanity. It was successful.[34] His lawyer, Jerry Giesler, credited the unwritten law: things which "are a part of no legally accepted code, but, no matter how we pooh-pooh them, they do exist in the minds of almost all people."[35]

In a few rare instances, a trial can be sensational even without a jury. The clearest example comes from 1924, when Richard Loeb and Nathan Leopold were tried in Chicago for the murder of Bobby Franks. This has been called "the crime of the century" (there are, of course, other candidates for this title). The two defendants were rich, young, brilliant, and Jewish; they killed young Franks, apparently, just for the thrill of it. For this reason, perhaps, their crime fascinated and horrified the country: it seemed to encapsulate some sort of twentieth-century malaise. Loeb and Leopold imagined that they could commit the perfect crime; but they were, in fact, blundering amateurs. They were caught fairly quickly; and they quickly confessed. The only issue to be decided, then, was their punishment: would they be hanged or not? Clarence Darrow argued for their defense; there was no jury, but the ladies and gentlemen of the press jammed the courtroom nonetheless. Darrow made an impassioned argument, insisting that the two young men were abnormal, emotionally immature, poisoned by reading too much Nietzsche, and the product of forces beyond their control. The judge did save them from the gallows, for whatever reason; he sentenced them to prison instead, to serve for the rest of their lives. It is unclear whether Darrow's eloquence made any difference. The judge stressed how young the defendants were; and Leopold himself (although he loved Darrow's speech) remarked that he found the whole psychiatric defense rather pointless: "We need only have introduced our birth certificates in evidence," and that would have been enough.[36] Loeb died in prison; a vindictive fellow prisoner stabbed him to death in the shower. Leopold served until the brink of old age, was released, and died a few years later.[37]

Sentencing

Crime leads to punishment; and punishment meant, increasingly, a "jolt" in prison. Except for some lifers, men who died in prison (there were quite a few of these), and men who were executed, all prisoners were eventually set free; hence (in theory) it was important to take steps to make sure they were cured of their evil inclinations. Of course, some criminals were beyond any hope of redemption, or so it was felt. The late nineteenth century invented the indeterminate sentence, as a way of separating wheat from chaff among prisoners. Under this system, a prisoner would be sentenced to some minimum term (often a year); at the end of the year, prison officials, who had him under their eye, would decide how long he needed to be locked up. After all, as an anonymous prisoner put it, in 1911, when a man goes to a hospital, he stays there not for a fixed period, but "until cured" (this was in the days before HMOs).[38] In the early twentieth century, more and more states shifted to the indeterminate system. New York in 1901 made it mandatory for all first offenders.

The states also adopted systems of parole and probation. Parole is a form of conditional release—the prisoner gets out early, on his promise of good behavior. Probation is an alternative to prison: it is a kind of preprison parole. These two were nineteenth-century reforms that became general in the early twentieth century. California, for example, passed an adult probation law in 1903.[39] The federal government adopted a parole law for federal prisoners in 1910. In each federal prison, a board of three would decide on paroles. In 1913 the law was extended even to lifers: they were eligible for parole after they had served fifteen years.[40] Forty-six of the forty-eight states had parole laws by 1925; and the two exceptions, Mississippi and Virginia, fell in line by the time of the Second World War.

Both parole and probation were, as we have said, conditional. They were ways of humanizing criminal justice, but they were also deeply discretionary. If a defendant asked for probation (after conviction, of course), his case was assigned to a probation officer, who looked around, talked to people, and made a report. The report was usually decisive. The judge almost always followed its recommendations. The report, then, was crucial in determining whether a man or woman went free or was shipped off to prison. But the reports, in California at least, were filled with gossip, neighborhood tittle-tattle, and a weird mixture of information thought to be somehow relevant. Good family background helped a lot. John Martindale, in Alameda County, got a negative report in 1907. Martindale had "practiced masturbation," and visited prostitutes "about two or three times a week"; he was also a drinker. Another loser, in the same year, had "masturbated since about 14," had gone "three times" to a brothel, was "fond of theatre," and had "no library card."[41] Parole conditions were also rather harsh: in Illinois in the 1940s it was a parole violation to drink or use drugs; in Minnesota it was a violation to buy goods on the installment plan; in California parolees were not to go in for "public speaking" or political activity; in Massachusetts it was a violation to "live with any woman" other than a "lawful wife."[42] Anybody who violated parole could be sent promptly back to prison—without further trial, or even without a chance to defend himself. Most men on parole were not sent back to prison, however: they either stayed clean, or stayed out of sight. Before the 1920s there was, in fact, very little formal supervision.[43]

Another innovation of the twentieth century was the juvenile-court system. The first juvenile-court law was enacted in Illinois in 1899, and applied to Cook County, Illinois (Chicago and some of its suburbs). Soon Denver had its juvenile court, too, under the leadership of Judge Ben Lindsey. The idea caught on. More than twenty states adopted the Illinois model, or something similar, within ten years; and by 1920 juvenile courts were almost universal.[44]

The juvenile court was, in theory, a family court for troubled kids. The law applied not only to "delinquents" (young people who had committed crimes) but also to neglected and abandoned children. In theory, this was no criminal court at all; even young delinquents were not to be tried and punished, but instead put under some sort of supervision; or sent to institutions where they would be, presumably, reformed and equipped for a better life. When one Frank Fisher of Philadelphia was committed to the House of Refuge under Pennsylvania's law of 1903, he complained that his rights had been violated: no trial, no jury, and "different punishments for the same offense . . . according to age." The appeals court brushed all these arguments aside. The law was not "for the punishment of offenders, but for the salvation of children"; its benign provisions put children under the "protecting arm" of the court.[45]

What was a delinquent? As the statutes defined it, this was a most expansive term. The Alabama law, as of 1907—and this law was by no means unique—was potentially vast and sweeping. A child under fourteen is delinquent, the law said, if, for example, he is "incorrigible"; or "knowingly visits or patronizes any . . . pool room, billiard room, bar room" or "habitually smokes cigarettes." A child is also delinquent, Alabama declared, if he "habitually wanders about any railroad yard or tracks; or jumps or hooks on to any moving engine or car"; or if he "habitually uses vile, obscene, profane or indecent language, or is found in possession of any indecent or lascivious book, picture, card, or paper." Proceedings in juvenile court, according to the statute, "shall be so conducted as to disarm the child's fears and win its respect and confidence"; these proceedings were to go on "without any form or ceremonies," so as to "elicit the true state of mind and morals of the child . . . and determine what is best for [his] . . . welfare."[46]

It would be good to know how wide the state in fact cast its net in Alabama, and elsewhere. We do know that most of the delinquents were boys. A study of Los Angeles County for the year 1912 found 502 delinquent boys and only 179 delinquent girls. ("Dependent" children were about equally divided among the sexes.) The youngest delinquent boy was eight; but most of them were fifteen, sixteen, and seventeen years old. The most common offense for boys was petty larceny (98 cases), followed by burglary (84), and incorrigibility (72). Girls got in trouble, for the most part, because they were "lewd and dissolute" (114).[47] The double standard, in short, was in full bloom.

In a controversial book, Anthony Platt has claimed that the reformers (the "child savers") more or less "invented" delinquency. Despite the rhetoric, the juvenile court was not as high-minded as advertised, according to Platt. The court was rather a means of socializing and oppressing the children of immigrants and the poor.[48] Certainly, this impulse existed. Contemporary literature, and the early reports out of the courts, are somewhat alarming: Judge Lindsey warned about "unchaperoned rides" in automobiles, about jazz, about the perils and "stimulations" of modern life.[49] A clash between middle-class and working-class cultures was definitely a factor in the way the courts operated. Juvenile courts and juvenile judges had enormous discretion; and they sometimes abused it. Not deliberately, to be sure. Most of the boys and girls who came into court were from poor families—predominantly immigrant families. In 1925 in

New York City, 71 percent of the young people had foreign-born parents. The judges' authority did come to "bear most heavily on the bottom sectors of society."[50] This, of course, was true of the whole criminal justice system.

On the other hand, we also know that, in some places at least, these courts were genuinely popular. Sometimes the true culture clash was between parent and child. In Alameda County, California, for example, a widow, Minnie Young, brought her young son George, age seventeen, into court. George, she said, was "vicious," and paid her "no respect." Bartolomeo Comella, a widower, had lost control of Salvatorio, who was fifteen: the boy stayed out "late at night and . . . [did] not explain where he has been"; he also stole $100 from his father's trunk.[51] In Utah in 1908 a sick mother told an investigator that her boy was "absolutely incorrigible"; he would gather with other boys in her house and "smoke cigarettes and read dime novels," threaten her, and stay away at night; he was "always running away."[52]

And what about the institutions themselves—the reform schools, the homes for troubled boys and girls? What were they like? Here, too, the picture is murky and mixed. There were genuine reformers, like Miriam Van Waters in Los Angeles, who wanted to avoid a harsh and punitive regime, and who tried to turn their charges into decent, upstanding citizens.[53] In other cases, the homes turned into prisons for the young—with iron bars and iron discipline.

The Crime of Imprisonment

Inside the prisons and jails of the country, conditions ranged from fair to abominable. This was, of course, nothing new. Prison was typically a "drab and lifeless world of granite, steel, and cement," often without a blade of grass, whose architecture expressed, in physical form, the very concept of brutality.[54] Penny-pinching by the state made conditions worse. In the 1920s, in Pennsylvania's Eastern Penitentiary, prisoners were crammed together so tightly— sometimes three or four to a tiny cell—that, according to one critic, there was "less room per prisoner . . . than a dead man has in his coffin."[55] Joseph Fishman, who published a scathing exposé of the jails in 1923, called them "human dumping grounds," a "putrid mire demoralizing to body, mind, and soul." He told a story of filth, vermin, disease, inhuman conditions. Prisoners were cut off from any sort of normal family life, and deprived of legitimate sexual outlets. As a result, according to Fishman, "homo-sexuality," both for men and women, was a "real problem in every prison."[56]

Of course there were from time to time attempts at change, amelioration, humanization. Thomas Mott Osborne became chairman of the New York State Commission on Prison Reform in 1913. Osborne was no airy theoretician; to get the flavor of prison life, he had himself admitted to Auburn prison, where he spent a week to see what it was like. He even spent a night in the "cooler" (the punishment cell)—sandwiched in between "the death chamber" on one side, and "on the other the prison dynamo with its ceaseless grinding, night and day." In this bare room, a "vaulted stone dungeon," prisoners slept on a floor of solid sheet iron, studded with rivets—an airless, dark hell. After only one day and night Osborne came out "feverish, nervous, completely unstrung."[57]

Unlike other critics and reformers, Osborne later had a chance to do something about prison conditions, when he himself became warden of Sing Sing in 1914. Osborne was full of fresh, high-minded ideas. He gave the prisoners a chance to enjoy a certain amount of self-government, for example. But Osborne did not last; he was forced out of office. In the words of his successor, Lewis Lawes, Osborne had let the pendulum swing too far, "from severity to liberality"; and the result was "chaos."[58]

Prison life was never a bed of roses, even in the North and West; even under a man like Lewis Lawes, it was regimented, degrading—and the food was bad. But there were amenities in Sing Sing in the 1920s: chicken twice a year, a library, extension courses. In the South, conditions were much worse, especially for black prisoners. And both north and south, some of the worst conditions were in the local jails and lockups, which lacked even the barest rudiments of professional management. Oscar Dowling, of Louisiana's State Board of Health, condemned the local jails of the state as "ill-ventilated, foul-smelling" places, and completely unsanitary. Prisoners complained of crowding, of bedbugs and mosquitoes, of unbearable heat. The food was inedible. One prisoner wrote that the bedding was not changed or aired for long periods; that there were no screens on the windows; that the stench was horrific. Breakfast was coffee and rice and bread and salt meat; the only other meal, the prisoner asserted, consisted of "White Beans or Black eyed Beas with fat Boiled meat and corn Bread the Beans create Such volum of Gas in my Stomach tel it causes me to suffer." The prisoners were supposed to bathe once a week, but one jailer sneered at the idea: "We bring them here to work not to bathe." The jails, Dowling concluded, were in fact "places of torture."[59]

Most appalling of all were conditions in southern chain gangs. Most of the prisoners were black. They worked under inhuman conditions, and in chains. The southern chain gangs, however, became a national scandal only because a white man, Robert E. Burns, told his story in a famous book: *I Am a Fugitive from a Georgia Chain Gang* (later made into a movie). Burns had been convicted of a crime in 1922 and sent to the chain gang (his gang, in segregated Georgia, consisted of about a hundred white men). Later he escaped. He was free for seven years; then a woman "betrayed" him by revealing his identity. He "voluntarily returned" to Georgia, expecting "justice." Instead he was sent to the chain gang again; he escaped for a second time in 1930.[60]

Life on the chain gang, as Burns described it, was a living hell. The men woke at 3:30 A.M., ate greasy fried dough, sorghum, and fried pork with coffee "by lamp light," then set about their backbreaking work—long, killing hours under the terrible, boiling southern sun, all the time shackled like animals, weighed down by heavy chains, even sleeping in chains, chains that were "permanently riveted on them, and were worn every minute of the time."[61] They were brutalized by illiterate, savage guards, and lived in crude barracks, in conditions of indescribable filth, eating rank, paltry, wormy food, day after endless day. Yet Georgia's reaction to the bad publicity was (at least at first) not outrage but rather anger and denial. The chain gang was not abolished in Georgia until the late 1940s.[62]

From time to time, a muckraker like Burns ripped open the walls, so to speak, and showed the horror of life inside the prison system. Another of these was Kate Barnard, who in 1908 exposed massive brutalities and inhumanities in the Kansas prison system: floggings, water torture, confinement in a chamber called the "crib." "Sodomists and masturbators" had to submit to a "surgical operation" in which a "brass ring was inserted through the foreskin of an offender's penis." But the public was indifferent; and the response of the governor of Kansas was perhaps typical: "Kate would like to see the prisoners . . . treated as if they were guests at the Waldorf Astoria."[63]

Not everybody suffered as much as the Kansas prisoners, or the black chain-gang prisoners. The prisons were not only harsh; they were frequently corrupt. When George Remus went to prison in Atlanta in 1923, this important bootlegger traveled in his own private railroad car. The warden, Albert E. Sartain, took bribes in exchange for giving big bootleggers special living quarters, better meals, and weekends of freedom. Sartain himself went to prison in 1927.[64] But in many prisons, contraband was smuggled in; and prisoners who had connections were able to use them to advantage.

As we saw, there *were* prisons that made an effort to treat prisoners as human beings—to give them a degree of freedom (as much as is possible behind bars), some meaningful work, religious life, a chance to learn. Nathan Leopold, at Stateville Prison in Illinois in the 1920s, records how grateful he was for the privilege of "the yard" on Saturdays. Turned loose from their cells, the men played baseball and handball: "There was a complete lack of formality. . . . You could smoke; you could go where you liked and talk to whom you liked; you could take off your shirt and get a sunburn."[65] Over the years, this freedom tended to increase. But it eventually paved the way to a strangely dual system— repression and high walls surrounding the prison, but a weird sort of anarchy inside, in the prison yard, in the cells, as if the prison were in fact a kind of penal colony, ruled by the inmates themselves. In such a society, the toughest and cruelest of the "cons" would rise to the top—the worst of the lot would become kings of a netherworld of violence. But much of this lay in the future.

The War Against Vice

America is said to suffer from (or glory in) a "Puritan" tradition; but any such statement has to be taken with a large grain of salt. The Puritans, after all, are long since gone; and not many living Americans are their descendants—far more of them come from very different backgrounds and cultures. Puritan ideas about vice, pleasure, sexuality have passed into history. In fact, the story of the war on vice is full of zigs and zags. In the early nineteenth century, the war sputtered to a halt, or was, at best, reduced from a boil to a simmer. At the end of the nineteenth century, there was an eruption or outburst of new morality—a flock of new laws heating up the war against sin and debauchery.

What exactly caused this shift is debatable. It is tempting to put some of the blame on a kind of cultural panic—a sense that America was under siege and had to defend its soul and its germ plasm from cultural enemies. On one side was solid old-fashioned, rural Protestant America. On the other side, the millions of immigrants, the debris of eastern Europe; the lowlifes and degenerates who were flooding into the country and breeding like rabbits; the vice and effeminacy of the big cities; the decay of family and church, and so on.

In any event, the old bourgeoisie took a stand against rank immorality. Legislatures peppered the statute books with fresh laws against obscenity, sex, sodomy, and gambling. With what effect is unclear. Satan was a crafty fellow, and he had many disguises. The purity movement extended into the early twentieth century as well; indeed, it heightened.

One particular object of horror was the so-called "social evil"—that is, prostitution. Prostitution had always been under a legal cloud; but many cities had evolved a cozy arrangement between the police on one hand, and those who bought and sold sex and other forbidden commodities on the other. Often enough, this arrangement required the greasing of official palms. The result was a kind of protozoning. Brothels and houses of assignation were tolerated, so long as they stayed in their place; their place was in the so-called red-light districts. This was usually established informally, although a Texas law of 1907, directed against "disorderly houses," specifically provided that the act would not "interfere with the control and regulation of bawds and bawdy houses" in cities in which these houses were "actually confined . . . within a designated district" of the city.[66] In Cheyenne, Wyoming, prostitutes paid a fee, were examined for "communicable diseases" and "personal cleanliness"; if they passed this test, they were given an official certificate.[67] In Chicago in 1910 the superintendent of police even issued "rules" regulating "vice." For example, "no swinging doors" on brothels; no "house of ill-fame" within two blocks of a school or church; no short skirts or "transparent gowns" in "the parlors, or public rooms."[68] These were rules and regulations for a business that was, in fact, itself illegal.

This comfortable system, naturally, offended many decent citizens; and in the early years of the century it came under vigorous attack. A number of cities created "vice commissions" to look into the situation, issue reports, and recommend what should be done. One notable example was the report of the Chicago Vice Commission (1911). According to the commission, the "honor of Chicago" and the "physical and moral integrity of the future generation" demanded an end to "public prostitution." The "social evil" left in its wake "sterility, insanity, paralysis, the blinded eyes of little babes, the twisted limbs of deformed children, degradation, physical rot and mental decay." The commission called for "constant and persistent repression of prostitution" in the short run, with "absolute annihilation" as "the ultimate ideal."[69]

The vice commission reports provided chapter and verse about the extent of the "social evil." The Philadelphia commission found 372 parlor houses, call houses, and other places where "immoral conditions" flourished; also 127 "disorderly saloons," for a total of "499 disorderly and vicious resorts"; they counted some 3,700 women who sold sex in Philadelphia, not to mention "kept women" and "casual prostitutes."[70] These reports were fodder for the crusaders who launched the so-called red-light abatement movement. The point was to put some teeth into the battle against vice. Specifically, it was a movement to get rid of the vice districts, and the payoffs that made them possible. Segregated districts merely spread the "cancer" of vice. They had to go. City after city— places as diverse as Minneapolis, Omaha, Des Moines, and Boston—tried to shut down the houses and drive the prostitutes out of town.[71] Severe "abatement" laws were passed; under these tough laws, an ordinary citizen could bring an action to "abate" a vice house as a nuisance. This made a detour around the corrupt police departments and politicians who were on the take. At the same time, massive pressure on the police and the city fathers from the clergy and the aroused bourgeoisie forced some cities to take action. The famous old districts—Storyville in New Orleans, Happy Hollow in Houston, the Barbary Coast and the Tenderloin in San Francisco—were closed down tight; the women were arrested or driven out of town.

Yet vice had a way of bouncing back. After all, these fallen women and wicked saloons did not make a living in a vacuum; they had real customers, thousands of them, and these customers were men from all walks of life. Nobody spoke out in favor of prostitution; but there was a silent army of customers, and when the drums and the gospel shouting died down, when the storms ceased and the sky cleared, vice came creeping back out of its hideaways; and perhaps with renewed strength. An investigation in San Francisco in 1935 found 135 brothels going full blast in the city—many of them houses that supposedly had been put out of business in 1917.[72]

Along with red-light abatement, there was a national uproar—almost a hysteria—over so-called white slavery. There were sensational claims that evil men in the sex business lurked in movie houses, dance halls, and dark passages to lure innocent country girls to their ruin, using trickery, force, or even "poisoned darts or hypodermic needles"; the girls would then be held as virtual slaves of sex. No one could tell "when his daughter or his wife or his mother would be selected as a victim."[73]

What was to be done? There were state and local laws, of course. Illinois, for example, had a law against pandering (1908). It was a crime to "cause, induce, persuade or encourage a female" to become an "inmate in a house of prostitution" by "promises, threats, violence, or any device or scheme."[74] In July 1908 one George Gibbs got a year in prison for attempting to sell a twenty-year-old woman, Minnie Peterson, to a brothel owner in the notorious Levee district of Chicago.[75] But on the whole, the state and local laws seemed ineffective, for one reason or another. Congress bestirred itself, responded to the clamor over white slavery, and passed the famous Mann Act, which made it a crime to "transport . . . any woman or girl" across state lines "for the purpose of prostitution or debauchery, or for any other immoral purpose."[76] James Mann, the representative whose name was immortalized in the Mann Act, came from Chicago's Hyde Park district, and was familiar with the pandering law.

Was there any truth to the hysteria over white slavery? Some, no doubt. But not a great deal. It was certainly right to worry about the sexual oppression of women; and about syphilis and gonorrhea. Yet perhaps the most important problem underlying the "social evil" was the economic inequity that faced women in big cities. Many women turned to prostitution on their own, without any hypodermic needles or drugs; they were desperate for money. This was a hard idea to swallow—especially in the light of traditional notions of the purity and innocence of women. The white-slave propaganda shifted the blame from the economy to evil, sinister, dark-haired men, who preyed on naive, virtuous women and ruined their lives. Outrage over these villains was more comfortable than outrage over what shopgirls took home as their pay.

The Mann Act was supposed to help crush white slavery, but the Supreme Court gave it a much broader reading. A key case involved two young men from Sacramento, California, Drew Caminetti and his buddy Maury Diggs. They were in their twenties, married with children, and from somewhat prominent families. Fidelity was not their strong suit. They went gallivanting off to Nevada with two young women in tow. This trip created something of a scandal; and the two men were arrested and, eventually, tried for violating the Mann Act. Of course, there was not a hint of white slavery, or prostitution, or commercialized vice in the case; no indication that the women were the least bit unwilling to have their fun. Nonetheless, the two men were convicted of violating the Mann Act. The Supreme Court affirmed: Caminetti and Diggs had crossed the state line for an "immoral purpose," and this was enough to satisfy the act.[77]

The Justice Department claimed that it was interested in commercialized sex, that for the most part it left alone the amateurs at the debauchery game— that is, people like Caminetti and Diggs. But the record shows otherwise. All sorts of cases were tried in the courts, cases which ranged "from seduction and betrayal, to casual romantic trips, to serious relationships of living together." From 1922 to 1937 the FBI looked into 50,500 alleged violations of the Mann Act. Many of the investigations started with complaints sent in by busybodies, people with grudges, outraged husbands, wives, parents, and miscellaneous others. For example, a woman calling herself "a mother" sent a letter to the Department of Justice from West Palm Beach in 1927, in which she claimed "There is a J.S. Nouser liveing at 727 Kanuga drive with a woman that he not married to and they was on a trip this summer to california and new York they stoped at the pennsylvania Hotel in new york as man and wife."[78]

The Mann Act was applied to women, too, if they violated the sexual code; a study of women in federal prison between 1927 and 1937 found that about a quarter of the Mann Act violators were simply unmarried women who dared to travel about with married men. Scandalized and angry wives sometimes blew the whistle on their husbands.[79] More sinister was the prosecution of the black boxer Jack Johnson, whose sex life crossed the state line *and* the color line. He was tried in 1913 and sentenced to prison. The rock-and-roll singer Chuck Berry was sent to prison similarly in 1960; and Charlie Chaplin, whose real sin was his leftist leanings, was tried but acquitted in 1943.[80] Critics had warned that the Mann Act was a fertile breeding ground for blackmail. Sure enough, in January 1916 detectives arrested a gang of alleged Mann Act blackmailers. These men supposedly would "shadow" rich men, following them across state lines with their girlfriends. They would then confront the men, claim to be United States marshals, and demand payoffs. Sometimes the gang "employed . . . attractive women to assist in creating evidence."[81] The victims, naturally enough, were reluctant to step forward.

The Mann Act was only the most notorious of the laws that broadened the war against illicit sex. Since the 1870s it had been a federal crime to send obscene stuff through the mail—and anything to do with contraception was by definition obscene. Under some state laws, too, contraception itself was taboo: in Connecticut it was a crime to use any "drug, medicinal article, or instrument" for this purpose.[82]

Obscenity itself was, of course, outlawed almost everywhere; and, according to some statutes, so was anything that was indecent, impure, or likely to corrupt the young. Connecticut added a ban on any printed stuff, including newspapers, which might be "devoted to the publication of . . . criminal news, police reports or pictures, and stories of deeds of bloodshed, lust or crime."[83] Kentucky had a similar statute, and added a ban on printed material whose "principal characteristic is to depict by illustrations men and women inflamed by alcoholic beverages, drugs, or stimulants."[84] In many states, it was also at least a minor offense to use indecent language in public.

Starting in the late nineteenth century, too, the states changed their laws in such a way as to make virtually all teen-age sex a crime. The key concept here was the so-called age of consent. If a male had sex with a woman or girl who was too young, legally speaking, to say yes, it was "statutory rape," a serious crime— even if she had, in fact, said yes; and even if the male himself was young. The common-law age of consent was ten—very low, to our tastes; and in 1885 it was no higher than twelve in any state. Many states had begun to raise the age considerably by 1900. In a handful of states, it was eighteen—which is, to our tastes, uncomfortably high. The trend continued: Florida jacked up the age of consent to eighteen in 1900, California did so in 1913, Georgia in 1918; in no state was the age of consent lower than sixteen in the early years of the twentieth century.[85]

The net result, of course, was that young love and young lust now carried the danger (for him) of prison. Needless to say, the laws did not put an end to hormonal longings. Undoubtedly, many young lovers did their thing when the parents were gone, or in hotel or motel rooms, or in the back seats of cars, and no one was the wiser (or no one cared). But the statutes were hardly dead letters. Mary Odem found 112 prosecutions for statutory rape in Alameda County, California, between 1910 and 1920. In twenty-five cases, the man was sent to state prison; in ten, he went to county jail. In most of these cases, the sex was entirely consensual. In 72 percent of the Alameda cases in the decade between 1910 and 1920, and 77 percent of cases in Los Angeles in 1920, according to Odem's study, the women said "they had consented to sexual relations with their male partners." In one case, a fifteen-year-old girl had a sexual relationship with a nineteen-year-old man. They met at the Majestic Dance Hall in Oakland. When the girl's mother found an incriminating letter, she "beat her daughter, reported her to juvenile authorities, and had the young man arrested for statutory rape."[86] Between 1930 and 1939 in New York City, 1,948 men were indicted for statutory rape, and a fifth of them suffered felony convictions.[87]

In general, however, the sex laws were sporadically enforced. There were millions of offenders, and most of them never got caught in the web of the law. There were occasional arrests, for example, for selling condoms and other such devices; yet the Sears, Roebuck catalogue of 1902 offered thirteen kinds of douching syringes, including one, a "Hard Rubber Stem Syringe," which was "highly recommended . . . to married ladies."[88] A study of 256 boys who were classified as "sex offenders" and treated at Children's Court clinics in New York is disconcerting to say the least. Seventy-one of the boys were accused of "excessive masturbation," forty-seven of "speaking or writing obscenity," twenty-three simply of "heterosexual experiences." Many others were accused of "sodomy" (seven of "sodomy with girl"), and forty-seven of "fellatio." One boy was accused of "attempted incest with mother."[89] The enemies of the tight sex laws were correct to talk about blackmail and bias in enforcement. They might have added sheer bad luck.

Whether enforced very much or not, these laws were on the books, and they give rise to an obvious question: what social factors lay behind this eruption of official morality? It is hard to say exactly; and probably there was no single cause. Clearly, there was a sense, among respectable elites, that American values were in danger. There were some objective reasons for alarm—venereal diseases, for example, and the development of more dangerous forms of drugs, like heroin; and certainly, respectable people were right to be concerned about police corruption, vicelords sitting on city councils, and so on. But beyond these more rational factors, as we have seen, there was also a sense of general culture unease—one might even say a kind of culture war. Immigration was changing the very face of America. Millions were pouring in from southern and eastern Europe: Catholics, Jews, Slavs. The country was more urban, less rural; more industrial, less agricultural. New ways of thinking and new ideologies were in the air. Technology was transforming the country. To many of the old-line, respectable, Protestant majority, the value system that they cherished was under attack. They turned to the legal system in a desperate attempt to buttress their moral code.

Men and women of the early twentieth century believed quite strongly in progress. Many of them defined progress as a long historical journey away from the animal nature of the human species—thus, away from vice—toward a purer, more respectable, more civilized style of life. Jane Addams envisioned a future without prostitution: a future free from "the survivals and savage infections of . . . primitive life." Mankind—with the help, to be sure, of science—was going to *evolve* toward a higher state.[90]

The Noble Experiment

Beyond a doubt, the climax of the moral fervor of the early twentieth century was the "noble experiment," national Prohibition. The Eighteenth Amendment prohibited the "manufacture, sale, or transportation of intoxicating liquors" within the United States, and any import or export of these commodities "for beverage purposes." It got the necessary number of state ratifications in 1919, and went into effect in January 1920. Congress and the states had "concurrent" authority to enforce the amendment through "appropriate legislation."

Of course, Prohibition did not come out of the blue.[91] There had been a strong temperance movement in the nineteenth century. The movement had its ups and down, but it won some notable successes; and a number of states were already legally dry by 1900—North and South Dakota, Kansas and Iowa, Maine, Vermont, and New Hampshire. The Anti-Saloon League, founded in the late nineteenth century, was a powerful and tireless lobbying group. By the early twentieth century, it had branches in almost all of the states. The league had strong allies among American Protestant churches. It worked to get "dry" laws passed at the local level, then at the state level; and, finally, to achieve the impossible dream, national prohibition.

The efforts of the league and its allies were successful, perhaps more than they could have imagined. By 1913 a group of southern states and Oklahoma had joined the ranks of the dries. But as in the case of child labor reform, prohibition ran into the ancient problem of federalism. The flow of liquor into dry states from other states kept these states "semimoist"; and yet the states had no power to put an end to interstate commerce—in liquor, or in anything else, for that matter.[92]

The drys increased pressure on Congress to do something about the problem. In 1913 Congress passed the Webb-Kenyon bill; this prohibited the shipment "of any spirituous . . . or other intoxicating liquor of any kind" into any state, if the liquor was "intended" to be used "in violation of any law" of the receiving state. President William Howard Taft vetoed the bill; he disliked handing power to the states over interstate commerce, even in the liquor trade. But the tide was running strongly against the wets. Congress overrode the veto, and the bill became law.[93]

The Webb-Kenyon bill put pressure on express companies and railroads. The dry states were quick to take advantage of the law. Mississippi, for example, enacted a law in 1918 forbidding any common carrier from shipping liquor into the state. There were to be "no property rights of any kind" in liquor; liquor could be seized by local officials, and then destroyed. It is interesting that the act made it a separate crime for the local officials to drink the stuff themselves.[94] The Kansas law of 1917 (officially called the "bone-dry law") made it a crime to own or possess any liquor, even for personal use.[95] Arkansas made it illegal to advertise liquor in dry areas of the state.[96] In 1917 America's entry into World War I made it easy to fight liquor as a way of conserving resources. In September 1917 the government prohibited the making of distilled spirits; the ban on making beer and wine came two years later.[97] And in December 1917 Congress sent the Eighteenth Amendment to the states for ratification.

After ratification, Congress duly passed the Volstead Act (1919) to provide Prohibition with its federal teeth.[98] The Volstead Act made it illegal to "manufacture, sell, barter, transport, import, export, deliver, furnish or possess any intoxicating liquor"; there were exceptions (medicine, sacramental wine), but even these were stringently regulated. Under the act, it was also unlawful to make or sell any "utensil, contrivance, machine, preparation, compound, table, substance, formula direction or recipe" for use in making liquor. Liquor making or liquor selling tainted any room, house, boat, or structure in which this indecency went on; any such place was a "common nuisance," and anybody who maintained a common nuisance was guilty of a crime.

Many states passed their own mini-Volsteads; the California version, the so-called Wright Act, was adopted by referendum in 1922.[99] It specifically provided that the "penal provisions" of the Volstead Act were "hereby adopted as the law of this state." From 1920 until 1933, when the Twenty-First Amendment put an end to the miserable career of Prohibition, the "noble experiment" was an object of controversy, praise, derision—and widespread evasion if not downright disobedience. Prohibition arrests and prosecutions filled the jails; yet millions drank and went on drinking. Prohibition is widely (and perhaps unfairly) blamed for the rise of the gangster culture—for Scarface Al Capone, the Chicago mobster, and his counterparts in other cities—blamed, in short, for the spread of organized crime. Organized crime would have emerged in any event; but Prohibition certainly gave it an opening, a market, and a wonderful, popular product to sell.

Prohibition is held up as the textbook example of an "unenforceable law." It may have been, in fact, more effective than most of its critics admit. City people, particularly rich ones, guzzled away in their speakeasies; but there were many "dry" strongholds in rural areas and small-town districts. Saloons and bars were illegal, selling liquor was illegal—even though millions violated the law, the law had an impact on the time, manner, and amount of violation. There is some evidence that this impact was far from zero. Deaths from liver disease and drunken driving dropped significantly during Prohibition, at least in the early years.

Prohibition certainly had its nasty side effects; and not just Al Capone. There was municipal corruption before and after Prohibition; but Prohibition provided a staggering array of incentives to bribe, cheat, and undermine the normal forces of law and order. Prohibition may have saved some lives that would have been lost to cirrhosis of the liver or splattered on the highways; on the other hand, it cost lives too. Liquor was an illegal product; it was peddled in the shadows, and it was manufactured by dubious people in dubious ways. In 1928, we are told, there was "an epidemic of deaths from wood-alcohol poisoning"; desperate people were drinking horrible concoctions made from antifreeze, rubbing alcohol, liquors contaminated with all kinds of poisons, with names like Old Horsey, Soda Pop Moon, Squirrel Whiskey, Cherry Dynamite, and a "fluid extract of Jamaica ginger, popularly known as Jake"; even "small quantities nearly always caused a terrible form of paralysis."[100]

In the end, Prohibition was a political failure—of this there can be no doubt at all. Millions hated it from the start, and the ranks of the wets gained more and more political recruits as the decade dragged on. Looking back, we tend to see Prohibition as the last gasp of the dour anhedonic culture of old-line America. It was a crusade led by small-town, solid, respectable Protestant worthies. It "symbolized the superior power and prestige of the old middle class in American society."[101] But this old middle class was, alas, swimming against the tide. The broader public, on the whole, saw nothing wrong with a nip or two, at least once in a while; or a glass of wine; or a friendly beer at home or in a tavern. The "public" here was Catholic and Jewish and ethnic, and it was closely allied to the big-city middle class. Prohibition was a fight between two cultural strains, and it is clear which one won out in the end.

Despite the enormous literature on Prohibition, there is a lot left to learn about enforcement on the ground. Most people who drank got away with it. Yet we know from official figures that there were thousands and thousands of arrests and prosecutions. In 1920 the federal district courts had a caseload of 7,291 Prohibition cases; in 1930 the numbers had gone up to 56,992. To be sure, most defendants pleaded guilty, paid a fine, and went home. In the Southern District of Texas, during the court term of February 1921 in Houston, there were twenty-three liquor cases; all of them paid fines except one man, who went to jail for six months.[102]

Nobody was satisfied with the level of enforcement. For the wets it was too much; they told horror stories of abusive enforcement, and of what almost amounted to warfare between agents and drinkers and suppliers. The exact figures are in dispute, but a newspaper in 1929 estimated that some 1,360 people had been killed, and another thousand wounded, in the course of enforcement of the laws.[103] Then there were the raids and the seizures in a vain attempt to end the flood of liquor pouring in from Canada, from home stills, from Caribbean ports, and from countless other sources. Yet for the dries, the rate of enforcement was far too low. By the end of the twenties, the smell of rot and decay was unmistakable. Prohibition was doomed. In 1929 President Hoover appointed a National Commission on Law Observance and Enforcement, the so-called Wickersham Commission. Among other things, it studied the question of how to enforce Prohibition. But the commission's conclusions were weak and namby-pamby; it satisfied neither wets nor dries. Tougher enforcement was in fact impossible—politically, if for no other reason.

The election of 1932 sealed the fate of Prohibition. The Democratic convention adopted a plank calling for the repeal of the Eighteenth Amendment. Roosevelt won the election in a landslide, and in 1933 the states ratified the Twenty-First Amendment to the Constitution, which sent the Eighteenth Amendment to an early grave. The "noble experiment" ended in failure.

The Second Prohibition: Drugs and Drug Laws

The first quarter of the twentieth century was a fateful period, too, for what became the war on drugs, one of the great law-enforcement disasters of the twentieth century. In the nineteenth century, neither drug trafficking nor addiction was, essentially, a criminal act. Not that anybody thought it was a good idea to be hooked on drugs; addiction was a disaster for most people, and almost everybody knew it. It was a slippery slope leading downward to complete ruin; it destroyed family life, smashed any hope of a meaningful career, and threatened early and pitiful death. But the state had not yet wheeled in the heavy artillery of criminal justice.

All this changed in the twentieth century.[104] In 1909 Congress passed an Opium Exclusion Act, making it illegal to import opium, or opium derivatives, except for "medicinal purposes."[105] The real turning point, however, was the Harrison Narcotic Drug Act of 1914.[106] This was not, in form, a criminal law. It was a registration and tax law. Those who made or distributed narcotics had to keep certain records, and register with the federal government. Buyers and sellers of drugs also had to pay a tax. The act also provided that you could not buy drugs without a doctor's prescription. The statute covered opium and opium products, and "coca leaves" and their derivatives as well.

Webb v. United States (1919) was an important test case.[107] Webb was a doctor who practiced in Memphis, Tennessee. He prescribed morphine for addicts who needed a fix; and Goldbaum, a druggist, filled these prescriptions. Were these men violating the Harrison Act? In a short, almost casual opinion, the Supreme Court said yes. Prescribing drugs so that an addict could be "comfortable" and maintain "his customary use" was a "perversion" of the law, said the court. The decision put an end to the career of "dope doctors," who made a living by prescribing drugs. In April 1919 a group of New York City doctors and druggists who had been supplying drugs to addicts were arrested in raids.[108] Tactics of this sort in effect made outlaws of everybody connected with the drug trade. Addiction itself became, in reality, a crime. Many cities established clinics, trying to wean addicts from their habit—with dubious success. The stick tended to prevail over the carrot.

By 1925, indeed, there were 10,297 federal arrests for narcotics law violations, and 5,600 convictions.[109] This was only the beginning. The Bureau of Narcotics was established in 1930. The federal drug authorities—notably Harry Anslinger, the first commissioner of narcotics (1930)—tirelessly argued for strict enforcement, and warned the nation incessantly of the drug menace. Anslinger and his minions were, in the opinion of some, "righteous zealots," who terrified the country with their horror stories and created "a great public hullaballoo" about the "dope menace" and "dope fiends."[110] Partly due to Anslinger's efforts, the Marihuana Tax Act added another drug to the list of the banned in 1937. Marijuana was associated in the public mind with Mexican immigrants; this "killer drug" was blamed for all sorts of violent crimes, and for causing Mexicans to run amok.[111] The propaganda of men like Anslinger, it has to be admitted, apparently fell on fertile soil.

The federal drug effort was echoed in the states, which passed their own drug laws—often piggybacking on the federal provisions. Thus Oklahoma in 1919 made it a state crime to buy, sell, or make drugs, except as authorized and licensed under the federal act.[112] Under Oregon's drug laws of 1923 any habitual user of drugs was declared a "vagrant," and could be punished accordingly.[113] In 1932 a Uniform Narcotic Drugs Act was drafted and offered up to the states. They responded eagerly: by 1952 the law had been adopted in forty-one of the states; and the few holdouts had drug laws of their own, more or less along the same lines.

The Uniform Narcotics Act made it unlawful to make or possess "narcotic drugs"—basically opiates and cocaine derivatives. Doctors and dentists could prescribe drugs, but only "in good faith and in the course of . . . professional practice." Any shop, house, or building "resorted to by narcotic drug addicts," or used to keep or sell drugs, was declared a "common nuisance." Violation of the act was a crime: in the South Carolina version, for example, a first offense carried a fine up to five hundred dollars, imprisonment up to six months, or both. Second offenses could earn a fine of two thousand dollars and up to two years in prison, or both.[114]

Long after Prohibition itself had been hooted off the stage, the "war on drugs" has continued; over the years it has, in fact, gotten more and more violent and desperate. The punishments for violation have become stupefyingly draconian; repeat drug offenders in some states can be punished more severely than murderers. Billions of dollars disappear down a rat hole. Yet the war never seems to get won. This is in many ways America's internal Vietnam.

Born Criminals and Other Enemies of Society

Every generation, it seems, has its own theory about what makes people do crimes, and why. Hardly anybody in 1900, say, believed that selling one's soul to the devil was an important source of criminality. They did, however, strongly believe that some people were born criminals; that crime was in their blood. These defective human beings constituted the new "dangerous classes." It was not a new idea. It went back to the work of Cesare Lombroso in Italy in the late nineteenth century.[115] Lombroso's ideas had a kind of climax of acceptance in the first part of the twentieth century. Henry Goddard in 1925 published a sensational book about the "Kallikak" family (a fictitious name). Goddard was director of research at a New Jersey institution for the feeble-minded. He traced the genealogy of a whole crew of prostitutes, degenerates, and petty criminals; the line went back to "Martin Kallikak," a soldier in the Revolutionary War, who fathered a bastard child. Kallikak later married a respectable woman, and produced a line of "good" people. Thus his sex life set in motion a kind of "natural experiment." The laws that Gregor Mendel had discovered in his work on "the ordinary garden pea" also applied to human beings.[116]

The ideas of men like Goddard seemed to have wide appeal. As Dr. William J. Hickens, director of the Psychopathic Laboratory of the Municipal Court of Chicago, put it in 1921, "A cabbage will produce a cabbage and a rose a rose, in spite of all." He pooh-poohed the idea of environmental causes of crime: "moral defectiveness" was the problem, nothing more. What could one expect from the likes of N.J., a male, aged twenty-one, a "low grade moron," a "hunchback," who did not walk or talk until he was four, a "heavy cigarette smoker," with two arrests, seven stays in a mental institution, and two alcoholic aunts?[117] Men like these were defectives, they would inevitably commit anti-social acts; and (worst of all) would breed true.

The science of "criminal anthropology" rested on the notion that criminal types betrayed themselves with physical signs. As late as the 1930s, Earnest Hooton, after a "nation-wide investigation of criminals," reported that criminals had "relatively shorter and broader faces. . . . The nose is relatively shorter and broader . . . ears with less roll of the helix or rim," along with "stunted growth and inferior development."[118] Other experts and penologists were skeptical; Thomas Mott Osborne, for one, sneered at the notion that there was such a thing as a "criminal nose."[119] But millions of people believed that crime was biological destiny. It was a curse of the blood.

Could anything be done about it? Leo Stanley, chief surgeon at San Quentin, thought he could improve the men in prison with glandular tinkering. Between 1918 and 1940 he performed ten thousand "testicular implantations." It seems that "goldfish, fed on a diet of ground testicular substance from the ram, increased their activity by four hundred per cent over those fed on . . . ordinary dried shrimp." Why should humans do any worse than goldfish? His subjects, Stanley thought, became more active and energetic, and had better appetites, after he had done his work.[120]

Adding "testicular implantations" was much less popular than the idea of getting rid of these offensive organs altogether: cut off the rotten branches and keep them from propagating. If you believed in born criminals, it made perfect sense to stop "perverts" and the mentally defective from having babies, by hook or by crook. The nation, after all, was "in danger of race degeneration because of the rapid increase in the ranks of the defective," as one writer put it.[121] Indiana passed a pioneer sterilization law in 1907: the preamble declared that "heredity plays a most important part in the transmission of crime, idiocy and imbecility."[122] Any institution in the state which housed "confirmed criminals, idiots, rapists and imbeciles" was authorized to hire two "skilled surgeons." If a "committee of experts" decided that "procreation was inadvisable" for an inmate, the "skilled surgeons" were to sterilize the creature.

California followed in 1909: its statute called for "asexualization" of convicts who had chalked up two sex crimes, or three serious crimes of any sort, and any convict who gave "evidence" in the prison that "he is a moral and sexual pervert."[123] About half the states eventually had some sort of eugenics statute.[124] The Washington State statute required all state institutions to report those under their care who were "feeble-minded, insane, epileptic," as well as "habitual criminals, moral degenerates and sexual perverts," whose "offspring," because of the inheritance of "inferior or anti-social traits," would likely become "a social menace or wards of the state." These were then candidates for sterilization.[125]

Some states were more enthusiastic than others about sterilizing. California went about this dreary task with great gusto, especially for the "feeble-minded"; 5,820 people had been operated on by 1929, a figure said to be four times as great as the total in the rest of the world.[126] Not everybody joined the chorus of praise for these laws. State courts struck down a fair number of them—for example, New Jersey, in a 1913 case involving an epileptic woman in a state hospital—usually on the grounds that they inflicted a cruel, degrading, and humiliating punishment, and without due process.[127] In some ways, the high (or low) point of this movement was reached in *Buck v. Bell,* a Virginia case that brought the issue before the United States Supreme Court.[128] Carrie Buck, described as a "feeble minded white woman," was eighteen years old and lived in the State Colony for Epileptics and Feeble Minded. She was said to be the "daughter of a feeble minded mother," and in turn the mother of an "illegitimate feeble minded child."

Oliver Wendell Holmes, Jr., wrote the opinion; and it is one of his most famous (or notorious). Holmes approved of the Virginia law, without hesitation; and he saw no constitutional barriers. After all, if the state could force children to be vaccinated (the Supreme Court had said so), and if it could force young men to die in battle, why should it not be able to order a woman to be sterilized? Sterilization here was fully justified. The eugenic nightmare of America demanded radical surgery. "Three generations of imbeciles," Holmes said, "are enough."

The irony is that what Holmes faced, really, was no generations of imbeciles at all. Neither Carrie Buck, nor her mother, nor her child (who died of measles in childhood) was actually retarded, as far as we know.[129] The child, in fact, had been considered quite bright. Hence the case was based on an appalling misconception. It was not three generations of imbeciles, but three generations of poor, inarticulate women; three generations of white trash, three generations at the bottom of the heap in society. To Holmes, and so many of his contemporaries, the decision was progressive. From the standpoint of the year 2001, *Buck v. Bell* looks entirely different. It seems like a heartless and gratuitous act of cruelty: Carrie Buck and her daughter were innocent victims, sacrificed on the altar of cultural and sexual hysteria.

5

Race Relations and Civil Liberties

In many ways, the period before the New Deal was the high point of American apartheid, the flowering of Jim Crow. A dense network of laws and ordinances in the southern and border states kept the races apart—and the whites on top. Behind the laws were the "unwritten laws," the code that made up the so-called southern way of life. If a black (in particular, a black man) stepped over the line, and acted insolent or "uppity" to a white person, he was at serious risk. If, God forbid, he was accused of molesting or raping a white woman, his life was not worth a nickel: torture, mutilation, and death, by lynch law, stared him in the face.

So firm was the dogma of separation that society and the law did not allow even consensual relationships. Sex between the races was taboo—formally at least. Marriage between black and white was strictly forbidden (this was true in many other parts of the country as well). This social taboo was strengthened by "scientific" arguments about higher and lower races; and the dire results of "mixing" or mongrelization. Any tincture of black blood was an offense against white purity. State statutes defined how much black blood it took to expel a person from the ranks of whitehood; more than one-sixteenth was a typical amount, but even one-sixteenth was too much blackness for Virginia. A law of 1924 made it a crime for a white person to marry anybody except a partner "who has no trace whatsoever of any blood other than Caucasian."[1]

In Mississippi around the time of the First World War, one Antonio Grandich and his wife sued Hancock County, Mississippi, which refused to let his children attend a school for whites. Antonio and his wife had married as white people, but the school officials thought the children were actually "colored." Great-grandmother Christiana was the problem; some said she was "an Indian," but others said she was "a negro, and that she was classed and associated with the negroes at church," that she had "negro hair" and "was dark or ginger-cake color." The children could pass for white; but the court held that any admixture of black blood made a person black.[2] In a will contest (from California, no less, and as late as 1939), a court declared the marriage of Marie Antoinette Monks invalid, because she was black and had married the deceased, Allan Monks, who was white, in Arizona, which did not tolerate such marriages. To prove that Marie Antoinette Monks was not white, a hairdresser testified about the "moons of her fingernails" and the "kink" in her hair; an anthropologist found "negroid" features in the cast of her face, the "color of her hands," and her "protruding heels"; a surgeon noted the "contour of her calves and heels," as well as the "wave of her hair."[3]

The "one-drop" rule owed much of its force to the traditions of slavery. Under slave codes, the child of a slave woman was itself a slave. Slave owners often slept with slaves, producing a class of light-skinned slaves—and eventually even slaves who could pass for white. A contrary rule, which would recognize white fathers, would have freed too many slaves. Slavery was long since gone; but the caste system remained, and blackness was so stigmatized and demonized that any trace of it was considered enough to cast a "white" into the class of the American untouchables.[4]

Position in society, economic opportunities, social mobility—all depended on race. Race was a southern obsession; somewhat less so (and less legally mandated) in the North. Race was also a key issue with regard to immigration and naturalization: these benefits were for white people only. The segregation laws were in full force in the first half of the century. Georgia law, for example, required separate schools for "white and colored races," and separation on railroads and street railways.[5] An Arkansas law of 1903 required "separate apartments . . . for white and negro prisoners" in all prisons and jails; and separate "bunks, beds, bedding . . . dining tables." It was against the law to handcuff or chain any white man to a "negro prisoner."[6] The law also required separate voting and tax rolls. In North Carolina factory owners were required to provide "separate and distinct toilet rooms" for workers, "said toilets to be lettered and marked in a distinct manner, so as to separate the white and colored males and females"—four toilets in all. Moreover, these toilets had to be "separated by substantial walls of brick or timber."[7] In North Carolina, as in the rest of the South, schools were, of course, segregated; but in this state, even books had to obey the segregation laws—books were "not . . . interchangeable between the white and colored schools"; they were confined to the use of the "race first using same."[8]

All this was only the tip of the iceberg, of course. The school and railroad laws solemnly promised that the facilities, though separate, would be "equal" for the races; but no southern state took this promise seriously. In fact, equality had to be avoided at all costs. The system was a caste system; and any situation in which blacks and whites could be or would be treated as equal members of society, or in which, God forbid, a black could come out on top, was a violation of the code. Hence the prohibition against intermarriage—aimed especially at black men who might want to take a white wife. Hence the 1915 ordinance of Fort Worth, Texas, that made it "unlawful for any white person and any negro to have sexual intercourse with each other, within the corporate limits of Fort Worth."[9] Hence the Texas law of 1933 which prohibited any "fistic combat match, boxing, sparring or wrestling contest between any person of the Caucasian or 'White' race and one of the African or 'Negro' race."[10] Elsewhere, of course, blacks and whites did fight in the ring; and Jack Johnson, a black man, had been heavyweight champion. When Johnson knocked out the "Great White Hope," Jim Jeffries, in 1910, a fight that generated enormous excitement, riots broke out all over the country; blacks in major cities North and South paid with broken bones for their "victory"; seven people died in the ensuing uproar.[11]

Parks and all public amenities were also strictly segregated in the southern states; whites had the best or only facilities; blacks were thrown a bone, or had nothing at all. The federal courts showed no sympathy for the black cause in the first decade of the century—no signs of backing away from *Plessy v. Ferguson;* or of interfering with segregation in any way. A case in point was *Berea College v. Kentucky* (1908).[12] Kentucky made it a crime to run a school or college "where persons of the white and negro races are both received as pupils for instruction." Berea College was interracial; it was fined for violating the statute. The Supreme Court saw nothing wrong with the law or the fine. In *Chiles v. Chesapeake and Ohio Railway Company* (1910), a black man bought a first-class railway ticket from Washington, D.C., to Lexington, Kentucky.[13] In Kentucky, where Chiles changed trains, he was forced into the colored section of the train, which he protested, claiming his rights as an interstate passenger. The Supreme Court cited *Plessy* and called the Kentucky rules "reasonable"; they reflected "the general sentiment of the community." What they meant of course, was the white community.

Any avenues to political change in the South were effectively blocked. Blacks simply lacked political power. No blacks held state or county offices in the states of the old Confederacy. Very few blacks voted—though not from apathy or choice. In the late nineteenth century, the southern states started the process of getting rid of black voters; they finished off the job in the twentieth. The states used every trick and stratagem in the books, and some outside the books, to keep blacks out of voting booths. Anyone who wanted to vote had to go through an obstacle course. In South Carolina voters had to pay a poll tax, own three hundred dollars' worth of property, and "both read and write any section" of the South Carolina Constitution.[14] In Mississippi prospective voters had to be able to read sections of the federal and state constitutions, and also give a "reasonable" interpretation of what they had read. No blacks ever seemed to be able to pass these tests; whites sailed through routinely (or were not even asked). Troublesome or persistent blacks were given rougher treatment. As an Alabama official put it: "At first, we used to kill them to keep them from voting; when we got sick of doing that we began to steal their ballots; and when stealing their ballots got to troubling our consciences we decided to handle the matter legally, fixing it so they couldn't vote."[15]

Unsurprisingly, the tactics worked. In 1906 in Alabama, 85 percent of all male whites of voting age were registered—and 2 percent of adult black males. In other states the story was much the same. By 1910 blacks of the South were effectively disenfranchised, through various devices.[16] The United States Supreme Court at first showed little interest in the voting rights of blacks. In *Giles v. Harris* (1903), the plaintiff, a "colored man," brought suit on behalf of himself and "more than five thousand negroes," complaining that they were wrongfully barred from voting in Montgomery County, Alabama.[17] The Supreme Court, in a decision both technical and smarmy, turned them down. Holmes, who wrote the opinion, added insult to injury: the complaint, he said, "imports that the great mass of the white population intends to keep the blacks from voting." But if this were true, then it would be pointless to register black voters: "a name on a piece of paper" would not defeat the "conspiracy." Holmes's rather cynical advice was to seek "relief" from the state of Alabama itself, or the government of the United States—exercises, of course, in total futility.

One notorious device for keeping the voting process white was the so-called grandfather clause. It was invented in Louisiana, at the very end of the nineteenth century, and spread from there to other southern states. The grandfather clause was a provision that exempted the descendants of voters from this or that prerequisite to voting. The issue of the grandfather clause came before the Supreme Court in 1915, in its Oklahoma version. Oklahoma, a freshly minted state, had amended its constitution to limit voting to those able to "read and write any section of the constitution of the State of Oklahoma." The registrars would make sure, of course, that no black ever passed such a test. And whites? Well, everyone was excused who was "entitled to vote under any form of government" on January 1, 1866; or lived in a foreign country at that time; or was a "lineal descendant" of anybody who fell into one of these categories. That, of course, covered just about every male except blacks.

This was a paper-thin subterfuge; and when it was attacked in the federal courts, in *Guinn v. U.S.* (1915), the Supreme Court did strike it down. There was only one reason, said the Court, for picking 1866 as the crucial date: that it came before the Fifteenth Amendment, which gave blacks the right to vote. Hence the clause violated the rights which that amendment guaranteed.[18]

This was, in a way, a great victory. It seemed to signal that the attitude of the Supreme Court was changing. But it meant little or nothing in practice. The Court had no power to enforce its decision, to affect what happened on the ground, at the polling booths and registries, and in the humid southern climate of general repression. The white South remained adamant; the federal government, under Presidents Taft and Wilson, showed no interest in helping out. To the contrary, Wilson, a white southerner in origin, was an avid fan of segregation in the federal capital.

Most blacks lived in the South, and most were farmworkers—sharecroppers, or contract workers. They were desperately poor; and totally dependent on white landowners. They were, in many ways, as tied to the land as they had been under slavery. In the Mississippi delta, which was overwhelmingly black, the blacks worked primarily as sharecroppers on big white plantations. They lived in rude cabins, and whole families worked long, killing hours in the cotton fields, from before dawn until sundown; the landowner gave them the cabin, some tools, cottonseed, water, firewood, a mule team—and took half of the crop. The workers were perennially in debt to the plantation store.[19]

Bailey v. Alabama (1911) mounted a rather direct attack on the southern labor system.[20] Lonzo Bailey, the plaintiff, a black farmworker, had signed a contract to work as a "farm hand" for a white-owned company; his pay was to be twelve dollars a month, and fifteen dollars was paid in advance. Bailey quit after about five weeks. In doing so, he ran afoul of a nasty and mean-spirited statute that made it a crime to defraud an employer by entering into a labor contract, getting an advance, and then failing to live up to the contract (or give back the money). This failure would be "prima facie evidence" of intent to defraud, according to the statute; and the defendant would not be allowed to testify "as to his uncommunicated motives, purpose or intention."[21] This all reads rather blandly; but the point of the statute was to tie black workers to their jobs—to make them virtual serfs. It was a criminal statute; hence violation would expose a poor black worker to the dreaded chain gang, or perhaps condemn him to work for his old boss for nothing, paying off his debt to the boss through the sweat of his brow.

This statute went too far for the United States Supreme Court to swallow. The Court struck it down (despite a tasteless, cynical, and sneering dissent from the great Oliver Wendell Holmes, Jr.). The statute created a form of "peonage," meaning (as the Court defined it) "compulsory service in payment of a debt." Congress had banned peonage in 1867.[22] The statute was within the power of Congress, said the Court, under the Thirteenth Amendment (which abolished slavery and "involuntary servitude").

The statute never said it was aimed at black workers (and black workers only), or had anything to do with race. But race and black farm labor were, in fact, what the statute was all about. It was part of a network of southern laws that tied black workers to their jobs.[23] Under Alabama law, for example, anyone who "entices, decoys, or persuades any apprentice or servant to leave the service or employment of his master" committed a crime; it was also a crime to "entice away" any "renter, or share-cropper" under contract to a landowner.[24] Perhaps even more crucial were the dreaded vagrancy laws. In Alabama any person "over the age of twenty-one years, able to work, and who does not work, and has no property sufficient for his support, and has not some means of a fair, honest, and reputable livelihood," was a "vagrant"; and vagrancy was a crime.[25]

Thus any unemployed black could be charged with a crime—and, once again, put to the choice between the chain gang and work for his regular "master."

This was, in general, a tough and abiding system, deeply entrenched. The *Bailey* case, like *Guinn,* changed nothing on the ground, altered nothing in the labor system. Some of the southern states made cosmetic changes in their statutes. But that was all. There was no follow-through; no *will* to follow through. Blacks, everywhere in the South, were treated as a pool of expendable labor. During the great Mississippi flood of 1927, black men were simply pressed into service on the levees—in Greenville, Mississippi, for example, blacks were ordered to do the job or go hungry. The men were "herded like cattle"; they had to work long, hard hours for zero wages, subject to "mean and brutish treatment" that amounted to "downright slavery."[26]

The labor system was tied to the larger, social system; a caste system, in which any and all whites outranked any and all blacks; in which all blacks were social pariahs, as far as whites were concerned. As we have seen, blacks could not legally marry a white person in many parts of the country. But in the South, the harsh code of white supremacy meant that no black man could act "indecently" or insolently or familiarly with a white woman. A black man who touched a white woman, even accidentally, was in deep trouble. The punishment for gross violations of the code was death. *A fortiori,* a black man who killed, raped, or assaulted a white woman, or was even suspected of such a crime, was as good as dead.

This period was the high-water mark of lynch law. In Paducah, Kentucky, a black man, Brock Henley, was accused of assaulting and robbing a white woman, Mrs. George D. Ross, in her own home. Henley was arrested. George Ross led a crowd of men to the jail; they sawed through the steel bars, seized Henley, walked him three miles to the Ross home for identification, then hanged him and another black man, in broad daylight. The bodies were "riddled with bullets and then burned beyond recognition." Mrs. Ross thanked the crowd: "I did not know I had so many friends." Nobody tried to stop the lynching; and the coroner's verdict was the usual one: death at the hands "of a mob composed of unknown persons." In the same state in 1908, a mob of "night riders" surrounded the home of a black named David Walker, who had been "involved in a dispute with a white woman, which of course was more than enough of a transgression." They poured oil on the house, set fire to it, and shot

Walker, his wife, her baby, and three other children as they appeared at the door, begging for mercy. Another child probably burned to death inside the house.[27] According to an NAACP report published in 1919 and covering a thirty-year period, there were on average more than one hundred victims of lynch mobs each year; 78 percent of the victims were black, and more than 90 percent of the incidents took place in the South.[28] A careful study published in 1933 claimed that 3,724 people had been lynched in the United States through 1930. As late as 1930, twenty-one lynching deaths were recorded; twenty of the victims were black. In one case, at Ocilla, Georgia, the victim suffered incredible torture: "His toes were cut off joint by joint. His fingers were similarly removed, and his teeth extracted with wire pliers." After more mutilation, the man was soaked with gasoline and set on fire; as thousands of people watched, his body was also pumped full of bullets.[29] This was no isolated case: dozens of blacks were tortured, burned, mutilated; and about the time of the First World War, a pregnant black woman in Georgia who protested against the lynching of her husband was herself murdered by a mob, tortured and burned; the baby was ripped from her belly and crushed to death.[30]

Almost nobody was ever punished for these hideous acts of barbarism. Most white southerners thought lynching was justified—often they blamed the justice system, which they condemned as too slow, too inefficient, too lax. In fact, the system was far from lax when black defendants were brought to trial. In some cases of blacks accused of rape, it was hard to tell the difference between lynching and "regular" justice. Will Mack, a black man, was indicted, tried, convicted, and sentenced in Rankin County, Mississippi, in just six hours in 1909. Then he was hanged in public, in front of more than three thousand people eating ice cream and watermelon; women and children were there, and the spectators howled as the trap door was opened and Mack's neck was broken on the gallows.[31]

The formal system was not usually this swift; and it did not allow as much physical suffering and torture as some people wanted. And it apparently did not convey a harsh enough message to the black population. Lynch law was the mailed fist of white supremacy. It enforced the southern "code" through sheer terror. Obviously, formal, official law could never give that code its full recognition; nor could it approve of the ways the code was transmitted and given flesh.

There were voices raised against lynch law—white voices as well as black ones—and even in the South. But on the whole the white community either approved of lynching or was at best indifferent to it, especially in small towns and rural areas. Blacks were outraged and black organizations were active in the struggle against lynching; but blacks lacked political power. Lynching was, to be sure, quite illegal. In some states, even southern states, there were specific statutes outlawing lynching. In Alabama, for example, lynching (or aiding and abetting lynching) was a crime punishable by death; any mob member who was even present at a lynching could be sent to prison for up to twenty-one years. Moreover, any jailer or sheriff who, "negligently or through cowardice," allowed a mob to take a prisoner out of the jail and put him to death could be fined and imprisoned.[32] Needless to say, this law was a dead letter. Federal legislation, often proposed, was politically out of the question. Congressman Dyer of Missouri introduced an antilynching bill in 1920; it passed the House in 1922, but southern senators talked it to death in the Senate.[33]

Generally speaking, the criminal justice system in the South was hopelessly biased against black defendants, especially those accused of crimes against whites. Such defendants had virtually no chance of acquittal—no chance even of fair trial. Black-on-black crime was treated, on the whole, with indifference. Rape of a black woman apparently was almost never punished. Even the occasional act of clemency to a black reeked of white supremacy. Stake Morris of South Carolina was convicted of killing another black. He was sentenced to death. The governor of the state, Cole Blease, commuted his sentence: "I am naturally against electrocuting or hanging one negro for killing another, because, if a man had two fine mules . . . and one went mad and kicked and killed the other he certainly would not take his gun and shoot the other mule"; similarly, "when one negro kills another . . . he should be put in the Penitentiary and made to work for the State."[34]

And work they did. In the late nineteenth century, some southern states leased their prisoners to private businesses, which almost literally worked them to death. The system continued into the twentieth century in Florida, for example. Florida had no state prison; it leased its convicts out—many of them were "good husky" black men, rounded up for petty charges or no charges at all, and put to dirty, dangerous work for private companies. In Alabama convicts mined coal under hellish conditions; 128 of them were killed in a mine explosion in 1911. But what replaced the leasing system was little better: chain gangs, forced labor for the state (instead of private businesses), and the same litany of inhuman treatment and miserable conditions. At Parchman, Mississippi's vast penal colony, the black convicts lived in terror of "Black Annie," a long leather strap, with which they were mercilessly whipped.[35]

Some stirrings of revolt, and signs of change, were seen in the 1930s. A famous instance was the notorious Scottsboro case in Alabama.[36] Nine poor young black men who had been riding the rails were accused of gang-raping two white girls. In fact, the charges were fabricated—the girls were lying, as one of them soon admitted. But that did not seem to matter. The trial was a scandal— quick, slapdash, with only the most feeble attempt to defend the frightened defendants. The jury was, naturally, all white. Eight of the nine were sentenced to death. The Alabama Supreme Court affirmed seven of the convictions. By this time, the case had become notorious, and the NAACP and the Communist Party vied for the right to defend the Scottsboro defendants. The case went to the United States Supreme Court, which reversed the convictions in 1932; the defendants, the Court said, had not received a fair trial.[37] The defendants were tried and convicted again, in a full blaze of publicity. Ultimately, the Scottsboro defendants got out of prison. They had wasted long years behind bars for a crime they did not commit; but their lives, at least, were spared.

Lynching, the labor system, political disfranchisement: in general, the period between 1890 and 1930, and especially up to 1915, was a dark and dismal period in the South (and in the country in general) for black Americans.[38] Race radicals were in control; they treated their black fellow citizens with cruelty and callousness; they defined blacks as beasts—savages, criminals, potential rapists; or as lazy and shiftless, worthless, ignorant, responding only to force or the threat of force. Why this occurred, and so systematically, is not easy to say. Clearly, the white South felt threatened; but by what? Blacks were a cheap pool of labor. The white South profited from exploiting them. Segregation and the southern code got rid of potential competition for good jobs. The caste system allowed even the poorest whites to feel superior. Any signs of rebellion and mobility—any sign of the emergence of a black middle class—merely fueled the resentment.

Yet these economic motives hardly seem adequate to explain the intensity of race hatred. Maybe it is pointless to look for rational explanations. At the end of the twentieth century, the century of the Armenian genocide, Pol Pot, Adolf Hitler, the slaughters in Rwanda, and Bosnia, and Kosovo, and countless other examples, should we still be surprised at how much savagery lies just beneath our human skin?

Housing

In the cities of the South, blacks were somewhat freer than in rural areas. In the early part of the century, many blacks did leave the country backwaters, and settle in the cities—in Richmond, Baltimore, St. Louis, Louisville, and others. White majorities hardly gave them a warm welcome. After 1910 many cities passed segregation ordinances—ordinances designed to keep blacks in black neighborhoods and away from white ones. Baltimore was a pioneer; but other cities followed—cities as large as Atlanta, Georgia, and as small as Greenville, South Carolina.[39]

Under the Louisville ordinance—an ordinance passed "to prevent conflict and ill-feeling between the white and colored races"—a black family was not allowed to move into any residential block with a white majority; nor could a white family move into a black-majority block. This symmetry probably fooled no one. In *Buchanan v. Warley* (1917) the United States Supreme Court unanimously struck down the ordinance.[40] The Court "freely admitted" that there was a good deal of "race hostility"; it admitted, too, that the law was "powerless" to control this, and that race hostility was a "serious and difficult problem." But the ordinance went too far: the Fourteenth Amendment did not allow local government to interfere with "property rights except by due process of law"; and this kind of race-based ordinance failed the test. *Buchanan v. Warley* was another famous victory that, in the end, accomplished precious little. True, states and cities could no longer segregate overtly, blatantly, and under color of law. But segregation continued almost unabated. There was more than one way to skin this particular cat.

It takes money and organization to bring a case like *Buchanan* to the Supreme Court. Moorfield Storey argued the case against the ordinance. His expenses were paid by a new organization, the National Association for the Advancement of Colored People. The roots of the NAACP went back to 1909.[41] In the immediate background was a horrendous race riot in Springfield, Illinois, in 1908. Mobs of whites ran amok in a black neighborhood for two days; several blacks were killed, and thousands fled the city. The riots moved people like Oswald Garrison Villard, grandson of a famous abolitionist, to form an interracial organization that might do something for the cause of racial justice. Ultimately, the NAACP adopted litigation as one of its key strategies—a decision which led to some of the most important cases of the century, and, finally, to *Brown v. Board of Education.*

The Other Americans: Asians

A strong strain of nativism runs through American history. To be sure, Americans have always thought of themselves as tolerant people, and perhaps they were, compared to others; but in the nineteenth century there were riots against the Irish, the Mormons, the Catholics, and the Chinese, as well as the scandalous history of relations between black and white and between Native American and white. Nativism was quite strong at the end of the nineteenth century, and in the first part of the twentieth. We mentioned a kind of cultural panic among old-line Americans. On the West Coast, where most Asians lived, the Chinese were subject to all sorts of legal and social indignities. By law, they were not allowed to immigrate; and no Chinese person could become a naturalized citizen. Consular officials in San Francisco and other ports rigorously enforced the anti-Chinese laws. They were also deeply skeptical of any Chinese person who knocked at the door of the port, claiming to be a citizen by birth. They considered these claims mostly false, and denied them by the hundreds. The Chinese who protested, and who got as far as the federal court system, occasionally won out. But the regulations grew tighter and tighter, until it was almost impossible for any claimant to wriggle through.[42]

The legal system (and society) discriminated against Asians, but there were many zigs and zags in the process. In the nineteenth century, for example, Chinese children in San Francisco went to segregated schools; but segregation, southern-style, did not flourish in California, and the policy lapsed in the twentieth century. As early as 1905 the San Francisco Board of Education gave up the idea of keeping Chinese students out of "white" high schools, when Chinese parents threatened a boycott. By the 1940s formal segregation no longer existed in the city.[43]

Japanese immigration began later than Chinese immigration. Many of the Japanese came to Hawaii and California as farm laborers; in 1900 there were twenty-five thousand on the mainland; by 1910 there were seventy-two thousand, the majority living in California. Whites in California were no friendlier to the Japanese than they had been to the Chinese, the other example of the "yellow peril." In San Francisco the board of education had originally tried to force Japanese students to go to the "Oriental school"; but here too the parents protested. The treatment of the Japanese then became a foreign policy issue. President Theodore Roosevelt in 1906 called segregation "a wicked absurdity." This was meant to mollify the Japanese government. In the so-called gentlemen's agreement of 1907–1908 between Japan and the United States, the Japanese government agreed to stop workers from moving to the United States; in exchange, the United States agreed to relax restrictions on the wives and children of Japanese laborers.[44] Still, the legislature in 1921 amended the California law to allow local districts to segregate Japanese students. Four school districts in Sacramento County did so, but no others. In Sacramento County at least one resident thought part of the problem was that Japanese kids "could play better baseball. . . . Well we couldn't stand for it."[45]

Race prejudice on the West Coast was quite strong. It was not as pervasive and deadly as race relations in the American South; but it was bad enough. It carried with it strong overtones of economic rivalry, sexual paranoia, and the usual vague fears of dark, unmentionable evils that might destroy (as it were) America's precious bodily fluids. The Japanese, as one California newspaper put it, "increase like rats."[46] As in the case of African-Americans, marriage between races was *verboten*. For example, under Oregon law, no marriage could take place between a white person and anyone with "one-fourth or more" of "Mongolian blood."[47] The land question was particularly touchy. Many of the Japanese had become farmers. In 1913 California passed a law to keep Asians from buying or owning land in the state.[48] A similar prohibition was embedded in the constitution and laws of Washington; and a law to the same effect was passed in Arizona in 1921.[49] Many of the Japanese, however, found ways to get around the Alien Land Law of 1913 in California. A law of 1920 closed many of the loopholes, and a law of 1923 was even more stringent.

Nativism and Immigration

Chinese exclusion laws constituted an early sign that the theory of the "melting pot" did not command universal respect. The melting-pot metaphor comes from the title of a play by Israel Zangwill (1908); Zangwill was himself a Jewish immigrant. America, he wrote, "is God's crucible, the great Melting Pot where all the races of Europe are melting and re-forming." He added, somewhat hyperbolically, "Germans and Frenchmen, Irishmen and Englishmen, Jews and Russians—into the Crucible with you all! God is making the American."[50]

Zangwill's idea of the melting pot was not everybody's idea. Most Americans, though they may have agreed that the country was a melting pot, had a different concept of what was supposed to melt and what would come out of the pot. Their notion was that immigrants should become real Americans, 100 percent Americans, not "hyphen-Americans"; immigrants were expected to get rid entirely of their old ways, and adopt the language, customs, habits, and manners of the older Americans. The Old World was nothing more than slag at the bottom of the pot.

Most immigrants found it hard enough to do the melting. For some groups, melting was just plain impossible—at least so the "real" Americans thought. The Chinese, for example, were (supposed to be) so different, so exotic, so through-and-through different, that they would always remain undigested. This was one reason why the country was better off without them.

In addition, the Chinese and Japanese were considered economically dangerous. They worked for peanuts, it was said, and this threatened the standard of living of American workers. Huntington Wilson put it this way in 1914: "We cannot maintain the wage scale of American labor and admit particularly cheap foreign labor any more than one can maintain two connected reservoirs at different levels." Wilson was also worried about "races which tend to live apart in groups and are not easily assimilable to the American nation in blood, traditions, sympathies, and ideals."[51]

The Chinese failed on both scores. So did the Japanese. In *Ozawa v. United States* (1922) the question was: were the Japanese eligible to become citizens? The answer depended on whether a Japanese could be a "free white person." Ozawa's lawyer argued that the Japanese were "white persons," who had "Caucasian root stocks; a superior class, fit for citizenship"; and, moreover "assimilable."[52] But the Supreme Court was not buying this line; in their view, the Japanese were clearly not Caucasian. Curiously enough, some non-Caucasians could be naturalized: Africans, and persons of African descent. This was because of constitutional amendments and statutes adopted after the Civil War. But very few Africans ever applied; and American blacks did not have to be naturalized; they were citizens by birth.

Thus it was Asians primarily who were barred; they were neither African nor white. But who was an Asian? In 1909 one Najour applied for citizenship; he came "from Mt. Lebanon, near Beirut." He was "Syrian," and "not particularly dark"; he had no "Mongolian" features. The government opposed his application (one wonders why), but a federal court let Najour become a citizen.[53] He did a lot better than one Shahid, another Syrian, who applied for citizenship in South Carolina. Shahid was fifty-nine, could not write English, and seemed to know very little about America. "In color, he is about that of walnut, or somewhat darker." A district judge decided Shahid was an Asian; moreover, he was not the sort of person who would "benefit . . . the country" if allowed to become a citizen; his application was denied.[54]

The Supreme Court faced the issue of defining an Asian when one Bhagat Singh Thind, who described himself as a "high caste Hindu," applied for citizenship. The people of India, his lawyer argued, "belong to the Aryan race." A "high-class Hindu" looks down on the "aboriginal Indian Mongoloid," whom these "high-class Hindus" had conquered. But the Supreme Court refused to buy the argument.[55] The "blond Scandinavian and the brown Hindu," said the Court, might have had a "common ancestor in the dim reaches of antiquity"; but the "average man knows perfectly well that there are unmistakable and profound differences between them today." The opinion contains a long disquisition on race, citing such authorities as the Encyclopedia Britannica. But popular opinion was the bottom line. And popular opinion (meaning, as well, the opinion of the justices) drew a line between the "children of English, French, German, Italian, Scandinavian, and other European parentage" and the likes of Bhagat Singh Thind; the European children "quickly merge into the mass of our population and lose the distinctive hallmarks of their European origin." Not so Mr. Thind: "It cannot be doubted that the children born in this country of Hindu parents would retain indefinitely the clear evidence of their ancestry." That evidence, presumably, was a dark and distinctive skin. This was a "racial difference"; and the "great body of our people instinctively recognize it and reject the thought of assimilation."

In these cases, the popular idea of race was dominant. An Asian was an Asian. It was the popular (social) definition of black that prevailed as well—the "one-drop" rule is a rule not of science but of public opinion. Asians were not fit for the melting pot. Other groups, presumably, could assimilate (even the "dark-eyed, swarthy people of Alpine and Mediterranean stock"); but there was a limit to national tolerance of swarthiness.[56]

There was also a growing fear that many new immigrants were choosing not to melt in the melting pot—they were living in private enclaves, in their little Italys and little Bohemias and little Polands. It was, after all, a time of troubles in the land—or at least, it felt that way. The frontier was closed, opportunities were shrinking, class war seemed to loom over the horizon. Nativism fed on these fears; and on the idea, or myth, that immigrants had no intention of giving up their foreign ways. This in itself seemed un-American. So was failure to speak English. In 1917 the state of Utah, hardly a hotbed of exotic foreigners, passed a statute to establish schools for "Americanization." Every alien in Utah between the ages of sixteen and forty-five who did not command English at the fifth-grade level had to attend an evening class "for at least four hours a week" during the normal term. The school districts were authorized (or required) to set up evening schools to teach "English, the fundamental principles of the Constitution of the United States, American history, and such other subjects as bear on Americanization."[57]

Guardians at the Gate

The immigration laws, from the turn of the century on, were not only restrictive, they were also arbitrary: they vested enormous power and discretion in the men who administered the laws.[58] The process was fast, sloppy, and callous. The records make clear that many administrators and consular officials felt their job was to keep out the riffraff, at all costs. If a few mistakes were made, so be it. Aliens and those who claimed to be citizens had little or no chance to prove their case, if they had one.

The courts were sometimes sympathetic to claims of immigrants, and sometimes not. In *U.S. v. Ju Toy* (1905) a Chinese man, temporarily out of the country (he said), was stopped at the port of San Francisco.[59] Ju Toy claimed he was a citizen; the port officials thought he was lying, and ordered him shipped back to China. Ju Toy protested; he appealed to the secretary of commerce and labor (immigration matters were in his jurisdiction). The secretary upheld the local consular official. Ju Toy then turned to the federal courts. The district court decided that Ju Toy was in fact a "native-born citizen," and had a perfect right to stay. But the Supreme Court, speaking through Oliver Wendell Holmes, Jr., reversed the lower court. The decision of the secretary was absolutely final. Ju Toy had no right to a "judicial trial," even though he claimed he was a citizen, unfairly banished from his native land. Congress could "entrust" the decision in cases like this to "an executive officer," and make his decision the first and only word.

The rules of the game, in a case like Ju Toy's, were heavily tilted against the Chinese applicant. Justice Brewer, who dissented in *Ju Toy,* quoted from the immigration rules—the Chinese who claimed a right to enter was not allowed to get in touch with anybody, the examination was in private, totally controlled by the immigration officer; appeals had to be made within two days, and, in all cases, the "burden of proof . . . rests upon Chinese persons claiming the right of admission"; in "every doubtful case the benefit of the doubt shall be given by administrative officers to the United States Government."

Not all the reported cases, by any means, were as tight and unyielding as *Ju Toy*. The law itself was complex. It distinguished between alleged citizens who stood at the gates in, say, San Francisco, and alleged citizens about to be deported from inside the country.[60] In any event, few aliens had the resources and the courage to fight against the government. Most must have given up and gone home—or, rather, to the "home" decreed by the U.S. government.

In theory, the states had no power to decide questions of immigration; that was reserved to the federal government. But some states and local groups found ways to make their mark. In 1898 in New Orleans, a group of 408 Italian immigrants arrived on a French boat with the unlikely name of *Britannia;* the boat had sailed from Palermo, Sicily, by way of Marseille. Local officials, playing on resentment against Italian immigrants, refused to allow them to land. The excuse was the state's quarantine laws. The ship, its cargo, its crew, and its passengers all had a clean bill of health; but under Louisiana law, local boards of health could declare the immigrants unwelcome, because New Orleans itself was full of noxious diseases. The Italians went to Pensacola, Florida, and the ship company went to court. That the board acted because its members wanted no more Italians, and not because of any valid notion of hygiene, seems obvious, but the Supreme Court refused to intervene.[61]

Closing the Gate

The history of immigration law in the first part of the twentieth century is a history of increasing restrictions—and restrictions which had a strong racial flavor. We have already mentioned the special rules with regard to Asians. But this was only part of a general thrust: undesirables had to be kept out. The Statue of Liberty said, "Give me . . . your huddled masses"; but the acts of Congress spoke more loudly: no huddled masses, thank you; at least none from undesirable places. The immigration law of 1903 sounded the new themes; it contained a long list of undesirables, who were not to be let in the door: "idiots, insane persons, epileptics, persons who have been insane within five years previous," or had had "two or more attacks of insanity at any time previously."[62] Prostitutes were excluded, along with "paupers; persons likely to become a public charge; professional beggars; persons afflicted with a loathesome or . . . dangerous contagious disease," persons convicted of any crime "involving moral turpitude." Polygamists were also definitely unwelcome, and so were "anarchists," and those who "believe in or advocate the overthrow by force or violence of the Government of the United States." This was an ominous move: the first time the immigration laws had contained a political test for admission. The act specified that people who did not "believe in organized government" had no right to be naturalized. The law also forbade importing contract labor, except for actors, artists, singers, ministers of the gospel, professors, members of "any recognized learned profession," or "personal or domestic servants." Still, the act made clear that the United States no longer wanted masses of foreign bodies, masses of foreign workers.

The march of legislation continued. In 1907 "imbeciles, and feeble-minded persons" were added to the list; and those whose mental or physical condition was such that they might become a burden on the welfare system, in the opinion of the examining doctor. Now, too, it was not only actual polygamists for whom the door was shut, but even "persons who admit their belief in polygamy."[63] Not that hordes of polygamists were knocking at the doors; but here once again, ideology or belief was the basis for exclusion—a fateful note.

The Immigration Act of 1917 established an "Asiatic barred zone"; it covered essentially all of south Asia, including India, Burma, what is now Malaysia and Indonesia, and the Pacific islands.[64] The countries were not named, but were defined in terms of latitude and longitude. The act also set up a literacy test; all aliens over sixteen were barred "who can not read the English language, or some other language or dialect, including Hebrew or Yiddish." The statute even prescribed the way immigration inspectors were to test literacy: "slips of uniform size" were to be printed, with thirty to forty ordinary words in all the relevant languages; the immigrant had to pick his language, and then read the slips. The act also added to the power of the government to expel aliens who were already in the country—those who had committed offenses, or advocated "anarchy" or the overthrow of the government.

In 1921 Congress passed an emergency immigration act. It limited immigration to 3 percent of the "number of foreign-born" persons of each nationality living in the United States as of 1910. Asians were still barred. The Western Hemisphere was not subject to the ceiling. The statute aimed at keeping immigration down to about 350,000 a year, with most of the spots reserved for people from northern Europe.[65] Then came the crucial immigration law of 1924. This was an outright rejection of the melting-pot idea. It put a cap on the numbers of immigrants, and made sure they would come from the right places. The statute continued the idea of national quotas, fixed in terms of the 1890 census: if 2 percent of the people who lived in the United States in 1890 hailed from Italy, then Italy would get 2 percent of the quota of immigrants. Why 1890? That was before the biggest flow of huddled masses from southern and eastern Europe. Under the 1924 act, more than two-thirds of the immigration spots were reserved for immigrants from Germany, Great Britain, and Ireland. About 17,000 Greeks had been entering the country each year; the 1924 act gave Greece a quota of exactly 307. Italians had been flocking to the United States— more than 150,000 a year; their quota was now 5,802.[66]

Not everybody, to be sure, approved of this demographic game. Industrialists did not think cheap imported labor was a bad idea, even if the unions did. Immigrant groups opposed the law, and many of them were bona fide voters. In the debates in Congress, Fiorella La Guardia, the "little flower," later to become a charismatic mayor of New York City, denounced the law, speaking out eloquently against it and in praise of his constituents, who were Italian, Jewish, and the like. But the law had the majority behind it, and it went into effect.

It was basically a law about Europe and Asia. Somewhat surprisingly, it did not apply at all to immigrants from Canada, Mexico, Cuba, Haiti, the Dominican Republic, and any "independent country of Central or South America."[67] As far as the law was concerned, the whole population of Guatemala or Nicaragua could simply travel north and settle down in the United States. This was certainly not because of any great love for the natives of these countries. Truly impoverished, truly traditional people do not emigrate. Hence Bolivia was not a problem; and Italy was.

One country of Latin America did call for special treatment. Bolivia was far away; Mexico was on our doorstep. And Mexicans were here already. The United States had inherited quite a few when it won the Mexican War and annexed about a third of Mexico's land mass. The borderlands were mostly barren desert, inhospitable, even dangerous. Yet people moved freely across the border; Mexican laborers, for example, left home to sweat away in the mines of Arizona. By about 1910 there was a substantial railroad net in Mexico; now it was fairly easy for Mexicans from the central plateau to reach the Rio Grande. Mexicans came on the railroads, and they also worked on the railroads. Nine Western railroads in 1929 employed more than twenty-two thousand Mexican workers—almost 60 percent of their force of laborers.[68]

Then things changed. Irrigation made the desert bloom—not with flowers but with crops. The Imperial Valley of California, the Salt River Valley in Arizona, and the valley of the Rio Grande turned into tremendous factories of food. The stoop labor was heavily Mexican. Revolution, hunger, and general instability drove thousands of Mexicans from their homelands, into the arms of agribusiness. The growers welcomed these Mexicans; they were better than whites at this work, the growers felt: whites, as one businessman put it, were "entirely unfitted for labor which requires bending, crouching, or elasticity." The "oriental" and the "Mexican," because of their "crouching and bending habits," could adapt to conditions which no white man could tolerate.[69]

The growers and the railroads wanted Mexican immigration. Not everybody sympathized. There was no Mexican quota; but there were restrictions—if the law of 1917 barred illiterate Hungarians, it barred illiterate Mexicans as well. This rule alone would have prevented the entry of many poor Mexicans. Yet they came, illegally; or were smuggled across the border. In 1925 Congress created a Border Patrol; by 1928 there were more than seven hundred patrol inspectors on the Mexican border, fighting smugglers and illegal aliens. And from 1928 on, consular officials began to deny visas to most Mexicans who wanted to enter the United States—on the grounds of illiteracy, or as "LPCs"—that is, liable to become a public charge.[70]

The Great Depression hit Mexican immigrants with a double blow. Mexicans lost jobs by the droves, and thousands of them streamed back across the border. Those that hung on were targets of a campaign to get rid of them. This campaign, launched during the last years of the Hoover presidency, was aimed at all illegal aliens; but the main thrust was against the Mexicans in southern

California and elsewhere. Los Angeles led the way; but thousands of Mexicans from Texas, Arizona, and Illinois also left the country. In Los Angeles many illegal aliens were bagged in swooping raids on public places. In some cities, gentler methods were used—by the welfare bureau of St. Paul, Minnesota, for example, in 1932. After 1932 the campaign tapered off, but there were sporadic attempts to clean out illegals until the outbreak of the Second World War.[71]

The war soaked up American manpower, and unskilled labor became a scarce commodity. In 1942 the United States entered into an agreement with Mexico under which Mexican workers, the so-called *braceros*, were allowed into the States. Legal and illegal immigrants from Mexico poured into booming Los Angeles. Ethnic relations were tense, especially between Chicanos and the Los Angeles Police Department. In 1942 came the famous "sleepy lagoon mystery." A young Chicano was found dead near a water reservoir in East Los Angeles. His death might have been an accident; or might not have been. The police rounded up and grilled hundreds of young Chicanos, and more than a dozen were convicted of murder, although there was hardly a shred of evidence against them.[72] The so-called zoot suit riots followed the next year; mobs, made up mostly of sailors and marines, ran amok for ten days, attacking and beating young *pachucos*, Mexican-American boys and men.[73] Official policy was schizophrenic; the bracero program continued in the 1950s and 1960s; on the other hand, Operation Wetback in 1954 was a program to tighten control of the border. Immigration law dumped the national quota system in 1965; from this point on, preferences went to people with family in the United States, or who had needed skills. But the Senate forced the Kennedy administration to compromise and agree to limits on immigration from the Western Hemisphere; there was to be a Western Hemisphere quota (roughly 120,000 a year) from 1968 on.[74]

Troubles in Mexico itself—economic, political—drove thousands and thousands of Mexicans over the border, in search of jobs and a haven in the United States. Illegal immigration rose dramatically in the 1970s; and the Mexicans were not alone any more: they were joined more and more by men and women from Guatemala, Nicaragua, Panama, the Dominican Republic. Cultural barriers and the isolation of traditional society had broken down in the age of TV; and once there were national enclaves in every big city, and perhaps a cousin with a flat in Los Angeles, a neighbor who knew about a dishwashing job in Denver, or an uncle in San Diego, the pull of America grew ever stronger.

The First People: The Law and Native Americans

For Native Americans, like blacks, the beginning years of the twentieth century were a low point. To be sure, armies and settlers were no longer killing Indians—there was no need to. But it looked as if the curtain would soon fall on native languages, cultures, religions, and ways of life. The Dawes Act (1887) gave the government authority to destroy the Indian land-tenure system.[75] The theory of this law was that Indians could become citizens—regular Americans— if they gave up tribal tenure systems, owned their lands outright, and farmed them as individual tracts, like the rest of the country. In practice, the Dawes Act did not emancipate the natives, or even assimilate them; on the contrary, it led to an orgy of cheating and divestment; in the process, much of the remaining land was stripped from the tribes and passed into the hands of the whites. Some of the tribes, not surprisingly, opposed the Dawes Act from the beginning, along with the land-grab processes that took place under its auspices. The Kiowas, who lived in southwestern Oklahoma, resisted general allotment. Under their treaty, Indian land was not to be ceded unless at least 75 percent of the adult males on the reservation agreed. In the waning years of the nineteenth century, a commission, headed by David Jerome, haggled with the Kiowa over an agreement to buy out more land. The commission dealt with the Kiowa in a high-handed way; ultimately, the commission presented Congress with an agreement that was basically fraudulent—full of fake signatures, supposed signatures of Kiowa who actually did not want to sign, and also signatures of non-Kiowa. Congress, however, accepted the agreement in 1900. The Kiowa protested in court—but, in the landmark case of *Lone Wolf v. Hitchcock* (1903), they lost badly.[76] Congress, said the Supreme Court, had plenary power over the native tribes. The claim of the Kiowa "ignores the status of the contracting Indians and the relation of dependency they bore and continue to bear towards the government of the United States." The decision, as John Wunder has remarked, was "devastating, as it justified the unilateral termination of treaties." It ushered in a period of "new colonialism."[77]

Indian rights were thus inherently precarious. The law that pertained to these rights was also extremely complicated. Three separate powers could claim jurisdiction over native people: the federal government, the states, and the native peoples themselves. *United States v. Sandoval* (1913) is a good illustration of how entangled questions of jurisdiction could become.[78] New Mexico had been admitted to the union in 1912. The Enabling Act outlawed the selling of liquor in "Indian country," including "lands now owned or occupied by the Pueblo Indians." New Mexico was also required to give up its claims to Indian lands. Sandoval was accused of selling liquor in the Santa Clara pueblo—but the larger question was whether Congress had any right to encroach on state authority, with regard to the Pueblo people. The Pueblo Indians had been, under the Mexican government, "full fledged citizens"; and they held legal title to their land. In other words—so ran the argument—the Pueblo people had a status, in law, different from the treaty Indians of other states.

The Supreme Court disagreed: and why? Because, in the words of Justice Van Devanter, an Indian is an Indian is an Indian, even though "sedentary rather than nomadic . . . and disposed to peace." Indians in general adhered to "primitive modes of life, largely influenced by superstition and fetishism"; they were "a simple, uninformed and inferior people." It was the very strength of Pueblo culture that made it so suspect in the eyes of the court, in the days when the only good Indian was an assimilated Indian.

From time to time, Congress bestirred itself to slow the loss of Indian land. Far more often, Congress bestirred itself to hasten the process. It is hard to make sense of the laws passed between 1900 and 1910.[79] Under the Burke Act (1906), Indian trust land became in essence inalienable: the native could not sell it until he or she had full title.[80] The point was to make it harder for whites to cheat Indians out of their land. But on the other hand, a law of 1902 gave the states the right to condemn Indian land for such things as roads and telephone lines—and without paying compensation. In 1908 the Burke Act was repealed; and in 1910, a law gave the secretary of the interior more power over tribal lands. All these decisions, of course, were made by a far-off Congress, and without the participation of the tribes. The "domestic dependent nations" were powerless, and without rights, under the control of a bureaucracy in Washington which cared nothing for their culture, religion, and way of life.

Once in a while the courts showed sympathy with the Indian cause. In *United States v. Winans* (1905) the Supreme Court upheld the salmon-fishing rights of the Yakama people against whites who were encroaching.[81] In 1919 the Supreme Court affirmed this right. But it was ominous that the issue kept on appearing in court; and in fact, commercial fishermen continually ignored the rights of the Yakama, and went right on scooping millions of salmon from places which belonged, by solemn treaty, to the tribe. It is good to have the Supreme Court on your side; but it is never enough.

Colonial America

At the end of the nineteenth century, the United States fought a "glorious little war" with Spain, and ended up with a colonial empire, of sorts. This was, after all, the heyday of imperialism. The sun never set, as the saying went, on the British Empire; and the French, the Portuguese, the Dutch, and the Germans all had fine, flourishing empires of their own. America was never part of the scramble for Africa, which was almost completely carved up and dished out among the colonial powers in the nineteenth century. America had expanded across its own continent; it had bullied and manipulated various banana republics; and it had acquired, in somewhat dubious manner, the Hawaiian Islands, which had become a "territory." Now, however, it found itself, at the dawn of the century, with something more imperial than a chain of Polynesian islands: Puerto Rico, Guam, and the Philippine Islands. These were booty from the war with Spain; and the question soon arose, exactly how this new empire should be governed; and on what legal and constitutional principles.[82]

The Foraker Act, passed in April 1900, dealt with Puerto Rico. The president was to appoint a governor and a council; the people of Puerto Rico would elect a legislature. But the legal status of the island remained ambiguous. The issue came before the Supreme Court in the famous "insular cases," decided shortly after the turn of the century.[83] The precise issues in the cases were rather obscure, even trivial. In *Fourteen Diamond Rings v. United States* (1901), a man named Emil J. Pepke, a soldier who hailed from North Dakota, was charged with a customs violation. Pepke had served in Luzon, and came home with rings he acquired in the Philippine Islands. Custom agents seized them, claiming that they had been brought into the country illegally, without payment of duty. Pepke argued that he owed nothing, because the Philippines were not a "foreign country." The Supreme Court agreed; but this left open the underlying issue. In *Downes v. Bidwell,* the most notable of the cases, the immediate question was whether a cargo of oranges, brought from Puerto Rico to New York, was subject to tax.[84] The Foraker Act had imposed special customs duties on goods from Puerto Rico. The Constitution, on the other hand, required that "all duties, imposts and excises shall be uniform throughout the United States" (art. I, §8). Was Puerto Rico part of the United States, in the constitutional sense, or was it a kind of colony?

This was the issue: or, as the phrase of the day put it, did the Constitution "follow the flag"? That is, did every word of the Constitution, every clause of the Bill of Rights, apply automatically to conquered territory? The Supreme Court said no, in a sharply divided opinion. Justice Brown, writing for the majority, was concerned about the future of the American empire. Successful wars, or the "natural gravitation of small bodies toward large ones," might bring about "annexation of distant possessions." And these possessions might be "inhabited by alien races, differing from us in religion, customs, laws, methods of taxation and modes of thought." For this reason, "the administration of government and justice, according to Anglo-Saxon principles, may for a time be impossible."[85]

The opinions in the "insular cases" were shot through with turn-of-the-century ideas about race. The Philippine people, the people of Guam, of Puerto Rico, were not ready for American civilization. Perhaps they never would be. If there was going to be an American empire at all, then it had to be on the same terms as other empires. The Constitution must not, therefore, follow the flag—at least not all of the Constitution. This was, apparently, what the bulk of the country felt. It was one way of reading the election of President McKinley. This led to the famous dictum of Mr. Dooley, the fictional Irishman in Finley Peter Dunne's humor columns: "No matther whether th' constitution follows th' flag or not, th' supreme coort follows th' illection returns."

Of course, not everybody agreed with the results of the insular cases. There was dissent—on the Supreme Court as well. John Marshall Harlan objected to the idea that "Congress may . . . engraft upon our republican institutions a colonial system such as exists under monarchical governments." If some "particular race" could not "assimilate with our people," then the country ought to think twice about acquiring such lands in the first place.[86] But this was a minority view. The Supreme Court decisions cleared the way for Congress and the president to decide on governments for these faraway places. In 1902 Congress laid down a framework for American government in the Philippines.[87] The framework included some aspects of the Bill of Rights, but not others: trial by jury, for example, was not extended to the country. William Howard Taft, the governor of the Philippines, explained that "ninety percent of the people are so ignorant that they could not sit on the jury to begin with and understand anything."[88]

Puerto Rico is still under the American flag; but the fate of the Philippines was to be different. The so-called Jones law of 1916 solemnly recited that it was "never the intention of the people of the United States in . . . the war with Spain to make it a war of conquest." The law announced a decision to "withdraw" from the Philippines and to "recognize their independence as soon as a stable government can be established."[89] Meanwhile, the United States promised to give the Philippines "control of their domestic affairs." The act also extended to the Philippines a bill of rights of the standard type (with some additions—a ban on polygamy, for example). There would be an elected legislature, with power to pass laws. But the executive would be a governor-general, appointed from Washington; and Congress reserved the power to nullify laws passed in Manila. In 1934 the Tydings McDuffie Act offered total independence, after a ten-year period of transition. The Second World War interrupted these plans, but in 1946, the Philippines did become a sovereign nation.

Puerto Rico never got a similar offer. But it did become less of a traditional colony. Under the Organic Act of 1917, the residents of the island became American citizens.[90] At this point, did the Constitution *now* follow the flag into Puerto Rico? One Jesús M. Balzac, an editor, was arrested and prosecuted for criminal libel. He demanded a jury trial. The island's law called for a jury in felony cases, but not in misdemeanors, and Balzac's request was turned down. He was convicted and appealed. Did he have a constitutional right to a jury?

The Supreme Court said no. Yes, the islanders were citizens; yes, they could "move into the continental United States," and there, of course, they would enjoy every last one of the rights in the Bill of Rights. The legislature of Puerto Rico had chosen not to give Balzac this particular right. The law of 1917 had not altered the situation. After all, the Court said, the jury system "needs citizens trained to the exercise of the responsibilities of jurors." It is not an easy system for "people not brought up in fundamentally popular government." The language was a lot more polite than Taft's language at the turn of the century. But the underlying tone was not all that different. Nor was the authorship. The opinion in *Balzac* was written by the chief justice: William Howard Taft.[91]

Many years later, in the age of plural equality, attitudes toward Puerto Rico and its culture began to change. This included respect for both language and legal culture. That culture, as the Supreme Court remarked in a case from 1970, was "impregnated with the Spanish tradition." It had to be handled accordingly. Hence federal courts were not to "construe" the laws of the commonwealth "in the Anglo-Saxon tradition." This would leave too little space for the "overtones of Spanish culture." The national courts should interfere with the workings of the Puerto Rican judiciary only when those courts were absolutely wrong.[92] By this time, Taft was long since dead.

The process of loosening the bonds over Puerto Rico continued. After the Second World War, Congress gave Puerto Ricans the right to elect their own governors. And in 1953 the island became an "estado libro asociado," a commonwealth in "free association" with its big and dominant neighbor. There have been a number of plebiscites on the island; independence never gets much of a vote, and most Puerto Ricans seem to accept things as they are. A large minority would like to become a state; but whether Congress could be talked into swallowing the idea of a Spanish-speaking state is somewhat doubtful. The island is poor, compared to the mainland, but better off than many of its neighbors. Millions of Puerto Ricans have made use of one of their rights as citizens—they have moved to the mainland, especially to New York City. Because they are citizens, no visa or passport is needed; a simple plane ticket will do, and the flight from San Juan to New York City is an ordinary domestic flight. This privilege is definitely not a trivial one.

The smaller imperial booty was sometimes dealt with in a more high-handed way. Guam was ruled by the Department of the Navy for more than fifty years after it was acquired. The people who lived there repeatedly asked for citizenship, and were repeatedly turned down. Guamanians, according to the Navy Department in the 1930s, had "not reached the state of development commensurate with the personal independence, obligations, and responsibilities of U.S. citizenship." Guam got an Organic Act, citizenship, and a local legislature only in 1950.[93]

Civil Rights

The ultimate test of a free society, perhaps, is how it deals with people who hold radical, unpopular, or disgusting points of view. And the ultimate test of this test is how the state behaves toward dissenters during wars or times of stress. Freedom of speech is guaranteed by the Constitution—or to be exact, by the

Bill of Rights. Congress is not to make any law abridging the freedom of speech, or of the press. State constitutions invariably have a similar or identical clause in their own bills of rights. The words have not changed very much, if at all, since they were written, in the late eighteenth century. But ideas about the scope and meaning of freedom of speech do expand and contract with the times. At the moment, we live in an age that is very permissive, both legally and socially, on a wide range of subjects from Karl Marx to kinky sex. This has not always been the case. Things that even children freely see and read and hear today—writings, pictures, words—would have been banned as just plain obscene, even for adults, as recently as the middle of the twentieth century. Even talk about politics had its limits.

In 1873 Congress passed the so-called Comstock law, named after Anthony Comstock, whose life's work was a battle against smut; this law made it a crime to send any "obscene, lewd or lascivious book" through the mail; or any "article or thing designed or intended for the prevention of conception or procuring of abortion."[94] Under the Comstock law, it was possible to seize all sorts of books and materials that argued in favor of "free love," on the grounds that these books were obscene; and of course, information about contraception was strictly taboo. There were, to be sure, people who argued against this policy on free speech grounds; but these arguments got short shrift in the courts.[95]

There is a Latin maxim, *silent leges inter arma:* in war the laws are silent. In point of fact, law is quite noisy and intrusive during modern wartime, but the maxim, alas, has a certain resonance as far as civil liberties are concerned. Of course, there is an argument for *some* suppression of speech. The country has to defend itself against its enemies. Loose lips sink ships. Military secrets have to be safeguarded. But during the First World War, suppression went far beyond anything the war could possibly justify. An outburst of anti-German feeling sometimes took absurd forms: sauerkraut became "liberty cabbage" on some menus, and some people even wanted to call German measles "liberty measles." There were schools that dropped German from the curriculum; the *New York Times* applauded this idea, and recommended Spanish instead, or perhaps French, which was "more cosmopolitan and urbane."[96] Four county councils in Missouri banned anybody from speaking German on the telephone; and some towns tried to banish it on the streets. The town of Potsdam, Missouri, changed its name to Pershing.[97]

The language of Goethe and Schiller survived this onslaught; other forms of xenophobia had more serious results. In a burst of fervor, Congress passed an Espionage Act in 1917.[98] The law understandably imposed severe penalties on people who passed secrets to the enemy. But it also made it a crime to "willfully make or convey false reports or false statements" with the aim of interfering with the "operation or success of the military or naval forces" of the country, or to "promote the success of its enemies"; or to try to foment "insubordination, disloyalty, mutiny, or refusal of duty" among the armed forces; or to "willfully obstruct the recruiting or enlistment service of the United States." The Trading with the Enemy Act (1917) did what the title suggested; but it also provided that nothing could be published or printed "in any foreign language" about the government of the United States, "or of any nation engaged in the present war, its politics, [or] international relations," unless a full translation was lodged with the postmaster general.[99] These provisions were barely discussed in the sometimes heated debates over the Espionage Act and the rest of the legislative package; in practice, they proved to be pregnant with trouble for anybody who fell short of 100 percent red-blooded patriotism, and in particular, for Americans of the left-wing persuasion.[100]

The war generated heat and paranoia. The government found it easy to smear speech that opposed the war or denounced capitalism or the like as dangerous talk which interfered with the war effort. The Sedition Act of 1918 was another truly drastic statute. Under this law, it was a crime to spread "false statements" that might hinder the war effort, obstruct the sale of bonds, or incite mutiny and disloyalty in the army. The act also criminalized saying, printing, or writing any "disloyal, profane, scurrilous or abusive language" about the government, the Constitution, the flag, the army, the uniform; or saying anything that would bring the government or the Constitution "into contempt, scorn, contumely, or disrepute." Anything written which violated the act was "nonmailable," and could not be sent through the post.[101]

In short, only total jingoism was acceptable—or legal. German-Americans in some parts of the country had a particularly tough time. In front-line South Dakota—a state with a large German population—zealous officials raided the offices of a German-language newspaper, the *Deutscher Herold,* where they found some truly dastardly objects, including a paperweight with an image of the kaiser. The editor, Conrad Kornmann, was charged with espionage, mostly because of a private letter he wrote to a friend, in which he was lukewarm about the war, to say the least. That this was an attack on vital war interests or the armed forces was totally absurd, but a jury found Kornmann guilty. The appeal court reversed; still, Kornmann's life was a shambles.[102]

South Dakota was not the only state in danger. Rumors flew about in remote Montana of German spies poised to invade from Canada. Local "liberty" or "defense" committees rounded up "slackers," reds, Wobblies, and other bad elements; Montana whipped itself into a froth and conducted a major witch-hunt.[103] In Illinois, a Granite City man got two years in Fort Leavenworth for shooting off his mouth in a saloon—to the effect that he liked the kaiser, and would fight for him.[104] In 1918 the Rev. John Fontana, a Lutheran minister in Salem, North Dakota, a German community, went on trial for violating the Espionage Act by obstructing the draft and fomenting insubordination. The evidence was flimsy, to say the least—some testimony that Fontana was unenthusiastic about the war, refused to buy liberty bonds, and prayed for the "old Fatherland." In wartime, the prosecutor said, "the unbridled tongue is more dangerous than the arms of the enemy, more stealthy than the submarine." The jury convicted him. The judge fulminated against Fontana for not putting away his German soul; he criticized immigrants in general ("these thousands of little islands of foreigners"), and sentenced Fontana to three years in Leavenworth.[105] On appeal, the case was reversed—but it seems incredible, today, that it was brought in the first place.

More than jingoism was involved in the bitter struggle against the Wobblies, the Industrial Workers of the World (IWW). This was a genuinely radical, even revolutionary organization. They were widely condemned as Bolsheviks, anarchists, vermin to be snuffed out mercilessly. The Wobblies fomented a strike in the copper mines of Bisbee, Arizona, in 1917.[106] There were threats and violent acts on both sides. The IWW, unlike Reverend Fontana, openly denounced the "Wall Street War" and reviled the government, the flag, and the employers alike. Local law enforcement people rounded up more than a thousand Wobblies, and shipped them by railroad car to an internment camp in New Mexico. This put an end to the Bisbee strikes.

This was certainly high-handed behavior, and some of those responsible were charged with kidnapping; Harry E. Wootton, who had to answer to this charge at trial in Tombstone, Arizona, defended himself on the grounds that the Wobblies deserved to be destroyed. They threatened the peace, the property, the very lives of the community. They flew the red flag while, under the

American flag, "American boys were dying in a foreign war." Their intent, the jury was told, was "the overthrow of your government and the bringing in of the red dawn."[107] It took the jury less than an hour to acquit. All in all, the wartime years and those immediately following seemed a grand opportunity to clean house and get rid of union organizers and other troublemakers.

The witch-hunts of the war period were followed by the "red scare" and mass deportations. These were responses to the panic over Bolshevism, the Russian Revolution, anarchists, Wobblies, and other alien threats to the American way of life. The goal was to purge and destroy the American Left in general. In 1920 the Department of Justice, under the direction of Attorney General A. Mitchell Palmer, a first-class jingo and bigot, arrested thousands of enemies of the people: communists and other radicals.

There was, of course, not the flimsiest excuse for this blatant violation of what were supposed to be basic constitutional rights. Not everybody approved—there were strong voices in opposition—but as far as we can tell, most of the public liked the war against the "reds."[108] Judges less blinded by prejudice and fear undid some of the worst cases, however. And the Supreme Court, for the first time, began to build up a body of decisions on freedom of speech—a subject which the Court had hardly dealt with before.

This is not as surprising as one might think. The Supreme Court can only decide cases and controversies; it does not debate abstract propositions. Free-speech cases do not come out of nowhere. Before World War I, most cases were state cases; and the "overwhelming weight" of the decisions "offered little recognition and even less protection of free speech interests."[109] Of course, there *was* free speech in the United States—and a lot of it, compared with dictatorships. But there were invisible and almost subconscious limits. Speech was free within the confines of an American elite consensus—speech that crossed over certain subtle, normative barriers had no real protection, in court or in society. Southern states, for example, before the Civil War had banned books, newspapers, and pamphlets that advocated abolition of slavery, on the grounds that these fomented uprisings of slaves.[110]

The case law that began in 1919 marked the beginning of the end for the nineteenth-century consensus; ultimately, what we have called plural equality undermined it, and by the end of the twentieth century, many limits on freedom of expression had vanished into thin air. There would be, of course, many detours along the way: McCarthyism, the oppression of Jehovah's Witnesses, political trials during the cold war, and others, as we shall see. We begin with a look at ground zero, the period of the First World War.

The wartime agitation and counteragitation, the crackdown on dissenters, naysayers, and radicals, soon reached the United States Supreme Court. In *Schenck v. United States* (1919), the defendants were accused of violating the Espionage Act.[111] They had mailed circulars to men about to join the army. In these documents, they claimed the war was a conspiracy of the capitalist class; the draft, they said, violated the constitutional rights of Americans. They were convicted, and appealed. The Supreme Court affirmed. Oliver Wendell Holmes, Jr., wrote the opinion; in his view, freedom of speech was not absolute—the "most stringent protection of free speech would not protect a man in falsely shouting fire in a theater." The question is, he added, "whether the words used are used in such circumstances and are of such a nature as to create a clear and present danger that they will bring about the substantive evils that Congress has a right to prevent."

This phrase "clear and present danger" was a huge success, and was mentioned, cited, argued thousands of times in the decades after *Schenck;* it has even gone into English idiom. This was small comfort for the defendants, of course. Holmes was, after all, writing for the majority, and in his judgment, the defendants in *Schenck* actually *were* a "clear and present danger." But afterward he did some soul-searching, and in the next free-speech case, *Abrams v. United States,* Holmes changed his mind somewhat; in this case he wrote a strong dissent.[112]

The defendants in *Abrams* were Russian Jewish anarchists—all of them aliens. Three of the defendants were men, one was a young woman, Mollie Steimer, a passionate firebrand for what she saw as social justice. They were charged with violating the Sedition Act. Russia had had its revolution, quit the war, and made peace with Germany. Within Russia, "whites" (loyal to the old order) were waging civil war against "reds." America had intervened—with troops—on the side of the whites. The defendants distributed leaflets—in Yiddish and English—protesting intervention in Russia. We were not, of course, at war with Russia at all; we were at war with Germany. But the government's theory was that the leaflets could bring about strikes in munition plants and otherwise hurt the war effort. This seems far-fetched; but it was enough for the judge, Henry DeLamar Clayton, Jr. (author, incidentally, of the Clayton Act), whose conduct at the trial was scandalous, and for the jury, which convicted the defendants. After the jury verdict, Clayton threw the book at the defendants, and delivered a long tirade against them, blasting their "insidious and despicable work," in furtherance of a "Bolshevik Revolution in this country."[113]

The Supreme Court affirmed the conviction, by a 7–2 vote. There was evidence, said the court, from which a jury could conclude that the defendants really did want to interfere with the war. The pamphlets were a "clear and present danger," because they were distributed "in the greatest port of our land," where "great quantities of war supplies . . . were . . . manufactured for transportation overseas."

Holmes wrote a short but brilliant dissent. He referred to the defendants as "poor and puny anonymities"; they were punished "for the creed that they avow." He found the creed ignorant and immature; but they had a right to believe in it. He ended with a passionate plea for freedom of speech. Time "has upset many fighting faiths." The theory of the Constitution is "free trade in ideas. . . . It is an experiment, as all life is an experiment." The defendants "were deprived of their rights," and should go free. But only Justice Brandeis agreed.

Abrams, Schenk, and others were political trials in every sense of the word. But the most famous political trial of the period was, in form, not a political trial at all, but an ordinary case of robbery and murder. This was the Sacco-Vanzetti case. It arose out of a holdup on April 15, 1920, in South Braintree, Massachusetts. Two men, Frederick Albert Parmenter, a paymaster, and a guard, Alessandro D. Berardelli, were killed by gunfire as they carried two boxes with the payroll of the Slater and Morrill shoe factory. A car with three other men in it picked up the killers and raced away. According to eyewitnesses, the men had dark complexions, and looked somewhat Italian.

Nicolà Sacco and Bartolomeo Vanzetti were anarchists; one was a shoemaker, the other a fish peddler. They were arrested and charged with the crime; after a sensational trial which lasted seven weeks, Sacco and Vanzetti were convicted, and sentenced to death. In the process, they became symbols and icons of the Left; they turned into a cause; millions of people came to believe that Sacco and Vanzetti were innocent men, railroaded because they dared to oppose a wicked and oppressive system. The far Left backed them almost reflexively; but there were thoughtful liberals who thought they were innocent; or, if not innocent, that the trial had been unfair, and a mockery of justice. In the years following the red scare, it was not hard to whip a jury into a frenzy of flag-waving zeal, especially when the defendants were foreign born and anarchists to boot.

Nor was the judge, Webster Thayer, a model of neutral propriety. Felix Frank-furter found the trial hopelessly biased; the district attorney, he felt, exploited the "unpopular social views" of the defendants, their "opposition to the war," to create a "riot of political passion and political sentiment; and the trial judge connived at—one had almost written, cooperated in—the process."[114]

In the end, however, despite all pleas, appeals, and protests, Sacco and Vanzetti went to their deaths. Whether they were, in fact, innocent is still a matter of lively debate.[115] Perhaps at least one of them was not quite as innocent a martyr as liberals thought at the time. Nonetheless, even if one (or both) had a hand in the crime, it seems clear that the trial itself was fatally flawed. Fear, prejudice, and unfairness pervaded the whole process, from arrest through conviction through execution. The trial of Sacco and Vanzetti is not something American justice can be proud of.

Doctrinally, the case law of the World War I period, and just afterward, laid the foundation for a body of free-speech law with teeth. But the *behavior* of the Supreme Court—the actual results of their decisions—was far from coura-geous. The Court did nothing to stand in the way of the Palmer raids and the arrest and persecution of leftists. Civil liberties are not just theories; they are systems of behavior. What the Supreme Court decides may be important; and may have an impact on society at large. But more often the Court reflects and refracts; in any event, the Court is only a piece of the government, and the government is only a piece of society. The Justice Department in the first part of the twentieth century was no friend of civil liberties. State and local govern-ments joined lustfully in the search for reds and other un-Americans. J. Edgar Hoover began his long, baleful career as a red-hunter. And the climate in the country was hostile or worse to "anarchists" or Wobblies or "reds."

There were other threats to civil liberties and civil rights, unconnected with the war on the Left. In 1915 the Ku Klux Klan was reborn, under the leadership of one William Joseph Simmons.[116] In the immediate background was the runaway success of *Birth of a Nation*. This movie, directed by D. W. Griffith, had its esthetic virtues, but politically it was a horror show. It glorified the Ku Klux Klan of the Reconstruction period, and it showed blacks as lustful and villainous barbarians, except for the occasional Uncle Tom. Millions saw the movie. The second Klan, which gained real power in the 1920s, was, of course, a bastion of white supremacy; unlike the first Klan, it was also bitterly anti-Semitic, and anti-Catholic. The Klan fulminated against black-robed priests who owed their allegiance "to a Dago Pope in Rome," and warned of evil plots to crush America and destroy the "purity of our women for the sake of the Dago on the Tiber." In many states the Klan gained significant political and legal power. Indiana became a hotbed of Klan hysteria in the early 1920s; citizens of a little town, North Manchester, became convinced that the pope was coming by train to take over; a mob met the train, and scared a visiting corset salesman half to death before they let him go.[117] Mercifully, in the late 1920s the Klan, rocked by scandals, began to lose its influence. The Klan was to flare up again in the years after *Brown v. Board of Education*.

Thus the period after the First World War was a period, as we have seen, of xenophobia. There was special fear of bearded, bomb-throwing foreigners. Immigration laws excluded "anarchists" and anybody who advocated the violent revolution.[118] The states had their own wave of superpatriotism; indeed, they competed with each other in passing laws against red flags, criminal syndicalism, and other dire threats to the republic. An Arizona law of 1919 made it a crime to display any "red or black flag, or banner"; only Old Glory, or the state flag, could be displayed. Twenty-four states passed red-flag laws in 1919, and eight more followed in 1920.[119]

Although the worst of the red scare was over by the 1920s, the states continued to prosecute leftists with some gusto. Benjamin Gitlow was indicted in New York for "criminal anarchy." Gitlow was a member of the Left Wing Section of the Socialist Party, organized in 1919. New York law made it a crime to advocate or teach the "duty, necessity or propriety of overthrowing . . . government by force or violence." The Left Wing Section published a manifesto full of "fervent language" about the proletarian revolution and the like. The Supreme Court in 1925 upheld Gitlow's conviction; Holmes and Brandeis dissented.[120] But the decision did contain one important new concept—somewhat buried in the text: freedom of speech was a "fundamental" right; and it was protected by the Fourteenth Amendment to the Constitution. That meant, in practice, that federal free-speech law was binding on all of the states.

But the glory days of free speech were far in the future; and two years after *Gitlow*, the Court upheld the conviction of Charlotte Anita Whitney. Whitney had been a member of the Communist Labor Party of California, and had once been an alternate member of its executive committee. At the time of her arrest, she had actually resigned from the party.[121] She was a middle-aged woman and not the usual suspect; her ancestors came over on the *Mayflower*. Nonetheless, she was charged with violating California's Criminal Syndicalism Act. The law defined "criminal syndicalism" as "any doctrine . . . advocating, teaching or aiding and abetting" crime, sabotage, force and violence, or terrorism "as a means of accomplishing a change in industrial ownership or control, or effecting any political change." It was also a crime to organize or "knowingly become a member" of any organization which advocated these dreaded doctrines. The statute also recited that the law was "necessary to the immediate preservation of the public peace and safety," because "large numbers of persons" were "going from place to place in the state, advocating, teaching and practicing criminal syndicalism."

Criminal syndicalism laws were products of the red scare. Idaho began the trend in 1917. California's law (passed in 1919) grew out of panic caused by a bomb that went off on the governor's back porch; the *Los Angeles Times,* under Harrison Gray Otis, beat the drums of rabid propaganda for tougher laws. Charlotte Whitney never had a chance. The prosecution brought in evidence to show what a dangerous organization the party was; and the jury convicted her of the infamous statutory crime. There was no place for reds in California. The Supreme Court upheld the conviction unanimously. Freedom of speech, said the court, did not mean an "absolute right to speak"; and the state had authority to protect itself against threats to its peace and security. Whitney, apparently, was one of those threats.[122]

As part of the surge of "one hundred percent Americanism" after World War I, some thirty-seven states restricted the teaching of foreign languages in public schools.[123] In *Meyer v. Nebraska,* decided in 1923, the Supreme Court confronted the Nebraska statute (1919) which made it illegal to teach in a foreign language in any elementary school, public or private.[124] Only students past the eighth grade could study a foreign language. The main target of this law was German; a similar statute in Ohio applied only to German, which was not to be taught to grammar school students. Nebraska argued that its law would "insure that the English language shall be the mother tongue and the language of the heart of the children reared in this country," replacing "foreign languages and foreign ideals."[125] A Congregational pastor back home in Nebraska felt that the language of Goethe and Beethoven was so loaded down with the "weight of infamy" that the "only appropriate place for it would seem to be in hell itself."[126]

The Supreme Court struck down the Nebraska law. It was "arbitrary," and unrelated to "any end within the competency of the State."[127] Four years later, the Court confronted a law of the territory of Hawaii regulating "foreign lan-guage schools," which were mostly after-hours schools teaching Japanese. Such schools were not allowed to enroll very young children (below fourth grade); and the state controlled the choice of textbooks, among other things.[128] The Court struck down this law, too. It is hard to tie these cases into a single, satisfying pattern—at least in a logical, or "legal" sense. The Court was hardly liberal, but neither was it a monolith of reaction. There seems little doubt that the Court came down hardest on laws that infringed rights of comfortable, respectable people; and that it had least sympathy for the lowly and disreputa-ble among us.

II

The New Deal and Its Successors

6

The Roosevelt Revolution

The Great Depression began, most dramatically, with the stock market crash of 1929. There had been signs of danger and impending crisis; but this event set off a chain reaction, like the first shots of a revolution. The economy went into total eclipse. The period of "normalcy" exploded. The great parade of the 1920s ended. The country spiraled downward into a deeper, blacker hole than most living Americans could ever remember. At the worst of the Depression, about a quarter of the working population was jobless. Businesses failed by the tens of thousands. Banks collapsed like tenpins. All over the country, people lost their money, their homes, their farms, their jobs—their hope of the future. Mortgages were foreclosed. People were evicted in the cities and camped on the streets. Hunger and misery stalked the land.

In this period of crisis, the cries for help—and the center of legal gravity—shifted, relatively speaking, from the exhausted, bankrupt governments of cities and states to Washington, D.C. The president, Herbert Hoover, failed to solve the problem. Not that Hoover, Congress, and the federal government were entirely inert. Hundreds of millions were poured, for example, into emergency relief and public works under a statute of 1932, the last year of Hoover's administration.[1] But politically and economically, it was not enough; and Hoover had to take the blame for forces over which he, in fact, had little control. The president was reviled: hobo encampments and shantytowns were called Hoovervilles; freight cars that tramps rode were Hoover Pullmans.[2] Hoover's day was done. In the crisis, the country turned to a different party, the Democrats, and to a new leader, a charismatic, buoyant soul, Franklin Delano Roosevelt, who swept into office in a landslide. There followed a period of intense lawmaking, a cascade of dramatic new laws, passed by Congress but masterminded by Roosevelt and his men—laws which seemed to many contemporaries almost revolutionary.

Though perhaps not quite. In some ways, the modern legal and social worlds begin with the New Deal; in other ways, the New Deal was only a spike on a graph that was going up in any event. The New Deal sucked power into Washington; but it was flowing in that direction anyway, for reasons we have already explored. Government employment went from about 240,000 in 1901 to 655,000 in 1920. Another 300,000 had been added by 1939; but the fact remains that Hoover already presided over a vast federal bureaucracy.[3] The New Deal made a difference—a big difference—but it is hard to imagine that, under any circumstances, a weak, decentralized, do-nothing ideology of government could have survived the massive social forces that were pushing society in one master direction.

Roosevelt was the spirit behind the New Deal, and its political genius; but of course he was not the man who wrote the laws or defended them in court or carried out the policies. The New Deal, among other things, was a full-employment deal for liberal lawyers; they flocked to Washington to do the spadework for the New Deal. Never before had government lawyers been quite so important. They came from all over, to take up positions in the capital, the place where the action was.[4]

The New Deal rushed, helter-skelter, into the great social void that the Depression had created. The country was hungry for action. And action was what the country got, in the New Deal's first "hundred days." There was a bank moratorium, and laws to try to solve the crisis of money and banking. One law (of June 13, 1933) established the Home Owners Loan Corporation, to stem the epidemic of foreclosures.[5] Three days later, as part of a banking act, Congress established the Federal Deposit Insurance Corporation, to prevent runs on banks and give depositors a sense of security.[6]

The New Deal also attacked the problem of unemployment with some vigor. If the private sector could not put people to work, the government would. The Civilian Conservation Corps took young people who were jobless and gave them work on rivers, parks, and forests. The National Industrial Recovery Act of 1933 included a Public Works Administration, to give jobs to the unemployed. A Civil Works Administration, created in 1933, provided work for almost four million people, who labored on roads, sewage systems, parks, and the like. But the CWA ended in 1934, and the problem of unemployment still haunted the country. The Works Progress Administration took the CWA's place. The WPA was created in 1935 by an executive order, but the Emergency Relief Acts, from 1935 on, gave it more formal authority.[7] The WPA grew to gigantic size. At its peak, it had millions of people on its rolls.

The WPA literally left its mark on the country. All over the country, for example, small and large post offices are adorned with WPA murals—works of art created by unemployed artists. In all honesty, most of them fall pretty far short of the standards set, say, for Florence or Siena in the days of the Medicis. Quite a few have the dreadful flavor of "socialist realism." But they were better than nothing—and provided work for hungry artists. WPA writers wrote guidebooks to the states. Humbler workers built thousands of miles of roads and culverts, drained swamps, cleared slums, promoted public health. WPA projects, conceived and sponsored by cities and local governments, reached into every part of the country.

The WPA was not universally popular. To many conservatives, it represented some of the worst vices of the New Deal. They sneered at WPA as a source of useless make-work: men leaning on shovels. They carped and chipped away at its activities. Some aspects of it fell victim to the grand strain of philistinism that lies just beneath the surface—or *on* the surface—of American political life. The yahoos of Congress banned theater projects in 1939; they were wasteful, they competed with private productions, and (this complaint came from some southerners) black and white actors sometimes appeared on the stage together. The projects also attracted, as one magazine put it, "a horde of out-at-elbows Communists," averse to honest work.[8] There was also the usual horror of socialism—in the sense of government enterprise. Any hint of competition with private businesses brought down wrath on the heads of WPA officials.

What right-wing critics overlooked was the profoundly conservative bent of WPA—and, in a way, of much of the New Deal effort. Roosevelt and most of his advisers had absolutely no interest in social revolution. Nor did they *make* one. The New Deal distributed a lot; but it was not (on the whole) *redistributive*. The "income profile" of America in 1940 was very much like that of 1930—or even of 1920.[9] It is no accident that WPA reproduced the existing structure of society. It gave artists work doing art; it gave writers work doing writing; it gave skilled mechanics work as skilled mechanics. It trained women to be maids and cooks; but it also gave librarians work as librarians, roofers work as roofers, locksmiths work with locks. It was aimed at the poor and the downtrodden, yes; but also and perhaps primarily at what one might call the submerged middle class. It was a rejection of the dole, and an affirmation of the work ethic. It was supposed to provide work for people "at occupations which will conserve their skills."[10] This was because, as one official put it in 1935, it was not good for morale if a "doctor of philosophy, or a mechanic" was set to work "digging ditches"; this was even worse "than to give him a dole, and let him remain idle."[11]

The submerged middle class was at the heart of other New Deal programs as well—the public housing program, for example. Building houses seemed like a great idea, because, in addition to the housing itself, it made jobs for construction workers. The Public Works Administration began to build houses as part of its program; but it soon faced legal obstacles, in the form of disapproving court decisions. In 1937 the Wagner Housing Act was passed. It was opposed by the National Lumber Dealers' Association, the National Association of Real Estate Boards, and other business interests. Partly because of the opposition, the act, as passed, was far from radical. Housing would be controlled by local housing authorities; the tenants would pay rent; this meant, originally, that tenants would be drawn from the honest, working poor, and from the submerged middle class. In fact, it was not until 1949 that welfare tenants were even allowed in public housing. The New Deal also tinkered with the idea of building whole new communities—towns with names like Greenbelt (Maryland), Greendale (Wisconsin), and Greenhills (Ohio).[12] A number of these communities were actually built; but many Congressmen found the whole idea of government housing and towns "un-American," if not, as Senator Harry Byrd of Virginia put it, reeking with the "stench" of "Russian communism." The communities ended up in private hands within a decade or so.

The Tennessee Valley Authority had a more lasting effect. This was one of Roosevelt's pet projects. It was a huge enterprise (authorized in May 1933) to shock one of America's vast rural slums into modernity. The Tennessee Valley, an area of forty-one thousand square miles, sprawled across parts of seven states. It was dirt poor, scourged by malaria and ravaged by floods. The soil was weak and eroded. The TVA built dams, generated hydroelectric power, worked on flood control projects, and brought light and hope to a region that had so often been left behind.[13] Roosevelt imagined the TVA as a model for similar great works around the country; this did not happen, but the TVA itself was a major achievement.

Too Much and Too Cheap

In some ways, the National Industrial Recovery Act of 1933 was the cornerstone of the early New Deal.[14] The act began by declaring a "national emergency," which was certainly true. The act encouraged trade associations—organizations made up of businesses in some particular line—to draw up "codes of fair competition." The president had power to approve these codes. Once the seal of approval was placed on a code, it was binding on the whole industry, like it or not. One of the key ideas here was to control production, and to shore up prices.

This might seem, on the surface, rather odd. Millions were out of work; countless millions had been reduced to grinding poverty. Why should the country want to make prices higher, when so many people could not afford to buy anything even at rock-bottom prices? But the answer seemed clear. Dazed and despondent, people all over the country were asking themselves: what went wrong? Whatever it was, there were now too many goods and services, and they were selling at prices far too low. The stock market was not the only institution that had crashed. Consumers, no doubt, had a liking for low prices; but storekeepers and farmers could not survive if prices were too low. And the New Deal, for all its populism, was no enemy of small business and the farmer. Nor was it really an enemy of medium and big business—provided business was willing to play ball. The NIRA, indeed, was in some ways a program to help even (or especially) the very largest businesses. The problem, as big business saw it, was that there was too much competition, and too little in the way of profits.

Under the NIRA, then, businesses were directed to get together, to cooperate, to put an end to overproduction and the other sicknesses that plagued the economy. They were also supposed to work things out with their employees. Section 7(a) of the NIRA told companies to guarantee minimum wages and maximum hours, and to allow their workers to join unions. Businesses hated 7(a), but they were forced to swallow it.[15]

It was a messy and chaotic process to get companies to join together and hammer out the "codes"; but it did eventually get done, for hundreds of industries, from iron and steel to the making of pretzels. Under the lumber and timber code (approved in August 1933), for example, companies in this industry agreed to set up a Lumber Code Authority; the authority had power to set production quotas and to set minimum prices. Codes typically also fixed minimum wages; the Corset and Brassiere Association of America agreed to pay employees at least fourteen dollars a week ("cutters" were to get at least twenty-five dollars), and not to "employ anyone under sixteen years of age." In the pretzel manufacturing industry, there were maximum hours fixed, and no "factory or mechanical worker or artisan [was to] be paid less than 30 cents per hour."[16] Despite the tumult and confusion, hundreds of codes were adopted, covering millions of workers.

Big business, labor, Chambers of Commerce were in general in favor of the NIRA plan—essentially, a plan for "publicly sanctioned cartels."[17] It represented the thinking of one essential faction of New Dealers in the program's early years: the faction that saw economic salvation in a kind of corporatism. Even those who regarded big business as a giant, evil, hydra-headed monster disagreed on what was to be done. Some believed in chopping the beast into bits, and ending the "curse of bigness" (Brandeis's phrase). Other people thought this was Utopian. There was no going back. The beast could not be killed; it had to be controlled. The NIRA appealed to this wing more than the others. The labor provisions would raise consumer purchasing power. The curb on competition would raise profits, and encourage new investment. This was the theory. But the practice was inconsistent, chaotic, imprecise—as was so much of the New Deal program. And, as we shall see, the NIRA was to die an early and inglorious death—at the hands of the "nine old men."

On the Farm and at the Store

Low prices were the bane of the farmer as well as the businessman; and life on the farm was if anything more desperate than life in the cities. The Agricultural Adjustment Act of 1933 was a cornerstone of early New Deal policy.[18] The trouble (as farmers saw it) was too much food at too low prices and too few buyers. Under the AAA, farmers were encouraged to grow less wheat, corn, and other crops. Plowing acres under would stabilize prices; the farmers who agreed to let their lands go fallow would be paid by the government; these funds would come from a tax on food processors.

For the beleaguered neighborhood grocer, in his white smock, working long hours for pennies in his corner store, the enemy was the chain stores. The Atlantic and Pacific Tea Company (A&P) was founded in the nineteenth century; but it took off only in the twentieth century. Chains had 8.3 percent of the grocery market in 1899, but 20.4 percent by 1909, and 32.8 percent in 1929. By that time, A&P had fifteen thousand outlets, with sales of over a billion dollars a year.[19]

Something had to be done. Small merchants could not compete in the marketplace, but they were voters, and they had a voice in state and local government. One solution was to tax the chain stores. Between 1927 and 1941, laws were passed in twenty-eight states to put special taxes on chain stores. Some of these laws—in Georgia, Maryland, and North Carolina, for example— were killed in the courts; but the majority survived.[20] In 1931 the Supreme Court upheld the Indiana law, passed in 1929, which put a tax of $3 a year on storekeepers who owned only one store, rising to $25 a year per store on companies that owned more than twenty.[21] The Indiana tax seems fairly modest; under the Texas law of 1935, on the other hand, one store cost $1 a year, but each store over fifty would set the owner back $750.[22]

The New Deal looked for other ideas that would shore up prices and help out the mom-and-pop store. A Senate resolution of 1928 asked the Federal Trade Commission to investigate chain-store practices. The commission spent time and money, and produced its report in 1934. The Robinson-Patman Act, in form an amendment to the Clayton Act, was passed in 1936.[23]

The Robinson-Patman Act was hardly a model of clarity. But the guts of it lay in a clause that made price discrimination between buyers of goods illegal, if the discrimination had an impact on competition. The basic idea was this: the chain stores, which had centralized and professional purchasing departments, and vast economic power, could squeeze lower prices out of suppliers than the little guy could, and thus would drive the little guy out of business. And, in fact, between 1926 and 1933 the chains gained enormously—their share of the retail market went from 9 percent to 25 percent; at the same time, independent retailers went out of business at an alarming clip.[24]

Another idea whose time seemed to have come was resale price maintenance. The maker of a product could insist on a fixed price both wholesale and retail, and control "cut-rate" retailers. But contracts for resale price maintenance had run afoul of the United States Supreme Court in 1911. The Dr. Miles

Medical Company of Indiana produced "proprietary medicines, prepared by means of secret methods and formulas and identified by distinctive packages, labels, and trade-marks"; to protect these wonderful products from cheap retailers, the company insisted on contracts to enforce the suggested retail price. But the Supreme Court held that the practice violated the Sherman Act; it was an "obvious" restraint of trade.[25] The retail codes under the NIRA had minimum price provisions, but the NIRA, as we shall see, was guillotined by the Supreme Court. The states began to pass their own resale maintenance laws, and the Miller-Tydings Act of 1937 gave these laws its blessing: an agreement which fixed a minimum resale price, for trademarked goods, was not a violation of the Sherman Act if it was legal in the state where the resale took place.[26]

These laws were bitterly criticized at the time; and the criticism became more strident with the years. Robert Bork, writing about Robinson-Patman, called it "the misshapen progeny of intolerable draftsmanship coupled to wholly mistaken economic theory."[27] But the "wholly mistaken economic theory" was probably not an economic theory at all. These laws were, to be honest about it, anticompetitive, and if economic efficiency were the measure of all things, they could be labeled "mistaken" or worse. They were reactions of panic and desperation, in a time of crisis, a time of collapsing values. There was a profound loss of faith in the market, in free competition, in the pillars on which America once had stood.

The Nine Old Men

The National Industrial Recovery Act was typical of the early New Deal. It was corporatist, yes; and, in its own way, like the WPA programs, it was aimed at restoring, not revolutionizing. It was meant to preserve business, not nationalize it; it handed over power to people who already had power, or who already had a stake in society, but were losing their grip because a tornado of destruction had torn the roof off the national economy. The NIRA gave a lot to big business; and in a sense, it had a philosophy different from those (later) programs— Robinson-Patman, anti–chain store taxes—which were drafted on behalf of the little guy in business, the small local shops of the nation. But all of the laws, of whatever stripe, were a far cry from Bolshevism, whatever the anti–New Dealers felt.

At the time, however, the New Deal programs certainly seemed bold, dramatic, risky. They also seemed unprecedented—certainly at the federal level. They frightened the old elites. Once enacted, the programs faced what had become by now almost a tradition in the legal system: that is, they had to run the gamut of the federal courts; their constitutionality had to be tested.

At the apex of this system sat the Supreme Court, and its "nine old men." None of them, of course, were Roosevelt's men at the time he took office. They were holdovers from earlier, mostly conservative, presidents. And the Court, in a dramatic series of decisions, struck at the very heart of the New Deal. On "Black Monday," May 27, 1935, the Supreme Court destroyed, by unanimous vote, the National Industrial Recovery Act, and the Frazier-Lemke Act, which provided for mortgage moratoriums.[28]

Schechter Poultry Corp. v. United States was the case that undid the NIRA.[29] In this, the so-called "sick chicken" case, the Schechters had run afoul of the Live Poultry Code. The Supreme Court thought Congress had no power to authorize such a code, under its commerce power; and the fact that shipping chickens within New York State might have an "indirect effect upon interstate commerce" was not enough to save the law—the Constitution did not provide for "a centralized system" of the sort the law contemplated. Moreover, the Supreme Court thought that the statute gave too much away: it empowered the industry groups, in effect, to make law. This "delegation of legislation power" was "unknown to our law" and was "utterly inconsistent with the constitutional prerogatives and duties of Congress."

This was a stunning setback for Roosevelt's New Deal. The next year, in *United States v. Butler,* the Agricultural Adjustment Act (AAA) was added to the casualty list.[30] The AAA assessed a tax, which was then spent to bribe farmers to cut down production. But Congress (said the Court) had no power to tax and spend to "induce action in a field in which the United States has no power to intermeddle." The use of a tax here was a mere "pretext." When the dust cleared, it was obvious that the "nine old men" had knocked out some of the main props of Roosevelt's New Deal.

Roosevelt was not about to take this lying down. He was reelected in 1936, in a landslide even greater than that of 1932. Now he was at the height of his power—idolized by the public, and with huge majorities in both houses of Congress. He decided to do something about the problem of the Supreme Court. What he came up with was the infamous court-packing plan, which he unleashed in 1937. He denounced the old justices—men whose view of the world was "blurred" by "old glasses fitted . . . for the needs of another genera-tion." He proposed adding one new justice for each justice who was six months past the age of seventy. That would have given him six new justices, and would have effectively neutralized the anti–New Deal bias of the Court.

But it was not to be. His proposal "generated an intensity of response unmatched by any legislative controversy" in the century. He had, somehow, profaned the holy of holies. Of course, fervent New Dealers were in favor of the plan (or said they were); but the opposition was even more powerful. The plan was denounced and condemned as a threat to the integrity of the courts. The tide ran strongly against the plan, which died with a feeble whimper.[31]

This was an amazing defeat for an amazingly popular president. But though Roosevelt lost the battle, in the end he won the war. Even in the short run, the situation changed, despite devastating criticism against the court-packing plan. The Supreme Court in 1937 began to uphold New Deal legisla-tion. In *National Labor Relations Board v. Jones & Laughlin Steel Corpora-tion,* the Supreme Court, by a narrow 5–4 margin, sustained the National Labor Relations Act.[32] In this and several other cases, Justice Roberts changed sides—or seemed to, converting 5–4 votes against New Deal measures to 5–4 votes in favor. This was the famous "switch in time that saved the nine." Was this in fact a reaction to the court-packing plan? Was there actually a switch, or was Roberts simply a middle-of-the-roader? The matter is still vigorously debated. The Court was in the process—had been in the process—of rethinking the way it understood the Constitution. The Court was once deeply committed to a firm, bright line between state power and federal power; between businesses that were so vital to the public that the government had broad authority to regulate them, and those that were strictly private. It once felt that the federal government could regulate commerce but not "production" (manufacturing).[33] Its tissue of doctrines tended to limit the power of states, and the federal government, to tell private businesses what to do, what to charge, what to pay.

All this was changing. In *Nebbia v. New York* (1934), the Court narrowly sustained a New York law regulating the milk industry. The New York law set up a Milk Control Board, with power to fix prices. The board decreed that milk should be sold in stores at nine cents a quart, no more and no less. Leo Nebbia, of Rochester, New York, sold two quarts of milk, plus a loaf of bread, for eighteen cents, and was fined. The Court talked about how important milk was, for babies and other people, how desperate a state the industry was in, and pointed to a long history of comparable regulation.[34] There were other straws in the wind—cases which pointed in a new direction.

In any event, time was on Roosevelt's side. He was elected four times, and the "nine old men" died off or resigned; they were replaced with stalwart New Dealers: men like William O. Douglas and Hugo Black. In the later Roosevelt years, and afterward, the Supreme Court renounced its economic activism. It gave its stamp of approval to all the programs of the New Deal. It simply abandoned the whole line of thought that *Lochner v. New York* epitomized. The Court, for example, stretched the concept of interstate commerce to the very limit. The Constitution gave Congress power to regulate commerce "among the states." This meant (according to the Court) commerce moving across state lines. But the Court had in some instances given the clause quite a narrow reading—in the child labor cases, for example. The Court also now dropped the flimsy distinction between "production" and "commerce." Now the Court allowed Congress to impose almost anything on anybody, as long as there was a hint, a trace, a soupçon of an argument that what the anybody did had some effect, direct or indirect, on interstate commerce. This was more than an act of retracting its horns; the Court was redefining the very structure of government—it was redrawing the map of freedom.

Wickard v. Filburn (1942) came up under the revised Agricultural Adjustment Act of 1938—a New Deal law that tried to keep farm prices up by controlling supply.[35] Roscoe C. Filburn was a farmer in Montgomery County, Ohio; he was a dairy farmer, but he raised a small amount of wheat. He had a quota of eleven acres and 222 bushels of wheat; he planted twenty-three acres, and produced 461 bushels. Filburn incurred a penalty of forty-nine cents a bushel, for growing too much. He sued to enjoin enforcement of the act. The problem for the government was what Filburn did with his wheat. He fed some to his chickens, used some for flour for his family, and saved some to use as seed for next year's crop. It was not clear whether he sold *any* of his wheat on the open market. How on earth could Filburn's wheat be under federal control? Where was the interstate commerce? It all seemed terribly local, terribly Ohio. The idea that Congress could tell Filburn what to do, on his own farm, with his own wheat, would have struck earlier Courts as completely incredible. But the Court upheld the law, and the quota system. The wheat industry was "a problem industry." True, Filburn's position in the wheat market was "trivial by itself"; but his "contribution, taken together with that of many others similarly situated, is far from trivial." There were tens of thousands of Filburns, all over the country; and their home-grown, home-consumed wheat, in the aggregate, cut the market demand for wheat and depressed the price. And this did affect the interstate commerce in wheat. This possibility was enough for the Court to sustain the law.

Filburn was a case of federal power. How far would the Court ride herd over state regulation? Hardly at all, it turned out. One case often cited as Exhibit A for the notion of judicial abdication is a later (1955) one, *Williamson v. Lee Optical Co.*[36] The subject was eyeglasses in Oklahoma. An Oklahoma law essentially discriminated against opticians: it gave a kind of monopoly to ophthalmologists or optometrists. A lower federal court thought that the law violated the equal-protection clause. But the Supreme Court reversed, unanimously. Douglas wrote the opinion. No more, said the Court, would the justices stand in the road blocking social and economic legislation. They would defer to the states (and federal government) on issues of regulation.

One might have thought, at the time, that the Supreme Court had taken a kind of monastic vow, a vow of legal chastity, retreating into a cloistered world of quiet deference. Looking back, we now see that they were merely shifting gears. In a case in 1938, *United States v. Carolene Products Co.*, Justice Harlan F. Stone remarked, in a footnote, that the Court had a duty to be vigilant on behalf of "discrete and insular minorities"—those who could not rely on "political processes" for their protection.[37] This proved to be a most accurate prediction; but the Court's work along these lines lay mostly in the future.

The most vigorous of the battles over New Deal law made headlines. Behind them was a change that was both deep and real. It was more than a change in doctrine. The New Deal transferred power to the federal government. At every level, it stimulated acceptance of an active, program-making, ubiquitous government. People still talked about limited government, federalism, states' rights (sometimes as a code for white supremacy), and so on; but something new had emerged, and was gaining general acceptance. This was the idea of strong, active government—government that could respond to the kind of crisis the Depression had brought on the country.

Bulls and Bears

Nobody forgot that the Depression had seemed to begin with a stock market crash. That crash took with it the life savings of thousands and thousands of people; and it left in its wake a lot of raw anger at the robber barons of Wall Street. The idea of taming Wall Street—or big business in general—was nothing new. The Sherman Act and the Clayton Act are examples of earlier efforts. Before the New Deal, occasional and sporadic state laws aimed their arrows against securities fraud.

The most important of these laws were the so-called blue sky laws, a somewhat mysterious term. Kansas passed the first blue sky law in 1911, after J. N. Dolley, the Kansas commissioner of banking, lobbied vigorously for the bill.[38] Dolley was a retired grocer, with some local banking experience. Kansas had had its share of stock scandals; and Dolley spoke (he said) for widows and orphans who had been bilked by evil and conniving stock promoters, vultures who preyed on their weakness. Under the Kansas blue sky law, nobody could market stocks and bonds in the state without a license, and without reporting on the financial condition of the company.

The blue sky laws were popular with bankers, especially small bankers; investment bankers were mostly on the other side. There was also a certain element of local protectionism: when Kansas people invested their money in stock schemes, the money almost always left Kansas for distant parts. As Dolley put it in one of his press releases, the point was to "keep Kansas money in Kansas."[39] Naturally, the idea of keeping Vermont money in Vermont, or Tennessee money in Tennessee, was pretty attractive to these states, too; and a positive epidemic of blue sky laws followed the Kansas example. Most of them were actually modeled on the Kansas statute; and by the early 1930s every state except Nevada had its own blue sky law.

The case for regulation was a strong one. There were frauds enough to go around, bucket shops, and fancy-talking salesmen who bilked the public. Many people felt that some dark and sinister forces, in far-off Wall Street, pulled the strings that ran the economy. Their misdeeds were responsible for depressions, unemployment, falling farm prices, rising railroad rates, and probably other things as well. In the twenties many ordinary people with a little spare cash jingling in their pocket displayed a growing appetite for investment in the market. If the robber barons could get rich through stocks, why not you and me? You can't cheat an honest man, as the old saying goes; and many "widows and orphans" (and others) who lost money to bucket shops, or in the stock market crash, had been seduced by the lure of easy money. That did not mean they were any less victims of misfortune.

The blue sky laws were popular; but probably did little good. Many were full of loopholes; in any event, in a federal system, they could do nothing about securities sold by mail, or across state lines. The blue sky laws could be a help against local sharpsters in Kansas, but they had no chance at all of curbing Wall Street.

Wall Street, in fact, was also worried about stock fraud. The New York Stock Exchange ran its own (private) system of securities regulation. Any company that wanted to list stock on the exchange had to file financial information, and provide independent legal opinion, about the company and its securities.[40] But companies could get around these requirements by registering stock on some other exchange. The New York Stock Exchange itself never had enough staff to double-check the information; many companies engaged in creative bookkeeping and accounting—which the stock exchange was powerless to detect.

The disaster of depression reinforced the political demand for drastic action. A rising tide raises all boats; a sinking ship sets off a search for scapegoats. The Senate Banking and Currency Committee began an investigation in 1933–1934; the chief counsel and major figure in the investigation was Ferdinand Pecora. The Pecora hearings produced sensational headlines, and scathing exposés of the doings of the House of Morgan and others. All this fanned the rage that the wrecked economy had engendered. Surely these rich, corrupt bankers and promoters were responsible for the hemorrhage of wealth, the destruction of small workers and farmers.

The demands for action produced the Securities Act of 1933.[41] The aim was to promote "full and fair disclosure," and "prevent fraud," in the sale of stocks and bonds. Roosevelt had asked for such a bill. The House Committee on Interstate and Foreign Commerce, which reported the bill out, talked about fifty billions in new securities "floated" in the country in the postwar decade, half of them "worthless. These cold figures spell tragedy in the lives of thousands of individuals who invested their life savings." Untold harm had been done by dishonest underwriters and securities dealers, by "irresponsibility" and greed, "abnormal profits," a "fantasy of security selling" reminiscent of the "days of the South Sea bubble."[42]

The actual bill was in fact essentially a disclosure law. People who sold securities had to register them with the Federal Trade Commission. They had to disclose a wealth of information about the securities, the underwriters, and the issuing company, including balance sheets and profit-and-loss statements. Any prospectus dangled before the public also had to contain much of this information.

The business community was far from happy with the Securities Act; brokers, underwriters, and stock exchanges fought it to the end. Because of the Depression, and the noise about scandal and chicanery, they were fighting a losing battle; nonetheless, they made their influence felt, and the act, in the end, was something of a compromise. The same could be said for the next of the great regulatory laws, the Securities and Exchange Act of 1934. This law replaced the FTC's role with an independent commission, the Securities and Exchange Commission; the new organ was also vested with broad powers to regulate stock exchanges. Stock exchanges, including the mighty New York Stock Exchange, had to register with the SEC, and the SEC had power to approve and monitor rules of the exchange.

The Securities and Exchange Commission Act also tried to discourage some of the wilder forms of market speculation. It imposed limits on margin trading. It tried to deal with the problem of insider trading—for example, big stockholders in any particular company were forced to disclose what they held, and to report any buying and selling.

The act was controversial, and went through many changes as it worked its way through Congress. It ended up much weaker than when it began. Nonetheless, it made a big difference to Wall Street (and to the country). Most significantly, it created an agency to regulate the financial markets—and it gave that agency a great deal of discretion. On the day President Roosevelt signed the bill, one of his advisers put it this way: the SEC law would be "good or bad . . . depending upon the men who administer it."[43]

Roosevelt surprised some and inflamed others by naming Joseph P. Kennedy his first SEC chairman. Kennedy certainly knew Wall Street—he was rich, Catholic, somewhat vulgar, a manipulator who was adept at "all the tricks of the trade." Some liberals called the appointment grotesque. But Kennedy was not just a political appointment. In office, he was tough but conciliatory. He told Wall Street that "we of the SEC do not regard ourselves as coroners sitting on the corpse of financial enterprise." Instead, "we regard ourselves . . . as partners in a cooperative enterprise." Businessmen were not all "crooks."[44]

Despite a lot of talk about malefactors of great wealth, despite a radical fringe, the essence of the New Deal was as Kennedy described it. It was conservative in the literal sense: meant to preserve the American system, not transform it. Yet in the event, preserving *meant* transforming. The world, after all, was transforming itself; it was a world of political upheaval, rapid change, social turmoil. Hitler had just come to power in Germany. Mussolini strutted on the stage in Italy. Stalin ruled the Soviet Union with an iron hand.

There were American socialists and radicals, and certainly the Depression swelled their ranks. But most of the New Dealers were neither socialist nor radical. They believed in saving capitalism, and what they considered the American way of life; but with many necessary changes. No serious thought was given to seizing the banks or other major industries. Nobody wanted to nationalize the economy. Yet banking and finance had to be controlled, tamed, regulated—for its own good, and for the good of the nation. One of the major statutes of the early New Deal was the Glass-Steagall Act of 1933.[45] In essence, this law tried to cut the cords that tied banks to the securities business. No bank was to trade in corporate securities of any sort; investment banks were not to accept deposits, and no officer or director of a commercial bank was allowed to manage a company which was mainly in the securities business.

In 1935, too, Congress passed the Public Utility Holding Company Act.[46] This act aimed to regulate gas and electric holding companies—huge, complex corporations, balloonlike structures whose sole asset was the stock of their subsidiaries, the working companies that actually supplied light and power and heat. The act gave the Securities and Exchange Commission authority over these companies. In particular, the "death sentence" clause of the act empowered the SEC to limit each holding company to a "single integrated public utility system," and to modify and simplify the structures of these companies, balanced on top of each other like acrobats in a circus.

In general, the New Deal took many forms. Its inconsistency is legendary. It writhed and squirmed and scrambled for policies. It was both for and against big business. The Securities and Exchange Act, the Federal Deposit Insurance Act—certainly, the government did not intend to let the invisible hand run the country. Still, regulating a stock exchange is a far cry from Bolshevism.

In the NIRA, after all, the New Deal had handed power to big business on a silver platter. Even some liberals—men like Brandeis—disliked the corporatist element of the early New Deal. After this stage of the New Deal collapsed, policy did become somewhat more hostile and regulatory. Thurman Arnold, in the Justice Department, began a vigorous trust-busting program. The Temporary National Economic Commission (TNEC) was formed in 1937 to find out what was really wrong with the economy, which was still sick, sick, sick despite all the New Deal medicines prescribed and taken. The TNEC issued forty-one volumes of reports. The bottom line was this: big business was too big; it controlled too much of the economy; it stifled the individual. What was needed was more government regulation and more trust-busting.[47]

In its final report, the TNEC argued that "political centralism is largely the product of economic centralism."[48] The chief argument, then, was an argument about bigness. Big business produced big government. Both the first and the second New Deals, in short, acted on the belief that the old days of small shops, farms, and the rugged individual were gone, and gone forever. Bigness was destiny. It had to be contained and controlled. A bruised and battered country agreed. They voted New Deal by the millions.

The New Deal and Labor

The Wagner Act of 1935 was another landmark. It was meant to begin a bold new era in labor relations.[49] The Wagner Act put the government firmly on the side of the unions. Strikes and labor unrest, the act recited, were burdens to "the flow of interstate commerce"; and strikes occurred when companies denied workers their right to organize. The preamble also referred to the "inequality of bargaining power," and announced (in a phrase that would have enraged the likes of Rufus Peckham) that workers did not really have meaningful "liberty of contract." The act created a National Labor Relations Board (NLRB) of three members. The board had power to intervene in conflicts between labor and management. The act ordered employers to "bargain in good faith" with unions. It prohibited "unfair" labor practices—mainly, antiunion activity.

There was good reason to suppose that the Supreme Court would strike down the law, in the light of what the Court had been doing to the rest of the New Deal programs. But in fact the Court sustained the NLRA—this was, as we saw, the famous case described as a dramatic "switch" in the Supreme Court, from no to yes on the New Deal. Chief Justice Hughes, writing for the majority, called the right of employees "to self-organization" a "fundamental right." Union was "essential to give laborers opportunity to deal on an equality with their employer." The legal heart of the case, however, was its expansive reading of the power of Congress to regulate industry, under the banner of the commerce clause.[50]

Business groups fought the Wagner Act bitterly: the act put the government firmly on the side of unions. It assumed that collective bargaining was the way for industry and labor to go. But the Wagner Act itself did not dictate the terms of any bargain. Nor did it bring about harmony in the workplace. Beginning in late 1936—just after Roosevelt's landslide reelection—a wave of sit-down strikes swept over the country. Eventually, the strikes engulfed the whole vast enterprise of General Motors, more than 140,000 workers and fifty plants. The core was in Flint, Michigan, where bodies for GM cars were produced.[51] Strictly speaking, the sit-ins were illegal—the workers were trespassing, and the police could have thrown them out. This is what GM wanted; but the Democrats in charge in Washington and Michigan were not eager to do so. In the end, GM gave way: it promised to recognize the United Auto Workers, and not to interfere in any way with unionization. In the same year, there were other sit-down strikes by the hundreds. And United States Steel gave in to the unions, without a strike. In 1937 unions recruited more than three million new members—they almost doubled in size.[52]

It was not the Wagner Act as such which made the difference, but the political facts of life that produced the Wagner Act. Business could not rely on government, the police, scabs, or the United States Supreme Court to hold back the power of organized labor. The Fair Labor Standards Act (1938) was another blow to the old order.[53] It established a minimum wage—twenty-five cents an hour, going up to forty cents after a period of years; and maximum hours—forty-four hours a week, going down to forty. Anything more than the maximum hours earned overtime pay of time and a half. The law also struck a blow at goods that were the product of "oppressive child labor." These goods were banned from interstate commerce. The law applied to workers in industries "engaged in commerce or in the production of goods for commerce." In *United States v. Darby* (1941), the Supreme Court unanimously held the law constitutional.[54] Moreover, the Court repudiated *Hammer v. Dagenhart,* and specifically overruled it as a "departure" from sound principle whose "vitality, as a precedent . . . has long since been exhausted."[55]

What followed was a kind of golden age for American unions. Labor unrest did not end—the strikes, lockouts, sit-downs, boycotts, and the like—but the rules of the game had changed; and the balance of power had shifted in signifi-

New Deal: Factors that made it possible
· Radio
· News
· Movies
· change in culture
· Roosevelt

cant ways. Union membership continued to grow. It rose to 10 million in 1942, and 15 million by 1951.[56]

In labor, as in many other fields, people talk about the New Deal as a revolution. But in many ways, the real revolution was not in court battles, won or lost, or even in the bold, innovative new laws, the alphabet soup of agencies, and the rest. Most "revolutions" in fact are not really revolutions; they erupt with a huge, explosive noise, but never out of the blue. A change in culture, in expectations, made the New Deal possible. The Depression was certainly a factor; but there had been depressions before. Roosevelt was a factor; he was a great politician, and a magnetic speaker; but his cousin Theodore had been equally charismatic. Partly it was radio, it was newsreels, it was the movies, it was all those technologies that focused attention on the center, that pulled national attention away from the neighborhoods and into Washington, D.C. And (also both cause and effect) it was a willingness, even an eagerness, to expand the scope of government—on the part of both the rulers and the ruled. Coolidge had been a do-nothing president, as a matter of both personality and ideology; Hoover had tried to do what he could, but he was hamstrung by a narrow conception of the role of government, especially the federal government. The days of a weak and tinny central government now came to an end. The country was in anguish. Washington looked like the only source of help.

Even more fundamental was the changing nature of the economy. The NLRA was upheld, as we have seen, in a case that involved the Jones and Laughlin Steel Corporation. Here is how this company was described: it had nineteen subsidiaries; it was a "completely integrated enterprise, owning and operating ore, coal and limestone properties, lake and river transportation facilities and terminal railroads. . . . It owns or controls mines in Michigan and Minnesota. It operates four ore steamships on the Great Lakes. . . . It owns coal mines in Pennsylvania. . . . It owns the Aliquippa and Southern Railroad Company"; it had warehouses in Chicago, Detroit, Cincinnati, and Memphis, and steel fabricating shops in Long Island City, New York, and in New Orleans; it had hundreds of thousands of employees, in various states.[57] Only the federal government had any hope of controlling such a behemoth. And a concept of "interstate commerce" which excluded the labor relations of such a company would convert the federal government into a toothless, night-watchman state. During the Depression, during world war, and during the age of globalization, finally, such a concept was simply not tenable.

Taming Leviathan

The New Deal, popular though it was, never lacked for opponents. It seemed to some to signal the end of the federal system, and the beginnings of a powerful, centralized autocracy. The New Deal, after all, did scoop up enormous amounts of power for the federal government; and it created an awesome array of new boards, agencies, and bureaucracies. The agencies had power, too; they had an impact on business and on life in general; they made rules and enforced them; they seemed to be lawmakers, prosecutors, judges, and juries, all rolled into one. The agencies decided thousands and thousands of controversies, big and small; and came to countless courtlike decisions each year. Anybody who wanted to sell a headache remedy, or run a radio station, for example, had to get permission; and if permission was not granted, had to fight for the right within the agency. The agencies told farmers how much wheat they could grow. They told businesses how much they had to pay their workers (at a minimum), and they laid down rules that generated miles and miles of red tape.

There had been, of course, administrative agencies, and an administrative apparatus before the New Deal. The New Deal was not, as we have seen, a total revolution, it turned nothing upside down; but it was a dramatic quickening, a ratcheting upward, that pushed the boundaries further and further into a kind of beyond. The shapeless, relatively weak American government, the "state of courts and parties," evolved, as Stephen Skowronek has put it, into a "hapless administrative giant," a state that "could spawn bureaucratic goods and services but that defied authoritative control and direction."[58] In some Western countries, the bureaucracy became an elite, technocratic corps, detached from the hurly-burly of political life—and safe from the intrusions of courts, litigants, and even politicians. This was much less true in the American experience.

The new administrative state created a multitude of problems. Obviously, not all decisions were fair, not all were honest, not all were sound. The New Deal was after all not run by angels or by the infallible. All power can be abused; all power *is* abused. Naked abuse, in fact, is probably less of a problem than rank stupidity, stubbornness, lack of empathy, human error, and other sicknesses that are endemic to any human agency. Here now was Leviathan. Who would control it, especially after the courts seemed to become lapdogs of Roosevelt's New Deal?

Conservatives, lawyers' groups, and others all proposed reforms.[59] They raised the specter of dictatorship: of an all-powerful administrative state, a central-planning state, in which the little man would be crushed into dust. Perhaps they wanted to reserve the right to crush little people into dust for themselves. New Dealers, for their part, resisted even the smallest reforms; they felt that they needed power, discretion, flexibility, ability to act. As long as Roosevelt sat in the saddle, there were only modest reforms. One idea—which came to nothing—was to set up a special administrative court, which would handle cases that came out of the administrative state.[60] In 1935, however, Congress did pass a law, creating a Federal Register. It was to contain all executive orders; and all agency documents that were of "general applicability and legal effect."[61] The very first entry (1936) was an executive order "enlarging Cape Romain migratory bird refuge" in South Carolina. The Federal Register runs to thousands of pages every year, full of mind-numbing detail; it is nobody's bedside reading, but it is nonetheless an essential instrument of governance, and a big step toward transparency. All rules, regulations, orders and decrees of big government appear in this central repository.

The next lurch forward in administrative reform was taken, however, only in 1946, when the Second World War was over and Harry S. Truman was president. At this point, Congress passed the Administrative Procedure Act.[62] A law on administrative procedure, the Walter-Logan bill, passed both houses in 1940, but the administration thought it gave the courts too much power; the president vetoed the bill. It took six more years of tinkering before the APA became the law of the land.[63] This extremely significant law set up more orderly, and fairer, procedures, for agencies, boards, and commissions to follow. The act also required every agency to give public notice of any proposed new rules; and to give "interested parties" a chance to put in their two cents. These notices would appear in the Federal Register. So in December 1947 the secretary of agriculture announced, under the Sugar Act of 1937, that he intended to propose new rules about sugar quotas. "All persons who desire to submit written data, views, or arguments" about the draft rules could "file the same in quadruplicate with the Director of the Sugar Branch, Production and Marketing Administration, United States Department of Agriculture," in Washington, not later than fifteen days after the notice appeared in the Federal Register.[64] In other cases, agencies held hearings out in the country, where the particular regulation was going to have its impact. So an announcement on December 24, 1948, told readers that proposals to make changes in a milk-handling order for the Clinton, Iowa, marketing area, would be discussed at the Clinton County Courthouse on January 10, 1949, at 10 A.M.[65]

The Administrative Procedure Act was meant to bring some kind of order and fairness to the machinery of bureaucracy. Rules were not simply to issue from the mouths of officials; the people and businesses affected must have their say. But what if the agencies disobeyed, or misinterpreted their mandate? Who would have the last word? The obvious answer had to be: the courts. The APA, among other things, helped create what was practically a new field of law, administrative law. This was the law about judicial review of administrative proceedings: how much power courts would have to control, limit, or second-guess the agencies.

Of course, judicial review was nothing new. Litigants had always had the right to go to court, whenever the post office or the ICC or any government agency misbehaved. But in many ways this was a hollow right. In most cases, the courts simply deferred to the agency. They accepted, too, the right of Congress to delegate the final word to officials. In extreme circumstances—the Chinese immigration cases are an example—the deference was also at times extreme.

On what basis were courts supposed to second-guess an agency? One significant case from the 1920s turned on the misdeeds of one Fred Leach, who advertised that his "Organo tablets" could cure many ills, including insomnia, urinary disorders, and "sexual decline or weakened manhood." The postmaster general issued a fraud order against Leach, and told him to stop using the mail to promote these dubious tablets. Leach went to court to protest this decision. But the Supreme Court sided with the postmaster general: the courts were not going to overturn an administrative decision, provided the decision was "fairly arrived at and has substantial evidence to support it"; only when the decision was "palpably wrong" and "arbitrary" would a court send it back to be redone.[66]

This was a high hurdle for anyone who wanted relief in the courts. A lot depended on how friendly the judges were to the law in question. The Chinese did poorly; the railroads did not. Courts had in many ways gutted the Interstate Commerce Act, and the Sherman Act, too, in its early days. The public utility commissions that tried to fix rates for gas, electric, and water companies did not find extreme deference from state courts. Still, on the whole, the field was underdeveloped. With the arrival of the New Deal, the issue became more salient; the agencies multiplied like rabbits, they affected more people; and they

[margin annotation: Judicial Review]

acted under vast and sometimes vague grants of authority. The early New Deal cases were hostile to the agencies; but by the end of the thirties, deference was in the saddle again. As James Landis, writing in 1938, put it, the old and "simple tripartite form of government" was not capable of dealing with "modern problems." Judges were simply not experts in all the fields that the administrative process had to deal with; "policies to shape such fields" had to be "developed by men bred to the facts."[67] This was the liberal faith of the day. It was soon to be tarnished and tattered; but that story belongs to later times.

The New Deal in the States

The New Deal, as we have seen, revolutionized relations between the states and the federal government.[68] It tilted the balance of power away from the states; that power and responsibility flowed into Washington; it was as if a war was under way. And indeed, there was a war: a war against a silent, invisible enemy, but a deadly one. Relatively speaking, then, the states lost some of their authority. Washington was now the center of gravity. The president himself was a charismatic figure. But government in general grew so rapidly, that the absolute role of state and city governments, if not their relative power, increased during the 1930s. And in many regards, the states were partners in the New Deal.

What the states actually did, and how they did it, of course, varied tremendously from state to state. In some states, there were "little New Deals." Some states tried their hand at relief, unemployment compensation, old-age pensions. There was also a flurry of copycat statutes, or statutes that marched in the same direction as the federal government. The federal government, for example, encouraged the states to adopt "little Wagner Acts," to make sure that workers had union rights in situations which the federal law did not cover. A number of states—New York and Pennsylvania among them—did so. After all, the landslide that brought Roosevelt to power also led to landslides for liberal Democrats in many states. In Maryland, for example, the legislature in 1935 passed a law against labor injunctions and yellow-dog contracts. The preamble declared that "negotiations" between labor and management should be "voluntary"; but that the "individual unorganized worker is helpless to exercise actual liberty of contract."[69]

Some federal programs specifically enlisted the states. The Federal Emergency Relief Act of 1933 asked the states to match federal poor relief. The act

(margin annotation: States loosing authority)

allocated $500 million; and the states were supposed to contribute three dollars for every dollar of federal money they got. Other laws, however, bypassed the states entirely. When the United States Housing Administration was created in 1937, the federal government deliberately created a federal-local partnership, to avoid dealing with the states (thought to be under the thumb of rurally controlled legislatures).[70] The New Deal reshaped and remodeled the country's federal structure.

The Great Depression created what we have called the submerged middle class. These were the millions who had lost their investments and their jobs, whose farms and homes had mortgages they could no longer pay, whose bank accounts had vanished like snow in summer, or who could not pay the rent on their apartments in the city. These millions were also voters, and their voices were heard in city hall, and in the state capitals.

The situation in the cities was quite desperate. Tens of thousands of families faced eviction because they had no money for the landlord. The landlords were not always rich; and, in any event, could not allow families to stay on without paying rent. Time and again bailiffs came to throw a family out onto the street, along with their miserable sticks of furniture. A rent riot occurred in 1931, for example, on the South Side of Chicago. Meanwhile, desperate landlords shut off gas, heat, water, and light to try to force families out who could not pay their rent; some Chicago landlords even took out window frames, to freeze out tenants in the cold of winter. The housing stock deteriorated as landlords stopped making repairs, and as destitute families doubled up and tripled up; "respectable" apartment houses turned into seething warrens of misery.[71]

Debt relief and mortgage relief, not surprisingly, became important legislative themes. There were all sorts of schemes, especially in farm states. A Minnesota law of 1933, one of the milder versions, declared an emergency and allowed the postponement of foreclosures on farms and homes effectively for two years; the farmer or homeowner could keep on living and working on the land, paying a reasonable rent to the creditor.[72] A New York law of the same year was more drastic: it suspended foreclosure altogether during the emergency—a period of "abnormal credit and currency," and "abnormal deflation of real property values." And a Texas law of 1933 dealt with a related problem.[73] Because few people were buying in these hard times, the creditor might buy the home or farm for a piddling price—less than the debt, so that the poor farmer or homeowner still had a crushing debt burden even after losing farm or home.

The law recited that "many honest, hard working and worthy city home owners and farm owners are being foreclosed in these hard, stringent and depressed times"; the buyers at foreclosure sales bid "unconscionably low prices," and an "unwarranted" judgment now hangs over the heads of these "honest, worthy people . . . further depressing their spirits when calamity overtook them through no fault of their own." The cure was to provide that, whatever the sale price, the debtor would be credited with the "actual value" of the property, and if that was equal to the debt, the creditor could collect nothing.

Passing these statutes was one thing; getting them by the courts was another. The federal Constitution, and state constitutions as well, had provisions forbidding states to "impair the obligation of a contract." This was intended beyond a doubt to curb the wilder forms of debtor relief. A Texas court struck down the Texas provision.[74] But the Minnesota provision survived, and provided one of the more dramatic of the cases in which the Supreme Court confronted the New Deal.

The Minnesota case came even before the famous "switch," and it was a clear sign of flexibility—a sign that the Court recognized how deep was the crisis. Minnesota's law essentially gave courts power to postpone and stretch out mortgage payments. The clause in the Constitution forbidding "impairment" of contracts was obviously aimed at just such laws as Minnesota's.

Nonetheless, the Court upheld the statute, 5–4, in *Home Building & Loan Association v. Blaisdell*.[75] Chief Justice Hughes wrote the opinion. "Emergency," he said, "does not create power"; but the Court's actions belied these words, as Hughes immediately added that "emergency may furnish the occasion for the exercise of power." The contracts clause was not "an instrument to throttle the capacity of the States to protect their fundamental interests." There had to be a way to "safeguard the economic structure upon which the good of all depends." The law was reasonable, and had to be upheld. The "four horsemen"—the conservative bloc on the Court—dissented: the Constitution, they insisted, meant what it said; and its provisions were to be followed "when they pinch as well as when they comfort." But this was a case where the Constitution was pinching too tight: the wave of foreclosures, the farm unrest, the pitiful scenes in cities, where evicted families huddled with their pitiful lot of possessions on the sidewalk; this had moved the swing members of the Court to bend the Constitution, fearing that otherwise it might crack in two.

The farm crisis was particularly acute; and the moratorium laws were, above all, aimed at protecting the family farm. The laws were responses not just to political pressure, but to unrest that verged on riots in the countryside. Masses of farmers often tried to prevent foreclosures and eviction by force. In North Dakota, Governor William Langer gave the National Guard authority to stop foreclosures of farms and small businesses. "Shoot the banker if he comes on your farm," he said. "Treat him like a chicken thief." Langer also declared a "white embargo" in fall 1933; no number one dark north spring wheat or number two amber durum wheat were to be shipped from the state until the price of wheat went up enough to cover the costs of production. In January 1934, not surprisingly, a federal district court declared this embargo unconstitutional.[76]

The Rise of the Welfare State

The New Deal is usually given credit, too, for the modern American welfare state. Undoubtedly, the ferment of the New Deal, the mobilization of hundreds of eager, reform-minded, talented lawyers and others who flocked to Washington, was crucial in the process.[77] The Depression was crucial, too, because it created a vast new clientele, the submerged middle class—the families who felt the bottom drop out from under them, families in shock at their sudden descent into poverty. The welfare state was also a long, slow outgrowth of basic changes that had taken place in the social structure, and in the culture. This was now an industrial society, an urban society, a highly technological society—and a society which was committed to a vast extension of social justice.

In any event, no achievement of the New Deal was more important than the Social Security Act of 1935.[78] In one stroke, the federal government decisively entered a field once the exclusive turf of the states. The federal government had no historic mandate to worry about the poor. That was the role of the states. Before the age of the Great Depression, welfare was almost entirely a state and local matter. The federal government kept its distance. But the Depression flattened state and local governments like a giant bulldozer. Money was scarce, and the needs were overwhelming. Desperate, the states and the cities turned to Washington for help.

The states had had systems of "poor relief," a niggardly, callous, and archaic mode of dealing with "paupers. In the nineteenth century, nobody glamorized or exalted the poor or humbly washed their feet; they were despised and stigmatized. In states as dissimilar as Rhode Island and South Dakota, deep into the twentieth century, it was an offense knowingly to import "any poor or indigent person" into a new town, if the "pauper" did not have a legal settlement in that town.[79] State policy was dominated by a positive horror of anything that might, even by the most twisted and unrealistic logic, encourage people to stop working and live off the dole.

A major move in the nineteenth century was to replace "outdoor" relief (relief given to people in their own homes) with "indoor" relief—the poorhouse, or poor farm, in short. If you wanted public money, you had to pack your pitiful belongings and move into this place—regimented, segregated, usually squalid and filthy as well, a shabby warehouse for the old, the sick, and the destitute. Anybody who possibly could avoided this place. Toward the end of the nineteenth century, some of the states began to do something about the poor laws. They set up state boards of charity, to provide some sort of centralized supervision and control. The poorhouses and poor farms survived, however; and many were still run as if they were prisons for the poor. In Ohio's county homes, inmates were supposed to perform "reasonable and moderate labor"; no free ride for anyone was to be tolerated; and the statute, rather ominously, allowed authorities to recapture inmates who escaped, and who, in the judgment of the state, were better off locked up in the county home.[80]

Welfare policy did try to separate the "worthy" from the "unworthy" poor. After all, even when federal welfare was taboo, the federal government ran an enormous welfare program, only by a different name: veterans' pensions. In 1913 veterans' pensions accounted for 18 percent of the federal budget; and in some states in the North, half of the elderly white men, and many of their widows, were getting these pensions.[81] There were state pensions, too; South Carolina, for example, paid pensions to Confederate veterans and their widows. In 1921 the state appropriated six hundred thousand dollars for this purpose.[82] There was no means test for these veterans, of course. After all, they *deserved* the money they were getting. In Ohio in 1930 veterans were eligible for general relief, and county commissioners had to make sure that veterans who had no money were buried "in a decent and respectable manner," and in a respectable cemetery. The same went for their wives, mothers, and widows, and for Army nurses.[83]

There were other categories of the deserving poor. In Ohio in 1930 the state gave aid for the needy blind, on a county basis.[84] The state also ran homes for indigent soldiers and sailors, the feeble-minded, and "deformed and crippled children." There were schools for the deaf and the blind, hospitals for the insane, and a state sanitarium for victims of tuberculosis. This was, of course, in addition to the system of general relief.

As this list indicates, the states put special emphasis on children; and, by association, on their mothers as well. Here there was some action at the national level. In 1912 Congress passed a law creating a Children's Bureau in the Department of Commerce and Labor. Florence Kelley and Lillian Wald (so goes the story) dreamed up the idea, at a breakfast together in 1903. What inspired them was not eggs and toast, but grim newspaper articles they had been reading. One story was about dying babies; another was about the secretary of agriculture and his role in the battle against the boll weevil. There was no program for the dying children. Why, they wondered, was the government so concerned about the "cotton crop," and not at all about the "child crop"?[85]

There was, of course, a simple answer to this question: cotton and its growers constituted a loud and pushy interest group; the hungry, ragged children of the poor were politically invisible, and nobody heard their sobbing in the hubbub and clatter of Washington affairs. Kelley and Wald tried to give these children a voice. It took nine years of struggle to persuade Congress to do anything at all. The first step was the establishment of the Children's Bureau; it began with a budget of $25,640 and a staff of fifteen—still far behind the boll weevil. The first head of the bureau was Julia Lathrop, who gave it vigorous leadership and strong direction.[86]

From the standpoint of the twenty-first century, the battle against child labor and for child welfare looks like the eternal struggle of good against evil, or the war of enlightenment against the forces of regression. The truth is a lot more complicated. Attitudes toward childhood and children had changed. The child was once an ordinary and productive member of the household; but by the late nineteenth century on, the child was redefined as something "priceless," or "sacred"; children were to be "kept off the market, useless but loving, and off the streets, protected and supervised."[87] As we have seen, the battle against child labor was in part an economic struggle *for* male heads of household. When the child became "priceless," it also became less of a threat to its daddy's job.

If children were sacred, then so too were the mothers who gave birth to these children, and nurtured them. Mothers' aid laws were politically appealing for a number of reasons. They tapped into fears of race suicide—the idea that only the immigrant women were making babies, while "American" mothers suffered from all sorts of disincentives. Also, anything that helped keep women (and children) off the job market was attractive to organized labor. It is only fair to add that this strategy was attractive to a lot of women as well. Twenty states enacted mothers' pension laws (or "widows' pension" laws) in 1911–1913, and forty states before 1920. The goal was to keep the children out of foster homes or orphanages, where poor, desperate women might otherwise dump them.[88] Women's groups made effective use of the image of the struggling mother, widowed or abandoned—the very epitome of the worthy poor. It was the direct opposite of the modern bogeywoman: the welfare mother as degraded, non-white trash. In practice, mothers' aid fell far short of the ideal. For one thing, the money was almost never enough—a pittance at best. It went mostly to the "respectable" poor—white widows were definitely preferred. In a few states, the statute was explicitly limited to widows. In Illinois, under a law of 1913, only a woman "whose husband is dead" or "permanently incapacitated for work" was eligible.[89] No divorced women, in short, need apply. And, of course, no unmarried mother was even to think about getting her hands on state money.

In fact, even in states less formally restrictive than Illinois, few unmarried women ever collected a penny. There was, in most states, a lot of snooping and harassment. This was almost inevitable: the Illinois law, for example, handed the matter over to the juvenile courts, and provided that any mother benefiting had to be "a proper person, physically, mentally and morally fit, to bring up her children."[90] Then, too, there was the equivalent of "workfare": poor women were often pushed into "low-wage drudgery," taking in washing, or cleaning houses, or working at home making lace or sewing buttons.[91] And the poorest women of all—black women—were radically underrepresented. In Houston, Texas, where blacks made up more than 20 percent of the population, not one black family got mothers' aid.[92] Still, mothers' aid, for all its faults, its niggardliness, its petty tyrannies, was certainly better than nothing.

Meanwhile, the Children's Bureau was one of the prime movers behind the Sheppard-Towner Act of 1921, an act for the "promotion of the welfare and hygiene of maternity and infancy."[93] In some ways, the law was an astonishing achievement—an "innovative federal welfare undertaking" which "slipped through during a period of intense conservative reaction."[94] It was the "first federally funded social welfare measure"; and a notable example of a law that had the women's movement behind it.[95] Yet it was also a very modest law. Sheppard-Towner appropriated money, to be parceled out among the states, to be used in promoting the health of mothers and infants. Its goals, and its accomplishments, were limited. It was, in practice, largely an education program. Ohio, for example, used its money to conduct health surveys, run demonstration projects, and provide information. The money paid for a "health mobile," a truck that went around the state, visiting county fairs and touring the countryside, spreading a message of health care for mothers and babies.[96]

Even within its limited sphere, Sheppard-Towner was controversial; and, in fact, it did not last very long. The American Medical Association, sworn enemy of government meddling in health systems, led the attack. Other voices on the right condemned the law, raising the old bogey of communism and the new bogey of feminism. Sheppard-Towner was allowed to lapse in 1929.[97]

Who would have predicted, when this mild, limited law died in Congress, that in a few short years the federal ship of state would sail full stream into the dark, uncharted waters of the welfare state? But then came the Great Depression, Franklin D. Roosevelt, and the New Deal. The circumstances were different, and the huge new constituency, the submerged middle class, destroyed the smug complacency of the American elite, and unleashed the political power of the ordinary citizen. The submerged middle class was vast and articulate; its members demanded help from the government—something to lift them out of their troubles, and back into the middle class where they belonged.

This was the climate that produced the Social Security Act. Old age pensions were an idea whose time had come. No problem of the Great Depression was more serious than unemployment. There was a vast, mutinous army of unemployed women and men. One primary goal of the New Deal was the making of jobs. Public works programs constituted part of the answer. Pensions for the elderly provided another. Not only was the pension an attractive idea in itself, it also promised to ease thousands out of the labor market, into comfortable retirement. The young and unemployed could take their place.

The Social Security Act, of course, did not come up out of nowhere. As is often the case, the first substantial moves took place in the private sector—a few large corporations instituted private pension plans—and in the states. Arizona passed the first old-age pension law (it was declared unconstitutional). Alaska adopted a pension law in 1915. There was more action in the 1920s—three states (Pennsylvania, Montana, Nevada) enacted pension laws in 1923; but the Pennsylvania courts set the guillotine to the Pennsylvania law. A number of states, mostly in the West, acted in the next few years; and nineteen states made the move between 1929 and 1933, after the Depression had begun.[98] Delaware's law (of 1931) established an Old Age Commission. People of sixty-five or older who had no one to support them and who needed "assistance" to "enjoy the essentials of life" could apply for help to the commission. The commission, in turn, after "careful inquiry," could give grants, but not more than twenty-five dollars a month. Inmates of almshouses were ineligible, and so were "professional" tramps or beggars.[99] In every state that had a program, you had to be poor to collect. In most states, there was a property limit of three thousand dollars, and an income limit of three thousand dollars a year. And not all states participated: no state in the Deep South had any program at all.[100]

The state laws were not, in any event, roaring successes. Businessmen (of course) denounced them as socialistic and claimed that they would encourage people to be paupers. The money was never enough. But the laws were responses to a deeply felt need. This was also the period of the Townsend movement, founded by Dr. Francis E. Townsend.[101] Townsend was a man with a plan: pensions of two hundred dollars a month for everybody, starting at age sixty. The pensioners would have to retire; and they had to spend every penny every month. The Townsend plan was not means-tested. You did not have to be poor to collect. And it was very seductive. The plan was far beyond the financial means of the states or the federal government; but it sounded terrific to millions of desperate people. These millions joined local Townsend Clubs. Politically, Townsend had become a menace, a threat to state and federal governments. Something had to be done. The states themselves lacked the money and the will to set up programs of social insurance. Only the federal government could save the day.

The Social Security scheme was radically different from plans like Delaware's (or from the Townsend plan). It was sold as a form of "social insurance." Workers would pay a bit out of their wages; employers would add their share. The pension would be automatic—rich and poor alike. Only workers were eligible. However: if they wanted to collect, they had to leave the workplace. The program had to do this double service.

Hardly any law has had a greater impact on American life—socially, economically, culturally. More than sixty years later, it still has a powerful economic and political grip on the population. The "crisis" in Social Security was a hot topic at the end of the twentieth century. Was Social Security solvent? If not, what was to be done? But in the debate, Social Security itself remained the "third rail" of politics—untouchable, sacred, deep-rooted.

What made the system untouchable was that nobody thought of it as welfare. You earned it, through payroll deductions. It was not a dole. It was a kind of insurance policy, backed up by the government. The average person imagined that somewhere, in Washington, he had an account—something like a bank account—which was solid, and tangible, and grew every year. In fact, Social Security was not at all like an insurance policy, and not at all like a bank account. But whatever the realities, this is the way Social Security *felt* to the public.

In any event, getting a Social Security check was not and is not a disgrace; everybody who works, rich and poor, becomes entitled (in varying amounts). There was and is no means test. This was the secret of the law's tremendous success. It was, in the main, a program for the submerged middle class. Indeed, the most downtrodden American workers—farmworkers, casual laborers, and "domestic labor in a private home"—were simply left out of the act. They did not qualify. Leaving out farmworkers was especially harmful, especially to blacks. But the conservative southerners in Congress, "anxious to retain control over their plantation labour force," insisted on this exclusion.[102] Despite its gaps and deficiencies, when all is said and done, the act was a tremendous achievement; and it worked. There was, however, a side effect: millions of middle-class Americans collected their checks, yet felt entitled to despise other people who got different checks (from "welfare") as lazy loafers, parasites, good-for-nothings. There was no sense of kinship and common entitlement. The act continued, and maybe even deepened, the rift between the deserving workers and the undeserving poor: between "social insurance," on the one hand; and welfare, charity, the dole, on the other.

The Social Security Act was basically a program of old-age benefits for retired workers; but this long, detailed law also included many classic welfare provisions. There was a program of Old Age Assistance—this was for old, needy people who needed help *now*, not in some future year when Social Security would kick in. In fact, for the first years, and up to the 1950s, more people got money from OAA than from the act's pension provision.[103] The act also included Aid to Dependent Children—essentially, federal support for the old programs of widows' pensions; and it also gave grants to the states to help "needy individuals who are blind."[104]

Significantly, too, the act tackled the problem of unemployment insurance. There had been some important precursors in the states and in the private sector here too. The pioneer in this regard was the Dennison Manufacturing Company, in 1917; other companies which had plans included Procter and Gamble (1923) and General Electric (1930, 1931). Typically, both employer and employee contributed to a fund from which workers could collect, for a spell, during layoffs.[105] There were also some joint union-management plans. But these covered only a tiny fraction of the country's workers. Wisconsin adopted a state plan in 1931.

As with many other issues, the Great Depression and the epidemic of unemployment added a real sense of urgency. A horror of idleness had long dominated welfare policy: myths about tramps, sturdy beggars, vagrants, men simply too lazy to work. Give money to unemployed, able-bodied men, and they would suffer an immediate moral meltdown and turn into bums. Here, too, the new class of unemployed people, the submerged middle class, was crucial. Now there were millions who said, not "There but for the grace of God go I," but "There without the grace of God I actually am."

The federal plan, after long debates, wrangling, reports, and arguments, became Title IX of the Social Security Act of 1935. Essentially, it put a tax on employers (provided they had eight or more workers on the payroll for twenty weeks or more during the year). The tax was fixed at a modest amount: 1 percent of the payroll in 1936, rising to 2 percent in 1937 and 3 percent in 1938. Small, time-limited benefits would be paid to workers who lost their jobs. Another room had been added to the house of the growing welfare state.

7

War and Postwar

Prosperity and the Flowering of the Welfare State

T he New Deal had shifted power from the states and localities to Washington; and fighting a major war only accelerated this trend. On December 7, 1941, the Japanese bombed Pearl Harbor; and within a week, the United States was also at war with Germany and Italy. Congress very quickly enacted a War Powers Act, which gave the president carte blanche to shift government agencies around, modify or amend government contracts, and deal with problems of enemy property and foreign exchange, for the duration of the war.[1]

The Second World War was a hard, desperate struggle—a two-ocean war. The whole country was put on a war footing. Even before the war began, the dark shadows of European and Pacific events had fallen across the country. The United States was officially neutral after Hitler plunged Europe into war in 1939. But Roosevelt wriggled and squirmed to get around this neutrality, trying to help the beleaguered British—the famous Lend-Lease program was perhaps the most important of his moves. In September 1940 a Selective Service Act passed Congress. All males between twenty-one and thirty-six had to register for possible service. The SSA was administered by "little groups of neighbors" (the local draft boards). The first draftees were selected by lottery. In October 1940, Secretary of War Henry Stimson, blindfolded, drew numbers out of a fishbowl. The fishbowl was filled with capsules containing numbers; Stimson stirred the bowl with a ladle "made from the wood of one of the rafters of Independence Hall." Number 158 was the winning (or losing) number first chosen.[2]

These draftees were supposed to serve for one year only; and could not be sent overseas. But then came an actual shooting war. Now the draft was used to suck millions of men into the armed forces to fight that war. In theory, the draft was race neutral, and profoundly democratic. Modern war demands this theory; it is total war, and only a rough equality of suffering can give it legitimacy with the public. During the American Civil War, a man could buy his way out of the fighting. This was an impossible idea in 1941. In theory (and in formal law), every man of draft age, rich and poor, high and low, had to be treated the same. Reality fell far short of the ideal, of course. This was, perhaps, inevitable with so decentralized a law; in practice, the impact of selective service did vary, at least somewhat, by social class and by geography.[3]

The Second World War was a greater event in national history than the First; it lasted longer, far more men and women were mobilized, and it cost vastly more in money and, alas, in lives. The draft, however, and mobilization (not to mention help for the struggling Allies) had begun, as we have seen, some time before. Like the First World War, the Second generated much new law. In 1940 Congress passed a Soldiers and Sailors Relief Act, which, in effect, postponed lawsuits against men and women in the armed forces.[4] The law made it hard to collect a debt from a soldier, sailor, marine, or airman; or to get a divorce by default; or to evict him or his family. All these were pushed off to the end of the period of service (plus a three-month grace period). Legislation gave the War Production Board enormous power. The president, as commander in chief, ran the war; and Congress also granted him almost limitless authority on the domestic side as well. The United States won the war on the assembly line as much as on the battlefield. Industry converted to a wartime basis; automobile manufacturers made tanks instead of cars; civilian production was curtailed; and war factories soaked up what was left of the Depression's surplus labor.

An Emergency Price Control Act was passed in January 1942.[5] An Office of Price Administration, run by a price administrator, had power to issue regulations or orders fixing maximum prices, supposed to be "fair and equitable," for any commodity. Later there were price freezes as well. The act also provided for rent control. "Defense-related" areas were subject to these controls. Fairly soon the whole country (more or less) became a "defense-related" area. Every city with a population of more than one hundred thousand, with the exception of Scranton, Pennsylvania, came under rent control.[6]

The OPA went to work with a vengeance, issuing a blizzard of orders and rules. There were more than six hundred price and rent regulations; the OPA regulated the prices of more than 8 million goods and services; there were also twenty categories of rationed commodities; and the distribution of various essential products was tightly controlled. Probably the OPA did dampen rising prices; one less desirable result was a "black market of immense proportions." Exactly how big a black market is hard to say; one survey of butchers in Chicago, in February 1944, found that 27 percent of the meat was sold "above ceiling"; some estimates were even higher. The OPA never had enough staff to police the law properly; that would have required something close to an army. Still, the OPA was not a paper tiger; from 1942 to 1947 the office imposed 259,966 sanctions; there were almost 14,000 federal prosecutions; and in New York City alone in 1944, there were 18,875 prosecutions of retailers and 4,000 of wholesalers. The government won most of its cases, but most defendants got off with a fine; about one in four went to jail.[7] In some ways, the situation resembled Prohibition; or perhaps King Canute commanding the waves. Market forces pressed against the wage, price, and rent controls like a vast flood held in by a flimsy dam. Without the sanctions—and, more significantly, without patriotic zeal, during this "good war"—the situation would have been, no doubt, even worse.

The war was won, of course, on the battlefield; but the enormous productive capacity of the Allies—especially the United States—was what sealed Hitler's doom, as we have seen. Factories and mines worked full throttle to turn out tanks, guns, ships, and the fuels that kept the engines going. But labor relations were far from smooth. The National War Labor Board was supposed to work to keep both workers and bosses happy. The basic bargain—not always achieved—was to give the unions the power they had always wanted, in return for a kind of unspoken promise that there would be no stoppages and strikes. But the United Mine Workers, under John L. Lewis, broke the no-strike pledge and called the workers out of the pits, in 1943. Roosevelt seized the mines and turned them over to the secretary of the interior, with orders to make a deal. The dispute raged on; Congress got into the act, and passed a punitive War Labor Disputes Act over Roosevelt's veto. In the end, however, the miners got what they wanted—more or less.[8]

After the First World War, the dominant slogan was: back to "normalcy." The Second World War, which extracted more from the public in the way of sacrifice, again produced a hunger for ordinary times. Price controls ended relatively quickly. Rent controls survived somewhat longer; in 1948 millions of units were still subject to control. Supply and demand curves seem especially nasty when your home or apartment is the issue. Landlords, of course, were bitterly opposed to peacetime rent control, and wanted it gone. The Property Owners Council of Nashville, Tennessee, in 1949 denounced rent control as "un-American," as "against God and the Bible," as "atheist and Communist in origin; it makes "slaves out of owners," and gives the tenant "more money . . . to buy whiskey, to gamble, and to throw to the wind."[9] The Korean War, which began in 1950, put new life into rent control, but by the mid 1950s, when that war was over, rent control was largely dismantled; New York City remained the major exception.

In between the two world wars had been the Great Depression, a long and traumatic nightmare. World War II had finally killed the Depression; or at least it seemed that way. Everybody who wanted to work found work during the wartime boom—meaningful work; high-paid work. Housewives became riveters. Blacks found jobs in factories that had refused to hire them before. The end of the war seemed to pose a huge new danger: millions of soldiers, sailors, marines, and airmen would be dumped back on the labor market—a market without the artificial stimulus of war.

The Employment Act (1946) announced boldly that the federal government had a "continuing . . . responsibility" to "promote . . . conditions under which there will be . . . useful employment opportunities . . . for those able, willing, and seeking to work"; the goal was "maximum employment."[10] There were those who had wanted a law with real teeth. The original title was the Full Employment Act. The text never went so far as to propose the (radical) idea of a right to a job for everybody; but it did call for a strong government program of spending to make jobs. This was too much for conservatives in Congress. As passed, the act was all talk and no action; it did create a Council of Economic Advisers, to "formulate and recommend national economic policy to promote employment," though "under free competitive enterprise." But nobody was forced to actually do anything about the council's recommendations.[11] Still, the government was acutely aware of the problem. And it did take some action. The main engine of economic stimulus was the so-called GI Bill of Rights.[12] The law was enacted even before the war ended. No doubt it did express sincere gratitude to the veterans; but it was also meant to keep the economy roaring.

In fact, this law had an incalculable impact on American society. It authorized a "readjustment allowance" of twenty dollars a week, for up to fifty-two weeks, while the veteran looked for a job. More significantly, GIs could have loans to start businesses, buy houses, or go to school. The results were dramatic. The GI Bill paved the way for the flight to the suburbs; for the creation of new communities—places like Levittown.[13] No doubt the rush to the suburbs would have happened in any event; but the GI Bill hurried the process along.

The GI Bill also democratized higher education; with tuition paid, and a monthly stipend, veterans flocked to schools they would not have dreamed of going to before. And they went in numbers that were much greater than predicted. By 1947 more than 1.1 million veterans were registered for college; they made up about half of all the students in higher education. All told, more than 2 million veterans got a higher education under the GI Bill; and millions more got vocational training, or went to art, music, or business schools.[14] Socially, the veterans transformed higher education—the colleges and universities were bursting at the seams; but, more important, they lost much of their elite, white Protestant flavor. The influence on professional schools—including law schools—was also immense.

The Postwar World

Roosevelt ran for president, and won, four times. The fourth time he was elected, Roosevelt was already a tired man, and mortally ill besides. He died in office in April 1945. The vice president, Harry S. Truman, succeeded him. Roosevelt had remade the Democratic Party in his image—in the New Deal image; he had dominated American politics for more than a decade. He was revered by masses of people. In thousands of homes, his picture (and that of his wife, Eleanor) hung on the walls. Franklin was the only president many young people had ever known. Now the question was: how much of the New Deal would survive its founder?

Most of it, as things turned out. There was in general no retreat from the big, important laws that were part of the Roosevelt revolution. Some aspects of it—Social Security, for example—had entered into a kind of legal pantheon, and were now totally unassailable. Postwar Congresses did not repeal any of the major laws; they did not even amend them drastically. Congress became more conservative. It left the social safety net alone; but it gave up entirely on programs some New Dealers had dreamed of—programs of vast planning and reform. Some New Dealers had been eager to cut deeply into the diseased body (as they saw it) of corporate capitalism, and perform major surgery. By 1945 even many liberals had given up on this goal. It was no longer needed. The big corporate beasts had gotten ever so much more tame. The New Deal had domesticated them. Other issues now took precedence: individual rights, consumer issues, the cold war.[15]

Not all New Deal legislation proved to be completely untouchable. Labor law was a partial exception. The unions had flourished under the New Deal; but their enemies had never given up the battle. In 1947 Congress enacted the Taft-Hartley Act.[16] There was a widespread feeling that the unions had gotten too much power during the Roosevelt years. Taft-Hartley outlawed secondary boycotts, and defined certain union activities as "unfair labor practices." The point was to equalize the balance of power between employers and employees; and to improve the rights of individual workers. Whether Taft-Hartley had much impact—or even changed very much of the body of labor law—has been disputed. Organized labor did, however, bitterly oppose the law, calling it a "slave labor" bill; and President Truman vetoed it. Congress overrode his veto; and, like the Labor Relations Act itself, the act proved extremely hard to kill. Truman won reelection in 1948, in an upset; the unions had given him their full support; yet in 1949 an attempt to repeal Taft-Hartley came to nothing.

Another landmark labor law was the Landrum-Griffin Act (1959).[17] This was an attempt to regulate the internal affairs of unions, to get rid of corruption, and make unions more responsible to their membership. New Deal labor law had rested on a different philosophy. Big business was organized and powerful. Labor needed its own big, powerful organizations. It was the bosses who talked about "freedom of contract," or the "rights" of individual workers; these were seen as code words for union-busting tactics and for Lochnerism.

Post–New Deal labor law, however, picked up the theme of individual rights once more. Big labor was a reality, and so was corruption and abuse of power. The New Deal had also, unwittingly, set in motion long-term trends that ultimately sapped the power of the unions. Union membership peaked at 35 percent of the nonagricultural, private workforce, in 1955; it never went beyond this, and after the 1970s it entered a period of long, serious decline. There are many reasons why; but surely one of them was the feeling, of many workers, that they did not *need* a union. Worker health and safety laws; minimum wage laws;

unemployment compensation—all these provided a social safety net; they made it possible for people to think that unions had outlived their usefulness. Was the worker getting her money's worth for her union dues? More and more people began to ask this question, and to answer it in the negative.

The Workers Who Came in from the Cold

January 5, 1959, was a bitterly cold day in Baltimore. The low was 11 degrees Fahrenheit. When some workers for the Washington Aluminum Company came to work, they found the shop floor colder than Siberia. The oil furnace had broken down and had not been fixed. There had already been many complaints about cold working conditions; but this was just too much. Some of the workers decided it was "too damned cold to work." Against the foreman's advice, seven of them simply got up and left. When the boss arrived, he summarily fired these workers.

The National Labor Relations Board ordered the company to give the workers back their jobs. Firing these workers was an "unfair labor practice." The workers had the right to "engage in . . . concerted activities for the purpose of collective bargaining or other mutual aid or protection." The company argued that walking off the job was hardly the kind of "concerted activity" the law had in mind. The board disagreed and, ultimately, so did the United States Supreme Court. The workers got their jobs back.

In many ways, the facts of this case are more interesting than the actual decision. These workers were not downtrodden serfs; they had a sense of entitlement—and a government agency to which they felt they could turn. And they could appeal to a rich, multicolored, complex fabric of law—a network of doctrines, rules, regulations, and attitudes that tied the hands of the boss, who had once been all-powerful. Moreover, they could appeal to a growing consensus that the age of imperial management was over. People had a right to a decent work environment. Some work conditions, the Supreme Court said, could not be "tolerated in a human and civilized society." A bone-cold workplace certainly fell into this category.

Nobody was or is actually entitled to a job. Union power has eroded since the 1950s. Firing and downsizing are rampant in American industry. But workers more and more felt entitled to justice on the job. A striking development in postwar labor law was the decay of the boss's absolute right to hire and fire. In the first place, many workers are protected by a union or a union contract. Others are technically "at-will" employees: they have no contracts, and they can be let go at any time. But in a dramatic series of cases, many courts have chipped away at the at-will doctrine. A worker fired in bad faith or for a bad reason has a cause of action against the boss.

Some courts turned against the employers one of their own weapons: employer handbooks. Many companies gave these out to employees; these usually boasted of how progressive and fair-minded the company was, so who needed a union, anyway? Some courts read these handbooks to imply a kind of promise not to fire except for good cause. Civil rights law, too, put more restrictions on bosses. If someone is fired because of race, sex, religion, age, or handicap, she has a legal cause of action. All of this dramatically restricts the right of the employer to fire a worker on a whim, or for a reason a court is likely to disapprove of.

Yet these doctrines are most helpful and applicable for employees above the level of the shop floor or the mining shaft. And they do not alter the fact that American law permits the boss much more latitude than the law of most European nations. Mass firings were commonplace in the 1980s and 1990s: tens of thousands of workers let go by giant corporations trying to become "lean and mean" or made redundant by some monstrous merger. Indeed, this is supposed to be one of the glories of American capitalism, one reason why (it is said) the economy so far outpaced the more sluggish economies of Europe. There is a paradox. What law (and custom) permit, and justify, is the *mass* layoff: a layoff for reasons of economy and competition. But the individual worker more and more demands, and gets, the right to be treated fairly *as a person.*

Public Housing

The public housing program was one aspect of the New Deal that fell on tougher days after the end of the war. Naturally, no houses were built for the poor during the war itself, as the submerged middle class fattened its wallets. The returning veterans had the GI Bill, which gave hope of a house and a yard and a rosebush in the suburbs. The GI Bill financed a massive resettlement program, which created a whole new suburban world. The city core became more and more the home of the dependent poor—and many of these people were black.[18]

Policy now took a fateful turn. Public housing might have become, as in some countries, a large stock of working-class housing—low-cost, subsidized housing for working families, those whose incomes were at the lower end of the spectrum. The Right, however, had always hated public housing, always snorted at it as "socialistic." In the postwar period, nothing was to compete with private developers and the construction and housing industries. Anybody who rose a bit in society, whose income went past the income limit, was forced to get out of public housing. This therefore became, more and more, last-resort housing, dead-end housing, housing for the hopeless and the disenfranchised. By 1963 nearly 40 percent of the families moving into public housing were on welfare; in St. Louis, 50 percent; in Detroit, 63 percent.[19] Public housing was supposed to be basic, minimal, no frills or extravagance. This soon turned out to mean huge, barren, ugly towers of concrete. "The projects" became dreary, degrading, and soulless neighborhoods; and dangerous to boot. Mothers on the twentieth floor could not control their children playing on the concrete far below. The projects were disasters almost from the day they were built. They became jungles of drug addiction, crime, filth, sexual assault. In some cities they became so infamous that the local authorities felt that nothing could be done but blow them to bits. This was, for example, the fate of the Pruitt-Igoe project, in St. Louis. This huge complex of thirty-three buildings, eleven stories high, "pock-marked with thousands of broken and boarded windows" and largely abandoned by tenants, was consigned to the wrecking ball in 1972.[20] In 1973 President Nixon ordered a freeze on new public housing.

Second and Third Waves

It would be a mistake to think of the postwar period solely in terms of retention and partial retrenchment. President Truman proposed a Fair Deal, a cluster of bold programs including health insurance, civil rights laws, and so on; a conservative Congress scuttled this and all other deals. The fate of health insurance is particularly instructive. This, after all, was a keystone in the arch of the English welfare state; at the end of the war, England had introduced a system of "cradle-to-grave" social insurance. Truman proposed a vastly expanded program of national health insurance. But the Truman plan ran up against a buzzsaw: the American Medical Association called it socialized medicine; it would turn doctors into "slaves"; the Truman plan, tarred with the brush of an alien ideology, sputtered and died in a hostile Congress.[21]

Thus major social legislation more or less hibernated until John F. Kennedy was assassinated and Lyndon Johnson became an accidental president. Kennedy had talked the talk; but there was very little action on the legislative front. Johnson, on the other hand, was a domestic ball of fire. In his first state of the union address, in January 1964, Johnson called for a War on Poverty. The Economic Opportunity Act of 1964 was a major weapon in this war.[22] Its aim, according to the preamble, was to "eliminate the paradox of poverty in the midst of plenty."

This was big and bold; but, typically, it was not at all revolutionary. It was a law about "opportunity," not about robbing the rich to give to the poor; or changing the basic structure of the economy. People were to have the "opportunity" for "education and training"; the "opportunity" to work, and to live in "decency and dignity." The idea was to open doors and clear away obstacles; nothing in it suggested that the economy was a zero-sum game; that some would have to give, in order for others to get.

The act scattered money in all directions: for a Job Corps, aid to migrant workers, adult education, and the like. The Office of Economic Opportunity was created to finance and direct the war. The office would support local community efforts to fight against poverty. The OEO begat a number of programs in its brief, intense life. One was Volunteers in Service to America (VISTA), something like the Peace Corps, only on the domestic side; and Upward Bound, which helped poor children aspire to college. Head Start was a preschool program for children from poor families. Some of the programs—Head Start, for example—were extremely popular, and lasted long after the government had given up the war and sent its troops back to their barracks.

Another offspring of the war, and of OEO, was a Legal Services Program.[23] Legal aid was not a new idea. There had been local legal-aid programs, of one sort or another, since the nineteenth century. More recently, various foundations had supported experiments in neighborhood legal offices. The OEO program of legal service won the endorsement of the American Bar Association in 1965; the ABA announced its "deep concern with the problem of providing legal services to all who need them," and resolved to "cooperate with the Office of Economic

Opportunity" in developing legal services for the poor.[24] The program got off to a good start; but it soon ran into trouble. A lawyer helps somebody *against* somebody else; and the somebody else turned out, very often, to be the city, the bureaucracy, the state, the government itself. This made Legal Services politically dangerous—and led, in the end, to severe cutbacks and restrictions.

In January 1965 President Johnson, in his state of the union speech, announced what he called the Great Society—another dramatic package of legislation. He wanted to step up the war on poverty. He wanted to fight disease through the National Institutes of Health, give more money for education, and rebuild the decaying cities. Congress established a Department of Housing and Urban Development in 1965. Even more significant—and long-lasting— were add-ons to the country's social insurance policy, Medicare and Medicaid. These became law in July 1965.[25] Medicare promised "basic protection" against hospital costs for almost everybody over age sixty-five. The program covered up to ninety days in a hospital for any one "spell of illness." A wage tax would supply the money. The elderly could also get their doctor bills paid, in exchange for a modest premium. The program would not pay for orthopedic shoes, eyeglasses, dental work, hearing aids, and cosmetic surgery; and it was not entirely free. But it was, nonetheless, an enormous step toward a more complete welfare state. Medicaid, part of the same statute, provided matching funds for the states, to help pay the medical bills of the blind, the disabled, and dependent children. Medicaid had the potential to cover all the needy poor, since the states were allowed to take the money they once used for the elderly poor (now covered by Medicare), and use it for this purpose.[26]

These were real changes in law and practice; and Medicare, in particular, was wildly popular almost from the moment it started. Like Social Security, any program that helped senior citizens also helped their middle-aged children. It was a special boon to the middle-class members of the "sandwich" generation—people struggling to pay off their mortgages and send the kids to college, and at the same time saddled with sick, elderly parents and their astronomical medical bills. The government had stepped in to ease this burden.

In 1964, too, Congress enacted a Food Stamp Act.[27] Food stamps started out, under Kennedy, as a pilot program; the Food Stamp Act expanded the program and put it on a permanent basis. The preamble promised to use the "abundance of food" to "raise levels of nutrition among low-income households." Under the law, eligible households would receive coupons, which they could redeem at grocery stores. Families had to pay for the coupons, but at a subsidized price. Like most truly successful welfare programs, there was something in it—a lot in fact—for people who were definitely not the suffering poor. The program sought to strengthen the "agricultural economy"; and the definition of "food" in the act excluded liquor, tobacco, and "foods which are identified . . . as . . . imported." It was a period of huge food surpluses and expensive agricultural support programs. The law was, of course, popular with farmers, with food companies, and with retailers.

In many ways, the Johnson initiatives were the high-water mark of federal activism. His leadership produced real breakthroughs in civil rights legislation. In general, nothing was beyond the reach of the federal government: not education, not crime, not culture. The federal government had the money and the muscle to provide for the general welfare; and under Johnson, it chose to use these. The government had been playing a larger and larger role in subsidizing research. It paid for the Manhattan Project, which built the atom bomb. It supported space research. The National Science Foundation was established in 1950. By the 1960s it was getting well over $100 million to support research.[28] Now, during the Johnson presidency, Congress also created the National Endowment for the Arts, and a National Endowment for the Humanities. A "high civilization," the statute proclaimed in its preamble, "must give full value and support to . . . man's scholarly and cultural activity." "World leadership . . . cannot rest solely upon superior power, wealth, and technology, but must be solidly founded upon worldwide respect and admiration for the Nation's high qualities as a leader in the realm of ideas and of the spirit."[29] This was, of course, fluff; but even fluff can be meaningful. Vermont or South Dakota cannot provide anything like "world leadership"; that has to come out of Washington.

The War on Poverty and the Great Society promised a bold new beginning; a great leap forward. But in retrospect, these were the crest, the peak; there was soon a definite falling off. The Great Society itself, in many ways, was one more victim of the war in Vietnam. It was caught in the battle between guns and butter. Johnson, exhausted and unpopular, declined to run for president in 1968; Richard Nixon was elected. In most regards, Nixon did not dare to (or want to) turn back the clock. Medicare, for example, was untouchable. But the welfare state did not go forward, as many enthusiasts thought it would and should.

The War on Pollution

The second wave of regulation was, in a way, a logical extension of the New Deal. The third wave, which came of age in the 1970s, was quite different. It was not concerned with the Depression, or with income distribution, but with social justice, rights, health and safety, style of life. It was legislation suited to a rich country, a striving, self-involved country—concerned with the quality of its civilization.

Nothing more plainly characterized the legislative program of the third wave than laws about the environment. This was made up of equal parts of worry about health, and a more romantic concern with the rape of Mother Nature. The environmental movement mixed hardheaded fears about air and water pollution, with softer appeals about the beauty of mountains, deserts, rivers, and natural wonders. Environmentalists were most effective politically when they raised the flag of public health. Many people cared not at all if the whooping crane or the California condor flew headlong into extinction; but nobody wants to choke to death breathing God's air, or be poisoned by a glass of water.

Clean-air and clean-water laws belong, of course, mostly to the health half of the movement. Air quality had, for some time, been a concern of some cities: what kind of stuff were people forced to gulp into their lungs?[30] A few cities had smoke ordinances as far back as the nineteenth century. Los Angeles became infamous for its smog—a noxious haze that smothered the mountains, hid the blue sky, and made people choke and wheeze. As is often the case, a dramatic tragedy was a strong catalyst for the clean-air movement. On October 29, 1948, a heavy fog or smog—the "Donora death fog"—enveloped the town of Donora, Pennsylvania. In Donora there was literally darkness at noon. People began to gasp for breath; they suffered from nausea and abdominal pains. The basement of a community center became a temporary morgue. A temperature inversion conspired with pollution from zinc and steel factories to choke off the breathable air supply and replace it with a thick, acrid, poisonous cloud. By most accounts, twenty people ended up dead, and seven thousand people—half of the town's population—had to be hospitalized. It was a national wakeup call. Federal and state health agencies launched an investigation—the first important effort to pin down the facts and dangers of air pollution.[31]

The federal government entered the picture somewhat gingerly, as was its habit. An act of 1955 offered grants to state and local agencies for research and training and demonstration projects.[32] In 1963 Congress enacted a more substantial law, the Clean Air Act. It began with a typically sonorous preamble, about the problem of air pollution, and its harm to people, property, and crops. Naturally, out of sensitivity to federalism (and local politics), the act declared that states and local government had "primary responsibility" for "prevention and control of air pollution at its source." The act provided more research money; it also allowed the secretary of health, education, and welfare to step in to abate air pollution in dangerous situations, but only after a long process of local failure. The statute also told the secretary to "encourage" efforts to control the exhaust fumes that belched out of automobiles, and to make reports to Congress.[33] In 1965 Congress enacted the Motor Vehicle Air Pollution Control Act; this gave the secretary of HEW authority to draft regulations and set standards for emissions.[34] Cars which violated the standards were not to be sold. Regulations were in due course issued. The Air Quality Act of 1967 expanded the role of the federal government; but the states were still supposed to be the major actors.[35] They were to set "ambient air quality control" standards on their own; if they fell down on the job, HEW was to come out with its own standards, and impose them on delinquent states; similarly, if the state simply failed to enforce its laws. Auto emission standards were waived in 1971, 1973, 1974, and 1976; ultimately, however, a much tougher law, the Clean Air Act of 1990, was enacted.[36]

Meanwhile, some states also acted on their own. New York, for example, created an Air Pollution Control Board in 1957.[37] The board had power to formulate codes and enforce them. It was a nine-member board: five state officers, and four appointed members: a doctor "experienced and competent in the toxicology of air contaminants"; a pollution engineer; a representative of industry (also supposed to be an expert); and a final expert drawn from the ranks of local government. By the 1970s, almost all states had some sort of clean-air law.

The Clean Air Act of 1970 decisively shifted the balance of power to the central government. In 1970, too, Congress enacted a National Environmental Policy Act. The point was to get all government agencies, and the whole executive branch, marching to the same drummer. Every important agency action that might affect the environment had to be covered by an "environmental impact statement."[38] Agencies had to make these statements public; this, of course, gave environmentalists something to shoot at, if need be. But the EIS proved to be a powerful weapon as well within the bureaucracy; every regulatory agency had to stop and think, had to take the environment into account, and the act guaranteed that each agency would have to harbor in its bosom a staff, or stafflet, of environmentally conscious employees.[39]

President Nixon also signed an executive order creating an Environmental Protection Agency (EPA). The EPA was cobbled together from other agencies that had been scattered throughout the government. Such tasks as setting national air standards were now in the hands of the EPA.

Nor Any Drop to Drink

Before the late twentieth century, the federal government had as little to do with clean water as it had to do with clean air.[40] It was a matter for the states. But a good many states had no provisions about water quality whatsoever, and most of the laws in force were meek and ineffective.

Practically speaking, federal concern with water began with the Water Pollution Control Act of 1948; under this law, the government offered loans to states for water treatment. (In 1956 the act was amended to include grants instead of loans.) This was a modest step indeed. In the 1960s, the issue became much more salient. Rachel Carson published an article in 1961 with the scary title "How Safe Is Your Drinking Water?" The Water Quality Act of 1965 reflected the rise of a strong "green" movement. The Clean Water Act of 1972 (in form, this amended the 1965 act), made clean water a national goal, insisted that lakes and rivers must be "fishable and swimmable" by 1983, forbade dumping crud into these waters, and gave new power to the EPA. Nixon vetoed the bill, but it passed over his veto. In 1974 the Safe Drinking Water Act gave the EPA the job of setting standards to make sure good, clean water comes out of America's faucets; local water utilities were supposed to make sure that these standards were met.[41]

Silent Spring

Chemicals and pesticides had been an issue at least since 1962, when Rachel Carson published *Silent Spring*. The book begins with a grim picture of a town once green and beautiful, now blighted as if by some "evil spell"; everywhere,

Carson saw the "shadow of death"; no birds were singing, the vegetation was withered and sere, the streams were lifeless, and all the fish were dead; children and adults sickened and died from mysterious ailments; a noxious white dust settled over all the houses. What had brought this plague about, and silenced "the voices of spring in countless towns?" Carson's answer was: we did it to ourselves. With DDT and other toxic chemicals and pesticides, with "elixirs of death," America and the world were poisoning themselves—they were spraying their crops with deadly chemicals. These chemicals would last, would spread, would blast and cripple the ecosystems of the world. The remedy was obvious: get rid of these chemicals, and turn to other ways of controlling pests. Fight worms with other worms, fight sawflies with shrews and voles, fight Japanese beetles with parasitic wasps.

It was a message whose time had come. The book created a sensation. The environmental movement was already strong. On "Earth Day" (April 22), millions celebrated and carried on, all in the interests of Mother Earth. In 1976 Congress enacted an elaborate Toxic Substances Control Act.[42] It gave the Environmental Protection Agency vast new powers to control chemicals and pesticides. The EPA was to require testing, looking for risks of "carcinogenesis, mutagenesis, teratogenesis, behavioral disorders, cumulative or synergistic effects." The EPA could require warning labels; and even ban or restrict substances which turned out to be too risky, in terms of health or the environment.

Consumers

The expanding consumer movement also produced its share of legislation. The preamble to the Consumer Product Safety Act of 1972 recited that there were an "unacceptable number of consumer products" that carried with them "unreasonable risks of injury."[43] You could not expect the helpless public to "anticipate risks" and do what was needed to protect themselves. A new Consumer Products Safety Commission had power to set safety standards for consumer products, and to ban "hazardous products" from the market altogether.

Consumer safety was paramount, too, in food and drug regulation. In 1937 a new scandal erupted that affected the scope of food and drug law. This involved the sulfa drugs. These were the first antibiotics; they were powerful and wonderful weapons for fighting disease. One company, the S. E. Massengill Company of Tennessee, hoped to get rich on the fact that people hate swallowing pills.

They marketed sulfa in a liquid (elixir) form—a nice, pink preparation, tasting of raspberries. No tests were performed; the product was simply rushed into market. As it turned out, there was one small problem: 70 percent of the elixir consisted of diethylene glycol, and it was a deadly poison; more than one hundred people died in agony (including thirty-four children) before the FDA pulled the product from the market.[44]

The FDA had had the power to seize bad drugs and get them away from the public; but in the uproar that followed the sulfa scandal, they gained even greater power: the power to keep these drugs off the market in the first place. After 1938 no "new drug" could be "introduced . . . into interstate commerce," unless it had the stamp of approval of the FDA. And the FDA would give this approval only to drugs that had proven themselves through scientific tests.[45]

At this time, too, the notion of prescription drugs became part of the law. From 1938 on, drugs would be divided into "over-the-counter drugs," which anybody could buy in any store; prescription drugs, which required the doctor's approval and his written authorization; and forbidden drugs, which nobody could buy legally at all. And FDA was given power over cosmetics, as well as over food and drugs.

Health and Safety

This was a century of centralization: power, as well as responsibility, was more and more concentrated in Washington. Washington became more and more responsible for the health and safety of the general public; and also, for particular groups that, for one reason or another, merited special attention. Government had long been concerned with the safety of railroad workers, for example, as well as merchant seamen.

Federal regulation of mining comprises a series of extremely complex laws. These are, first of all, concerned with the health and safety of the miners themselves—described in the preamble to the Federal Coal Mine Health and Safety Act (1969) as the "most precious resource" of the coal mining industry (a sentiment few mine owners in the nineteenth century would be likely to express).[46] This law gave vast powers to the federal government to inspect coal mines and enforce safety standards. These standards were spelled out in great detail in the law. For example, all "electric conductors" were to have "adequate current-carrying capacity," and to be so constructed that "a rise in temperature resulting from normal operation will not damage the insulating material." There were rules about coal dust, chest X rays for miners, roof support and ventilation in underground coal mines, fire prevention measures, regulation of blasting and explosives, of hoists and trolleys and elevators. Another elaborate law of 1977 dealt with strip mining.[47] Here the main concern was with Mother Earth: rules and regulation requiring mine owners to restore the land to what it was before the great jaws of the strip-mining machines had chewed it up.

The government is not only a regulator; it is also a pulpit and a school—it gives out vast amounts of information, most of it (we hope) true. The government handed out, and hands out, pamphlets and brochures by the million dealing with health and safety. It issues reports and studies. None has been more significant than the surgeon general's report of 1964. This report, written in drab but compelling language, as cool and impressive as a doctor's white lab coat, named cigarettes as one of the country's greatest killers. Cigarettes caused lung cancer, emphysema, heart disease. Smokers died of lung cancer at a rate 1000 percent higher than nonsmokers, and contracted chronic bronchitis and emphysema at rates 500 percent higher.[48] Cigarettes were truly (as the old phrase went) "coffin nails."

It is impossible to measure how much impact the surgeon general's report actually had. Whatever it was, it dwarfed the impact of any actual legislation. Congress passed a toothless bill in 1965, requiring all packs of cigarettes to carry the words: "Caution: Cigarette smoking may be hazardous to your health."[49] As people became aware of the dangers of smoking, many of them gave up the habit. Probably none of them were persuaded by this mealy-mouthed phrase in small print.

Safety and health legislation added up, in the aggregate, to a massive amount of law. Whether effective with the public or not, the laws certainly made a lot more work, and red tape, for American business. The number of federal agencies tells the story: fewer than ten before 1900; fifty-three major regulatory agencies in the 1990s. The increases since 1970 have been particularly dramatic. Between 1970 and 1975, the amounts spent by regulatory agencies on consumer safety and health, job safety, the environment, and energy rose from about $1 billion to almost $3 billion; the amounts spent on economic regulation went from less than $1½ billion to almost $3½ billion.[50]

There was, of course, opposition to every one of the new forms of regulation. Obviously, people and businesses who felt the bite of rules and regulations often felt like victims—harassed, put upon by a massive, intrusive government. Was Leviathan getting too big—and too incoherent—for the good of society? The growth of government set the stage for a reaction, a backlash, which, as we shall see, produced a kind of counterrevolution in the 1980s.

The Care and Feeding of Leviathan

The New Deal had created big, important agencies; and the post–New Deal legislation had added immeasurably to the supply of "alphabet soup." In the latter half of the century, vast amounts of law and legal process had no contact with courts, judges, juries, police, jails, or even, at times, with lawyers. It was law within the huge subterranean world of the administrative agencies, as they cranked out thousands of rules and regulations, administered their huge bureaucracies, and made their infinite decisions: about the butterfat content of ice cream, radio station licenses, issues of debentures, pensions for war veterans, and so on and so forth.

Each agency was a little world in itself. Many of the big ones had field offices—sometimes dozens and dozens of them. The Soil Conservation Service, part of the Department of Agriculture as of 1970, was directed by an administrator in Washington; fifty "state conservationists" answered directly to him, and underneath them, 245 "area conservationists" directed the work of 2,845 "district conservationists." From there, the locals worked with farmers: in 1937 they helped grape growers in Cucamonga to solve the problem of their "coarse-textured surface soil," soil blowouts, and wind erosion; they also lent a hand to the growers of Tabasco peppers in Evangeline County, Louisiana, putting in a diversion ditch to prevent harmful runoff.[51]

Each agency had a mission to perform. In order to deliver the goods, the agency, no matter how big, had to find a way to get the word to each local branch and worker; and from there out into the field. Coordination depended on a blizzard of directives, manuals, orders, loose-leaf folders, conferences, visits from division chiefs. Some agencies, like the Soil Conservation Bureau, mostly provided service. Others were tough regulators (or were supposed to be). The Federal Trade Commission published dozens of guides in the 1960s, some covering specific industries, some "general practices such as deceptive pricing." It also rendered scores of advisory opinions. The commission also heard complaints, issued cease-and-desist orders, and entered into settlement agreements.[52] Other agencies were downright intrusive: investigating, snooping, sending agents to visit plants, factories, and places of business.

Why were these agencies created in the first place? Each had its own purpose; but they had in common the idea of bringing constant, meticulous, expert opinion to bear on some problem. Congress set general policy. Agencies were supposed to carry it out. If Congress said (in effect), get rid of quack medicines, the job went to the FDA; and the FDA had to hire chemists and pharmaceutical experts to do the job. The agencies were full of lawyers; but they were also full of engineers, economists, and Ph.D.s in all sorts of sciences, depending on the mission. Thus the EPA had a heap of toxicologists within an Office of Pesticides and Toxic Substances; and in 1976 the EPA formed a Carcinogen Assessment Group to investigate whether this or that chemical was apt to cause cancer.[53]

How well did all this work? Impossible to say. Each agency had its own story. Some were efficient. Some were sloppy. A few were downright corrupt. Some—the Interstate Commerce Commission, very notably—were said to have been "captured" by the industries they regulated. But *capture* may not be the right word. Regulated businesses had money, clout, lobbies, and persuasive voices. They also had an enduring, constant interest; they could nag and wheedle and complain. The public was more fickle and distant. Moreover, the goal was to regulate, not to paralyze or drive out of business. Many businesspeople hated the agencies that controlled them; the regulations were like parasites, sucking their blood. But the ideal parasite is one that keeps its beast alive; and the agencies quickly learned not to draw too much blood. No doubt in many cases they drew far too little.

Regulation in the States

One of the major stories of American law in the twentieth century, as we have seen, is the dramatic expansion of the federal government. As a regulator, it is a colossus; it dwarfs the efforts of the particular states; or even the states as a whole. But there are still huge areas of law and life which are mainly regulated by the states—land-use planning, education, workers' compensation; the states give out driver's licenses and deal with traffic and traffic law. The states also regulate and control their public utilities—gas companies, electric companies, and the like. Occupational licensing and business licensing are chiefly matters for the states. The states are also partners with the central government in running welfare programs. In many programs, the federal government confines itself to handing out sacks of money; the states do the actual job.

The states on their own pass hundreds of health and safety laws. Many of the laws parallel federal laws: if there is a federal food, drug, and cosmetic law, then there is likely to be one at the level of the states. Every session of every state legislature adds to the corpus of health and safety laws, and regulation of business. The Michigan session laws of 1974, for example, begin with an elaborate law on the state's public service commission—the agency responsible for "coordinating" action relating to the "energy supply" of Michigan. The next law amends a state law of 1965 on the certification of "horologists" (a fancy name for people who fix watches).[54] But this is only the beginning. The thick volume, representing the work of one session, contains literally dozens of regulatory laws. One law amends an earlier act which licenses horse racing, and creates the office of racing commissioner.[55] There are statutes controlling the sale of fireworks, and of hazardous substances (including dangerous toys); there are regulations about nursing homes, provisions about excavations which might interfere with utility lines, and so on. There is a particularly rich harvest of laws about occupational licensing—amendments to laws about accountants, architects, and auto dealers, all the way through marriage counselors, plumbers, private detectives, osteopaths, and veterinarians. The 1974 session also created a new licensing board, to regulate "myomassologists." This turns out to mean people who practice the art of "body massage," by hand or machine, or who use "oil rubs, salt glows, hot and cold packs, and baths." Only people who passed a test, and met the requirements for a license, would be allowed to do these things in Michigan.[56]

Below the level of the states is another vast area of regulation, by towns, cities, counties, and other subdivisions of the state. The ordinance book of a New York or a Los Angeles is volumes long. Much of this local law concerns land use: zoning, building codes, and the like. But health and safety are also prominent subjects of regulation.

8

Crime and Criminal Justice in the Postwar World

T he fate of criminal justice in the period after the Second World War was dominated by a single, brute fact: an explosion of crime, especially violent crime. The murder rate had been high in the late 1920s and early 1930s—reaching slightly less than 10 per 100,000. Then it declined steadily. In 1955 it stood at 4.5 per 100,000. From then on, it rose steadily, once again reaching 10 per 100,000 in the 1970s; and there it remained, more or less, until the 1990s, with small fluctuations.[1] These are very high rates—much, much higher than those of European countries (Russia excepted); and staggeringly higher than, say, Japan. All violent crime seemed to skyrocket during this period. The crime rate, not surprisingly, was front-page news in the newspapers, and on the TV news programs.

Crime and crime policy became a national issue from the 1950s on. This had not been true before, except for the dubious instance of Prohibition and the Wickersham report. In the 1950s, there was high national anxiety over juvenile delinquency. In 1964 Barry Goldwater, in his race for president, made political noise about "violence in the streets."[2] Goldwater went down to defeat in a torrent of votes for Lyndon Johnson; but the message survived. In 1965, while Johnson was president, Congress passed the Law Enforcement Assistance Act and officially launched a federal war on crime.[3] Later, under President Richard Nixon, came the Omnibus Crime Control and Safe Streets Act.[4]

Since then, crime has never left the national stage and the national agenda.

Yet criminal justice was almost as local as it had been before. These federal laws did not, in fact, attack crime directly. Mostly, the rich national uncle poured money into state and city agencies and police departments. It remains true that the federal government, mighty as it is in many regards, is a puppy when it comes to criminal justice. Candidates for Senate or for the presidency huff and puff and threaten to blow the house down; but once elected, what they actually can do about crime is quite limited.

This is certainly true of the president and Congress. The federal courts, in at least one regard, are another matter. They are guardians of the Bill of Rights; and the Bill of Rights is, more than anything else, a little code of criminal procedure. The Supreme Court, under Earl Warren, who became chief justice in 1953, expanded the constitutional rights of criminal defendants. And the Court made these rights truly national. Technically, this was done through the so-called incorporation doctrine. The original Bill of Rights did not, in fact, apply to the states at all; it was a curb on the federal government, and that was all. The Supreme Court said so in the nineteenth century.[5] The states, of course, had their own bills of rights. They were very similar, on the whole, to the federal Bill of Rights. But what they meant was what the state high court said they meant. There was no instrument of national coordination.

The incorporation doctrine rests on the words of the Fourteenth Amendment. This amendment most definitely did apply to the states. No state could take away a person's life, liberty, or property without "due process of law." What did this vague language mean? In a bold series of cases, the Supreme Court held that these words meant to swallow up *most* of the Bill of Rights—"incorporated" those amendments within the Fourteenth, so that they were, in effect, now *part* of the Fourteenth Amendment, as if they had been put there in the first place. This meant that these parts of the Bill of Rights now applied to the states as well as the federal government.

The Supreme Court was, at first, rather cautious about this business of incorporation. In *Palko v. Connecticut* (1937) the defendant, Frank Palko, was indicted for first-degree murder; the jury found him guilty of second-degree murder instead. The state appealed.[6] The state usually has no right to appeal in criminal cases; but under Connecticut law, an appeal was allowed "upon all questions of law . . . with the permission of the presiding judge." The Connecticut Supreme Court ordered Palko retried. This time he was convicted and sentenced to death. This was not at all to Palko's liking. The second trial, he claimed was "double jeopardy"—that is, trying a defendant twice for the same crime. Double jeopardy is outlawed under the Fifth Amendment of the Bill of Rights. Did the Fourteenth Amendment "incorporate" the Fifth?

In this case, the Supreme Court said no. Justice Cardozo wrote the opinion. Some of the provisions of the Bill of Rights were, indeed, incorporated—he conceded as much. Which were they? Those that were "of the very essence of a scheme of ordered liberty," provisions so deeply rooted in "traditions and conscience as to be ranked fundamental." Freedom of speech (the First Amendment) met this test; it was "the matrix, the indispensable condition, of nearly every other form of freedom." Palko's claim did not rise to this level. The Connecticut law was no "seismic innovation"; the "edifice of justice" still stood; consequently, "ordered liberty" (in Cardozo's view) did not require incorporation. Palko lost.

For the rest of the century, the Supreme Court generally adhered to the basic formulation in *Palko:* some of the rights in the Bill of Rights are now national rights, thanks to the Fourteenth Amendment. But not all of them. Yet since *Palko,* the Court's view of the "essence of . . . ordered liberty" has gotten steadily more expansive. In *Mapp v. Ohio* (1961) three Cleveland police officers had come bursting into the home of a woman named Dolly Mapp.[7] They had no search warrant. They ransacked the place, and found some "obscene" material. Under Ohio law, it was OK to use this material at the trial, despite the warrantless search and seizure. It was in fact used. This time the United States Supreme Court reversed. The rules in the Bill of Rights on warrants and on searches and seizures, along with their federal interpretation, were incorporated by means of the Fourteenth Amendment. Ohio's rule had to give way; and Dolly Mapp's conviction could not stand.

The process continued; in fact, *Palko* itself was overruled in 1969.[8] Probably the two most notable Warren Court cases on criminal justice were *Miranda v. Arizona* (1966) and *Gideon v. Wainwright* (1963).[9] Ernesto Miranda was arrested for rape. After the police gave him a thorough grilling, he confessed to the crime and was convicted. The police insisted they had not beaten Miranda, or seduced him with promises. But the Supreme Court nevertheless reversed. A person held for questioning has to be told of his rights: the right to be silent, the right to consult a lawyer. This gave rise to the famous "Miranda" warning, which the police now read to everyone they arrest; and which every couch potato knows from TV, if nowhere else. It was read, for example, in both

Spanish and English, to a man arrested in 1976, after a fight in which another man had been stabbed twice. The victim died on the way to the hospital. His name was Ernesto Miranda.[10]

Clarence Gideon, the unlikely hero of *Gideon v. Wainwright,* was a classic loser: a loner, a drifter, constantly in trouble with the law. The charge: breaking into a Florida poolroom. Gideon, for all his failings, had a certain spunk, a gritty obstinacy. He insisted that he was innocent. Nobody believed him. He demanded a lawyer; but under Florida law, he was not entitled to a lawyer unless he could pay; and money was exactly what Gideon did not have. He ran his own defense, lost, and insisted on trying to appeal. The Florida Supreme Court turned a deaf ear; and Gideon appealed to the United States Supreme Court. Abe Fortas, a prominent Washington lawyer, later a member of the Supreme Court, argued Gideon's case (without fee).

Unanimously, the Supreme Court reversed; and, in the process, overruled an earlier case, *Betts v. Brady,* decided in 1942.[11] The Sixth Amendment to the Constitution gave a right to counsel. This meant, the Court said, that a penniless defendant, charged with a serious crime, had a right to a state-appointed lawyer. And the Fourteenth Amendment, the Court also felt, imposed this rule on the states. At the second trial—this time with a lawyer—Gideon won his case and went free.

The decisions of the Warren Court were quite controversial. Civil libertarians praised them; the police denounced them or were skeptical; and they fed into the popular notion that the courts were "coddling" criminals. But in the first place, the decisions were less revolutionary than they seemed. Take the *Gideon* case. Under Florida law, Gideon had no right to a state-furnished lawyer. But Florida was an exception: most states, by 1960, did provide free lawyers for people accused of felonies. This had been true in California, for example, since 1872. In the *Gideon* case, some twenty-two states filed briefs with the Court, asking it to overrule *Betts v. Brady*. The *Gideon* case did smooth out the bumps, it got the outliers in line—it created a national standard. It completed a system which was already mostly in place, but with some glaring exceptions.

We have little or no knowledge about the impact of these decisions. Did Miranda hamstring the police? Did it make crime control more difficult? Some of its critics have thought so; and some are still arguing that it does and did, and are trying to get rid of it. But the evidence is conflicting and dubious. There are those who think the Miranda warning is essentially toothless—a formula that the police routinely mumble. The police, in this view, still have their ways to induce defendants to come clean. They still "lie . . . cajole . . . and manipulate in the process of obtaining confessions"; they act "as confidence men." Moreover, enough time has gone by to make the Miranda warning part of ordinary police practice, part of their routine; the police are, in some senses at least, "progressively more oriented to the rule of law."[12]

The *Gideon* case, too, was a famous victory; but how much did it actually accomplish? It certainly helped Clarence Gideon. But who else has it helped? The states have to provide lawyers; and, in theory, these should be earnest and effective lawyers. But does this happen? In many states, greatly overworked public defenders have to do the job. Most states do not spend enough money for them to do the job right. The lawyers are not well paid, and there is certainly not enough money for investigations, finding witnesses, checking DNA, and so on. In some states, there are no public defenders, and the court appoints lawyers—sometimes incompetent ones, or business lawyers out of their depth in a murder trial. It is (or should be) a national scandal that even men on trial for their life get a hurried, slapdash defense. The situation is particularly bad in Texas, the Saudi Arabia of executions. One lawyer who had flunked criminal law in law school was a favorite of the judges in Harris County, Texas, in the 1990s. This lawyer was a champion in one regard: more of his clients had been sentenced to death than was true of any other lawyer in the United States.[13]

Which brings us to a third point. Criminal justice has been changing, evolving, since these landmark cases were decided. We honestly do not know how much credit (or blame) to give to Supreme Court decisions. The world does not stand still. Society and culture change rapidly. In the nineteenth century there were thousands of Gideons, thousands of tramps, deviants, losers, drifters, who fell into the hands of the system. Their wants, needs, and rights were ignored. If one dared to open his mouth (few did), the police shut it up for him, and quickly. Nobody gave men like Ernesto Miranda a warning about rights; on the contrary, the police were likely to beat a confession out of their hides. Ernest Jerome Hopkins, writing about the "lawless police" in 1931, painted a dismal picture of "the third degree." A police "genius" had discovered the plan of beating with a "rubber hose"; it strikes a "terrible blow but . . . it does not cut the skin"; this was the "most fashionable confession getter of all," supplemented by a "blow of the fist in the pit of the stomach, or in the hollows above the hip-bones"; or "arm-twisting," or the simple use of starvation and exhaustion.[14] But these techniques became less acceptable over time. In the age of the civil rights movement, and of plural equality, even the downtrodden drink at the fountain of the culture of rights. It was Clarence Gideon himself, a man at the bottom of the heap, who squawked and demanded his rights. Abe Fortas argued the case; but Gideon's own stubborn insistence set the process in motion. The *Gideon* case, then, is not just about the Supreme Court; it is also about Gideon himself. Nor do police behaviors and attitudes take place in a vacuum. Police brutality is still, in the year 2001, a serious problem; but its victims are less likely to take it lying down.

State Courts

In the latter part of the twentieth century, criminal justice was also a growing issue on the level of state high courts. Thirty-one percent of the business of the Illinois Supreme Court between 1940 and 1970 consisted of criminal cases; and in a third of these cases, some issue of procedural due process was present.[15] Similar increases took place in other states as well.

Some of the ferment in the states was the direct result of cases like *Miranda* and *Gideon*. The Warren Court influence on the states was obvious and measurable: more cases, more constitutional decisions, and hundreds of citations to federal decisions. It would be wrong to think that the state courts were reluctant partners, dragged kicking and screaming into the new world of defendants' rights. Some were reluctant and some were not. The Supreme Court led the way, but some state courts were eager to follow. Of course, in constitutional cases, they *had* to follow; but the same culture of expansion of rights infected the state courts too, though of course with significant variations. The news also filtered down as well to people with a real and immediate interest: defendants and prisoners. In Wisconsin, for example, four prisoners filed petitions for habeas corpus in the 1959 term of the Wisconsin Supreme Court; by the 1969 term the number had swollen to 134.[16] Habeas corpus (the "great writ" of history) is the device a prisoner uses to try to persuade a court to let him go free because his trial was tainted or unfair. The Warren Court decision led to such a traffic jam of prisoner petitions that many states—including Wisconsin—passed sweeping new laws to govern "postconviction remedies."

Sometimes state courts went beyond the federal decisions. In one Michigan case, for example (1974),[17] James Jackson tried to rob a bar. He failed; but he did manage to steal a credit card from a vending machine collector in the process. Jackson was arrested when he tried to use the credit card. During the trial for attempted robbery, one key witness was the barmaid, who identified Jackson from photographs and at a lineup. Jackson was convicted and raised a whole series of objections on appeal. One issue was whether he had a right to a lawyer at the photographic display. The Supreme Court of the United States had said no. But the Michigan Supreme Court felt otherwise; if the man was already under arrest or in custody, he did have such a right. For Michigan, clearly, Supreme Court doctrine on this point was not a ceiling but a floor.

Sentencing and Corrections

Liberalization was the theme of the Warren Court innovations. But outside the courts, policy and practice were going in quite a different direction. In this period, the states began to back away from the indeterminate sentence. Both the Right and the Left were unhappy with this system. As usual, the Right wanted toughness; the indeterminate sentence seemed flabby—seemed to allow dangerous criminals to get off lightly. The Left, on the other hand, felt that the indeterminate sentence was unfair and arbitrary. To Judge Marvin Frankel, writing in the early 1970s, "the almost wholly unchecked and sweeping powers" of judges in sentencing defendants were "terrifying and intolerable." He also flayed the indeterminate sentencing system: "a hated regime of uncertainty"; it breeds in prisoners "a sense of helpless rage."[18]

Maine adopted a new criminal code in 1975, and used the occasion to change to determinate sentencing. The Maine law divided crimes (other than first-degree murder) into six classes, each with a prescribed sentence.[19] Minnesota established a sentencing commission in 1978. Its charge was to produce sentencing "guidelines." The guidelines appeared, and were enacted into law. Under the Minnesota plan, a judge, faced with a convicted defendant, would consult a complex grid and arrive at the defendant's "score." One factor was the crime itself. Murder, naturally, scored higher than check-forging. A repeat offender also had a higher score. The defendant's score determined his sentence. The judge was left with very little wiggle room.[20]

The idea caught on. Congress in 1984 set up a Sentencing Commission, to draft guidelines for federal judges. The guidelines went into effect in 1987. In this plan, too, crimes were ranked on a scale: murder, at the top, got a score of 43; blackmail got a mere 9. Many other factors pushed scores up or down. Amendments, and amendments to amendments, turned the guideline system into a nightmare of complexity. This was probably unavoidable. The system was trying to be both fair and objective. So, for example, robbery in the early 1990s had a base score of 20; robbing a bank added two more points; shooting a gun added seven, but if you only "brandished" the gun, a mere five. And so it went.[21] By the end of the century, most of the states (and the federal government) had some form of a guideline system.

There was also a reaction against parole. Many states, in fact, abolished parole altogether: Illinois, for example, in 1977. Men and women already in prison in 1977 could choose to stay on the parole system or accept a fixed release time. New inmates had no such choice. Other states—including most of the guideline states—opted for mandatory minimum sentences and got rid of parole.

Toughness was all. The idea was: lock them up and throw away the key. So-called "truth in sentencing" laws tried to ensure that when a man went to prison for twenty years, by God, he would *serve* twenty years; or close to it. A federal statute of 1994 offered money to states that got rid of parole, and required inmates convicted of serious crimes to serve at least 85 percent of their sentences.[22] The money would be used to build new prisons—which of course such a law made necessary.[23]

Bad Kids

The movement to toughen up criminal justice affected juvenile justice as well. In the early part of the century, as we have seen, there was a strong, and successful, movement to take kids out of the regular courts, and give them special courts of their own. Juveniles were not to be labeled as criminals at all. Every state moved to this system. In 1948 the New York legislature decriminalized all juvenile offenses, including murder; nobody under fifteen could be tried even for homicide; in 1956 nobody under sixteen.[24]

But this was a high-water mark. Another high-water mark, of sorts, came in 1967, when the Supreme Court decided the famous Arizona case of *In Re Gault*.[25] Gerald Gault was fifteen. A woman neighbor accused him of making indecent phone calls. Gault was taken into custody, and the juvenile court declared him a "delinquent child." Gault ended up in the Arizona State Industrial School. An adult would have paid a small fine, or spent a month or two in jail for this offense. Gault was shipped off for a possible six-year term—that is, until he became an adult. The proceedings were informal, to say the least: no real trial, no lawyer, none of the usual procedural safeguards.

On appeal, the Supreme Court ruled in Gault's favor. In some ways, it was a typical Warren Court decision. Yet another area responded to their broad reading of the Bill of Rights. The "condition of being a boy," said the Court, "does not justify a kangaroo court." Gault had a right to counsel, to notice, to due process, and he had a right to appeal. The Court did not abolish, or want to abolish, all differences between juvenile court and adult court; but it recognized that, if the consequences looked like punishment (whatever these consequences were called), certain safeguards were required. Some states, in fact, had anticipated *Gault* and made juvenile proceedings more like ordinary trials. They recognized that juvenile court was a serious place, where young people were sometimes accused of serious crimes; and that juvenile halls, detention homes, and "industrial schools" were not always as benign and therapeutic as they were supposed to be.

Gerald Gault's offense was relatively trivial; it was easy to argue that he was no criminal, only a mixed-up kid. The trouble was, the kids were getting more mixed-up, and in dangerous, ominous ways. If we read the classic study of youth gangs in Chicago, written by Frederick Thrasher in the 1930s, what strikes the reader in the twenty-first century is that gang delinquency was small potatoes then.[26] Thrasher makes virtually no mention of guns, drugs, or extreme violence of any sort. Truancy, petty theft, and the like dominate the study.

The popular press, in the 1950s and beyond, painted a very different picture: young thugs, dangerous boys who respected nothing and nobody, teen-aged hoodlums who would stop at nothing, and who laughed at the police, in part because they felt they were immune from real prosecution. At least this was what people believed. An article in the *New York Times Magazine* in 1975 carried this provocative title: "They Think I Can Kill Because I'm Fourteen." The reporter, Ted Morgan, spoke of young "murderers and rapists returned to the street in no time."[27] And in truth, young offenders *were* getting more violent, more alienated, more threatening. Ordinary people were afraid to walk the streets because they were afraid of armed, sinister gangs of young hoods; and if the gangs were black or Mexican or Puerto Rican, so much the worse.

Since *Gault*, the trend to shove young offenders into juvenile court has reversed itself in a crucial way: now, more and more, juveniles can be tried as adults. As the slogan goes: old enough to do the crime, old enough to do the time. Kids who kill or rape can be tried as adults if they are over a certain age. Under Oregon law, the juvenile court can transfer any young person older than fifteen to adult criminal court, if the crime was serious, and if the young person was "of sufficient sophistication and maturity" to know what he was doing. The court can even transfer somebody younger than fifteen if he or she was charged with murder, rape, or sodomy "in the first degree," or "unlawful sexual penetration in the first degree." The minimum age is twelve.[28]

"A Dark and Evil World": Prisons and Jails

In prison life, there is a constant cycle of scandal, mild attempts at reform, and a relapse back into barbarism. The public, frankly, seems indifferent to prison conditions (except when they complain about "country clubs"). After prison riots in 1968 in Ohio, Ysabel Rennie of Columbus reported that the state's prisons "corrupt, pervert, and dehumanize" their inmates. One story she told was of guards at Chillicothe Correctional Institute who dashed out the brains of prisoners' pet cats, in full view of the prisoners themselves. According to Rennie, cat lovers all over the country rose up in righteous wrath at this horrible deed; the "murders and beatings of prisoners," on the other hand, caused scarcely a murmur.[29]

In the 1960s a new phase began: the prisoners' rights movement. Like blacks in the civil rights movement, prisoners looked for relief in the federal courts. And the courts, beginning in the late 1960s, proved surprisingly receptive. In *Holt v. Sarver* the District Court of Arkansas declared the whole prison system of the state unconstitutional.[30] Chief Judge Henley recounted stories of rape, violence, filth, forced labor; a sentence to the Arkansas penitentiary, he said, "amounts to a banishment from civilized society to a dark and evil world," a world of "peril and . . . degradation." And a world of physical danger too— from other prisoners. The inmates, said the judge, "ought at least to be able to fall asleep at night without fear of having their throats cut before morning." Life in prison in Arkansas, he concluded, amounted to "cruel and unusual punishment," forbidden by the Eighth Amendment to the Constitution. It had to be radically reformed.[31]

There were other cases equally dramatic, also (at times) involving whole state systems. Far more common, however, were cases in which prisoners complained about something more local and specific: poor food, overcrowding, assaults by guards, inadequate toilets or showers, and the like. In 1966 there were 218 of these claims; by 1992 there were 26,824. Almost always the prisoner lacked a lawyer; and the prisoner almost always lost: 2 percent of the claims actually went to trial, the rest were dismissed.[32] Despite this dismal record, it would be wrong to conclude that the complaints have had no effect. Prison authorities are aware that the courts might hear at least a few of these cases. At the very least, the cases are bad publicity. In some instances, prison officials actually liked getting sued (or learned to like it): this was shrewd strategy, if you were reform minded and saw no chance of getting more money and more staff and better conditions out of a hostile and niggardly legislature. Thus the sheriff of Alameda County, California, got a sparkling new jail in the 1980s out of a lawsuit that he initially resisted.[33]

There is no question that conditions at some prisons and jails have improved since the 1960s. Some federal courts, drunk with the heady wine of the rights movement and judicial activism, moved boldly into a vacuum of reform. But they were not alone. The prisoners themselves had been galvanized. And the litigation drew strength from and gave strength to a strong movement, by professionals and for professionals, to clean up prisons, modernize them, and make them more congruent with the rest of the bureaucratic state.[34] A lot was accomplished. Yet there is an irony here. Prisons became, unquestionably, somewhat less harsh, less arbitrary. The food got better. Within the prison walls, there was at least some measure of internal freedom, some room to breathe, some way to live a life. But partly as a consequence, many prisons became, paradoxically, tougher and rougher places: dangerous, anarchic. The outside world had a way of filtering through the iron bars and scaling the walls. A kind of "community" had developed within prisons, with leaders and followers. Donald Clemmer in 1940 described such a community, its language, its code; but it was much less organized than those described in later prison studies.[35]

In the late sixties and early seventies, a strong gang culture began to appear within prison communities, in Illinois, in the Western states, and elsewhere. Violent, brutal, and desperate men led the gangs; sometimes they terrorized and dominated the rest of the inmates. The prison gangs split along racial lines: they had names like the Aryan Brotherhood, the Mexican Mafia, the El Rukns, the Black Guerrilla Family.[36] The gangs were responsible for hundreds of assaults and even killings in prisons.

Prisons had always seethed with repressed sexuality. Parchman, the dreadful Mississippi prison farm, was, oddly enough, one of the few institutions to do something about the problem. It began a system of so-called conjugal visits. At first the visitors were black prostitutes, who serviced black men in crude wooden shacks; by 1930 white inmates also had the right to get these visits, and not only from prostitutes.[37] But Parchman was exceptional. Men in prison were men without women. Women in prison were women without men. No surprise that some men turned to the only sexual outlet that was available—other men. And women turned to other women.[38] A few accounts of male prison life, like Joseph Fishman's, published in 1934, lifted the veil on sexual practices, in elaborate if somewhat prudish detail. Fishman refers at times to "coercion"; he describes a few cases in which men were forced into sex by threats; but most of his story is about consensual sex, the product of loneliness and frustration; or plain masturbation—still regarded as a problem. Some men, Fishman claimed, were able to conquer their impulses. He told how a banker, in jail for embezzlement, struggled gallantly against the urge to masturbate, and finally learned to control himself by sheer force of will.[39]

Already, in some prisons, sex had taken a more violent form. Hayword Patterson, one of the Scottsboro defendants, described a wholesale pattern of rape in Alabama's Atmore State Prison in 1937. And in the later, more anarchic stage, when the rough and strong governed the prisons internally, violent rape became more widespread. Mass rapes were said to be "routine" in Cook County Jail in Chicago in 1968.[40] Most of these rapes were interracial: black rapists and white victims.[41] Some scholars think the problem has been overblown, that most sex in prison is still consensual. But it seems clear that at least some younger men are exploited and brutalized, or even turned into sex "slaves." A good proportion of the incidents seem to be gang rapes. Few rapes are ever reported to authorities. In fact, guards and prison officials often turn a blind eye. They may even encourage the practice. Some guards are only too happy to let the strong prey on the weak, in exchange for an implicit promise to cooperate in keeping the lid on in general.[42]

What happened to prisons is eerily reminiscent of Russia after the collapse of the Soviet Union. A system of total tyranny ended; and in a vacuum of power, what rose to the top was not the cream but the dregs. It was a dog-eat-dog world; the most ruthless dominated a society in which morality was turned upside down.

Riots and Rioters

Prisons had always been places of unrest. There is a long history of riots, uprisings, mass attempts to escape. For a year and a half after April 1952, a "tidal wave of prison riots," some forty in all, swamped the prison system.[43] In 1971 a riot at Attica, in New York, ended with forty-three deaths; during a bloody riot in New Mexico in 1980, rampaging prisoners tortured and murdered "snitches" and settled other old scores. These were periods of turmoil and high crime rates; the riots no doubt reinforced the public view that prisoners were animals, and that toughness and crackdowns were the best, in fact the only, policy. There were probably as many causes of riots as there were riots. But most of them were protests against bad conditions, brutality, insensitivity, and inhumanity. They were also products of a period in which racial awareness had heightened; and in which the idea of "rights," even for prisoners, had a tighter grip on people's consciousness. For the public, though, the answer was often tougher and tougher crackdowns.

The Death Penalty

No development in the period after the Second World War was quite so dramatic, perhaps, as the fall and rise of the death penalty.[44] The death penalty had had its ups and downs even in the nineteenth century; and there were states (Wisconsin, Michigan) that had abolished it. There were changes in methods, too. Hangings were once big, open-air public shows. Most states in the nineteenth century moved them out of the town square into the more cloistered atmosphere of the prison yard. Public executions survived only in the South in the twentieth century. In 1915 a crowd of five thousand people watched two black men hang in Starkville, Mississippi, described as a "pleasant little town of two thousand souls down in the cottonseed-oil district." According to reports, there were sandwiches, free soft drinks—lemonade and soda water—and speeches by political candidates; right after the hanging, "the clattering of knives and forks arose" as five thousand spectators began eating their picnic lunches.[45] One Rainey Bethea, who went to the gallows in Owensboro, Kentucky, in 1936, had the honor of being the last man to be hanged in public. Thousands and thousands came to see this great event; every hotel room in town was taken; hundreds slept on cots, outdoors, the night before. Vendors sold hot dogs, popcorn, and soft drinks to the crowd. Early in the morning, Bethea, a long black hood covering his face and neck, dropped to his death while the vast crowd watched.[46]

But most states, as we have seen, had rejected the idea of public hanging. Science had come to the rescue in the late nineteenth century, in the form of the electric chair, hailed as a more humane way of killing. It was also more private: death in "the chair" was death in a small, claustrophobic room, deep in the bowels of the prison. Fifteen states had switched by 1913 from hanging to the electric chair; twenty-six by 1949.[47] In 1921 Nevada passed a Humane Death Bill, which replaced the electric chair with the "administration of lethal gas."[48] Gee Jon, convicted of murder, was the first to die in a gas chamber, in Carson City, Nevada, on February 8, 1924. Arizona and Colorado passed gas chamber laws in 1933.[49] Eleven states were using lethal gas by 1955. Later the method of choice became lethal injection. As of 1997 this was the exclusive method in twenty-one states, and an option in twelve others. Six states still used electrocution. Hanging was still possible in Montana, New Hampshire, and Washington State; the firing squad in Idaho and Utah. Whether any of these methods is actually humane is a question. Opponents of the death penalty report scenes of cruelty, pain, and suffering: sizzling flesh, bodies in flames, moaning, gagging, drooling, convulsive movements, twitching, botched injections, executions that lasted ten or fifteen minutes or more.[50]

Civil rights and civil liberties groups had long led a legal attack on the death penalty. The number of executions reached a peak in 1935, when 199 men and women were executed. From then on, the numbers fell steadily. In the 1950s fewer than one hundred a year suffered capital punishment; in 1961, forty-two people; in 1963, twenty-one. In 1968 there was one lonely execution.[51] The public—at least according to the polls—was turning against the death penalty.

In 1937 about twice as many people favored the death penalty as opposed it (61 percent to 33, according to a Gallup poll). But in the late 1950s and 1960s, support for the death penalty declined; and in 1966 (but only in that year) there were more people against the death penalty than for it (47 percent to 42). These figures reversed themselves in later years, and spectacularly; and the death penalty became (if the polls are to be believed) wildly popular. Seventy percent were in favor by 1986, and only 22 percent against.[52]

In *Furman v. Georgia* (1972) the Supreme Court weighed in on the question of the death penalty, and in a dramatic way; it wiped out all the existing death penalty statutes, and in one massive legal blow, spared the lives of all the men and women on death row.[53] But exactly what the case decided was not so easy to decipher. The Court was deeply divided; every justice expressed his own opinion on the subject. At least two justices thought the death penalty was so "degrading," so pockmarked with bias and whim that it was beyond redemption—it was inherently "cruel and unusual" (which meant that the Eighth Amendment forbade it). Three justices—enough to make a bare majority—thought *existing* death penalty statutes and procedures were totally unacceptable; the process was random, arbitrary, unfair—a death sentence, said Potter Stewart, was like being "struck by lightning." But these three were unwilling to make a blanket assertion that *no* statute could meet constitutional needs. Four justices dissented; they were willing to uphold the current crop of statutes.

Furman v. Georgia could not and did not end the matter. The states mulled over the decision; they scanned the long, bloated text for hints; and then proceeded to pass statutes that they *thought* might meet the objections of the *Furman* majority. Four years later, the Supreme Court dropped the other shoe. Two groups of statutes came to them for review. One group started out from the idea that the way to avoid an "arbitrary" or "random" death penalty was to make the death penalty automatic: the punishment for first-degree murder would be death—period. The Court struck down these statutes. Another group—headed by Georgia—came up with a plan that the majority felt it could live with. The Georgia law contained elaborate procedures and special rights of appeal.[54] After the Supreme Court put its stamp of approval on the Georgia law, other states eagerly rose to the bait. In California, for example, a man or woman found guilty of first-degree murder could get the death penalty only if the jury found one or more "special circumstances." It was "special" to use a bomb or poison, or to kill more than one person, or to torture the victim, or to kill a police officer. California divided a capital trial into two phases: a guilt phase, and then a sentencing phase. The sentencing phase was almost a second trial: but now the jury's job was the question of life in prison, or death.

Most states have stuck with the death penalty, with statutes more or less like California's. At first, there were few executions. Gary Gilmore broke the ice in Utah, on January 17, 1977; this was the first execution in more than ten years. John Spenkelink followed on May 25, 1979. The pace went up considerably in the late 1980s and 1990s. By the end of 1999, well over five hundred men (and a few women) had been put to death. More than four hundred of these executions took place after 1990.

According to the polls, as we have seen, vast majorities favor the death penalty, almost everywhere; it seems to be political suicide for any candidate to breathe a word against it. At least this is what politicians think; and they may be right. Nonetheless, the legal situation at the end of the twentieth century was quite complex. About a dozen states do not have the death penalty at all; these include old New England states like Massachusetts, a clutch of states in the upper Midwest (Michigan, Wisconsin, Minnesota), and, in the Far West, Hawaii. In addition, some states have the death penalty in theory, but between reinstatement after 1976 and the end of the century, they put absolutely nobody to death. New Mexico, New Jersey, Connecticut, and (surprisingly) Tennessee were in this category. Kansas joined the ranks of death penalty states in 1994, New York in 1995; but no New Yorker or Kansan has made it all the way to the death chamber as yet. Ohio lost its virginity in 1999; before this, none of the two hundred or so people on death row had been executed.

In all, as of late 1999, some thirty states had actually put somebody to death since the death penalty itself came back from the dead. But many northern and western states used it very, very sparingly: three executions in Pennsylvania, seven in California, two in Oregon, one in Colorado. Only a few states of the Old South, like Virginia and Florida, have a real passion for the death penalty, and use it frequently. Missouri, a border state, also falls in this category. Virginia's toll was sixty-eight, Florida's forty-four, Missouri's forty. The South accounted for 80 percent of the nation's executions—449 out of 562, as of July 1999. But the South is hardly a monolith. Mississippi has had, surprisingly, only four executions; Tennessee, as we saw, none at all. And Texas is in a class by itself, at the other end of the scale. Texas began slowly, with the execution of Charles Brooks, on December 18, 1982; then gathered steam. Texas soon became the death state, par excellence. One out of every three executions takes place in Texas, way out of proportion to its share of the population.[55] Whether this has any effect at all on the murder rate in Texas—it is comparatively high—is extremely dubious.

Everywhere, even in states like Texas and Florida, there is a cruel irony in the situation. Many men and women on death row had quick, sloppy trials, and were defended by incompetent, bungling, or poorly trained lawyers, as we have seen. The dying itself is only a matter of minutes. What comes in between sentencing and dying is incredibly, painfully slow. Death on death row is a lingering death. This was not always the case. Giuseppe Zangara shot at President-elect Roosevelt on February 15, 1933; Zangara missed, but he hit the mayor of Chicago, Anton Cermak. Cermak died of his injuries on March 6. Zangara pleaded guilty, and died in the electric chair on March 23—less than a month after trial. In the early part of the century, even defendants who put up a fight, and pursued the maximum in appeals, could count on a year or two at most.[56]

No longer. The process began to slow down even before *Furman*. Caryl Chessman, sentenced to death in California on June 25, 1948, spent almost twelve years on death row, wrote three books, and became a symbol of resistance to the death penalty. (The queen of Belgium, Dr. Albert Schweitzer, Pablo Casals, and the Vatican, among others, begged for his life.) He died in the gas chamber on May 2, 1960.[57] This was an unusual case; but it is now the norm. Indeed, Chessman's twelve years would be nothing special today. Brian Keith Baldwin was executed in Alabama, in the electric chair, on June 18, 1999. He was eighteen when he committed his crime—he murdered a sixteen-year-old girl. When he died, he was forty and had been on death row for more than twenty years.

Why does it take so long to put a man to death? There are technical answers: automatic appeals, shortages of lawyers to handle these appeals, writs of habeas corpus, petitions for retrial, and so on. But underneath may be a genuine ambivalence, a kind of social hesitation, even though the public claims to love the death penalty dearly. A small band of zealots fights the death penalty tooth and nail. Those who defend it concede, at the very least, some procedural safeguards. Any legal battlefield so contested, so bitterly fought over, develops pathologies of pace and convolution. The conflict itself brings about spastic, halting doctrine; breeds complexities and irrationalities. Robert Weisberg, indeed, has talked about a "culturally optimal" number of executions: enough "to keep the art form alive, but not so many as to cause excessive social cost."[58]

The rate of executions has been going up; but it is still much slower than the rate of convictions that carry the death sentence. One result is a kind of population explosion on death row. As of April 1, 1999, there were 3,565 men and women under sentence of death in the United States. California had 536 of these wretched creatures, Texas 437, Florida 390, Pennsylvania 225. A disturbingly high percentage of these men and women were black—more than four out of ten.[59]

The murder rate is high in some states that use the death penalty (Texas), some that do not (Michigan); very low in some states (Maine) that lack it entirely. Does the death penalty make a difference to the crime rate? The evidence is conflicting; on the whole, the no's seem to have the better of the argument. But why should this be the case? Common sense tells us that criminals, like everybody else, are afraid to die, and prefer not to die. Most men and women on death row in fact prove this point: they fight desperately, from court to court, from writ to writ, appeal to appeal, in their painful, drawn-out struggle to stay alive. In theory, then, the death penalty should be a powerful deterrent.

But matters are not that simple. The real question is not whether death deters, but whether it deters more than, say, life imprisonment. After all, nobody suggests, as an alternative to the death penalty, a gold medal, a pension, or a slap on the wrist; the alternative is a lifetime locked up like an animal behind bars, often life without possibility of parole; in any event, long, tough, dreary years in prison. Very few murders would be worth the penalty, on a raw cost-benefit basis, even without the death penalty. Would killing a store clerk ever be worth twenty years in prison, if you thought about it? Nobody seriously denies that the threat of severe punishment might act as a deterrent; or even that it actually deters some people. Besides, most people are already deterred: by conscience, by fear of prison, and the like. The question then is, does capital punishment add anything extra to the strong deterrents already in place. And it is not at all clear that it does.

The public thinks otherwise. Or perhaps the public thinks that these criminals simply *ought* to die; because of their crimes, they have forfeited the right to live. This, perhaps, was a much more powerful motive driving the capital punishment revival than any arcane discussion of deterrence. Kill the bastards! Because of this, the long, drawn-out process was an irritation, a stench in the nostrils. The public was angered, annoyed at the constant stream of appeals, claims, petitions. It irked the proponents of the death penalty that the cases yo-yo'd between state and federal courts. The Supreme Court and many other courts also showed impatience. Why did it take so long to put a man to death?

The Antiterrorism and Effective Death Penalty Act of 1996, a strange mixture of material, as the title reflects, made it much harder for criminal defendants to get into federal court through the writ of habeas corpus.[60] The point was to speed up the process, and get rid of some of the endless procedural steps.

On the other hand, the death penalty got something of a bad press in the last year or two of the century. In a number of disturbing cases, men sitting on death row turned out to be innocent. DNA evidence came to the rescue in some of these cases—five times in Illinois alone. The American Bar Association, hardly a radical junta, was disturbed enough to call for a moratorium in 1997: until states were willing to provide "competent legal counsel at all stages," eliminate race discrimination, and stop the execution of retarded people and killers who were under eighteen, the ABA thought it was best not to carry out the death penalty at all.[61] At the time, nobody much listened. But in 1999 in Illinois, site of some of the most dramatic exonerations of men on death row, the public began to have second thoughts; the House of Representatives called for a complete halt in the process. The Nebraska legislature (not a big death penalty state in any event) actually voted a moratorium; the governor vetoed this act.[62]

White-Collar Crime

A sociologist, Edwin Sutherland, introduced the phrase "white-collar crime" in 1949. He defined the term to mean "nonviolent, economic crimes that involve some level of fraud, collusion, or deception." White-collar workers, or even people higher up, commit most of these crimes, but by no means all of them. A coal miner is hardly in a position to violate the antitrust laws; but he can cheat on his income tax just like anybody else.

The phrase "white-collar crime" may be fairly recent; the thing itself is not. Embezzlement, mail fraud, passing bad checks: these are hardly novelties. Neither are bank and insurance scandals; or bribery. But the regulatory state creates dozens and dozens of brand-new crimes; each law that adds a tax or regulates something also adds a new crime to the books. Before the New Deal, there was no such crime as "insider trading." Under the Emergency Livestock

Feed Assistance Act of 1988, a person who improperly disposes of feed furnished under the law (meant for owners of starving cattle in times of flood,
drought, or the like) was guilty of a misdemeanor.[63] Under a typical occupational licensing law of a typical state, it is an offense to practice, say, optometry
without a license.

OPA and price and rent controls during World War II were a fertile source
of white-collar crime. Most violators did not think of themselves as criminals—
at least not real criminals. Donald Cressey studied embezzlers around 1950;
many of them said they were only "borrowing" the money; one said, "I needed
money very badly. . . . I was in a bit of a spot. . . . I reasoned that I was going to
pay it back."[64] The idea that these are not bad guys, like street criminals, seems
fairly widespread. The same people who scream and agitate for tougher sentences on drug dealers, more use of the death penalty, and an iron fist for thugs
and holdup men may themselves go in for a little genteel cheating on their
income tax returns. There is some evidence that judges and juries have a sort of
there-but-for-the-grace-of-God-go-I feeling about white-collar crime, and that
sentences tend to be less harsh than for "real" criminals.[65] This may, of course,
also reflect the fact that many white-collar defendants can afford to buy the very
best in the way of lawyers.

Some white-collar crimes, however, can produce real indignation. The
Teapot Dome scandal, during the 1920s, sent President Harding's secretary of
the interior, Albert Fall, to jail in 1931 for bribery and fraud. Samuel Insull, a
Chicago millionaire who headed a public utility empire, was charged with mail
fraud and embezzlement after the stock market crash (he was acquitted). The
savings and loan scandal of the 1980s cost the country megabillions.[66] There
have been other high-profile arrests and trials. Michael Milken, the junk bond
king, who earned billions from his financial deals, was sentenced to prison in
November 1990; he had pleaded guilty to six criminal counts after a federal
investigation of insider trading on Wall Street.[67] Ivan Boesky, another Wall
Street financier, was convicted of insider trading in 1987.[68] The crimes of these
men, and others like them, are so arcane that not one person out of a thousand
has the foggiest notion what a Milken or a Boesky has done. But the prosecutors
give off the impression of some vast, sinister financial conspiracy, which (perhaps) brings misery and ruin to millions. Most of this is in the realm of fantasy.

It is hard to work up much sympathy for Boesky, or for Leona Helmsley,
the "queen of mean," a woman who, with her husband, built up a real estate and

hotel empire, and then went to jail for tax fraud. Yet ambitious and unscrupulous prosecutors have sometimes misused the power of their office to bring down the mighty, meanwhile getting their names in the paper and their faces on the evening news. Many people thought that Kenneth Starr, the special prosecutor, overstepped the mark when he pushed to have President Clinton impeached for perjury about what one might call white-zipper crime. Another special prosecutor, Donald Smaltz, spent years of effort and $17 million in a vain attempt to pin charges of corruption on Mike Espy, who had been secretary of agriculture under Clinton. A federal jury in December 1998 "took barely 10 hours to reject 30 counts" of the charges; Mike Espy went free, but only after "four years of harrowing investigation," a two-month trial, and, of course, the complete ruin of his career.[69]

Healthy skepticism about *some* prosecutions for recondite crimes, or the excesses of special prosecutors, does not mean that white-collar crime is unreal, or that it is not a problem in society. Bank robbers rob banks because (as the famous quotation goes) that's where the money is. And the same motive inspires those who want to rob the bank from the inside, rather than tunneling in, or bursting in with a ski mask and gun. Business as a whole is, after all, about money, about profits, about the bottom line; and the social system rewards and honors high rollers, big spenders, the people with money—and never mind its source. The political system, too, floats on a sea of money. The line between "contributions" and bribes or expected payoffs can be thin. Politics sometimes opens the door and practically invites white-collar robbers in. This was the case with the savings and loan scandal: in 1980 Congress removed restrictions on interest rates, but it increased deposit insurance. This "selective application of the principles of free enterprise," which was "spearheaded . . . by members of Congress with ties to the thrift industry," paved the way for vast and "risk-free fraud."[70]

Political Crime

There is no exact definition of a political crime or a political trial. Some crimes, like treason or espionage, are inherently political. And a state must defend itself against these political enemies. But in a democratic society, ordinary dissent or opposition is not supposed to be a crime. Of course, no country, including the United States, lives up to the ideal. Many trials have as a primary or secondary goal smashing a political movement, or gagging some voice of radical dissent. We have seen this motive in the Sacco-Vanzetti case.

Angelo Herndon, a black organizer for the Communist Party, went on trial in Georgia in 1932. A Georgia statute, passed just after the Civil War, made "insurrection" a crime (the punishment could be death). "Inciting insurrection" was also a crime, and so was circulating "insurrectionary papers."[71] Herndon was charged with violating this statute.[72] The trial jury was, of course, all white. The Communists, according to the prosecution, wanted to grab land from white people and give it to blacks; and they were also in favor of racial intermarriage. This was, apparently, insurrection. The prosecutor demanded that the jury "send this damnable anarchistic Bolsheviki" to the electric chair. The jury convicted Herndon, but recommended "mercy," which in this case meant a mere eighteen to twenty years in prison. The Supreme Court, in *Herndon v. Lowry*—a 5–4 decision—struck down the Georgia statute.[73] Justice Roberts described it as a "dragnet which may enmesh anyone who agitates for a change of government," so long as the prosecution could convince the jury that the defendant "ought to have foreseen that his words would have some effect."

Most political trials in the United States have been aimed at the political Left. Many grew out of the cold war—like the sensational espionage trial of Julius and Ethel Rosenberg. There were occasional exceptions. During the Second World War, the government indicted a motley crew of anti-Semites, nativists, and pro-Germans; the trial, in 1944, dragged on for months. The government tried to link the defendants to a worldwide Nazi conspiracy. The judge died of a heart attack in late November 1944; and a mistrial was declared. The trial eventually fizzled out.[74]

The government also often tries to make a political drama out of a trial of dissenters—to use the trial as a propaganda platform. But two can play at this game; and in some notable instances, defendants have turned the table on the government, and made their own political circus out of the trial. Perhaps the most notable example was the trial of the "Chicago Seven," which began in September 1969.[75] In the background were riots at the Democratic Convention of summer 1968. Protesters against the war in Vietnam converged on Chicago; the police broke up the demonstrations with force and violence—it was, in fact, as an investigating commission reported, a "police riot" more than anything else.

Nonetheless, the Chicago Seven were indicted under a law passed in April 1968—aimed really at black militants—which made it a crime to cross state lines, or even to send mail or messages across state lines, in order to "incite a riot," or to organize or promote a riot, or "aid or abet" somebody doing these things. To be convicted, the defendant also had to have committed some "overt act" in furtherance of the riot or scheme for a riot.[76] The Johnson administration and its attorney general, Ramsey Clark, refused to prosecute. But a new, more conservative administration, headed by Richard Nixon, took office early in 1969. It was the Nixon administration that pushed the trial of the Chicago Seven.

The trial was long and stormy. The judge, Julius Hoffman, exhibited "blatant bias" against the defendants and even "ordered the gagging and hog-tieing" of one of them. The defendants reacted by staging guerrilla theater in the courtroom: they jeered and mocked the judge at every turn. One day the defendants "brought in a Vietcong flag. . . . Another day, [they] entered the courtroom wearing robes covered by Stars of David," then "removed the robes, threw them on the floor, and wiped their feet on them." One defendant told the judge he was "synonymous with" Adolf Hitler. The defendants "sat at their table, often reading, writing speeches, munching jelly beans, making faces, or laughing. Sometimes they slept. Litter piled up on their table and the carpet underneath it."[77] The point was to oppose not only the war, but society in general: to proclaim a "new life style in America." Defendant David Dellinger refused to say "your Honor"; he called the judge "Mr. Hoffman," because Dellinger believed in "equality."[78] To Tom Hayden, one of the defendants, the courtroom was a "sterile horror," and the judge a "bizarre puppet"; the defense table, on the other hand, was a "liberated zone," and the "ultimate defiance of a court system that demands the repression of people into well-behaved clients, advocates, and jurors."[79]

These goings-on probably turned off more people than they converted to the cause. As an antiwar tactic, the behavior of the Chicago Seven was a failure; as an advertisement for the counterculture, it had less clear results. A generation later, rappers and rock bands rake in hundreds of millions of dollars for behavior every bit as bizarre, every bit as defiant of conventional morality. Trials have always had a theatrical element; even more so in the age of television. At the end of the twentieth century, there was guerrilla theater to be seen, day in and day out, on TV dramas, or on the popular "judge" shows—and weird behavior, defiant, raucous—all this long after the original Chicago Seven were either dead or disguised in three-piece suits.

Victimless Crime

As we have seen, the fight against "immorality" and victimless crime reached a kind of crescendo in the early part of the century; and Prohibition was its crowning achievement. Moral crusading had already lost some of its force when Prohibition passed into history. From roughly 1930 on, the worm slowly turned. Morals and mores changed; and though laws against victimless crimes never lacked for defenders, they never again reached the level that they reached in the period that ended around 1930.

Between the 1930s and the end of the century, the United States underwent profound cultural change. Twentieth-century affluence emancipated millions of people from lives of hand-to-mouth drudgery. This was a society with growing amounts of leisure. It turned out that people did not necessarily spend their leisure time reading Shakespeare or studying the Bible. Some did; many did not. People had time and money; they were consumers on a grand scale; and they actively sought out pleasure. The market for vice increased—for sex, for gambling, for liquor, and for drugs. And the demand, even when it was covert, even when people were too shy or embarrassed to express their wants openly, put constant, implicit, unremitting pressure on the law.

The state was the mouthpiece of articulate, respectable people, middle class and up. They had the ear of Congress and the legislatures. The state did not of course give up its role as regulator of leisure and morality. Liquor stepped out of the criminal closet; but liquor regulation never ended. The market for liquor never evolved into total laissez-faire. The world of sports had long been in a kind of shadowland; lower-class sports, like boxing and wrestling, were illegal or suspect; tennis and golf were never under the ban. Horse and dog racing carried the stigma of gambling. The suspect sports were gradually legalized; but sometimes, like liquor, with tight regulation, ostensibly in the interests of fairness or public morality. Thus West Virginia in 1931 created a State Athletic Commission to control boxing and wrestling.[80] The law was full of detailed provisions—no boxing match was to go more than twelve rounds of three minutes each, with a one-minute intermission between rounds; the boxers had to wear gloves weighing at least six ounces. And there was to be no boxing on Sunday. The commission did not have a comparable rule for more genteel sports.

Gambling was also decriminalized, and with a vengeance. Once Las Vegas had been the only really open sin spot. Now it began to have rivals. Some states began to take a few tentative steps: New Mexico, for example, enacted a Bingo and Raffle Act in 1981, to allow charities and churches to run these games.[81] Then Las Vegas developed a powerful rival in Atlantic City. In the nineteenth century, the federal government had crushed the lottery business. In the late twentieth century, the lottery business came roaring back. State after state, hungry for revenue, passed lottery laws—and advertised them heavily. There were the usual moral and policy complaints, but they were drowned out in the rush to make money and appease the public hunger for lottery tickets and dreams of easy money. Lottery laws turned state governments into high-class bookies. Casinos, too, proliferated: on the Mississippi River, on Indian reservations. Gambling became one of the country's leading industries.

Another symptom of the leisure society was the decline and fall of Sunday blue laws. At one time, statutes and ordinances outlawed most kinds of work on Sunday, plus most sports and games. Well into the twentieth century, there were statutes on the books which seemed to make official what one might call the Puritan Sunday: a day of prayer and quiet, devoted solely to virtue and to God. Thus in Vermont, in the second decade of the century, it was against the law to do "any business or employment" on Sunday, "except works of necessity or charity"; or to hold a "ball or dance," or engage in any "game, sport, or play," or "resort" to a "house of entertainment for amusement or recreation"; hunting was also prohibited.[82] In Mississippi, under its 1927 Code, "farces," plays, games, "tricks, ball-playing of any kind, juggling, sleight of hand, or feats of dexterity" were prohibited on Sunday.[83] The Ohio statute against "desecration" of the Sabbath as late as the 1950s added a ban on any "rope dancing or sparring exhibition, variety show, negro minstrelsy, living statuary, [or] ballooning" in the "forenoon," and "ten pins or other games of similar kind" all day; also "hunting, fishing or shooting."[84]

The political power of these laws was not just a matter of religion; unions also wanted a guaranteed day off. Nobody yet dreamed of the modern Sunday—a day for church, to be sure, for millions; but also for sleeping late, for family shopping, and (above all) for fun. Even in the early part of the century, some courts either interpreted their Sunday laws to allow baseball and movies, or struck down laws which were too harsh on these innocent pursuits. Oregon, in fact, repealed its Sunday laws by referendum in 1916.[85] By 1947 Vermont had exempted "winter sports, tennis or golf" from its statute; and other sports were allowed, so long as they did not charge admission. Voters of Vermont towns could also vote to permit "baseball, moving pictures, lectures or concerts" on Sunday, but not until two in the afternoon (six o'clock in the case of the movies).[86] The morning, apparently, was still reserved for church.

But the laws continued to crumble. True, the United States was and is a deeply religious country. Many of its churches are jammed to the rafters on Sunday—in the morning. But what happens later is another story. The Puritan Sunday is dead. To begin with, the country is a religious melting pot; Sunday is no longer the only sacred day. More significantly, families in which everybody works do most of their shopping on Sunday. The stores are eager to sell on Sunday, and people are eager to buy. And after they pray, and shop, they want to enjoy. Even the descendants of Puritans no longer want the Puritan Sunday. The Puritan Sunday is no fun.

The struggle in states like New Jersey over blue laws was basically not a religious struggle; it was a struggle between, say, supermarket checkers and their union, on the one side, and the owners of stores on the other. Ohio repealed its Sunday laws in 1973. By the end of the century, in many parts of the country, some stores were open not only on Sunday, but all night, and 365 days out of the year. Shopping had triumphed. Some states, like Alabama, deep in the Bible Belt, retained Sunday laws, punishable even with jail time. But Alabama's law was riddled with exceptions: drug stores, naturally, but also places that sold gas, or newspapers; auto repair shops, florists, fruit stands, ice cream parlors, and restaurants could stay open; and, for some reason, motorcycle and auto racing on Sunday was allowed.[87] The laws were fitfully enforced at best. In one of the rare reported cases, the department store Kmart kept its doors open on Sunday; it was challenged, but Kmart won its case. The judges saw clearly that the law had become an anomaly; and an unfair one, at that. A drug store could stay open on Sunday; but drug stores had become, in effect, little department stores. They sold everything from pencils to milk. If so, how could you punish a real department store for staying open—and a department store which, in fact, along with everything else, also happened to sell drugs?[88]

The Sexual Revolution

The most dramatic changes of all, perhaps, were part and parcel of the so-called sexual revolution. *Sexual Behavior in the Human Male,* the first part of the famous Kinsey report, appeared in 1948. It burst into public view like a Roman candle on the Fourth of July. Alfred C. Kinsey was a biologist, whose early work was on gall wasps, not people. He intended his report on sexual behavior to be dry and objective; and to a certain extent it was—it bristled with charts, graphs, and figures. The subject was sex; but the treatment was humorless, clinical; Kinsey reported, for example, with a perfectly straight face, statistical evidence on the angle of the penis when erect. (The average position, it seems, was "very slightly above the horizontal," though some 8–10 percent "carry the erect penis nearly vertically, more or less tightly against the belly").[89]

The angle of the penis was not what Kinsey was after. He had a definite mission. He meant to unmask the hypocrisy of America's sex laws; these laws, he thought, were worse than futile; they were perverse. They made crimes out of behaviors that were rampantly common. Kinsey claimed that 59 percent of American men had "some experience in mouth-genital contacts"; more than a third had had "some homosexual experience"; as many as 17 percent of the "farm boys" had experimented with "animal intercourse." All these acts were crimes—many, in fact, were grave crimes, infamous crimes, crimes that could get you years and years in prison, according to the various penal codes. In fact, Kinsey said, 95 percent of "the total male population" had committed one or more of these statutory crimes. All of these men were technically "sex offenders"; they could all, in theory, sit in prison, guarded by the 5 percent of the male population at large who were innocent of such crimes. His follow-up book, on the sexual behavior of women, was less shocking only because it came after the book about men, and was therefore not such a surprise. American women were not as wildly criminal as American men; but they were bad enough.[90]

The Kinsey report was an instant best-seller. It was, naturally, declaimed and denounced from dozens of pulpits and in all sorts of respectable places. Its methodology was analyzed and criticized and ripped to shreds; the data were drawn (it was said) from weirdly unrepresentative samples. Did the Kinsey report get the facts right, after all? Probably not—at least not totally; some of its statistics have failed to stand the test of time. But the essential message was far more important than the statistics; and this message really hit home.

In retrospect, it seems clear that Kinsey's books were just one burst of artillery fire in the new sexual revolution. The sexual revolution became also, most definitely, a legal revolution. This legal revolution did not, of course, take place overnight. But the laws were modified gradually, in state after state. In most states, fornication disappeared from the penal code. In New Jersey the state supreme court declared the fornication law unconstitutional—as a gross intrusion on "personal autonomy." An expert witness, Dr. Richard Green, testified that the sex drive was "central" to "personality development"; repression could lead to dreadful consequences—guilt, anxiety, "inability to achieve erection" in males, and "frigidity" or "painful intercourse" in women.[91]

In some states, adultery went into the legal trash heap along with fornication; and in a number of states, including California and Illinois, after the penal codes were housecleaned and reformed, any sexual relations between that randy pair, "two consenting adults," no matter what these relations were, or how they were, or who the parties were (same sex or opposite sexes), carried no penal sanction whatsoever. Kinsey's dream had come true. The Mann Act, too, traveled down the road to oblivion. As late as the 1940s the government had used the law to sensational effect against no less a celebrity than Charlie Chaplin. Chaplin had gotten involved with a young woman named Joan Barry; they quarreled and split up; she brought a paternity action against him (blood tests cleared Chaplin), and was later the complaining "victim" in a Mann Act case. Chaplin, it was alleged, paid her to go to New York and have sex with him.[92] The evil genius behind this far-fetched case was J. Edgar Hoover, who considered Chaplin a dangerous radical. Chaplin was acquitted. The Mann Act was now slowly dying. By the end of the 1960s, there were only a handful of convictions. In 1978 and 1986 the law was drastically amended; "white slavery" and "debauchery" disappeared from the text; the act became unisex; and the crime was redefined. Now it consisted only of transporting for purposes of "prostitution," or "any sexual activity for which any person can be charged with a criminal offense." This meant, for example, that crossing over into Nevada from California, for ordinary lust and consummation, was no longer an illegal act.[93]

For most of the century, there were stringent laws against pornography and obscenity. Most respectable people firmly believed (or said they believed) that pornography was sinful, disgusting, and a danger to society. Hardly any one questioned the idea that pornography and obscenity were beyond the pale. States and cities had a perfect right to regulate, control, and ban all forms of "dirt." Free speech stopped at the border of naked bodies doing their naked thing.

Works once ran afoul of the censor that would in 2000 be considered great literature or, sometimes, harmless family entertainment. New Haven, Connecticut, banned George Bernard Shaw's play *Mrs. Warren's Profession* in 1905.[94] A few judges took a more enlightened view: in one famous case in 1933, a federal judge courageously decided that James Joyce's *Ulysses* was not obscene, despite its "dirty words" and its vivid descriptions of sex.[95] But until the 1930s, the U.S. Customs Department, boldly protecting our shores from foreign filth, banned works by such notorious peddlers of smut as Aristophanes, Balzac, Defoe, Flaubert, and Voltaire.[96]

Most people (if asked) would insist that pornography—words and pictures depicting sex acts graphically and without a figleaf—was disgusting, filthy and even perverted. Should we believe them? Probably not (or at least not all of them). After all, the underground market for sex, and for books and pictures of sex, had always been enormous. In the postwar period, what had been underground pushed its way more and more into plain view. Not without opposition, of course. The official line was that obscenity led people, especially young people, straight down the path to degeneracy. Pennsylvania in 1956 passed a law against selling obscene comic books and magazines to minors. The preamble is worth quoting. It began:

> WHEREAS, we believe that the destructive and adventurous potentialities of children and adolescents are often stimulated by collections of pictures and stories of criminal deeds of bloodshed or lust so massed as to incite to violent and depraved crimes . . . [and] we believe that such juveniles . . . do, in fact, commit such crimes at least partly because incited to do so by such publications . . . [97]

This belief, according to the legislators, "even though not capable of statistical demonstration" was "supported by our experience" (and the "opinions of some specialists").

Children, to be sure, have always been a special case. Arguably (and the Pennsylvania statute so argued) an act that merely regulated "the access of children" to obscene publications did not infringe on freedom of speech. But what about the access of adults? The question became more and more pointed. The Supreme Court did not decide a single case on pornography and free speech until after the Second World War. The first case (1957) was *Roth v. United States*.[98] Here the Court upheld the right of the states to punish people who made and sold obscenity. But where was the boundary line? What *was* obscenity? Clearly, the definition was shifting rather drastically. In 1966 the Supreme Court faced the issue again. It confronted that formidable woman of the eighteenth century, Fanny Hill, heroine (if that is the word) of John Cleland's rather wonderful piece of erotica, *Memoirs of a Woman of Pleasure*. This book was written about the same time as the First Amendment itself; but nobody before the late twentieth century even dared to suggest that a decent publisher should be able to sell such a book—or that decent folks could or might read it. The Supreme Court gave Fanny a clean bill of health. The state could ban a book only if it was "utterly without redeeming social value." Presumably Fanny had a lesson to teach us; or some literary value. Justice Douglas noticed that when the book came out of the closet in 1963, "universities and libraries" placed "an unusually large number of orders"; and the "library of Congress requested the right to translate the book into Braille."[99] This may not be a striking legal point, but it does say something rather telling about the decline of Victorian prudery.

The Supreme Court never did work out a coherent theory of obscenity. It struggled with the problem in case after case. On the other hand, the general public (with obvious exceptions) did work out a theory of sorts. Essentially, in 2001 the rule is: in most places anything, absolutely anything, goes. To be sure, not every state has gone all the way. Obscenity laws remain on the books in some states—probably, for the most part, fitfully enforced, if at all. The Bible Belt states have, not surprisingly, resisted the general trend. To this day, sodomy and adultery are also crimes in many of these states—although the courts have been hostile to them. Even fornication is not an extinct crime: in Mississippi, it is a crime for a man and a woman to "unlawfully cohabit, whether in adultery or fornication."[100] Jail time is possible. But certainly not probable, even in Mississippi.

Obscenity and pornography are still controversial, of course. One branch of feminist thought, led by Catharine MacKinnon, is actively at war against pornography; MacKinnon sees pornography as a vital prop of male domination. MacKinnon would ban any sexually explicit material that portrays the subordination of women. She drafted a strong ordinance to this effect; Indianapolis adopted it, but the federal courts threw it out on free-speech grounds.[101] Antipornography campaigns make strange bedfellows: millions of deeply religious people who would find MacKinnon's brand of feminism abhorrent would agree with her that pornography should not be allowed.

Pornography may be free speech; but it tends to be tacky speech; and it resides in tacky stores and tacky places. Like tattoo parlors, an "adult bookstore" is not a sign of an upscale neighborhood. Many cities, having given up trying to ban pornography, have tried instead to confine it to vice ghettos; or at the least, to keep it away from children and churchgoers. The city of Minot, North Dakota, adopted an ordinance imposing license fees on "adult" shops, and telling them not to locate within 1,250 feet of a church, school, or residential district. This ordinance was aimed directly at the Last Chance Bookstore in Minot (its one and only pornography shop). A federal court upheld the ordinance in 1981.[102] It says something about society in 1981 that little Minot, North Dakota, had an adult bookstore; and it says even more that the city fathers (and mothers) must have felt it was hopeless to try to get rid of it entirely; the most they could do was to harass it, and perhaps to keep it in its place.

It says something, too, that the Supreme Court of the United States, in 1991, had to solemnly adjudicate the affairs of the Kitty Kat Lounge in South Bend, Indiana, which featured women doing "go-go dancing," completely nude, and the Glen Theatre, also in South Bend, where customers could put money in a slot and look at "live nude and seminude dancers" through glass panels. The issue was an Indiana law that banned public nudity; the dancers (under this law) had to wear "pasties" and "G-strings." The Kitty Kat and the Glen claimed that the law infringed their rights of "freedom of expression." They lost—but barely. Four members of the Supreme Court agreed. So did the majority of the judges of the Seventh Circuit. Judge Richard Posner's opinion was particularly striking and perceptive. Nudity, he pointed out, "as titillation or outrage is relative rather than absolute"; in Victorian England, "even the legs of furniture were sometimes clad for the sake of decency," and "a bare ankle was a sensation."[103] In Posner's view, nudity itself was less erotic than before; but in any event, the erotic too was entitled to constitutional protection. Both aspects of social life had changed, in short; what was acceptable as nonerotic, and what was acceptable as openly erotic. But the Supreme Court—or five of them at least—was not willing to go quite that far. G-strings and pasties survived in Indiana.

The general lines of development seem clear: a retreat from Victorian sensibilities, and Victorian laws, at first orderly, then in a total helter-skelter rout. But it would be wrong to assume that the lines of movement were always in one direction. As the Indiana case indicates, public nudity is still a no-no. Along the way to the permissive society, there were many zigs and zags. As late as 1962 the comedian Lenny Bruce was arrested for obscenity and dirty words in his performances. Eventually, Bruce was exonerated—after he had died of a drug overdose in 1966, bankrupt and bitter.[104] There is some evidence that repression of gays increased after the end of the Second World War; some scholars have talked about an "anti-homosexual terror," or a campaign against "perverts"; and indeed, there were arrests and crackdowns in many cities: in Washington, D.C., for example, the police made five sodomy arrests in 1942; perhaps seventy-eight or more in 1950.[105] Congress enacted a law for the District of Columbia on "sexual psychopaths" in 1948. The statute included severe sodomy laws: anyone convicted of "taking into his or her mouth or anus" a "sexual organ" or who was convicted "of having carnal copulation" in any "opening of the body except sexual parts" could receive up to ten years imprisonment.[106]

Leslie Reagan, in her study of abortion practice, has pointed out a similar trend in the 1950s: a war on abortion, which put a number of rather well-known doctors in jail. In New York a "sharp crackdown" made abortions more difficult and expensive. Abortion, which had been a more or less open secret, now went underground; there were stories of women who were driven in blindfolds to a hidden location, where the operation was carried out. Quality declined, as the better class of doctor shrank from the practice: one "doctor" smoked a cigar while doing the job; another, in Chicago, worked "in a dirty T shirt"; another one was drunk, and performed the abortion in his kitchen.[107]

This was also, of course, the period of McCarthy and McCarthyism. It was a period of furious reaction against enemies within and without, a period of strenuous witch-hunts. The hunt for subversives, as is well known, often included a hunt for "perverts" in the government. Both communists and homosexuals were supposed to be eager to recruit and corrupt the young. A connection with abortion laws may seem a bit more arcane. But danger to the moral fabric of the country was perhaps the link. McCarthyism and the war on the reds also provided cover for a wholesale attack on everything that smelled of liberalism (and hence of Godless Communism). The witch-hunts and the anti-abortion campaign shared some traits, as Leslie Reagan has pointed out: "Silencing, forced speaking, naming names, and public exposure of subversive behavior and beliefs."[108]

The war against abortion soon took a different and dramatic turn, in *Roe v. Wade*. And by the end of the century, the war against dirty books and pictures had been essentially lost—for consenting adults, though emphatically not with regard to children. And the definition of obscenity had altered, socially if not legally. The Minot, North Dakota, ordinance defined "adult cinema" in terms of "specified sexual activities or specified anatomical areas"; the "areas" included the "female breast below a point immediately above the top of the areola," and "male genitalia in a discernibly turgid state"; the "activities" included masturbation and sexual intercourse.[109] Only triple-X material was covered—and even that, as we have seen, was regulated, not banned. It was a long, long way from Anthony Comstock.

The War on Drugs

Despite these ups and downs, the period between 1930 and 2000 was one in which laws against victimless crime lost most of their validity and force. There were battles over abortion and the sexual minorities; but the battles against gambling and pornography, as we have seen, virtually collapsed. One great exception to this parade of permissiveness was the "war on drugs." Here was no surrender, no armistice, no treaty of peace. The war has become more and more important—more and more money, artillery, more and more casualties. And it has kept its popularity. There are very few public figures who dare to advocate making drugs legal, or anything close to this.

The laws have become tougher and tougher, both on the state and federal levels. A law in Congress in 1951 (the so-called Boggs Act) punished importers of narcotics. Third offenders could get up to twenty years.[110] The Narcotic Control Act of 1956 was a real get-tough law. The minimum sentence for selling narcotics was five years; second offenses got ten years; there were harsh provisions on smuggling drugs; and suspended sentences, probation, and parole were ruled out for drug offenders.[111] The Drug Abuse Control Amendments of 1965 added "depressant or stimulant drugs" to the list of the damned.[112] In 1968 the Federal Bureau of Narcotics was transferred to the Department of Justice.

The Comprehensive Drug Abuse Prevention and Control Act (1970) had a different tone—as if the country were catching its breath and thinking aloud about where it was going. This law eliminated mandatory minimum sentences, which, according to the Senate report, had not achieved results; in fact, "severe drug laws, specifically as applied to marihuana have . . . contributed to the alienation of youth."[113] A law of 1972 created a National Institute on Drug Abuse to carry out programs of education and research; this was specifically an agency for "prevention" of drug abuse.[114]

The pause did not last very long. In 1973 Congress created the Drug Enforcement Administration; and in the 1980s Congress enacted a number of mandatory minimum laws for drug abuse—the same kinds of law that had been abandoned as ineffective in 1970. The keystone act was the Anti–Drug Abuse Act of 1986.[115] More money and men were thrown into the battle from then on. The Drug Enforcement Administration had a budget of $74.9 million in 1973; by 1999 this had risen to $1.4 billion, and the agency had more than nine thousand employees.[116]

The war has produced an enormous body of law in the states as well as on the federal level. Here too, in general, the statutes have gotten harsher and harsher. Politicians sensed, perhaps correctly, that toughness was a box-office hit. Governor Nelson Rockefeller of New York pushed a draconian law through the legislature in 1973. A person convicted of a serious drug offense could get life in prison. Parole carried with it lifetime supervision. Rockefeller crowed that this was the country's "toughest" law; a real weapon against "pushers." But the law, in practice, was a disaster: the trial rate went way up, burdening the courts; the whole process slowed to a crawl, because the harshness of the law gave defendants every incentive to fight conviction; and the law in action produced its share of injustices and anomalies: a thirty-eight-year-old woman, for example, with no record, sentenced to life in prison for possession of one ounce of cocaine. In 1979 the legislature repealed this unhappy law.[117] But even in New York, the laws that remained were terribly severe.

The failure of the Rockefeller law was a rare setback for drug warriors in the states. In general, the trend has been in the other direction. In Michigan, under a law of 1978, a person who makes or delivers a narcotic drug (heroin and cocaine, among others), provided the amount in question weighed 650 grams or more (this is somewhat more than a pound) was to be "imprisoned for life." This punishment was, incidentally, the same as the maximum for first-degree murder in Michigan, which has no death penalty.[118]

The drug codes have also gotten more and more elaborate. Most states now have "drug paraphernalia" laws, which criminalize owning or dealing in the equipment people employ to make, deliver, or use illegal drugs. These laws come in a number of versions. One common version, which outlaws such things as "roach clips," "chillums," and "bongs," also includes (somewhat alarmingly) in its definition of drug paraphernalia "scales and balances," bowls, spoons, "capsules, balloons, envelopes," and containers in general, so long as they were "used, intended for use, or designed for use" in compounding, packaging, or storing and concealing "controlled substances."[119]

Very few people, I imagine, are arrested simply because they own a sinful spoon or a delinquent envelope. But the law gives the police another excuse to arrest addicts and pushers, even when they cannot be caught red-handed with actual drugs, or in the actual act of selling them; more significantly, it gives the authorities a weapon for cracking down on "head shops." The reported cases are mostly about such head shops; and they generally uphold the statutes. One Roger Munson, owner of the Impulse General Store in Springfield, Missouri, sold roach clips and cocaine kits to a man who was, unfortunately for Munson, a member of the police force. Munson posted signs in his store that the articles he sold were "not intended for illegal use"; but this slogan was not enough to save him from conviction, and a sentence of eight years in prison.[120]

Again, in this age of permissiveness, the drug laws are a jarring, jangling exception. There is no easy explanation. Of course, in the history of the drug war, there are heroes (or villains, as you see fit): moral entrepreneurs—like Harry Anslinger, Governor Rockefeller, and President Richard Nixon—who made the war on drugs their own, and who did their best to enlist the general public (or send the public into panic). But their propaganda seemed to reach very eager ears. Why were drugs different from other vices? For one thing, nice people drank, and had sex, and gambled a little; but nice people (on the whole) did not take drugs. Drugs were a scourge of low, weak, inferior people. And minorities: it was associated with black people, Hispanics, the Chinese. It was easy to demonize the addict; and (above all) the men and women who made and sold the drugs.

There was also the problem of the kids. Parents were terrified of pushers— evil men who would turn their children into zombies. In this light, drug laws were not really so exceptional. Drug abuse was "contagious and criminal." It corrupted the values people wanted to teach their children: "values that hinged on the authority of parents, the state, and the law."[121] It came to be associated with hippies, with rebellion against society. For all these reasons, children had to be protected from drugs. The world could be a wicked, dangerous place. Childhood was supposed to be a period of innocence and vulnerability. For little kids, the worst bogeyman was the dirty, perverted stranger, offering candy and a ride to hell in his car. For bigger kids, the pusher took his place. As taboos dropped like flies in the adult world—sex, liquor, gambling—it was more and more important to save the children, to insulate them from the horrors of an unregulated world.

Probably no aspect of the war on drugs has been so disturbing as the color line it draws. Of course, no drug statute explicitly targets black people. But this has been the result, conscious or unconscious, of some of the more pitiless drug laws. The most notorious example is the famous (and often misrepresented and misunderstood) "one hundred to one" difference between powder cocaine and crack cocaine. Under the 1986 Anti-Drug Abuse Act, a ten-year mandatory penalty could be triggered by five kilograms of powder cocaine, or 50 grams (1 percent of five kilograms) of solid (crack) cocaine. There had been a media blitz about the horrors of crack—the crack epidemic was labeled by *Newsweek* as the "issue of the year" in September 1986. The public got the idea, which was not entirely far-fetched, that crack was especially loathesome, dangerous, and addictive. Congress followed the crowd. The racial results were dramatic. According to the United States Sentencing Commission, 88.3 percent of the defendants charged with trafficking in crack cocaine in the 1990s were black; 4.1 percent were white; 7.1 percent were Hispanic. Among those charged with trafficking in powder cocaine, 27.4 percent were black.[122]

In general, drug laws have also played a major role in filling up the prisons. Between 1947 and 1950, an average of 115 prisoners a year entered California prisons on drug charges. The figure for 1985 was 3,609; for 1990 it was 13,741.[123] In 1996 in the state courts, there were 347,774 *felony* convictions for drug offenses—more than a third of all convictions. And 135,270 of these were for simple possession. More than 90 percent of the defendants pleaded guilty. Seventy percent of the men and women convicted of possession went to prison or jail.[124]

Prison populations in general have skyrocketed since the 1980s. The drug laws are a major cause, though not the only one: a general campaign of toughness also makes a major contribution. In 1980 there were 329,000 state and federal prisoners; in 1997 there were more than 1.2 million—and climbing. California's prison population went from about 25,000 to 157,000. The number of people entangled in the web of criminal justice has become absolutely staggering: 5,690,000 either incarcerated or on probation or parole as of December 31,

1997—more than the population of Wisconsin.[125] And there was no end in sight to this boom. The men in prison, except for a noxious riot once in a while, are truly invisible. The public knows very little about prison policy; but what little it knows, it probably approves of. After all, if you lock up the scum, they can hardly rape, rob, pillage, and murder *us*. The *costs* of the program—in dollars, in wasted lives, in blighted communities—are rarely, if ever, taken into account.

The War on Guns

Permissive sex laws are an aspect of late-twentieth-century individualism, and are darlings of the Left. Some people on the Right are engaged in furious (and losing) battle against these laws and nonlaws. Permissive gun laws are another aspect of late-twentieth-century individualism, and are darlings of the Right. The Left is in furious battle against *these* laws; with decidedly mixed results.

Many Americans, especially in the South and West, are passionate about their guns, and are positively in love with the Second Amendment, which gives them (they think) an absolute right to bear arms. Americans think of themselves as historically a gun-toting nation; but in fact most nineteenth-century murders were not committed with guns, and cheap, reliable handguns were not available until late in the century. Today we think of Texas as a gun owner's heaven; but Texas passed a law in 1907 putting a whopping tax on all wholesale and retail dealers in pistols: 50 percent of "gross receipts from sales of all firearms." Under an Oregon law passed in 1913, you needed a permit and two written affidavits of "good moral character" to buy a "pocket pistol or revolver" from a dealer; and all dealers had to record the buyer's name and the serial number of the weapon, and give this information to the county sheriff.[126] New York was another leader in the struggle against handguns. The campaign was particularly directed against foreigners, especially the sinister Italians. No noncitizen "shall have or carry firearms or dangerous weapons in any public place at any time," according to a law of 1905.[127] In 1910 an attempt to assassinate the mayor, William J. Gaynor, put handguns into the headlines. The Sullivan Law of 1911 tightened the control laws, made it illegal to own a weapon without a license in any city or town, and required gun sellers to keep records and to demand a permit from any buyer.[128] Similarly, Michigan in 1925 made it a crime to carry a concealed weapon without a license; the licenses were to be given only to "suitable" people, and for a "reasonable cause." Dealers had to be licensed and keep records; and the law also added an extra jolt in prison (two to five years) for any felony committed with a gun.[129]

Even the federal government got into the act. The National Firearms Act (1934) imposed a tax of two hundred dollars on the transfer of "firearms" (rifles and shotguns), and called for application forms, revenue stamps, and other devices plainly meant to establish some kind of rather stringent gun control.[130] The law was attacked as a violation of the sacred Second Amendment, but the Supreme Court in 1938 brushed this argument aside. The Second Amendment begins by referring to state militias; this gun-control law had nothing to do with these militias. The guns in question were not "ordinary military equipment," and militias were apparently all that the Second Amendment dealt with, according to the Court.[131]

There is squabbling in the scholarly literature about what the Second Amendment meant in the first place. Did it, in fact, mean only that the states had a right to a citizen militia, or did it carry a broader meaning?[132] The National Rifle Association insists that the meaning is very broad indeed—that the Constitution guarantees the right to own and carry guns. Of course, the NRA and its fellow travelers do not really care about "original intent" (what the Constitution meant to the men who wrote it), any more than prochoice people or gay rights advocates really care. Gun owners are convinced that *their* right to bear arms is precious and fundamental. History has very little to do with the case.

The canonization of the right to bear arms is, in other words, a form of late-twentieth-century rights consciousness—a bastard cousin of the civil rights movement. Politically, of course, there is no relationship at all between people who are passionate about guns and those who are passionate about prisoners' rights, affirmative action, abortion rights, and the like. But on one level, these passions derive from the same social source.

In March 1981 John W. Hinckley, Jr., waited for President Reagan outside a Washington hotel. As the president came out, Hinckley shot him, wounding him severely. The bullets also shattered the body of James Brady, the president's press secretary. The event galvanized Brady's wife, Sarah, into action. She became one of the leaders of the gun control movement. By 2000 there was a fairly dense network of laws and regulations on the sale and ownership of guns, though they were, on the whole, of dubious effectiveness. The so-called Brady bill of 1993 tried to put more teeth into regulation.[133] The NRA is a powerful lobby; but now there is something of a counterforce. Pressure on both sides of the issue continues to be intense.

The Insanity Defense

Hinckley's bullets had an impact on another area of criminal law: the insanity defense. Hinckley had (he said) a psychotic obsession with the actress Jodie Foster. What all this had to do with the president was always murky. A jury found Hinckley not guilty by reason of insanity; the verdict touched off a storm of protest. Huge majorities in the country thought the decision was an outrage. Dozens of bills were introduced into state and federal legislatures to do something about the insanity defense, that blot on the face of the law.

The insanity defense had been a bone of contention for some time.[134] Under old and standard doctrine, a defendant has to be sane to stand trial at all; and a defendant who was insane when he committed the crime is not responsible for his acts. But what does the law mean by *insane?* The traditional test was the so-called McNaghten rule, an English formulation dating from 1843. Under this test a person is insane if, because of mental disease, he does not "know the nature and quality of the act he was doing, or if he did know it," did "not know he was doing what was wrong."[135]

This so-called "right or wrong" test became standard doctrine in the United States. Psychiatrists thought it was meaningless or worse. Some states added another test, the "irresistible impulse" test—the defendant was insane if his mental disease made it impossible for him to control what he was doing. It was never clear, in any event, what juries understood of these formulas: any test, after all, is basically just words, intoned to the jury by the judge. The jury then goes into a locked room and comes to its own decision. Still, enlightened medical and legal opinion disliked the McNaghten rules. In *Durham v. United States* (1954), a District of Columbia case, Judge David L. Bazelon tossed McNaghten out the window.[136] Under Bazelon's new test, an accused was not criminally responsible if his "unlawful act was the product of mental disease or mental defect."

The *Durham* rule was hailed as a great advance, at least by psychiatrists. But only one state (Maine) actually adopted it; and it was so vague and open-ended that it provided little or no help for a jury (assuming a jury wanted this kind of help). It was in bad odor almost immediately. By the early 1970s even the District of Columbia had abandoned it.[137] Most states kept, or returned to, a modified form of the old McNaghten rules. The "right and wrong" test is alive and well in California and elsewhere.[138]

Millions of people seem to feel that the insanity defense is some sort of scam—just one more way in which vicious criminals get away with murder. The Hinckley trial drove the point home.[139] Hence the great rush to toughen up the law. In the Insanity Defense Reform Act of 1984 (part of a comprehensive crime-control bill), Congress restricted the defense to those who were "unable to appreciate the nature and quality or wrongfulness" of their acts—a very McNaghten formulation. More than thirty states made some response to the Hinckley case in the next few years. And a few states (Idaho and Montana, for example) abolished the insanity plea altogether.[140]

This is less drastic, in a way, than it seems. Nobody in Idaho is allowed to plead "not guilty by reason of insanity"; but a defendant still has to be sane to stand trial at all—sane enough to understand what is going on, and to mount some sort of defense; if not, there will be no trial while the condition lasts.[141] Everywhere, most of the people who are obviously crazy never get to trial; they go straight to some sort of institution. And because the definitions of most crimes assume some sort of intent, a man on trial for murder in the first degree, even in Utah (another abolition state), is entitled to show that he was too deranged to form the cold-blooded intent which makes murder murder and not something else.[142]

The point of these laws, then, is political and symbolic. They are responses to the general demand for tough, tougher, toughest. This demand in turn is related, no doubt, to actual crime rates, though the exact relationship is pretty obscure. It is also no doubt related to the steamy publicity about crime that saturates the media. This publicity reaches ears that are all too willing to listen. The public does not believe in social theories of crime. It believes in total, unbridled free will (at least for other people). It accepts few if any excuses as valid. It does not want to hear about abusive parents, broken homes, and other such claims in mitigation. (It does not accept these excuses for poverty, either, as the stark, punitive attitudes toward welfare show.) All this stands in sharp contrast to the prevailing public attitude toward "accidents," toward catastrophes that are "nobody's fault."

In California the Dan White case played a role somewhat analogous to the Hinckley case. White, a former San Francisco supervisor, shot and killed the mayor of San Francisco, George Moscone, and supervisor Harvey Milk, who was openly gay. The trial took place in 1979. White had killed the two men in broad daylight and in City Hall; his defense had to be based on his mental condition. After a sensational trial, the jury found White guilty, but only of voluntary manslaughter. It was impossible to argue that White was insane in the legal sense; but sunny California recognized an in-between category, "diminished capacity." The meaning of this term was somewhat mysterious and rather technical; but the root idea was simply this: some people who were not really insane were also not quite normal, and deserved some lesser punishment. After the verdict, there were riots in the streets of San Francisco, and the legislature did away with the whole concept of diminished capacity. White served his time in prison, got out, and promptly killed himself.[143]

Badfellas

One war on crime which seemed, on the whole, to have somewhat more success than the war on drugs was the war on organized crime. During Prohibition, and in the years afterward, the great crime families had attained enormous power (and enormous publicity). To be sure, the government did ship "Scarface" Al Capone off to Alcatraz, and other big-time gangsters went to prison or were packed off to Sicily; but the American Mafia nonetheless seemed to be thriving.

The twentieth century was a century of big crime as well as big business. The Mafia had Italian roots, of course, but most gangsters were not Italians. In the 1920s there were Jewish gangsters (like Meyer Lansky) and Irish gangsters (the Hill Mob in Boston) as well.[144] Just as legitimate businesses had economies of scale, so too did crime families: there was power in numbers. Ties of kinship and blood—and machine gun bullets—supplemented and replaced the contracts, deals, and mergers of legitimate businesses.

In time, the Italian crime families came to dominate. They corrupted governments, controlled some labor unions, and reached their tentacles into many industries and businesses. The Kefauver Committee (1950–1951), led by Senator Estes Kefauver of Tennessee, threw a lurid spotlight on the doings of the mob; the committee made dramatic use of the new medium, television. In the 1960s Attorney General Robert Kennedy made the fight against organized crime one of his top priorities. (J. Edgar Hoover, head of the FBI, had stead-

fastly denied that there was such a thing as the Mafia in the United States.)
Joseph Valachi, a turncoat Mafioso, testified in public about the Cosa Nostra to
a thrilled audience of millions. Kennedy set up an Organized Crime Section
inside the Justice Department.[145] The 1968 Omnibus Crime Control and Safe
Streets Act made it possible for the FBI to "spin a thick web of wiretaps and electronic bugs around the organized-crime families." Another important weapon
in the battle was the statute known as RICO, Racketeer Influenced and Corrupt
Organizations Act, passed in 1970. This is a complicated statute, but it gave the
government tools for smashing the connection between organized crime groups
and their business enterprises. The Witness Security Program, also initiated in
1970, allowed prosecutors to protect witnesses by promising them a "new
identity and a new life."[146] By the end of the century, many big-time gangsters
were in jail, and the grip of the mob on New York's Fulton Fish Market, on
Kennedy Airport, and on various businesses seemed to have been finally and
rather decisively broken.

This was the domestic war. There were also two international wars. One
was an extension of the war on drugs, waged at the borders, complete with
sniffing dogs and Coast Guard cutters; and overseas as well, in the form of
money poured into foreign countries like Bolivia or Colombia to help them
stamp out the growing or processing or trafficking in drugs. The other was the
war against international crime: as crime transcended borders, so did the efforts
of law enforcement agencies, which formed organizations like Interpol, in an
effort to deal with transnational crime.[147]

Gender and Justice

Criminal justice has always been mostly a man's world. Men ran the system; and
it was men who did the crimes, especially violent crimes. In 1950 only 3.5
percent of the inmates of adult prisons, federal and state, were women; a quarter
of a century later, the figure was still just 3.6 percent. The rate went up somewhat in the 1990s; women accounted for 5.7 percent of all prisoners in 1990,
and 6.4 percent in 1998, still far below women's share of the population.[148]
Between 1930 and 1973, 3,827 men were executed—and 32 women.[149] After
Gregg v. Georgia (1976), executions of women continued to be very rare. Karla
Tucker, put to death in 1997 in Texas, was only the second woman since 1976 to
die at the hands of the state; her impending execution touched off loud cries of

anguish, and a protest from the pope. She went to her death anyway. Few male executions had created such a fuss.

In the nineteenth century, women intersected with the criminal justice system mostly as victims and witnesses. Their consciousness, their voice, their slant—very little of this percolated into the halls of justice. In the period after the Second World War, this situation changed dramatically: women now voted, they served on juries, and there were, increasingly, women lawyers present; and women judges presiding in the courtroom. Moreover, the women's movement, especially in the 1970s, began to speak out forcefully on areas of law and practice that vitally affected women—notably rape and domestic violence.

One goal of the women's movement was to force or persuade the police to take domestic violence seriously. There is no question that domestic violence is a serious problem. Wife-beating, to be sure, had been a crime in every state—it was a crime to beat up anybody—but the police were reluctant to do much about family matters. Many women who ended up dead had called the police time and time again after awful sessions of abuse from drunk or angry husbands or boyfriends; the police either did not intervene, or intervened only feebly. The police stepped in only as a last resort. Some departments had a "stitch rule": only if the woman needed stitches would there be an arrest; otherwise, the police were just supposed to "break it up," or calm people down.[150] In the 1970s women's groups began opening shelters for battered women. They also agitated for better police work and more protection for women. There were also more women serving as police officers. All this has brought about some changes, in attitude and behavior, among police departments in many parts of the country.

Another significant legal change was the appearance of the "battered woman" defense. Women do not go in for homicide very often; and when they do kill, it is perhaps when they feel trapped in an abusive and hopeless situation. A survey of women in a California prison in the late 1970s found that twenty-nine of thirty women convicted of killing a partner had been abused by the "victim."[151] At about this time, some women on trial began to advance the argument that their violence was really a form of self-defense; and courts began to agree that there was merit to the argument. Of course, no woman before the late twentieth century could have claimed self-defense if she killed her husband or lover, say, in his sleep. In *State v. Norman*, a North Carolina case from 1988, the defendant did exactly this: she shot her sleeping husband to death.[152] She was convicted of the crime, and appealed. The dead man, an abusive alcoholic, had beaten his wife mercilessly, time and again, using "his fist, a fly swatter, a baseball bat, his shoe, or a bottle; he put out cigarettes on defendant's skin; . . . he . . . once smashed a glass in her face." The Court of Appeals of North Carolina ordered a new trial. A jury could well believe that "decedent's sleep was but a momentary hiatus in a continuous reign of terror." If so, there was perhaps enough legal "provocation" to allow the woman to claim that she killed in self-defense.

But why not just run away? Many battered women do: but others, as the court recognized, are afraid to. There is no place to go, and no place to hide—nowhere that a violent, angry, and deadly mate cannot find her and kill her.

No changes in the law were more dramatic than those in the law of rape, one of the most serious (and common) offenses against women. Figures on rape are notoriously hard to come by; many women, for one reason or another, never report that they were raped. There is a sense of shame; and women may dread the publicity and the ordeal they would have to go through. The formal law of rape was, historically, somewhat forbidding. In many states, a woman could not complain of rape unless she resisted with every inch of her strength—an honorable woman, after all, would rather give up her life than her virtue. (At least this is what some judges liked to say.) In 1969 there were 2,415 complaints of rape in New York, 1,085 arrests—and eighteen convictions.[153] Harry Kalven and Hans Zeisel, who studied jury verdicts in the 1960s, found that juries did not take rape very seriously; they had a tendency to let the defendant go free unless the rape was unusually violent, or it was gang-rape, or somehow "aggravated"; "simple" rape tended to go unpunished.[154] What we now call date rape was rarely reported and even more rarely punished. Most rapists were boyfriends—or relatives—of the victim; but this was not the dominant image of rape, or the image that most moved juries.[155]

Moreover, juries were reluctant to convict a man of rape, if they thought the woman "asked for it," which could mean that she wore a short skirt, or hung around bars, or was something other than an unsullied virgin. On top of that, the law allowed the defense to rummage around in the woman's sex life, digging up dirt. Many rape trials, then, became classic cases of trying the victim.

Not that trying the victim is rare in the criminal justice system—or even necessarily a bad thing. After all, in the "battered woman" cases, the defendant's only hope is to try the victim—that is, to put the dead man on trial, blacken his reputation, describe him as a vicious, drunken ape; the dead husband or boyfriend, after all, is not around to defend himself against these charges. But in rape cases, trying the victim had a particularly vicious edge; and it rested on some ancient stereotypes—that an "unchaste woman" has no virtue, and is probably a liar as well; and that a woman who had sex with men before will surely do it again; and in any event, she is not much better than a whore, and a criminal court should not bother to protect or vindicate her bodily integrity.

These attitudes changed dramatically in the last decades of the twentieth century. The women's movement played an important part. Sex and gender roles in the late twentieth century made the old assumptions underlying rape law completely out of date. Virginity and chastity were no longer treated as sacred, to say the least. In the 1970s the states began changing the rules substantially. Almost every state passed a so-called rape shield law, in one form or another. The point was to prevent the defense in a rape case from scrutinizing the victim's sex life. The statutes vary from place to place, and they are far from absolute. They usually let the defendant show that he had had sex with the victim before. Some statutes give the judge wide latitude to admit "relevant" evidence of sexual behavior.[156] Still, for all their faults, these laws reflect improved sensitivity to the rights and the feelings of women.

The old rule, that a woman had to fight her rapist to the death, or close to it, is long since gone. A California court in 1942 called this notion "primitive"; facing a rapist, a woman "need not resist to the point of risking being beaten into insensibility."[157] Did she have to resist at all, physically speaking? Yes, in California (for example), under the statute as it read up to 1980: it was rape only when her "resistance" was "overcome by force or violence." But in 1980 the legislature dropped all reference to resistance: rape was sex imposed against a woman's will, and if she had a reasonable "fear of immediate and unlawful bodily injury," there need not be actual violence.[158]

Still, most states clung to the notion that the crime of rape had to have some element of force, or at least some threat of force. In 1982 a California law defined *consent* as "positive cooperation in act or attitude pursuant to an exercise of free will."[159] A striking New Jersey case (1992) held that any "act of sexual penetration" is a "sexual assault" unless there is "affirmative and freely-given permission."[160] Most courts, however, have been very reluctant to hold flatly and absolutely that no means no. To do so would make sexual intercourse a serious crime unless there was a strong and eager yes.

At common law, a wife could not accuse her own husband of rape, no matter what the circumstances. The rape-reform movement largely put an end to the marital exemption; it survives only in a few recalcitrant states.[161] Modern statutes, too, tend to be gender neutral. Men rape other men, especially in prison—prison rape may be positively epidemic, as we have seen; but this form of rape is even more drastically underreported than the rape of women by men. The stigma is enormous. Raped prisoners also feel that nobody cares, least of all the prison guards, which is probably true; and in most prisons, snitching is a sure way to earn a knife in the back.

Rape statistics are notoriously poor, and always have been, as we have seen. Also, the definition of rape has changed over the years—legally, and, even more significantly, socially as well. As a result, it is extremely difficult to say whether the rape rate is going up, going down, or staying put. It is also hard to say whether the reform laws have had any impact. Michigan's reform law did seem to increase convictions for rape, according to a study published in 1982; but prosecutors still seemed influenced by older ideas—like whether the woman "asked for it."[162]

That rape is a serious problem hardly anybody questions. The most serious and dangerous crimes are acts that take "normal" behavior, accepted behavior, and push it beyond an invisible line. Society allows competition, aggressiveness, strength, forcefulness, ambition; these are highly valued traits, highly rewarded. Society punishes fraud and assault because they cross the invisible line into forbidden territory. Sexual etiquette, historically, called for men to take the lead. Men asked women out on dates; women waited to be asked. Men proposed, women said yes or no. Moreover, men were supposed to be always hungry for sex, always seething with lust, while women were supposed to be coy and resistant; and to have much less appetite for sex. One prosecutor in Michigan put it this way, in 1980: "I feel that there's an obligation for healthy males to do whatever they can with every girl they come across." This behavior, he felt, was acceptable so long as the "healthy male" didn't get too "physical."[163] Men like this are unlikely to change their behavior toward women until they change their attitudes. And because the living law of rape and sexual assault closely tracks the attitudes of men (and women), *it* will change only if and when these attitudes change.

9

Courts, Trials, and Procedures in the Twentieth Century

C ivil procedure is the ugly duckling of law. It is a field only a lawyer can love; and even most lawyers find loving it a struggle. Procedure, in the older common law—the system inherited from England—was a maze, a mess, a tangle of arcane and tricky rules. Pleading—drawing up the papers that would begin a lawsuit—was a science in itself; and a murky and difficult one at that. A lot of this arcane rubbish was swept away in the nineteenth century, though some states were more progressive than others. The so-called Field Code, adopted in New York in 1848, was a famous example of procedural reform. But even in the "code" states, there was plenty of room left for improvement. The twentieth century, in its own right, and in many ways more impressively, was a century dedicated to procedural reform.

What was the problem? The problem was complexity, waste, and injustice. One symptom of the problem was the astonishing number of reported cases that turned not on the merits of the case but on tiny points of procedure or pleading; or even on whether the plaintiff had picked the right court to bring his suit in. "Our system of courts is archaic and our procedure behind the times," wrote Roscoe Pound in 1906. He cited some impressive facts and figures to back up his claim: nearly 20 percent of a sample of Missouri cases in the higher courts of that state turned on "points of appellate procedure." All of this focus on procedure, in his view, was "sheer waste." Missouri was nothing special in this regard; and the federal courts, no less than the state courts, were hardly models of efficiency and rationality.[1]

In New York in 1912 and 1913 the legislature directed the Board of Statutory Consolidation to draft a new civil practice act; in 1920 the legislature enacted a law calling for a convention at which judges and lawyers would meet "to consider and adopt rules of civil practice." The underlying idea was to turn procedure over to an expert, impartial, nonpartisan body of jurists.[2] The result was a set of shiny, new, up-to-date procedural reforms, which took effect in the 1920s. The Illinois Civil Practice Act of 1933 modernized a system which was one of the most archaic in the country.

Beyond a doubt, the climax of the movement for procedural reform was the adoption of the Federal Rules of Civil Procedure in 1938. The federal government had done almost nothing to reform procedure in its courts; the rules were a complex and ramshackle mess. The so-called Conformity Act instructed federal courts to "conform" their practices and procedures, in civil cases, "as near as may be, to the practices, pleadings, and forms and modes of proceedings" of whatever state the federal court happened to be sitting in. The Conformity Act did not apply to equity or admiralty cases—and the federal courts rigorously preserved the distinction between law and equity. The phrase "as near as may be" was also a problem: exactly what did it mean? The result was a messy soup of "conflicting decisions," which clouded the subject of procedure "in hideous confusion and shifting uncertainty."[3]

The movement to reform procedure was perhaps a legal echo of a more general revolt in the law against formalism; and a widespread feeling that law should become less technical, more just, and more efficient. This was an appealing notion for the business community. One proponent of reform, Thomas W. Shelton, put it this way in 1922, speaking to the House Judiciary Committee: it "frequently" happens that a case brought by a "sensible man, a businessman, a practical business man," gets "thrown out on a technicality"; this, according to Shelton, in something of a stretch, is "one of the things that is making Bolshevists in this country."[4]

The deformities of civil procedure were probably not producing many Bolsheviks; but there was nonetheless pressure on Congress to make some changes. In 1934 Congress passed an Enabling Act, which authorized the Supreme Court to "prescribe by general rules . . . the forms of process, writs, pleadings and motions, and the practice and procedure" in civil cases in federal courts.[5] Charles E. Clark, dean of the Yale Law School and an expert on procedure, was appointed reporter of the Supreme Court Advisory Committee—the body that actually wrote the rules. Clark's philosophy was simple and direct: procedure was a means to an end, nothing more. Old technicalities merely clogged the pipes. Clark wanted the rules to be clear, flexible, uncluttered, but definite enough to be workable. One senses the influence of the legal realist movement, perhaps even of progressivism; certainly of a general belief in progress, in the evolution of law (like everything else) from lower to higher, from primitive to modern. And the days of the New Deal were the perfect background and climate for this movement of legal reform.

Clark was an expert on nineteenth-century procedural reforms, on code practice, the Field Code, and the like. One of the chief aims and accomplishments of the Field Code had been to merge law and equity. English law, which was notoriously complicated, had over the centuries evolved not one but two quite separate systems of law. "Law" (the common law proper) was the indigenous system. But side by side with it was a quite different system, "equity," with its own courts, its own procedures, its own rules. Equity, as the name suggests, started out as a corrective to the common law, which was rather austere, rigid, and formalistic. Equity courts could modify or bend stubborn rules of the common law which sometimes worked injustice. But equity developed, in time, its own brand of rigor mortis; it was equity and its courts of Chancery that Dickens flayed alive in *Bleak House*.

Equity had a strong dash of Continental (civil) law in its makeup. Equity cases never went before a jury. Equity preferred written documents to oral testimony. But equity did have a powerful battery of procedural remedies—the injunction, for example—that the common law lacked. These remedies, at least potentially, gave equity a power and suppleness that the common law could only dream about.

The Field Code melded the two systems into one. Gone was the system of two separate courts, with different criteria—a system that forced the poor plaintiff to choose or to guess which court to try; and woe unto him if he made a mistake. When the systems were spliced together, "equitable" remedies were imported wholesale into the surviving unisystem. As we have seen, this happened in New York before 1850; certain other states either merged law and equity—this was one of the results of the Illinois reforms of 1933—or never had separate systems in the first place. In the federal courts, however, law and equity were distinct and unmerged well into the twentieth century. The new Federal Rules blended the two systems. As in the Field Code, the broad, flexible procedures and remedies of equity (many of them embodied in the Federal Equity Rules of 1912) were given pride of place over common-law pleadings. The common-law ideal had been to frame and refine a single issue; to limit the domain of the dispute, perhaps rather narrowly—and rather technically. The equity ideal had been different: it was to cast a broad net, to employ all sorts of techniques of evidence and remedy, in order to reach a just result. This was Clark's goal. Consequently, in the federal rules, as Stephen Subrin has put it, "equity had swallowed common law."[6]

The federal rules were hailed on their adoption in 1938 as a great advance on the past. The rules owed almost nothing to the text of the Field Code, but they rested on similar premises. Niceties of pleading were abolished. The plaintiff was supposed to set out "a short and plain statement" of his claim, and to tell exactly what he wanted by way of relief; the defense was also to be "short and plain." Every aspect of pleading was to be "simple, concise, and direct."

The federal rules, like rules of procedure in general, may seem like boring and arcane stuff, interesting only to specialists with peculiar tastes. But some of the rules had rather wide implications. For example, rules 26–37 were about depositions and "discovery." Under rule 34, any party to a lawsuit, on "showing good cause," could ask for an order from the court to inspect and copy "any designated documents, papers, books, accounts, letters, photographs, objects, or tangible things," which "constitute or contain evidence" for the case.

"Discovery" was an old equity practice. So was the notion of taking depositions (or submitting written questions to the other side, through "interrogatories"). Here they got new life. Discovery became more and more important. At its worst, discovery and similar practices permit wildly expensive and inefficient fishing expeditions, letting one party rummage about in the files, documents, and working papers of his enemy; or pestering corporate officers and employees with endless rounds of depositions. At its best, they make for more streamlined and efficient trials—trials without surprises or waste motion. Or they may lead to a situation in which both sides learn enough to realize they had better settle their dispute out of court.

Discovery was part of a trend in which pretrial proceedings—those things lawyers do before a trial begins—started to overshadow the trial itself. Rule 16 of the federal rules, indeed, gave the court power to order both sides to come together in court for a "conference." Here they would consider, under the judge's prodding, how to simplify the issues, how to streamline the proceedings, and any "other matters as may aid in the disposition of the action." All of this goes along with an emphasis on "diversion," on avoiding trials, on settlement, negotiation, mediation—anything to avoid the old-fashioned courtroom battle. Plenty of these battles remain; but they are survivors, die-hard or uncompromisable claims, that resist all efforts to forestall or to settle or divert. Even for these cases, the phase of discovery and deposition may be as important as what happens before judge and jury, or more so.

The classic trial, at least as it was pictured, was a battle between two tricksters, or a contest between two silver-tongued orators. It was open, oral, dramatic, full of twists and turns. Daniel Webster was the beau ideal of the nineteenth-century lawyer. The modern business lawyer is a problem solver, not an orator; even litigators prefer to keep clients out of trouble. Litigation is trouble. Going to court at all is an admission of failure of sorts. The best lawyers would rather vaccinate than cure a disease.

Not that the trial is dead; far from it. Indeed, it has had something of a rebirth since 1975: more effort goes into litigation in law-firms than was true before then. And the twentieth century produced some new, startling, significant ways of making and handling lawsuits. Rule 23 of the federal rules dealt with so-called class actions—lawsuits brought in the name of a whole class. It rested on an earlier Equity Rule (number 38), but broadened its scope.[7] In 1966 rule 23 was thoroughly revamped. One or more persons could bring an action on behalf of a whole class of people if there were "questions of law or fact common to the class," and if the people who brought the suit were in a position to protect the interests, and speak for the interests, of the whole class.

This new rule 23 is a powerful beast because, as Stephen Yeazell has put it, it creates "litigative power"; under rule 23, "claims by unorganized groups" can be presented "as if they were those of organizations."[8] If thousands of people feel that they were cheated out of a few dollars each by a bank or a conniving retail chain, a class-action suit can be brought on behalf of this class. If a woman worker thinks that her company, a giant enterprise, discriminates against women (and against her), she can bring a claim on behalf of herself—and on behalf of all the other women who work at her place. The great mass tort cases are class actions. Civil rights cases are often class actions.

Class-action cases are complicated and difficult. There is the problem of defining the class. There is the problem of keeping all the members, or potential members, informed; and giving them a chance to come in, or stay out. There is the problem of the dissenter: people who disapprove and refuse to join; and people who prefer to go it alone. Class-action cases can be a gold mine for the lawyers who manage them—assuming they win. A lawyer "whose work produces a recovery benefiting a class" can earn a juicy fee if the aggregate recovery, the "common fund," is large.[9] There are lawyers who specialize in class actions; and some who specialize in smoking out *possible* class actions. It is claimed (by those on the losing end) that unscrupulous lawyers scrape together classes out of nothing, simply to line their own pockets. From the very start, businesses have hated and feared class actions. It was a monster; and it was growing fast. Perhaps they exaggerated; but the number of class actions did, apparently, increase, and "at a dramatic rate," after 1966.[10]

An open window lets in bugs as well as fresh air. It is a question which is more important. Class actions are group cases, but they are (paradoxically) fueled by the spirit of the age, a spirit of individualism and rights consciousness. Litigation in late-twentieth-century America became a political and economic instrument, a tool, a locus for strategic behavior. The class action was an important way to involve courts in battles over civil rights, corporate governance, protecting the environment, and consumer protection. And class action is central in the society of "total justice." Class actions depend on quirks and accidents of procedural history, and the peculiarities of the American legal order—many legal systems have no such beast as the class action at all. But the class action has long since transcended its origins. It grew fat on the fodder of late-twentieth-century culture.

The State Court Systems

As we have seen, there was reform action in the states even before the adoption of the federal rules in 1938. After 1938 the federal rules proved extremely seductive as models. Arizona adopted them, essentially, in 1939, Colorado in 1942, New Mexico in 1943. At least half of the states eventually made the federal rules their own, or modified their local rules under its powerful influence.

The state systems remain, however, quite diverse—both as to rules of procedure, and (very much) in terms of court structure. Little Delaware still has a "chancery court," administering rules of "equity"—this living fossil continues to exist more than a century after the Field Code merged law and equity in New York, and more than fifty years after the adoption of the federal rules. Indeed, it would be wrong to label this court as a quaint and harmless vestige. Hundreds of huge corporations are chartered in Delaware; and many issues of corporation law, for historical reasons, go before the courts of chancery. Hence the chancery, in this tiny and powerless state, has an influence far beyond what one might expect.

Many states, however, revamped their court systems during the twentieth century. For one thing, many states went from a two-tier to a three-tier system.[11] Population growth made this seem like an absolute necessity. In a state with a small population, like Idaho, appeals go directly from trial court to supreme court; and every loser at trial can bring an appeal. This system would be impossible in New York or Texas or California. As their populations grew, more states added another level of courts—intermediate appellate courts. California took this step early in the century, as we have seen. In North Carolina the state supreme court wrote 473 opinions in 1967. Then the state created a tier of intermediate appellate courts, and gave the supreme court power over its docket. In 1969 and 1970 the North Carolina Supreme Court averaged fewer than one hundred opinions—but they were twice as long as before; and dissents and reversals were also more frequent.[12]

These were on one level purely structural changes. But they may have had a deeper impact. They gave top courts more power to control what they heard; now they could turn down most appeals, and consider only those cases they considered truly significant. What they defined as truly significant, of course, changed over the years. They reflected social norms the judges were probably hardly aware of. Criminal cases and constitutional cases tended to gain a bigger share of the dockets. Did the structural change affect the self-image of high courts? Possibly. It reinforced the notion that they were important institutions; tribunals that handled society's tough cases, and only the toughest and the hardest at that.

Adding another tier of courts was an important reform. But it was hardly all that was called for. Well into the twentieth century, some of the state court systems were badly in need of reorganization. A textbook case was New Jersey. Its court system in 1930 was described as a "hydraheaded monster of confusion for litigants and a legal maze for lawyers."[13] New Jersey still had courts of equity. It had a flock of special courts, with functions that overlapped in a mystifying way; some cases bounced from court to court, as if the real question in the case was not one of justice, but of which door to go in and come out of. Arthur T. Vanderbilt, lawyer, and chairman of the New Jersey Judicial Council, ABA activist, worked tirelessly for reform. A new reform constitution went down to defeat in 1944; but in 1947 it was adopted overwhelmingly by public vote; and Vanderbilt became the first chief justice of New Jersey under the new constitution, and head of the streamlined system of courts.[14]

Decades of reform have resulted in procedural systems which, on paper at least, are far more rational than anything in the nineteenth century. Yet hundreds of cases still turn on points of procedure and appellate review, questions of jurisdiction, and the like. In a court-centered legal system, this may be in some ways inevitable. "Rationality" may not be a realistic goal. Technicality is a nuisance. But it also can be, and often is, a protective device. This is most obvious in criminal trials. Before you can send a man to his death or put a woman in prison for twenty years, you had better dot every i and cross every t. This is, at least, the ideal; and abuses, which are real and pervasive, come from slapdash procedures more often than from the opposite, the coddling of crooks (despite what the public thinks).

Procedure is also a way of keeping a political struggle alive. Many cases turn on points of procedure, because litigants have no other bullets left in their gun. If you lose at the trial-court level, or if an administrative agency issues a ruling against your interests, you may want to appeal. But on what grounds? An appeal court, under our system, does not hear evidence. It does not try a case again. You can appeal only by arguing that the court below, or the agency, made some sort of "error"; and the error has to be an error of law—very often, some mistake of procedure, a mistake in letting in bad evidence, keeping good evidence out, a misstatement of law by the judge, or a violation of the agency's own internal rules.

For this reason, controversial subjects, in our system, tend to become proceduralized. There is no other way. The people on death row (rather, their lawyers) fight for years and years on one technicality or another; only occasionally do they have a chance to claim innocence; for the most part their struggle is a struggle dressed up in procedural disguise. Big environmental cases, huge administrative cases—cases in which billions may be at stake—often turn on points of administrative procedure. And at least partly because of this, *within* the agencies the steps and processes are highly technical. Every step of the way is difficult. Each action has to be exactly right, procedurally.

Robert Kagan has described, in painful detail, the saga of the Port of Oakland, in San Francisco Bay, and its plans to deepen its harbor. This was a badly needed move to modernize the port. The plans were initiated in the 1970s. In 1986 the Army Corps of Engineers issued an Environmental Impact Statement. It called for dredging, and had a scheme for getting rid of the dredged-up sands. Environmental groups were unhappy. State and local regulatory agencies objected to the dumping site. More impact statements. More tests. More plans. In 1988 the Half Moon Bay Fishermen's Marketing Association sued to stop the latest plan—calling for dumping in the Pacific Ocean. The federal courts turned the association down. One day of dredging actually took place. But then a state court judge, in another lawsuit, decided to call a halt to the dredging: the California Coastal Commission had not issued the necessary certification. More moves and countermoves. Finally, a plan was approved—after eight years of wrangling. The port was dredged, finally, in 1995.[15]

That agencies and courts sometimes do pay attention to small points of procedure—that they decide on "technicalities"—does not mean that the judges and administrators are petty sticklers for detail. They simply reflect the same kind of social ambivalence that underlies, say, environmental cases (shall we save jobs, or save nature?), or capital punishment cases (victims' rights versus defendants' rights). The Oakland harbor needed dredging—nobody argued it did not. But how, and where, and what to do with the debris? These were controversial questions; and controversies, in the main, tend to wear procedural dress: this step was wrong, this kind of notice not given, this hearing was mistaken, this certificate never issued, and so on.

American procedures are complicated—but relatively transparent. Everybody is invited to have their say. The process works well in some cases. All interests get represented. But the costs (of all sorts) are high. The procedures are surrogates for other, deeper issues; and the use of the procedures is deeply rooted in American legal culture. For these reasons, procedure is difficult, if not impossible to reform. And a clean, surgical, no-fuss procedural regime is probably not within our grasp—and not only because we do not know how to design one on the drawing board.

Jurisdiction of the Federal Courts

The United States, from the very beginning, had a double system: state courts and federal courts. Most cases went to state courts. Federal courts decided federal issues—issues under the federal Constitution, or under some federal statute, or concerning the territories; some areas of law (bankruptcy, admiralty, copyright and patent) were, under the Constitution, specifically handed over to the federal courts. The main area of overlap was in so-called diversity cases (cases in which a New Yorker, say, sued someone from Delaware: that is, cases between citizens of different states). But the federal courts were not supposed to hear petty cases. There was a jurisdictional floor, expressed in terms of money. At the turn of the century, the "matter in controversy" had to be worth two thousand dollars; it went up to three thousand in 1911; it jumped to ten thousand in 1958, then to fifty thousand in 1988; since 1996 it has been seventy-five thousand dollars.[16]

The theory behind diversity jurisdiction was simple. The framers of the Constitution were afraid that a New York resident who sued a Delaware resident in New York's local courts would have an unfair home-court advantage. Was this true? People certainly thought so. In railroad accident cases, for example—and there were thousands of these—the mangled victims were eager to try cases in state courts, where friendly hometown folks would sit on the jury. Railroad corporations, for their part, were just as eager to "remove" the case to the federal courts. These courts were often farther away; and they were more expensive, which was in itself a valuable way to wear a plaintiff down. The two sides battled over this issue of jurisdiction in hundreds of cases in the first third of the twentieth century. State jurisdiction was therefore important to some accident victims; in fact, some were willing to scale down their claims, so that they were less than the federal minimum, in order to keep the railroad from dragging them over into federal court.[17]

The End of Federal Common Law

Whatever else the New Deal accomplished, it focused power and attention on Washington, on the central government. As the federal government grew, so did the significance of the federal courts. Yet in one important way, the federal courts in the 1930s gave up an important wellspring of power and autonomy. In 1938 the Supreme Court overruled *Swift v. Tyson*—a case almost a century old.[18]

Under the *Swift* doctrine (1842), federal courts in diversity cases had the right to ignore the common-law decisions of the state they were sitting in; they could decide according to their own, federal common law.[19] The early cases—and the *Swift* case itself—concerned commercial law. A strong tradition insisted that the basic rules of commercial law were not local anyway; rather, they rested on an international body of customary law, built up by merchants and traders. The *Swift* doctrine, however, began to expand beyond commercial law cases. How far it should go was a matter of dispute, and a source of considerable confusion.

Critics of *Swift*—and there were many of them—had a list of horror stories to tell. One of their favorites was *Black and White Taxicab and Transfer Company v. Brown and Yellow Taxicab and Transfer Company* (1928).[20] The Black and White cabs, operating in Kentucky, entered into an unholy alliance with a Kentucky railroad. Black and White would get a monopoly of the business at the depot in Bowling Green. Unfortunately, this kind of arrangement was illegal in Kentucky. What to do? Black and White dissolved itself, reincorporated in Tennessee, and went ahead with the deal; it then sued in federal court to throw the Brown and Yellow people out of the depot business. Federal law (unlike Kentucky law), the company insisted, allowed this kind of exclusive deal. And Black and White won. The Supreme Court refused to ask about the "motives" that led the cab company to get itself chartered in Tennessee. The Kentucky rule was contrary to general common-law "principles"; and the federal courts did not have to follow it.

Scholars, and (increasingly) judges found this kind of result totally obnoxious. Finally, in the famous case of *Erie Railroad Co. v. Tompkins* (1938), the Supreme Court reversed itself, discarded *Swift v. Tyson* (after ninety-six years!), and put state law back in the saddle.[21]

As often, a big legal change came out of rather humdrum facts. *Erie* was the tragic but all too familiar case of man against machine. An unemployed worker, Harry James Tompkins, twenty-seven, was walking home, in Hughestown, Pennsylvania, on a path near the Eric's railroad tracks. As a train passed by, something on the train—a door, perhaps—smashed into Tompkins and knocked him down. He was found unconscious on the ground, his right arm cut off and lying next to him.

Tompkins recovered from his injuries, as best he could; and sued the railroad. Did he have a case? Under Pennsylvania law, probably not: technically, he had been trespassing at the time of the accident. The railroad, under Pennsylvania law, owed no particular duty of care to trespassers; so long as the railroad had not been "wantonly negligent," a trespasser had no right to recover damages for any injury. But Tompkins's lawyers took the case to federal court. Under the rule of *Swift v. Tyson,* the federal courts could ignore Pennsylvania law and come to their own conclusion. At the trial the jury returned a verdict for Tompkins, and awarded him thirty thousand dollars. But Tompkins, alas, was never to see this money. The Supreme Court seized on poor Tompkins's case as the occasion to get rid of *Swift v. Tyson,* once and for all.

Justice Brandeis wrote the majority opinion. Experience, he said, had revealed many defects in the *Swift* line of cases. These cases were supposed to produce uniformity—to smooth out bumps and idiosyncracies in the law, as applied in different states. But the line of cases after *Swift* did nothing of the sort. Rather, they sowed confusion. Nobody knew, or could know, what the "general law" was, or when the federal courts were likely to apply it. *Swift* also led to an anomalous situation: out-of-state claimants and in-state claimants had different rights and duties; and too much turned on which court you chose to sue in. For these reasons, *Swift* had to go. The federal courts, in all diversity cases, would be bound to follow the common-law rules of the states in which they sat. This was, indeed, the new conformity.

The case caused a sensation among lawyers and judges, and its fame has lasted to this day. The language of the case was in part technical, in part based on jurisprudential ideas. But as Edward A. Purcell, Jr., has persuasively argued, there was a deeper political meaning to the case—a meaning Brandeis actively pursued.[22] The federal courts in 1938 were still considered bastions of conservatism—famous for issuing injunctions against strikes, and looking at social legislation with a bleary eye. Brandeis meant to restore power to states and to legislatures. His goals were the goals of progressivism. Ironically, to reach these goals, he had to shut the door on poor Tompkins with his severed arm.

Erie had a profound, immediate effect on the federal courts. Hundreds of cases each year applied the doctrine. The federal courts were now, in effect, subordinate to state courts in common-law matters—even to lower state courts. Difficult legal questions arose under *Erie:* suppose there is no state decision? or suppose the state courts have a muddled and inconsistent line of cases? But on the whole, *Erie* sank deep roots into the system; there was never any thought of going back.

How much power did *Erie* give back to the states? Probably not very much. First of all, it made a difference only if federal common law diverged from state common law; and this was not the usual case. And it applied only to "diversity" cases. These are hardly rare; but they are not the heart of the federal caseload. For the year ending September 30, 1980, federal district courts disposed of about 160,000 cases; a quarter of these were diversity cases, about evenly split between cases of contract and of tort.[23] For the year ending March 31, 1999, these same courts disposed of 270,000 or so cases; 65,000 of these were diversity cases, most of them personal injury suits.[24] So much of the law is statutory, and so much litigation turns on federal questions, that the significance of *Erie,* though real enough, is not at the heart of federal decision making.

The federal courts are still minority courts—most of the business goes on in state courts. But the volume of their work has steadily increased; and (though this is hard to measure) so too of their share of significant cases. Like the state courts, the nature of their dockets has changed. We have data for the Courts of Appeals since 1925. In the period 1925–1936, criminal cases were 11.8 percent, civil liberties cases 0.5 percent, civil rights cases 1.2 percent; the rest were "economic" cases (government contracts, diversity cases, and so on). For the period 1970–1988, however, 32.3 percent were criminal cases, 5 percent civil liberties cases, and 13.5 percent civil rights cases; the "economic" cases had fallen to just under one-half.[25] Of course, these figures do not tell the whole story—one huge antitrust case may outweigh dozens of prisoner petitions—but they do suggest the rising importance of cases growing out of the civil rights revolution and other trends of the second half of the century.

Trial by Jury

The jury in civil cases is something of a stepchild as far as the public is concerned. It gets little or no attention. Books, plays, movies, and TV endlessly parade the criminal jury before us. The civil jury works in the shadows. Yet paradoxically, the criminal jury is not controversial. Nobody talks about getting rid of it. It is a constitutional right. The civil jury, on the other hand, *is* controversial; and has been so, for most of the past century.

This is, in large part, because of personal-injury and similar cases. The charge is that the civil jury has a deep-seated prejudice against defendants, who are usually companies, and in favor of plaintiffs, who are usually just plain people. Edson Sunderland, writing in 1915, thought that the judge should play a stronger role in civil cases. He should act as "a real adviser" to the jury. That might get rid of the tricks, the artifices, the "appeals to passion, sympathy, and prejudice."[26] In fact, judges have always had a great deal of control. Judges who considered a case too weak to go before the jury could simply dismiss the case. This happened quite frequently in tort cases. In 1910, according to Randolph Bergstrom's figures for New York City, the trial judge threw out some 16 percent of the personal-injury cases; another 21 percent were dismissed for "plaintiff's lack of prosecution, or default."[27] Even cases that went all the way were hardly automatic victories for the plaintiff. Charles E. Clark and Harry Shulman's sample of Connecticut cases in the late 1920s shows this dramatically. Of 233 cases tried before a jury, the plaintiff won 137, the defendant 95. In negligence cases—where juries are supposed to be so proplaintiff—plaintiffs won 94 cases and lost 63. This hardly suggests blind prejudice.[28]

Civil trial by jury had, in any event, a declining share of the time and attention of the system. In the twentieth century, trial by jury touched bottom. In the Clark and Shulman study, in New Haven and Waterbury, Connecticut, between 1919 and 1932, fewer than 4 percent of the civil cases went to a jury.[29] In 1994–1995 in North Carolina, 4.2 percent of the civil cases went to trial by jury. In the huge state of California in 1991–1992, there were only about ten thousand jury trials; they amounted to 1.7 percent of total dispositions in the regular trial courts. This figure included criminal cases; only 1.8 percent of the personal-injury cases went to the jury.[30]

The jury of 1900 was a rather different beast from the jury of 2000. To begin with, it looked different. No women served on it, for example. This was by law. In the South, no blacks served on the jury—not by law, but by "custom" (often backed up by force, real or implied). There was also a somewhat different theory of selection. In Kentucky, to take one instance, a juror was supposed to be a "housekeeper, sober, temperate, discreet and of good demeanor."[31] In Maine, municipal officers drew up the jury lists. Selection was hardly random: jurors had to be men of "good moral character, of sound judgment and well informed."[32] By law, in Connecticut, men "esteemed in their community" were supposed to make up the jury.[33] Under the New York Code of Civil Procedure, early in the century, the jurors in New York City were required to be "intelligent."[34] The code did not offer a definition of the term. As one New York judge put it (in a criminal case), it was important to get smart, honest men on the jury, people who read newspapers—and to keep out the "ignorant classes."[35] Alabama vested power in jury commissioners (three per county, appointed by the governor), who (as of the 1920s) were required to list, in a "well bound book," all "male citizens . . . who are generally reputed to be honest and intelligent men, and are esteemed in the community for their integrity, good character and sound judgment."[36] Needless to say, no black man ever met this description. In New York a court could order a "special" jury for "intricate" or important cases—and these juries were heavily weighted with businessmen and professionals. Women, laborers, and service personnel rarely appeared. The Supreme Court upheld the practice in 1947.[37]

In many states, in other words, the jury had a blue-ribbon flavor, either explicitly or otherwise. Nobody could quarrel with the general principle that jurors should have a decent stock of brains. But the system certainly opened the door to class bias, if nothing else.

Oddly enough, despite the blue-ribbon tilt of jury laws, state laws in the first part of the century lavishly exempted whole classes of people from jury duty. In Illinois, for example, in 1921, the list started with the governor and went all the way down the ladder of government to local officials and schoolteachers. The exempt list also included lawyers, ministers of the gospel, "constant ferry-men," police, pharmacists, firemen, embalmers and undertakers, and people who worked for newspapers. North Carolina added to the usual suspects "millers of grist mills," brakemen and pilots, and members of the North Carolina National Guard. Virginia threw in "all persons while actually engaged in harvest or securing grain or hay or in cutting or securing tobacco," not to mention the six "lock keepers of the Dismal Swamp Canal Co."[38] Rich and powerful people, in any event, had ways of wriggling out of jury duty. Jurors, in short, probably tended to be the middling sort: not vagrants or ditchdiggers, but skilled workers, small merchants, and the like.

In the late twentieth century, the trend ran strongly in the other direction; the exemptions shrank to almost nothing—in Iowa, for example, you could get yourself excused if you were "solely responsible for the daily care of a person with a permanent disability," or were the "mother of a breastfed child"; but that was just about it.[39] Presumably, even the governor would have to serve, if called. Of course, people still find ways to get themselves off the jury; but on paper at least the system is more egalitarian. It is certainly more diverse: women serve equally with men, and the all-white juries of the South have disappeared.

The rise of what we have called plural equality has had an impact on jury selection, as it has on almost everything else. There has been a shift in the theory of the jury in the latter part of the century. The jury is no longer a blue-ribbon panel. Now it is supposed to be diverse—representing the community in all its many forms and guises. Courts have never gone so far as to say that the jury must reflect the class composition of the community. Race, gender, and ethnicity, however, are significant. Underlying the new jury is a kind of pop version of postmodernism. There is no such thing as objective truth. There is white truth and black truth and Asian truth and Hispanic truth. There is male truth and female truth. Probably there is young truth and old truth, and rich truth and poor truth, too. If not truth, then at least point of view. In any event, ideas along these lines are at least implicit in the thinking of millions of people—whether or not they have ever heard of postmodernism or the social construction of reality or similar theories.

The Law of Evidence

Alexis de Tocqueville thought that the jury, especially the civil jury, was a school for politics and democracy in America. The jury is important, granted; its actual impact on society, though, is a difficult and open question. On one point, however, there can be no doubt: the jury has a massive impact on the law. It is thanks almost entirely to the jury that we have a huge, lumbering body of doctrine and practice called the law of evidence.

The law of evidence in the United States is probably the most complex, maddening, and rule-bound in the entire world. John Henry Wigmore (1863–1943), the great master of this lush and flamboyant field, produced a vast treatise on the subject; the first edition, running to a mere four volumes, appeared in 1904–1905. A second edition, in five volumes, came out in 1923; the third edition, in 1940, had swollen to ten volumes; and the current (fourth) edition, still carrying Wigmore's name, and perhaps guided by his spirit from the afterworld, runs to eleven volumes, not to mention supplements.

Why all this lore, all these decisions, statutes, distinctions, doctrines? Why so much controversy over what kind of facts, testimonies, documents, exhibits, and the like, can be "admitted into evidence"? Wigmore put it succinctly: the whole system "is based on the purpose of saving the jurors from being misled." It is there solely because of the jury's "inexperience in analyzing evidence, and their unfamiliarity with the chicanery of counsel."[40] A trained judge would not need all these rules; and, indeed, the law of evidence in systems that lack a jury is short, sweet, and clear.

Not so in American law. Everybody who watches trials on TV or in the movies is familiar with the rituals: one lawyer tries to sneak in some damning piece of evidence, the other lawyer leaps up and cries out, in wounded dignity, "objection"; and the judge overrules or sustains. The rules are strict; they encourage lawyers, therefore, to find some artful dodges to get around the rules; or to shoehorn into the courtroom, and into the tender ears of the jury, bits of fact and opinion that strictly speaking are verboten. The other side will of course object. Even when the judge says, "objection overruled," that does not necessarily end the matter. If the lawyer who objected loses her case, she can, after all, appeal the case, and try to put the objection to good use. That means persuading a higher court that the trial judge made a mistake; and that the case must be shipped back down to be tried again. But not every error is a "reversible error"—an error serious enough to influence the jury. There is also "harmless error," and the appeals court must decide which is which. American courts (said Wigmore) were far too prone to reverse for the "most trifling error," a practice he called a superstitious relic, a useless piece of "technical trumpery."[41]

The common-law system is also extremely keen on the spoken word. It likes testimony—testimony in open court, in the form of questions and answers. (Most European systems are far less interested in talk, and "procedure tends to become primarily a written matter"—that is, a matter of documents.[42]) And it assigns an enormous value to cross-examination. Indeed, the point of the famous "hearsay rule," perhaps the most elaborate rule in the arsenal of the law of evidence, is exactly this: if at all possible, we should be able to quiz a witness directly. We do not want a witness to say that Joe said this or Mary said that; we want Joe or Mary to say it themselves, so that they can be grilled on the stand by the other side.

Of course, this formulation hardly does justice to the hearsay rule, which is not in fact a single rule, but a whole cluster of rules; it is a jumble of rules, a crazyquilt of rules. Or rather, it expresses a tendency, a general proposition, but that proposition comes encumbered with dozens of exceptions, some of them extremely broad, some fairly narrow. Indeed, in the big treatises on evidence, there are probably more pages about hearsay and its exceptions than about anything else; Wigmore spends hundreds and hundreds of pages on the subject. Recent cases and statutes have nibbled about the edges of the rule—and added more exceptions—but the core remains amazingly firm.

Still, the law of evidence has not been immune to change and reform. It is a reform even to try to reduce the rules to a code, and make it more knowable and accessible. California codified its rules in the 1960s. The federal rules of evidence were an incoherent mess until 1975, when Congress codified them. Many states adopted the new federal rules for their own use, though sometimes in modified form.

Reforms in the substance of the law of evidence go mainly in one direction: toward making the rules less strict, toward letting more evidence in. Until late in the nineteenth century, for example, the parties to a lawsuit—the people most intimately involved—were (believe it or not) simply not allowed to testify. When the rule was abolished, an important vestige remained, in the form of so-called dead man's statutes. If I had a business deal with a man who then died, and I sued his estate, I was not allowed to testify about that deal. Scholars denounce this exception as another archaic leftover; but it stubbornly survives in most states. A few, however, have abolished it (Arizona, California), and others have cut it down considerably.

At common law, husband and wife were not allowed to testify, for or against each other. This was another rule that has gone by the boards, usually by statute. The Supreme Court swept it away for federal courts in 1933; a man named Funk was on trial on a Prohibition charge; he wanted his wife to testify for him; the trial court refused. The Supreme Court called the rule "outworn and antiquated" and put it to sleep.[43]

This was a rule about competency—rules about who is and who is not forbidden to testify. Rules of competency must not be confused with rules about privilege. Funk wanted his wife to get on the stand and help him out; if he wanted to keep her off the stand, he had that right, as part of his marital privilege. Pillow talk between spouses is privileged; and so is what a client says to his lawyer. What about sins confessed to a priest, minister, or rabbi? These were not privileged at common law. In Minnesota in 1931, Gladys Sundseth sued husband Arnold for divorce. She said he was an adulterer, and to prove it, she wanted to call the Rev. Emil Swenson, a Lutheran clergyman. Arnold, she believed, had sobbingly confessed his sins. Swenson refused to talk, and was held in contempt; but the Minnesota Supreme Court reversed. People who seek "spiritual advice" should be able to do it without fear that a confession will come back to haunt the confessor in court.[44] Other states granted the privilege by statute.

Most witnesses are literally witnesses: they saw, with their own two eyes, something relevant to the case. But in many trials, there is important testimony by people who had nothing to do with the case: testimony by "experts." Doctors, engineers, fingerprint and handwriting analysts, forensic psychiatrists, economists—all of them have paraded before judges and juries, peddling their informed opinions. In many trials, there are experts on both sides, often (or usually) contradicting each other. Experts may testify, under the law, only on subjects where a layperson cannot be expected to form an intelligent judgment. This is hardly, as you can imagine, a rule with crystal clear boundaries. And this is a society full of skepticism about experts. A society where the battle between evolution and "creation science" still rages is not a society that defers blindly to experts (compared, say, with most European countries).

And who exactly is an expert? The world is full of quacks and pseudo-scientists, peddling "junk science." Many of them have their corps of true believers. What is good science, and what is bad? In a case in the District of Columbia in 1923, one James Alphonso Frye was on trial for murder. He wanted to bring in an expert to testify about the "systolic blood pressure deception test." This was a kind of lie-detector test which showed (Frye said) that Frye was innocent. The court refused. Expert testimony has to be based on science which has "gained general acceptance." The "systolic blood pressure deception test" had not crossed this line, and it was perfectly legitimate to exclude it.[45] Fringe science was out.

This was not an easy rule to apply; and it was also a controversial rule. It did not stop plaintiffs from parading their own versions of junk science into court, whenever they could. In court, "science" turned out, often enough, to be a battle between experts. "Adversary science" is a far cry from what scientists consider real science. Trials become "orgies of deconstruction," in which (at times) good scientists unraveled and decomposed on the stand, under withering cross-examination.[46]

Yet in theory, at least, the *Frye* rule lasted, more or less, for seventy years. It was abandoned in an important case in 1993, *Daubert v. Merrell Dow*.[47] Young Jason Daubert was born with severe deformities; his parents sued Merrell Dow, a drug company. They claimed that a drug, Bendectin, which Jason's mother had taken for morning sickness, caused these physical deficiencies. Millions of women had used this drug; whether it caused deformities was subject to debate. (The company did, however, yank it from the market in 1983.) The lower (federal) court heard from one Dr. Steven Lamm, who reported on some thirty scientific studies, none of which found Bendectin guilty of causing deformities.

Not to be outdone, the plaintiff tried to bring in eight experts to argue the opposite. The court, citing *Frye,* refused to allow these "experts" to testify. Their point of view was not part of the scientific consensus; their studies did not have the benefit of peer review, and so on. The Supreme Court reversed. Scientific evidence was admissible so long as it was scientific and would "assist the trier of fact." The test of "general acceptance" was no longer the law. Peer review and consensus and all of that were certainly relevant; but they were not absolutely controlling.

On one level, *Daubert* was simply a reading of texts—an interpretation of words in the new Federal Rules of Evidence (1975). Nothing in the rules demanded that the court stick with the *Frye* test. But it might not be too far-fetched to read a deeper meaning into *Daubert.* It put in legal form the skepticism and pluralism of the 1990s. These fit the *Daubert* rule much more than they fit the rule of *Frye.* Of course, science is still a kind of god. But especially in the 1990s, it had become more like a Greek god than almighty God; it has its sphere and its limits, and it is all too human. Millions of people believe in astrology, millions are open to alternative medicine, everything from acupuncture and holistic medicine, to ginseng root; it is an age which, when it wants to, doubts the ultimate truth of any consensus, including the consensus labeled "science." Of course, the *Daubert* rule also put more power into the hands of the judges—an unintended but important consequence.

The Practice of Judging: Appellate Opinion

In a rather well-known essay on judging, Karl Llewellyn introduced the idea of "period style." Judges in the late nineteenth century, he argued, used what he called "formal" style. Their opinions were dry, legalistic, mechanical. They rested exclusively on purely legal logic; their opinions never cited broad principle or discussed the social context.

Of course, this does not mean that the judges thought this way (that is, using strict, dry legal logic); but this was the way they framed their decisions. Llewellyn contrasted this style with another, which he called "grand style." This was the style of the great judges of the first half of the nineteenth century: men like John Marshall or James Kent. They were not formal and hidebound; they tested their outcomes against "principles" and considerations of policy and the public good. In Llewellyn's (optimistic) view, a new style was emerging by the 1930s or so—a "style of reason," less formalistic, more willing to use "sense in the remodeling of doctrine."[48]

"Style" is difficult to measure. Most legal scholars feel, intuitively, that courts *have* changed in the twentieth century. Opinions are more personal, more individual; judges are less likely to hide their feelings behind a mask of legal logic; they are more likely to write dissents and concurrences; more willing to overrule earlier cases; more likely to cite law review articles, social science materials, even newspapers and literary sources, in addition to citations of law.

These developments are real, but should not be exaggerated. On the level of the great cases, decided, say, by the United States Supreme Court, dissents and concurrences are as common as houseflies. The Supreme Court also is not shy about overruling older cases. The Warren Court overruled 3.7 cases per term, for a total of forty-three; the Burger Court overruled forty-six cases, or 3.3 per term.[49] Court opinions (which are long and getting longer) bristle with citations to everything under the sun. But the Supreme Court is not typical. A study of sixteen state supreme courts did find an increase in concurrences and dissents from 1900 to 1970; this increase was real but rather modest. In these courts, 92.5 percent of the decisions were unanimous in 1900–1910; 83.5 percent in 1960–1970. And there was enormous variation among the states. In Maine the dissent rate went from about zero in 1900–1910 to 5.6 percent in 1960–1970; in Michigan from 3.7 percent to an astonishing 44.4 percent. Courts almost never cited law reviews in 1900–1910 (there were few of them to cite); in 1960–1970 they did so in 12 percent of their cases. Again, there was great variation: the New Jersey Supreme Court cited law reviews in more than one-third of its cases.[50] The citation of law reviews doubled in California between 1950 and 1970.[51] Law reviews are not standard authority—they are not cases or statutes; and law reviews, especially today, contain all sorts of articles on all sorts of subjects. Some are drily legal; some are social-scientific, some are humanistic flights of fancy. Citation of nonlegal authority—books in the social sciences; or newspapers; or emanations of popular culture—were still very rare in 1970 in state supreme courts.

In short, the style of the judges is still quite formal, quite "legal," on the whole; though less so than a century ago. Some scholars think the style reflects a reality: judges honestly and sincerely look for the best legal answer. Other scholars feel sure that social variables—background, class, political party, and other such factors—explain decision making better than the idea that judges simply follow legal rules.

The evidence is slippery and elusive. Most cases in most courts are decided without dissent. Republicans and Democrats, blacks and whites, men and women: no difference. Many judges will give you, if you ask them, a formalist line. Or they say that only a few, tough cases really test their judgment—only a few cases make them think about changing the rules or bending a line of decisions. Mostly, they follow the rules and abide by prior cases. Henry R. Glick interviewed high court judges in New Jersey, Massachusetts, Louisiana, and Pennsylvania in a study published in 1971.[52] He asked the judges, among other things, whether nonlegal factors were important for them in deciding cases. Yes, very important, said the judges in New Jersey; no, not important at all, said the judges in Louisiana. On the whole, though, a modest role—following the law—corresponds to what judges say they do. There is no reason to think that these judges are lying; and it would be arrogant for an outsider to say that they are totally blind to what they do day in and day out.

But the fact is that judge-made law does change, has changed, keeps on changing, and that these changes do not fall from the sky; they come from the judges themselves. In a way, this is not surprising. Judges are creatures of their society; they live in this society; they breathe the same air, read the same books, watch the same programs, think the same thoughts, as other members of society. The very doctrines they expound are, inevitably, manufactured out of the cultural stuff of society. Judges of the nineteenth century, whatever their background, had nineteenth-century views—what else could they have? A "conservative" judge today is liberal—is downright radical—on certain issues, compared to his forebears: race, women's rights, freedom of speech, the scope of government. There are right-wing and left-wing judges, to be sure, but the whole context, the whole climate of opinion, has shifted underneath their feet.

They are like men and women standing on opposite sides of a ship; their position relative to each other does not change, but the boat may have gone a thousand miles since they left home port.

Most cases seem routine to judges: predetermined. Precedent governs; or the plain, flat text of a statute. In most cases, discretion, imagination, creativity, have little or nothing to do with the outcome. These cases (judges think) are controlled by "the law." They are cut-and-dried. But what makes a case seem obvious, routine? This judgment is itself extremely variable—it is, in fact, a product of the times. What seems obvious and routine is itself culturally determined: it is a function of the society in which judge and judgment are embedded. Nobody in 1800 thought that pictures of naked people doing naked things were protected by the First Amendment. Nobody thought that the federal government had the right to tell schools to admit students regardless of race; or the right to tell builders they had to put in ramps for people in wheelchairs. Conversely, everybody (certainly every judge) thought the state had the power and indeed the duty to make adultery and fornication crimes, not to mention same-sex relations.

A common-law system places great stress on the individual judge—his or her skill, philosophy, and style. High court judges have a personality; they have an ideology, a point of view, a distinctive voice. European judges for the most part are faceless, anonymous; in many countries, there are no dissenting opinions; the judges, on the whole, hide behind a velvet curtain of bland technicality. This is a style of self-abnegation.[53] The common-law style is quite different. Even the most formalist judge has a legal personality—and a name. The very fact that judges sign their opinions tells us something important about the role of the judge in a common-law society.

This "common law" system, however, is less and less pure common law: that is, concerned mainly with judge-made law. The statute books got bigger and bigger in the course of the twentieth century. This meant that more and more courts were interpreting statutes. It is hard to measure this trend precisely. A rough survey of the work of the Tennessee Supreme Court illustrates the point. In 1900 about 6 percent of the cases concerned the (state) constitution, about 15 percent were statutory, and more than three-quarters were pure common law. By 1930 constitutional cases had risen to 15 percent, statutory cases to 39 percent, and the common-law share had fallen below 47 percent. In 1999 constitutional cases amounted to 17 percent, more than half of all the cases construed statutes, and the common-law share had dropped to a little more than a quarter of the caseload.[54]

In the nineteenth century, most of the "grand style" judges worked on state courts. In the twentieth century, few state court judges were well known; the spotlight had passed to the United States Supreme Court. Benjamin Nathan Cardozo was perhaps the most noteworthy exception.[55] Cardozo, born in 1870, made most of his reputation in New York, as a judge on the New York Court of Appeals. He was an austere, remote man who never married; his prose was perhaps a bit too purple for present-day tastes, but his craftsmanship was subtle and sophisticated. Another example of a notable state court judge was Roger Traynor of California. Traynor (1900–1983), was born in Park City, Utah, educated at the University of California, Berkeley, and earned a Ph.D. in political science. He taught law at Berkeley until 1940, when he was appointed to the California Supreme Court; he became chief justice in 1964, and retired in 1970. Traynor was an innovator, pragmatic but forward-looking; and he left his mark on many fields of law. Arthur Vanderbilt, of New Jersey, was an important figure in court reform, as we have seen.

The lower federal judges also labored in obscurity, relative to their brethren on the Supreme Court. Learned Hand is one of the few exceptions—his work is still studied and admired.[56] Hand (1872–1961) became a district judge in New York in 1909; from 1924 on he served on the 2d Circuit Court of Appeals, writing more than three thousand sane, lucid opinions. Later in the century, Ronald Reagan appointed Richard Posner, a professor at the University of Chicago, to the (federal) Seventh Circuit. Posner was perhaps more famous for the books he wrote before (and during) his tenure, particularly his role in the law and economics movement, than for his work as a judge. But his crisp, thoughtful opinions stood out like a pool of clear water in a judicial desert of dreary, bloated prose.[57] The southern federal judges who, in the face of tremendous scorn and even physical danger, enforced the *Brown* decision and its progeny, are another special case. Some became famous or notorious, though hardly because of craftsmanship or style. But courage is also a virtue worth honoring.

Almost all American judges are political figures, in one way or another. In most states, this is literally true: they are elected, in ordinary elections. Many others are appointed—to fill a vacancy, for example—and then elected. In any case, they get on the slate, or get appointed, initially at least, because they have been active politically, or have done something to attract a sponsor in the Senate, in the statehouse, or in city government. Political life, of course, is a rough and tumble business; and there have been plenty of judicial scandals in United States history. Most concerned lower-court judges in the states. Federal judges also come out of political life. Yet they have been, on the whole, squeaky clean. Probably the worst scandal involved Martin Manton, chief judge of the Second Circuit (which includes New York). Manton resigned in 1939, after Thomas E. Dewey, district attorney of New York County, made the sensational charge that Manton was a judge who took bribes. Manton was put on trial, was convicted, and spent seventeen months in federal prison.[58]

Supreme Court justices, unlike state court judges, are almost bound to be famous; and this has become increasingly the case. There have been many powerful and significant figures on the court—justices who stood out in one way or another. Any short list would have to include John Marshall Harlan at the beginning of the century, later Louis D. Brandeis, Felix Frankfurter, Hugo Black, William J. Brennan, Thurgood Marshall, among others.

Brandeis was born in 1856 in Louisville, Kentucky, to affluent Jewish parents. He went to the Harvard Law School and practiced law in Boston with a partner, Samuel Warren. Brandeis took on many important and delicate cases, and earned a reputation as a fair and progressive lawyer—a lawyer with a penchant for acting in what he at least considered the public interest. The "Brandeis brief" in *Muller v. Oregon* was an example of Brandeis's role in fighting for his causes. Brandeis was no radical, but he hated what he considered the excesses of the capitalist system. Woodrow Wilson nominated him to the United States Supreme Court in 1916. He was confirmed, but only after a bitter struggle, marred with discreet and not-so-discreet anti-Semitism. He sat on the Court until 1939, anchoring the liberal wing of the Court, often joining forces with Oliver Wendell Holmes, Jr.

The chief justices of the twentieth century have been a varied lot. Some have been rather obscure, such as Edward D. White, appointed by President Taft in 1910. Taft himself was appointed chief justice by President Harding in 1920—the first and only ex-president to occupy this seat. Taft was a strong, conservative force on the Court, as well as by far the fattest person ever to serve as chief justice. His successor, Charles Evans Hughes, was a more moderate figure—more rounded in every way except in body.

Among the chief justices, a special place has to be assigned to Earl Warren.[59] Warren has often been criticized as a poor craftsman, an indifferent technician; but he was nonetheless a mighty figure, and a defining one. "The Warren Court" has a meaning, a resonance, which "the White Court" or "the Vinson Court" or "the Burger Court" or "the Rehnquist Court"—still going strong—simply does not have. A bumper sticker that said "Impeach Edward White," or Fred Vinson, or even William Rehnquist, is somehow unthinkable; but these signs sprouted like weeds, particularly in the South, during the high days of the Warren Court.

Earl Warren was born in 1891 in Los Angeles. He went to college and law school at Berkeley. He served as a deputy district attorney in Alameda County (Oakland is the county seat) in 1920; in 1925 he became district attorney of the county, and made a reputation as a crusading, clean-'em-up prosecutor. He ran for attorney general of California in 1938, and won; and in 1942 he was elected governor. He served three terms, and was enormously popular. He was Republican candidate for vice president in 1948, but the ticket lost the election. In 1953 President Eisenhower appointed him chief justice. Warren resigned in 1969 and died in 1974.

Warren's background did not suggest a firebrand liberal; or a man with advanced views on questions of race. During the Second World War, he was a zealous advocate of Japanese internment. But on the Court, he was boldly creative and impatient of technicality. Of course, the chief is only one of nine justices. The "Warren Court" is also the court of William O. Douglas, of William Brennan, and of Hugo Black; but Warren's influence, his personality, and his loose-jointed, nonlegalistic style set the tone for one of the most revolutionary periods in Supreme Court decision making.

The famous Supreme Court justices have been important and influential men. Virtually all of them, however, were less famous for forceful style than for forceful views, and the power to influence other justices; or for their historical importance; or simply that the time has come to honor what were once lonely voices of dissent. Occasionally, one of these dissents has a kind of cranky eloquence, but on the whole, the Court does not produce anything that could honestly be described as literature. Indeed, from a literary point of view, the Court has gone seriously downhill. The opinions of Supreme Court justices today tend to be bloated, overblown, disgracefully long. They also lack style.

Most high-court judges, state or federal, seem to write a kind of English that would not be out of place in an insurance policy.

Perhaps the outstanding exception, and perhaps the most famous of all Supreme Court justices, was Oliver Wendell Holmes, Jr.[60] Holmes was a Civil War veteran, and the son of a famous American man of letters, Oliver Wendell Holmes. The younger Holmes wrote an important book, *The Common Law*, in 1881; he served on the Massachusetts court and then was appointed to the United States Supreme Court by President Theodore Roosevelt in 1902. Holmes sat on the Court for twenty-nine years, and was ninety years old when he retired. He died in 1935. His opinions are brief, pithy, full of memorable phrases; he had no peer in writing agile, pungent English. He was also a prolific letter writer, and a powerful intellect.

Holmes has a reputation as something of a liberal. It is more accurate to call him a skeptic. He had a kind of cool, intellectual detachment, colored with a deep-seated pessimism. He was, on the one hand, the justice who devised the "clear and present danger" test in the freedom of speech cases; and who warned the justices not to embrace laissez-faire theories as if they were gifts of the Founding Fathers. This makes him seem like a progressive and a prophet. But just as often, perhaps, his opinions seemed blind to the needs and wants of the dispossessed. In many ways, he felt the country was going to hell; but he saw no reason for the Court, and no power in the Court, to stand in the way of decline and fall. No one more brilliant and protean has ever graced the Supreme Court. Holmes, more than sixty years after his death, continues to enthrall biographers, and the literature on Holmes, his work, his career has ballooned to massive size.

Settled Out of Court

Legal education and legal scholarship focus on trials, and on appellate opinions. A law student might get the impression that this is how most disputes get resolved. Of course, this would be entirely wrong. Only a tiny handful of disputes go all the way—the vast majority never make it to court. They are dropped, ignored, mediated, or otherwise settled out of court.

Until fairly recently, little was known about the life cycle of a dispute. The Civil Litigation Research Project, carried out in the late 1970s by scholars at the

University of Wisconsin, tried to shed light on this issue. Researchers took a sample of grievances, in various parts of the country, studied how many of these turned into claims, how many of these claims turned into disputes, and how many disputes ended up in court. It is a process, as they put it, of naming, blaming, and claiming. The general pattern—no surprise—showed that few grievances end up as court filings; the aggregation of disputes can be pictured as a pyramid, with a broad base, and a very pointy top. For every thousand grievances, only fifty reach this point—the point of actual trial. Different kinds of grievances have different life cycles: almost half of all postdivorce grievances (visitation problems, money problems) end up in court; but only thirty-eight of every thousand tort grievances, and a dismal eight of every thousand grievances that involve discrimination; most of these lost grievances never find any outlet at all.[61]

Other research confirms the idea of a dispute pyramid. Curtis J. Berger and Patrick J. Rohan studied condemnation—the taking of land for public purposes—in Nassau County, New York, between 1960 and 1964. During this period, the county took title to 2,409 parcels of land. These parcels were taken against the will of the owner, for the most part. The county would have the land appraised, and then make an offer to the owner. Overwhelmingly, the two sides settled out of court. In fewer than 10 percent of the cases was there a trial.[62] Laurence Ross, in a classic study, first published in 1970, looked at insurance claims adjustments in cases of automobile accidents. Here too, the overwhelming majority of incidents led to settlement out of court.[63] Most criminal cases end up in plea bargaining; and most divorce cases go by default (which means the dispute, if there is one, is ironed out long before anybody files the papers in court).

Do these studies refute the idea that Americans are litigious, or claims conscious? Yes and no. They certainly suggest that Americans (like everybody else) do not run to lawyers or to courts or both at the drop of a hat. Most grievances are swallowed, lumped, mediated, or settled. It is another question whether Americans are more claims conscious than other peoples; and also whether their willingness to litigate is going up, going down, or standing still.

Yet there was widespread public feeling, in the latter part of the twentieth century, that there was entirely too much litigating; and because litigation is wasteful and time consuming, that there has to be a better way. The average lawyer and judge probably agree. There has been an eager search to find substitutes for litigation. There was, in a way, nothing new about the concept: the whole idea of juvenile courts, family courts, and the like represents a retreat from strict litigation. But an alternative dispute resolution (ADR) movement developed in full force in the 1970s. In 1976 in St. Paul, Minnesota, a conference was convened on the Causes of Popular Dissatisfaction with the Administration of Justice (borrowing from the title of a famous talk by Roscoe Pound, early in the century). The conference helped push the idea of cheaper, quicker, fairer methods of dispute settlement.[64] The Civil Justice Reform Act of 1990 required all federal district courts to adopt a "civil justice expense and delay reduction plan," which would include ADR techniques.[65] The Administrative Dispute Resolution Act of 1990 required all federal agencies to "adopt a policy that addresses the use of alternative means of dispute resolution and case management," in the quest for "more creative, efficient, and sensible outcomes."[66] The states, too, have jumped on the bandwagon; many of them have passed laws to encourage ADR.[67] Businesses have been enthusiastic about this new idea. There are private companies which provide ADR services. In some places, with particularly long queues for trial time, parties can run their own private trials, with a private referee, who is often a retired judge—a procedure nicknamed "rent-a-judge." Renting a judge is not only faster and cheaper than waiting for a trial—it also allows businesses to avoid washing their dirty linen in public.[68]

It is hard to quarrel with the idea of efficiency; or to be against quicker and better ways to settle quarrels. In some ways, ADR and the idea of ADR are variations on time-honored themes. People have used arbitrators since the beginnings of American history. Communities and businesses have often preferred mediation and other informal ways of settling quarrels. ADR has its fans and admirers; but there are also some who ask what gets lost when cases are shunted away from the regular legal system.

10

Race Relations and Civil Rights

No changes in the law in the latter half of the twentieth century were more dramatic than the changes in the laws and legal practices with regard to race. The law started from a very low base. As we have seen, the American system of apartheid was firmly in place in the first half of the century; and in some ways was more stringent and oppressive than ever. *Plessy v. Ferguson* had been decided in the last years of the nineteenth century. Blacks in the South were disenfranchised and subordinated. Their situation in the North was at least formally better; there was no overt segregation, no drinking fountains that said "whites only"—and no pervasive pattern of lynching. But even in Chicago or Detroit countless stores, hotels, and neighborhoods excluded black people; and they were barred from many of the best and best-paying jobs.

After the Second World War, the situation began to change, and rather rapidly. Good war jobs and a shortage of labor pulled thousands of blacks up north. Here they were at least able to vote, and this gave them a certain amount of political clout, especially in the biggest cities. Racist ideology was on the defensive. Social scientists and anthropologists had turned against the idea of higher and lower races—indeed, they threw cold water on race as a meaningful category altogether. In the war Hitler had been America's archenemy—a man with lunatic ideas about race, who slaughtered millions of Jews. The Nazis would no doubt have done the same to blacks, but they had very few of them at hand to kill; they had to make do with the dark-skinned Gypsies.

Still, the army, navy, and air force that fought Hitler were strictly segregated. The majority of Americans were quite able to hate Hitler while believing in white supremacy. They had their own styles of racism; and after all they were also fighting the "Japs." The Japanese were the target of the most blatant violation of civil rights in America during the Second World War. In February 1942 President Franklin D. Roosevelt issued an executive order authorizing internment of Japanese and Japanese-Americans on the West Coast. The military authorities, who had eagerly pressed for this power, made their move in May 1942. In essence, they drove the Japanese out of their homes and businesses—whether they were citizens or not did not matter. Japanese-Americans ended up in "relocation centers"—parched, dreary, soulless camps in the barren wastes of the western deserts.

The war was the excuse for this drastic move. There were more than one hundred thousand ethnic Japanese living in the coastal states, especially California. They were farmers and small businessmen; many of them were doing well—working hard and getting ahead. This earned them the jealousy and hatred of local nativists. The attorney general of California, one Earl Warren, was among the officials who demanded action. The Japanese were dangerous. True, nothing had yet happened—no sabotage or any sign of it. But this was, to some, perhaps the "most ominous sign of all"; it must mean that the Japanese were lying low, planning a sneak attack.[1] Bigotry fed wild rumors, and greed fanned the flames. And when the issue reached the Supreme Court in 1944, the Japanese-Americans did badly, even in those cool, insulated precincts. The Court meekly upheld the "exclusion orders" on the grounds of military necessity.[2]

In 2001 it would be hard to find anybody who defends the case—or the internment itself. In fact, in 1988 Congress passed a law officially apologizing "on behalf of the people of the United States" for the "grave injustice" done to Japanese-Americans, injustice "motivated largely by racial prejudice, wartime hysteria, and a failure of political leadership." Congress did more than talk: it awarded each survivor of the camps the sum of twenty thousand dollars.[3] More than $1.5 billion was eventually allocated.

Much less well known, but equally dubious, was the wartime situation in Hawaii—where some 40 percent of the residents were of Japanese ancestry. After the attack on Pearl Harbor, the territorial governor, Joseph B. Poindexter, declared martial law and turned judicial matters over to the army. The civil courts were closed; the army "instituted a comprehensive and restrictive military regime," complete with military tribunals. What followed has been called "arbitrary and capricious," and a "wholesale and wanton violation of constitutional liberties." There were those who thought it would be a great idea to lock up the Hawaiian Japanese as well as the mainland Japanese; but in the end they were mostly left in place—perhaps because the islands would have been depleted of skilled workers; and because there were simply too many Japanese on the islands. Still, under martial law, the army put into place draconian labor policies, and trials were conducted without even the most rudimentary procedural safeguards—"drum-head" justice, quick, sloppy, but in its own way efficient: the conviction rate was 99 percent.[4]

To be sure, martial law was gradually relaxed, and the civilian courts reopened for business, even during the war. Still, in February 1944, when one Duncan, a civilian shipfitter working in the navy yard at Honolulu, got into a brawl with two marine sentries, he faced a military tribunal; and he was accordingly tried and sentenced. Duncan appealed all the way to the Supreme Court; the Court took his case, along with the case of one White, a stockbroker in Honolulu, charged with embezzlement in August 1942, tried by a military court, and sentenced to five years in prison. In *Duncan v. Kahanamoku* (1946) the Court set both men free.[5] The opinion was cautiously worded (and the war was already over), but it did hold that the "awesome power" of the military had in these cases definitely gone past the border of legitimate authority.

There was no "liberty cabbage" during the Second World War, and nobody tried to kick Goethe, Schiller, and Beethoven out of public life. Still, the fate of the West Coast Japanese reminds us that there was plenty of bigotry afoot. The passions of the war gave cover to some spectacular incidents of intolerance. Among the worst victims were members of Jehovah's Witnesses. This was a small but fervent band, very active in trying to spread the word of God, as they saw it. Witnesses went from door to door, selling or giving away their literature, especially their organ, *The Watchtower*. Witnesses also refused to salute the flag: they considered the flag salute rank idolatry. This behavior threw American Legionnaires and other superpatriots into an utter frenzy. It lent credence to the ridiculous claim that the Witnesses were fifth columnists, spics, Nazi sympathizers. The flag salute issue came to the Supreme Court in 1940, in *Minersville School District v. Gobitis.*[6] In a small town in Pennsylvania, three students, children of Witnesses, refused to salute the flag and were summarily expelled from school. Felix Frankfurter, writing for the majority, upheld the expulsion; only Justice Stone dissented. The flag, Frankfurter said, "is the symbol of . . . national unity." "Religious convictions" do not excuse a citizen from the "discharge of political responsibilities" if these "convictions . . . contradict the relevant concerns of society." Frankfurter also was willing to give the legislature a great deal of deference in matters of "educational policy."

The world was in flames as Frankfurter wrote; and he was, in a sense, carried away. He personally meant no harm to the Witnesses. But the decision gave a green light to small-town chauvinists; dozens of riots and mob actions against the hapless Witnesses followed. Local law enforcement officers stood by, or actively pitched in, as mobs beat and harassed Witnesses, or even tortured them. In Rockville, Maryland, a crowd sacked the Witnesses' meeting hall. In one particularly gruesome incident, a Witness in Nebraska was castrated.[7] In many communities, the American Legion egged on or led the rioters. The American Civil Liberties Union, on the other side, fought gamely for the rights of the Witnesses; the ACLU lobbied, cajoled, and litigated in an attempt, often unsuccessful, to safeguard the rights of this group.

The battle was waged in state courts as well as federal courts; on the whole, the Witnesses and the ACLU did better in state courts than in federal courts, at least at first. The persecution was pervasive: Witnesses lost their jobs at the height of the hysteria, were hectored out of towns, and arrested on trumped-up charges, or on paranoid claims of insurrection and sedition. The courts, to their credit, sometimes granted injunctions and overturned groundless arrests. Witnesses were also persecuted for their refusal to fight in "manmade" wars. Even though the text of the law clearly respected the rights of conscientious objectors, and exempted ministers from service altogether, about four thousand Witnesses went to jail for violating the draft laws. Even after the war was over, more than a thousand Witnesses stayed in prison for crimes against the Selective Service Act.[8]

The end of the war put an end to the most rabid persecutions. And the Supreme Court itself had second thoughts about its decision. A mere three years after *Gobitis*, the Court overruled that decision. Justice Jackson wrote for a six-man majority, in *West Virginia State Board of Education v. Barnette* (1943).[9] It is, he said, a "fixed star in our constitutional constellation . . . that no official, high or petty, can prescribe what shall be orthodox in politics, nationalism, religion or other matters of opinion." The Constitution protected the right of the Witnesses not to salute the flag.

Jackson's words were eloquent, persuasive. They were not entirely accurate. What he called a "fixed star" in the constitutional scheme was historically no such thing. Officials had always prescribed—at least implicitly—what was orthodox and what was not. Nor was religion historically considered a "matter of opinion" at all, but rather a form of divine truth (the *right* religion, that is). But the times were definitely changing. The stubborn fight of the Witnesses—and the ACLU—may have helped the Court to see things in a different light. Behind this was a deeper source of change: new ideas of equality, new forms of pluralism, new concepts of individual rights and individual worth. These were fighting their way through the thickets of inherited culture.

Black and White

In 1937 the Carnegie Corporation invited Professor Gunnar Myrdal, an eminent Swedish social scientist, to come to this country and undertake a "comprehensive study of the Negro in the United States." Myrdal arrived in 1938, and went to work. The study, *An American Dilemma,* was published in 1942.[10] Carnegie's money was well spent; Myrdal and his associates had produced a masterpiece: comprehensive, dispassionate, and rigorous. Beneath its narrative calm lay a fervid and devastating critique of America's racial record. The "Negro problem" was "America's greatest failure," Myrdal wrote. He documented that failure in careful but telling detail. And Myrdal held out some hope: if the country could only learn to "follow its own deepest convictions," race relations might turn the corner, and become an "incomparably great opportunity for the future."[11]

Myrdal's book was not, of course, mainly about the law of race relations. It did show the ways, legal or not, in which blacks were kept "in their place," especially in the South. Poll taxes, educational requirements, and "character" requirements in the southern states kept blacks from voting: devices which were "seldom applied to whites but almost always to Negroes." In addition, "Violence, terror, and intimidation [were] . . . effectively used to disfranchise Negroes in the South." The law was a two-edged sword: it enforced the subjugation of the race, and it looked the other way when blacks were victims. "A white man can steal from or maltreat a Negro in almost any way without fear of reprisal"; the "justice" system in the South was effectively closed to blacks. The typical southern policeman was a "promoted poor white with a legal sanction to use a weapon. His social heritage has taught him to despise the Negroes"; he remained profoundly prejudiced against all blacks.[12] In both the South and the North most blacks were desperately poor; they lagged behind whites in health and education; they were stigmatized and oppressed; and they lived out lives of stunted opportunities.

Yet Myrdal also saw signs of change in the wind; and change was indeed on the way. Perhaps the most important catalyst was the civil rights movement—the work of militant blacks who decided, at great personal cost (and danger), to rebel against white supremacy. They found some support in the North. The white North was racist enough on its own. But there were important differences between northern racism and southern racism. The typical white northerner was no friend of blacks, and wanted nothing to do with them; but this same northerner found actual, formal segregation repulsive—separate toilets and drinking fountains and that sort of thing—and felt smugly superior to the primitive, redneck South.

Moreover, racism was or had become an international embarrassment. The Second World War was a war against a vicious, racist regime. During the cold war, American apartheid was a weapon in the hands of the Soviet Union. Most of the world was nonwhite. Africa, in particular, was breaking free of its white colonial masters. The British and French empires were dissolving. India became independent. To southern segregationists, any talk about racial equality was communist propaganda, and utterly abhorrent. But to the state department, and to many Americans, civil rights were a weapon *against* communist propaganda, a way to polish the international image of the country. As Secretary of State Dean Acheson put it in 1952, discrimination gave the Soviets "the most effective kind of ammunition for their propaganda warfare." It was an embarrassment, too, when "dark-skinned foreign visitors," including ambassadors, were humiliated in hotels and restaurants in Washington, D.C. (at least until they proved they were foreigners).[13]

The civil rights movement was, however, the crucial factor. It did not come out of a vacuum. Not only did it have a political value, but a dramatic, growing sense of rights was characteristic of the period as a whole. Whether this sense was a cause or an effect of the movement for black liberation is hard to tell. Probably both. In any event, pressures were building up, demographic, cultural, political, economic; and the citadels of white supremacy came more and more under siege.

How was this citadel to be attacked? There was no doorway for blacks to enter politics in the South. Blacks had no political power whatsoever. Whites suppressed any "uppity" impulses on the part of blacks; sometimes with murderous violence, as we have seen. There was absolutely nothing to be gotten from all-white legislatures and city councils. There was no hope from southern registrars and police chiefs. The administration in Washington was indifferent or worse. White southern Democrats wielded enormous power in Congress. Some of them were obscenely rabid on the subject of race. The "moderates" kept quiet. There was, however, one slim ray of hope: the federal courts. Already there were signs that the courts were at least willing to listen. After the Second World War, the federal courts became, reluctantly perhaps, champions of a new age of racial equality.

Shelley v. Kraemer (1948) was an important legal victory—a straw in the wind.[14] The issue was housing segregation—in some ways, the very heart of apartheid. As we have seen, the Supreme Court had struck down, earlier in the century, actual segregation ordinances in various cities. One substitute for these ordinances was the restrictive covenant. Covenants were private agreements in the text of deeds to houses. These covenants aimed to protect the value and quality of whole neighborhoods, subdivisions, or developments. Deeds could contain all sorts of covenants—that owners, for example, were not to use the land for anything but a family home (no boarding houses or tanning factories). Notoriously, covenants often also provided that land and house were for Caucasians only. These covenants spread like weeds. By one estimate, up to 80 percent of Chicago was covered by racial covenants. And the courts had enforced them—rigorously.[15] These covenants "ran with the land"—that is, they stuck to the land like glue, no matter how often it was transferred; and any neighbor, anyone in the same subdivision or development, could go to court and enforce them.

It was this system that came before the United States Supreme Court in *Shelley v. Kraemer*. Black families had bought homes in defiance of the covenants. The lower courts (in Missouri) sided with the (white) neighbors, and ordered the black families off the land. The Supreme Court reversed. No court should enforce such a covenant. The Fourteenth Amendment outlawed race discrimination by any state or state agency. Chief Justice Vinson, writing for the court, pointed out that enforcement of the covenant required "the active intervention of the state courts, supported by the full panoply of state power." This could not constitutionally be done.

Shelley v. Kraemer struck a blow against housing segregation, but not a decisive one: the door opened by a crack, nothing more. Powerful norms and customs—and the habits of real estate brokers and others—still kept cities divided into black zones and white zones. Still, without *Shelley,* America's vast new suburban empire would have been closed to nonwhites, completely and forever. The case was also an important straw in the wind. The Supreme Court found American apartheid repulsive.

The Court had also given an unmistakable sign that it had lost its faith in school segregation. The old doctrine of "separate but equal" showed real signs of wear. A black woman, Ada Lois Sipuel, applied for admission to the University of Oklahoma Law School—the only law school in the state. She was turned down cold—state law made any mixed-race education illegal. The Supreme Court (1948) ordered Oklahoma to provide Sipuel with a legal education. The state board of regents "angrily created a law school overnight, roping off a small section of the state capitol . . . and assigning three teachers" to deal with Sipuel. She—and many students at the university—denounced this as a farce; but on reappeal, the Supreme Court timidly refused to intervene any further.[16]

The Court, however, inched forward in two subsequent cases. In *McLaurin v. Oklahoma State Regents,* sixty-eight-year-old George W. McLaurin was grudgingly admitted as a graduate student to the University of Oklahoma (he wanted a doctorate in education).[17] But McLaurin was black. He had to sit alone, eat alone, and use a special, separate desk in the library. At one point, officials of the university "surrounded his seat with a railing marked 'Reserved for Colored.'" White students, to their credit, tore the sign down.[18] The Supreme Court took McLaurin's case, and at the same time heard and decided *Sweatt v. Painter* (1950).[19] Sweatt was a black mailman, whose ambition was to attend the law school of the University of Texas. Alarmed by the Sipuel case, Texas hastily created a new law school, for blacks only. But it "consisted of three small rooms in a basement, three part-time faculty members," and a tiny library.[20] It was hard to argue that this was "equal" to the law school of the University of Texas. The Supreme Court certainly did not think so. The University of Texas had great qualities, qualities "incapable of objective measurement"—its traditions, its prestige, and so on. The Court ordered Texas to admit

Sweatt to the law school of the University of Texas; and it ordered Oklahoma to end McLaurin's indignities.

The two cases were unanimous. They signaled, fairly clearly, that *Plessy v. Ferguson* was losing its force. The emphasis on "intangibles" in the Texas case showed impatience with tokenism and phony equalities. The great, dramatic moment—the turning point—came with *Brown v. Board of Education* in 1954.[21] The case was a direct, frontal attack on school segregation. The NAACP spearheaded the fight. Prominent black lawyers guided the NAACP in its careful but determined struggle in the courts. One of these lawyers was Charles Houston, Jr.; after Houston died, Thurgood Marshall, later the first black Supreme Court justice, took his place at the head of the legal army. It was Marshall who more than anyone else determined the strategy that led to *Brown*.

In *Brown*, Marshall decided to go for broke—to stop the piecemeal approach, and ask the court to put an end to school desegregation, once and for all. The case was closely watched as it worked its way up the judicial ladder. (Some southern states, afraid of what might be coming, suddenly began to pour money into black schools, to make them more "equal.") The case was argued before the Supreme Court, put off, then reargued in 1953. Thurgood Marshall presented the black case forcefully: school segregation was "odious and invidious"; it was humiliating and degrading to the children. On the other side, John W. Davis, a distinguished southern lawyer and one-time Democratic candidate for president, nearing the end of his career, defended the right of southern states to segregate their schools; race differences, after all, were "implanted" in human beings, and could not be wished away. Black children, moreover, would be happier and better off in segregated schools.[22]

It was not clear at first what the Supreme Court would do. The Court was, in fact, deeply divided. A bare majority seemed ready to consign segregation to the dustheap of history. The chief justice, Fred Vinson, was more doubtful—fearful of taking so drastic a step. At this point, destiny stepped in and dealt the cards. Between the first and second rounds of arguments, Chief Justice Vinson died quite suddenly of a heart attack, at the age of sixty-three. President Eisenhower appointed a new chief justice: Earl Warren of California. Warren was a distinguished Republican, and he had campaigned vigorously for Eisenhower's election. In appointing him, Eisenhower was repaying a political debt.[23]

Later on, Eisenhower—no great friend of civil rights—came to regret what he had done; but too late. Warren quickly decided that segregation was wrong;

and he set about, successfully, to build not just a majority (that he had), but a strong, unanimous opinion—an opinion in which the Court would speak forcefully and as one. It took some doing—the last holdout was Stanley Reed—but Warren got his way.

On May 17, 1954, at 12:52 P.M., the new chief justice began reading, "in a firm, clear, unemotional voice," the Court's short, trenchant, and unanimous opinion.[24] No decision, perhaps, in all of American history has been quite so momentous. The Constitution, said the Court, did not allow states to segregate children by race. That was a violation of the Fourteenth Amendment. Separate schools, in the southern context, were inherently unequal. To separate children "from others of similar age and qualifications solely because of their race generates a feeling of inferiority"; segregation, when it carries with it "the sanction of law," can "retard . . . educational and mental development." Putting black children in separate schools denied them the "equal protection" of the law.

Brown was a case about schools, and only about schools; but the message had far-reaching implications. And in fact, *Brown* was only a beginning. The decision itself set off an explosion of ranting, raving, and posturing throughout the white South. This, of course, was not unexpected. The Court itself was reluctant to push the South too far too fast. The Court in *Brown* did not decide the next step: should the states immediately end their segregated systems, did they have time to work out plans, or what? The matter was deferred for a year, to give both sides a chance to argue how to end segregation.[25]

The second case, *Brown II* (1955), was somewhat mealymouthed.[26] The Court did not order an immediate, surgical end to segregation. Rather, it sent the matter down to the lower federal courts; it ordered those courts to enter "such orders and decrees consistent with this opinion as are necessary and proper" in order to end segregation "with all deliberate speed." This was a cryptic phrase, to say the least. What exactly did it mean? The South took it to mean what they wanted it to mean: obstruct, obfuscate, and delay.

If anybody believed that the white South would bow its head and accept the decision of the Supreme Court, they quickly learned how wrong they were. Southern political figures fell all over themselves to denounce the *Brown* decision, and the decisions that came after it. All over the South, politicians and ordinary citizens heaped obloquy on the Court—on an institution that had dared to attack the "southern way of life." Ninety-six southern members of Congress signed a declaration on integration in 1956, calling the *Brown* decision

"unwarranted"; it was, they said, with unconscious irony, "destroying the ami-
cable relations between the white and Negro races that have been created
through ninety years of patient effort by the good people of both races."

The white South fought back in the courts, as best it could; and it fought
back extralegally as well. Despite the Court's decree, not a single black student
entered a white school for years in states like Mississippi. Even at the university
level, it was a long and sometimes violent struggle to force even the slightest
degree of integration. When a young woman of color, Autherine Lucy, armed
with a federal court order, tried to enroll at the University of Alabama in
February 1956, a mob "roamed Tuscaloosa for several days, burning crosses,
waving Confederate flags, and attacking cars driven by blacks." The university
drove Lucy off the campus, and then formally expelled her.[27]

James Meredith was a stubborn and courageous young black who dared to
dream of going to "Ole Miss," the University of Mississippi, in the early 1960s.
The white leadership of Mississippi reacted with fury and threw whatever
obstacles it could in Meredith's way. The governor of Mississippi, Ross Barnett, vowed to "interpose" the "sovereignty" of the great state of Mississippi to
keep its university white. He denounced the "unlawful dictates of the federal
government"; Mississippi would refuse to "drink from the cup of genocide."[28]
Eventually, Meredith entered the university, but only after bloody riots, the
intervention of federal troops, countless writs and orders from the federal
courts, and the citation of Barnett for contempt.

But scuffles and court battles were not the worst of it. The southern caste
system had always had its ugly, violent side. In 1955 Emmett Till, a fourteen-
year-old boy from Chicago, was visiting relatives in Mississippi. Till bragged
that he had a white girlfriend up north; in part because his cousins dared him,
he went into a grocery store, squeezed a white woman's hand, whistled at her,
and asked her for a date. He paid for this insolence with his life. His naked body
was pulled out of a river three days later, mangled almost beyond recognition.[29]
It was pretty clear from the start who killed him—the woman's husband and his
half-brother; but a jury of twelve white men acquitted these two after sixty-seven
minutes of deliberation. This was business as usual for the South; but the *Brown*
case and other factors had made southern race violence more newsworthy; and
Till, after all, came from the North. In the North, this was a scandal, a shock, an
outrage—and a shot in the arm for the civil rights movement.

The Till affair showed how deep the wellsprings of hatred ran in the South.

The Ku Klux Klan, like a vampire imperfectly impaled, popped up out of its coffin. The Klan had had its day in the 1920s, as we have seen, but it lost strength after that; the *Brown* decision gave it a new burst of strength. By 1958 the Klan had about forty thousand members. Intimidation and assaults of civil rights workers took place all across the South; and in some cases, there was outright and cold-blooded murder. The Klan was responsible for bombing four black churches in Montgomery in 1957; one "Klavern" of the Klan seized a black handyman near Birmingham, castrated him, and tortured him by pouring kerosene and turpentine on his wounds.[30] The Klan was probably responsible, too, for what was perhaps the worst atrocity of all, the bombing of the Sixteenth Street Baptist Church in Birmingham, killing four little girls.

Many white southerners, of course, deplored the violence. Yet lawlessness had its champions at the highest levels of southern government. The White Citizens Councils, which sprang up all over the South, were meant to provide "responsible" (that is, non-KKK) leadership in the fight against integration. The councils were, however, racist to the core; they often went in for boycotts, or "cruelly intimidated free-thinking blacks." Grover Hall called their actions "manicured Kluxism," and pronounced them guilty of "economic thuggery."[31] The state of Mississippi created a State Sovereignty Commission, as a kind of supercouncil; the commission used "spy tactics, intimidation, false imprisonment, jury tampering," and other methods to fight the civil rights movement. It was, in the words of a Mississippi journalist, the "K.G.B. of the cotton patches." The commission harassed civil rights leaders in their jobs and businesses, and in their lives in general. The commission went out of business in 1977; its sorry records were unsealed in 1998.[32]

The civil rights movement produced its share of martyrs, black and white. In Martin Luther King, Jr., it also produced a vital and charismatic leader. In the end, on the balcony of a motel in Memphis, King became a martyr as well.

And what of the federal courts? The Supreme Court had spoken; had announced rules binding on the states. The rules, of course, were also binding on the federal system—on the lower federal courts; and on the federal executive. Some federal courts in the South showed great courage and understanding, but by no means all of them. On the one side, there were the "unlikely heroes"— federal judges who did their duty and defied the community; others, however, were rabid segregationists and white supremacists.[33] President Dwight D. Eisenhower—though hardly a fan of the civil rights movement—had appointed many of these hero-judges, moderate Republicans committed to the rule of law. Their white friends and neighbors shunned them; they worked under the shadow of death threats, at times; but they stuck to their guns. President Kennedy, on the other hand, had a mixed record of court appointments. In part because he felt politically dependent on southern Democrats in Congress, Kennedy appointed some federal judges—Harold Cox was the most notorious—who were frankly racist, and frankly a disgrace to the bench.

At first, the federal government was, to say the least, less than eager to enter the battle for racial equality. For the first few years, President Eisenhower dithered and delayed. But a crisis came at Little Rock in 1957. A federal court had ordered Central High School to admit black students. The governor of the state, Orval Faubus, was determined to block integration. He ordered the Arkansas National Guard to march to Central High; the Guard turned away any black students who tried to get in. The governor claimed he did this to prevent violence. Ultimately, a reluctant President Eisenhower federalized the Arkansas National Guard, and sent paratroopers into Little Rock. Eisenhower swallowed his dislike for *Brown;* whatever he felt about that decision, he could not ignore the fact that Faubus was defying national authority—including the authority of the president of the United States.[34]

The school board did not give up; it went to court, trying to persuade the court to kill the desegregation order. The board talked about "extreme public hostility"; as a consequence, a "sound educational program at Central High School" was "impossible," unless the "Negro students" were "withdrawn and sent to segregated schools." The district court agreed; it found a completely "intolerable" situation of "chaos, bedlam and turmoil." But the Eighth Circuit reversed, and the Supreme Court, in a sharp, unanimous opinion, sustained the Circuit Court.[35] "Violence and disorder" could not be allowed to trump "constitutional rights." Central High School had to open its doors.

Brown, more than forty years later, has clearly entered the pantheon of Great Decisions. Only a lunatic fringe would want to go back to a system of segregated schools—at least legally segregated schools. But there is still some controversy over *Brown* itself. How much impact did the case actually have? The border states moved quickly to implement the decision; but the South, as we have seen, resisted tooth and nail. Ten years after *Brown,* only 1.2 percent of black schoolchildren in southern states went to schools with white children.

Outside of Texas and Tennessee, the percentage was less than one-half of one percent.[36]

The strongest argument on behalf of *Brown* is that it acted as a catalyst; it stimulated and encouraged the civil rights movement. On the other side, some say that *Brown* itself was ineffective—as we have seen, very little actual desegregation of schools took place for years and years. Only the Civil Rights Acts (of 1964) broke the logjam. Worse yet (so the argument goes), *Brown* polarized the country, created a tremendous backlash, and may have even retarded the civil rights cause.[37] There was, in fact, what Michael Klarman has called a "dramatic rightward lurch" in southern politics—and *Brown* may well be one of the causes. The fuss over *Brown,* he argues, masks evidence of real progress toward moderation in the South taking place before *Brown;* moreover, the Supreme Court did not give birth to the civil rights movement; the movement was alive and well long before *Brown*.

There was, indeed, some progress before *Brown*. But it was wrung from bitter, intransigent, and often violent white opposition. When a shipyard in Mobile, Alabama, dared to hire twelve black welders during the Second World War, white workers assaulted them with bricks, hammers, wrenches, and crowbars.[38] This is not much in the way of progress. There was, to be sure, some countervailing evidence: President Harry S. Truman issued an order abolishing segregation in the armed forces after the war, and some elements of show business and sports were slowly integrating. Perhaps *Brown* did fan the flames of hatred in the South. But southern white fury and violence, beamed to the whole country on TV, horrified millions of people in the North. They watched police dogs with dripping fangs attacking demonstrators, tiny girls in neat dresses walking to school while howling mobs shrieked and spit on them, young people and religious leaders beaten with clubs. Thus TV was a major ally of the civil rights movement, just as it was to be a major ally of the antiwar movement during the conflict in Vietnam. And the change in the climate of opinion—mostly, but not entirely, in the North—set in motion a process that ended with a "national commitment" to bring Jim Crow to an end.[39]

The Supreme Court, for its part, never wavered or turned back. It hacked away at segregation wherever it found it. *Brown* was a case about schools; Warren's opinion stressed the importance of education in modern life and modern society. But the Supreme Court soon made it clear that any official segregation was unlawful, school or no school. Unlike many earlier civil rights cases, *Brown* was not destined to stand alone. The NAACP and its allies kept up the pressure; and the Supreme Court seemed almost eager to make decisions that put nail after nail in the coffin of legal segregation. Segregation, the Court made clear, was illegal in every sphere of life, not just in schools; it was illegal in parks, swimming pools, and all public facilities; and the law would not tolerate any line-drawing that put down the minority races.

Some of these new cases were *per curiam,* that is, "by the court": short, almost perfunctory, and without any written opinion. *Dawson v. Mayor and City Council of Baltimore City* (1955) dealt with segregated beaches and bathhouses; the Fourth Circuit held this system unconstitutional; the Supreme Court affirmed the judgment, in an opinion exactly one sentence long.[40] Some legal scholars—notably, Herbert Wechsler, in a famous article—criticized these per curiams, because they were not "principled," because they did not ground what they did in reasoned argument.[41] But the Supreme Court knew what it was doing. It wanted to make as little noise as possible, under the circumstances. And the "principle" was plain enough for anybody with eyes to see: segregation and race discrimination, through law, rule, ordinance, or regulation, was an evil, and was going to be struck down by this Supreme Court wherever it appeared.

In *Loving v. Virginia* (1967) the Supreme Court confronted what had once been the third rail of race relations: interracial marriage and sex.[42] Virginia's law, like the laws of many states, made it a crime for any white person to "intermarry with a colored person." Loving was white; his wife was black. They were charged with violating this law. Virginia's courts upheld the law, citing earlier cases that talked about "racial integrity," "corruption of blood," "racial pride" and a "mongrel breed of citizens." Virginia also argued that the law did not really discriminate—its burden fell just as much on whites as it did on blacks.

But the Supreme Court would have none of this; it struck down the statute, unanimously. Earl Warren saw no "legitimate" purpose in miscegenation laws; the statutes were nothing more than measures "designed to maintain White Supremacy." No state could infringe the "freedom to marry, or not marry, a person of another race." *Loving* was a kind of climax: segregation as a legal policy could not survive, even in this most sensitive of areas. There was total firmness at the level of the United States Supreme Court.

But racism and white supremacy were not easily killed. The southern system was like some primitive beast, a crawling, creeping creature low on the scale of evolution, growing new bodies from old ones that had been hacked to bits. And the white South had power: it was in almost total control of the machinery of southern states. There were forces which, as we have seen, were willing to play very rough. The main tactic of the South, as far as schools were concerned, was simply to do nothing. Delay, evade, dither; force the NAACP and its allies, and the federal government if necessary, to spend time, money, effort, on every school district, in every state; make it prohibitively costly and slow to shoehorn each black student into a white school or college. Integration thus proceeded in the Deep South at a snail's pace. Finally, the Supreme Court itself showed impatience. The original *Brown* decision had called for integration "with all deliberate speed"; but for ten years, said the Court in *Griffin v. County School Board* (1964), there had been "entirely too much deliberation and not enough speed."[43] The case arose out of Virginia, which had a strategy of "massive resistance."[44] In *Griffin,* Prince Edward County, Virginia, had tried to dodge integration by a simple, brutal move: it closed down all the public schools. The blacks were left with nothing; the whites went to private schools, hastily cobbled together and supported by state grants of tuition. The Court held this plan unconstitutional.

In the end, "massive resistance" proved to be futile, and it collapsed under the pressure of politics and court orders. Nonetheless, in most cities of the South, integration came grinding to a halt. What killed school integration in the end was not segregationism and its tricks, but simply white flight. Segregation in housing doomed integration in schooling. In *Swann v. Charlotte-Mecklenburg Board of Education* (1970), the Supreme Court put its stamp of approval on a plan to disperse the black students of Charlotte, North Carolina.[45] The plan involved putting kids on buses and sending them here and there, so that the ratio of blacks to whites would be the same all over Charlotte. The decision was unanimous, but there was heated disagreement behind the scenes, which the decision papered over. *Swann* was not the first, or the last, battle over busing. In general, busing was desperately unpopular among whites in city after city. *Swann* came out of North Carolina; but this was no longer a southern problem or a southern issue. In few places was the school bus a more explosive topic than in Boston, in the heart of Yankee country. Massachusetts had passed a Racial Imbalance Act in 1965; but attempts to use school buses to make integration a reality led to one of the stormiest and most acrimonious confrontations between races in the history of the city.[46]

In truth, the North now had to confront its own dark and dirty secrets. Northern schools were not segregated by law—at least not openly. But they were segregated in fact. Northern prejudice was more subtle and less violent, on the whole, than southern prejudice; but it was stubborn, deeply rooted, and pervasive. Of course, in Mississippi, not a single black child attended school with white children in the 1950s, and this was never true of New York or Chicago or Denver. But the vast majority of black students in the North and West went to schools that were all black; and the vast majority of whites went to schools that were entirely white. The issue, then, was the issue of de facto segregation. The lawsuits were not long in coming. The first to reach the Supreme Court, in 1973, came out of Denver—a city far from the Deep South, in a state that had never had a policy of segregated schools.[47] It had, in fact, banned racial discrimination for decades. But the school board had gerrymandered school districts and manipulated boundaries—enough so that the Supreme Court was able to find an intent to discriminate, and it held Denver responsible.

At this point, however, as the integration issue became national, the Supreme Court for the first time drew back. The key case came out of Detroit. A federal district judge, Stephen Roth, found the Detroit Board of Education guilty of Denver-like tactics. What was startling was his remedy: he tied the city (mostly black) in with its suburbs (mostly white), and ordered a plan to bus children back and forth on a fairly massive scale. How else, asked Judge Roth, could you "desegregate a black city, or a black school system?" How else, indeed. Whether the country was ready for such a step seems dubious. In any event, the Supreme Court was not. In *Milliken v. Bradley* (1974), a 5–4 decision, the Court disapproved the plan; the suburbs could not be lumped in with Detroit in the local decree on desegregation.[48] The world was made safe for white flight. White suburbs were secure in their grassy enclaves. This was the first time in twenty years that blacks had lost a school case at the level of the Supreme Court. It was also, in a way, the end of school integration; and housing integration as well. Official, legal segregation indeed was dead; but what replaced it was a deeper, more profound segregation, a segregation of home, neighborhood, and ways of life. Tens of thousands of black children attend schools that are all black, schools where they never see a white face; and they live massed in ghettos which are also entirely black. To be sure, the new segregation, unlike the old segregation, was not a universal system; there were blacks who escaped from the ghetto and lived in mixed neighborhoods. But these were mostly more affluent blacks—a minority within a minority.

Making Rights Real: The Civil Rights Laws

Some scholars, as we have seen, have expressed doubts over whether *Brown* had any real impact; but there can be no real argument about the Civil Rights Act of 1964. This clearly made a difference. The great constitutional cases may get more headlines, and generate more excitement; but the dogged, day-in and day-out work of making civil rights real belongs to institutions which this law brought into being.

The Civil Rights Act was a breakthrough in many ways. It was, to begin with, a political breakthrough. Congress had passed a mild civil rights law in 1957. President Eisenhower was lukewarm at best about this issue; and powerful southern senators and congressmen, in key positions, did their best to bottle up civil rights bills; or, if any of them managed to escape to the floor of Congress, to talk them to death. These men paraded under the flag of states' rights; but their real goal was white supremacy. They regularly denounced race mixing and other horrors of integration. Under Kennedy and Johnson, their position became somewhat weaker; and public opinion in the North gradually turned against the segregationists. Martin Luther King, Jr., had emerged as a powerful and charismatic leader. In September 1963 the 16th Street Baptist Church in Birmingham was bombed. Four little African-American girls at Sunday school died in this horror. This outrage was beamed across the country on prime-time television. A kind of consensus developed that something had to be done.

Still, the 1964 act crawled slowly and tortuously through Congress.[49] A last-ditch filibuster failed when the Senate voted, 71–29 for cloture—that is, for cutting off debate. In the House, a bipartisan coalition made an end run around the House Rules Committee, which was controlled by Chairman Howard Smith, a diehard southern Democrat from Virginia. President Johnson signed the bill into law in July 1964.[50]

The act was long, detailed, sweeping, and comprehensive. Title II outlawed discrimination in public accommodations—no hotel, motel, inn (with five or more rooms), no restaurant, cafeteria, or lunchroom, no gas station, no theater or sports stadium could discriminate on the basis of race or color. Title IV dealt with public education. Title VII—a crucial part of the act—forbade race discrimination in hiring and firing; it applied to all employers of twenty-five or more workers, provided that they were "engaged in an industry affecting commerce." This turned out to be almost everything. The act also gave power to an administrative agency, the Equal Employment Opportunity Commission (EEOC), with five appointed members, to hear complaints. The EEOC was supposed to make every effort to work things out—to get more or less voluntary compliance. But if this failed, it had the power to haul an employer into court. Any "aggrieved" person could do this as well: the victim of discrimination could bring a civil suit on her own.

In the late twentieth century, every major statute was bound to run the gamut of litigation. The Civil Rights Act was promptly challenged in court. On what basis did Congress have the right to tell a motel or a restaurant who they could or could not accept as a customer? The so-called Civil Rights Cases (1883) said flatly that Congress had no such power; the Fourteenth Amendment prohibited a state government from discriminating; but ordinary people could do exactly as they wished.[51] Those who drafted the 1964 law were aware of this problem. They tried to get around it by hitching the act to Congress's power to regulate interstate commerce. The Supreme Court unanimously upheld the act, in two cases decided in 1964. One of these came out of Birmingham; the owners of Ollie's Barbecue, a restaurant "specializing in barbecued meats and home-made pies," refused to serve blacks. Some of this barbecued meat had crossed state lines. Besides (said the Court), discrimination against black people means that they buy less, and in this and other ways bigotry impedes the flow of commerce.[52] A nineteenth-century court—or even a court in the first half of the twentieth century—would have found this reasoning preposterous. But the heart of the law knows reasons which reason (or "neutral principles") knows not of.

The EEOC was busy from the very start. It expected 2,000 complaints the first year (ending in June 1966); it got 8,854. This was more than twice as many as all the state antidiscrimination agencies put together received in a year. Blacks brought about half of the complaints. Most of these were from the South: 709 from North Carolina, for example, compared with 33 from Massachusetts.[53] Many complaints were farmed out to state agencies; many were dropped or dismissed; a good many were settled or conciliated; but even so, a fair number of lawsuits came out of the agency's work.

When the EEOC began its operation, race discrimination was positively epidemic in the job market. In the next thirty years or so, the situation improved dramatically. But the sheer number of complaints did not decline. In the 1990s the number of complaints of race discrimination on the job hovered around thirty thousand. About two-thirds of these were dismissed, because the agency found "no reasonable cause"; in only about one case out of four was there some sort of positive resolution.[54] Complaints were not clustered in the South anymore; they had gone national. The rise in complaints cannot mean that discrimination has increased—in fact, the opposite has surely happened. But blacks are now exposed to race prejudice in fields where they had once been totally excluded. More significantly, rights consciousness, and claims consciousness, had risen with the years.

The Civil Rights Acts produced tons of rulings and regulations; and a large amount of case law. Crass, brutal, overt discrimination was forced to go underground. A good deal of the litigation dealt with claims of evasion and subterfuge. *Griggs v. Duke Power Co.* (1971) was a crucial decision.[55] The company, in North Carolina, had hired blacks only for jobs like sweeping the floor. Good jobs all went to white folks. By 1971 the company realized that this blatant policy would have to go. It opened jobs to blacks as well as whites; but to get these jobs, workers had to have a high school diploma, and had to pass an ability test. Most local blacks had never finished high school, and had trouble passing the test. Still, the company claimed that it was acting in good faith; and the lower federal courts took the company at its word.

The Supreme Court did not. The Civil Rights Act, said the court, disallows "practices, procedures, or tests," even if they are "neutral on their face," when their effect is to "freeze" the status quo. These tests and prerequisites had to be justified—the company had to show that they were necessary, that they had some real relationship with the job itself. (The company had never seemed to need them before.) Otherwise, they were violations of law. The *Griggs* case, in other words, dealt a severe blow to the more subtle forms of discrimination—some of which might even have been unconscious or unintended. Job requirements like tests and prerequisites that had a "disparate impact"—in other words, screened out more blacks than whites—were permissible only if the company could show some tight relationship between the requirement and the job. You can demand a college degree for some jobs; for ditchdiggers, definitely not.

The *Griggs* case was exceptionally important on issues of procedure. In cases on employment discrimination, procedure, evidence, burdens of proof are not trivial matters; they are make-or-break factors in a lawsuit. It was significant, then, that *Griggs* shifted the burden of proof onto employers, as long as a disparate impact was shown. At this point, the employer had to bring in evidence to explain why it did as it did, or lose the case. Later cases nibbled at the edges of the *Griggs* doctrine; there were moves and countermoves between Congress and the Court; but the core idea remains more or less intact. Job discrimination cannot hide behind tests and standards, unless they are clearly germane. Some of the cases, precisely because the alleged discrimination was subtle and covert, turned on difficult questions of proof, and on elaborate statistical analyses. Businesses disliked these cases, of course; but they learned to live with them.

In some ways, the Voting Rights Act of 1965 may have been the most important step of all in the march of liberty. The Reconstruction amendments had given blacks the right to vote—in theory. But as we have seen, white governments in the South had stripped this right away. In some counties not a single black was registered, not a single black cast a ballot. Anyone who tried was soon taught a lesson in humility. The 1957 Civil Rights Act gave the attorney general the right to challenge race discrimination in the voting process.[56] But this and later acts were ineffective. The government had to work case by case, in each state, county, town, or township. Moving against the tough, adamant, South under this law was like trying to bail out a sinking ship with a teaspoon.

The Voting Rights Act of 1965 was different.[57] It contained some ingenious, and practical, provisions. Its point was to sweep aside all those tricks and traps that kept blacks from voting—the poll tax, literacy tests, requirements of "good moral character," demands to interpret the Constitution, and so on. (The Twenty-Fourth Amendment to the Constitution, adopted in 1964, did away with the poll tax requirement in federal elections.) The Voting Rights Act also contained a "triggering" mechanism: any state, and any county, where fewer than half the people of voting age actually were registered on November 1, 1964, or where fewer than half had actually voted in the presidential election of November 1964, fell into a special category. These jurisdictions had to reform their practices; moreover, any new voting qualification or prerequisite, any change in any "standard, practice, or procedure with respect to voting," had to be submitted to federal authorities for "preclearance." Six whole states in the South—Alabama, Georgia, Louisiana, Mississippi, South Carolina, and Virginia—fell under the ban, along with forty of North Carolina's one hundred counties, the whole state of Alaska (oddly enough), four counties in Arizona, Elmore County in Idaho, and Honolulu County in Hawaii. (Alaska and the Idaho county got themselves rather quickly excused.)[58]

Because the Justice Department was now serious about enforcement, and the civil rights movement was even more serious, and because the provisions of the act were drastic and hard to evade, the Voting Rights Act did not join the long list of dead-letter laws. On the contrary, it turned southern politics upside down and inside out. Southern legislatures, city councils, and the like could no longer keep themselves lily-white. Southern sheriffs, judges, mayors, and other officials could no longer ignore their black constituents. Within a ten-year period, more than a million black voters registered to vote. In Mississippi, for example, only 6.7 percent of the eligible blacks were registered in the early 1960s; by 1980 the figure had risen to 72.2 percent.[59] Blacks began to appear in southern legislatures, and, for the first time since Reconstruction, the South began to send blacks to Congress. Not all of this change was due to the Voting Rights Act—white supremacy was already under siege when the act was passed; but it undoubtedly speeded up the process in a dramatic way.[60]

Jones v. Alfred H. Mayer Co. (1968) was a startling case.[61] Joseph Lee Jones wanted to buy a home "in the Paddock Woods community of St. Louis County"; the defendant, he alleged, refused to sell, "for the sole reason that petitioner Joseph Lee Jones is a Negro." Jones invoked a law of 1866, left over from Reconstruction, which provided that "all citizens . . . shall have the same right . . . as is enjoyed by white citizens . . . to inherit, purchase, lease, sell, hold, and convey real and personal property."[62] This provision had been gathering dust for a century. Now the Court resurrected it. Did Congress really have the power to prohibit purely private acts of discrimination? Yes, said the Court, under the Thirteenth Amendment (which abolished slavery), Congress can also abolish the lingering effects of slavery. It can ensure that a "dollar in the hands of a Negro will purchase the same thing as a dollar in the hands of a white man." If Congress had no power to do this, then "the Thirteenth Amendment made a promise the Nation cannot keep."[63] Here too, Congress and the court were by now marching together. A Fair Housing Act (1968) basically outlawed discrimination in the real estate business, with only minor exceptions.[64]

If Gunnar Myrdal came back to life to write about the American dilemma as of 2001, he would no doubt see these changes as nothing short of revolutionary. There have been black cabinet officers; black mayors and other political figures occupy positions of power; black lawyers, doctors, businesspeople—and black plumbers, carpenters, police, and salespeople—hold down jobs they never could have dreamed of in 1950, south or north. The army, navy, air force, and marines are desegregated. A black man (Colin Powell) has served as chief of staff and secretary of state. The Metropolitan Opera has black singers. There are black pitchers and catchers and quarterbacks; and black players utterly dominate professional basketball. There are blacks on Wall Street and LaSalle Street and black movie stars—sometimes romantically linked on the screen with white movie stars. All this is on the plus side. Yet most blacks would agree that the United States is still not a colorblind society. Blacks with money can go just about anywhere they want, and even live just about anywhere they want; but millions of blacks have no money and live in squalid black slums. The public accommodations law has been an almost total success, for those who can afford these public accommodations. Universities are open to all races. Housing and jobs are more complicated. No housing development can simply slam the door in the face of blacks who want to live there. Still, there is a good deal of muffled discrimination. In many regards, the United States is still two nations—and unequal ones at that.

Sex Discrimination

The Civil Rights Act of 1964 did not deal only with race. It outlawed discrimination on the basis of religion, too; but this was hardly controversial in the late twentieth century. More significantly, and more dramatically, it outlawed sex discrimination. Legend has it that congressmen from the Deep South, in a last-ditch attempt to kill the bill, threw into it provisions on sex discrimination; this, they felt, would be the kiss of death. Here too they misread the temper of the times. The act became law—and the provisions on sex along with it.

No major legal change comes out of thin air. Women had agitated for their rights for more than a century. The great social and technological revolutions of the nineteenth century had shaken the foundations of the traditional family. The legal position of women had improved. The Married Women's Property Acts in the nineteenth century largely wiped out distinctions between the property rights of married women and those of men (married or not). Women had entered the workforce in great numbers. Five million women were in the labor force in 1900—but this was less than one-fifth of the total. In 1950 women were about a quarter of the workforce; and in 1970 more than a third—an army of more than 31 million women were on the job.[65] By 1970 women were entering the professions in some numbers—the legal profession, for one.

The most dramatic victory for women was passage of the Nineteenth Amendment, and its ratification in 1920. The amendment provided that neither the state nor the federal government could deny or abridge the right to vote "on account of sex." A few states had already granted women the right to vote; others had granted at least limited rights: in Connecticut, for example, women could vote in school board elections. After 1920 a few women began to appear in Congress and in state legislatures. There were never more than a few. During the Depression, many women lost their jobs; the idea was that the husband was and ought to be the family breadwinner, especially at a time when there was little bread to win. Women clustered at the bottom end of the pay scale; the Social Security Act of 1935 excluded farmworkers and domestic servants; this left most women workers (and the vast majority of black women workers) uncovered. "Rosie the Riveter" and her sisters had good factory jobs during the Second World War, because the men were off fighting; but many of these jobs ended when the war ended.

Statute books still contained lots of "protective" statutes—about women's hours, conditions of work, and the like. In New York, for example, a statute of 1912 provided that no factory, store, or mill could "knowingly employ a female or permit a female to be employed therein within four weeks after she has given birth to a child."[66] Pennsylvania, in the early part of the century, had an elaborate statute on "female" labor. Women were not to work more than a fifty-four-hour week, or more than a ten-hour day. No night work in "any manufacturing establishment," except for "clerical or stenographic work." Women had to have at least a forty-five-minute lunch break. Companies had to provide seats, and "suitable wash and dressing-rooms and water-closets, or privies." They had to supply "clean and pure drinking water." No women were to work in coal mines.[67] No women were allowed to sell liquor; and no hotel, tavern, or restaurant was to "employ any female" as a "lady conversationalist," or hire women to attract men to such places.[68] The Connecticut statutes—right up to the time of the civil rights laws—refused to let hotels, taverns, and restaurants serve women at bars.[69] No state required women to wear a shadur or dress modestly; but Michigan, for example, made it unlawful for a woman to work as a barkeeper, or to serve liquor, "or to furnish music," or dance in any saloon or barroom.[70]

These statutes exalted women, or imprisoned them, depending how one looks at it. Interestingly, the Pennsylvania statute on vagrants and tramps stated specifically that the act was not to apply to any "female."[71] It was acceptable, after all, for a woman not to work, or to depend on a man for her bread and butter; and the idea of a woman hobo was, apparently, unthinkable. All these statutes, mixing sentimentality and suppression, began to have a distinctly archaic ring, especially as more and more women were earning their living—and demanding their rights. Then, too, family structure (and family law) were changing. Step by step, attitudes began to shift, to match new social realities. The law trailed along. In 1963 Congress amended the Fair Labor Standards Act to give women (on paper at least) equality with men on the job—equal pay for equal work.[72]

The Supreme Court, up to this point, had never shown much interest in gender issues. In a 1961 case out of Florida, a woman was tried for smashing her husband's head with a baseball bat. The jury—twelve men—convicted her. Women were eligible for jury duty in Florida, but they served only if they wanted to serve, and only if they signed up for service, which few of them did. The Supreme Court saw nothing wrong with this law, constitutionally speaking. After all, despite a certain amount of "enlightened emancipation," women were still "the center of home and family life"; and unless the women themselves stepped up and volunteered, a state was entitled to decide that women "should be relieved from the civic duty of jury service"—presumably so that they could do their all-important home thing.[73]

Three years later, in 1964, the Civil Rights Act included women in Title VII; discrimination against women in the job market was now a violation of law. Then in 1971, seven years later on, the Supreme Court made one of its great periodic discoveries, or revelations. It found, hidden deep inside the Fourteenth Amendment, where nobody had been able to see it before, a principle that made sex discrimination unconstitutional. To be sure, the men (and they were, of course, all men) who wrote the words of the Fourteenth Amendment almost certainly had no such thing in mind—certainly not equal rights for women. After all, women in 1868 did not vote, serve on juries, or hold office.

There were no women judges, and no women lawyers to speak of. Married women, indeed, did not yet (in many states) have full property rights.

But the Constitution that the Supreme Court reads is not a text frozen in time; it is not the Constitution that sits in a glass case in the National Archives. The Supreme Court has its own edition of the Constitution, its own text—a moving, shifting, protean, evolving text. Whatever the theory of constitutional law, whatever the rhetoric or the justification, this is the plain fact of the matter. And so, in 1971, almost a century after the Fourteenth Amendment was adopted, the Court began to read it as a charter against sex discrimination.

The first case was *Reed v. Reed* (1971).[74] The problem here was not exactly earthshaking: it concerned the succession laws of Idaho. Under these laws, if somebody died without a will, and no surviving wife, but, say, two grown children, a son and a daughter, the son, not the daughter, had first crack at administering the estate. A unanimous Court said that this was invalid. Chief Justice Warren Burger wrote the opinion: it was short and punchy. This gender classification was "arbitrary" and was "forbidden by the Equal Protection Clause."

Of course, this change in Idaho's succession laws made a difference to very few people. But the case sent up an important signal: sex, like race, was covered by the Fourteenth Amendment. In the next years, the Court struck down several laws and arrangements on gender grounds. In *Stanton v. Stanton* (1975), a Utah law required parents to support their sons until age twenty-one; their daughters only until eighteen.[75] After all, Utah argued, girls "tend generally to mature physically, emotionally and mentally before boys." The Court refused to accept this reasoning. In *Frontiero v. Richardson* (1973), the law in question arguably favored women.[76] A man in the army or navy could automatically claim his wife as a dependent (and get better housing that way). A woman in the army or navy was in a different position. To get the benefits, she had to show that her husband was actually dependent on her, and for more than half his support. The Court struck this down; it was the product of "gross, stereotyped distinctions between the sexes." The opinion denounced "romantic paternalism," which put women "not on a pedestal, but in a cage." In Oklahoma, women could buy 3.2 percent beer at eighteen, men at twenty-one. This was bad (according to the Court) because it discriminated against men.[77] Feminists, though, were on the whole glad to see the end of "protective" legislation. They were opposed to these forms of "romantic paternalism," after all—opposed to the pedestal that turned out, as the Court had said, to be a cage; and the symbols of the pedestal-cage.

Thus the walls of "protection" came tumbling down; and the thesis of *Muller v. Oregon* was turned on its head. Factory laws that put limits on women's hours of work, or forced employers to give them places to sit down and rest no longer looked benign. None of these laws survived the push for equality of the last third of the century. The (presumed) delicacy of women was a trap—a trick to keep them out of the rough and tumble of men's world.

The Supreme Court never carried gender as far as race. Any law that discriminated against blacks faced "strict scrutiny" in the Supreme Court, which meant it was almost certainly doomed. Gender faced a somewhat less beady eye: "intermediate" scrutiny. Tons of paper and oceans of legal ink have been spent in arguments about these levels of scrutiny. Much of this seems like arid hairsplitting. But underneath the verbal arguments is a genuine dispute. Civil rights law aimed to obliterate all legal distinctions based on race. There are no real differences between the races—nothing that would justify a law that would draw the race line. But no such theory could be applied quite so rigorously to gender: men and woman *are* different; and the differences may be such as to justify *some* differences in treatment, in custom or law.

Cleveland v. La Fleur (1974) was not, on the surface, an ordinary case of gender discrimination.[78] Jo Carol La Fleur, and two other women who brought these cases, were schoolteachers. They had also been pregnant. La Fleur worked for the Cleveland school system. Cleveland had a rule that no pregnant teacher could stay on the job after "five months before the expected birth of her child." La Fleur was healthy and vigorous, and wanted to keep on teaching. The Supreme Court struck down the rules, which, the Court said, had no "rational relationship" to any "valid state interest"; and which burdened the "women's exercise of constitutionally protected freedom."

The decision rested, in part, on rather murky premises; and the Court later backed off with regard to some of them.[79] But the Court did show a certain sensitivity to women's position in society. The "constitutionally protected freedom" mentioned was the freedom to get pregnant and have a baby. Why did Cleveland, and the other districts, adopt these rules in the first place? The school boards talked publicly about the health of the women and continuity of instruction; in private, they talked about "giggling schoolchildren," and the need to get the teachers out of the classroom before they "began to show," when the kids would say that "teacher swallowed a watermelon, things like that." Thus, ultimately, the case was about the intersection between sexuality and gender; and the Court was really taking a stand against what it considered Victorian prudery.

In any event, in the early 1970s gender was definitely on the map, as far as the Supreme Court was concerned. The Court was not as straightforward as in race cases; it sometimes wobbled and weaved like a drunk trying to walk a straight line. In *Geduldig v. Aiello* (1974), decided shortly after *Cleveland v. La Fleur,* a California state program of disability insurance for working people failed to cover the hospital cases of an ordinary pregnancy and childbirth.[80] Carolyn Aiello and other women workers claimed sex discrimination. The Court had a sudden attack of blindness, as if the justices had fallen into some dark unfathomed cave. They saw no sex discrimination here at all. The statute merely drew a line between pregnant and nonpregnant people. Of course, the class of pregnant people is fairly one-sided, genderwise (a fact the Court presumably knew), which made the distinction a bit ridiculous. Congress showed its contempt for this decision by passing a Pregnancy Discrimination Act (1978), which swept the case into the dustbin.[81]

Another troublesome case was *Michael M. v. Superior Court* (1981).[82] Here the Court confronted a California law on statutory rape. As we have seen, a male who has intercourse with an underage girl commits this crime, even if the girl says yes, even if she positively lusted after him; and even if he himself was underage—which, in fact, Michael M. was. This would seem, in the context of the 1980s, a pretty clear instance of sex discrimination—and one which rested on ancient stereotypes to boot. The Court, however, upheld the law. It saw a plain difference here: she could get pregnant; he could not. That, they felt, justified the difference in the statute. Here too the legislature stepped in and changed the law. "Statutory rape" is now "unlawful sexual intercourse." The statute is unisex. And the sex is criminal only if one of the two is very young, or if one is a minor, and the other is more than three years older.[83]

Finally, in *Rostker v. Goldberg* (1982), the Court came face to face with a thorny issue: whether women could fight and die for their country.[84] Young men, but not young women, had to register for the draft. But this was acceptable, said the Court, because women were not "eligible for combat"—a point on which all the justices agreed. Why were women, in fact, less fit to shoot a bazooka, or throw ta hand grenade, than to be on the police force, or fight fire, or mine coal, or act as umpires? The Court never answered. This may be because the answer had nothing to do with formal laws, but with a deep and powerful gender taboo.

There were many sex discrimination cases, most of them rather ordinary cases of bias in the workplace. Bias here too learned how to disguise itself. Thus the *Griggs* doctrine could be, and was, used in sex discrimination cases. Dianne Rawlinson wanted to be a prison guard in an all-male Alabama prison. Alabama wanted its prison guards to stand tall: they had to be more than five feet, two inches in height; they also had to weigh more than 120 pounds. The weight requirement would exclude 22 percent of the women but only 2 percent of the men; the height requirement would exclude a third of the women and only 2 percent of the men. The Supreme Court struck down these requirements in 1977—Dianne, however, lost her case on other grounds.[85]

The EEOC had jurisdiction over sex discrimination cases. In the very first year of its existence, more than two thousand complaints were filed under this heading. Complaints and lawsuits have kept on growing. In the 1990s the number of complaints reached twenty thousand a year or more. Most of them died at the agency, presumably because they were groundless (at least in the judgment of the EEOC). In fiscal 1995 the EEOC found "reasonable cause" in only 2.3 percent of the complaints; a small number in addition were successfully "conciliated" or settled.[86]

Most claimants, then, got nowhere; but there were so many who tried that even the small percentage of surviving suits and administrative actions were enough to erect a vast, ballooning body of law on sex discrimination in the workplace. Sex cases were not like race cases in one key legal regard. A business could turn down a woman (or a man) for a job if gender was a "bona fide occupational qualification," or BFOQ. There was no such exception in race cases. A theater looking for somebody to play Hamlet could presumably pass up women who applied for the job. In other regards, the court read this exception very narrowly. In *Diaz v. Pan American* (1971), a man, Celio Díaz, Jr., wanted a job as an airline flight attendant. All domestic flight attendants were women ("stewardesses"). Pan American claimed that customers preferred women; the airline brought in a psychiatrist as an expert witness. This expert, Dr. Eric Berne (author of *The Structure and Dynamics of Organizations and Groups*) explained why women were better at the job: an airplane, he said, is a "sealed enclave," an "enclosed and limited space," in which people suffer the "unusual physical experience of being levitated off the ground . . . out of touch with their accustomed world." Women would do better in this situation than men; male passengers "would subconsciously resent a male flight attendant perceived as more masculine than they."[87] The trial court accepted this argument; but the appeal court reversed; this was not a legitimate BFOQ.[88] In another case, brought against Southwest Airlines, the defendant, as Deborah Rhode has put it, "presented woman as temptress rather than nurturer"; the airline's "sexy image" made women attendants in "hot pants and high boots" more desirable. But the "flying bordello" was as unsuccessful in court as the "flying womb."[89] Stewardesses passed into history, and flight attendants (of either sex) replaced them.

In these airline cases, men won the victory; but arguably, in a deeper sense, it was women who won. The cases tried to break down old stereotypes about women. These stereotypes were barriers to women, in the job market, and elsewhere, even when they were couched in flattering terms, and were supposed to benefit women in some way. The courts made it clear that employment ghettos, whether male or female, were no longer legally acceptable. To let men serve coffee on airplanes, then, was a step toward letting women do brain surgery, ride in police cars—or, for that matter, serve as CEOs of big corporations. Thus when the Court told the Mississippi University for Women in 1982 that it could not exclude men from its nursing school, women were entitled to cheer.[90]

One important development was the law of sexual harassment. This has been defined as "the imposition of unwelcome sexual demands or the creation of sexually offensive environments."[91] Women began bringing complaints about sexual harassment on the job in the 1970s; an important book by Catharine Mac-Kinnon, published in 1979, discussed these complaints and made a powerful argument that harassment ought to be considered sex discrimination, and therefore prohibited by Title VII.[92] In 1980 EEOC agreed, and defined sexual harassment as discrimination. The Supreme Court approved in a later case (1986).[93]

Sexual harassment came in two versions: the first, more literal kind included fondling, propositioning, demanding sexual favors, and the like; the second, less obvious, consisted of acts that created a "hostile work environment," workplaces where men called women bitches or whores or worse, plastered the place with pinup pictures, and in general made life miserable for women.[94] Many men, some women, and some judges have sneered at these developments—called them fussy overreactions and manifestations of "political correctness."

Nonetheless, the claims continue, and grow. In the last years of the century, claims of harassment, filed with EEOC itself, or with state and local Fair Employment Practices agencies, amounted to about fifteen thousand a year. About 10 percent of these complaints were brought by men.[95] Many of these complaints, of course, went nowhere. But they were all part of a larger movement, slow, conflicted, multiplex, redefining the relationship between men and women in the family, the marketplace, the workplace, and in life in general.

Civil Rights in the States

So far, we have focused on the federal government and the federal courts. Civil rights laws were imposed on the states of the Deep South. It took a kind of revolution, led by black people, and the whole force of the federal government, to drag these states into the world of racial equality, kicking and screaming.

The situation in the rest of the country was quite different. There was, to be sure, plenty of race prejudice everywhere. But the official doctrines, at least, were color-blind. And many of the states enacted civil rights laws, years before there was federal legislation. In California, for example, the Civil Code (§51) had, since 1905, accorded all citizens "full and equal accommodations" in "inns, restaurants, hotels, eatinghouses, barber shops, bath houses, theaters, skating rinks, and all other places of public accommodation or amusement." In 1919 public conveyances were added; and in 1923 ice cream parlors. How effective this law was, is another question. In 1941 one Joseph Suttles brought an action against the Hollywood Turf Club; Suttles bought two box seats for the races, but was told, "We do not allow Negroes in this place"; he was offered seats in the grandstand instead.[96] Suttles won his case; but the attitude of the turf club was probably more typical than Suttles's tough refusal to put up with it.

Employment was touchier than public accommodations. In 1945 New York enacted a Fair Employment Practices Act, and established a Fair Employment Practices Commission. Other states followed—by 1963 there were some twenty-five such state laws.[97] The New York law was not entirely toothless: it stressed voluntary compliance and conciliation, but state authorities could force obedience, if it came to that. In 1952 New York added public accommodations to the law, and in 1955 public housing. During the first ten years or so, the New York State Commission against Discrimination proceeded very cautiously indeed; after *Brown,* the climate of enforcement became more vibrant, and the authorities were far more vigorous. New Jersey had its own civil rights agency. Here, too, the agency proceeded, at first, with extreme caution. In the early 1960s a study found, for example, that the agency granted relief in only 14 percent of some 120 complaints about employment discrimination; most complaints were dismissed.[98] By the end of the century, of course, the whole climate had changed, even in the South. North Carolina passed an Equal Opportunity Practices Act in 1977; it covered "race, religion, color, national origin, age, sex or handicap."[99] South Carolina passed a fair housing law in 1989.[100]

Reshaping Democracy

Voting rights were an issue not only for blacks. Most states, as of the 1950s and 1960s, were "malapportioned." Population was leaving the countryside for cities and suburbs; but legislatures, dominated by small-towners and farm districts, dragged their heels at changing the lines of electoral districts. In Tennessee, for example, the district lines (for elections to the General Assembly) had been frozen in place since 1901, with only minor changes. Members of the legislature simply refused to reapportion themselves out of business. But in *Baker v. Carr* (1962), the Supreme Court stepped boldly into the Tennessee tangle.[101]

The Court faced one big obstacle: the "political question" doctrine. On a number of occasions, the Court had invoked this doctrine to avoid certain touchy, politically charged questions—including the very sort of question presented in *Baker v. Carr*. In *Colegrove v. Green* (1946), the issue was the way Illinois drew the lines of congressional districts.[102] The Court (speaking through Justice Frankfurter) refused to do anything about it, refused to "enter this political thicket." But in *Baker v. Carr*, the Court changed its mind. It decided that this *was* a case the Court could hear; that there was a genuine issue of equal protection in the case; and it sent the case back down for decision. Frankfurter, old and about to retire, dissented passionately.

The case sent a clear signal to voters; and within a year, there were lawsuits in more than thirty states. In 1968, in cases involving Alabama, Colorado, Delaware, Maryland, New York, and Virginia, the Court set down what came to be called the principle of one person, one vote. Legislators represent "people, not trees or acres. Legislators are elected by voters, not farms or cities or economic interests."[103] Districts had to be roughly equal in population.

Baker v. Carr, and the cases that followed it, redrew the electoral map dramatically. The Supreme Court had made a stunning difference: the cases applied the doctrine to congressional districts, and, in the states, to both houses, lower and upper. The federal Senate was certainly not based on "one person, one vote"; after all, Wyoming or Vermont had the same number of senators as California or New York; but the Supreme Court insisted that state senates were different. There was some agitation for a constitutional amendment, so that states could apportion at least one house on some basis other than population; but nothing came of it.[104]

The Supreme Court had acted boldly, and changed the face of political life. Whether there was a real change in what legislatures did, is another, more difficult question. The cities and suburbs got more representatives in Springfield, Illinois, or Sacramento, California; but whether they got more political output from these representatives is less clear. What is clear is how the Warren Court flexed its muscles. The Supreme Court had taken on the job of making democracy, as the Court saw it, more real. The slogan about people and trees, about voters and economic interests, tells us a lot about the mind-set of the Court. Legislatures were not protecting trees as such, or farms as such; but rural, old-fashioned, Protestant America. In the end, if anybody gained, it was not the urban masses but the middle class in suburban bulges ringed around the midriff of metropolitan areas.

The Rights Revolution Rolls On

An active, involved Supreme Court, in the Warren era and the decade or so following, had breathed life in the equal-protection clause—made it an all-purpose weapon against "discrimination." The Court had ordered reapportionment. It tried to beef up and nationalize a menu of rights for people accused of crime. The Supreme Court had always been an activist court. In part, this was an American tradition. American judges are not meek civil servants. They are, by habit and background, politicians. Politics and policy flow through their blood vessels. The only question is what sort of activism. And the Warren Court came at a time of pluralist ferment.

Race, gender, ethnic origin, religion: these were clear categories that the Court protected, under the umbrella of the Fourteenth Amendment. Were there other categories? Quite a few groups of the dispossessed or disfavored—bastard children, for example, and men in prison—tested the limits. With mixed results.

One group consisted of aliens. The Court, as we saw, had disapproved of the laws restricting land ownership by noncitizens. But these were racist laws, directed against the Japanese and other Asians. All sorts of other state laws, big and small, limited the rights of noncitizens. Perhaps the most extreme were Pennsylvania's game laws of the 1920s; under these laws, no "unnaturalized foreign-born person" could hunt birds or animals, possess "a shotgun or rifle or pistol or firearm" or even a "dog of any kind, at any place outside of buildings." No alien could go fishing in Pennsylvania.[105] More commonly, states simply excluded aliens from state jobs.

In *Nyquist v. Mauclet* (1977) a bare majority of the Supreme Court struck down a New York law on state scholarships and loans for college students.[106] Only citizens were eligible, or aliens who had applied to be citizens (or who could swear that they intended to do so). In 1973 the Court, in another New York case, said that New York could not bar resident aliens from becoming civil servants. Nor could Connecticut block resident aliens from taking the bar exam and practicing law.[107] Resident aliens, like citizens, "pay taxes, support the economy, serve in the Armed Forces." In 1984 the Court told Texas that it had to let resident aliens act as notaries public.[108] But in all these cases, the Court was far from unanimous; Justice Rehnquist, for example, dissented in every one of them. Is an alien, he asked (irreverently and irrelevantly), "who, after arriving from abroad in New York City, immediately purchases a pack of cigarettes, thereby paying federal, state and city taxes, really no different from a citizen?"[109] Rehnquist finally had his day in 1978. California allowed only citizens to be peace officers. Two Spanish-speaking men from Los Angeles, noncitizens, wanted to be deputy probation officers, applied, were turned down, and appealed. The Court upheld the California rule. Peace officers "symbolize" the sovereignty of the state; a state can require these symbols to be citizens.[110]

Tinker v. Des Moines School District (1969) was a students' rights case.[111] In the background was the unpopular war in Vietnam. Certain antiwar students in an Iowa high school, in December 1965, proposed wearing black armbands to school. They wanted to express their "grief over the deaths of soldiers and civilians in Vietnam." The school board, anxious (it said) to avoid "a disturbing situation," said no to the armbands. Tinker and others defied this order; they were sent home and suspended from school. The case found its way, eventually, to the United States Supreme Court, which upheld the students. Constitutional rights are not "shed . . . at the schoolhouse gate." Vague fears of disturbance are "not enough to overcome the right to freedom of expression."

Hugo Black wrote an angry dissent. Among other things, he argued that the "original idea of schools" was that "children had not yet reached the point of experience and wisdom which enabled them to teach all of their elders." This idea was not "worthless or out of date." Taxpayers send children to "learn, not teach"; and he decried the decline of school discipline. The decision would encourage students to "defy their teachers"; and he painted a grim picture of rebellious students, "already running loose, conducting break-ins, sit-ins, lie-ins, and smash-ins."

Black's dissent can be dismissed as an old man's longing for some golden age; as the angry wails of a onetime liberal icon, marooned in a raucous and permissive culture, which had engulfed his standards of gentility and rationality. Yet Black had put his finger on the heart of the case. The case was not about free speech, in a sense: it was about discipline and authority. The lesser liberation movements—students, prisoners, aliens, for example—were not about discrimination in the same sense as the civil rights movement; they were indeed about discipline and authority. And they were signs of deep change, for better or for worse, in the culture of discipline and authority—signs of a steep decline in the vertical power of teachers, parents, and leaders in general.

Tinker grew out of a rights-consciousness mentality—a mentality in which at least some students balked at what teachers and principals told them to do, if they thought it impinged on their "rights"; and in which some parents backed their children. There were very few such cases before the 1960s; in one of these, in 1921, young Miss Valentine, graduating in Iowa, refused to wear a cap and gown because of its "offensive odor." The school withheld her diploma. She protested, and won.[112] But before the Second World War, not a single case of students' rights appeared in a federal court.[113] Suddenly, between 1969 and 1978, there were no fewer than 118 federal cases—and no fewer than 87 of these concerned an issue that nobody had ever imagined, or thought significant in the past: dress codes and hair. Or, to be exact, male hair: sideburns, moustaches, beards. Was there a constitutional right to hair on your face? The federal courts spluttered and vacillated, and split almost evenly on this great issue.

Some judges did complain that these were trivial matters, unworthy of their time. One judge in 1969, mentioning the "crisis" over the "monumental" mustache question, wondered why an "overloaded" judge had to decide when the "fuzz or down above the lips of a teenager becomes a mustache." This judge thought teachers had rights, too; and "unkempt faces" staring at them were a violation of these rights.[114] But in the late twentieth century, no aspect of your personal freedom was truly trivial, provided that you yourself defined it as a right, as an aspect of the self, the personality. This was the *Tinker* issue once again: authority, in the broadest sense, the right to dictate to the young. Young people—and people in general—were kicking against the traces. And, more and more, in the days of the Warren Court, they found a court system, especially the federal court system, that would give them a chance to be heard.

The courts decided earthshaking cases; but they also dealt with what we might call big issues in little places, like the issue of students' beards. Here too we would place the lawsuit of Terry Dean Eaton, who used the word "chickenshit" under cross-examination in the Municipal Court of Tulsa, Oklahoma, and was cited for contempt of court; or the man accused of wearing an American flag sewn on the seat of his pants; or the man arrested for wearing "a jacket bearing the words 'Fuck the Draft' " in the Los Angeles County Courthouse; or two passengers who objected to canned music on public buses.[115] All these cases, in fact, went up to the highest court in the nation. In *Wooley v. Maynard* (1977), the burning issue before the Supreme Court was New Hampshire's license plates.[116] From 1969 on they carried the noble motto "Live Free or Die." George Maynard, a Jehovah's Witness, covered up the motto on his Toyota Corolla and Plymouth station wagon; he considered these words offensive, on religious grounds. The Supreme Court agreed with him. New Hampshire could not require its people to become a "mobile billboard" for the state's "ideological message."

The federal courts, in short, showed a strong vein of sympathy for dissenters, naysayers, even cranks. In some ways, these people constitute one of the "discrete and insular minorities." The phrase, as we have seen, comes from a footnote in *United States v. Carolene Products Co.* (1938).[117] The case itself had nothing to do with race, religion, sex, or any minority or identity group; at issue was an act of Congress, passed in 1923, on the interstate shipment of skimmed milk. The Court, speaking through Harlan Fiske Stone, upheld the statute; the Supreme Court had a duty to defer to Congress, said Harlan Fiske Stone. But, he added in the footnote that has since become famous, a different standard might apply in statutes aimed at minorities. Prejudice against "discrete and insular minorities" might "call for a . . . more searching judicial inquiry."

The Court used this more "searching judicial inquiry" above all when race was the issue; but the concept expanded to include many other "suspect classes," as we have seen. It had definite limitations: the Court's sympathy for underdogs and the unpopular hardly extended to Communists and fellow travelers—or even, in some cases, people suspected of these tendencies. And the question remained: how far would the Court carry this idea, of helping the helpless? What, for example, about the poor? If you have no money, if you are at the bottom of the American heap, does that make you part of a "discrete and insular minority"? Are you under the Court's special wing of protection? In some senses, yes: the *Gideon* case, as we have seen, told the states they had to provide legal counsel to people accused of serious crime.[118] In *Boddie v. Connecticut* (1971), the issue was divorce—specifically, court fees and costs amounting to about sixty dollars.[119] Boddie said he couldn't scrape up the money. The Court was sympathetic. Marriage in this society was "basic" in the "hierarchy of values"; getting out of a marriage was therefore pretty basic too; it was the only way to dissolve the relationship. Connecticut therefore could not deny Boddie his divorce simply because he had no money to pay for it.

How much further was the Supreme Court willing to go? Not very far, it turned out. Two years later, the Court upheld a section of the bankruptcy law which demanded costs and fees of about fifty dollars from potential bankrupts. Getting out of a crushing burden of debt turned out to be less "fundamental" than getting out of a wrecked marriage.[120] In the same year, the Court considered an Oregon law on welfare benefits; if the state denied or reduced your benefits, you had the right to ask a court to review this decision. But going to court would cost the usual filing fee, which was twenty-five dollars. The Court upheld this requirement, though by a narrow margin.[121]

With some exceptions, then, the Court has been exceedingly skittish about using the Constitution to iron out inequalities of income and wealth. This is, after all, a capitalist society. Some things (in the Court's view) should be free for everybody—these were things that money should not buy; but in the American system, these have to be kept within bounds.

The Sound of Distant Drums: Military Justice

It is easy to forget that millions of Americans—during wartime, tens of millions—fall under another, special legal system—the system of military justice.[122] The Articles of War, on British models, were in effect from 1776 on. Military justice always had something of a kangaroo court aspect; army commanders, and ship captains, had enormous, almost unrestrained power to discipline their men. War is cruel and tough, and this power was supposed to be necessary. But the long-term trend has been toward granting more rights, more due process, to servicemen and -women. The process began after the First World War. After the Second World War, the Department of Defense set up a committee, with orders to draft a Uniform Code of Military Justice. The UCMJ went into effect in 1951. The code created a United States Court of Military Appeals—a court made up of officers, but structurally independent; a court which was not to be cowed and controlled by commanding generals and admirals. Essentially, under the code, men and women accused of crimes against the military code had many of the same constitutional rights as civilians.

It is probably no accident that the code took form in the early 1950s—a decade of ferment, a decade of rights revolution in the civilian courts. Since 1951 military justice has continued to evolve in the same direction—that is, toward some kind of convergence with civilian justice; more like ordinary courts, less like the traditional court-martial.[123] Differences remain—and perhaps will always remain; military justice is still *military* justice. Military courts are still subject to the overall military mission. The code contains provisions that have no counterpart in civilian justice—going AWOL or deserting, for example; these are obvious enough, but there is also "conduct unbecoming an officer and a gentleman" (art. 133, CMJ), or the crime of using "contemptuous words against the President" or other high officials; or behaving "with disrespect" toward a "superior commissioned officer" (arts. 88, 89). And Article 134 allows the punishment of "all disorders and neglects" which prejudice "good order and discipline," or which "bring discredit upon the armed forces," even though the acts are "not specifically mentioned" in the code. Nevertheless, military justice has come a long way from the quick, summary, brutal system of past times.

First Nations

The period up to the New Deal was a low point for Native Americans. The Depression hit the reservations very hard. Indians were, in general, dirt poor; in 1930 Navajo income was $150 a year per person; and by 1935 annual per capita income on the Sioux reservations had sunk to some $67. Robbed and cheated and oppressed by one policy after another, including the Dawes Act, most native Americans had become "destitute"; "landless, homeless, and mired in poverty."[124]

The Bureau of Indian Affairs had never demonstrated much sympathy or insight or efficiency. Change came under a new commissioner of Indian affairs, John Collier, appointed by Roosevelt in 1933. Collier was something different: a man who wanted to preserve Indian culture, not destroy it. An order he issued in 1934 sounded a fresh note in policy: it was "desirable," according to the order, "that Indians be bilingual—fluent and literate in English, and fluent in their vital, beautiful, and efficient native languages"; Indian religions and cultures were also to be respected.[125]

Thus Collier turned his back on the policy of assimilation; and, more significantly, on the idea that the native tribes were primitive savages, who would be best off giving up their primitive ways. The Indian Reorganization Act of 1934 gave native peoples the right to organize, and to "adopt an appropriate constitution and bylaws."[126] The act also put an end to the allotment policy of the Dawes Act. The Code of Indian Tribal Offenses (1935) clarified the criminal jurisdiction of the various peoples.[127] Many tribes did indeed adopt constitutions, and many created indigenous penal codes.[128]

A drumbeat of criticism of the Collier policies was present from the outset; and the noise only grew louder over the years. In the 1950s another major about-face occurred. Policy reverted to assimilation—which meant, in practice, destroying tribal custom and tribal life. The goal was (according to Congress) putting native peoples under the same laws, and "entitled to the same privileges and responsibilities" as were "applicable to other citizens," and to end, as soon as possible, their "status as wards of the United States."[129] Under a law of 1953 the states could assume jurisdiction over civil and criminal cases inside "Indian country," even if both sides of the case were members of the tribe.[130] In 1954 Congress voted to "terminate" a whole long list of tribes—for example, the Klamath of Oregon and the Menominee tribe of Wisconsin. When a tribe was "terminated," the individual members were to divvy up tribal assets. All federal housing, education, and welfare programs were also "terminated." The tribes were thus handed over to the tender mercies of the individual states.[131]

In the 1960s and 1970s the pendulum swung back to a policy of self-determination; and termination was itself terminated. No doubt the civil rights movement, and the whole concept of plural equality, played a vital role in this process. Termination had been, in many cases, a disaster. When the Wisconsin Menominee were terminated, they suddenly found themselves liable to pay property taxes, and when people failed to pay, they lost some of their lands. Unemployment increased; public health suffered. From 1969 on the Menominee lobbied to be un-terminated; and in 1973 Congress enacted the Menominee Restoration Bill, to undo the calamity of termination.[132]

Like other minorities, the first nations organized, and they produced their own brand of militancy. The American Indian Movement was founded in 1968; it burst into the headlines when activist Indians seized Alcatraz Island, in San Francisco Bay, in November 1969. The Indians stayed on the island until June 1971. In 1973 a group of Native Americans convened in Wounded Knee, on the Pine Ridge Indian reservation. This was the site of a nineteenth-century massacre of Sioux Indians. At Wounded Knee, they issued some demands—new hearings on old treaties, "investigations and exposures of the Bureau of Indian Affairs," and so on. The government response was negative and heavy-handed; roads were blocked, and armed federal officers surrounded the site. The Indians dug trenches and built bunkers, and a two-month siege began—a kind of stalemate, punctuated with acts of violence. Two Indians were killed, and a federal marshal paralyzed. In the end, the siege fizzled out, the federal government arrested hundreds of protesters; and some of the activists were put on trial.[133]

Yet militancy, in the end, paid off; it raised the consciousness of the general public, and, perhaps more significantly, the consciousness of native Americans. In an age of rights consciousness and identity politics, their time had finally come. Claims that would have had no chance of success got hearings in court—and sometimes ended in victory. The whole tone of legislation changed. The Indian Self-Determination and Education Assistance Act of 1975 began by reciting that "prolonged Federal domination of Indian service programs has served to retard rather than enhance the progress of Indian people."[134] Three years later, Congress made it official policy to protect and "preserve" the "traditional religions of the American Indian, Eskimo, Aleut, and Native Hawaiians," an idea which would have astounded and appalled generations of missionaries; the executive branch took steps to protect "sacred sites." The Indian Child Welfare Act of 1978 gave tribes jurisdiction of child custody cases.[135]

Self-government and autonomy increased on the reservations, particularly for larger tribes. One sign of this was the growth of tribal courts. There were 119 in 1978; perhaps 500 by 2000; and they handled tens of thousands of cases. The Muscogee nation, for example, has a Supreme Court made up of six justices, appointed by the principal chief of the nation. Still, the relationship between these courts, the national courts, and the state courts remains complex and subtle; and constantly shifting in principle and tone. The tribal courts apply, in theory, tribal law. But the reports of the Navajo Supreme Court do not differ that much from reports of local courts anywhere else; most of the law they apply is ordinary American law. Nevertheless, the court does insist on the right to apply what it calls Navajo common law, in those spaces left open to it—mostly cases of property rights, family law, and inheritance.[136]

Autonomy is now, in short, basic policy for the first nations. Autonomy means that the tribes can, within limits, run their own affairs, maintain their own traditions. But those traditions cannot contradict what Americans consider "fundamental" principles. So the Indian Civil Rights Act of 1968 extended much of the federal Bill of Rights to tribal governments. No Indian tribe, for example, was to abridge freedom of speech or religion; and the familiar bans on double jeopardy and cruel and unusual punishment were also included in the list.[137] Any "tradition" that contradicted these principles had to go.

At the end of the twentieth century, some of the first nations showed a strength no one would have predicted in 1900. The march toward extinction had halted. True, native culture was under siege. Some small tribes were not likely to survive. Dozens of native languages were either extinct, or spoken only by a few old women and men. Assimilation was still an ever-present danger. The threat no longer came from a cruel and indifferent government; it came from a more powerful and implacable enemy: American mass culture, TV, and the seductions of modernity. But the bigger tribes—the Navajo, the Cherokee— had definitely turned a corner. Their populations were growing. Their languages and religions seemed, for the moment, secure. A number of tribes, too, had been able to get out of the rut of poverty. Some tribes exploited valuable mineral rights; other exploited their sovereignty, by running casinos or selling fireworks in places where these businesses were otherwise illegal. Despite these gains, poverty still stalked many reservations—grinding, miserable, abject poverty, along with its deadly concomitants: alcoholism, family disintegration.

The Other Americans

For most of American history, nonwhite America consisted of the masses of blacks, and the native tribes. Hispanics and Asians became a significant part of the fabric in the nineteenth century; and more significant, socially and legally, in the twentieth.

In California, a few grand old Hispanic families were left over from old Mexican days; but far more significant were the thousands of poor Mexican immigrants in dusty citrus towns of southern California, stoop-laborers, dishwashers, hired hands. Like the black farmworkers of the South, they were despised but essential. The Chicano population of California grew rapidly in the twentieth century; by 1927 nearly 10 percent of the state's public school population was of Mexican descent—some sixty-five thousand pupils, concentrated in the southern part of the state.[138] As the population grew, school boards began to force Mexican kids into segregated schools. The city of San Bernardino went further: it barred people of "Mexican or Latin descent" from certain swimming pools, bathhouses, parks, and playgrounds. A federal court declared the practice unconstitutional in 1944.[139]

The Chicano experience was in some ways like the experience of southern blacks; but there were also crucial differences. In Orange County, in the town of El Modena, poor Mexicans went to one school; the Anglos went to another, separated from the Chicano school by a common playing field.[140] The line between the schools was not as stark and either/or as the black-white line in the South. Lighter-skinned Mexicans from better-off families went to the "white" school, and never mixed with the other Spanish-speakers. The "one-drop" rule never applied to Hispanics; instead, class, race, and social status mixed in a single, potent but complicated brew. People with some Hispanic ancestry, but light-skinned and mostly Anglo, could and did fade into the majority population.

For most Mexican-Americans, however, in the 1920s, segregation was a reality in towns like El Modeno. School segregation for Chicanos had a fairly shaky foundation in state law; and, after the Second World War, Chicano activisits brought a class-action lawsuit in the federal court, complaining about segregation in El Modeno and other districts in Orange County. One of the plaintiffs was Gonzalo Mendez, who lent his name to the case. The plaintiffs won. The district court found a system of discrimination "against . . . pupils of Mexican ancestry," and granted relief; and the Court of Appeals affirmed.[141] It was a significant victory, and it came before *Brown v. Board of Education.* Interestingly, both sides "conceded" that there was "no question of race discrimination" in the case. And the courts treated the case accordingly, as one of ethnicity, not race.[142] In 1947 the legislature of California repealed the laws which authorized school segregation; and the governor, Earl Warren, signed the bill.[143] Segregation of Chinese and Japanese kids in San Francisco had also never been as rigid as the segregation of blacks. The law permitted segregation, but long before *Brown v. Board of Education*—in fact, in the late 1920s—the system had already broken down.[144]

In the 1990s, issues of segregation and busing took on quite a different look in San Francisco. Black organizations like the NAACP wanted busing to continue—although not all black parents agreed. The city now had a large Chinese-American population. Many Chinese parents loathed the idea of busing. They wanted compact school districts in which their kids could have specialized language training; and they wanted their kids as close to home as possible. The young Chinese were high achievers: rules establishing quotas for elite public high schools, meant to produce "diversity," had the perverse effect of discriminating *against* this minority race.[145] At the end of the century, this dilemma remained unresolved.

Who Am I?

The civil rights movement had many consequences; one of them, perhaps paradoxically, was to increase people's consciousness of race, nationality, or, in general, their "roots." Of course, nobody needed to explain to black Americans that they were part of a group—the white majority imposed this lesson on them every day in every way. The civil rights movement fought for the proposition that group membership should not subject you to humiliation, shame, or downright oppression. The idea caught on. In *Saint Francis College v. Al-Khazraji* (1987), a Supreme Court case, the plaintiff, Al-Khazraji, was an American citizen, born in Iraq, who taught at the college.[146] The college denied him tenure. He suspected bias: against him, as an Arab-American. If he was right, did this bias count as race discrimination? Technically, the case turned on how one read a particular federal law; but the Court (which ruled in favor of Al-Khazraji) redefined *racial discrimination* in very broad terms. The Court spoke about discrimination against "identifiable classes of persons," people who suffered this "intentional discrimination solely because of their ancestry or ethnic characteristics." And in a companion case, the Court used the same broad reading, in a case brought by a Jewish congregation, against people who sprayed the synagogue walls with "red and black paint and with large anti-Semitic slogans."[147]

Indeed, the successes of the civil rights movement also lent a certain cachet to victim status. Or perhaps a better way of putting it is that it took away some of the stigma—to be a victim was not a matter of shame, not a mark of Cain, but a mark of the sanctity of suffering, and a defining event, like the Holocaust for Jews. It also encouraged comradeship and pride: black pride, feminist pride, pride in *la raza*, gay pride, and so on. The pride vogue rubbed off on other groups, groups that had vaguer claims of victimhood, or none at all. If there was black pride, then why not Armenian pride or Irish pride? Why not Norwegian pride? Why not, indeed. Ethnic politics was nothing new; it had been a staple of local politics for at least a century. But nobody in the nineteenth century wore a T-shirt saying "Kiss Me, I'm Irish."

People felt—more and more, perhaps—that group identity mattered, and ought to matter. It should be a source of strength. It should also be a source of downright entitlement, at least for victims of the dark and dirty past. This underlay the moral claim for "affirmative action"—a much-maligned phrase, whose zigzag course we shall explore. Affirmative action is, in a way, the flip side of race discrimination: group members become more and more conscious of their groupness as a basis of claims for benefits rather than a locus of oppression.

Age Discrimination

For most of American history, old people (senior citizens, if you will) were not a clear-cut interest group.[148] They became one, in a way, during the Great Depression. Millions of people were unemployed; there was enormous pressure to spread the work; male heads of families were the ones who most needed jobs. The Social Security Act was supposed to kill two birds with one stone.

The heart of this law, as we have seen, was a kind of Faustian bargain: to get your pension, you had to retire at sixty-five.

Throughout the century, lives have been getting longer (and healthier). There are more senior citizens, absolutely and proportionately. They are also more organized than before. They form a powerful lobby. A retired educator, Dr. Ethel Percy Andrus, founded the American Association for Retired People (AARP) in 1958. Membership by the end of the century ran into the millions. Like blacks, members of ethnic groups, and the sexual minorities, senior citizens had their consciousness raised. They complained, with some justice, that society was suffused with ageism. Beauty and strength belonged to the young. That was, perhaps, inevitable. But what about jobs? Men and women over forty found it hard to get hired when they needed work. Complaints led to some legal results: New York added "age" to its fair employment law in 1958, as one of the categories of discrimination the statute outlawed.

Congress passed an "Older Americans Act" in 1965; it created a new federal official, the commissioner on aging (inside the Department of Health, Education, and Welfare), and it appropriated money for community planning, research, and the like.[149] This was part of Lyndon Johnson's Great Society package. Much more significant, of course, for the elderly, were two massive new health programs, Medicare and Medicaid, as we have seen.

To be sure, Medicare was not just for the elderly; it helped their children and grandchildren, too. On the other hand, ADEA (the Age Discrimination in Employment Act) was a big step in a new direction.[150] Congress passed this law in 1967—three years after the crucial civil rights act of 1964. ADEA created a new offense: age discrimination. Under the law, it was illegal to refuse to hire a worker because of age, or to fire because of age, or to discriminate in "terms, conditions, or privileges of employment" because of age. All employers whose industries "affected" commerce were covered, if they had twenty-five or more workers. On the other hand, the law was limited to a particular age band: people older than forty but younger than sixty-five. This meant, of course, that the original act was hardly a bone thrown to the "gray lobby." It protected, in the main, people of middle age.

This situation did not last. The top age was raised to seventy in 1978; and finally, in 1986 the cap was removed altogether. This was the end of mandatory retirement—at any age. Today, then, it is possible (if unlikely) to work as a coal miner at ninety, or to teach school at ninety-five. A company can shove you out if you cannot do the work; but no company can adopt a blanket rule forcing retirement at some particular age. There are a few exceptions under the law: police officers and firefighters, commercial airline pilots (they have to go at sixty), drivers of long-distance buses, high corporate executives.[151] But for the rest of us, retirement comes when we want it to—or when health or fate steps in.

Age discrimination was another category handed over to EEOC. The supply of complaints is rich and growing. For the fiscal year that ended in 1992, there were nearly twenty-thousand age complaints before EEOC. Here, too, only a small percentage got what they wanted—or got anything at all; about 80 percent of the complaints either were dropped or ended with a finding of "no reasonable cause." By fiscal 1999 the number of complaints had eased somewhat, to just over fourteen thousand.[152] But it is still a substantial number.

Disabilities

The most recent development, and a quite dramatic one, in the law of civil rights, was the passage of the Americans with Disabilities Act (ADA) in 1990.[153] The ADA was not entirely a bolt from the blue. The Rehabilitation Act of 1973 also prohibited discrimination against the handicapped; but the law applied only to federal agencies, and federal contractors. The earlier act had neither muscle nor money behind it.[154] The ADA made up for this lack. Restaurants and hotels could not discriminate against the disabled; new trains and buses had to be fitted so as to accommodate them. But most significantly, the act made it a wrong for an employer to refuse to hire a person with disabilities, or to discriminate on the job in any way, or in benefits, job classifications, and the like, unless the disability really prevented a person from doing the job (no blind truck drivers); moreover, the employer had to make "reasonable accommodations" (ramps for wheelchairs, for example) to let disabled people do the work. The act was a sweeping one: it applied to employers who had fifteen or more employees—that is, almost every employer except mom-and-pop operations. It also defined *disability* in a quite broad way—any impairment (mental or physical) that "substantially limits" one or more "major life activities." The statute does not define what this means; but the EEOC regulations spelled it out somewhat more, referring to "functions such as caring for oneself, performing manual tasks, walking, seeing, speaking, breathing, learning, and working."[155] There are very few exceptions; but Congress was careful to specify that the act did not include homosexuals and bisexuals, people with "gender identity disorders," or compulsive gamblers, pedophiles, kleptomaniacs, and pyromaniacs.[156]

As is often the case, the preamble to the statute is significant. Congress "finds" (said the text) that "some 43,000,000 Americans have one or more physical or mental disabilities"; the number was growing as the population aged. Historically, society "has tended to isolate and segregate" these people; and they "occupy an inferior status in our society." They were, in fact, a "discrete and insular minority" (quoting from the famous footnote in the *Carolene Products* case). What the preamble (and the statute) do, in short, is to establish an identity group out of the congeries of Americans with disabilities. It recognizes—and helps to create—a new "pan-ethnicity." It takes a whole raft of "discrete and insular" minorities, and it lumps them together—the blind, the deaf, people in wheelchairs, diabetics, and even the mentally ill. It thus creates, in a sense, a new political and social unit. No doubt this was already happening (though slowly) in the outside world. No doubt, too, that this act was yet another reflex of the civil rights revolution.

The statute was big news, and especially to those who were in fact disabled. The EEOC received fifteen thousand complaints as early as the fiscal year ending in 1993, and the numbers have gone up a bit since then. As with other forms of discrimination, only a small number of the people who complain end up with any kind of victory.[157] There is no question, however, that the act has made its mark: the architectural landscape, for example, has permanently changed, with ramps, lifts, Braille in elevators, closed-caption broadcasts, and the like. Life has become, perhaps, a bit more easy for people with disabilities; and their consciousness, and the consciousness of the rest of us, has also been raised.

The Right of Privacy

Hardly any development of the period was quite so dramatic as another right that the Supreme Court "discovered," hidden like code writing in the text of the Constitution—the so-called right of privacy. In general, the word *privacy* suggests the right to be left alone, the right to shut the door of the bathroom, the right to some "personal space," the right to keep some secrets, the right to have the sole, exclusive chance to read your mail. In tort law, the right of privacy, as we will see, has something of this meaning. But the constitutional right of privacy is quite different. On the surface, it seems to have only a dim point of contact with privacy in its common-sense meaning.

In hindsight, *Skinner v. Oklahoma* (1942) seemed to point the way.[158] Skinner was a three-time loser; he had been convicted for stealing chickens, then twice for armed robbery. Under Oklahoma law, this made him a "habitual criminal." In Oklahoma a habitual criminal of Skinner's sort could be "rendered sexually sterile." Skinner found this idea unappetizing, to say the least. The Supreme Court of the United States agreed with him. William O. Douglas wrote the opinion; he leaned heavily on the fact that the statute exempted embezzlers, and people who violated Prohibition and revenue laws. This was an irrational classification; and irrational classifications arguably are unconstitutional; they deny some people the equal protection of the laws.

Of course the law usually lets states have wide latitude to draw lines between classes of criminals; nobody could complain if burglars got longer prison terms than embezzlers. What, then, made this case so special? It was special, Douglas said, because "marriage and procreation" are "fundamental to the very existence and survival of the race." Sterilization laws were dangerous, especially in "evil or reckless hands" (Douglas was no doubt thinking of Adolf Hitler here). Such laws, therefore, had to pass a stringent test of constitutionality; and this statute, in Douglas's opinion, failed.[159]

Skinner looks like a pioneer case today; but at the time, it seemed somewhat isolated; a case that pointed in no particular direction. The case that (legally speaking) actually put the ball in motion was *Griswold v. Connecticut* (1965).[160] This was another Douglas opinion, more than twenty years later. The issue here was birth control. In the twentieth century millions of people were using birth control. There was religious opposition, to be sure. The Roman Catholic Church considered contraception a sin. Most states had loosened any restrictions on the sale or use of condoms and the like before the 1950s; as early as the 1930s most people in the country, according to polls, believed that birth control ought to be legal.[161]

Connecticut was a holdout. It had one of the most severe statutes in the country—the only one which made it a crime even to use a "drug, medicinal article or instrument for the purpose of preventing conception." And any kind of family planning or counseling, if it gave advice on contraception, made one an accessory to this crime. Family-planning clinics were simply taboo in Connecticut—at least theoretically. In actual fact, anybody who wanted to buy a condom in Connecticut had no trouble doing so: in the 1950s Professor Vern Countryman of the Yale Law School, eager to provoke a challenge to the law, went with a reporter to a Liggett Drug Store in Hamden, Connecticut, bought a package of Ramses condoms for three dollars, then marched to the local police station. He showed the officers what he had bought, and demanded that charges be brought; the police showed no enthusiasm, and Countryman gave up.[162]

Countryman was not the only person who tried to challenge the law. In the legislature, however, it survived every test; and all court challenges had failed. *Poe v. Ullman* (1961) came close.[163] The plaintiffs wanted the Supreme Court to decide whether the statute was constitutional. But the Court dodged the issue: Felix Frankfurter rather feebly argued that nobody ever enforced the statute; therefore there really was no case. Perhaps the Court hoped the issue would simply go away.

It did not. *Griswold* was the case that broke the deadlock. Estelle Griswold, executive director of the Planned Parenthood League of Connecticut, had been fined as an "accessory" for giving out birth control information (to married people). In a rather weird opinion, Douglas, writing for the Court, reversed Griswold's conviction, and declared the statute void. The words of the Constitution, Douglas said, implied a "zone of privacy." The guarantees of the Bill of Rights had "penumbras, formed by emanations from those guarantees." Privacy was apparently one of these penumbras or emanations. Douglas also invoked the bogeyman of police searching the "sacred precincts of marital bedrooms for telltale signs of the use of contraceptives"; and closed his opinion with a ringing hymn of praise for marriage, that blessed state, "intimate to the degree of being sacred."

Sex (and marriage) were now, to some degree, "sacred"; and some aspects of sex (and marriage) were protected, to some degree, by the Constitution—or at least by the Constitution as Douglas and others read it. Later cases carried the idea somewhat further. They made it clear that this right of privacy was not confined to married people. Other bedrooms, too, were apparently also sacred. And the principle of *Griswold* provided one of the legal props under *Roe v. Wade,* the famous 1973 case on abortion rights.[164] No decision since *Brown v. Board of Education* created a more immediate furor; or a more lasting one. Twenty-five years after *Brown,* that decision had been at least beatified, if not canonized; but getting rid of *Roe v. Wade* is still a major political goal of millions of people—while millions more have made up their mind to defend it to the death.

A long history of controversy over abortion was in the background of *Roe v. Wade*.[165] Abortion had been essentially criminalized since the late nineteenth century. There was, to be sure, a significant abortion underground; and in some states, it was not very far under ground. After World War II, however, some states tightened up their enforcement. Legal abortion became more difficult to get in many places. The troubles of Sherri Finkbine, a television hostess in Arizona, twenty-nine years old and pregnant, made headlines in 1962. Her husband, Bob, had brought back some headache pills from a trip to Europe. Sherri Finkbine discovered, to her horror, that the pills contained thalidomide. This drug had been widely used in Europe, but the FDA had never cleared it for use in the United States. And a good thing, too: the drug savagely attacked the helpless unborn, and produced a crop of severely malformed children—the so-called thalidomide babies. When Sherri Finkbine became aware of this, she began a desperate struggle to get an abortion—no easy task in Arizona. Her struggle ended when she and her husband fled to Sweden. There, thirteen weeks into Sherri Finkbine's pregnancy, doctors removed a malformed fetus from her body. All this took place in a blaze of publicity.[166]

It was, for Sherri Finkbine, a bittersweet ending; or at least a resolution. For many other women, illegal abortions brought painful, bloody death. Here was a dual system, like prostitution, pornography, and divorce: a sharp divide between the official law, and the working reality. There was a vast, subterranean demand for abortion, but it was blocked by men and women whose disapproval was intense, white-hot, and informed by moral passion. The result was a stalemate. In *Roe v. Wade,* the Supreme Court cut this Gordian knot.

Exactly what did the case decide? To begin with, it threw out all existing abortion statutes. Justice Harry Blackmun, who wrote the majority opinion, invoked the right of privacy; this right was "broad enough to encompass a woman's decision whether or not to terminate her pregnancy." But the right was not absolute—at least not past the first trimester. Abortions in the first trimester were medically routine, and the state had no particular interest in regulating them, although the state could, of course, make sure that abortions were "performed under circumstances that insure . . . safety for the patient." In the second trimester, the state "may, if it chooses, regulate the abortion procedure," but only in the interests of the mother's health; for the last stage of pregnancy, the stage of "viability," the state's regulatory power would be greater, and might even extend to prohibition.

This was a carefully crafted plan. Undoubtedly, Blackmun considered it a compromise—and a reasonable one. Some women's groups wanted the law to recognize a woman's right to an abortion absolutely—that is, anytime, anywhere, and up to the moment before birth. Some people, to the contrary, would have liked to see a total ban on abortion. Blackmun no doubt thought he was splitting the difference. But many Americans with deep religious beliefs on the issues, Catholics and Protestants alike, were not interested in compromise. To them, abortion was murder—a crime against God and humanity; a slaughter of innocent children. A compromise with murder is impossible.

The decision was controversial from the start; and the controversy has never ended. Many states—and Congress—took the "prolife" position, in whole or in part, and tried either to subvert *Roe* or to limit its impact. The Hyde Amendment, first enacted by Congress in 1976, banned the use of federal Medicaid funds for abortions, except for victims of rape or incest (a tiny group), or where the "life of the mother would be endangered if the fetus were carried to term." By a one-vote margin, the Supreme Court upheld this statute: government, according to *Roe,* cannot "place obstacles in the path of a woman's exercise of her freedom of choice," but the government does not have to "remove" obstacles that it did not create; and being poor was one such obstacle.[167] Poor women now had no access to federal money, for the most part. Prochoice people predicted a grim return to the system of back-alley abortions. The worst horrors did not, in fact, come to pass, mostly because private agencies moved in to fill the gap, as much as they could. But some states continued to battle *Roe v. Wade,* and to nibble it to death with exceptions and provisos. Most of these nibblings—but not all—an increasingly conservative Court eventually accepted.

The Cold War and Political Justice

The story of the Warren Court, the triumph of the civil rights movement, the invention of constitutional "privacy," the abortion cases, and the like—all these give the impression of a general age of enlightenment (as liberals defined it) between 1950 and 1980. Even Congress joined in; on the streets and in the business world, prejudice was on the defensive.

But as far as freedom of speech and what we might call political justice were concerned, this was a darker and more ambiguous period, especially in the early years. After the First World War, there had been the infamous Palmer raids, and the red scare. After the Second World War, there was the cold war, and the war in Korea (which broke out in 1950). The war made the communist menace much more palpable. American boys were dying in a struggle against communists half a world away.

The late 1940s began a period of hysteria over communism and communist fellow travelers. The low point was the self-seeking ranting of Senator Joseph McCarthy and his followers. McCarthy has given his name to the period; he burst onto the national stage like a skyrocket after a famous speech in February 1950 at Wheeling, West Virginia, in which he stated that he had in his hand a list of fifty-seven people who were "either card carrying members or certainly loyal to the Communist Party," and who worked in the State Department. These traitors were supposedly selling out the nation.[168] McCarthy in speech after speech insisted that the government was riddled with communists and communist dupes. He was the most obvious, most visible of the witch-hunters, federal and state. But there were many, many others. McCarthyism at its height created a kind of reign of terror against anything that even remotely smacked of "reds." The government was purged and repurged; universities, private industries— and even Hollywood—truckled under and swept away everybody who could be considered a communist or fellow traveler.

McCarthy's sensational charges certainly ratcheted up the stakes and the hysteria. But there was McCarthyism before McCarthy. The House Un-American Activities Committee had been established in 1938. The Smith Act— a strong anticommunist law—was passed in 1940. The Second World War had hardly ended when the cold war began. Truman instituted a federal loyalty program in 1946, and strengthened it in 1947. When China fell to the communists, the fear and suspicion heightened: the question was, who lost China? Spy incidents and trials—the trial of Alger Hiss for perjury in 1948 was one example—increased the pressure. After war broke out in Korea, the cold war with communism became a tough, brutal, dangerous, killing hot war.

Now an epidemic of witch-hunting, paranoia, and political grandstanding infected the whole country. States and local governments got into the act. Fifteen states passed laws in 1949 against subversive activities; forty-four jurisdictions had laws by 1955 to punish sedition, criminal anarchy, criminal syndicalism, advocating the overthrow of the government, and so on. Some of these laws were incredibly draconian: in Michigan subversives could be imprisoned for life; in Tennessee the death penalty was theoretically possible for anybody who dared advocate the violent overthrow of the United States government. Many states outlawed the Communist Party. New Hampshire's attorney general, Louis C. Wyman, was a particularly notorious zealot, out to get Marxists, fellow travelers, "dupes," and "apologists" for the communists. A number of states created committees and commissions to carry out investigations (essentially witch-hunts), searching for radicals secreted in the nodes of business, government, and academia. Washington State, Illinois, California, and Maryland had legislative committees especially keen on ferreting out reds. Ohio was another state with an Un-American Activities Commission. After all, as a congressman from Ohio warned, there were 1,300 actual Communists in Ohio; and consequently there "can be no real peace or security . . . for Communism is the devil's own instrument of hatred, war, chaos and ruin."[169]

It is impossible to measure the damage done to individual lives, and to the fabric of civil liberties. In some regards, however, the bark of the law was worse than its bite. Nobody was put to death in Tennessee as a subversive. Some of the laws were more or less dead letters. Some governors, like Adlai Stevenson in Illinois, were willing to veto the most obnoxious proposals. State courts declared a fair number of laws—the most egregious ones—unconstitutional. Teachers and public employees hounded out of their jobs or forced to resign after reckless charges, occasionally went to court and got their jobs back. Yet, undeniably, a hurricane of intolerance swept across the country. There were no murders, but there were a handful of desperate suicides; lives were wrecked, careers broken; and rights, liberties, and many decent liberal impulses were trampled to death in the stampede to crush the reds.

The cold war was serious business; it was also a godsend to the right wing of American politics, frustrated so long by Roosevelt's New Deal. Now the Right flexed its muscles. Red-baiting was a useful tool to smear anything even mildly to the left. The Right seized eagerly on the crusade against communism to wage war on unions, on racial equality, and whatever else they could tar with the communist brush—the whole legacy of the New Deal, for example.

There was opposition, of course. The American Civil Liberties Union, though it conducted its own purge of communists, stood up for a more expansive reading of constitutional rights.[170] Some American procedures, laws, and institutions not only survived the hurricane but somewhat mitigated the storm. The Supreme Court of the United States was not, at first, among these. The Court continued its tradition of bending and bowing its head during foul weather. The Smith Act had made it a crime to "knowingly or willfully advocate, abet, advise, or teach the duty, necessity, desirability, or propriety of overthrowing . . . any government in the United States by force or violence." Congress passed this law as the right stuff for smashing the Communist Party. Truman's administration was under pressure to show that it was serious about reds. In 1949 the government indicted eleven leaders of the party and brought them to trial. They were charged with conspiracy to advocate the overthrow of the government.[171]

The defendants may or may not have been guilty of the crimes they were charged with. They were definitely guilty of emoting and posturing, in the ridiculous belief that they served either their own cause or the toiling masses or the greater cause of the party in so doing. The trial lasted from January to October 1949. Throughout it was raucous and tumultuous. It was also blatantly unfair. The federal judge who presided, Harold Medina, was hardly a model of impartiality; he apparently believed, quite sincerely, that the Communists and their lawyers were trying to drive him crazy, or even that they were trying to put him into a hypnotic trance.[172] J. Edgar Hoover fed information to the prosecution. Shouting matches, recriminations, manifestoes punctuated the trial. The evidence against the defendants was hardly overwhelming—dubious testimony from ex-Communist witnesses, and a parade of inflammatory quotations from Communist writings. But no one was surprised when the jury came back with its verdict: guilty as charged.

Naturally, the defendants appealed. In *Dennis v. United States* (1951) the Supreme Court confirmed the convictions.[173] The defendants were in a way unlucky; the outbreak of the Korean War undoubtedly hurt their cause and their case. In *Dennis,* the Court held the Smith Act constitutional; it also held that the act, in effect, outlawed the Communist Party. The defendants' lawyers argued that the statute "stifles ideas and is contrary to all concepts of . . . free speech." Chief Justice Vinson, speaking for a majority of the Court, disagreed. The Smith Act was "directed at advocacy, not discussion." The United States had the right to defend itself; it need not "wait until the putsch is about to be executed." Violent overthrow is a "sufficient evil for Congress to prevent." The clear-and-present-danger test was met. World conditions were "inflammable." The party was a "highly organized conspiracy, with rigidly disciplined members."

Was the American Communist Party in fact a threat to the country? William O. Douglas, who dissented, argued that the Communists, as a political party, were "of little consequence." They were "miserable merchants of unwanted ideas." And the Communists had been "destroyed . . . as an effective political party" *because* of and by means of free speech. The idea that the Communists presented a "clear and present danger" of revolution, and therefore had to be "suppressed," seemed patently absurd. Fifty years later, in the cold, hard light of historical hindsight, it is hard not to agree with him.

The Communist Party had been, in fact, nearly destroyed by then; but not entirely by free speech. The fight against communism was much more than words and arguments. The FBI had thoroughly infiltrated the party. Open members were harassed wherever they lived or worked, and not only by the FBI. The *Dennis* case gave a green light to further threats and persecutions. It legitimated these actions, but, more important, it gave a clear signal that the courts would not stand in the way.

During the McCarthy period, loyalty oaths multiplied like flies, and it was inevitable that this issue, too, would come before the Supreme Court. It did, in 1951. The state was California, the city Los Angeles: under a state law, the city asked all of its employees to swear that they "do not advise, advocate or teach . . . the overthrow by force, violence or other means, of the Government," and had not done so in the past. Each employee also had to execute an affidavit stating whether he was or ever had been a member of the Communist Party. The Supreme Court upheld the law, ordinance, oath, and affidavit.[174] The oaths were only one device in a thorough purge of the civil service. In New York City about 320 schoolteachers and 58 college teachers lost their jobs during this new red scare.[175]

A series of dramatic spy trials seemed to buttress the argument that there *was* an internal communist menace. The most sensational of these was the trial of Julius and Ethel Rosenberg. They were accused of turning over vital atomic secrets to the Russians. The trial began in March 1951, in New York. It was, relatively speaking, quite short—it took only about three weeks. The Rosenbergs were found guilty; and on April 5, 1951, Judge Irving Kaufman sentenced them to death. They had committed, he said, a crime "worse than murder." The Rosenbergs appealed; but the federal court of appeals affirmed the conviction and the sentence. The Supreme Court denied certiorari, on October 13, 1952.[176] They were executed on June 19, 1953.

Of course, there *were* spies—Julius Rosenberg was perhaps one of them—professionals, or amateurs, who passed documents and tidbits of information to the Soviet Union for one reason or another. The Soviet Union, especially under the iron hand of Joseph Stalin, was a stubborn, aggressive, implacable, and paranoid enemy during the cold war. And like all major powers, it made an effort to spy on other countries. There was, for example, Judith Coplon, a political analyst in the Foreign Agents Registration Section of the Department of Justice. Coplon fell in love with the wrong man—Valentine A. Gubichev, a Russian who worked (ostensibly) for the United Nations. She passed documents to Gubichev during their furtive meetings. Coplon was arrested, and tried not once but twice: in New York, on conspiracy charges; and in Washington, on espionage charges. Both times she was convicted. But both convictions were reversed: in New York, because the arrest was made without a warrant; in Washington, because the government allegedly tapped her phone conversations with her lawyer.[177] Judith Coplon, a lucky woman, went free, and vanished into obscurity.

Much more sensational was the trial of Alger Hiss, once a high official of the State Department, later president of the Carnegie Endowment for International Peace. Whittaker Chambers, himself an ex-Communist, fingered Hiss as a secret Communist, and in fact a Soviet agent.[178] Hiss denied the charges under oath. He was tried for perjury in 1948. The case evoked enormous passion on both sides. Liberals felt in their bones that this was vile, right-wing slander. The right wing saw in this case a confirmation of what they felt in *their* bones: the whole elite, striped-pants, eastern establishment was a nest of traitors and spies. The trial was dramatic, full of surprises and elaborate hocus-pocus, with tales of microfilm hidden in pumpkins, and fascinating details from the underground world of the far, far Left. A mistrial was declared; Hiss went to trial again in 1950, was convicted, and sentenced to prison. To the end of his long life (he died in 1996, at age ninety-two), Hiss insisted that he was an innocent man. More likely than not, Hiss had in fact been a Communist, and perhaps something of a (minor) agent of the Soviet Union.

But very few Americans were actually Communists; most who sympathized with communism had gotten off the bus by the 1950s; even some of the secret Communists who passed documents during the war—and the Soviet Union was America's ally at the time—were no longer active in the 1950s. As the McCarthy era lurched into darker and deeper modes, emphasis shifted. The government, at first, announced the quite reasonable goal of getting rid of people who were actually disloyal, if not downright traitors. But later the target became not spies, but "security risks," a far broader and more nebulous category. A man whose brother-in-law was a communist, or who had been a member of some left-wing group, or who lived next door to a communist, or who was a suspected homosexual—he might not be actually disloyal, but there was a shadow, a possibility, a doubt; and this made him a "security risk." Obviously, the search for security risks heightened the atmosphere of paranoia.

"Security risks" were not only people who, say, worked for the Atomic Energy Commission, or handled secret documents for the army. They might be schoolteachers, employees of the Department of Agriculture, chemists with the Food and Drug Administration. Were left-wing janitors or pink army dentists really a threat to the nation? Obviously not. But it did not matter. They were evil, people whose souls were in hock to the devil, sources of moral contagion. The right wing, egged on by the likes of J. Edgar Hoover, turned up the heat, set the cauldron of fear and anxiety on high—to score political points, to clean out New Dealers, and to weaken any tendency toward liberal programs and doctrines.

Only when the worst of the crisis was over, and McCarthy was a fallen idol, did the Supreme Court come creeping around to a more balanced view. In general, during the McCarthy era, the Court backed and filled and equivocated; it is hard (probably impossible) to make the cases fit any single, coherent pattern.[179] In 1957, on "Red Monday," the Supreme Court turned away from its cold war stance, in a dramatic way.[180] In *Yates v. United States* the Court set aside the convictions of second-tier leaders of the Communist Party, charged (as before) with conspiracy to evade the Smith Act.[181] People who simply advocate overthrowing the government, even if they utter words in the hope that their speech will "ultimately lead to violent revolution," the Court ruled, cannot be convicted of a crime. Such words were too "remote from concrete action" to allow for actual punishment.

Despite Red Monday, the Court remained deeply divided—and somewhat timid—on cold war issues. The Subversive Activities Control Act of 1950 required all "Communist-action organizations" to register with the attorney general, and open up their membership lists. In 1961, in *Communist Party v. Subversive Activities Control Board,* a narrow 5–4 majority upheld the statute. After all, the communists (said the Court) were a "world-wide integrated movement"; and they used every means, fair and foul, "to destroy the government." Congress, the Court felt, needed a lot of discretion in deciding how to meet the communist threat consistently "with the safeguarding of personal freedom."[182] Personal freedom obviously came in second here. Yet four years later, in *Albertson v. Subversive Activities Control Board,* the Court seemed to do a flip-flop.[183] The Communist Party had refused to register and turn over its membership lists. The Court held that the government could not force them to do so. If the party registered, it might lay members open to the threat of prosecution, under the Smith Act. Registration, then, in a sense forced them to incriminate themselves, and this would violate their Fifth Amendment rights. And in 1966, in *Elfbrandt v. Russell,* the Court confronted an Arizona law under which state workers had to take a loyalty oath, and swear that they were not communists or members of any organization committed to overthrowing the government.[184] The Court felt the state could not punish mere membership in these organizations; even if the organization had an unlawful purpose; only a member who actually intended to pursue this goal actively could be considered a threat to society.

When the Supreme Court speaks, on civil liberties, it acts in an authoritative manner—at least as far as the court system is concerned. Its mandate must be obeyed; and it is obeyed—at least on the surface. Yet Red Monday and the decisions which at least cast doubt on cold war excesses did not always have the impact the Court intended. J. Edgar Hoover, rabid leader of the FBI, was not to be deterred by such things as Supreme Court decisions; he waged his own, continuing war on reds. He ran a massive, secret, and quite illegal program of harassment, spying, and infiltration. As usual, he aimed his artillery not just at communist organizations, but at anybody and everybody he deemed a fellow traveler; or who advocated programs that Hoover was against. Hoover apparently had trouble telling the difference between a Soviet agent and, say, Martin Luther King, Jr.

McCarthyism, and Hoover's actions, illustrate once more the point that liberty is not a document, not a set of doctrines, not a collection of court cases, but a system, a process, a climate of life within a country. A stifling, bigoted community, which shuns deviants, which makes their life miserable, which is intolerant of dissent, is of course far better than the Third Reich or Stalin's Russia; but it is oppressive enough in its own right. The powerful, volcanic emotions of the McCarthy period would have overwhelmed the courts—even assuming that the courts were in the mood to resist. In this regard "law" and "society" cannot really be separated. The Court can show more "enlightenment" than the general population—and in many ways, during this period, it did—but it does not feel able to get very far out in front of the pack. Nor does it usually want to: the justices are, after all, creatures of society themselves. The cold war justices were not immune to the cold war mind.

Almost fifty years have gone by since the second great red scare of the century. The cold war is officially over. To many people, the age of McCarthy seems as remote, as foreign, as the age of the first great American witch-hunt, a search for real witches, not metaphorical ones, in seventeenth-century Salem, Massachusetts. Millions of respectable, responsible people in the McCarthy age joined the crusade against leftists; yet today, only a few revisionist historians, and a few unregenerate red-baiters, have a kind word to say about McCarthyism; it lingers in historical memory like a bad smell. What possessed us, in those days?

We have already mentioned some answers. The Soviet Union was, unquestionably, a dangerous enemy. And the war on reds was also a grand political opportunity to settle a score with the New Deal. Central casting could hardly have found a better enemy than communism as a foil for American rage and fear. Communism sneered at religion; and this was a deeply religious country. It preached racial equality, and this was anathema to the South. The three Ku Klux Klans were only the most obvious signs of a powerful, ultraconservative tendency within American society—something that emerges from time to time, like the creature from the black lagoon. For many Americans what was new, what was foreign always seemed dangerous, corrupt, satanic. It was easy to see the Rosenbergs—small, dark, Jewish, with mournful and shifty eyes—as traitors, parasites, secret agents sapping the vital bodily fluids of America; they replaced Sacco and Vanzetti, the dark and crafty anarchists of the 1920s. Almost equally baleful were the aristocratic spies: the Alger Hisses of the world—remote, aloof, vaguely effete, disdainful of the American masses. McCarthy, in his Wheeling speech, sneered at the "bright young men who are born with silver spoons in their mouths"; those were the worst of the traitors; and he referred to Dean Acheson, the secretary of state, as a "pompous diplomat in striped pants."[185]

McCarthyism drew some of its sinister power from the darker side of American populism: the crude, vulgar populism that fed white supremacy in the South, and nativism and race prejudice elsewhere. Scholars have pointed out that only America had McCarthyism; other countries—England, notoriously—had to deal with whole nests of Soviet spies, many of them in high places; but England never fouled itself with witch-hunts and right-wing crusades. America, compared with its rivals in Europe, is informal, nonhierarchical, lacking in deference, suspicious of elites and intellectuals, distrustful of upper classes. This is one of its strengths. But it is also a weakness; America at times lies naked to the worst impulses of mass thought.

Speech, Media, the Press

In the cold war cases, the Supreme Court, as we have seen, showed a certain timidity; it seemed reluctant to unleash the full power of free-speech doctrines against the laws and practices of the McCarthy period. Its attitude toward other issues of free speech—pornography, for example—was also somewhat halting and ambivalent.

The Court seemed boldest, in some ways, in race cases. And race was in the background of one of the Court's most significant decisions on freedom and the First Amendment, *New York Times v. Sullivan* (1964), although the legal issue was quite different.[186] The "Committee to Defend Martin Luther King, Jr." bought an ad in the *Times*. Its headline read, "Heed Their Rising Voices." The ad bitterly criticized city officials of Montgomery, Alabama (without naming names); "they" had "bombed Dr. King's home," they had harassed him, they had arrested him seven times, and now they had charged him with "perjury, a felony under which they could imprison him for ten years." The ad asked for money to help in the fight for racial equality.

In fact, there were some mistakes in the ad. Dr. King had been arrested four times, not seven, for example. The ad said that protesting students sang "My Country, 'Tis of Thee" at the Alabama capitol; in fact, they sang "The Star-Spangled Banner." None of the mistakes seemed particularly earthshaking; but they were in fact mistakes. A city commissioner of Montgomery, L. B. Sullivan, sued the *New York Times* for libel; a jury of twelve white men in Montgomery found for Commissioner Sullivan (no big surprise), and awarded him half a million dollars in damages. The Alabama Supreme Court affirmed this decision. No Supreme Court case had ever considered the issue of libel laws and freedom of speech. It was pretty much assumed that the First Amendment did not protect libel and slander. But the Supreme Court overturned the verdict against the *New York Times*. A "public official" could not recover damages for a lie or misstatement about his official conduct, unless the statement was made with "actual malice." A newspaper was protected, constitutionally, for "erroneous statements honestly made." In other words, unless the *Times* knew that the statements were false, or had acted with "reckless disregard" of whether the statements were true or false, its work was "privileged." The great wings of the Constitution now sheltered the press against libel actions, even when what a publication printed turned out not to be true. Free speech has to be "uninhibited, robust, and wide-open"; mistakes in such robust, freewheeling speech are "inevitable."

The Court had shown sensitivity before to censorship of the press. In *Near v. Minnesota* (1931) the Court struck down a Minnesota statute (the "Minnesota gag law") which allowed the county attorney of any county to move to suppress ("abate"), as a "public nuisance," any "malicious, scandalous, and defamatory newspaper."[187] Chief Justice Hughes sang the praises of a free press, though he also pointed out in that case that the libel laws remained in effect. The "newspaper" in question (it hardly deserved the name) was the *Saturday Press* of Minneapolis. This was a scurrilous rag which made vicious attacks on Jews— "Every vendor of vile hooch . . . every snake-faced gangster and embryonic yegg in the Twin Cities is a JEW"—and it made constant references to "Yids," and to people "with a hook nose" who ate herring; there were thinly veiled calls for action against these horrible specimens. But the Court clearly felt that the statute was a case of overkill. The Court hated the idea of "prior restraints"— that is, censorship in advance of what a newspaper puts in print.

Near left open the question which *Sullivan* attempted to close. Certainly, the advertisers in the *Times* were a more sympathetic lot—heroes, in fact. The lawsuit against the *Times* was a threat to the civil rights movement; the Court was surely aware of this point. But the *Sullivan* case tapped even deeper cultural veins. *Sullivan* protected reports about public officials, but later cases extended the protection to all discussions of "public figures"—that is, celebrities, famous people in general. In one case, it was enough to be "Elvis Presley's 'No. 1 girl'" (and have something of a show business career) to become a public figure.[188] It is even possible to be an "involuntary" public figure: somebody thrust into the limelight by calamity or some stroke of enormous luck, like winning the lottery.

As the *Near* case shows, and the history of the "yellow press" in the late nineteenth and early twentieth century confirms, wild, irresponsible journalism is nothing new. The content changes somewhat over time. Supermarket tabloids, *People* magazine, and celebrity gossip vehicles are politically neutered and show few signs of race hatred; they feed on the vices and weaknesses of the "stars": heroes of stage, screen, radio, TV, and music; sports figures; political figures thrown in to the bargain only insofar as they qualify as celebrities. In the late twentieth century, the market for celebrity news had become voracious. In a way, *New York Times v. Sullivan,* a case of somber nobility, a shield for the brave and the virtuous against white supremacists and other racial predators, turned into a Magna Carta for the celebrity society—a society hungry for every last crumb of gossip and dirt about famous people. Today, legally speaking, almost anything goes. The public, we are told, has a legitimate (and constitutional) interest in everything—certainly in the sex life of President William Jefferson Clinton, including the shape of his penis—and is entitled to know or hear about everybody of any significance, and even people of no significance, as long as their lives could possibly be considered "public," during their proverbial fifteen minutes of fame. *New York Times v. Sullivan,* of course, did not create the raucous, intrusive, scandal-mad hunger for "news." It did not create reality TV or "trash talk shows." And if the cases had gone in some other direction, that would probably not have been able to stop the explosion of morbid curiosity. This was inevitable in a society saturated with images day and night—images that give the illusion of reducing the social distance between the ordinary Joe and Jane, on the one hand, and the rhinestone glitter of celebrity life on the other; images that blur the line between fact and fiction, between truth and fantasy. The *Sullivan* case became one part of a mighty current of events.

Immigration

The cold war deeply affected immigration policy. Millions were slaughtered in the Second World War, millions were left homeless, hungry, and drifting in the rubble of Europe. Even before Germany surrendered, there were cracks in the alliance between the Western democracies and their rather strange bedfellow,

Joseph Stalin. Immigration policy, almost immediately, offered shelter to victims of communism in preference to victims of Hitler. Even the act of 1948, allowing entry to "displaced persons," made special provision for natives of Czechoslovakia who fled persecution after January 1, 1948 (when the Communists seized power in that country).[189] The act also reflected another postwar fear: unemployment. It asked for "assurances" that a refugee would not cost any American his job, or become a "public charge," and would have "safe and sanitary housing without displacing some other person."

Legislation in the 1950s continued to reflect the hot breath of the cold war. Under the Internal Security Act of 1950 an alien who belonged to a "subversive" organization could be deported.[190] The McCarran-Walters Act of 1952 revamped and restated American immigration law in a narrow, mean-spirited way, drenched with xenophobia and political intolerance.[191] The act kept the quota system; it removed the absolute ban on Asians, but gave them absurdly low quotas—one hundred persons or so per year.

President Truman vetoed this law; it passed over his veto. But the racist twist of the law was becoming an anachronism. The Immigration and Nationality Act (1965) was an important change in policy and direction.[192] President Lyndon Johnson signed the bill into law, ceremoniously, at the Statue of Liberty, symbol of immigration and the "huddled masses yearning to be free." The new law, however, did not open any doors to huddled masses. It junked the virtual ban on Asians, and got rid of the quota system; but it replaced these with a low lid on immigration (170,000 immigrants a year). And it looked toward a cap on Western Hemisphere immigrants. What people were entitled to the slots under this new system? The law listed priorities: first, close relatives of citizens; next, workers with needed skills; third, refugees; everybody else had to get in line and wait their turn. The Refugee Act of March 17, 1980, solemnly referred to the "historic policy of the United States to respond to the urgent needs of persons subject to persecution in their homelands." It borrowed its definition of a refugee from the United Nations: a refugee was somebody who was afraid to go home because of "persecution, or a well-founded fear of persecution on account of race, religion, nationality, membership in a particular social group, or political opinion."[193] The act authorized admission of fifty thousand refugees a year. A well-founded fear of starving to death was, naturally, no part of this law.

The United States is an immigrant country (like Australia or Chile), and continues to be. Many countries do not have quotas; they have no general policy of letting in outsiders at all. Millions of American citizens—and millions more who simply live in America—were born elsewhere; in 1990 they amounted to about 8 percent of the population, or some 20 million people; and the numbers and proportions have been rising in recent years.[194] There is an insatiable world demand for places in America.

Not that America was the only magnet for immigrants: millions of the world's poor people were and are desperate for a foothold in any developed country, Germany, Sweden, Italy, anything. America is probably the most glamorous and attractive. It is also, despite nativism, hate crimes, barbed wire, and the like, in many ways the most hospitable. This was and is a loose, mobile, formless society; less tight and impenetrable than, say, Sweden—certainly more so than Japan, a country that shrank with horror from the prospect of letting anybody in who was not "Japanese." The United States is big, protean, a land of endless possibilities. Or so it seemed. What was, perhaps, even more important: by the end of the twentieth century there was hardly any nationality so small that it could not find an enclave of its own in some American big city. In how many countries could a Tongan or an Icelander or a Nigerian find a coven of countrymen, perhaps a newspaper in his native language, familiar foods, churches, ways of life?

Poverty, hunger, war, and despair were powerful motives for immigration. Travel had gotten cheaper and easier in the twentieth century. Population pressure in third-world countries drove people from the countryside. Even more powerful than the push of poverty was the pull of opportunity and culture. The decline of traditional society killed off a major barrier to emigration. Isolated peasants and tribespeople, deep in some forest, unaware of the world outside their villages, do not move to Los Angeles or Stockholm. As we have seen, the real barrier that protected the United States from Western Hemisphere immigration in the first half of the century was precisely traditional culture. Nothing so stimulated emigration as the message of modernism and mass culture, the message of consumer goods and Hollywood glitz, the message of McDonald's and rock-music guitars, spread above all by the ubiquitous beam of TV.[195]

State Constitutional Law

The Supreme Court of the United States gets the headlines and the glory—and, perhaps, the toughest and most significant cases. But there are fifty states, and fifty state constitutions. These constitutions are significant documents in their own right. California, Texas, and New York, for example, have huge populations; and for many purposes, the state constitution is the supreme law of these subnations. The high courts of the states decide dozens of cases on state constitutional law. It goes without saying that many of these cases are extremely important for the people who live in the state.

But the world of legal scholarship does not pay much attention to the state constitutions. Legal education ignores them almost entirely. So does the public. A survey in 1991 found that only 52 percent of the respondents even knew that their state had a constitution; 11 percent thought it did not have one, and 37 percent either did not know or gave no answer.[196] State constitutions, and constitutional case law, are like Cinderella, sitting in the ashes, as far as legal education and legal culture are concerned. One partial excuse for the scholars— a rather lame one—is that it is hard to say much about them in general terms. No two state constitutions are alike. They all have bills of rights, and they share some bits of text with the federal Constitution; but they are also, often, wildly different—from each other, and from the federal Constitution, too. They are also much more changeable. There has been one, and only one, federal Constitution. There has not been a constitutional convention for the country as a whole since the 1780s, when James Madison and other men with breeches and quill pens got together in Philadelphia. The states have been much less shy about changing. Some states (about twenty of them), to be sure, have made do with a single constitution. But others have molted constitutions like a snake molts its skin. The champion, apparently, is Louisiana; it has had either eleven or twelve, depending on how one counts. The latest version was adopted in 1974.

The pace of constitution making slowed down in the twentieth century. There were new constitutions in only twelve states in the century. (Five other states—Oklahoma, Arizona, New Mexico, Hawaii, and Alaska—came into the union and adopted a first constitution.) There were sixty-four constitutional conventions during the century, less than half the number that took place in the nineteenth century. And there were long fallow periods: no state adopted a new constitution at all between 1922 and 1944.[197] Still, sixty-four constitutional conventions is a lot more than zero. In the 1960s, for example, there were conventions in Rhode Island, New York, Maryland, Hawaii, New Mexico, Arkansas, and Illinois.[198] These conventions drafted new constitutions and presented them to the public. The public was not very impressed; five out of seven went down to defeat. New York's proposed constitution was a particular disaster: more than 70 percent of the voters said no. Only in Illinois and Hawaii did the voters approve of the hard work of the conventions. Rhode Island, after 143 years with an old constitution, some forty amendments, and a history of failed conventions, finally adopted a new constitution in 1986.

The states also amend their constitutions with gleeful abandon. The United States Constitution was amended only twelve times in the twentieth century. The states, on the other hand, do an enormous amount of tinkering and retinkering and patching and sewing and revising. This is especially true of states whose citizens can stitch new sections into the state constitution by way of referendum. So California has had the "same" constitution throughout the twentieth century (the constitution that went into effect on January 1, 1880). But not the same text. The constitution has been amended and amended and amended; and the process still goes on. Each election brings in a new flock of amendments. The Arkansas Constitution dates from 1864; but it has been amended seventy-six times, almost all of these in the twentieth century. Kansas has had only one constitution (adopted in 1859), but, like other state constitutions, it is hardly an eternal and unchanging text. For example, art. 15, §3 forbids lotteries; this was amended in 1974 to open the door to church bingo. In 1986, another amendment authorized horse and dog racing "and parimutuel wagering," in counties that voted to have such things; and in the same year, still another amendment allowed the state to run its own lottery.

According to one estimate, by the end of the 1960s, the fifty state constitutions had been amended 4,883 times—a staggering total. Georgia was the champion here, with 654 amendments.[199] As a result of all this amending— mostly adding and only a little bit of subtracting—the state constitutions tend to be very long, very bloated, and detailed. Louisiana's constitution, at 254,000 words, is almost as long as this book. The federal Constitution, on the other hand, is a model of crispness and brevity. So were many of the early state constitutions.

Why are state constitutions so long? Why are they amended so often? For one thing, they lack the magic of the federal Constitution. They symbolize nothing in particular. Nobody gets choked up at the thought of these documents. Nobody preserves them in shrines under glass. The average citizen knows little enough about the federal Constitution; Joe and Mary Smith are, as we saw, blissfully ignorant about their state constitution. No structural or ideo-logical obstacles stand in the way of loading up these texts with all sorts of material: stuff which arguably does not belong there. Whatever some interest group wants to put beyond legislative reach goes into the state constitution. Because these constitutions are not at all sacred, they are brittle as well: the federal Constitution, flexible and majestic, bends and flows subtly along with the times. But when times change, the temptation in, say, Louisiana, to junk the whole thing seems irresistible; in other states, increasingly, the constitution stays put in the formal sense, but the text is altered almost beyond recognition.

The National Municipal League, formed in 1894, was a group that pushed for reforms in state constitutions. They lobbied for the initiative system, which thirteen states adopted between 1902 and 1918. It has been a fertile source of constitutional change. The Municipal League also published a Model State Constitution in the 1920s; it got nowhere, but later versions had an impact on constitutions in the new states of Hawaii and Alaska.[200] Many changes the league proposed—and many amendments to state constitutions—were de-signed to streamline government, to make it more rational and efficient. Old restrictions on legislative and executive power were pruned away.

But in recent years, in particular, there has been movement in the other direction: toward adding restrictions on legislative power. This is easiest in states with the referendum process. In California, for example, interest groups with money scrabble together enough signatures to put their pet projects on the ballot in the form of proposed amendments. The notorious Proposition 13, adopted in California in 1978 by referendum, cut the property tax radically; it also made it extremely hard ever to raise the rates again; in the process, it put the state's finances into a straitjacket. Antitax groups put tax cut laws on the (constitutional) agenda in other states, too; some plans succeeded, some failed. The tax revolution was a conservative drive—linked, ideologically, to the idea that government is inherently wicked, a song Ronald Reagan sang with enor-mous skill. The idea of term limits was cut from the same cloth: throw the rascals out of office after a certain number of years. This too won some major victories; California, once more, was a bellwether state; it adopted term limits for state legislators in November 1990.

The fifty state supreme courts decided thousands of cases in the twentieth century on questions of constitutional law. Because state court judges live in the same society, and are part of the same world, it is no surprise that their case law shares on the whole the same long-term trends—with notable exceptions (questions on race, before *Brown*, in the South). William E. Nelson, for example, looked at the "changing meaning of equality" in the high courts of New York.[201] Here the movement, on the whole, has been toward minority rights and plural equality. New York's courts expanded the concept of free speech to cover expressive behavior, including actions that would have horrified Thomas Jefferson. In one case in 1967 the police arrested (pretty much at random) members of a crowd on the grass in Tompkins Square Park on Memorial Day—people playing bongo drums and the like, whose behavior was "unconventional," and whose dress was "bizarre." Their convictions, for disorderly conduct, were overturned: New York's courts were not about to "deny the equal protection of the law to the unwashed, unshod, unkempt, or uninhibited."[202] These were sentiments the Warren Court would have shared; and reflected attitudes that went in tandem with those of the federal courts.

In the late nineteenth century, many leading constitutional decisions came out of state courts; many of the most powerful constitutional doctrines were devised, elaborated, and hammered out in state courts. In the twentieth century, leadership passed to the federal courts, or, more accurately, to the United States Supreme Court. But the state courts retained a great reservoir of power. One source, more and more important, is the doctrine of independent state grounds. Federal courts cannot and do not overturn state decisions, if these decisions can be grounded in the text of the state constitution. After all, as far as these texts were concerned, the state high courts had the last and most authoritative word.[203] For the most part, the states tend to follow the lead of the United States Supreme Court. In the period from the 1960s to the end of the 1980s, according to one study, this was egregiously the case—state supreme courts, in criminal procedure cases, played follow the leader with the United States Supreme Court.[204]

But not always were state supreme courts content with this role. For example, in *Pruneyard Shopping Center v. Robins*, a case out of California (1980), the issue was free speech in that most typical of modern locales, the shopping mall.[205] The Pruneyard shopping center, in Campbell, California, was an ordinary suburban mall, with sixty-five stores, ten restaurants, and a movie theater. High school students set up a card table, passed out pamphlets, and asked passersby to sign petitions protesting against a United Nations resolution which condemned Zionism. A security guard told the students to go; and they went, but only as far as the nearest courthouse.

The United States Supreme Court had wrestled before with shopping center cases. Was a big mall of the Pruneyard type a kind of company town? If so, it could not restrict free speech. Or was it simply private property (which meant that it could)? After considerable waffling, the Court had decided against the theory of the company town. Malls were just sprawling collections of private shops; the owner of the mall could exclude, if it wished, the kids in *Pruneyard* or other petitioners. But the California Supreme Court held otherwise. That state's constitution protected free speech in shopping malls; and never mind what the federal Constitution and the Supreme Court said. The United States Supreme Court bowed to California. A state has a "sovereign right to adopt in its own Constitution individual liberties more expansive than those conferred by the Federal Constitution." And that was that.

11

The Liability Explosion

Personal-Injury Law in the Twentieth Century

Tort law—a lawyer's term—is the law of civil wrongs. When we do harm to somebody else, that is a tort. It is "civil" to distinguish it from criminal wrongs. If I carelessly back into your car in a parking lot, I have probably committed a tort, and I may have to pay for your repairs; but I will certainly not go to jail, especially if it was simply an accident.

Tort law is a grab bag of behaviors; slander is a tort, and so is trespassing on somebody else's land. But the heart and soul of tort law is the law relating to personal injury. This was essentially a creation of the nineteenth century—a creation, to be more exact, of the railroad and the factory. For the first time in history, injury to the body caused by machines became a major social problem. The industrial revolution, like most revolutions, shed a lot of blood: the blood of factory workers, railroad passengers, and sometimes bystanders. Society offered up their shattered bodies as sacrifices to the gods of the new machines. Out of the many lawsuits that followed, a whole new body of law—tort law—was constructed, built up (mainly by the courts) piece by piece, and case by case.

In essence, nineteenth-century tort law was a law of limitation: a law that set boundaries to the liability of enterprise; a law that made it difficult (especially for workers) to collect for personal injury.[1] In the twentieth century, the old tort system was completely dismantled; the courts and the legislatures limited or removed the obstacles that stood in the way of plaintiffs; and a new body of law developed, law which favored the plaintiffs—to the point where people spoke about a liability "explosion." Some of the changes were slow and incremental; some were dramatic. Some were inventions of judges; some were embodied in complicated statutes.

Generally speaking, already at the beginning of the twentieth century, courts were more responsive to the claims of injured people than they had been, say, some fifty years before, though this is hard to document precisely. In *Kambour v. Boston & Main Railroad,* a New Hampshire case decided in 1913, Edward B. Kambour, who was "less than fourteen years old," lived in Blair, New Hampshire, and went to school in Plymouth, by train.[2] At a crossing near the school, the train "usually slackened speed"; and at that point, Edward and his friends would jump off. The boys presumably knew this was a bit on the dangerous side. So did the railroad. And sure enough, Edward jumped one morning, fell under a car, and was injured. He sued the railroad. A jury decided in his favor.

On appeal, the railroad argued, not illogically, that the boy knew what he was doing (he "assumed the risk"); he was "guilty of contributory negligence"; the railroad claimed that it had done nothing wrong. The court rejected all these arguments—the plaintiff was a "boy"; doing something a bit risky does not make a boy a legal "outlaw"; and anyway the railroad, which knew about the practice, should have done something about it. The exact logic is not important; the court's attitude is. It signaled an evolution, a slow change—pointing in the direction of enterprise liability. The typical tort case pitted an injured individual against a corporation (often a big corporation). The corporation, more likely than not, carried insurance. Under these conditions, the courts lost whatever zeal they once had for protecting the erosion of capital through lawsuits.

The change did not take place overnight. What is startling, from the standpoint of the year 2001, is how little money the tort system then provided for accident victims. There was a belief—almost an article of faith—among businesspeople (and some judges) that juries gave away money like candy. But this was largely legend. In New York City in 1910, plaintiffs won fewer than half of their personal injury cases in court, although they did better against railroads (winning 63 percent) than against other defendants. The average amount these winners got was $958—though here too railroads fared the worst ($4,200 was the average in these cases).[3] In Alameda County, California, too, plaintiffs won only half of the tort cases that went to trial.[4] It must also be remembered that most cases never got to trial; they were dismissed by the jury or settled out of court—often for tiny amounts.

Particularly startling is how stingy the system was for victims of great disasters. In 1904 the *General Slocum,* an excursion boat, burned in the East River, in New York. The crew abandoned the burning ship, leaving the passengers to their fate. There were life preservers; but many of them were in terrible condition, and essentially useless. Hundreds drowned, hundreds more died in the flames. The captain went to prison. The families of the dead collected nothing. Another great disaster was the fire at the Triangle Shirtwaist Factory in 1911. The fire started in a bundle of oil-soaked rags. The fire hoses were rotten and improperly connected. Escape doors were locked; the fire was too high to be reached by fire-engine ladders. Many young women burned to death; others jumped to eternity from the windows of the doomed company, desperate to earn a quicker, easier death, as hundreds of people on the streets watched in horror. The gutters on the streets ran with blood. One hundred forty-five workers died, almost all young immigrant women. There were a few civil cases against the owners of the building; but they got nowhere. The company claimed the women had assumed the risks of work, and it also invoked the fellow-servant rule. In the end, the wrongful-death claims settled for $75 each.[5]

A similar story can be told of other great disasters: the 1942 Coconut Grove nightclub fire, for example. In this great Boston catastrophe, 491 people died, the defendant went bankrupt, and the yield was about $160 per victim. When an iceberg sank the *Titanic* in 1912, more than a thousand people died—mostly because there were not enough lifeboats. Nobody collected more than fifty thousand dollars, and the life of each immigrant in the bowels of the ship was valued at one thousand dollars each. Everywhere, as Marc Galanter has put it, we find a story of "hapless victims encountering ineffectual and sometimes predatory lawyers, unflinching antagonists, unresponsive law, callous lawmakers, and a largely indifferent public."[6]

Why so little, when liability seemed so obvious? Sometimes the law stood in the way. Even when the law was no barrier, the legal system was effectively stacked: corporate defendants were rich, or were well connected, or had good lawyers, or all three. They were able to stall, to manipulate, to obfuscate; victims often gave in or gave up. But undoubtedly tort law was responsive here to deeper social attitudes. After all, juries were made up of ordinary people. People felt, apparently, that "accidents" were an unavoidable part of life; that they were "nobody's fault." If there was fault at all, that fault was not systemic; it was the "carelessness" of individuals—often of the victims themselves.

Owners of coal mines, for example, passionately believed that 99 percent of all mine accidents were "due absolutely" to the sloppiness or ignorance or "wilful negligence" of the miners themselves.[7] Indeed, there was some truth to this charge. The cruel pace of work in mines and factories was at least partly to blame. Workers were often impaled on the horns of a dilemma: between a slow and cautious pace that would save their skins, and a faster, crueler pace that would give them enough money to live on. People who took shortcuts across railroad tracks, or hitched rides on streetcars, or were careless in other ways had to bear some of the blame as well. But the harshness of the law, and of its institutions, was in process of evolution; and blame was to be, as we shall see, redefined.

Workers' Compensation

One of the first pillars of the old system formally to go was the so-called fellow-servant rule. Few rules of law were so hated by working people. Under the fellow-servant rule, an injured workman could not sue his employer if the negligence of another employee (a "fellow servant") caused his injury. This meant, in effect, that most human casualties of the industrial revolution collected not a farthing for their mangled bones.

Already in the nineteenth century, and increasingly in the early twentieth century, the states began to nibble away at the fellow-servant rule. Some courts stretched a point, when they could, to let a worker win some particular case. Some states—for example, New York in 1902—enacted laws that restricted the rule somewhat. Under New York's law, an employer had a duty to avoid any "defect in the condition of ways, works, or machinery"and was liable for any negligence of a superintendent or subboss.[8]

The Federal Employers' Liability Act (FELA) of 1906 abolished the fellow-servant rule completely for railroad workers. The statute was declared unconstitutional; but Congress came back with a new version in 1908. This law made the railroad liable for any death or injury resulting from the "negligence of any . . . employees . . . or by reason of any defect or insufficiency, due to . . . negligence, in its cars, engines, appliances, machinery, track, roadbed, works, boats, wharves, or other equipment." Even if the worker himself had been

careless, that did not "bar a recovery"; it only lowered the damages, "in proportion" to the worker's negligence.[9] Employers attacked this law, too, but the
Supreme Court upheld it in 1912.[10] Congress followed up in 1920 with a statute
that applied the same rules to "any seaman who shall suffer personal injury."[11]
The FELA and its sister statutes are still in force today. Essentially, these laws
embody old-fashioned tort law, but stripped of the tough defenses that stood in
the way of workers who tried to collect damages for injuries.

In the states, however, and for the overwhelming majority of workers, what
replaced the fellow-servant rule was an entirely new system—a system that
broke completely with the tort law tradition. This was workers' compensation.
It was a plan to get rid of all tort actions, and simply insure workers against
accidents that took place on the job.[12] The British had done away with the
fellow-servant rule and embraced this system in 1897. (A similar plan had been
adopted, even earlier, in Bismarck's Germany.) A number of states passed early
versions of workers' compensation by 1910. New York was one of these pioneer
states. The Court of Appeals (New York's highest court) struck down the
statute in 1911—the court denounced the scheme as "radical"; it was legislation
"taking the property of A and giving it to B," which (the court said) "cannot be
done under our Constitutions."[13] But in other states, the courts were more
receptive. New York amended its constitution to permit a workers' compensation plan; a new law was passed, and it successfully ran the judicial gamut. The
United States Supreme Court upheld the law in 1917.[14] By 1920 most states had
a workers' compensation law. The stragglers were in the South. In the 1930s,
some of them—Florida, South Carolina, and Arkansas—got on the bandwagon.
The last holdout was Mississippi; and it succumbed in 1948.[15]

What lay behind these laws? Of course, organized labor hated the fellow-
servant rule. Employers had long defended it; but they too began to have their
doubts. As a report to the Ohio legislature, in 1911, put it, the system was
"intolerantly [sic] wasteful." It "forces the employer to fight the widow and
children of his injured employe; results in such a magnitude of misery and
wretchedness to the homes of the injured workmen; is entirely devoid of uniformity and consistency, no more than a great gamble where a very few get a large
settlement, a few more secure insignificant amounts, while the great army of
injured workmen are getting nothing whatsoever."[16]

Studies of work accidents, and how they were compensated (or not
compensated) bore out these conclusions. In Allegheny County, Pennsylvania

(Pittsburgh), out of 235 instances of married workers killed in accidents in 1906–1907, fifty-nine families got absolutely nothing; another sixty-five got one hundred dollars or less; and only forty-eight families collected more than five hundred dollars (which was about one year's income for the lowest-paid workers).[17] Each year, Pittsburgh, according to the report, sent out "from its mills, railroad yards, factories, and mines, 45 one-legged men; 100 hopeless cripples . . . 45 men with a twisted, useless arm; 30 men with an empty sleeve; 20 men with but one hand; 60 with half a hand gone; 70 one-eyed men—500 such wrecks in all." The human toll was vast: "suffering, grief, bitterness, thwarted hopes incalculable."[18]

This despite the fact that the courts, and legislatures, were showing displeasure with the system. Decisions and statutes chopped away at doctrines that favored employers. By 1911 some twenty-three states had passed laws limiting employer defenses.[19] Employers, too, were almost paranoid on the subject of juries: juries, they believed, nearly always sympathized with the worker, nearly always made the deep pocket pay. In fact, this was something of a myth, as we have seen: juries were much less likely to soak the rich than the companies thought. But this was a firm belief of employers, and it made them anxious to avoid litigation, at all costs.

Workers' compensation is usually thought of as a great victory for labor; yet a slight majority of employers surveyed in Ohio early in the century actually favored such a system. Why? Perhaps employers were thinking of the huge costs of the middlemen between workers and their bosses. The tort system was expensive: employers had to pay millions for insurance, for lawyers, for claims adjusters. Insurance premiums (liability and accident) cost employers millions of dollars.[20] It was a big expense to fight lawsuits—for both sides. Many millions were "wasted" in this way. Why not take all these millions in costs and split the difference, between labor and capital? Both sides might end up better off; and, in addition, there might be intangible gains—in worker satisfaction, in industrial peace.

In a sense, then, workers' compensation laws were compromises. Each side gave something up. Workers gave up the chance to win the lottery—that is, to collect a big pot of cash, a rare but real chance. Employers gave up their defenses, and agreed to compensate everybody, regardless of fault—to pay compensation for every last accident at work. Yet both labor and management were (arguably) ahead of the game, because the new system did not operate through courts, but administratively; it was supposed to work quickly, almost automatically, without muss or fuss; and in theory (in part also in practice) it got rid of the waste and cost of the creaking old tort system.

Each state had its own version of workers' compensation; but in texture and shape, they were all much of a sameness. The fellow-servant rule was abolished. Indeed, the whole fault system went by the boards; negligence was no longer an issue. Any accident on the job, no matter what caused it, gave the worker a claim. The Connecticut law of 1913, in typical language, applied to all injuries "arising out of and in the course of . . . employment." A careless employee collected as much as a careful one. The only workers who lost their rights were those who brought injury on themselves through "willful and serious misconduct" or "intoxication."[21]

What did the employer get in return? It got limitation of liability. For example, when a worker was killed on the job, Connecticut's law gave the family $100 for burial expenses, and, for his dependents, half his weekly wage (but no more than ten dollars a week; and for no longer than six years). Workers who were injured collected various sums of money, depending on whether they suffered "total incapacity to perform work of any character" or only "partial incapacity." These payments, too, were limited in amount and duration (ten years for "total incapacity"). In addition, there was a grisly catalog of body parts, and attached to it something resembling a price list. For example, loss of "one foot at or above the ankle" produced two and a half years of compensation; loss of "any toe except the great toe," thirteen weeks.[22] Connecticut established a board of five commissioners to administer the act.

The Connecticut pattern was typical. Typically, too, the scheme covered most workers—but not everyone. Household help, in general, had no rights; people who worked in small mom-and-pop shops were excluded; and in many states—South Dakota, for example, and Minnesota—farmworkers were left out of the system.[23] In other words, many states specifically did not cover the weakest of the weak in the labor market. Each state had its own list of exceptions. Still, by 1950 more than three out of four workers had some sort of coverage.

Products Liability

Workers' compensation was only a beginning. The tort system in general changed radically, especially after the 1940s; what developed was what Marc

Galanter has called a "high accountability–high remedy system."[24] Defenses have eroded, and courts (and legislatures) have expanded liability to a point that the nineteenth century would have considered sheer, utter madness. In fact, the liability explosion went so far as to engender a backlash of considerable proportions.

One of the most significant signs of change was the emergence of products liability. It was always true, under general tort law, that if a defective product hurt you in some way, you had some sort of claim against the maker of the product. Only in the twentieth century, however, did lawyers (and the public) come to think of this as a special and important category. The social background was the development of mass production and mass-produced goods. Consumers in general became more and more dependent on these products; they bought canned food, they bought medicine and drugs, they bought sewing machines and automobiles, they bought clothing off the rack.

MacPherson v. Buick Motor Company, decided by the New York Court of Appeals in 1916, was a landmark case.[25] This is one of Cardozo's most famous opinions. MacPherson bought a Buick from a dealer. One of the wheels was "made of defective wood, and its spokes crumbled into fragments." The car collapsed, and MacPherson was injured. He sued Buick. Under an old doctrine ("privity"), a buyer could sue whomever had actually sold him the product, but nobody else. In this case, that would mean suing the car dealer. Privity would not allow suing Buick directly. The rule made sense, perhaps, for hand-crafted products, but not for mass-produced goods. The natural inclination today, if you feel poisoned by a can of chicken soup, is to sue the soup company, not the grocery store where the soup was bought. Cardozo, in a crafty, subtle, and cautious opinion, undermined the old doctrine, and rendered it pointless. He laid down a new rule (while denying that it was new). Stripped of technicalities and circumlocutions, the rule meant that the buyer could sue the manufacturer directly. The privity doctrine was dead. Other states soon fell into line; and *MacPherson* became universal.[26]

Another significant case was *Escola v. Coca Cola Bottling Co. of Fresno* (1944).[27] Gladys Escola, a waitress, worked in a restaurant in Madera, California. She was hurt, and badly, when a bottle of Coca-Cola exploded and mangled her hand. She won a jury verdict, and the Supreme Court of California affirmed the trial court decision. The court's opinion was nothing special, but one of the judges, Roger Traynor, wrote a concurrence which sounded a rather radical note. Traynor wanted courts to apply a new, tough rule to manufacturers. When a product was defective, and somebody was injured, the maker should be liable—and never mind any question of "negligence." The manufacturer should "incur" an "absolute liability." The company, after all, was in a better position to avoid accidents—and to pay for them—than the innocent consumer.

At the time, Traynor's ideas made little stir. But there was something in the wind that was subtly but surely pushing toward greater liability. Two years after *Escola*, in *Bonbrest v. Kotz* (1946), a federal case in the District of Columbia, Bette Gay Bonbrest, "an infant," through her father, sued the physicians J. Kotz and Morton S. Kaufman "for injuries sustained by the infant when it was allegedly taken from its mother's womb through professional malpractice."[28] Up to that point, no child had ever won a tort case for injuries suffered before the child was born. This time was different. The court sneered at "myopic and specious resort to precedent"; why should the law permit "idiocy, imbecility, paralysis, loss of function, and like residuals of another's negligence to be locked in the limbo of uncompensable wrong" just because of "outmoded" doctrine. The common law, said the court, "is not an arid and sterile thing, and it is anything but static and inert."

In fact, the common law had never been "arid" or "sterile." The court assumed that the modern, progressive, even inevitable, trend was to expand liability; to dismantle the rules of the common law that stood in the way of vast liability. The court, as it turned out, was reading the tea leaves correctly. Within twenty years, virtually every state changed its mind on this particular issue. Texas was one of the last, but it did so in 1967. A pregnant woman, injured in a car accident, gave birth to a baby who died two days later. The court, citing an "impressive contemporary trend," allowed the lawsuit.[29]

In 1960, in *Henningsen v. Bloomfield Motors, Inc.*, a New Jersey case, Claus Henningsen bought a Plymouth as a mother's day gift for his wife, Helen.[30] The car had a defect in its steering mechanism, and it spun out of control one day. Helen was injured. The court held that "under modern marketing conditions," the car company gives the buyer an "implied warranty" that the car is "reasonably suitable for use." What about the contract of sale, which (in small print) made the company liable only for defective parts—and then only if the defective parts were returned to the factory, with transportation charges prepaid? Auto buyers, said the court, had "no real freedom of choice," no control over the small print; the sleazy warranty was a take-it-or-leave-it proposition. The disclaimer, which Chrysler had put in the contract, was "inimical to the public"; and the court refused to give it any effect.

Thus two paths opened up, each of which could make manufacturers more responsible for injuries caused by their products. The first was by stretching the concept of *warranty* like taffy; the second was Traynor's idea—that is, stretching strict liability to cover much of the classic domain of torts. In the event, it was the Traynor path that was taken. In part, this was because it appealed more to judges and jurists; and because the Restatement of Torts, a much-cited work sponsored by the American Law Institute, pointed in this direction.

Both paths, as we have seen, led to the same destination. And almost all changes in doctrine in the second half of the century expanded the liability of defendants. To take one instance: courts in the nineteenth century were loath to allow a plaintiff to recover damages for emotional distress (as opposed to physical injury). Illness because of shock, fright, and so on, was compensable only if it followed, and depended on, some physical injury. In the twentieth century, this doctrine began to unravel. In a Georgia case (1928), the plaintiff, described as "an unmarried white lady," went to the circus, and sat in a front row.[31] A horse, which was "going through a dancing performance," backed up and "evacuated his bowels into her lap." Everybody (naturally) laughed; this (she claimed) made her suffer acute embarrassment and "mental pain and suffering" to the tune of five hundred dollars.

It was true, said the court, that the law would not award damages for "mental suffering," without a showing of "physical injury." But any "unlawful touching," or "precipitation upon the body . . . of any material substance," was legally an injury. Because the horse had "evacuated" on the plaintiff, there was an "injury," and, on this slender thread, the court upheld the monetary award.

Here we see the common-law habit, still very much alive, of changing the law without admitting it; or changing it in a weird, incremental, slip-and-slide way. Perhaps the judges felt an urge to rise up in defense of the southern white woman—thought of as a delicate flower, and easily bruised by vulgarity. But attitudes toward mental distress were changing more generally. In *Orlo v. Connecticut Company* (1941), Angelo Orlo, the plaintiff, was a passenger in an auto, driving just behind a trolleycar.[32] The trolley pole, through some accident, came into contact with a flock of wires, which broke, and Angelo's car was in terrible danger. He sat there, terrified, with wires all about the car, "flashing, spitting and hissing." The electricity apparently never touched him, and there were no marks or bruises on his body. He claimed severe injuries nonetheless: "nervous shock and severe fright." This caused him to shake and tremble, aggravated his diabetic condition, put him in the hospital for a month, and so on. The trial court instructed the jury that he could not recover for any of this, unless he could show a "physical injury . . . of a traumatic nature." Hearing this, the jury gave him nothing. The appeal court reversed and ordered a new trial. The law showed a "definite tendency" to "enlarge" recovery for "damages resulting from fright or nervous shock." This "definite tendency" appeared in many other cases of the period.

Another doctrine that disappeared was the doctrine of charitable immunity: no tort actions against hospitals, churches, schools, and other such organizations. In a typical case, *Schloendorff v. Society of New York Hospital* (1914), a woman entered the hospital with a stomach complaint. Under ether, a tumor was removed—without her consent (or so she claimed). She developed gangrene, some fingers were amputated, and she endured "intense" suffering. She lost her case. It was the "settled rule," said the court, that "such a hospital is not liable for the negligence of its physicians and nurses." Any other rule would harm the hospital in its "beneficent work."

As late as 1940 almost all states clung to this rule. A few courts then began to waver: in an Oklahoma case (1940) a worker who fell from a scaffold, while working on a building owned by the Salvation Army, sued successfully.[33] In New York the end came in 1957. Isabel Bing entered St. John's Episcopal Hospital, "for correction of a fissure of the anus." An anesthetist "painted the lumbar region" of her back with "tincture of zephiran," a reddish fluid which was highly inflammable. When the doctor applied a "heated electric cautery" to the fissure, the tincture ignited, and Bing was severely burned. The New York court overruled the Schloendorff case; it was "out of tune with the life about us," and "at variance with modern-day needs."[34] By 1964, according to William Prosser, the reigning torts expert, a "deluge of decisions" had eliminated charitable immunity in nineteen states, the District of Columbia, and Puerto Rico; and it was "in full retreat"—frayed and restricted—in many others; only nine states still held onto the doctrine.[35] Almost all of these had joined the crowd by 1980 or so; and today charitable immunity is essentially dead.

Defenseless

Not only did courts and legislatures seem eager to widen the scope of liability, they also gradually stripped away the most potent defenses of defendants. One of these was the doctrine of contributory negligence. This sounds harmless enough in its core—X cannot sue Y for negligence if X was at fault himself, or if X contributed to whatever the problem or accident was. But the doctrine had been taken to rather extreme lengths. If somebody had been smashed to bits by a railroad, even the tiniest bit of negligence on his part was enough to keep his family from collecting a cent.

The retreat began as early as 1908; the Federal Employers' Liability Act, which covered railroad workers, laid down the rule that contributory negligence would no longer bar the right to recover. Rather, if the railroad worker was negligent, the jury would "diminish" his damages "in proportion to the amount of negligence" which could be attributed to him.[36] This is the core notion of what came to be called the comparative negligence doctrine. Mississippi in 1910 adopted a form of the doctrine. In 1920, the federal government extended the railroad rule to seamen, under the so-called Jones Act.[37] By the early 1980s, some version or other was the law in forty states; and by the end of the century, in almost all of them. In some of these states, the plaintiff loses if she shoulders more than half the blame; in others, however, a plaintiff who was 85 percent to blame might still recover 15 percent of her damages. (A jury, of course, has the job of deciding, through its usual magic, who is responsible, and for what, and in what percentage. Nobody has yet invented a machine to measure negligence or damages.)

The Puzzles of Causation

The tort story in the twentieth century is, as we have said, a story of ever-expanding liability. But not every plaintiff won every case. Among the most famous losers was a woman named Helen Palsgraf. Helen Palsgraf was an immigrant, and poor. She bought a ticket on the Long Island Railroad Company, planning to go to Rockaway Beach in New York. She was standing on the platform with her children. A train stopped at the station. A man, carrying a small package wrapped in newspaper, tried to jump aboard. It looked as if he was going to fall. A guard pushed him in from behind. The package fell on the rails. It contained fireworks, which exploded. The shock reverberated on the platform, and knocked over some scales, "many feet away." The scales hit Helen Palsgraf, and injured her. This was the basis of her claim.

The case worked its way up to the highest court of New York. Here Helen Palsgraf lost her case by a margin of a single vote; the chief judge, Benjamin Cardozo, wrote the majority opinion.[38] Perhaps the railroad's employee had been negligent; even so, Cardozo said, he owed no duty to Helen Palsgraf—perhaps because (as some commentators suggested) it was a freak accident. Her injuries were not foreseeable. Who could possibly guess that a package would fall, explode, and the scales would land on Helen Palsgraf?

Under one view, the case seems to stand for the idea that liability must have some limit. If you do something wrong, as the circle of harm unforeseeably widens, at some point responsibility stops. But the opinion, written by Cardozo in elegant shades and nuances, may mean more than this—or less. In any event, Cardozo's opinion has puzzled and exasperated generations of law students. Exactly why this case is so famous is also something of a mystery. It has become a kind of celebrity case: famous for being famous. It also has become part of law school tradition. Every first-year law student, wherever located, wherever educated, has racked her brains over Helen Palsgraf and the falling scales. No torts casebook would dare omit this classic; and none of them do.

The Liability Explosion Marches On: Workers' Compensation

As liability expanded in tort law, workers' compensation evolved in a similar direction. Compensation, according to the statutes, was limited to accidents and injuries "arising out of and in the course of employment": nine little words, taken from the British statute. Their core meaning was obvious: only injuries caused by the job ("arising out of" it) were covered; and they also had to take place on the job ("in the course of employment"). But the courts continually expanded the meaning of the phrases, including more and more kinds of harms and events.

The so-called "horseplay" cases are a good example. In the early cases, courts denied compensation if workers were hurt fooling around on the job. By 1940 the cases were going the other way.[39] The law gave protection even to playful, prankish, careless, loutish, and stupid workers. In one memorable Wisconsin case, decided in 1943, a truck driver's helper decided to urinate off the side of a moving truck—not the smartest thing to do. He fell off the truck and was injured. The Wisconsin Supreme Court held he could get his compensation.[40] Stupidity was the cause of his injury; but he did not forfeit compensation. There was no place in the system for contributory negligence.

The states had passed compensation laws to deal with "industrial accidents." In the background was the long, bitter struggle between labor and management. The issue was the factory, the coal mine, the railroad yard: huge, noisy, dangerous places, filled with destructive machines—machines that mangled bodies and bones; machines that manufactured widows and orphans. The laws were concerned with "accidents," in the literal sense; nobody dreamed of a worker who urinated off the side of a truck, or slipped and fell during horseplay.

Nor were they thinking of workers whose pain and suffering came on them gradually. Julius J. Young was a stonecutter, who operated a stone-surfacing machine in the granite shops of St. Cloud, Minnesota. The job put Young under "a great strain and jar"; his shoulder and back began to ache. Gradually, over weeks of work, his shoulder stiffened; the muscles atrophied, and the nerves degenerated. The Minnesota court (1922) was unsympathetic: there was no "accident" here. Nothing "happened suddenly or violently to plaintiff." The compensation act was "not designed to cover cases where injuries result from ordinary overwork or too long continued effort without any sudden or violent rupture or collapse."[41] This was typical of the attitude of the early cases.

Neither companies nor courts appeared to care if workers simply wore themselves out. In 2001 this seems unbearably callous. But the Minnesota case came before old-age pensions, before the developed welfare state; before the full flowering of the norm of total justice. Slowly, the attitudes of courts and agencies changed. An early straw in the wind was an Idaho case from 1934.[42] Lee Beaver had tuberculosis, but in a dormant state (his widow claimed). He did rock-crusher work, which released "thick clouds of dust." The plaintiff's theory was that the dust, which he took into his lungs day after day, caused his disease to flare up. It eventually killed him. The company claimed there was no "accident" here. The court disagreed. If a workman drives a car for years, "until he wears the tires down to the inner tube" and has a sudden blowout, and the car goes into a ditch and kills him, everybody would call this an accident; by the same token, it is an accident "if silica dust grinds on a workman's lungs for many months," until he has a pulmonary blowout; and then dies.

In short, courts and agencies became more and more liberal in granting awards, so that almost anything that happened on the job, which resulted in any sort of medical problem, became compensable—a secretary who twisted her neck, a salesman who slipped on the stairs recovered compensation. The courts also expanded the very idea of a job: workers changing into work clothes at their lockers, before punching in, a traveling salesman killed in a motel fire, an employee hurt sliding into second base at a company picnic on the Fourth of July—these too could receive compensation.

These were, of course, rare, freak cases. There were, however, more serious matters at the cutting edge: heart attacks and nervous breakdowns brought on by stress; and occupational diseases. These were hardly rare events. Heart attack claims, not surprisingly, failed in most of the early cases. The courts looked for unusual strains—something they could call an "accident." The daily grind was not enough. Later cases, on the whole, abandoned this idea; or were willing to find, on very slender evidence, that the job somehow brought on the attack.

The early statutes did not usually cover occupational diseases at all. (A rare exception was Illinois, but its statute was later declared unconstitutional.[43]) Diseases, after all, were not "accidents." Indeed, Oklahoma law was at first restricted to workers in "hazardous employments." The statute contained a list of these—factories, cotton gins, foundries, blast furnaces, gasworks, logging, lumbering, and steam heating plants, among others; and it also covered only "manual or mechanical work or labor"; "clerical workers" (and agricultural workers) were specifically omitted.[44] Some states did cover a few occupational diseases, which they dutifully listed. The New York statute (1920) mentioned twenty-three diseases, beginning with anthrax and lead poisoning, through glanders, "acute bursitis over the elbow (miner's beat elbow)," to "cataract in glass workers." In each case, the disease was connected with a particular industrial process: for example, anthrax compensation was only for workers who handled "wool, hair, bristles, hides or skins"; only those glassworkers with cataracts who had been exposed to the "glare of molten glass" could make a claim.[45] Workers who sickened and died because of pollution or other work conditions got little or no response from the compensation scheme in most states. This was, for example, the lot of the "radium girls," the young women hired to paint luminous dials on wristwatches, who began dying of cancer in the 1920s.[46] A few of the girls won settlements from their companies; others died without collecting a cent. Their case, however, played a role in consciousness raising. The Consumers' League, a women's reform group, took up their cause; the league lobbied hard in New Jersey, where many of the girls had lived; and New Jersey in 1949 amended its law to cover "all diseases arising out of and in the course of employment, which are due to causes and conditions . . . characteristic of or peculiar to a particular trade, occupation, process, or employment."[47] Other states joined in later—Louisiana, for example, in 1975.[48]

The liability explosion also affected maritime law. Under standard doctrine, a shipowner was liable to pay "maintenance" and wages, to a seaman injured on the job. This meant, historically, accidents on the high seas. But in one 1948 case the third assistant engineer on an American ship, on leave in Manila, hurt himself diving into a pool (after three beers) at the United Seaman's Service Club. In another case from the same year, a sailor was on shore leave in Split, Yugoslavia. He got into a fight with a prostitute, over money; and ended up jumping out a brothel window (to avoid a worse fate). Both men got their "maintenance."[49]

A Society on Wheels

Tort law in the nineteenth century was in many ways dominated by the railroad. Case after leading case came out of railroad accidents. Then the railroad faded slowly into history, and the twentieth century became the century of the automobile. Cars soon replaced streetcars and railroads as prime killers and maimers of Americans. In 1949 auto accidents killed 31,701 men and women; railway accidents, the king of torts in the nineteenth century, killed a mere 2,119.[50] This massive increase in accidental death dwarfed the potential of industrial accidents. The "visibility and the numbers of humans injured by automobiles . . . brought the mutilations and the corpses right into the center of American public life."[51]

Most auto accidents, even serious ones, never ended up in court; but enough of them did to dominate the dockets. According to a report on the problem published in 1932, in the Supreme Court of New York County, 30 percent of the "new issues placed on the calendar" between October 1928 and April 1930 were "motor vehicle accident cases"; the percentages in the Courts of Common Pleas of Philadelphia County in 1932 were quite similar. At this time fewer than a third of the cars in the country were "insured for public liability"; in the cities the figure was somewhat higher, and the injured could find an insurance company to sue in from half to two-thirds of the cases.[52] Massachusetts made insurance compulsory in 1925.[53] Many states, starting with Connecticut in 1925, passed "financial responsibility laws"—laws which imposed an insurance duty at least on some drivers (those who had, for example, broken the rules of the road).[54] But no other state followed Massachusetts all the way, for more than thirty years—the insurance companies fought compulsory insurance bitterly; they saw it as a camel's nose under the tent, the camel being the government. In the end they lost the battle. New York made insurance compulsory in 1956 and North Carolina in 1957.

Still, many victims of accidents never collected a cent from anybody, while on the other hand, the insurance companies wailed about fraud, racketeers, fake claims, gangs that simulated injuries with chicken blood, and the like.[55] Insurance companies also believed that the courts and juries were on the side of the victim. A Duke Law School student named Richard M. Nixon (who went on to bigger if not better things) expressed this opinion in an article published in 1936. The courts, he claimed, tended to stretch traditional rules "in order to insure recovery to an injured plaintiff."[56]

But by the end of the century what the courts did was in many ways irrelevant. Drivers and car owners had insurance; compulsory laws were widespread; and the real law of auto accidents was a mixture of statutes, doctrines, the occasional jury trial, and the actual practices of insurance companies. The companies settled almost all cases out of court, according to rules of thumb and company guidelines. Claims adjusters were the leading legal actors in this whole vast field. Insurance law had "drawn the sting from tort law sanctions on the insured defendant."[57] Insurance, accidents, drunk driving, road rage: there were still, of course, more than enough legal problems associated with cars; but the formal law of torts was no longer center stage.

Bad Medicine: Is There a Doctor in the Court?

In 1953 a man named Martin Salgo consulted Dr. Frank Gerbode at the Stanford University Hospital in California. Salgo, fifty-five, complained of cramps in his legs, and pain in various parts of his body. It was clear to the doctor that Salgo was a very sick man, with possible blockage of his abdominal aorta. Salgo underwent a procedure called aortography, in which a needle is inserted into the aorta, and X rays are then taken. This delicate procedure seemed to go very well; but a day later, Salgo discovered "his lower extremities were para-lyzed"; they never improved. He sued the doctor and the hospital for medical malpractice.[58]

Salgo was not alone. Medical malpractice was a growing subfield of the law of torts, roughly from the 1950s on. In one sense there was nothing new in the idea of suing doctors for bad medicine; a careless or negligent doctor was just as liable for his misdeeds as a careless truck driver or a careless maker of canned soup. In actual fact, malpractice cases were rare in the nineteenth century, and remained so well into the twentieth century. In Randolph Bergstrom's 1910 study of New York City courts, there were exactly eight such cases, or 1.1 per-cent of the 728 cases of tort.[59]

A study of San Francisco County and Cook County (primarily Chicago) between 1959 and 1980 showed a considerable increase over Bergstrom's fig-ures, especially in San Francisco County. There 7 percent of the civil jury trials were for professional malpractice (overwhelmingly medical malpractice); in Cook County the figure was 3 percent. Moreover, some of these cases brought in huge recoveries. For 1960–1964, the mean recovery in these courts was $89,000, the median $45,000; for 1975–1979, the mean was $457,000, the median $70,000. But these are figures for plaintiffs who actually won. Only 35 percent of the San Francisco plaintiffs were victorious; 33 percent in Cook County.[60] What this suggests is that juries were skeptical about a lot of these claims; when they were convinced, however, they were inclined to be generous. Many of these plaintiffs, after all, had suffered horrendous injuries—modern medicine is full of wild and wonderful machines and techniques; but when they go awry, the results can be fearful indeed.

As for Salgo, the jury awarded him a quarter of a million dollars. The defendants appealed, on various grounds—mainly, about the judge's instruc-tions. One of the disputed instructions had to do with the duty to "disclose"—that is, the duty of a doctor to tell all to her patient: the risks and the side effects of whatever the doctor planned to do. Sometimes, the court allowed, you can tell a patient too much: if you mention remote risks, this might "result in alarming a patient who is already unduly apprehensive." But the doctor has to tell the patient whatever is necessary for "informed consent."[61]

This was in 1957; by the early 1960s, the phrase "informed consent" had been picked up in the literature and was quickly hardening into doctrine. The *Salgo* court was cautious; later courts were much less so. A doctor must tell the patient absolutely everything. "Informed consent" became a crucial element in malpractice law. Bad medicine was not the only form of malpractice; so, too, was bad bedside behavior—not telling the client about risks, alternatives, and the like.

Doctrines do not grow on trees; they feed on the meat and drink of social approval. Medicine was becoming more scientific, but also more impersonal. The old family doctor who made house calls and sat at your bedside was on the verge of extinction. He was a friendly and lovable old doctor; of course, he never cured anybody, but suing him was as unthinkable as suing a devoted old friend. In the high-tech world of medicine, barriers against lawsuits crumbled. The "informed consent" doctrine, too, fit neatly with many other trends in modern law: part of a general right to know, to choose, to act independent of authority. This was the essence of late-twentieth-century culture.

There was also no question that doctors did make mistakes; and sometimes horrific ones. Study after study showed that malpractice was a fact, not a fantasy of paranoid or disappointed patients. Whether the law of torts was an effective way of handling the malpractice problem is another question. It did, arguably, make insurance for doctors very expensive. This in turn helped fuel a backlash, as we shall see.

Mass Toxic Torts

The desperate lawsuit of a dying man, Clarence Borel, began a new stage in the law of torts. Borel had gone to work as an "industrial insulation worker" in 1936. On the job he was exposed to "heavy concentrations of asbestos dust generated by insulation materials." In 1969 Borel, a sick man, was in the hospital; a lung biopsy found "pulmonary asbestosis." This later flamed into lung cancer. Borel was of course covered by workers' compensation; but he sued—not his boss, but the companies that made the asbestos that was killing him. He won at the trial; and, on appeal, the judgment was affirmed (1973).[62] By then, Borel was already dead.

The evidence, in fact, suggests that perhaps a quarter of a million people, and probably many more, died from exposure to asbestos. The *Borel* case started the trend; by the middle of the 1980s, more than 30,000 claims for damages had been filed against asbestos makers. According to an estimate for 1991, more than 115,000 asbestos claims were waiting to be resolved in the courts or through outside settlement.[63] Billions of dollars were involved; and the lawsuits had effectively destroyed the asbestos business. Asbestos companies had been driven into bankruptcy—bankruptcy became, for them, a kind of sanctuary.[64]

The asbestos cases were among the first of the so-called mass toxic torts. They blossomed like some rare, exotic plant in the 1970s and 1980s. One of the most famous was the Agent Orange case, a class action begun in 1979. The charge was that the United States government, and a major portion of the chemical industry, had caused "deaths and dreadful injuries to tens of thousands of Vietnam veterans who came in contact with herbicides" during the war in Vietnam.[65] Agent Orange was sprayed over Vietnam to clear the thick jungle growth and to destroy fields and crops used by the Vietcong. Many veterans blamed Agent Orange for cancers, birth defects in children, and other tragedies; they believed that the government and the chemical companies had systematically lied to them. Massive scientific evidence was presented; but in fact it failed to pin the blame decisively on Agent Orange—at best, it left the case open; at worst, it proved the plaintiffs were simply wrong.

Another gigantic, controversial lawsuit involved the Dalkon Shield. The A. H. Robins Company sold more than four and a half million of these intrauterine birth control devices from 1971 on. As a birth control device, it was a failure: many women became pregnant anyway. The real problems were more serious: miscarriages and babies born with congenital defects, some pelvic infections, even sterility; in a few, rare cases, the shield was even blamed for a user's death. The Food and Drug Administration intervened, and the company stopped selling the product in 1974; but a flood of lawsuits ensued. There was endless wrangling over procedures—should the lawsuits be aggregated into a single gigantic "class action," for example. A number of individuals also brought cases. The company won some and lost some. It then went into reorganization, transferred some billions of dollars into a trust, and eventually settled most claims.[66]

Still another megacase concerned diethylstilbestrol (DES), a drug used to prevent miscarriages that was blamed for certain kinds of cancer. This produced more spectacular lawsuits against many leading pharmaceutical companies. Most of these cases never got as far as a trial on the merits. The lawsuit got bogged down in procedural issues, and other issues at the threshold of liability. The controversy dragged on for years. In 1992 one company, Eli Lilly, reported that it had settled 250 such cases, and that 350 were still pending.[67] In the end, apparently, the companies settled all the cases.

At the end of the twentieth century, it was the turn of the tobacco industry—sued by cancer victims and state governments. The sums involved in these cases were truly astronomical. Up to 2000, the tobacco companies had succeeded in holding off the flood; but their grip was clearly weakening. Plans for gigantic settlements had been floated. Communities and individuals were also filing lawsuits against gun companies. In these cases, more was involved than compensation: these were struggles to the death against unpopular industries.

Privacy: The Birth of a Tort

Almost all tort cases that get to court concern either negligence or strict liability; they are accident cases—either personal injury or property damage. Along with divorce and a few other causes of action, these are the plankton of the sea of civil litigation. Other kinds of torts have always been rare—libel and slander, for example; trespass to real estate; false imprisonment.

Rare is not always the same as unimportant. One special twentieth-century tort, which never amounted to much, statistically speaking, can serve as a kind of cultural marker. This is the tort called invasion of privacy.

Most authorities on this tort trace it to a famous law review article, written by Louis D. Brandeis and Samuel D. Warren and published in 1890 in the *Harvard Law Review*.[68] Brandeis and Warren argued that the common law could and should protect people's privacy. The press, they said, "is overstepping . . . the obvious bounds of . . . decency. Gossip is no longer the resource of the idle and the vicious"; it had become an important business. This was, of course, the age of the "yellow press"; and it was, as Robert Mensel has pointed out, also the age of the Kodak—the first "candid camera." Before Kodak, nobody could take your picture without your permission, indeed, without your collaboration. You had to actually pose and sit still. Now, with fast cameras, it was possible to steal somebody's image—and even without his knowledge or awareness.[69] The threat to "decency" was obvious.

Courts were slow, however, to warm up to this idea. In New York, the Franklin Mills Company of Rochester used a trademark which featured a slogan, "Flour of the Family," and a picture of a young woman, Abigail Roberson— without her approval. The company distributed twenty-five thousand flyers in the Rochester area; Abigail, when she found this out, "suffered a nervous shock and was confined to her bed." She sued the company; the lower courts thought ...e had a case; but the court of appeals (1902) turned her down, 4–3—it found no basis in the law for any such claim.[70]

This was not a popular result, and the New York legislature in 1903 enacted a law "to prevent the unauthorized use of the name or picture of any person for the purposes of trade." Violation was a misdemeanor; more significantly, the victim could sue for damages (or get a restraining order).[71] This was, of course, much narrower than a general right of privacy. Two years later, however, the Supreme Court of Georgia embraced the ideas of Warren and Brandeis. This too was a commercial case: Paolo Pavesich was amazed to see his picture in an Atlanta newspaper as part of an insurance ad. He sued and won his case.[72]

The Red Kimono: The Rise and Fall of Decency

Gabrielle Darley, who made a cameo appearance in American legal history in 1931, was a woman who had led a colorful life. She had at one time been a prostitute. She had also been arrested and tried for murder; a jury acquitted her, however. At this point, in 1918, she "abandoned her life of shame," married Bernard Melvin, and lived a "righteous" life, earning a "place in respectable society." Many people in her new circle knew nothing about her checkered past. But in 1925 a movie appeared, The Red Kimono, based on her life and times—and using her real name. Her cover blown, Gabrielle Darley Melvin brought a lawsuit.

The California appellate court was sympathetic. It was wrong to destroy Gabrielle's reputation and her social standing; it was wrong to publish the "story of her former depravity" for no other reason than "private gain." Society's goal, said the court, should be to "lift up and sustain the unfortunate rather than tear him down." The defendants' actions were "not justified by any standard of morals or ethics." In fact, they violated Gabrielle's right, guaranteed by the California Constitution, "to pursue and obtain happiness." Whether one called her claim a "right of privacy," or gave it "any other name" was immaterial.[73]

This was, perhaps, the high-water mark of the tort—in its original meaning. It was a protection for "privacy" in the sense of respectability, honor, repentance, bourgeois decency. But these virtues themselves began a long retreat; and in so doing, "invasion of privacy" lost a great deal of its strength. By the end of the century not much was left of actual privacy, in the sense of immunity from the camera's prying eyes, or the leers of the media, or the breathless gossip of the tabloid press. In a celebrity society, *privacy* has no meaning for anyone at all public or notorious. This was the message, after all, of *New York Times v. Sullivan*. Pornography was wildly popular, in books, movies, and on the World Wide Web; "decency" had taken quite a beating. In the last two years of the millennium, the biggest and most sensational news concerned the sex life of the president, William Jefferson Clinton. This brought him, through a tortuous chain of events, to the brink of removal from office. People on television, on "trash talk" shows, washed their dirtiest linens in public.[74] Millions more were happy to watch them do it. The only protection for John and Jane Public was the fact that nobody cared about their lives—unless they exposed themselves voluntarily. In a society hungry for "news" and sensation, was anything about the private lives of public people, or the public lives of private people, out of bounds?

It was a question Mike Virgil asked the courts (through his lawyers). Virgil was a two-bit celebrity—a world-class body surfer. *Sports Illustrated* ran a story about him—detailing his surfing exploits, of course, but also revealing that he "never learned how to read," that he once "dove headfirst down a flight of stairs" because it was "groovy" and might impress "chicks"; and his wife's statement that he ate "spiders and other insects and things." A federal court in 1975 thought that body surfing, though "not hot news of the day," was of "general public interest." The court conceded that there were limits to "morbid and sensational prying into private lives," even for such luminaries as Mike Virgil; this was, in the court's opinion, a very close case. It was sent back down the chain of courts for fresh examination.[75] In the last quarter of the twentieth century, Gabrielle Darley would not have had the slightest chance of winning her case.

At the same time, as we have seen, the right of "privacy," in the constitutional sense, had expanded enormously. Here the meaning was not what Warren and Brandeis meant by the word; privacy rather had come to mean that certain life choices were beyond the reach of the government. Yet the two senses were culturally if not legally related. If there is a right to buy condoms, or to view pornography, or to have sex with any consenting adult—if these acts first

lose their criminality, then their stigma, then become constitutional rights—
then millions of people can, and do, come out of whatever closet they were
hiding in. Some of them come all the way out into the talk shows.

The Cause and the Meaning of It All

The dramatic extension of the tort system in the twentieth century is unquestionably real. People brought lawsuits which would have been unthinkable in
the nineteenth century, or even in the earlier part of the twentieth. Were they
winning billions of dollars? The evidence is ambiguous. There are data about
jury cases, which are, overwhelmingly, tort cases. Between 1960 and 1979, 88
percent of the 21,500 plaintiffs who had civil jury trials in Cook County had
bodily injury claims; 4 percent more sued for wrongful death.[76] Yet average
and median awards (by judge or jury) are probably more modest than most
people think. There have been a few very startling jury verdicts—verdicts in the
megamillions; but these are exceptional. They are, of course, the verdicts that
make news; losing, or collecting two thousand dollars, does not get your name
in the papers. And of course, the mass tort cases are an exceedingly significant development.

What lay behind these dramatic changes in tort law? No single factor can
account for it. Certainly, insurance has a lot to do with it. Businesses carry
liability insurance. Drivers carry insurance on their cars. Ordinary people carry
life insurance—a practice once condemned as almost immoral.[77] In 1905 the
three biggest life insurance companies had about $5 billion in policies in force—
forty years earlier, they had had $150,000.[78] An insurance society is a society
willing to spread losses. It is not a fatalistic, shrug-the-shoulders society, a
society that tells victims "that's the breaks," and that life isn't fair. It is a society
which is affluent enough so that ordinary people can afford to buy protection
for their loved ones. Death is, after all, natural; but accidents are interruptions,
incursions—and they too call for ways to protect the victims and their families.
Economic growth and (relative) affluence led to, and was influenced by, cultural
changes that made liability more palatable to society.

Different periods have different ideas, too, about what is "fair" and "just."
The fault system of the nineteenth century talked a language that sounded as if it
was concerned with ethics. After all, *fault* is a loaded term. Perhaps this was
only a cover. Tort law favored enterprise, growth, a booming economy.[79] A

rising tide lifts all the boats; and puncturing a hole in the bottom of the boat sinks rich and poor, boss and worker, alike. Unquestionably, attitudes changed in the twentieth century. Workers' compensation is one obvious example. The law of industrial accidents almost completely eliminated fault. Fault retreated, too, in products liability. William L. Prosser noted in 1941 that the law often forced defendants to pay despite "well-intentioned and entirely moral and reasonable conduct." And why? Because "it is considered to be good social policy"—that is, "enterprises should pay their way by bearing the loss they inflict."[80] This was essentially an insurance idea: the companies in a way were insuring their workers and their other victims. And they, the companies, could in turn buy insurance on the open market to cover their losses.

Mention should also be made of the personal-injury bar—the lawyers who threw the bombs during the liability explosion. This is a lively bunch indeed. The cast of characters includes such flamboyant figures as Melvin Belli, the "king of torts." Belli pioneered many tricks and techniques that later became standard operating procedure. He brought "demonstrative evidence" into the courtroom: in one case in the 1940s, a young woman had lost her leg in an accident. Belli walked into the courtroom with an "L-shaped package wrapped in cheap yellow paper." Slowly, he unwrapped it. Inside was an artificial leg: his client, he told the jury "will wear this . . . for the rest of her life in exchange for that limb which God gave her." In another case, his client was a sailor, twenty-one years old, a married man. He was injured in a streetcar accident. Belli told the jury the sailor was sterile and impotent; he also showed the jury a "thin plastic rod," and told them that his client would "have to pass [it] through his penis every ten days," as long as he lived.[81]

Lawyers like Belli no doubt played a role in the torts explosion. They were dramatic, outrageous, off the wall—and quite effective. Belli was not alone; there were others, too, men like Stuart M. Speiser, who specialized in airplane crashes, and literally wrote the book on the subject.[82] The dramatic techniques of Belli and others obscured the fact that these big cases took a lot of work—and a lot of money. Tort lawyers took cases on a contingent fee basis. When the lawyers won, they won big—they pocketed a quarter or more of the winnings. When they lost, they collected nothing.

The panjandrums of the bar hated Belli, hated those like him, and railed against them just as they had railed against the "ambulance chasers" earlier in the century. A personal-injury lawyer does not have repeat clients—clients on retainer. Nobody gets hit by a bus or smashed in a train crash year after year after year. A personal-injury lawyer is flamboyant almost by necessity. She thrives on publicity—she needs publicity, to ensure a steady flow of clients. Hence, unlike the gray, drab lawyers of Wall Street, hidden behind the genteel anonymity of wealth, the world of the "p.i." lawyer is a world of eccentricity and extravagance. It was functional to be like Melvin Belli; his many marriages, his antics, his madhouse of an office—all these helped, rather than hindered, his phenomenal career.

Belli and his cohorts won headlines and publicity; they garnered credit for big victories; but judges and juries were their quiet accomplices. Belli would have gotten nowhere if he had been swimming against the social current. He was not. The Bellis of the world seized an opportunity; but the opportunity came from a social revolution. They were more an effect of the liability explosion than a cause.

Behind it all was the "total justice" or "total compensation" society; a society in which millions of people expected justice, and defined justice as getting money when calamity struck.[83] In the nineteenth century life was insecure in ways we can hardly imagine today. Women died by the thousands during childbirth. Cholera and yellow fever and other epidemics carried off thousands more, men, women, and children. Doctors flailed about helplessly with nostrums, leeches, and tinctures of this and that. The "social safety net" barely existed. During the periodic crashes and panics, banks failed right and left, dragging down with them small businesses, merchants, and the lifetime savings of thousands. Drought, locusts, or torrential rains could spell ruin for a farm family. The average person, city or country, had no insurance of any sort. In a society of this kind, railroad disasters or streetcar accidents were just one more vicissitude of life.

All this had changed by the twentieth century. Because of advances in medicine, and in social arrangements (affluence, the welfare state), people no longer assumed that calamity was inevitable, or irremediable. As we mentioned, insurance became widespread. The deep pocket of business was deeper than ever before. People began to expect some kind of payment, some recompense, when disaster struck. There were, in fact, programs of disaster relief, for earthquakes, floods, and fires. All these social facts drastically altered the legal culture.

These factors also help explain the big toxic tort cases—from asbestos on. To be sure, procedural innovations made these cases possible; and they tapped the willingness of courts to listen to novel tortlike complaints. In the age of "total justice," people were willing to believe, and indeed wanted to believe, that somebody must have been at fault if their health failed disastrously; and, just as important, that somebody ought to pay for their harms. Many cases claimed (sometimes quite persuasively) that government or industry had lied, cheated, manipulated data, suppressed information, and used every dodge and trick under the sun to avoid liability. The mass toxic torts thus also depended on the general loss of faith in government—and in experts employed by government; and a willingness to believe the worst of other institutions, including big business.

Many factors just mentioned were common to the whole Western world. Modern medicine and accident insurance are not something special in America. Yet there was also something uniquely American about the liability explosion. No other country has a tort system quite like ours. In part, this may be because the American welfare system still operates in bits and pieces; it leaves holes that tort law and compensation law fill, at least in part. Another factor is the jury. But in the end, one has to fall back on a strain in American legal culture which supports (for some of us, at least) the idea of suing the daylights out of those we blame for our misfortunes.[84]

Leviathan Chimes In

Tort law was largely the creation of judges in the nineteenth century; in the twentieth century, judges continued to play a major role. But legislatures also made significant contributions. Some legislation bore directly on tort law, or replaced it. We have mentioned FELA and workers' compensation. Probably even more important have been legislative programs to prevent accidents from happening—health and safety regulation.

Congress began to pay attention to the safety of workers, and to the health of consumers, in the late nineteenth century. In 1893 Congress required railroads to use safety devices: power driving-wheels, brakes, and automatic couplers, and grab irons and handholds to use in coupling and uncoupling railroad cars.[85] In the first part of the century, Congress passed food and drug laws, and meat inspection laws; Congress also enacted more railroad safety laws. Clean air and water acts are also obviously laws on public health.

In the 1960s and 1970s, there was a quantum leap in the pace of enactment of health and safety laws.[86] Congress passed a Federal Coal Mine Health and Safety Law in 1969; this elaborate statute included a long list of interim standards for coal mines—on roof support, ventilation, coal dust, combustible materials, electrical equipment, trailing cables, fire protection, blasting materials, and hoisting and communication devices, and more.[87] A Federal Hazardous Substances Labeling Act of 1960 regulated "toxic" and "corrosive" substances, as well as "irritants" and inflammable material; Congress amended the law in 1969 to include, among other things, toys.[88]

In 1970 Congress enacted the Occupational Safety and Health Act (OSHA).[89] The preamble made the usual perfunctory bow to congressional power over interstate commerce: "Personal injuries and illnesses arising out of work situations" could be a "burden" on interstate commerce. This important new law set forth a striking goal: workplaces "free from recognized hazards." The secretary of labor could promulgate safety rules and standards, and impose them on businesses. On the same day, Congress passed the Egg Products Inspection Act, which gave the secretary of agriculture power to inspect centers of egg production, and to seize adulterated eggs.[90] And in 1972 Congress enacted a Consumer Product Safety Act.[91]

All this action has federalized control of health and safety, at least to some degree. But the states cannot be written out of the picture. They have also been busy legislating. Probably every state has its own laws on foods and drugs. Texas, for example, passed an elaborate meat inspection law in 1945.[92] OSHA was copied in a number of states; Tennessee, to take one instance, passed its own version in 1972.[93] There are elaborate statutes everywhere about fire safety, safety in school buildings, and so on. City building codes establish standards that contractors have to meet. The federal government, in other words, has no real monopoly on the protection of health and safety. It is, as of 2001, a concern of government at every level.

12

Business Law in an Age of Change

The New Deal flowered during the Great Depression. The period after the Second World War—roughly the second half of the century—was, despite some ups and downs, a period of great prosperity and economic growth. Business law of this period reflected that expansion; it also reflected the broader social movements that were in turn influenced by economic expansion. And, not least of all, business law reflected the development of a strong consumer movement.

The New Deal vastly increased the power of the federal government. States remained "sovereign," however. And so they are, within their domain, or what is left of it. On the other hand, from the very start, the United States has been a gigantic free-trade area. Moreover, in the twentieth century, a national culture and a national economy made the lines between states almost meaningless. Neither TV nor the market pays any attention to borders. A person who drives across the country on interstate highways hardly notices borders, except for signs that say Welcome to Nebraska, Obey the Speed Limit, and the like. The driver zips from state to state without customs barriers or hindrances of any kind. Passengers in jet airplanes never sense the borders at all. Meanwhile, the whole country sees the same movies, listens to the same radio programs, watches the same game shows on TV.

Congress has power to regulate interstate commerce, and the states cannot interfere with or "burden" this commerce. The states can regulate business inside the state. Contract law and contract cases are mostly state law; so is commercial law, though there has been a strong movement to make the law

377

uniform from state to state. And the power to regulate inside state borders inevitably spills over into other states. This may be only a pinprick here and there, a nagging little rule or ordinance or two; but sometimes it amounts to more—arguably to a "burden" on interstate commerce. And some rules may encroach on an area which the national government has "preempted"—that is, swallowed up and claimed for its own.

The Supreme Court dozens of times has had to decide issues of state versus federal power. The case law is difficult, and vacillating. States cannot discriminate against "foreign" (out-of-state) merchandise. In a key case from 1951, an ordinance of Madison, Wisconsin, forbade the sale of milk unless it was pasteurized within five miles of the state capitol; this effectively cut off all milk produced on farms more than twenty-five miles from downtown Madison. Milk from Illinois was thus banned, and the Supreme Court refused to allow the ordinance to stand.[1] A New Jersey statute in the 1970s prevented anyone from bringing any "solid or liquid waste" from outside into New Jersey without official approval (which was never given). Owners of private landfills protested; and won. The Supreme Court brushed aside arguments based on health or environmental concerns; the statute was naked discrimination against other states, and could not be sustained.[2] The Court reached a similar result in 1992, when Alabama imposed a "disposal fee" on hazardous waste brought in from other states to be processed in Alabama, and imposed no such fee on home-grown hazardous waste.[3]

Could South Carolina insist that no truck on its highways weigh more than ten tons loaded, or be wider than ninety inches? In 1938 the Supreme Court said yes. But the Arizona Train Limit Law (originally passed in 1912), which disallowed any trains longer than fourteen passenger cars or seventy freight cars, was unacceptable, as a "serious burden on interstate commerce" (1945). And in 1959 the Court struck down, on similar grounds, an Illinois law that imposed a special kind of mudflap on trucks.[4]

Of course, a glance at any state statute book would show hundreds of regulatory statutes, most of them never questioned in court. This means that there is a certain lack of uniformity in rules that govern business. The danger to businesses, if they operate throughout the country, is death from fifty tiny cuts. Fifty different sovereignties, and fifty different schemes of commercial law, constitute an inconvenience at the very least.

The Great Uniform Code

Despite the uniform laws movement, so successful in the early part of the century, legal scholars still felt, on the whole, that commercial law was backward, and, worse, unstandardized and chaotic. Businessmen in general tended to agree.

What was the solution? One suggestion was to draft a massive, comprehensive code unifying commercial law all across the country, and tying it together into a single, rational whole. Congress could conceivably enact such a code; this idea was floated in the 1940s, but came to nothing. If not Congress, then the states would have to make the code; and unifying the country would mean persuading the states, one by one, to adopt a uniform law. This looked like a really tough job; but in the end, it was substantially accomplished.

Karl Llewellyn, perhaps the country's most prominent, erratic, and productive legal thinker, was one of the brains behind the code. Uniformity was a crucial goal; but Llewellyn also wanted to make the law more rational. This meant, to him, making it conform to sound business practice. The basis of the code should be the "norms of merchant behavior"—that is, the unwritten rules that good businesspeople followed. Law should be made from the "folkways of merchants." Under Llewellyn's original scheme, a "merchant jury system" would be an important part of the system; this would be a panel of businesspeople, who would decide issues which only merchants, with their special knowledge, their feel for the business situation, could properly resolve.[5] But Llewellyn did not mean to abdicate all power to the merchants. He wanted the code to reflect ethical business practices; he wanted it to protect consumers as well as sellers and producers; and he wanted a considerable dollop of judicial oversight.[6]

Llewellyn led the team (which included his wife, Soia Mentschikoff) that drafted the code for the American Law Institute in the 1940s. The process was long and arduous; and the drafters had to abandon or compromise many of their ideas along the way. The merchant jury was an early casualty. In general, the world of business was less enthusiastic about some of Llewellyn's ideas than he had hoped. Business representatives did not like to give judges power to regulate or oversee mercantile contracts. They did not like the clauses that were supposed to protect consumers. The finished draft of about 1950 was far from what Llewellyn and Mentschikoff might have wanted, but it was still arguably an improvement over existing law.

The next job was to sell the Uniform Commercial Code to the states. The first convert was Pennsylvania, in 1953. A few years later came Massachusetts, then Kentucky. Progress was slow. New York was a key state, but a reluctant one. Then the dam broke. Fourteen states were in line by 1962; by 1967 every state except Louisiana had adopted the code, along with the District of Columbia and the Virgin Islands. Louisiana, despite its civil-law tradition, swallowed the bulk of the code in 1974. At that point, the United States had (more or less) achieved a kind of uniformity in commercial law. There were some minor divergences here and there; and of course no one could guarantee that the states would interpret uniform codes in a uniform way. It was not clear then—or now—whether the code had any real impact on commerce, or whether it improved the gross national product in any way. But it was a gold mine for law professors, giving them something to write about endlessly. And it did make a difference to the practice, in some branches of commercial law.

The code was divided into nine articles.[7] It superseded the uniform laws on sales, negotiable instruments, and bills of lading. Very notably, the code covered "secured transactions"—that is, commercial transactions backed up by security or collateral—including, of course, that most common of American habits, buying a car or a piano "on time." Here it replaced a jumble of local laws on conditional sales, chattel mortgages, and similar devices.

The code was, in a sense, "up to date"; and it brought some order into a multistate chaos. But what is up to date soon becomes dated itself. The code did very little in the way of what we would now call consumer protection. In the process of hammering out a code, clauses which required businesses to disclose their interest rates, for example, simply disappeared. Consumer interests were, by and large, not on the radar screen of business at that time. The early drafts, too, had had tough warranty provisions. These also died in the journey to passage.

But soon after the code was adopted, the consumer movement became strong enough to make a difference. Congress passed a Truth in Lending Act in 1968.[8] In 1975 Congress enacted the Magnuson-Moss Warranty Improvement Act.[9] Magnuson-Moss gave the Federal Trade Commission power to set federal standards for written warranties on consumer products; and it set out "minimum standards" for such warranties—the companies, for example, had to make good on products which turned out to be lemons. States passed their own "lemon" laws—California, for example, enacted one in 1970.[10] Other warranty and consumer protection laws followed. These applied to all sorts of products, but especially to cars. In California, indeed, not only does the dealer have to take back the lemon, but the car must thereafter bear the words "Lemon Law Buyback" on its ownership certificate; and a decal, like a sort of scarlet letter, is affixed to the car itself.[11]

The General Law of Contracts

The rules of contract law, in theory, govern any agreement—any exchange of goods or services, whether to sell a carload of lumber, to buy lessons in ballroom dancing, or to abstain from alcohol and tobacco in exchange for your uncle's estate. In practice, of course, most contracts—and almost all contracts of any great size—come out of the world of commerce and business. In many ways, the nineteenth century was the century of contract: Sir Henry Maine, in his famous book *Ancient Law* (1861), made contract a kind of centerpiece of evolution: the law of "progressive" societies moved from status to contract. In most premodern societies, rights and privileges inhered in the family, the clan, not the individual. Status determined rights and duties: were you a man or a woman? a commoner or a noble? a merchant or a peasant farmer? In modern societies, legal relationships tend to be individual, voluntary, and based on free agreements. Nobody is born a buyer or a seller (there may be born shoppers); men and women *assume* the role of buyer, seller, trader, or dealer, and they put these roles on and off as they might put on and take off clothes.

The nineteenth century believed in Maine's thesis. This was the age of laissez-faire in theory, if not always in practice.[12] It was also, for ideological (and practical) reasons, an age that exalted voluntary agreement. Legal education celebrated the regime of contract. The very first casebook for law students under the Harvard method in the late nineteenth century was C. C. Langdell's casebook on contracts. Every single first-year law student since Langdell's time has studied the law of contracts. Samuel Williston (1861–1963) of Harvard put together a massive treatise on contracts, first published in 1920, which influenced generations of teachers. Williston's treatise was dry, formalistic, and exceedingly "legal"; it reinforced an image of contract as a neutral body of law, a network of interlaced principles logically related to each other, and free from politics, culture, and social structure. This corresponded neatly (if unconsciously) with the view that law should support the free market without question. The sole duty of contract law was to enforce voluntary agreements, not to impose rules and provisions on people who had not chosen these for themselves.

The great anti-Williston was Arthur Corbin (1874–1967), who presided over contract law in the rival citadel, Yale Law School. His eight-volume treatise on contracts appeared in 1950; it breathed some of the air of the legal realist movement, and was more concerned with "the purposes and policies behind specific legal rules." Unlike Williston, Corbin did not "assume a timeless ahistorical law of contracts based on principles found in the cases."[13]

Corbin was probably closer to the working reality. In many regards, "contract law," the pure and beautiful entity that Williston imagined, never existed, or if it did, was in a state of disintegration and decay by the twentieth century.[14] Grant Gilmore of Yale proclaimed the "death of contract" in a highly regarded book published in 1974.[15] Already in the nineteenth century, contract law had begun to evolve in the direction of "laxity" or "paternalism," at least as the nineteenth century understood these terms. In the twentieth century, courts were even less likely to enforce a contract they considered one-sided or unfair. Friedrich Kessler, a refugee scholar from Europe, introduced, in an article published in 1943, the concept of a "contract of adhesion."[16] A contract of adhesion is a form contract—a take-it-or-leave-it contract—almost always drafted by business lawyers, to be signed by customers who never read the "fine print." In the nineteenth century, many courts were likely to say, if you signed it, you're stuck with it; but this was not the late-twentieth-century ethos.

Contract law, in general, became less "harsh." But harshness is a social judgment. The judges of the nineteenth century, strictly enforcing the terms of contracts (when they actually did), did not think of themselves as cruel, callous people. They thought that they were making decisions that, in the aggregate, were good for the country. A bargain was a bargain; and it had to be enforced. Otherwise, what would become of economic life?

Twentieth-century courts were more likely to look at the context of a case; or to listen to an argument that the contract was unfair. In some cases, the court enforced promises that nineteenth-century judges refused to enforce. Contract law insisted on two promises, not one. If, for example, a donor promised to contribute a million dollars to help build a new wing on a hospital, and the trustees hired contractors and started the building process, in classical theory, the donor could back out. Twentieth-century judges felt otherwise. This was a case of "promissory estoppel": if somebody had reasonably relied on a promise, the courts would enforce it, even if strict old-fashioned contract law would not have done so. The doctrine was enshrined in §90 of the Restatement of Contracts, drafted in the late 1920s; and this gave added strength to the idea.

"Unconscionability" was another new doctrine. An early, and striking case, was *Campbell Soup Co. v. Wentz* (1948).[17] Wentz and other farmers agreed to deliver all of their "Chantenay red cored carrots," at a fixed price, to the soup company. These were apparently marvelous soup carrots. Wentz tried to back out of the deal (probably because the market price of such carrots had climbed sky-high). Campbell tried to hold Wentz and the others to their deal. But the court said no; Campbell had struck "too hard a bargain." The contract had (naturally) been drafted by Campbell's lawyers, and it was fairly one-sided: Campbell, for example, did not have to take the carrots under certain conditions, but Wentz could not sell to anybody else without Campbell's permission. Equity, said the court, "does not enforce unconscionable bargains."

Unconscionability was embodied in the Uniform Commercial Code, in §2-305. In *Vokes v. Arthur Murray, Inc.,* a Florida case (1968), a childless widow in her early fifties, Audrey Vokes, went to a dance studio in Clearwater, Florida, for lessons.[18] The studio cajoled and flattered her, told her she had it in her to become a "beautiful dancer," and similar lies; eventually she signed up for 2,302 hours of dancing lessons, for a price of more than thirty thousand dollars, in the hopes of getting a bronze medal, then a silver medal, then a gold medal, eligibility for trips, and other items of bait. Eventually, Vokes woke up and realized that she had signed up for many lifetimes of dance lessons, at the cost of a small fortune. She went to court to get out of her contract. A lower court threw out the case, but the appeal court reversed. Generally speaking people should be held to their bargains, said the court, but not here. Audrey Vokes was entitled to show that she was bamboozled.

The Florida court never actually used the word *unconscionable.* But it was sympathetic to a gullible woman, and showed distaste for what it considered sharp business practices. The consumer protection movement no doubt influences judges; it certainly made a mark on legislation. We have already mentioned some consumer protection statutes. Under standard contract doctrine, a deal was a deal; once the parties signed on the dotted line, there was no backing out. But a California law of 1971 made an exception to this rule. The statute applied to door-to-door salespeople (or to any sale at "other than appropriate trade premises"); it gave the buyer the right to cancel up to "midnight of the third business day" after signing up.[19] Undoubtedly, this law was in harmony with actual social norms. People feel that they should have a reasonable chance to change their minds, after the high-pressure salesman goes out the door, and second thoughts set in.

In many ways, the market itself responded to changing norms. People had expectations, and business had to conform or lose out. Giant businesses were built more or less on the principle that the customer is always right. Department stores will freely accept returns. This does not mean that contract is "dead," whatever Grant Gilmore thought or wrote. Indeed, contract was probably far more alive in the late twentieth century than it had ever been—this was a gigantic, growing economy, which rested on a firm basis of private business, private enterprise, and private consumption. A regime of contract, then, survives and is hearty and hale. The market economy runs on contracts. What was dead was the nineteenth-century image of contract—and unrealistic assumptions about people, companies, situations, and events.

In the law, there was less and less space and scope for a general law covering all voluntary agreements. Instead, the law of contract shattered like a broken mirror, and splintered into subfields: into special rules applicable to this or that kind of contract. Many of these subfields had a past; they were older than the twentieth century—insurance law, for example. Courts (and legislatures) tended to sympathize with the insured, not with the company. Courts used doctrines of "waiver" or "estoppel" or similar devices, to force reluctant insurance companies to pay claims. It happened (often), that the insured had not exactly told the truth, the whole truth, and nothing but the truth, in applying, say, for life insurance; or had violated the insurance contract in some way. If the court felt that the lie or error was not exactly vital, it refused to let the company off. In this way, the judges, as Clarence Morris wrote in 1957, converted insurance "from a custom-made document . . . to a brand-name staple sold over the counter by mine-run salesmen to the trusting public."[20] The insurance companies had (and descrvcd) a bad reputation—they liked collecting premiums, but disliked paying claims. Many states began to insist, by law, that life insurance policies contain "incontestability" clauses. If the policy had been in effect for, say, two years, the company could no longer contest it, even if the insured had told a little lie or two. Some companies adopted such clauses voluntarily. In general, states subjected insurance contracts and companies to a blizzard of statute. The Wisconsin legislature, between 1906 and 1959, passed no fewer than eight hundred statutes on the subject of insurance.[21]

The New Deal labor laws, and labor law in general, helped make the labor agreement into a special subfield of its own. Commercial codes covered commercial law. Civil rights laws impinged on all sorts of contractual relationships—between bosses and workers, between hotel keepers and guests, between landlords and tenants, and so on. By 2000 a solid and thick pattern of rules modified, buttressed, and overlay the basic regime of contract.

The working rules of contract, moreover, are not necessarily the rules the casebooks talk about. Business has its own norms, its own ways of thinking and acting. A famous study, by Stewart Macaulay of the University of Wisconsin Law School (1963), explored the actual behavior of businesspeople in Wisconsin.[22] Macaulay's businesspeople were not eager to sue each other; nor were they quick to insist on their "rights" as the formal law of contract defined these rights. Networks of personal and business relationships developed between companies. People dealt with each other, relied on each other. A person who stubbornly insisted on sticking to the letter of contract law would put valuable business relationships at risk. A follow-up study of corporate counsel, published in 1992, supported Macaulay's insights.[23] The lawyers were asked: suppose there was a shift in the market price of some goods; and a supplier asked you to modify the contract price. Would your company consider it? Ninety-five percent of them said that they would. And 83 percent had themselves "requested relief from contractual obligations." Business cannot go on without contracts; but it also cannot go on without trust, understanding, and common sense. The real world of contractual behavior was far more complex than the lawbooks suggested.

Second Chances

In matters of contract and business behavior, the mentality of the twentieth century seemed more fluid and nuanced than the mentality of the nineteenth century—at least as far as legal matters were concerned. Not that people were smarter than before; or kinder and gentler. But as society changed, attitudes toward risk, chances, and calamity changed, as we saw in our discussion of tort law.

The welfare state itself—the social safety net—was a key element in this shift, whether you think of it as cause or effect. A key theme was security for people, money for old age, money to tide people over rough spots in life (like loss of a job); but the social safety net also embodied the idea of second chances in life. The culture did not much like irreversible misfortunes. A good example of this culture was the way modern bankruptcy laws developed.

These laws become especially important in times of easy credit. People buy all sorts of expensive goods on the installment plan. Business, after all, is eager to sell as much as it can; it spends billions on advertisements. It tries to cajole people, to stimulate them to buy, buy, buy; not to defer gratification, but to satisfy their desires right now. All those wonderful things they see advertised in the papers, magazines, on TV, and all around them—a brand new car, a power lawnmower, a houseful of furniture, a trip to Australia.

Easy credit is important in a market society, a consumer society. People have to be able to go into debt, they have to be able to buy "on time." But creditors also need tough, workable ways to collect; otherwise, the deadbeats would win every time. The law had to develop a delicate balance, between easy credit and hard laws on creditors' rights. The Uniform Commercial Code, in its provisions on secured transactions, tried to strike such a balance. Cars can be repossessed. Mortgages can be foreclosed. Courts can give judgments against debtors. But after all the hard goods have gone back to the seller, if debts still remain, the last resort is the law of bankruptcy.

As we have seen, the Constitution gave bankruptcy power to the federal government; but it was not until 1898 that a national law was passed that lasted more than a few years. This law—much amended, to be sure—is still in force. As we have seen, there are two main points to a bankruptcy law. The first is fairness to creditors—that is, the corpse has to be equally and honestly divided among waiting vultures. The second is a fresh start for the debtor. The Chandler Act (1938) made important changes in bankruptcy law.[24] Chapters 10 and 11 of the Chandler Act provided a way to keep bankrupt enterprises alive: they could regroup, revamp, and stay in business. In the Depression years, this seemed like an especially good idea. There was something similar in the old bankruptcy law, but for various reasons it was ineffective. Chapter 10 of the new act fell into disuse; chapter 11, however, was an immediate success. A corporation that went into chapter 11 would draw up a plan to restructure its debts (subject to court approval). Then it could get on with its life.

Chapter 13 of the Chandler Act set up a system for wage earners. It has been described as "bankruptcy on the installment plan." Chapter 13 was only for individuals, not businesses; it allowed a debtor to pay off his debts in a reasonable time; the creditors had to agree to the plan; the debtor had to agree to make regular payments. These payments would go to a trustee, who doled out a living allowance to the debtor, and paid the rest to the creditors. A Wisconsin study (1964) found that most individual debtors preferred straight bankruptcy: only 14 percent used Chapter 13—these were relatively high-income debtors, whose debt burdens were relatively low.[25]

Bankruptcy was a way out, when debt became unbearable. At the time of the Wisconsin study, far more workers—ten times as many as went bankrupt—were subject to garnishment of wages. A hungry creditor could get a court order telling the debtor's employer to withhold some of the debtor's wages and pay it directly to the creditor. A study of five cities in Ohio, published in 1933, found that garnishment actions made up 50.5 percent of the total civil caseload. Clothing stores accounted for a quarter of these; doctors, jewelers, and grocery stores were also big users of garnishment.[26] In the year ending June 30, 1968, in Los Angeles County, 148,773 orders for garnishment of wages were issued.[27] These were workers who bought cars and other expensive items, then fell behind in their payments. Many creditors preferred to garnishee wages rather than try to repossess. The creditor usually turned the matter over to a collection agency, which took over and got the court order. This meant that the debtor was saddled with extra charges: attorney's fees, collection charges, interest, and service fees.[28] The workers almost never contested. Employers, for their part, also disliked garnishments—it was a costly bother to administer, and it was bad for worker morale. Employers tended to fire workers who had too many parasitic growths on their salary checks.

Garnishment law was complicated. Nowhere was a creditor allowed to grab everything a worker made. Exemptions varied from state to state: Illinois, for example, as of 1947, exempted twenty dollars a week of the earnings of the "head of a family."[29] Some states were more generous—in Florida in the 1960s, for example, all of the earnings of the head of a family were exempt. Garnishment was politically unpopular, too; it fell victim to the American passion for giving second chances. In 1968 Congress, solemnly intoning words about "predatory extensions of credit," burdens on interstate commerce, and the ways in which the jungle of garnishment laws had "destroyed the uniformity of the bankruptcy laws," put a national limit on garnishment: 25 percent of the worker's disposable income could be garnisheed, and no more. And no employer was to fire an employee simply because his wages had been garnisheed.[30]

Bankruptcy remains a rather technical, arcane field of law. Complaints were heard that the system was slow, inefficient, and perhaps unfair. Congress established a Bankruptcy Commission in 1968; the commission held hearings and recommended an overhaul of the bankruptcy law.[31] The new law, enacted in 1978, created, in each judicial district, a United States Bankruptcy Court, as an "adjunct" to the regular federal district court. The president (with the usual advice and consent of the Senate) would appoint bankruptcy judges. Regular federal judges serve for life; but bankruptcy judges were to be appointed for fourteen-year terms.[32] Bankruptcy can be voluntary (the debtor makes the first move), or involuntary (the creditor pushes the debtor over the edge). Overwhelmingly, men, women, and businesses in bankruptcy are voluntary, although creditor pressure might lie behind many of these "voluntary" moves. The numbers of cases filed rose from fewer than 20,000 in the first decade of the century to more than 60,000 in the depths of the Depression. For the fiscal year that ended on June 30, 1942, there were 52,109 bankruptcy filings; only 1,337 of these were involuntary. The numbers fell rapidly with wartime prosperity—in the year that ended June 30, 1945, only 12,862 petitions were filed. Afterward, the numbers began climbing again, and reached 53,136 in 1954.[33] In recent years, bankruptcy has become incredibly popular. The statistics reflect a society that floats, as we have seen, on oceans of credit, a society of credit cards and bank cards; a society, moreover, in which there is no stigma to going bankrupt once in a while. For the twelve months ended September 30, 1990, there were 1,436,949 filings in bankruptcy. Well over 90 percent of these were classified as nonbusiness; only 47,125 were classified as business filings.

Under the Chandler Act, as we have seen, a business could stay alive through bankruptcy, and get "reorganized." In fact, most businesses that went into chapter 11 of the Chandler Act did not survive. In the 1978 law, a remodeled chapter 11 tried to eliminate problems that had plagued the old procedures. Companies in chapter 11 could propose their own plan of reorganization; creditors could vote the plan up or down. One of the ideas behind the new chapter 11 was to let companies file before it was "too late," before they were "too far gone." This would make it possible to "save" a lot of businesses from corporate death.[34]

Corporations (or their lawyers) have been quite ingenious, however, in thinking up uses for chapter 11 that Congress, perhaps, never intended. In 1983, for example, Continental Airlines filed "for protection" under chapter 11; Continental, which was in trouble, asked pilots and flight attendants to make wage and work-rule concessions. The workers said no. This "triggered" the application for chapter 11.[35] Under the old rules, a company had to show that it was insolvent; under the new rules, there was no such requirement. The change was probably made to avoid fuss and red tape; nobody expected solvent corporations to file "for protection." But this is exactly what the Manville Corporation did, in 1983, faced with a zillion potential claims of asbestos victims.[36]

Bankruptcy plays an obvious role in the economy; it is an important part of the debtor-creditor cycle. But some of its most important consequences are almost intangible. Bankruptcy is part of the psychological and cultural underpinnings of a society of entrepreneurs. Americans think of themselves as bold in business, as fearless risk takers; the vitality of small and new business owes a lot to the culture of independence, of taking a chance, of "owning your own business," of not having a boss. But it also owes something to the social safety net; to bankruptcy laws; to limited liability. Failure is not total catastrophe. Would people put their savings into a pizza parlor or an internet start-up if they thought debtor's prison, or a lifetime of grinding poverty, was the price of failure? If you want many people to walk on your tightrope, you had better provide them with a net.

Corporation Law

As we have seen, corporation law had evolved into a flexible, open system of nonrules. It allowed corporations to do whatever they wished, buy other businesses, sell them again, change the corporate name, change role, change focus, merge, unmerge; structure and restructure—do whatever, in short, the "business judgment" of the managers commended. It was a far cry from the classic idea that a corporation held a "franchise," and that its charter had to be construed as narrowly as possible.

This freedom for corporations may seem ironic, in a period which regulated them much more than the nineteenth century had; but as we have seen, the state gave up the attempt to regulate corporations as such. The new regulatory laws applied to corporations, of course—indeed, mostly to corporations. But they were specific—they were laws about certain kinds of corporations (insurance, for example), or about certain aspects of corporate life: labor relations, handling toxic wastes, hiring or not hiring women, and so on. Corporation law itself had, for example, no general rules making it hard for corporations to merge. But antitrust law did make some mergers illegal. And there were important new statutes about stocks and bonds, which the SEC administered.

In theory, stockholders owned the company; the managers were only their agents. The reality was perhaps rather different. In a 1933 book that excited a good deal of comment, Adolph Berle and Gardiner Means argued that the modern corporation sharply divided ownership and actual control.[37] The real bosses of the corporation—the effective owners—were the managers; the stockholders were powerless and inert.

The Berle and Means thesis has been severely criticized. Stockholders can vote with their feet, so to speak; and when share prices fall, and stockholders sell, management is in deep, deep trouble. Nor could Berle and Means foresee the power of big institutional stockholders: pensions and mutual funds, notably, owning millions and millions of shares. There is, of course, a core of fact in the authors' thesis. Scholars have noted that the American big business corporation is quite different from, say, the Japanese or German corporation. In these countries, stockholders are more likely to have actual control; but the stockholders are hardly widows and orphans; they are big banks and financial institutions. David Skeel has argued that legal restraints on banks and other financial institutions have prevented this from happening in the United States. The Glass-Steagall Act (1933) separated commercial and investment banking.[38] The Bank Holding Company Act (1956) made it unlawful for a bank holding company to own stock in "any company which is not a bank."[39] State laws discouraged insurance companies from owning big blocks of stock in other companies. These restraints—products of populism, and the lobbying of small-bank groups—worked to "minimize the role of financial institutions in corporate governance."[40]

Corporations are also, of course, subject to the antitrust laws, which remain very much alive. Policy, of course, tends to vacillate from administration to administration; the years right after the Second World War were years of high activity, followed by bouts of caution. When the Republicans returned to power in the 1950s, they did not abandon antitrust, and there were a few spectacular cases, including a price-fixing case against General Electric and other companies in the electrical industry.[41] Among the relatively few high-profile cases later on was the great battle to break up IBM. The government filed suit in 1969. It accused IBM of monopolizing the mainframe industry—it controlled over 60 percent of this market—and of various nasty tricks to keep out or crush competitors. IBM fought back, throwing everything it had into the battle—contesting every single point, burying the government under mountains of paper, documents, and depositions, filing umpteen motions. The actual trial started in 1975; it staggered on for years, before it sputtered and went out, like a spent candle. The government simply dropped the case in 1982. In its prime, this massive case consumed the efforts of hundreds of lawyers. Counsel for IBM deployed endless numbers of young attorneys, who were thrown into the fray like second lieutenants at Verdun in the First World War; these young lawyers tended to burn out after months poring over documents and files in some warehouse. On the other hand, the government did succeed in breaking up the telephone monopoly. The American Telephone and Telegraph Company ("Ma Bell") agreed, in a settlement, to hack itself into eight different pieces. This result was announced at the same time as the IBM dismissal. The severed pieces of the old telephone monopoly, in fact, prospered; and the pieces showed signs, in the 1990s, of regenerating, like primitive worms, into whole new animals. At the end of the millennium, the government was once again engaged in a massive antitrust suit, this time against mighty Microsoft.

Antitrust policy was and is a subject of fierce dispute and argument, among economists and lawyers. How important *is* antitrust law? Some insist that the market itself is the best trust-buster, especially in a time of innovation and explosive new technology. The government gave up its fight against IBM with a whimper and slunk away; but IBM was whipped and disciplined by its competitors; it could not, in the end, keep its stranglehold on the market. At least one economist has argued that IBM would have been better off—like AT&T—if it had lost its case.[42] The public has learned to live with big companies. They are no longer bogeymen. This may be especially true in a booming economy. Moreover, millions of people work for big corporations, and pin their future on the health of their companies. Already in 1951, a survey showed that 76 percent of the population thought that "good things outweigh the bad things" about big business.[43]

But antitrust law and policy should not be judged just in terms of these megacases. The government brings many small, local cases that, in the aggregate, probably make a difference, if not to the whole economy, then to this or that business, in this or that piece of the country. In 1950, for example, the government indicted Gimbel Brothers, which was (the government said) fixing department store prices in Philadelphia; Gimbel did not contest, and paid a fine. Another price-fixing case in that year targeted a corporation and seven individuals in the dry cleaning business in Anchorage, Alaska. A third attacked anticompetitive behavior among owners of cigarette vending machines in the San Francisco area; still another went after a monopoly on wire garment hangers in the eastern two-thirds of the country.[44]

The antitrust division monitors mergers, too, with an eye to their impact on competition. In the last third or so of the twentieth century, there was a tremendous wave of mergers. As always, big fish swallowed little fish, but there seemed to be much more swallowing than ever. Fierce competition led many companies to think their only mode of survival was to merge with rivals or complementary companies. During the 1980s, ten thousand merger notifications were filed with the antitrust division.[45] Some were gigantic—General Electric gobbled up RCA—others were not. The antitrust division challenged exactly twenty-eight of these ten thousand. The government obviously felt that companies had to merge or die. This was especially true in the face of competition from foreign multinationals (which were doing a lot of gobbling on their own). William Baxter, chief of the antitrust division under Reagan, argued that consolidation was on the whole a good thing: nothing was "written in the sky that says that the world would not be a perfectly satisfactory place if there were only 100 companies." Debate over "merger mania" continued to the end of the century, zigging and zagging with each administration. Huge mergers continued to take place, even across borders—Daimler, a German auto company, merged with (or gobbled up) Chrysler, the third-largest American auto company. (American companies, of course, were ravenously feeding on overseas companies as well.) Although few mergers are challenged, the mere fact that they have to be vetted may discourage some, and alter the shape of certain others. Once antitrust policy was headline stuff (and accomplished very little); now it provokes only yawns from the general public, but it has a real effect. As Richard Hofstadter put it in the 1960s, at one time "the United States had an antitrust movement without antitrust prosecutions"; now it has "antitrust prosecutions without an antitrust movement." Antitrust has left the world of high politics and gone over to the realm of economics, the dismal science.

Taxation

The federal income tax law, as we have seen, was a creature of the twentieth century. Tax policy during the New Deal was an important political issue. The federal government needed money to support its new programs. Some New Dealers liked the idea of soaking the rich and redistributing income; others were afraid of killing a goose that might lay a golden egg or two, even in a depression. There were struggles throughout the 1930s over income tax rates and doctrines; the tax became, on the whole, more progressive, meaning that the rich paid a higher percentage as they made more. But the Social Security tax was regressive—this was, in theory, social insurance, and it was supposed to pay for itself.[46]

The income tax affected mostly businesses and rich people. Not one American out of twenty paid the tax during the 1930s. The Second World War changed the situation totally. Incomes rose; and so did the voracious appetite of the government. Billions were needed to finance the war. Rates went up—and sharply. Some proposals were downright confiscatory—Roosevelt in 1942 even toyed with a proposal to limit all incomes to twenty-five thousand dollars, a comfortable income in those days; the rest would go to the IRS. Wartime tax rates included a surtax, which went from 13 percent on the first two thousand dollars to 82 percent on net income over two hundred thousand dollars.[47] Moreover, the war brought full employment, and good jobs in factories and businesses. Millions of people, for the first time, found themselves liable to pay an income tax.

In 1943 the treasury proposed a "pay-as-you go" plan: taxes would be withheld from paychecks, at the source. This would provide a more even flow of money, keep taxpayers current, and prevent sticker shock at tax time the following year. Social Security was already using a pay-as-you-go system. There was bitter debate about one aspect of the plan: should 1942 taxes be forgiven, as Beardsley Ruml, chairman of the New York Federal Reserve Bank, suggested?

Otherwise, citizens would pay twice in 1943: once for the year before and again, in the form of withholding, for the current year. After bitter debate, Ruml's idea won out over Roosevelt's opposition; essentially, the Current Tax Payment Act of 1943 forgave 75 percent of the 1942 or 1943 taxes, whichever were lower.[48] More significantly, the act "put wage and salary earners on a withholding basis of tax collection" from July 1, 1943, on; farmworkers, domestic help, casual laborers, soldiers, and sailors were exempted.[49]

The income tax was no longer a "class tax"; now it was a "mass tax," as one author has put it. Seven million Americans had to pay in 1940; by 1945 the figure was 45 million. Consequently, the social meaning of the income tax changed dramatically. It now confronted the general public with a perplexing, difficult, and onerous burden, in money and effort. The government launched a major propaganda campaign to sell the income tax as a war measure. Even Donald Duck was enlisted; Disney produced an animated short, which 32 million people watched in twelve thousand theaters. And Irving Berlin wrote a song to celebrate taxpaying, with these deathless words:

> I said to my Uncle Sam
> "Old Man Taxes here I am. . . .
> I'm proud as I can be
> I paid my income tax today. . . .
> I'm squared up with the U.S.A."[50]

This propaganda was probably effective during the war years; and, after a while, taxpayers simply got used to withholding, and to the income tax in general. But as more people had to pay, the fairness of the tax became an issue. In 1948 Congress allowed married couples to file a joint return. The treasury had been in favor of this move to keep rich men from fobbing income-producing assets off on their (nonearning) wives. In community-property states (southern and western), all income of the "community" (husband and wife) was already treated as half his, half hers. But most states did not have this system; to keep fairness between, say, California and New York, the new system, in effect, made every marriage a "community."[51]

As the rates rose, too, the tax laws became more and more significant for businesses, and called for more and more complicated planning. The early laws were complex enough—but they soon demonstrated a wonderful capacity for getting more so. High rates created huge incentives to find ways to get around the tax. Tax fraud is probably one of the commonest white-collar crimes. Even more popular than outright fraud is the game of finding a loophole. Rich people and businesses structured transactions with an eye to the tax laws; tax avoidance became a national pastime, perhaps even more popular than baseball, at least among the ranks of people with money, investments, and capital gains. The Internal Revenue Service and the taxpayers (more accurately, their clever lawyers or accountants) became locked in a kind of dance, a rhumba of avoidance and counteravoidance. Each time a rule or regulation or section of the code tried to plug a loophole, hundreds of lawyers and accountants began to search for a bright new loophole. It was a battle without victors or endings, a never-ending struggle, like the war between bacteria and antibiotics; the tricks, devices, schemes, and loopholes were constantly mutating in the search for ways to avoid the tight grip of the tax laws. The IRS reacted to each new tax-avoidance invention with more rules, regulations, and statutory amendments. Exceptions, exemptions, loopholes, and counterloopholes—they turned the law into a bloated, overgrown monster, the largest, most complicated, most difficult statute in the country, the most maddening and opaque, a huge, towering, jerry-built structure, a crazy-house of rules and counterrules, expressed in a language that seemed only vaguely related to standard English. Despite the incredible detail of the Internal Revenue Code, it has to be, and is, supplemented by a blizzard of regulations, rulings, and opinion letters, which rain down on taxpayers and their advisers like a tropical storm.

The Internal Revenue Code, despite attempts to streamline and reform, remained in 2000 in this state of petrified distortion: unwieldy, swollen, crammed with arcane, involute, and incomprehensible clauses and subclauses and sub-subclauses. Here, for example, is an excerpt from the code, as of the end of the century, on the subject of charitable deductions. The code sets a limit on the amount of money a person can deduct for gifts to charity in any given year. The limit is 50 percent of your "contribution base," which means, essentially, your gross income. If you contribute more, you are allowed to carry some of the extra deduction over to another year. Here is how the code puts it:

> In the case of an individual, if the amount of charitable contri-
> butions . . . exceeds 50 percent of the taxpayer's contribution base
> for such year, such excess shall be treated as a charitable deduc-
> tion . . . paid in each of the 5 succeeding taxable years in order of

time, but, with respect to any such succeeding taxable year, only to the extent of the lesser of the two following amounts:

(i) the amount by which 50 percent of the taxpayer's contribution base for such succeeding taxable year exceeds the sum of the charitable contributions . . . payment of which is made by the taxpayer within such succeeding taxable year (determined without regard to this subparagraph) and the charitable contributions . . . payment of which was made in taxable years before the contribution year which are treated under this subparagraph as having been paid in such succeeding taxable year; or

(ii) in the case of the first succeeding taxable year, the amount of such excess, and in the case the second, third, fourth, or fifth succeeding taxable year, the portion of such excess not treated under this subparagraph as a charitable contribution . . . paid in any taxable year intervening between the contribution year and such succeeding taxable year.[52]

The whole code is written, more or less, in this style. It gives employment to lawyers, accountants, and tax advisers; but ordinary human beings could never handle prose of this nature. It is terminally impenetrable. The Internal Revenue Code consists of hundreds of pages of similar material. Much of it, of course, is a reaction to the skill and nerve of tax specialists in developing their loophole. Beyond the maze of rules and regulations, some basics remained intact. The income tax was to be progressive. It would take the biggest bite from the wallets of the rich. There would also be a flat tax on corporate income (52 percent until 1964). But in Roosevelt's day, high taxes on the rich were more than a way to make money: they were instruments of policy—instruments of redistribution. In the last decades of the twentieth century, this policy goal faded into obscurity.

When all is said and done, the federal income tax is the greatest money machine in the country—probably in the world. In 1995 individuals paid no less than $590 billion to the federal government. Corporations threw in another $157 billion. Together, they produced three out of every four federal dollars. Estate and gift taxes contributed another $14.7 billion. Customs and miscellaneous taxes brought in the rest.[53]

The states, too, have increased their tax bite enormously. A great many states have income taxes on their own. Only a handful did so before the federal tax came into existence; but the Depression touched off a mad scramble for revenue, and nineteen states adopted income tax laws between 1929 and 1939, for a total of thirty-one states. California passed its law in 1935. Slightly more states had a tax on corporate net income; these, too, were mostly Depression babies. One state, Rhode Island, made its move in the 1940s; but no state added a personal income tax during that decade.

At the end of the twentieth century, forty-three states had some sort of personal income tax law, and forty-six had some sort of corporate income tax. Texas was a major holdout. Income taxes brought in some $125 billion for the states in 1995. Sales taxes, and a ragbag of excise taxes, brought in most of the rest. Some cities, too, had income taxes, but local governments continued to depend heavily on property taxes, to the tune of some $193 billion in 1995.[54]

In tax law, the progressive principle has eroded over the years. The top rates were very high during the Second World War; after that, they declined. President John F. Kennedy proposed a tax cut (it was enacted after his death); but the Reagan presidency produced the most dramatic cuts. The Economic Recovery Tax Act of 1981 dropped the top rate from 70 percent to 50 percent.[55] Even so, the tax was still quite progressive; there were fifteen brackets. The Tax Reform Act of 1986 flattened the income tax considerably.[56] The top rate fell to 28 percent, and there were only two brackets (15 percent and 28 percent). The country was getting close to the Emerald City of tax conservatives, an income tax which would be totally flat.

During the Reagan years, the country was also running a gigantic deficit. The money machine was not producing enough to cover what the administration felt it had to spend. Reagan, after all, never met an expensive weapons system he did not fall in love with. After Reagan departed, the rates began to creep up again: a third bracket, at 31 percent, was added in 1990. At the end of the century, the top rate was 39.6 percent. Tax cutting fever also hit the states during the Reagan years. California's "Proposition 13," one of the most notorious examples, gutted the local property tax in 1978. Prop 13 rolled back property taxes dramatically; moreover, these taxes could go up no more than 2 percent a year; and the legislature was barred from raising the rates without a two-thirds vote in both houses—something almost impossible to achieve.[57]

Soaking the rich was no longer a popular policy. It is, of course, fairly easy to understand why Californians would vote so eagerly to cut property taxes.

This tax sits on top of the urban and suburban middle class like a dead weight. As real estate prices go up, so do assessments, and so does the tax. It becomes a kind of great white shark, biting off huge chunks of homeowners' flesh every year. But this motive does not explain why California, in a striking move, voted by referendum to eliminate the state's death taxes. These taxes fell exclusively on the rich. Nor does it explain why the flat tax should have any political appeal at all, locally or nationally.

In the 1990s, nobody was talking anymore about "malefactors of great wealth." One reason, I suspect, was the changing image of the rich, in an age of celebrity gossip and television chatter. The glitter and glamour of wealth fascinated ordinary people. "Rich" no longer meant the callous robber barons; it no longer conjured up the image of Wall Street connivers, or a prune-faced John D. Rockefeller, giving tiny tips, and squeezing the life out of competitors. Now it meant the likes of basketball players, home run hitters, rock musicians, rapsters, movie stars. These were people just like us, people with talents that the ordinary person could appreciate—talents that ordinary people could even aspire to. Even the image of the businessperson had changed. The famous ones now were young, brilliant, self-made computer geeks and internet moguls. Moreover, to everybody's surprise, the deficit disappeared in the 1990s and even turned into a surplus. As the new millennium dawned, there was a golden glow on the horizon, brighter than a thousand suns: the dream of trillions and trillions of extra dollars, money for tax cuts, money to shore up Social Security, to pay off the national debt, with enough left over to buy prescription drugs for the old folks and perhaps do other new things. Whether the money would actually materialize was another question.

In any event, America was like a surfer riding the waves, thrilled by its vast, oceanic wealth. Some sort of tax cut seemed almost inevitable. The rich seemed almost certain to get richer. Some form of the flat tax was still on the agenda. A bill to phase out the estate and gift taxes passed both houses of Congress. President Clinton vetoed it. That it had gotten this far was an amazing fact. And in 2001, in fact, it became law—though postponed for a term of years.

13

The Law of Property

The United States is most definitely a free-market country; but for most people, whether in business or not, an absolute, unregulated free market might be good for the other guy; for one's self, help from the government is welcome, necessary, and of course richly deserved.

Zoning, land-use controls, and urban planning are cases in point; they are a story of mixed motives, a brew of culture, morality, and economics. In the nineteenth century, cities grew like weeds. In 1800 there was no Chicago, no Los Angeles, no Seattle, no Houston. In 1900 cities were huge—they were also shapeless, ugly, filthy, and frequently corrupt. The city fathers, as their cities matured, wanted something more than raw economic growth: they wanted parks, symphony orchestras, and other signs of culture and refinement. They also wanted to get rid of factories, slaughterhouses, and the like, or at least get them out of the better neighborhoods. The more socially conscious wanted tenement laws and better sewage systems. All these aspirations encouraged those who professed a brand new specialty: city planning. The Chicago World's Fair of 1893 is often connected to the ideal of the "city beautiful"; Chicago built a "shimmering 'White City'" on Lake Michigan, a community which "contrasted sharply with the dirty industrial city outside its gates."[1] The White City was a glimpse of a glorious urban future.

The Pig in the Parlor: Zoning Comes to America

Esthetic motives—the vision of the city beautiful—had a catalytic or symbolic importance; the hard core of city planning was economic and political. Zoning and land-use controls were, above all, devices to protect property values. This meant, among other things, keeping bad people and bad buildings out of nice neighborhoods. Benjamin Marsh of New York published a book on city planning in 1909; in the same year, a National Conference on City Planning met in Washington, D.C. Marsh had traveled in Europe, and had seen city planning at work in Germany. There cities were cut up into zones or districts; the maximum height of a building depended on its district or zone.[2]

New York City adopted the first comprehensive zoning ordinance. The merchants of Fifth Avenue, owners of elegant stores, backed it with enthusiasm; they had watched in horror as the tacky sweatshops and grimy workers of the garment industry crept north toward their district. The newfangled skyscrapers were another problem: these monstrous buildings shut off air and light for acres all about them. The city wanted zoning, and height restrictions. The New York legislature passed an enabling act in 1914. A Commission on Building Districts and Restrictions issued a report in 1916. The city, according to the report, had "reached a point beyond which continued unplanned growth cannot take place without inviting social and economic disaster."[3] The New York City Board of Estimate and Apportionment adopted the commission's recommendations that July.[4]

Specific problems and pressures led to the zoning ordinance in New York City. But zoning did not appeal only to high-class merchants on Fifth Avenue. Home owners came to see zoning as a way to protect their home—especially as an investment. Zoning spread like wildfire across the country. Legislatures passed enabling acts; and cities rushed to adopt these ordinances. Thirty-five cities had zoning by 1920.[5] By 1930 there were 1,100 cities with ordinances. Columbus, Ohio, to take one example, adopted zoning in 1923. It divided the city into five "use districts." The top category was restricted to one- or two-family houses; another district allowed apartment houses; other districts allowed commercial establishments; and there were "first [light] industrial" and "second [heavy] industrial" districts. Higher uses were allowed in lower zones; but not the reverse. There were provisions to control building height and density.[6]

As the practice spread, it was challenged in the courts in many states. Zoning, after all, though it protected some values, hurt others: it prevented a landowner from building, say, an apartment house if his district was not zoned for it. Zoning, in other words, has winners and losers. Land zoned for residential use is worth less than if a factory or a shopping mall could go on it. The courts, however, were on the whole extremely sympathetic to zoning. The Supreme Court of Wisconsin, for example, upheld the Milwaukee ordinance in 1923. It was within the power of government to act to prevent "deterioration" in residential sections; "deterioration" could result in "destruction of property values." Besides, the "home instinct" of the public "craves fresh air, sunshine, and well-kept lawns."[7] Of course, millions of people lacked fresh air and lawns of any kind; but the middle-class Milwaukee home owners who had these amenities found friends on the Wisconsin court.

In *Village of Euclid v. Ambler* (1926), the zoning issue reached the United States Supreme Court.[8] The justices upheld the ordinance of a Cleveland suburb in sweeping terms. They agreed with the "experts" that "segregation of residential, business, and industrial buildings" was a good idea; that it would "increase the safety and security of home life," reduce street accidents, decrease noises and other conditions "which produce or intensify nervous disorders," create a better environment for children, and so on. Apartment houses (Euclid barred them from the highest residential areas) could "destroy" a whole area for "private house purposes"; and one apartment house leads to another, interfering "with the free circulation of air and monopolizing the rays of the sun"; apartment houses bring traffic and take play areas away from children. An apartment house in a district of single-family homes was a "mere parasite," living off the amenities of the "open spaces and attractive surroundings" of the neighborhood. Under these circumstances, apartment houses "come very near to being nuisances"; and a nuisance, as the court pointed out, is "merely a right thing in the wrong place—like a pig in the parlor instead of the barnyard."

Thus zoning, in the Court's opinion, was good for society; it brought order and security out of chaos. As one author later put it, zoning was enacted "for the well-being of all"; we have moved away, he said, "from the archaic conception of man's right to indiscriminately hold and use his property for any purpose, regardless of the price to his fellow man."[9] *Price* is perhaps the right word. Zoning was a restriction on property rights; but for the benefit of the middle-class mass.

Zoning was, and is, genuinely popular. Almost every city (Houston is a glaring exception) and every self-respecting suburb ended up with a zoning ordinance. Zoning also produced a dense mass of law. Zoning ordinances were never absolute. Usually, the ordinance allowed "non-conforming uses" to continue; if the pig, in other words, was already in the parlor, he might stay. Thus, under Virginia law as of the 1940s, each city had a zoning board; and .. ove it a board of zoning appeals. The appeals board had power to authorize "variances" in "special cases," to avoid "unnecessary hardship," and to do "substantial justice."[10] This was, obviously, a mile-wide grant of discretion—if the board chose to use it.

Thus zoning, among other effects, made land development very bureaucratic, very political, and very complicated. It became standard to require a "building permit" before anybody could build, remodel, refurbish, or change his land-use plan; and cities had to have a corps of building inspectors. Closely connected was state control of subdivisions. Developers could no longer simply buy land and build houses. They needed permission from some local agency. Under a New Jersey law of 1930, cities and towns were given the power to create "planning boards." The boards could adopt a "master plan" for their town; once the plan was adopted, major construction had to fit the plan. The board could also adopt "regulations governing the subdivision of land within its jurisdiction." And the planning board could "approve, modify and approve, or disapprove" any such subdivision.[11]

A New Jersey case from 1938 is a good example of the pluses and minuses of the new regime.[12] A real estate company, Mansfield and Swett, Inc., bought a four-and-a-half-acre lot in West Orange, one of the tonier spots in northern New Jersey. The company tore down an old house and some outbuildings on the lot. It presented a plan to the town board, consisting of a subdivision of nineteen lots and two streets. The developers, who even in those ancient days attached fancy names to subdivisions, wanted to call this area Shadowlawn. The planning board turned them down cold; Shadowlawn was not in keeping with the character of West Orange, it would make for more traffic and otherwise disrupt the town's peace. But board members were also foolish enough to make the real reason clear. The fancy people of West Orange, sitting on large leafy lots, were against the plan. The big-lot people wanted no small-lot people in their town. The company appealed to the courts.

The developers lost a battle but won the war. The lost battle was over the statute. The New Jersey court ringingly endorsed subdivision control, planning boards, and the whole apparatus of the 1930 statute. But the court disapproved of what this particular board had done; its action was based on pure snobbery, on the objections of rich, big-lot owners, and the law did not allow that as a basis for decision. The judges sent the case back for rehearing; they hinted strongly how they wanted the case to come out. For their money, Shadowlawn deserved to be built.

The problem of Shadowlawn did not go away. Land-use controls were, above all, a tool of exclusion; and exclusion did not go unquestioned in the civil rights era. Two factors collided in the postwar period: the first was the rush to the suburbs, the passion of the (white) middle class for neat, safe houses with yards, rose bushes, and what they considered decent neighbors. The second factor was the rise of plural equality and the civil rights movement in its various forms.

Racially restrictive covenants met their Waterloo, as we have seen, in 1948, in *Shelley v. Kraemer*. Zoning and other forms of land-use control were less overt ways to keep neighborhoods lily-white and cosily middle class. The first of the famous *Mount Laurel* cases in New Jersey (1975) attacked the land-use policy of Mount Laurel Township, a "flat, sprawling township" of twenty-two square miles in southern New Jersey. The local NAACP chapter brought the suit.[13] Mount Laurel had once been largely rural: a cow township. But in the 1960s the population began to grow. The local ordinances were exceedingly restrictive: no apartments, no townhouses, no mobile homes, nothing residential except single-family homes on big lots. The Supreme Court of New Jersey found this unacceptable: Mount Laurel simply wanted to "build a wall around itself," to keep out "people or entities" which did not help with their tax base. Many of those who were excluded were black; all of the excluded had low incomes. The court ordered Mount Laurel to allow an "appropriate variety and choice of housing for all categories including low and moderate income."

The New Jersey Supreme Court may have thought of *Mount Laurel* as a kind of *Brown v. Board* of housing. The analogy is, alas, in some ways all too apt. *Mount Laurel*, too, met with massive resistance. Eight years later, Mount Laurel was back in court: "Ten years after the trial court's initial order . . . Mount Laurel remains afflicted with a blatantly exclusionary ordinance. . . . We believe that there is widespread non-compliance with . . . our original opinion." Mount Laurel township was not alone: other communities, too, were battling in court to keep the lower orders out. Just as in the southern states after *Brown*, this meant a "waste of judicial energy," "needless expenditure of talent on the part of lawyers and experts," and long, expensive, and "outrageous" trials.[14] The court issued stern orders. States passed fair-housing laws. Did anything really change?

In general, no. In American life, class and race are bound up inextricably together. Racism helps poison policy toward the poor; and fear and hatred of the underclass feeds American racism. We have already noticed the effect on public housing. In the *Gautreaux* case in Chicago, plaintiffs (all black) accused the Chicago Housing Authority of putting every project in a black neighborhood. The plaintiffs eventually won the case, after years and years of struggle. (Dorothy Gautreaux, the plaintiff who gave her name to the case, was long since dead.) But the main result of decisions like this, most probably, was not integrated, scattered public housing. Rather, these cases help bring on the death of public housing as a significant factor in the housing stock.[15]

The race-and-class issue was not just an issue of public housing or zoning. Its impact was felt in the history of urban renewal. In 1949 Congress embarked on this major new program. The preamble to the Housing Act of 1949 stressed curing the "serious housing shortage" and getting rid of "substandard and other inadequate housing through the clearance of slums and blighted areas." The goal was a "decent home and a suitable living environment for every American family."[16]

The goal got lost in the shuffle. The heart of the law was a program of loans and grants to local public agencies "for the undertaking of projects for the assembly, clearance, preparation, and sale and lease of land for development." "Private enterprise" was to "serve as large a part of the total need" as possible. The statute made no attempt to define *blight* or *slum*. It simply handed out money to clear bad neighborhoods, which would then be turned over to developers, who would build something nicer (for a profit). The law made reference to relocating people who were displaced, and it certainly was not intended to make the housing shortage worse. Nonetheless, urban renewal seemed all too often to degenerate into "Negro removal": cities eagerly pounced on urban renewal as a scheme for getting rid of black neighborhoods that were too close to white neighborhoods and showed signs of spreading.[17]

Like zoning itself, there was an esthetic and cultural element in the redevelopment movement; and a strong dash of social reform. But the hard core was greed and economic self-interest. Slum clearance and the fight against blight *sounded* as if they were sensible parts of a war on poverty. The reality was very different; slum clearance ended up as gentrification, or plans to put new life (and vigor) into the rotting downtowns of the cities. Under the law, renewal was supposed to be "predominantly residential"; but Congress enacted a 10 percent exception to this requirement in 1954, raised it to 20 percent in 1959, and 30 percent in 1961. Projects with grandiose names (Golden Gateway in San Francisco, Erieview in Cleveland) were rushed to the drawing boards.[18] The poor were, as usual, left out in the cold. Minorities were hit especially hard.

Urban renewal had never lacked for critics. One of the most powerful was Jane Jacobs; her classic study *The Death and Life of Great American Cities* (1961) was also a song of love for old-fashioned cities, with their bustling life, their crowds, their close communities, their richness in sound, smell, sight, and population. What Jacobs—and her fans—were up against, however, were powerful forces of intolerance and individualism. The city, as she (perhaps romantically) described it, was a cluster of real communities. But Americans did not want communities anymore. They wanted space, privacy, their own house and garden; they wanted fences, walls, gardens. Even the forced conformity of suburbia, the endless rows of ticky-tack houses, all more or less alike, the sheer homogeneity of these places, did not outweigh, for middle-class Americans, the value of a small, enclosed back yard, and neighbors who looked just like them.

And of course the cities did have problems: noise, filth, and crime. Some cities were perhaps beyond salvation. And politically, central cities suffered because they were becoming, in many cases, predominantly black: Detroit, Atlanta, Washington, D.C. There was, of course, progress in race relations, even in housing. Fair-housing laws meant that black brain surgeons and Hispanic stockbrokers could live just about anywhere they wanted to. But the minority masses remained unwelcome. And it is sad but true, as Charles Abrams put it in 1965, that cities "inhabited only by the poor are poor cities."[19] Meanwhile, billions had been spent to create a suburban belt that now strangled the central cities, and left them to choke in the debris of neglected problems.

In one significant regard, the ideology of development and redevelopment began to weaken later in the century. People no longer assumed that only the new, the sparkling, the up-to-date, was inherently good. Heritage and architecture were values in themselves. In 1931 the first "historic district" was established, in Charleston, South Carolina. In 1936 the Louisiana Constitution authorized the city of New Orleans to create a Vieux Carré Commission, and soon the Latin Quarter earned the label of a historic district. By 1950 there were about a dozen such districts, in 1965 about 100; by 1972 at least 133. In 1975 a survey found 421 local landmark or historical district commissions.[20] By the end of the century there were probably thousands. History was in. So was good architecture. Masterpieces like Louis Sullivan's Stock Exchange Building in Chicago had once fallen victim to the wrecking ball. (Nothing is left of it today except some fragments preserved in Chicago's Art Institute.) Such destruction is no longer so easily accomplished.

The courts almost uniformly upheld ordinances that protected history and architecture, even if they crimped the style (and hurt the pocketbook) of those fortunate or unfortunate enough to own a historic site. But there was money in tourism, too: the justices of Massachusetts, in approving a plan to preserve Nantucket Island as it was in the old days of whaling, praised the "sedate and quaint appearance" of Nantucket, its "unspoiled" nature; these virtues allowed the island to "build up its summer vacation business," its new economic base.[21] In the 1950s, too, the "scenic easement" appeared, as a way to make preservation cheaper and more widespread. Government or private interests would buy not the land itself but the right to keep it in its pristine shape.

Meanwhile, the federal government created a National Trust for Historic Preservation (1949).[22] The trust was authorized to receive donations of sites. A National Historic Preservation Act (1966) announced that "the spirit and direction of the nation are founded upon and reflected in its historic past."[23] This law, unlike the older law, included money: specifically, a program of matching grants to the states. History had come of age. America was no longer a country of raze and boom. Forces were at work which gave a different social and economic slant to old and beautiful places. They also fed the rise of the environmental movement.

Our House and Your House: Landlords and Tenants

The law of landlord and tenant grew up in an age of farms and farming. There were no apartment buildings or shopping centers in the Middle Ages. Even in the nineteenth century, landlord-tenant law was in fact mostly about farmland; the law was also strongly prolandlord. A tenant, for example, who "held over" (stayed past the end of the lease), even for a single day, automatically owed the landlord for a whole new period of rent. Common-law rules gave landlords very few duties toward tenants, and tenants had very little recourse against landlords.

In the twentieth century, of course, the conditions of tenure changed. The lease became a much more protean document. In big cities, millions of citizens and voters lived in apartment houses. Landlords were, on the whole, richer than tenants. But there were fewer of them. There was pressure on the law to bend in the direction of the tenants. The trend was particularly marked after 1970. Under traditional rules, a tenant had to keep on paying rent, or risk eviction, even when the landlord did not do his duty—by making repairs, for example. After 1970 case law and statutes overturned this doctrine, and imposed stricter duties on landlords.[24]

Housing is a commodity, but a rather special one. An apartment is not just a roof, a bathtub, a stove, and some furniture; it is also a home. Having a car repossessed is bad news; being evicted from a home is a disaster. The same forces underlying the "liability explosion" in tort law pushed the law of landlords and tenants in a similar direction—particularly because the "landlord" was often a big corporation, like the defendants in cases of tort.

Javins v. First National Realty Corporation (1970) was a landmark case.[25] First National owned apartments in the District of Columbia. The tenants in question held back on the rent. The landlord, they said, was not complying with the District's housing regulations. Under the older law, this was no excuse for a failure to pay rent. But times had changed. The judge, Skelly Wright, felt a lease was nothing but a contract between landlord and tenant. This contract implied that the landlord would keep the place in good shape. The tenant's promise to pay rent was conditional: if the lessor did not live up to its bargain, the tenant was excused.

The *Javins* case did not come out of thin air. The civil rights movement, the legal services movement—the whole atmosphere of the 1960s—helped transform the law of landlord and tenant. Skelly Wright himself had been "influenced by . . . the nationwide racial turmoil," and the fact that most tenants in District slums "were poor and black and most of the landlords were rich and white. There is no doubt in my mind that these conditions played a subconscious role."[26] At the same time, a quite different group—families that lived in luxury apartments—found the old rules equally obnoxious. The two groups made a powerful combination.

Indeed, after 1970 court after court discovered a "warranty of habitability" hidden between the lines of leases, and imposed this warranty on the landlord. The National Conference of Commissioners of Uniform State Laws drafted a

Uniform Residential Landlord and Tenant Act in 1972. The URLTA required landlords to comply with housing codes, keep up the premises, provide hot running water and plumbing and so on. About half of the states bought into the URLTA; and most of the rest passed laws along more or less similar lines.

The housing codes themselves became an important limitation on the rights of landlords. The ancestors of these codes were tenement laws, like the elaborate New York law of 1901. By 1920 about twenty cities had housing codes. But the codes became significant only in the 1950s, partly in response to the Housing Acts of 1949 and 1954. There were nearly five thousand housing codes in effect by the late 1960s. No two were the same; but typically they laid down minimum standards for space, light, and ventilation, dealt with plumbing and structural conditions, and the general state of repair. How strictly these codes were enforced is another question; but a landlord who did not keep his place "up to code" was vulnerable to rent strikes and other forms of tenant action.

Another important case, *Edwards v. Habib* (1968), also came out of the District of Columbia.[27] The tenant, Yvonne Edwards, went to the Department of Licenses and Inspections with complaints about violations of sanitary codes in her place. The inspectors came, looked, and found some forty violations. Habib, the landlord, promptly told Edwards, who had a month-to-month lease, to get out at the end of the month. She went to court, arguing that Habib had punished her for exercising her rights. Habib answered that a landlord can do what he wants when the lease is up; he can throw the tenant out for any reason, or no reason at all. This, too, was historically a powerful argument. But Habib reckoned without Skelly Wright. Wright found for the tenant; to allow "retaliatory eviction" would make nonsense out of the housing code. The landlord would surely toss out all complainers at the end of their lease.

Most states followed Wright's lead, either through court decisions or through statutes. New Jersey enacted a law against retaliatory eviction in 1970; it followed up with an even bolder law in 1974: no landlord could evict a tenant from his apartment, house, or mobile home, without "good cause." Good cause included not paying the rent, smashing up the premises, or acting in such a "disorderly" way as to "destroy the peace and quiet of . . . other tenants."[28] But the statute at least made a gesture toward giving tenants some kind of vested right in a rented apartment, a right otherwise unknown to American law.

In the 1960s and 1970s there was also a certain revival of interest in rent control. New York City had long since had it; now other cities (Berkeley, California; Cambridge, Massachusetts; Washington, D.C.) tried to control or "stabilize" rents. Typically, cities allowed landlords to raise rents—there was no total freeze—but only once a year, and only incrementally. Landlords, of course, hate rent control. Economists, almost to a person, hate them too. Rent control, they argue, distorts the rental market, stifles innovation, and discourages builders from adding to the housing stock. Most cities with rent control allow new housing more leeway than old housing. Rent control probably has little impact, one way or another, on low-income housing; nobody seems able to make money on this housing anyway. What cities with rent control have may be the worst of both worlds: protection for New Yorkers clinging lovingly to old, elegant, spacious apartments, for aging yuppies in their comfortable flats, but nothing much for the poor. A similar point could be made about the housing codes, rules against retaliatory eviction, and the like. All these have clearly been a response to tenant pressure and to the general atmosphere of the Great Society and its penumbras. Yet in some ways they are something of a fraud. No housing code ever created a single unit of decent, affordable housing. Actual enforcement, arguably, would have the opposite effect: it would reduce the supply of places where the poor could find a roof over their heads. The codes latched onto a convenient villain, the slumlord—they shifted all the blame for the miseries of the slums to evil landlords. Many of them richly deserved the blame, of course. But public housing programs stagnated, and more or less drifted into oblivion. Government was never willing to put up the money to build decent homes for people squeezed out of the market.

Commercial leases were of course as significant as residential leases. One innovation in the latter half of the century was the percentage lease.[29] This can be used for any business, from movie houses to grocery stores, but its major habitat and breeding ground is in shopping centers. In a percentage lease, the tenant agrees to pay not a fixed monthly rent but a certain percentage of the gross volume of sales in the store. (There are many variations on this theme; commonly, the lease does specify some minimum rent.) Scattered examples can be found early in the century, but the percentage lease really took off after the Second World War. This was also the period of the mallification of America: thousands of malls, plazas, "shopping villages," and the like sprang up all over suburbia.

Property and Space

The common law has always been clever and supple in creating a variety of types of interest in land. It sliced land up in ingenious ways: slices of space, time, and ownership. Several people can have interests at the same time in the same piece of land (as joint tenants, for example); or in the same piece of land at different times (landlords and tenants, people with life interests, and people with "remainder" interests, who inherit at the death of the life tenant); they can have rights to walk over somebody else's land, or to dig in it for coal or drill in it for oil; they can have rights underneath, or air rights (rights to build on top). Perhaps the most common way of sharing interests in property is the mortgage: the family lives in its little house and has an "equity," but each month they pay their dues to the bank which holds their mortgage.

The condominium, which entered the world of real estate around 1960, was added to all of these old and well-known interests. In a "condo," people own slices of a tall building; if you buy apartment B on the tenth floor, your property is more or less floating in space, though carried on the shoulders of whoever owns apartment B on the ninth floor, who in turn depends on the eighth floor, and so on. In 1961 the National Housing Act provided that NHA insurance could be extended to condominiums ("individually owned units in multifamily struc-tures"), a decision which gave those homes another kick forward.[30]

You own your condo, or your cooperative apartment; and ownership is a form of independence—or so it seems. A home of one's own is an American dream. This dream was reinforced by the post–World War II faith in perpetual motion—faith that real estate prices only went up. There was also the dream, as we have seen, of escaping the noise, dirt, and crime of the city—and of course leaving behind the undesirable poor. In the last decades of the twentieth century, there was a massive flowering of various forms of what Evan McKenzie has called "privatopia"—private developments, complexes, gated communities, and the like.[31] But privatopia is a realm of paradox. Families that live in these enclaves sign away their soul to homeowner associations; they must agree to whatever bundle of "covenants, conditions, and restrictions" the association writes into its deeds.

These "CCRS" enforce a kind of numbing conformity. Deviations are a threat to the majority, and, perhaps, are a kind of blasphemy against the great god of property values. The courts enforce these private rules, unless they are "unreasonable." In one notable California case (1994), Natore Nahrstedt moved into a condominium complex (of 530 units) in southern California. She brought her three cats with her. Cats were *verboten* under the rules of Lakeside Village Condominium (so were dogs and lizards; goldfish were acceptable). The condominium association, ruling body of the complex, told her to get rid of her cats. Nahrstedt stubbornly fought for her cats all the way up to the California Supreme Court. They were indoor cats, she claimed, and they bothered nobody. The rule was (she claimed) unreasonable. The court was unconvinced. It upheld this little bit of suburban tyranny. Nahrstedt had to choose: her condo or her cats. She could not have both.[32]

Municipal Government

No development of the nineteenth and twentieth centuries was more important than the rise of the cities. America once lived, essentially, on the land. No longer. Technically, cities and other jurisdictional fragments—counties, for example—had no inherent powers of their own. They could do only what the state allowed them to do. This was "Dillon's rule"—named for John Dillon, who published a treatise on "municipal corporations" in 1872. A municipal corporation, Dillon said, is a creature of the legislature; it has only the powers which the legislature gives it; and nothing more.[33] Formally, this remains more or less true. Practically, it began to weaken even in Dillon's days. What weakened it was "home rule," a vague phrase for various ways in which states gave increased rights and powers to their cities. Cities got home rule either through statutes or (more commonly) by amendments to the state constitution. Iowa's constitution (1968; art. 3, §38A) granted cities and towns "home rule power and authority . . . to determine their local affairs and government"; and specifically reversed Dillon's rule: "The rule . . . that a municipal corporation possesses and can exercise only those powers granted in express words is not a part of the law of this state."

Home rule cities sometimes were even allowed to draw up their own charters; but this hardly meant that they were truly independent from the state. A home rule city can govern itself as far as all local affairs are concerned; but what is "local"? In some states, home rule seems to make little or no difference; in others, the towns and cities are clearly more powerful than they were in the nineteenth century.

California in 1911 extended home rule to counties: any county could "frame a charter for its government" and run itself (within limits). It could provide for the election of local officers; and various other matters, like fixing the "compensation of . . . fish and game wardens." Washington State adopted a county home rule provision in 1947 (art. 11, §4 of the constitution, as amended). In the 1990s, more than forty states had some sort of home rule provision; and thirty-six states allowed some kind of county home rule.

Almost as important as the growth of the cities was the decline of the cities in the late twentieth century: power drained out of them, into the suburbs and the exurbs. The downtowns of many middle-sized cities became empty shells—deserts of parking lots, banks, and hotels, punctuated with vacant lots, tattoo parlors, and fast-food shops, all quite shabby and lifeless at night. Metropolitan areas grew and grew and grew. Central cities, especially the older cities, shrank. Some of them shrank catastrophically. The population of St. Louis was 856,000 in 1950; in 1999 it was 334,000. The older cities, on the whole, were trapped within their historic borders—strangled by a belt of suburbs that lay beyond their reach. Cities could, under the law, annex vacant land, and grow outward; but if the ring around the city was inhabited, annexation was not possible without the consent of people who lived in the area to be annexed. The new cities in the West seemed able to pull this off; the older cities could not. In California between 1951 and 1957, eighty-six cities carried out 1,876 annexations, adding 278,432 people to their populations. The annexing champion was Texas, where some big cities could annex without consent of the people in outlying areas. Houston and a few other Texas cities gobbled up half a million people. In the same period, New Jersey cities annexed exactly nobody, and New York cities almost nobody.[34]

Older central cities had problems they could hardly solve for themselves. The suburbs were no help. One solution, which a lot of experts liked, was to provide for metropolitan government: join cities and suburbs under a single political roof. But this went against the American grain. Middle-class America loved its enclaves. Villages stubbornly insisted on their independence, their right to control zoning, character, and (of course) property values. Some towns were nothing more than gated communities with an official name and a seal.

In the nineteenth century, there was no such thing as "urban policy" in Washington. That was a matter for the states. But the Great Society tended to funnel money directly into the cities, or to local organizations. There were all sorts of programs that bypassed the state governments and dealt directly with public or private entities. In 1996 New York City received almost $2 billion from the federal government. This was about 4 percent of the city's budget (Chicago's share was 7 percent). It was certainly not decisive. Still, money is money.[35]

The Dead

The law of succession—the transfer of property at death—rarely makes the headlines. It is, nonetheless, enormously important. Billions and billions of privately owned wealth turns over each generation. No matter how much you want to, and how much you delay, alas, you can't take it with you. The pharaohs tried, centuries ago. They failed.

American succession law subscribes, on the whole, to freedom of testation. That is, you can leave your money as you wish. The main exception, in twentieth-century law, is for married people: you cannot totally disinherit a surviving spouse. In the typical state, a widow or widower can claim one-half or one-third of the estate. In general, over the years, the spouse's rights and share has gone up; the claims of the "bloodline" have gone down. Children, for example, can be freely disinherited; at worst, a word or two in a will can do it, except in Louisiana, where the civil-law tradition still has influence.

In practice, "spouse" means widows more often than it means widowers; men marry younger women, and usually die before their wives. Most men leave most or all of their estates to their widows. A study of Bucks County, Pennsylvania, found that in the 1890s, in small estates (less than seven thousand dollars), fewer than a third of the people who died left everything to the spouse. Sixty-four percent left the spouse less than half. In 1979, however, for estates of less than $120,000 (we can treat these as relatively modest), 63.5 percent left everything to the spouse; and only about a quarter left the spouse less than half.[36]

Modern medicine and nutrition have added years to life in the twentieth century. A child born in 2001 can expect to live much longer than its great-great-grandparent born a century before. Long life has social and legal consequences. Inheriting money at twenty-five means something quite different from inheriting at sixty from a mother who dies at ninety-two. For the middle class, then, inheritance becomes less important than lifetime transfers—gifts to children for college, down payments on a house, and so on.[37] Well-to-do people who live long lives have plenty of time to indulge in the sport of estate planning. The sovereign document for transferring money at death used to be the will. In the twentieth century, more and more people with money in fact made out wills to ensure that they would die "testate." The richest of these, however, make sure that much or all of their money bypasses the will, which is sometimes a hollow shell, emptied of assets.

There has been, in short, a luxuriant growth of will substitutes. Thousands of people leave money behind in the form of "Totten trusts." These are savings bank accounts, set up "in trust for" so-and-so (the "beneficiary"). The Totten trust gets its name from a court case early in the century.[38] (Litigants sometimes get immortality this way, like doctors who name rare diseases, or astronomers who give their name to stars.) Logically, the Totten trust is not much like an ordinary trust. The so-called beneficiary has no rights whatsoever, and the person who sets up the account can close it, spend the money, change the beneficiary, shift the money to a different account, and so on. But the device is convenient, and useful: the courts quickly endorsed this form of "poor man's will."

Perhaps the most notable will substitute is the living trust. The creator of the trust (the "settlor") transfers some or all of her wealth to a trustee. The trustee will manage it during the settlor's lifetime (usually paying the income to the settlor herself), and then distribute it according to a fixed plan when the settlor dies. A living trust is almost always "revocable and amendable"—that is, the settlor can shift terms and beneficiaries, or even change her mind and take the money back. Functionally at least, a living trust acts very much like a will— or, to be more precise, like a trust with a will attached. It has some real advantages: somebody else (a bank, for example) has the headache of investing and managing the assets (for a fee); and the money moves smoothly at death, without the bother and expense of probate court. Hence the living trust is the heart of schemes to avoid probate: schemes that have created a whole new business, and spawned a cottage industry of how-to books. The most famous of these, by Norman Dacey, first appeared in 1965, and has gone through several iterations.[39]

The Law of Trusts

Trusts, of all sorts, became much more common in the twentieth century—they are devices for rich people, by and large; and there are more and more of these.

Banks and trust companies handle thousands of these arrangements. The trust is an old device of the common law, unknown in continental Europe. It is a device for managing property: a trustee has technical ownership, and runs the show, but all in the interests of one or more beneficiaries. Trusts are common, supple, and useful devices for all sorts of reasons. The trustee—like the guardian of a minor, or the executor of an estate, or the conservator of an Alzheimer's patient—is a "fiduciary," which means, among other things, that she is subject to strict and demanding rules of loyalty and fairness. The trustee cannot, for example, mix trust assets with her own; they have to be kept rigorously separate.

This general rule ran into some trouble during the Great Depression. Banks—which commonly acted as trustees for the wealthy—were supposed to earmark each individual trust fund. But the banks for a long time had ignored this rule. In one case, in 1936, the bank (a Connecticut institution) had taken mortgages in its own name; it parceled out shares of these mortgages to various small trusts, carefully listing on its books who had what share. This was, strictly speaking, a breach of the rules; some of the mortgages went belly-up in the Depression, and beneficiaries who lost money sued the bank. The court refused to let the plaintiff win anything but nominal damages: it was not the bank's practices, but the Great Depression, that stole the plaintiff's money. Any other decision, of course, would have driven the bank, and hundreds of others, to the wall.[40] Clearly, then, the court was reluctant to adhere to the older rule—one more instance of the responsiveness of American judge-made law.

The tax laws have been a particularly strong influence on the laws of trusts in the twentieth century. The law of trusts made it possible for the rich to keep their dynastic estate intact, and cut down on taxes from generation to generation. Most trusts, especially small ones, are caretaker trusts: a trust is a good way for a parent to leave money to a small child, if the parent dies young. Rarer, but quite important, are what we might call dynastic trusts. A rich man or woman can leave money in trust (often managed by a bank), ordering the trustee to pay income to his children, then his grandchildren, perhaps even his great-grandchildren, for as long as they live. This keeps the "estate" itself intact; the family gets money to live on, but has no power to waste the corpus on crazy investment schemes or Broadway plays or girlfriends or boyfriends or otherwise.

How long can a trust of this kind go on? How long can the dead hand control? The limit is set by the so-called rule against perpetuities, a weird and arcane doctrine. The general idea is fairly simple, but the devil is in the details.

These details, murderously technical, and full of pitfalls, have terrorized lawyers and law students for generations. The practical effect of the rule, however, is to limit trusts to no more than, say, ninety years or a century (most expire more quickly). States have revised and reformed the rule in the twentieth century, pruning away its crazier subrules—rules with wonderful nicknames like the "fertile octogenarian," the "unborn widow," the "precocious toddler," and the "magic gravel pit."[41] But most states have kept alive the essence of the rule. After a while, the dead hand has to relax its grip and relinquish its ghostly control.

In 1976, as part of a tax reform bill, the so-called tax on generation-skipping trusts entered the law. It was a cluster of rules of awesome technicality. But the main point was clear: to tax dynastic trusts each time a generation passed through the doorways of death. No longer could a billionaire defer taxes on the estates of his children, grandchildren, and so on, until the trust finally dissolved. Basically, each generation had to pay its toll as it passed into the grave. Generous exemptions meant that the bite of this tax fell only on the truly rich.

Charity and Law

The rise of the charitable foundation was a development of great social significance. A few trusts and foundations went back to the nineteenth century, but only a few. The law at the time was distinctly unfriendly. In a few states, such foundations were downright illegal. The twentieth century reversed this trend decisively. The law now favored gifts to charity. A person can set up a trust or foundation—tax-free, and perpetual—for almost anything conceivably educational or public, or for the relief of poverty, or the advancement of religion. The courts almost always approve; but there are limits. In a well-known case from 1951 in Virginia, the deceased set up a trust to hand out money at Christmas and Easter to all the students in the first, second, and third grades of the John Kerr School in Winchester, Virginia, rich and poor alike. This was not, said the court, a proper charitable object.[42]

Twentieth-century courts not only favored charitable trusts; they were willing to keep them alive even if their original purpose failed or became illegal or impossible. This is the so-called doctrine of *cy pres*. The court will modify the trust, to make it legal and keep it a going concern, so long as its new goal is as close (*cy pres,* in legal French) as possible to the original one. Universities, for example, have used this doctrine to modify old scholarship trusts and the like that were restricted to "whites" or "gentiles" or "boys"; the universities have argued, almost always successfully, that they cannot carry out such trusts anymore, and have asked the court to "cy pres" away the offensive condition.[43]

Under the estate tax laws, an estate left to charity pays no tax. This was an important incentive to set up charitable foundations. There were other motives, too. The Ford Foundation, perhaps the largest and most notable private foundation of the late twentieth century, rested on a scheme to let the Ford family keep control of its automotive company. The Fords divided the stock of the company into two categories—voting stock (only 10 percent of the shares), and nonvoting stock (the other 90 percent). As early as 1937 the family began transferring nonvoting stock to the foundation. Huge blocks of such stock went to the foundation when Henry Ford and his son Edsel Ford died. The family retained complete control of the voting shares.[44]

In the 1950s Congress, in a witch-hunting mood, turned on the great foundations, which were supposed to be dangerously radical. The Reece Committee (headed by Rep. B. Carroll Reece) conducted hearings in 1953; Reece wanted to know whether the funds of the "large foundations" were "aiding and abetting Marxist tendencies in the United States and weakening the love which every American should have for his way of life," a perfectly ridiculous idea. The committee report was somewhat less hysterical; it did accuse the foundations of such sins as promoting "moral relativity" and "social engineering," and, perhaps worst of all, blind faith in the United Nations.[45] In the 1960s there were proposals for curbing the foundations, or reforming them. The Tax Reform Law of 1969 did lay down some rather strict rules. Foundations have to pay out at least 5 percent of the value of their assets each year for charitable purposes; there were also provisions meant to curb the use of foundations to perpetuate family control over big companies.

These were pinpricks, as it turned out; the foundations have thrived and multiplied. In 1944 there were, according to one estimate, 505 foundations, with assets of $1.8 billion; by 1953 there were 4,029, and their assets had risen to $4.5 billion. In 1980 there were 22,000, and in 1995 there were more than 40,000; the Ford Foundation alone was worth $8.1 billion dollars; and the total assets of the foundations in 1995 amounted to more than $226 billion. The foundations made grants in 1995 of more than $6 billion.[46] In these profitable times, the foundations continued to grow rapidly. In 1997 it was reported that the foundations had $329 billion in assets, and grants were almost $16 billion.[47] In the arts, in education, in health research, foundations were clearly making a difference—at least to the lucky people and institutions who got the grants. The Ford Motor Company had long since gone public; and the Ford Foundation had long since sold off most of its Ford stock. In the life cycle of foundations, family control lasts a generation or two; then the institution falls into the hands of "philanthropoids." As in private trusts, too, dead founders and their ghosts have to give up control in the end.

Guardianship

Guardianship is an arrangement very much like a trust, except that there is no written document, and most guardianships are very short-term. In the twentieth century, there were fewer orphans, with or without money, than before; but, on the other hand, there was a vast increase in the need for help at the other end of life. Long life meant more people (some with money) who slipped slowly, or suddenly, into the darkness of mental confusion. Guardianship of these adults ("conservatorship" in California) was once a quite drastic step: the law stripped the elderly ward of all his rights. The trend is away from this severity; the law in many states now takes away from the ward only what is absolutely necessary. The ward is no longer legally as if dead.[48]

Only a court can appoint a guardian. The process is cumbersome and, at times, expensive. The numbers are significant, and rising. In New York state, from 1992 to 1998, the number of court-appointed guardians rose from fifteen thousand to thirty-two thousand. In Michigan guardianship petitions quadrupled between 1981 and 1998.[49] Because people (for good reason) do not like going to court, there has been a search for alternatives. One popular alternative is the durable power of appointment—you give someone you trust the right to handle your financial affairs. This can be drafted so as to go into effect only when you "lose it." There is also a rich flowering of such devices as the "living will"; instructions on what to do about a person's poor, racked, dying body, when to "pull the plug," and perhaps what to do with one's organs after death. These are responses to the technology of prolongation: to medical technique which can stretch us, like Lear, far too long on the rack of time.

Pension Law

Trust law is mostly for the rich. For the average person, pension law, and retirement provisions, loom much larger than the law of trusts, or even the law of wills. Besides the Social Security laws, there are thousands of private pension provisions. Unions lobby for pensions as part of their collective bargains. White-collar workers and middle management pay almost as much attention to fringe benefits (pensions, health care, dental benefits) as to salary.

Some large companies had pension plans even before the Social Security Act—which is, of course, a kind of national pension plan.[50] Railroads provided pensions for their employees. During the Great Depression, the federal government had to bail out the railroads, which were unable to make good on their promises. In the postwar period, there were repeated complaints about "abuses" in the private pension system. Congress passed a disclosure bill in 1958 (the Welfare and Pension Plans Disclosure Act). In 1963 the Studebaker Company, which made cars, but sold too few of them, went under; and thousands of workers lost their pensions. There were horror stories about companies that looted their pension funds, and about companies that liked to fire employees just before the point at which their pension rights would "vest."

It is unclear how many of these abuses there actually were; but the stories had a political impact. They led to a big, complicated federal law: the Employee Retirement Income Security Act (1974), known to one and all as ERISA. The heart of ERISA was a rule that pensions had to vest after ten years on the job (in 1986 this was lowered to five years). The federal government backed up this promise, in effect offering pension insurance. ERISA leans ideologically, in short, on the same social insurance ideology that lay behind the Social Security Act itself.

Wilderness, Public Lands, and the Great American West

Public land law was a central aspect of American property law in the nineteenth century. It was a complicated, Byzantine branch of law. At the heart of it, there were vast giveaway programs—millions and millions of acres transferred to the states, to railroad builders, and to settlers.

Some of these giveaway programs lasted into the twentieth century. But despite giving away or selling millions and millions of acres, the federal government remained, in the twentieth century, by far the largest lord of the land. More than a quarter of all the land in this huge country still belonged to the federal government at the end of the millennium—an empire of forests, deserts, and mountains, mostly in the West. At the end of the century, the federal government owned one-third of New Mexico, more than half of Oregon, 62 percent of Idaho, 64 percent of Utah, and a whopping 79 percent of Nevada.[51] The vast and barren federal stretches of Nevada were large enough to be used to test atomic bombs. In addition, the federal government owned national parks, government buildings, army bases, and the like, in every part of the country.

By the late nineteenth century, there was a feeling in the country that the frontier was at an end. The tide of settlement had long since reached the Pacific. This was the climax of what seemed like a natural development, although the native tribes (and perhaps Mexico) might have filed a dissenting opinion. In many ways, the closing of the frontier was more a metaphor than a statement of fact. For one thing, oceans were no barrier to American expansion—Hawaii, Puerto Rico, Guam, and the Philippines attested to that. Nor was there any shortage of empty land. The Territory of Alaska, as of 1900 a bleak, austerely beautiful domain, twice the size of Texas, had a tiny population (sixty-four thousand)—about one human being for every ten square miles. Nevada had a population of forty-two thousand. (This was before the boom in Las Vegas.) Not a single mountain, desert, or Pacific state had more than a million people, except California, which had a million and a half; most western states did not even come close. Much of the West, in short, was still big sky and open spaces. The population center moved steadily west (and south) in the twentieth century; but this was, in 1900, only a hope or a dream.

Millions and millions of acres were left in the public domain in 1900. But they were not, on the whole, the rich, well-watered land of Iowa or Indiana. They were dry, barren, and uninviting—at least for settlers. They were an obstacle, a challenge, a wilderness to be "tamed." This was the nineteenth-century attitude, and it persisted long into the twentieth century. In the nineteenth century, people believed (or acted as if) resources were infinite. Nature was in fact the enemy. It was something to be fought, something to be conquered. The destiny of a forest was to be chopped down and turned into timber or farmland. The destiny of a swamp was to be drained and planted and plowed. Many states paid money to people who killed wolves; there was no endangered-species act, no earth day, no talk about ecosystems. Even standards of beauty reflected the culture of boom, plow, and build. "Wilderness" was not a compliment; quite to the contrary. Deserts were ugly—and dangerous; they stood in the way of progress. Bedraggled armies of settlers, crawling slowly across the country in covered wagons, facing death from thirst, starvation, exhaustion, hostile tribes, could hardly be expected to admire the scenery—or wish to preserve it from "civilization." People in New Orleans, wracked with yellow fever and other miasmic visitations, had no appreciation of swamps. It took a century of wealth, vaccines, and antibiotics to turn swamps into "valuable wetlands." It took air-conditioning, a national highway system, and changes in consciousness to make the desert into a thing of beauty and a tourist attraction: to make Death Valley a place for vacations instead of a valley of death.

In 1900 western politicians (and citizens) were still mostly eager to promote growth, to exploit natural resources. Water law, mineral law, rules and regulations about oil and gas, grazing rights, damming the rivers, irrigation—these were the issues. Congress passed an important Reclamation Act in 1902. Under this law, the proceeds of public land sales in the West were mostly set aside in a "reclamation fund," to irrigate or reclaim "arid and semiarid lands." The act authorized public irrigation works on construction sites. Eight hours was to constitute a day's work, and "no Mongolian labor" was to be used.[52]

Reclamation is a significant word. The land was to be redeemed from its dry, useless state. Land with farms or ranches or herds of cattle was good land. Desert land was bad land. For more than forty years, since the famous Homestead Act of 1862, the government had offered public land, free, to settlers. A 1904 law offered a square mile (640 acres) of the arid lands in western Nebraska to anybody who farmed it for five years and put in improvements worth $1.25 an acre.[53] This was a much bigger chunk of land than the Homestead Act had allowed. In 1909 the Enlarged Homestead Act, which applied to Colorado, Montana, Nevada, Oregon, Utah, Washington, Wyoming, and the Territories of Arizona and New Mexico, offered homesteads of 320 acres. But only land that could be irrigated was eligible—the goal was still family farms—and a claimant had to show, by two "credible witnesses," that at least an eighth of the land "was continuously cultivated to agricultural crops other than native grasses."[54] (Whether crops *could* grow in these dry areas, on farms of such size, is another question.[55]) Congress regularly gave money to the Department of Agriculture to get rid of animal "vermin." As late as 1921, when Congress was already supporting bison ranges and national parks, it was also allotting funds "for experiments, demonstrations, and cooperation in destroying mountain lions, wolves, coyotes, bobcats, prairie dogs, gophers, ground squirrels, jack rabbits, and other animals injurious to agriculture, horticulure, forestry, animal husbandry, and wild game."[56] State-level policy was similar: Pennsylvania in 1923 still offered a fifteen-dollar bounty for killing a lynx, four dollars for a gray fox, two dollars for a red fox, and one dollar for each dead weasel.[57] A Minnesota law of 1931 empowered counties to offer gray fox bounties—and anybody claiming a bounty had to affirm "that he did not . . . spare the life of any grey fox he could have killed."[58]

This seems many lifetimes ago. Nobody today would dream of "destroying" mountain lions or wolves. Indeed, millions are spent on protecting these animals—and on reintroducing them to places from which they had disappeared. The first glimmerings of conservation came in the late nineteenth century. The government created Yellowstone National Park in 1872. Presidents Harrison and Cleveland set aside millions of western acres as forest preserves. And when only a pitiful handful of bison were left, this great animal won a kind of reprieve. They had a measure of safety inside Yellowstone; and in 1908 Congress also established a national bison range in Montana, within lands of the Flathead Indian Reservation.[59] Theodore Roosevelt, who fancied himself a great white hunter, expanded the national forests, and in March 1903 he created, by executive order, a wildlife refuge on Pelican Island, Florida.

It was already too late for the passenger pigeon, or the Carolina parakeet, both of which had flown into the darkness of extinction. But consciousness was changing, slowly but surely. A treaty of 1916 aimed to protect birds that migrated from Canada to the United States.[60] The Migratory Bird Treaty Act of 1918 made it a federal crime to catch or kill birds protected by that treaty; and in 1929 Congress passed a Migratory Bird Conservation Act, which gave the Secretary of Agriculture the right to buy or rent land, to set up "inviolate sanctuaries" for migratory birds.[61] The 1916 treaty proclaimed that many of these birds were "of great value as a source of food or in destroying insects which are injurious to forests and forage plants on the public domain, as well as to agricultural crops." The act listed game birds (ducks and geese, for example), and "migratory insectivorous birds," from bobolinks to wrens; there was also a miscellaneous list of favored birds, from auks and auklets to shearwaters and terns. There was, in short, not much romance and earth-worship in the law; but it was a step in that direction.

By the late twentieth century, the wilderness had finally become beautiful, and the mountain lion and the wolf were no longer ravening, hideous predators. They had become noble savages, creatures of God, living beings with as much claim to Mother Earth as humans; millions were spent trying to save the whooping crane and the California condor, even though nobody had ever served one on a plate or set them loose in a field to eat bugs. The black-footed ferret (the rarest mammal in the United States), and the fat little prairie dogs it loved to eat, were both granted asylum from extinction.

Bounties for timberwolves were ancient history. As early as the 1930s and 1940s, there were attempts to extend protection to grizzly bears and the bald eagle; a Bald Eagle Protection Act was passed in 1940. This bird was, after all, the symbol of America. In 1966 Congress solemnly declared that "one of the unfortunate consequences of growth and development in the United States has been the extermination of some native species of fish and wildlife"; this caused "serious losses" among animals with "educational, historical, recreational, and scientific value."[62] In 1964 Congress passed the Wilderness Act to protect wilderness as "an enduring resource"; it set aside "areas untrammeled by man, where man himself is a visitor who does not remain," and where the land retains its "primeval character and influence." A century before, trammeling was the whole point of national policy. Now the Wilderness Act banned from its lands commercial enterprises, permanent roads, motorized equipment, houses, and all the rest. Wilderness is to remain pristine, untouched—islands of spiritual purity in the cauldron of capitalist fury.[63]

In 1969 came the Endangered Species Conservation Act. Now it became illegal to import endangered species, or to sell or ship species on the critical list across state lines. In 1971 Congress passed a Wild Free-Roaming Horses and Burros Act. The preamble recited that these "fast disappearing" animals were "living symbols of the historic and pioneer spirit of the West." They also "contribute to the diversity of life forms within the Nation and enrich the lives of the American people."[64] In 1972 Congress extended its benevolence to the ocean, by passing the Marine Mammal Protection Act.[65] This law gave sanctuary to manatees, whales, seals, sea otters, and polar bears. It called them "resources of great international significance, esthetic and recreational as well as economic"; and referred to the "health and stability of the marine ecosystem."

In 1973 Congress put its money where its mouth was, and took a truly

decisive step, passing the Endangered Species Act. The act decried the consequences of unrestricted "economic growth and development" (heresy in the
nineteenth century). The act covered mammals, fish, and birds, but also am-
phibians, reptiles, mollusks, crustaceans, insects and spiders, and any "part,
product, egg, or offspring thereof." Lists of endangered species were to be
drawn up; once on the list, the species was sacred: no one could import it or
export it, sell it or ship it in interstate commerce; most significantly, it was
unlawful to "take" the species at all. And *take* was defined, very broadly, as
"to harass, harm, pursue, hunt, shoot, wound, kill, trap, capture, or collect"
the species.[66]

The Endangered Species Act has not had entirely smooth sailing. Most
Americans probably accept the general principle, especially for big, sexy animals and birds like the bison, the manatee, the sea elephant, or the whooping
crane (the so-called "charismatic megafauna"). This was undoubtedly what
Congress most had in mind.[67] But the language of the act included everything
else, including beetles, crabs, and salamanders; environmental groups were able
to latch onto the text and take it for a wilder and wilder ride.

The law in action almost necessarily stepped on some powerful toes. It was
easy for business interests to make fun of the law: to talk about jobs lost and
huge projects killed, in order to protect a worm, a snail, a fluttering moth, a bug-
eyed owl. If the local economy depended on clear-cutting a forest, there was
bound to be an outcry if a lizard stood in the way. After the ESA became law, the
snail darter—a tiny fish nobody had ever heard of before—became the excuse
for stopping construction on the Tennessee Valley Authority's mighty Tellico
Dam. Millions had already been spent on the dam; work had begun before the
ESA was passed. Environmental groups never wanted the dam in the first place—
there were powerful arguments against it on economic grounds. But the snail
darter gave the enemies of the dam a brilliant new strategy. The battle raged on
and on in the courts; finally, in 1978, the Supreme Court decided the case. Even
though one of the justices asked whether snail darters were "suitable for bait,"
the Court came down squarely on the side of the fish.[68]

This was not the end of the story. Congress was outraged. Senator Scott of
Pennsylvania quoted from an authority higher than the ESA, the book of Gene-
sis: God had given man "dominion over the fish of the sea." Senator Garn of
Utah reminded people that beavers build dams, and some are "destructive."[69]
The poor little fish had less power in Congress than it had in the courts; the ESA

was quickly amended in 1978, in a move intended to save the Tellico Dam and trim the sails of ESA. The new law created an Endangered Species Committee, consisting of seven members (among them three cabinet members); if five members agreed, then the committee could give the green light to a project, even if it would harm an endangered species. Congress expected the ESC to save the Tellico Dam; but that did not happen. The "God Committee," as it was nicknamed, looked like a way to weaken ESA; but the committee's mandate in fact made this difficult. In the end, the dam was built—not because of the "God Committee" or the courts, but because powerful men in Congress insisted on it. The "pork-barrel proponents" of the dam, not to be undone, slipped a rider onto an appropriations bill, ordering the project to be finished; over objections from Cherokee Indians, TVA completed its dam, and floodwaters ended the long and bitter controversy.[70]

At the end of the twentieth century, the same conflicts and tensions that plagued ESA continued. The tradition of exploiting the public domain, using it as an economic resource, an udder to be milked, had really never died; it simply coexisted with romantic preservation and love of the environment. The balance shifted from one side to the other. There was never a final victory. Clearly, friends of the environment themselves had enormous political power. But the public was fickle; and (like Congress), it was hard to get people to work up a sweat over obscure plants and river mussels. The big uproar of the 1990s on this front was the controversy over saving the spotted owl—a night creature of the forest whose preservation (if you believed the propaganda) threatened thousands of logging jobs.

The West was both a stronghold of conservation and a stronghold of exploitation of resources. Western stockmen, for example, felt that they had a God-given right to graze their cattle on the public domain. Ideally, they wanted the government to give them the land; what they got was the Taylor Grazing Act of 1934, which was almost as good. Under this law, the government leased the land to cattlemen at bargain prices. The lands still belonged to the U.S. government, but they were managed "as if they were private property": permit fees were very low, and the government used these to improve the range. The government, in essence, then, got no revenue from the lands; and the cattlemen got what they needed.[71]

In the last part of the century, states also passed laws to preserve farmland and open space. Maryland was the first state to do this, in 1956; there was a great flurry of activity in the 1970s, and ultimately every state followed, usually using some sort of tax gimmick.[72] There was some romance and nostalgia behind these laws; but also concrete interests. Farmers complained bitterly about property taxes. If a farm was close to the city, its market value shot up. This was great for farmers who wanted to sell, but a disaster for those who did not. Developers who gobble up land are easy to hate, and farm families can be romanticized as if they were characters in a Norman Rockwell painting. Cities, after all, do need to grow. Whether these farmland preservation laws have done any good—or done anything at all—is an open question.

Intellectual Property

The law of intellectual property gained enormously in importance in the course of the twentieth century. The growth of the American industrial empire, and the revolution in technology, practically guaranteed that this field of law would move into center stage.

The Constitution specifically gave the central government power over intellectual property. Under article 1, section 8 (8), Congress had power to "promote the Progress of Science and useful Arts, by securing for limited Times to Authors and Inventors the exclusive Right to their respective Writings and Discoveries."

Copyright is for "writings"; patent law is for "discoveries." Both terms have expanded in meaning. The framers of the Constitution had no cameras, not to mention photocopying machines and computer software. Courts in the twentieth century had to face issues tougher than anything the founders had in mind.[73] In a 1903 case the defendant had reproduced three posters advertising a circus. Was this an infringement of copyright? The old cases seemed to say that a mere advertisement could not be copyrighted; "writings" meant books, articles, essays. But the Supreme Court now held otherwise. Oliver Wendell Holmes, Jr., wrote the opinion; a picture, he said, "is none the less a picture and . . . a subject of copyright" even when used to advertise "soap, or the theatre," or, for that matter, the circus. Such pictures had "commercial value."[74] A picture did not have to be fine art to be protected. Soon, courts held that the Copyright Act applied to movies as well; then piano rolls and phonograph records.

It is new technology that touches off copyright wars. With the invention of radio, there was a battle over royalties for music, between ASCAP (the American Society of Composers, Authors, and Publishers), founded in 1913, and the broadcasters.[75] Photocopying devices set off the next big battle. There were also struggles touched off by VCRs and television and, at the very end of the century, the issue of "downloading" music for free from the World Wide Web. Copyright protection for software has been a recent "frontier" issue, and international copyright problems have become severe. Now that the United States is the leading exporter of intellectual property (if rap music or *Terminator 2* can be called "intellectual"), it has an obvious interest in spreading its system worldwide. The Asian pirates who copy books, movies, and the like, or who try to discover the secrets of some software code, seem to pose a greater danger to the nation, perhaps, than the patch-eyed pirates of the old high seas.

A patent is a monopoly, which the government grants to an inventor for a limited period. Monopolies, of course, are hardly favorites of law or policy. But the patent monopoly is arguably different: it would be a severe disincentive for invention if commercial jackals could steal and use and profit by the product of somebody else's sweat and brains. Of course, in the twentieth century, the typical inventor was no eccentric loner, toiling away in his basement lab. Most patents were issued to big corporations; the companies could use patents strategically to control some segment of the market. For this reason, the courts cast a somewhat beady eye on patents. In the first half of the century, the patent holder who brought an infringement suit usually lost his case. Courts held either that the patent had not, in fact, been infringed; or that the patent was no good in the first place.

The requirements for a patent, formally, changed very little in the twentieth century. The patent law was overhauled in 1952; but this law did not touch the basic system.[76] What did make a difference was a law of 1982, which created the Court of Appeals for the Federal Circuit.[77] This law took patent cases out of the federal circuit courts, abolished the Court of Customs and Patent Appeals, and gave the new court the exclusive right to hear patent appeals. And, wonder of wonders, the new court seemed to look on patents with a less jaundiced eye. Patent owners began to enjoy much greater protection—a much greater chance of winning infringement cases.

The structural change probably reinforced a change in legal culture. In the 1980s and 1990s the image of the patent holder shifted once more. The patent was no longer just a tool of big business; now it was a legal shield to protect the entrepreneur, the risk taker, the start-up company. Patents were seen as the key to winning the technology race. And high technology was America's hope and salvation in a changing economic world. Discovery and innovation were to America and its standard of living what oil was to Saudi Arabia or coffee to Brazil. Whether patent law in fact had shifted function is another question; that it looked different to judges seems plain.

People usually associate patents with new tools, machines, and devices; but all sorts of other things can be patented. The Plant Patent Act of 1930 allowed a patent to someone who had "discovered and asexually reproduced any distinct and new variety of plant."[78] In 1980 the Supreme Court heard a case in which a microbiologist (or rather, his employer, General Electric), had filed for a patent on a genetically altered "bacterium from the genus Pseudomonas." The biologist had found a way to change this bacterium so that it might possibly gobble up oil spills. The government resisted granting a patent; but a bare majority of the Supreme Court allowed it. The new creature was not "nature's handiwork," but the work of the scientist, a product of "human ingenuity and research."[79]

Trademarks and brand names have enormous significance in a consumer society; the growth in advertising magnified their importance. The media penetrated every American home, first with newspapers and magazines, then through radio and TV, all of these flush with ads, and indeed dependent on ads for their income. Brand names had value; and trademark law protected this value. The Constitution does not mention trademarks (a trademark is neither a "writing" nor a "discovery"). But Congress can regulate interstate and foreign commerce, and the trademark law of 1905 specifically rested on that basis.[80] Copyrights and patents have a limited life, but a trademark can be forever, or as long as it is used as a trademark. The 1905 law fixed a term of twenty years; but the term could be renewed and renewed by the owner of the work.[81]

The 1905 act provided that this owner could register his mark, for a fee of ten dollars, with the Commissioner of Patents. Someone else could contest the registration; but once registered, a trademark was assumed to be valid and worthy of protection. The owner could sue any imitator for damages, or ask for an injunction. Any mark could be registered, with some exceptions—the United States flag, or the portrait of a living person (without his written permission); there was also no protection for a mark which consisted "merely in the name of an individual firm, corporation, or association," unless there was something special about the way it was written or the like. Mere descriptions of the goods, or geographical terms, also could not be trademarked. As people in this exceedingly mobile society changed jobs, or roamed the country simply as tourists, brand names became ever more valuable. Businesses that were once strictly local became chains, or sold their goods all over the country. There were, of course, economies of scale in bigness; but the brand name was also a valuable asset. A traveler who stayed at a Holiday Inn or bought a hamburger at McDonald's felt that she knew what she was getting. Locals might be aware of a better hotel, or a better and cheaper hamburger at some local greasy spoon; but brand names were sovereign with strangers. And then with locals as well, as "independent" businesses withered and died. Grocery chains—Piggly-Wiggly stores and the A&P—were followed by Burger King and Kentucky Fried Chicken, then hotels and department stores; much later, national law firms and accounting firms, and real-estate brokerage firms. There was something of the same dynamic behind them all: the power of the trademark, the brand name, in a society always on the move.

The Lanham Act (1946) codified and strengthened trademark law.[82] The aim was to give businesses more protection against infringers. Trademark law was, necessarily, about boundaries. Imitation is the sincerest form of flattery; it is also a universal marketing strategy. How far could a company go in trying to snatch for itself some of the aura of a well-known product? If you called your soft drink Koka-Kola, was this a violation of Coca-Cola's rights? Probably. But what if you manufactured shoes, and called them Coca-Cola shoes? One test was whether a consumer was likely to be confused: in a 1917 case, the makers of Aunt Jemima self-rising flour got an injunction against a company that made pancake syrup and called it Aunt Jemima. Flour and syrup were different; but both were food, and a buyer of the syrup was likely to think that the flour maker had branched out into syrup.[83] In the case of, say, Coca-Cola shoes, the problem is similar: nobody could confuse a shoe with a soft drink, but one could still imagine that the soft drink company was now in the shoe business too, for whatever harm (or good) that might cause. At any rate, trademark protection was a vital branch of law in a global and competitive world, in which hyenas and vultures of trade eagerly snapped at any scrap of the market.

14

Family Law and Family Life

I n the twentieth century, family law underwent some fairly drastic changes. The family itself changed, in structure and in culture. In the old-model family (never as common as pictured) the husband was the "head of the family," the wife stayed home, cooked, darned his socks, and washed the children's mouths with soap if they said a dirty word.

Fewer families, as time went on, fit this picture. For one thing, more and more women had to work or wanted to work. They met with prejudice and discrimination, and were paid miserable wages; but millions of women went out to earn their bread. In 1932, in the depths of the Depression, Congress insisted that if both husband and wife worked for the government, and there was a "reduction of personnel," one of them had to go; and if one spouse already worked for the government, the other one would be bumped from the lists of job applicants.[1] This (like antinepotism rules in universities), in practice meant that wives lost their jobs. During the Second World War, when millions of men were in the army, women replaced them in factories and businesses. Many women joined unions, and agitated (through the unions) for "equal pay for equal work."[2] When Johnny came marching home again, looking for work, Rosie the riveter had to give way, as we have seen. Nonetheless, war, social change, and new technology were at work constructing a new kind of family. Birth control, feminism, and the sexual revolution were also at work, especially in the latter half of the twentieth century. Social forces were constructing a new kind of family; and family law was to feel the effects.

The Law of Marriage

The early part of the century was a period of deep unrest—a period of doubts about the future of the country. Immigration was changing the way America acted and looked. What was once a country of sturdy Protestant farmers was more and more a country of landless urban workers, drawn from many countries. A kind of cultural and social panic overtook old-line Americans—they worried about pauperism, degeneracy, and general loss of soul. This panic had an impact on the law of immigration, the criminal law, as we have seen, and also on the laws of marriage and divorce.

Marriage was the gateway to reproduction, and the pillar of family life. It had been taken more or less for granted; but now attention had to be paid, because of the issue of "biological fitness." States began to tighten marriage law, to keep undesirables from marrying and having babies. In Indiana (1905) no marriage license was to be issued to any male who had been, within the previous five years, "an inmate of any county asylum or home for indigent persons," unless he could show that "the cause" of his "condition" had been "removed," and that he was "able to support a family." This particular law was directed against paupers; pauperism was closely associated in the public mind with other kinds of degeneracy. Other statutes were more tightly linked to worries about reproduction. A 1909 Washington State statute on marriage prohibited the marriage of "a common drunkard, habitual criminal, epileptic, imbecile, feeble-minded person, idiot or insane person," or anybody "afflicted with hereditary insanity," or "pulmonary tuberculosis in its advanced stages, or any contagious venereal disease." The act applied only to women under forty-five, but to men "of any age," except those marrying women older than forty-five.[3]

The idea that the state ought to control marriage threatened an old American institution, the common-law marriage. In popular speech, "common-law" wife or husband is a sneering way to describe a couple who are simply "shacked up," as the slang phrase has it. The legal meaning is quite different. A common-law marriage is a marriage by contract, a marriage without ceremony—two people merely agree to be married, to live together as husband and wife; and that is that. In most states in the nineteenth century, the common-law marriage was a perfectly valid and proper marriage, even with no witnesses, no clergyman or judge, no marriage license, no ceremony—nothing but the naked words of woman and man to each other.[4] The two were just as married, legally speaking, as they would be after a church wedding with dozens of guests. Common-law marriage was a useful institution under frontier conditions, with a shortage of ministers, and poor record keeping. It saved the inheritances of thousands of women and children who could not prove a ceremonial marriage. It spared the children the stigma of bastardy.

The twentieth century changed direction. Nobody needed an informal marriage anymore. The formalities were cheap, easy to fulfill, and quite accessible. In a Texas case (1935) the court admitted that common-law marriages were still valid in Texas, but insisted on strong proof. Courts were entitled to be skeptical about a secret, informal marriage, "contracted in the shadow of the county-clerk's office and within the sound of church bells."[5] The courts, in short, doubted that anybody would contract such a marriage, when the other kind was so near and so easy. One by one, the states abolished the doctrine. In Nebraska, for example, under a 1923 law no marriage was valid without a license and a ceremony.[6] In the mid-1920s about half of the states recognized common-law marriage, and half did not. The trend continued. Oklahoma left the ranks in 1994. Twentieth-century courts (and legislatures) smelled blackmail in the doctrine—it was a way for scheming women to get their hands on the money of rich, dead men they had slept with. (Claims based on informal marriages were almost never brought by men.) Besides, if people could marry just by deciding to marry, there would be, as one judge put it, "no bar to the matrimonial entanglements of the immature or the mentally deficient," or of "those infected with syphilis and gonorrhea."[7] In the age of eugenics, this was an unacceptable loophole. Besides, common-law marriages were clouds on title: they were the bases for claims to land and property, without documentary evidence; this unsettled estates and put a question mark around the ownership of property. American law tends to disfavor such doctrines.

The New Deal period put further pressure on common-law marriages. Most cases after the 1930s, in states that preserved the doctrine, were claims for Social Security, or workers' compensation. Common-law marriages made trouble for the bureaucracy; most of the claims (so people thought) were false; these were not real marriages but "meretricious" relationships (in other words, sex, pure and simple). In recent years, of course, "meretricious" relationships have made a dramatic comeback.

The Heart Balm Issue

One sign of changing sexual mores was the fate of claims for breach of promise of marriage. If two people were engaged—that is, if they exchanged promises to marry—and one of them backed out, the other could sue for breach of promise. This was a well-established type of lawsuit. The plaintiff was almost always a woman, the defendant a man. The real issue was invariably sex, and often pregnancy. The woman had relied on the promise, and given up her virginity; then she was jilted. In one case from Wisconsin, in 1914, Elsie Luther, "a factory girl," sued Roy Shaw, "an iron molder" (whose father owned the company) for breach of promise; she won a verdict of three thousand dollars (later reduced somewhat), which was quite sizable for the times. Even though, as the court remarked, "it required no long siege or consummate strategy to induce the plaintiff to surrender the citadel of virtue," she had "yielded" because of his promise, and when he committed the "perfidy" of breaking his promise, she was left "to bear the loss, suffering, and shame alone."[8]

These were, technically speaking, odd cases—hardly contract cases at all. As one commentator in the early 1930s asked, what kind of breach of contract is it when "the injured party has assented" to the breach (that is, let herself be seduced)? But despite "modern theorizing about the equality of the sexes and the freedom of woman, in the relation of betrothal there is not and cannot be equality." Once a woman gives a man "full love and confidence," she has "entrusted herself to his honor."[9] If he leaves her in the lurch, she has lost social position, she is damaged goods in the marriage market, is often saddled with a bastard child—and has lost her chance for a home and social position.

By 1930 these assumptions were becoming somewhat anachronistic—excessively Victorian. The legal literature roundly denounced these "heart balm" cases. The plaintiffs were described as scheming women, intent on sexual blackmail. By the end of 1935, twenty-three states were considering laws to reform the system.[10] Seven states (including such big ones as New York and Pennsylvania) had gotten rid of it. Indiana in 1935 abolished all civil suits "for breach of promise to marry, for alienation of affections, for criminal conversation, and for seduction of any female person" (provided she was twenty-one or older).[11] (Criminal conversation, incidentally, does not refer to talk, but to action—adultery, in short.) Colorado joined the parade in 1937, California in 1938, Massachusetts in 1939. By the end of the Second World War, fifteen states had enlisted in the campaign against heart balm. Even where the cause of action survived, it had lost most of its strength.

Divorce

In 1942 Anna Kreyling brought a divorce action against her husband, Daniel.[12] Desertion was the grounds; but not the ordinary kind of desertion, where the husband simply walks out the door. Anna complained that her husband "insisted on using a contraceptive device during intercourse"; he refused even to think about having a child; he preferred, she said, "the luxuries of life like a car every year." For three years "they indulged in intercourse about twice a week"; but though she begged him "to have natural intercourse," Daniel refused. At that point, she brought a bed in from her mother's apartment, and slept in a separate room. After a year and a half of this, Daniel moved out.

The Court granted the divorce. The judges were disgusted with Daniel, who refused to have "natural" sex. Apparently, he "regarded the married state as mere licensed concubinage." The court admitted that contraception was "widely accepted"; and that even in states where there were "statutory prohibitions," these were "more obeyed in their breach than in their observance." If both husband and wife "willingly indulge" in this practice, well, that was a matter for their "individual consciences." But in this case, the husband was "selfish"; and Anna, "her maternal instinct clamoring . . . for the realization of her desire to become a mother," was "condemned" to a life of "frustration of that maternal instinct and desire." Such a "frustration" must lead to "deleterious physical, emotional and mental effects." Daniel's conduct was "a violation of both human and Divine law."

The facts of the case are distinctively twentieth century; and in a way, so are the results. It is as true in 2001 as in the 1940s that a marriage is probably doomed if husband and wife cannot agree on something so basic as whether or not to have children. What seems archaic is the tone, language, and ethos of the court. Sex is God's way of making children; nothing more. Contraception is "unnatural." Women have a maternal "instinct" and "clamor" to have children. Anybody (man or woman) who prefers a new car to raising children is almost a traitor to the human race.

In one sense, the case accurately reflected the official law of divorce. No divorce was possible without "grounds." Marriage (in legal theory) was a contract between man and wife; but unlike most contracts, once the two were in it, it was devilishly hard to get out. A contract to buy a horse can be called off if both buyer and seller want to call it off; but a marriage contract is not like buying a horse. Only a court could dissolve a marriage, and only when one party, herself quite innocent, could prove the other guilty of an offense against the marriage—the so-called grounds for divorce.

Admissible grounds varied from state to state. In South Carolina absolute divorce was not available at all, for any reason; divorce arrived in South Carolina only in 1948. In the other states, the common grounds were adultery, desertion, and cruelty; but there were all sorts of state idiosyncracies. Drunkenness, failure to provide, imprisonment, and impotence were grounds in some states. Leprosy was grounds for divorce in Hawaii; in Virginia a husband could divorce his wife if he discovered she had been a prostitute.[13] Cruelty became the grounds of choice in the twentieth century; it overtook adultery in 1922, and in 1950 accounted for almost three-fifths of all divorces.[14] Most states recognized cruelty as a valid reason for divorce—New York was a prominent exception.

What accounts for this outbreak of marital cruelty? Nothing. It was, in fact, an outbreak of collusion. Most "cruelty" cases were uncontested. The plaintiff (usually the wife) filed for divorce. The husband made no defense. Divorce was granted, by default. Collusive divorce had become common in the late nineteenth century; in the twentieth century, it was absolutely pervasive. In legal theory, a collusive divorce was void. Husband and wife had no right to agree to split. In practice, collusion was the rule, not the exception; and the judges all knew it. Their (implicit) motto was: don't ask, don't tell.

The precise form of collusion did vary from state to state. It mirrored the state statute; it was, in a sense, "cheating in the shadow of the law." In California, as in most states, cruelty was the courtroom favorite. In case after case after case, the wife complained that her husband cursed her and hit her, and made her life miserable. In San Diego in 1912, Maude E. Burke accused John Burke of using vile and abusive language, calling her "bitch" and "prostitute." In 1917 Mary Lee Scheider, also of San Diego, accused her husband of "cruel, unkind and unbearable conduct"; he called her "a damn fool" and said she had sex with "strange men." He also shoved her around, and even hit her. Mary Lee was, she said, a woman of "sensitive nature and delicate health"; his conduct caused "grievous mental suffering."[15] In 1921 in San Francisco, the wife was plaintiff in 70 percent of divorce cases; and she alleged cruelty in 40 percent of the cases.[16] By 1950 the percentage of accusations of cruelty had reached 70 percent.[17]

In New York divorce was available, practically speaking, only for adultery. This was an extreme situation; but any and all attempts to amend the law ended in shipwreck in the legislature. The demand for divorce, however, was as strong in New York as it was elsewhere. One end-run around divorce was annulment. Annulment is a declaration that a marriage never was valid, because of some kind of fraud or other impediment; in most states, annulment was a rare beast—usually fewer than 4 percent of all dissolutions of marriage. But New York was an annulment Mecca. By 1950 there were ten counties in New York which granted more annulments than divorces; and for the state as a whole, there were two-thirds as many annulments as decrees of divorce.[18]

New York also developed a weird form of collusive adultery—one might even call it soft-core adultery. A man would check into a hotel, a woman (usually a blonde) would appear, together with a photographer; the photographer would take pictures of the couple, in pajamas or underwear or even naked; the woman would get her fifty-dollar fee; and lo and behold! here was evidence of adultery. The flavor of this charade is neatly captured in the title of a magazine article from 1934: "I Was the Unknown Blonde in 100 New York Divorces."[19]

Collusion was by far the most popular, and practical, detour around tough divorce laws. But the federal system opened another door: the migratory divorce. There had been a number of divorce "mills" in the nineteenth century: states that attracted birds of passage with easy divorce laws. The clergy and respectable people usually objected to this rather tawdry business; and most divorce mills—South Dakota was one—were soon closed down.

The main survivor was Nevada, a barren expanse of sagebrush, an empty desert; a kind of moon landscape in the West, but with sovereignty. Nevada made a business out of divorce, as it would later make a business out of gambling, easy marriage, and other forms of pleasure (or vice); "going to Reno" almost became synonymous with "getting a divorce."[20] Nevada was the most popular divorce mill; but some spouses tried more exotic places—the American Virgin Islands, for example, or even Mexico. These were never so popular as Nevada, because there was even more of a question as to whether divorces in those places were valid.

Squabbles over migratory divorce pitted state against state. A kind of high (or low) point was reached in two cases called *Williams v. North Carolina,* decided in 1942 and 1944 by the United States Supreme Court.[21] O. B. Williams lived in North Carolina with his wife and four children. He left them in 1940 and hightailed it to Nevada. So did another North Carolinian, a Mrs. Hendrix. They both checked into the Alamo Auto Court, on the Las Vegas–Los Angeles road. They stayed there exactly six weeks—which is all Nevada required—then filed for divorce. The day they were divorced, the lovebirds got married, and returned to North Carolina.

They had a hot reception—no doubt at the instigation of two outraged ex-spouses. They were arrested, charged with bigamy, and put on trial. Convicted, they appealed to the United States Supreme Court. The Supreme Court, in *Williams I*, reversed their conviction: North Carolina had to give the Nevada divorce "full faith and credit." Under the Constitution, states were duty bound to honor the judgments of their sister states. But Williams and Hendrix were by no means out of the woods. They were retried and reconvicted; this time, conviction rested on a different basis. Now North Carolina held that Nevada never had jurisdiction in the first place; the domicile was phony from the start; the couple never intended to live there. And if Nevada had no jurisdiction, then North Carolina had no duty to honor the Nevada decree. This time the Supreme Court affirmed. Williams and Hendrix, presumably, would have to go to jail.

The Williams cases created a stir in the legal world; unsettled some migratory divorces; and probably made quite a few men and women nervous about their marriages. But for every disputed divorce, hundreds sailed blithely through the system. The divorce rate rose. More and more people, it seemed, wanted out of their marriages; wanted to start over again, with somebody new. It was not just an upper-class matter. Working-class divorce was common. In Muncie, Indiana, the divorce rate rose 622 percent between 1890 and the 1920s (the population rose 87 percent); in most of these divorces the "cover story" was "cruelty," just as in California.[22]

Many moralists and religious figures found this trend quite alarming. They read it as a symptom of the decline of the West, East, and just about everywhere. They opposed making divorce any easier. Hence easy divorce was political poison. The formal law of divorce in fact, changed very little in the first half of the century. Divorce had become a classic example of what one might call a dual system—a system with a radical disjuncture, or gap, between the official system and the living law. Of course, official law and living law are never perfectly congruent; but in a true dual system, the two systems are entirely separate, operating almost in two different worlds.

Divorce was not the only such system. Prostitution was another, and vice in general—illegal in theory, tolerated in fact, or even regulated. Dual systems arise from a number of causes. Divorce was a kind of stalemate. The forces that opposed it were powerful. Divorce was absolutely forbidden to Roman Catholics; other religions tolerated it, but barely. It carried a stigma. Yet the demand for divorce continued to rise; and it proved impossible to confine it within the narrow channels of the official law. An irresistible force (the popular desire for divorce) had met an immovable object (the opposition to easy divorce).

Yet ironically, divorce was not a sign of the breakdown of marriage, but almost the opposite. Divorce flows out of what has been called companionate marriage. It comes out of a conception of marriage as a genuine partnership. Of course, the man is the managing partner; but the woman is supposed to be his best friend, his confidant, his companion. The companionate husband does not go bowling with the boys, but goes on vacation with his wife; the companionate wife does not hang out with her sisters and her mother-in-law, but shares deeply in every aspect of her husband's life. A companionate marriage is obviously harder to sustain than a traditional marriage. It is easier for a man to find a good cook, a good mother for his children, or for a woman to find a good provider who drinks in moderation, than it is for either to find a soul mate, a life partner. Companionate marriage is an ideal. Reality often falls far short. If marriage means so much, if it is supposed to be so totally fulfilling, then by that token it can more easily fail. When it does, many men (and some women) want to break off and try again. Divorce is the clear way out.[23]

There were, of course, costs to the dual system. It was tawdry and unpopular; it was expensive; it degraded everybody who took part in it. Yet there was no easy way for the system to change. It was rotting from within; but the constant calls for reform made little headway. Some reformers wanted to get rid of the adversary system; and replace it with something more honest—and also more "therapeutic," more concerned with human and family values.[24] There were many proposals, and some action, to convert divorce courts into courts of "conciliation," courts that ignored the legalism and tried to save a broken marriage, if possible.[25] Marriages, like people, could be sick, and need a doctor. The courts could act as marriage doctors, as therapeutic institutions, with the help of social scientists, psychiatrists, and other experts.

The Court of Conciliation of Los Angeles County, which flourished in the 1950s under Judge Louis H. Burke, was an experiment along these lines. Couples were invited to take their marital problems to this court. The court had limited powers, but some of them were rather startling—because the court had "jurisdiction over *all persons having any relation* to the domestic controversy," it could call in "third party 'paramours'" and order them to quit their paramouring. In a few cases in which all parties did in fact sign on to such an agreement, the court sent violators to jail for contempt.[26]

The conciliation court tried to get husband and wife to execute a "reconciliation agreement." In a typical agreement, as Judge Burke reported it, the attitudes toward gender and marriage were hardly revolutionary: the husband was responsible for "financial support of the family," and took care of the "outside of the home"; the wife took care of "the inside of the home," including meals and clothing (though, if a wife worked, the husband "must share to a larger extent in the work of the home"). A wife was supposed to bear the greater share of "giving" during a marriage; the wife's lot is to "go through a great amount of sacrifice" for the sake of husband and family; but she is "happy" to do so.

The agreement was quite specific on some points. Both parties agreed not to give the other the "silent treatment." The husband promised not to "maintain late and unusual hours." He agreed to "take the wife out for dinner" or the like "at least once a week." He had to have reasonable "pocket money" for golf expenses and snacks; the wife got "pin money" for the beauty parlor and cosmetics. Mealtimes were to be "times of great peace and calmness." Both of them were to control their tempers, if at all possible. There were elaborate strictures about child rearing. Sexual intercourse, we discover, "provides a safe and healthy outlet for passion"; but should be done in "moderation." Twice a week, on average, "under normal conditions, should not be considered excessive." Neither husband nor wife should act selfishly, in bed. "Lovemaking" in the "first stages of intercourse" was essential; a woman is not "aroused" as quickly as a man; "her passion side is slow to make its appearance." The wife was supposed to "respond to the husband's efforts in lovemaking and not to act like a patient undergoing a physical examination." Both husband and wife should take care of their "personal appearance," and avoid "uncleanliness, overweight, vulgarity, or carelessness in dress." The passage of time, of course, brought "baldness, wrinkles, denture difficulties, arthritis" and the like; it was sinful to blame the partner for these ills; by implication, they were no excuse for falling out of love.[27]

These typical agreements seem retrograde from the vantage point of 2001; but they did strive for a rough sort of equality, as the likes of Judge Burke understood. When a man marries, the agreement provided, "he must cease to be one of 'the boys.'" The couple should make "mutual friends," and try to share each other's work and hobbies. Despite all the language of therapy and conciliation, the agreements reflected, as they had to, a changing conception of marriage; marriage as partnership, and perhaps even as a vehicle of fulfillment. But that conception undermined the conciliation court—and the law of divorce as well.

By the 1960s the climate was ripe for reform. The Catholic Church was still absolutely opposed to divorce, but ordinary Catholics, even many Catholics who considered themselves fairly religious, did not go along with the official line on divorce, and on contraception, too, for that matter. In 1966 New York— the adultery-only state—finally reformed its laws; it added other grounds, most significantly "cruel and inhuman treatment" that "endangers the physical or mental well-being" of the plaintiff, and "abandonment . . . for a period of two or more years."[28]

But the most dramatic change—an apparent revolution—began (no surprise) in California. In 1970 California adopted the first so-called no-fault statute. The new law swept away every vestige of the old system. There were no longer any "grounds" for divorce. There was, in fact, no longer divorce: it was now called "dissolution of marriage." Any marriage could be dissolved if there were "irreconcilable differences," causing the "irremediable breakdown of the marriage."[29]

No-fault was intended to be a mild, salutary reform, but like many revolutions, it took on a life of its own. During the long years of the dirty, dual system, divorce by consent was a reality; all that it took was a little white lie. Reformers agreed, above all, that the lying and the fraud and the disgusting dual system had to go; they wanted to bring consensual divorce into the sunlight, and legitimate it. Under the California law, courts were not supposed to grant divorces automatically; they were supposed to investigate whether the marriage had, in fact, broken down. Presumably, the sick marriage would be etherized upon the table, and a corps of experts would work over its body.

No such thing happened. The supporting institutions never got created or funded. Judges simply handed out divorces to anybody who wanted one. Thus, almost immediately, no-fault turned out to be something nobody had predicted. It went beyond consent. It became a system of unilateral divorce—if either husband or wife said, "I want out," that was it. There was no defense.

This seemed dramatically new. But there had been, in a limited way, a kind of creeping no-fault in some states decades before the new law. In some states, a couple could get a divorce, without grounds, if they had been separated for a number of years, with or without a formal separation agreement. This was, in effect, no-fault divorce. By 1950 some nineteen or twenty states had signed on to one form or another of creeping no-fault. But the waiting periods could be quite long—ten years in Rhode Island, five years in Arizona, Kentucky, Maryland, and Minnesota. This was hardly a practical solution. New Mexico, in another pioneering move, added "incompatibility" to its list of grounds for divorce. Two years later, Alaska Territory joined New Mexico; in 1953 Oklahoma followed, then Nevada, Delaware, and Kansas. All this was coming dangerously close to no-fault divorce.[30]

What followed California's move of 1970 was, however, nonetheless dramatic. No-fault "spread like a prairie fire," first to Iowa, then to state after state. By 1974 "forty-five states already possessed a no-fault procedure"; and the rest fell in line within a decade.[31] There were differences in detail, to be sure. Many states did not go the whole route; they simply added no-fault to their list of grounds, or stuck with a kind of creeping no-fault. Yet in many states the effect was the same as in California: surveys of trial judges in Iowa in 1972 and of Nebraska cases in the mid-1970s came to the same conclusion. Whatever the language of the statute, no-fault meant that either party could simply opt out, and the marriage was over. No judge in these states ever denied a demand for divorce.[32]

What brought about the no-fault revolution? What was its underlying cause? Companionate marriage lay at the base of consensual divorce: marriage as partnership. But there was an even more "advanced" concept of marriage, a concept that went beyond companionate marriage: marriage as an aspect of the journey toward self-realization, a stage on the road to individual fulfillment. A person's job in life is to choose a course that is personally satisfying; and he or she has the right to change the course of life, if necessary for personal growth. If that means molting spouses like a lizard molts skin, so be it.

The no-fault statutes were gender-neutral; they were supposed to be fair to both women and men. Were women better off under a no-fault system? The evidence is conflicting; some scholars say yes, some say no.[33] In fact it would be foolish to expect these statutes to bring about equality of the sexes. Women are worse off, in general, after a divorce: they are usually stuck with the kids; many dads are deadbeats; women earn less than men; and two households are more expensive to run than one. But the real question is, can we blame no-fault divorce for their predicament? Probably not. Under the old system, women did as badly, or worse.

No-fault removed one question entirely from the law: should X get a divorce? But divorces still get contested, on other grounds—money and kids. Family law specialists were certainly not put out of business by no-fault. They are, probably, more sought after than before. Where there is no property, no-fault divorce is as smooth as butter. Zero divided by two is still zero. But in an affluent society, the division of property is more often contested than before.

Child Custody

Divorce is hard on children. There are millions of children of divorce—unlike the good old days. Of course, the good old days (as usual) were not as good as some people suppose. Fewer homes were "broken" by divorce; but so many mothers died in childbirth, so many fathers were carried off by one disease or another, that the family world was full of orphans, foster parents, grandparents and aunts raising children—another empire of "broken" homes. When a marriage dissolves, where do the children go? Usually to the mother—by mutual agreement. Some women give up custody voluntarily; some men fight for the children, and win; but these are a minority. For the most part, mother raises the kids; father comes on Sunday and takes them to the zoo. Mostly, custody and visitation questions get resolved more or less peacefully. If not, the court has to decide. The test is the best interests of the child. This is the standard that is supposed to guide decisions about custody. A vaguer standard would be hard to imagine. Custody disputes remain troublesome, sometimes acrimonious. The judgment of Solomon would not be enough to solve some of the problems when the two sides battle for the children they say they love.

Custody, in a few rare but interesting cases, posed special problems— problems that came from new definitions of *child, mother, father, family*. In the old days, there were fathers and mothers, and, from the 1850s on, children by adoption. There were also foster children and wards. All of these categories survived through the twentieth century; but late in the century there arrived more complications and all sorts of mothers and fathers—in vitro fertilization, womb mothers versus egg mothers, surrogate mothers, children with two mothers and no fathers, or two fathers and no mothers; and other variations on what had once been a simpler scheme. Basically, there were mothers and fathers who based their claims on biology: they supplied the genes and the chromosomes, the eggs and the sperm. Others, in contested cases, based their claim on care, love, affection and sweat equity; they changed the diapers and pushed the strollers. Who had the better claim?

In some ways, modern law paid attention to both kinds of parents, in different situations: the affective and the biological. Adoption, by its nature, favors affective ties; and this is especially clear when children are removed from "unsuitable" parents and given to foster parents who later adopt them. But the biological aspect remains strong. There was once a taboo against letting adopted children find their "real" parents; it was not possible, practically speaking, for these children to discover the secrets of their birth. Toward the end of the century, attitudes and policies were rapidly changing; children had a "right" to solve the mystery of who they were. Here, then, is a case where biology could trump the claims of affective parenting, as we shall see.

As always, new family issues tended to find their way, sooner or later, into the courtroom. The case of "Baby M" made headlines in 1988.[34] Mary Beth Whitehead had agreed to be a surrogate mother for William and Elizabeth Stern—that is, she agreed to carry a baby for them (the sperm was William's), then give it up to the Sterns at birth. The Sterns paid money to Whitehead— rented her womb, in a way. But Whitehead "bonded" with her baby, and refused to give the child up. A sordid soap opera followed, with episodes of baby snatching, a flight to Florida, emotional scenes, threats of suicide, and finally, a major lawsuit. The trial court sided with the Sterns: a deal is a deal. Whitehead had signed her rights away, and that was that. The Supreme Court of New Jersey disagreed. The contract amounted to baby selling, and that was forbidden under New Jersey law. Once that issue was out of the way, the case became an ordinary case of child custody: a biological father and a biological mother squabbled over their respective rights. In the end, the court gave Baby M to the Sterns, but left Mary Beth with visitation and other rights. It was still her child.

In other states, too, surrogate motherhood ran into legal trouble. Case law in New York disapproved of the practice. Surrogacy for money was against the law in Kentucky, Arizona, and Nebraska.[35] In other states, surrogacy contracts were illegal under all circumstances.[36] But in other states, surrogacy was legal, either explicitly by law, or simply because no case or statute said no; in a few states—Florida was one—surrogacy was allowed but subject to regulations and strictures.[37]

Adoption

At common law, there had been no such thing as adoption. Most states enacted adoption laws in the latter half of the nineteenth century, some of them on the model of the pioneer Massachusetts statute of 1851.[38] These laws were, above all, concerned with inheritance. The crucial legal aspect of adoption was that it wiped the original, natal family off the map. The adopted child belonged to its new parents. They had all the usual parental rights. The child was also legally their heir, the same as a "natural-born" child.

Adoption served a number of purposes. Many children were orphaned. Families broke up in the nineteenth century with depressing regularity, as we have seen—mothers died in childbirth, disease carried off thousands of parents. There was plenty of young material to fill the orphanages. There were also children whose parents were alive, but (in the judgment of the state) were unfit parents: drug addicts, child abusers, "immoral" mothers, and so on. There were teenage mothers who got pregnant and gave up their children for adoption. Yet state intervention could be biased and intrusive. Prejudice against poor families, minority families—above all, as we have seen, American Indian families—led to pathetic situations in which children were taken from their homes and given to strangers. On the other hand, cases of rampant child abuse sometimes slipped through the cracks in lumbering, creaking, overloaded bureaucracies; every time a child was murdered by its parents, or starved to death, or was tortured by foster parents, the public raised a great hue and cry, blaming the struggling bureaucracy, and demanding incisive reform.[39]

The trend in the twentieth century has been for adoption law and practice to become more professional. It also became the practice to try to match adopted children to their new families. In the first part of the century, the statutes reflected fashionable ideas about eugenics. Minnesota was the first state to require an investigation before a child could be adopted (1917). The state board of control was to look into the "conditions and antecedents of the child," to see whether the child was a "proper subject for adoption" and whether the proposed new home was "suitable." There was also a kind of "lemon" law for adopted children. If, within five years, the child developed "feeble-mindedness, epilepsy, insanity or venereal infection as a result of conditions existing prior to the adoption," and if the adopting parents had "no knowledge or notice" of these problems, the new parents could petition the court to "annul the adoption" and ship the child back to the state board of control.[40]

The obverse of this return option was the situation in which a birth mother or father wanted to get back a child the state had taken away. This was not always easy. Cases sometimes reeked of class bias. In one New York case (1932), the court described the natural father as an "admitted adulterer and seducer"; the court felt that he wanted the child back only because it was "old enough to help . . . on his peddler's cart." The adoptive parents, on the other hand, lived "in a nicely furnished . . . apartment" and had "ample means." It is not hard to guess who got the child.[41]

Adoption was also clothed in secrecy. Adoption not only wiped out the birth parents, legally speaking; it also expunged them from the records. They became nonpersons. The Minnesota law of 1917 called for sealed records, and many other states followed suit from the 1930s to the 1950s. Under Illinois law in the 1930s, an adoptive family could ask for a fresh birth certificate, with their names on it instead of the original names. And no birth certificate in Illinois was ever to state "that the child has been adopted," or was illegitimate.[42] Secrecy was the norm and the standard.

After the Second World War, the adoption rate spiked upward. Petitions for adoption in 1944 were three times what they were in 1934.[43] In 1951 there were seventy-two thousand such petitions; this figure doubled by 1982.[44] Demand for fresh babies increased enormously. The sexual revolution had a tremendous, if indirect, effect on the law of adoption. The stigma attached to bastards, and to "unwed mothers," weakened considerably. After all, millions of mothers were unwed. More and more of them kept their babies. This drastically depressed the adoption supply.

But who controlled the supply? Sometimes, state agencies; or private but nonprofit charities. Other adoptions were "private" or "independent." There was, in fact, a kind of black market in babies. Prime sources were teenage girls from decent families who were "in trouble." Quite a few states, before 1950, tried to make it illegal to adopt a baby except through recognized agencies. There were occasional crackdowns: in 1949 two lawyers and a housewife in New York were accused of a "big-time business" in bringing babies from Florida and selling them for two thousand dollars per baby.[45] But generally speaking, the laws were ineffective.[46] And, of course, informal "adoptions" within families were always common: uncles, aunts, grandmothers, and cousins, who took in children when the parents died or landed in jail or were simply unable to cope.

A tricky issue was adoption that crossed religious lines. A newborn baby, practically speaking, has no religion; and nobody can inherit a religion, biologically speaking. Still, many statutes insisted on religious matching—babies of Catholic mothers to Catholic families, and so on—if at all possible. Adoption across race lines was rare before the 1950s. Early in the century, when (Catholic) babies from the East were placed with Mexican-American families in Arizona, a great uproar ensued; the babies were snatched away, in a kind of vigilante action; they ended up with "good white families." The courts approved.[47] A few states forbade interracial adoption altogether.

But after the Korean War, Americans adopted thousands of war orphans or abandoned Korean children; many American Indians were placed in white homes; and in the 1960s, white adoption of black children became much more common.[48] These last two practices aroused controversy: the Native American adoptions were condemned as a form of genocide, and the National Association of Black Social Workers in the 1970s denounced white adoption of black babies on similar grounds. The Native American situation was, indeed, a scandal: investigations in the 1970s showed that one Indian child out of four was likely to spend time in a boarding home run by the Bureau of Indian Affairs, or in a foster home. It was, according to tribal representatives, child stealing, plain and simple. Congress reacted by passing an Indian Child Welfare Act in 1978. One goal of the law was to prevent "the breakup of Indian families."[49] Tribes were given the right to decide custody cases involving members of the tribe. The act made it harder to take a child away from an Indian family. If an Indian child was up for adoption, its extended family had first choice; next came members of the child's tribe, then "other Indian families."

The last provision is worth a comment. Why should a Cherokee have more rights to adopt a Navajo baby than, say, an Italian-American? Underlying the provision is the concept of pan-ethnicity: the idea that the native peoples, despite differences in culture, religion, language, and ways of life, have some sort of overarching unity. The bias against "assimilation" extended, then, to native peoples, as a collectivity, as well as to each individual tribal nation. And underlying this, in turn, was the rise of plural equality, and with it the emphasis on ethnicity and "roots."

Now came a demand from adopted children for *their* roots: the demand, as we have seen, to know who they were and where they came from; the right to find their "real" mothers and fathers. They also felt a right to know something about their genes and their medical history. (On this point, their adopting parents might agree.) And because the concept of illegitimacy had lost its bite, there was less resistance (on everybody's part) to shining a light on the secrets of a person's birth. Historically, the only thing worse than being a bastard was giving birth to one. The twentieth century reversed these historical attitudes. A pioneer Arizona statute, passed in 1921, made every child "the legitimate child of its natural parents," with the same rights to support and education, and the same right to inherit, as if "born in lawful wedlock."[50] This was ahead of its time, but similar statutes began to appear after the Second World War—for example, in North Dakota in 1969 (with language very much like Arizona's).[51]

In *Levy v. Louisiana* the Supreme Court gave this trend constitutional approval.[52] Louise Levy had five illegitimate children, who lived with her. She worked as a "domestic servant" to support them, she took them to church, she enrolled them in private school at her own expense. Were these children entitled to collect damages for her wrongful death? Louisiana law said no— because they were bastards. But, said William O. Douglas, speaking for the Court, "illegitimate persons are not 'nonpersons.' They are humans." These were Louise Levy's children "in the biological and in the spiritual sense"; under the Fourteenth Amendment, the state had no right to discriminate against them. Justice Harlan dissented; the state had a perfect right not to recognize a "family relationship" not based on marriage.[53] But the sharp, dramatic line between orthodox and unorthodox families was breaking down. The spread of cohabitation, moreover, legitimated "illegitimacy." By 1985 mothers without wedding rings bore 22 percent of all children; by 1997 the figure had risen to 32 percent. More than one birth out of four to white mothers was "illegitimate";

among black mothers, the figure was an astonishing 69 percent.[54] Of course, the parents of some of these children lived in stable unions—they were conventional, bourgeois couples, who simply did not bother with ceremony.

Cohabitation and the Law

On the surface, few changes took place in the law of marriage in the years after the Second World War. One crucial change, as we have seen, was the end of laws against interracial marriage. The social meaning of marriage, however, seemed to change radically; and the same was true of divorce. Behind these changes was the so-called sexual revolution. This led to massive decriminalization of sexual behavior. And there was, as we have seen, a dramatic rise in "cohabitation."

At one time, cohabitation was a crime: fornication, or adultery. (These still are illegal in a few states.) In 1912, for example, one C. H. Hamilton of San Diego, a married man, was sentenced to one year in county jail for living "in a state of cohabitation and adultery with one Mary Doe," an unmarried woman.[55] Hamilton was ahead of his time. By the end of the century, there were millions like him; and nobody raised an eyebrow.

Cohabitation confronted the law in the celebrated case of *Marvin v. Marvin* (1976).[56] Lee Marvin, the defendant, was a movie star. Michelle Triola Marvin, the plaintiff, claimed that they had an "oral agreement" —they would live together, pool their earnings (he earned a *lot*); and she would render "services" to him as "companion, homemaker, housekeeper, and cook." The three-letter word *sex* does not appear in this list of duties, but everybody knew it was there. They lived together for a while, apparently happily; but then came trouble, and Lee Marvin eventually threw her out. She sued for her share of the money.

Lee Marvin thought he had a perfect defense. Courts had traditionally refused to enforce "immoral" contracts, contracts for "meretricious sexual services." The trial court accordingly dismissed the case. But the California Supreme Court reversed; it ordered a new trial. "We are aware," said the Court, "that many young couples live together without the solemnization of marriage." The Court also recognized that the "mores of the society have . . . changed," and "radically." The old rule no longer fit; and it had to be abandoned.

There was a lot of dry, technical stuff in the case as well—about such mysterious entities as *quantum meruit,* implied contracts, implied agreements of "partnership or joint venture." But the thrust of the case was plain: sex outside of marriage was no longer legally taboo. Cohabitors had rights. The richer cohabitor (usually the man) might, without knowing it, run the risk of a lawsuit, when the kissing stopped. The media had a field day with the case: editorials, jokes, commentary, cartoons. A new word entered the language: *palimony.* There was a flurry of legal activity—dozens of lawsuits and threatened lawsuits, and reactions of anger and disappointment by partners who felt they were unjustly "dumped." Soon, though, the situation regressed to normal, with only the odd lawsuit here and there. In 1979 the Illinois Supreme Court pointedly rejected the *Marvin* approach.[57] In a state like Mississippi, where cohabiting was still a crime, courts were disinclined to dish out "palimony."[58] A Minnesota statute, passed in 1980, limited *Marvin* rather severely: a contract between a man and woman living together "out of wedlock" was not illegal, even if "sexual relations" were "contemplated," but it could not be enforced unless the "contract" was "written and signed by the parties."[59] But most jurisdictions came to accept the idea behind *Marvin v. Marvin,* in various colors and shades.

Education

Family life is more than marriage and divorce. Family life is also children. Children figure in many ways in the law: in custody battles, in issues of guardianship or foster care. Most children, fortunately, do not have these problems. Almost every child, however, and almost every family, confronts the educational system. The newborn baby's world is the home; but from age five or six on, for the bulk of the country's children, many of the child's prime waking hours are spent in school; school competes with the home as a center of authority and learning.

Education is a state matter, and is heavily regulated. The statute books of every state contain huge, wordy, elaborate laws about education and the schools. This was so throughout the century. The Florida statutes as of 1920, for example, devoted about eighty pages of close-grained text to laws regulating education. There is material on teachers' certificates, compulsory attendance, organization of school districts, school bonds, school taxes and so on. There are minute provisions about school safety—fire drills, fire escapes, as well as a requirement that school doors must be hung so as to swing open to the outside. Florida also had a State Text-book Commission, which was authorized to take bids on textbooks, and to prescribe "uniform" textbooks for the whole state, for dozens of courses, from reading and writing to hygiene, bookkeeping, solid geometry and Latin composition. No textbook, however, was to "contain anything of a partisan or sectarian nature."[60]

In Florida, of course, a state of the Old South, education was segregated by race before the 1950s. And the ethos of the school was not what it was to become by 2000. Schools were not for creativity, or for questioning authority; such slogans as "do your own thing," or the practice of show and tell, had not invaded the schoolyard yet. Teachers, according to Florida law, were supposed to "labor faithfully and earnestly for the advancement of the pupils in their studies, deportment and morals"; they were to teach, by "precept and example, the principles of truth, honesty and patriotism and the practice of every Christian virtue." They were to "require" of all their pupils neatness, order, promptness, and "gentility of manners"; pupils were to learn "to avoid vulgarity and profanity, and to cultivate . . . habits of industry and economy." How successful the teachers were in these noble endeavors is hard to say.

As these laws make clear, statutes at the time faithfully preserved, like fossils in shale, the ideology that education is supposed to turn out copies of good grown-ups, with good habits, and traditional values and virtues, including patriotic zeal. Nevada required teachers to inculcate "thrift" in their students. A law of 1921 made it the "duty of all teachers in the public schools" to teach "lessons" about "thrift"—the "importance of industry, production, earning, wise spending, regular saving, and safe investment; also the importance of thrift in time and material."[61] Mississippi law, as of 1930, required all students to learn "the principles of morality," and also "good manners." The course was to "include what is known as the Mosaic Ten Commandments," although the statute went on to say, somewhat inconsistently, that no "doctrinal or sectarian teaching shall be permitted."[62] Schools also were required to teach citizenship, patriotism, Americanism, and personal hygiene. An Illinois law of 1909 made it the "duty" of every public school teacher to teach pupils "honesty, kindness, justice and moral courage," as well as "humane treatment and protection of birds and animals."[63]

These statutes have an archaic ring not because we no longer believe in honesty and kindness, or in gentleness to dogs and parrots, but because they assume a kind of consensus, a shared understanding of social norms. Such a consensus is still presumed by at least the language of the law, in some states. Louisiana requires all public high schools to give "instruction on the essentials and benefits of the free enterprise system" (a system in which "investments . . . are determined by private decision rather than state control"). The instruction has to "emphasize the positive values of profit and competition in a free economy and the enhancement of the worth and dignity of the individual under such a system."[64] Louisiana schools can (but need not) give "instruction in sex education"; but if they do, they have to put "major emphasis" on "sexual abstinence," except for married folks. The schools were not to distribute contraceptives, and there were to be no "explicit materials depicting male or female homosexual activity."[65] No doubt there are high school students in Louisiana who could teach the teachers a thing or two about sex, though perhaps not much about abstinence.

Life, and the school milieu, move faster than the Louisiana legislature; and perhaps the legislature knows it. Schools still have a tremendous effect on their students; they socialize students (a polite word for indoctrination), whether they intend to or not. Bland neutrality in education is as impossible as a total vacuum, and just about as desirable. But the emphasis, in education, has shifted from open, overt socialization to an emphasis on developing the self: from character to personality.[66] Moral preachment has given way to show and tell. This is a change far too profound to be captured in the words of the statute books.

The education budget is enormous—countless billions of dollars, spent by state and local governments. Money may not be the root of all evil, but it is close to the root of all politics. Local schools, traditionally, raised local money, usually in the form of a property tax, administered by the state. School finance was often a burning issue. There was a lot of inequality within the states. Rich districts had plenty of school money; poor districts had very little. More and more, in big cities, the poor districts were also black districts and Hispanic districts; the rich districts were white. As integration stumbled and came to a grinding halt, some activists brought a fresh wave of cases on the money issue. In *Serrano v. Priest* (1971) the suit was brought by parents in the Los Angeles area. According to them, there were wild disparities among the school districts in the amounts of money spent per child. The district that spent the least allocated $407 per child in elementary school; the district that spent the most budgeted $2,586 per pupil; the median was $672. These figures reflected even grosser disparities in assessed valuation: the poorest district had $103 behind each child, the median had $19,600, and the richest had $952,156.[67] The system, said the California court, was unconstitutional: a denial of "equal protection."

The *Serrano* line of cases was derailed by the United States Supreme Court in 1973, in *San Antonio Independent School District v. Rodriguez*.[68] Here the Texas system was under attack. But a majority of the Supreme Court refused to find a constitutional issue. This was not the end of the road, however. The Court simply bucked the issue back to the states—and the state constitutions. The results have been mixed. In Idaho, in a 1975 case, the state court refused to do anything about the disparities. The court felt disinclined to act as a "super-legislature," and, in any event, felt that money wasn't everything; less money spent, or more, did not mean that a constitutional right was at issue.[69] The Kentucky Supreme Court, on the other hand, threw out the whole state system, and ordered the legislature to try and try again. The Kentucky Constitution had a clause telling the state to provide "an efficient system of common schools"; this bland, empty phrase gave the court a text to hook its decision on.[70] Meanwhile, in California, "Proposition 13" gutted the local property tax system, pushing onto the state more and more of the burden of financing schools. The issue lives on.

Education was traditionally a matter for state and local government—above all, for local school boards; and for local parents. The federal government had little or nothing to do with education. In the nineteenth century, the federal government helped out with land grants, but that was about all. An Office of Education was established in 1867; but this was not a powerful agency, and its appropriation did not reach a million dollars until 1930; even then, three-quarters of its budget went to educate the Inuit in Alaska.[71] In 1917 the Smith-Hughes Act gave money to the states to support vocational education (training in "agricultural subjects," and in "trade, home economics, and industrial subjects").[72] In 1946 Congress passed a National School Lunch Act—states were to use the money to give good lunches to children who were "unable to pay the full cost."[73] The GI Bill of Rights of 1944 had a major impact on higher education; it opened the door to millions of veterans.[74] The Agricultural Act of 1954 appropriated money to buy milk for schoolchildren.[75] And the National Defense Education Act of 1958 provided money to support science, mathematics, and modern foreign languages, especially in higher education.[76]

All these were bits and pieces, and responses to particular lobbies and interests. Dairy farmers, for example, loved the idea of spending federal money to buy milk for schoolkids; and the school lunch program, too, was a way to get rid of farm surpluses (the Secretary of Agriculture administered the program). The NDEA of 1958 was a response to the Sputnik crisis: the Soviet Union had launched a satellite, and, horror of horrors, it seemed as if America had fallen behind the evil empire in science and technology. But all attempts to provide general aid to education, through federal grants, limped and sputtered, and went down to defeat. Conservatives resisted the idea of federal aid to education because they resisted anything at all that shifted responsibility to Washington. As President Eisenhower put it, giving the central government "additional power" was the goal of "believers in paternalism, if not outright socialism."[77] And race and religion—a powerful and almost lethal combination—were the two biggest stumbling blocks: what to do about aid to segregated schools, and what to do about aid to private (mostly Catholic) schools?

The Elementary and Secondary Education Act wrought a major change in the landscape.[78] It came during the palmy days of Lyndon Johnson's Great Society. The Civil Rights Act of 1964 had more or less neutralized the race issue. Johnson's landslide victory had reduced the ultraconservatives to a twittering minority. And the act skillfully finessed the issue of parochial schools by focusing on children (students), rather than on schools. The act aimed to "provide financial assistance" to local school boards whose districts had "concentrations of children from low-income families," children described as "educationally deprived."

Like crime, education now became (to a degree) a federal responsibility. The first steps were tentative and gingerly, as the federal government tiptoed about the bulky obstacle of states' rights, enfeebled but still dangerous, like a wounded tiger. The national government would sponsor research (who could object to that?), it would give help to districts loaded with low-income students, it would pay its share in "federally impacted" areas (districts next to big army bases, for example); it would lend a hand to the education of handicapped children.[79] Gradually, the federal role broadened. Washington threw more money at education. In 1965 federal support for education came to about $5.4 billion; in 1998 it was $107 billion. Education remains a profoundly local responsibility; but the federal contribution is no longer marginal.

The federal government, after all, had the money; and in the age of television, it had the attention of the public. No important issue could remain strictly local. A sign of the times was establishment of a cabinet-level Department of Education in 1979. The law creating the department made the usual bows to state and local control, but aimed to "ensure that education issues receive proper treatment at the Federal level." In the 1990s presidents and presidential candidates routinely shouted about their devotion to education, their commitment to education, and they shoved proposals about education, of one sort or another, to the head of the lists of things they proposed to do.

One key issue concerned the rights of handicapped children. This became salient because attitudes toward the handicapped were changing, in the era of civil rights and plural equality. The earlier picture had been mixed. Many states did make provisions for deaf or blind children. A New York law of 1917, for example, gave boards of education power to provide for these children, and for "crippled" children as well. In 1949 the Territory of Hawaii passed a law to provide "instruction, special facilities, and special services" for "exceptional children" (defined as children who "deviate" enough from the "so-called normal person" to need extra and different attention).[80] Many states enacted such programs in the years after 1950.

But there were counterindications as well. In 1919 the school authorities of Antigo, Wisconsin, decided to exclude Merritt Beattie, age thirteen, from public school. Beattie was described as a "crippled and defective" child; he had a "high, rasping and disturbing voice," drooled, had "uncontrollable facial distortion," and, in general, had a "depressing and nauseating effect upon the teachers and school."[81] A court upheld this action. In *Pennsylvania Association for Retarded Children v. Commonwealth of Pennsylvania* (1971), the Supreme Court held that Pennsylvania had an "obligation" to mentally retarded children; the state had to provide a "free, public program of education and training appropriate to the child's capacity."[82] This overturned a state law that allowed schools to turn away children who were "unable to profit from further public school attendance."

In 1975 Congress passed the Education for All Handicapped Children Act.[83] Local agencies, to qualify for federal money, were required, among other things, to establish for handicapped children "an individualized education program . . . at the beginning of each school year." Handicapped children were to be educated in the least restrictive environment possible. This came to be called "mainstreaming": no segregation, if at all possible. Mainstreaming was not mandatory; but it was strongly preferred.

There is, of course, deeper significance to the concept of mainstreaming. Mainstreaming is not the same as assimilation; it is a leveling of the playing field. It is part and parcel of the rights revolution. What is, after all, the point of the rights revolution, if not "mainstreaming"? The goal of *Brown v. Board of Education* was "mainstreaming"; the laws against sex discrimination, age discrimination, and the like are "mainstreaming"; ramps and elevators and Braille for the handicapped are "mainstreaming" too. The late twentieth century, in fact, was the age of mainstreaming, in countless areas of law.

Where Are Your Children?

If there was one constant in the twentieth-century history of the family, and family law, it was that parents were losing control over their children. School itself helped weaken the ties of parent and child. It was the state, not mom and dad, who decided what was taught and how it was taught. For the most part, parents went along, but certainly not always. Jehovah's Witnesses fought against flag salutes. Religious parents fought against Darwin. Secular parents fought against Bible reading. Sometimes parents won, sometimes they lost.

On the whole, of course, parents were only too glad to hand children over to schools where they would get an education. They were also forced to hand children over to a more subtle and dangerous enemy: modern mass culture, spread by radio, television, and the movies. At the same time, the family itself seemed to be disintegrating. Divorce and death created millions of "broken homes." Single-parenting rose at staggering rates in the latter half of the century, as we have seen.

American culture and society had a corrosive effect on the authority of immigrant parents. This was obvious, even at the beginning of the century. Shocked and unable to cope, some parents turned to juvenile courts for help. At the same time, people began to panic over white slavery: the way evil men in big cities lured innocent girls into lives of appalling vice. This moral panic gave rise to the Mann Act. The theme of loss of control was an important factor in the continued vitality of drug laws. There were so many dangers lurking out there: pushers, homosexuals eager to "recruit" fresh converts, sexual predators, monsters who fed on the blood of the children. There were even (it was said) Satanic groups—secreted even in nursery schools—that preyed on the bodies of young children. Each of these fears produced its harvest of law. Parents were losing their grip. They could no longer keep their children safe and sound. They needed the help of the state.

In the second half of the century, too, many old taboos broke down. This became a permissive society. Sex and pornography were everywhere. Children had to be protected; but this was harder and harder to do—for parents, at least. The very word *protection,* as Philip Jenkins has pointed out, suggests that children are in danger; that they need "safeguarding over and above what they would normally receive from the family." But protection also means control: children are not, after all, adults, and they have no right to choose a life of trouble, sin, or vice.[84]

There was also more and more recognition that the world was full of bad families. There were parents and foster parents who beat their children, raped them, tortured or murdered them. The love that dared not speak its name was no longer gay love, but incest. In the last quarter of the century, incest, child abuse, and related family crimes came roaring out of the closet onto the front page. States passed laws that made it mandatory to report these offenses. Between 1976 and 1986 reports of child abuse and neglect rose from 669,000 to more than 2 million, and to 2.9 million in 1993; more than eighteen times as many reports of sexual abuse were recorded in 1985 as in 1976. Many of these, of course, were unfounded.[85] But many, no doubt, were all too true. Horror, like charity, often begins at home.

15

Internal Legal Culture

The Legal Profession

T
he period after the Second World War was a period of enormous growth in the legal profession. In 1951 there were 221,605 lawyers in the country, according to a Bar Association survey. By 1991, forty years later, there were more than 800,000 lawyers in the United States; the 1995 estimate was nearly 900,000.[1] By the end of the century, if all went according to schedule, the number of lawyers should have easily passed the million mark. In 1994–1995, the country's law schools awarded 39,349 professional degrees in law.[2] Lawyers were, in a sense, breeding like rabbits—the profession was growing far faster than the nation. Few populations have grown quite so rapidly—computer programmers, perhaps, and of course people in prison.

The demography of the bar changed dramatically, too, in the last part of the century. Women had been members of the bar since the 1870s, when the first few were (grudgingly) admitted; but for decades, they were a tiny and token minority. Women could not hold office, or vote (except in a few advanced communities) until the Nineteenth Amendment (1920). And that was not the end of political disabilities for women. The amendment did not automatically put women on juries—and some states resisted as late as the 1940s—nor did it in itself push up the numbers of women in the legal profession. In fact, in 1955 there were only 5,036 women lawyers—1.3 percent of the total; in New Mexico, there were exactly four (six-tenths of one percent of the total), and in Delaware a grand total of three.[3]

Some law schools had admitted women (always in small numbers) since the nineteenth century. Others refused. Harvard, for one, strenuously resisted the idea. In 1948 Soia Mentschikoff spent a year at the law school as a visiting professor, a first for Harvard. Two years later the school admitted its first female students.[4] The few women who did go to law school often found it a painful experience. The schools were clubby and unwelcoming aggregations of men. Janet Reno, who in 1992 was to become the first woman to serve as attorney general of the United States, entered Harvard Law School in 1960. Her class consisted of 509 men and just 16 women. Some of the professors were openly hostile to women. W. Barton Leach, who taught property, used to schedule a special "Ladies' Day"; on that day women had to sit in front of the class and answer pointed questions. One of Reno's classmates put it bluntly: the women had to "put up with an incredible amount of shit."[5]

Yet a few years later, an avalanche of women hit the law schools. Four percent of the students in law schools in 1965 were women; in 1973 the figure was 16 percent, in 1979 it was 32 percent, and in 1995 it was 42 percent. Law degrees were conferred on 16,757 women in 1994–1995—not far behind the 22,592 men.[6] One out of four lawyers in the late 1990s was a woman; and as the older men die or retire, the "feminization" of the profession is bound to increase.

Women also began appearing, in some numbers, on the bench; and on the faculties of law schools. Progress was slow. Franklin Roosevelt appointed only white men to the federal courts. Truman appointed one woman as a district court judge; Eisenhower appointed none. Until Jimmy Carter's presidency, tokenism was the rule. But 14 percent of Carter's appointments to the district courts—twenty-nine in number—were women.[7] In 1981 President Ronald Reagan broke a historic barrier when he made Sandra Day O'Connor a justice of the United States Supreme Court. This fulfilled a campaign promise; but Reagan in fact appointed fewer women judges than Carter—twenty-four in all, in two terms in office. President Clinton was committed to putting women on the bench; he also appointed Ruth Bader Ginsburg to the Supreme Court in 1993; at the end of the twentieth century, two women sat on the Court.

Women also began to be represented on state courts. Rose Bird was chief justice of California (and a most controversial one) during the late 1970s and early 1980s. Minnesota in 1991 crossed a significant line; it became the first state in which women were the majority on the state supreme court. At one point in 1999 there were no fewer than twelve women serving as chief justices in their states: Colorado, Idaho, Kansas, Minnesota, Mississippi, Montana, New Jersey, New York, Oklahoma, Washington, West Virginia, and Wisconsin.[8] The bar was coming to look more "like America," at least in gender balance.

There was progress in racial representation, too; but it was even slower than the progress for women. In 1965 blacks made up 1.3 percent of the law students; half of these were clustered in a few all-black law schools, like Howard University's. At this point, however, doors began to open in other schools. By 1977 about 5 percent of the country's law students were black. Many law schools had affirmative action programs, though a reaction later set in.[9] Black judges began appearing on the bench as well. On the federal level, no black served as a district judge before the Kennedy administration.[10] Kennedy also appointed Reynaldo Garza of Brownsville, Texas, to the district court—the first Hispanic federal judge. Garza was later promoted by President Carter to the 5th Circuit.[11] Lyndon Johnson made a historic move when he appointed Thurgood Marshall to the United States Supreme Court. When Marshall stepped down, President George Bush nominated another black, Clarence Thomas (1991). Thomas was extremely conservative, and the nomination touched off an abrasive and sensational controversy. In the end, however, Thomas was confirmed. Toward the end of the century, state and federal governments had become conscious of a need to put Asians and Hispanics on the bench as well. Here too the numbers were small: in 1990 there were only 114 Asian-Americans on the bench, at any level—almost all of them in California and Hawaii.[12]

The push toward a broader base, and the huge increase in the number of lawyers, had a significant impact on the American Bar Association, and the local bar associations as well. No longer were these organizations clubs of elites: now they were open to everybody—all races, all genders, all ethnic groups. At one time, it was about as hard to get into the Association of the Bar of the City of New York, for example, as to get into Skull and Bones or some exclusive college fraternity. Six members had to recommend you. By 1972 this was down to one member, and even this had become a mere formality: if you did not actually know a member, the ABCNY would introduce you to one.[13] In the latter half of the century, the American Bar Association too opened its arms to all those entitled to call themselves lawyers. In 1951, with 43,000 members (out of 190,000 potentials), the ABA launched a "monumental" campaign to bring more in; the goal was to recruit "at least 50% of practicing American lawyers."[14] But nobody has to join the American Bar Association, or the local bars; the 50 percent goal has never been achieved by the ABA. Still, at the end of the twentieth century, it had about 350,000 members. This is a lot of lawyers; and they are much more diverse than the historical bar—and less likely to represent only one point of view, on almost any subject.

The move toward "diversity" reached the law firms too. As late as the 1950s, big Wall Street firms excluded women and blacks, and, for the most part, Jews. (Jews tended, as we have seen, to form their own law firms.) The barriers against Jews crumbled first, followed by the other barriers. As women poured out of the law schools in the 1960s and 1970s, law firms responded, at first reluctantly, to the change in the supply pipeline. But by the 1990s women in fact made up the majority of associates at the larger San Francisco law firms. Will these women eventually "make partner"? There is a lot of talk about the "glass ceiling." It still seems difficult for women to rise to the top in big firms. This is especially true for women who have children and take motherhood seriously.

Blacks remain fairly scarce in the higher ranks of the profession. But firms do not dare discriminate openly anymore; and black students who graduate from elite law schools have opportunities their grandparents could scarcely dream of. Other racial minorities are still thinly represented: Asians, Hispanics, Native Americans. In 1998 a survey of the 250 largest law firms found that 3.4 percent of the partners, and 13 percent of the associates, were members of minority groups: almost half of these associates were Asian, 4 percent were black, 3 percent Hispanic.[15] And in 1999 only ten Fortune 500 companies had a nonwhite as general counsel: this tiny crew consisted of one Asian, one Hispanic, and eight blacks.[16]

Big Fish and Little Fish

The legal profession was big, getting bigger, it was also more diverse; and it was diverse, too, in forms of practice. Many lawyers were still solo practitioners; many still practiced in small firms; an increasing number were partners or associates in the giant big-city firms. Other lawyers worked for corporations (as "house counsel") or for the government, at all levels. Lawyers seemed to be everywhere in society; they were active on every issue; they seemed to be (as before, only more so) society's jacks-of-all-trades.

There is a good deal of research about the background of lawyers: who their fathers and mothers were, where they went to school, and what kind of firms or businesses they worked for. Research on what they actually do in these businesses or firms is surprisingly thin. Lawyers are a notoriously difficult bunch to study. They do not like to be examined too closely. They also insist that everything they do for their clients is confidential. They have a point, of course; but this also provides much useful cover.

In general terms, of course, what lawyers do is no mystery. The public may think of them as courtroom warriors, but businesspeople know better. Lawyers, in the main, service business. They help form corporations, they advise on corporate affairs, they maneuver through tangles of red tape; they cope with federal, state, and local government; they help put deals together. Big-firm lawyers work for big business, small-firm lawyers for small business. Business clients occupy most of their hours. John Heinz and Edward Laumann, in their classic study of Chicago lawyers in the 1970s, divided lawyers (and their work) into two big sectors or "hemispheres." The "corporate client sector" accounted for 53 percent of the legal effort. These lawyers worked mainly for big business. The other hemisphere was the "personal/small business client sector"; this accounted for 40 percent of the legal effort. Almost half of this was also business law, but for the little guy. Only 22 percent of the total legal effort went to nonbusiness matters: criminal defense work, divorce and family law, civil rights, personal injury work for plaintiffs.[17] There was almost no overlap between the hemispheres. The business lawyers tended to work for law firms, some of them quite large; lawyers who worked for individuals were in smaller firms, or on their own.

Lawyers in private practice account for most of the bulge in the profession in the last decades of the twentieth century. But the profession has so swollen in size that the absolute number of lawyers who work for government, or for private industry as "house counsel," has also grown greatly, even if the proportions have not. In 1952 out of about two hundred thousand lawyers, 10 percent worked for the government (at all levels), about eighteen thousand in private industry. In 1960 there were twenty-seven thousand government lawyers, in 1980 almost fifty-four thousand, and by 1995 about sixty-five thousand. House counsel went from eighteen thousand in 1952 to more than eighty thousand in 1995.[18]

At one time, "solos" made up most of the bar. Over time, more and more lawyers practiced in firms—in partnerships. In Wisconsin 53 percent of the lawyers were in solo practice in 1935; in 1955 the number was 49 percent, in 1975 it was 30 percent, in 1995 just 26 percent. Firm lawyers went from 37 percent in 1935 to 51 percent in 1995; government lawyers from 4 percent to 12 percent; corporate lawyers from 1 percent to 9 percent.[19] The exact percentages vary somewhat from state to state, but Wisconsin's history is probably typical. Not all law firms, of course, were big firms. There were many small general firms, in towns or neighborhoods of big cities. A growing number of lawyers worked for so-called boutique firms—small but highly specialized law firms dealing with intellectual property, or tax law, or estates work, or food-and-drug law; or some other niche of the practice.

Still, the most phenomenal growth has been in big-firm practice. There has been a "general shift to larger units of practice." In the late 1950s there were only 38 law firms in the United States that had more than fifty lawyers. Most of these were in New York City. In 1985 there were more than 500 such firms. In 1968 the largest firm in the country had 169 lawyers; in 1988 the largest firm had 962 lawyers.[20] The 1,000-lawyer barrier was soon breached; in 1995 Baker and McKenzie, the largest firm in the country, had 1,754 lawyers on its staff. In that year, too, there were 702 firms with more than fifty lawyers; and 321 of these firms had more than 100 lawyers—in 1980 there had been only 87 of these megafirms.[21]

The biggest firms, of course, were in the biggest cities: in New York, Los Angeles, Chicago, Denver, and others. But there was growth everywhere. In 1935 the largest law firm in Wisconsin had 14 lawyers, and the size of the median firm was 6; in 1995 the largest law firm had 210 lawyers (in a single office), and the median firm size had grown to 21.[22] At one time, too, law firms were firmly planted in a single place: there were New York firms, Cleveland firms, Wichita firms, and so on. A few very big or cosmopolitan law firms might have a branch in Washington, D.C., but geographical expansion hardly went beyond that. The megafirms of the 1990s, however, were branching out right and left. They were a long way from McDonald's or the Gap, but they were moving in that direction. Megafirms typically had offices in a number of cities, some of them overseas. The giant, Baker and McKenzie, had branches or affiliates in more than fifty cities, all over the world (146 lawyers in Hong Kong alone; a single lawyer in Hanoi). Sullivan and Cromwell, with headquarters on Wall Street, had branches in Washington, D.C., London, Paris, Melbourne, and Frankfurt, among other places.[23]

The Wall Street lawyer of the 1950s was a steady, gray, and almost invisible man; he worked behind the scenes. He tried strenuously to avoid litigation. A good firm had good, solid clients—big corporations, major companies. The law firm handled work for these clients year in and year out, on retainer. A senior partner perhaps sat on the board of directors. The big law firms had "an enviable autonomy"; and competition among them was "very much a gentlemanly affair."[24]

All this changed rapidly after the 1960s. The law firms expanded; there was an astonishing increase in the scale and work of the big firms. And the practice became more volatile, more competitive. More people were suing the giant corporations—and the giant corporations were increasingly suing each other, when they were not trying to swallow each other whole. Mergers, takeovers, and big-time acquisitions are like bombs that explode in the marketplace; they require lawyerly skills that conservative old firms did not necessarily have. In the 1950s Joe Flom, a lawyer for the four-man firm of Skadden, Arps, "pioneered in hostile takeovers"; he thrived on the "scraps from law firms that were too haughty or too dignified to conduct hostile raids." But in the 1970s Morgan Stanley dropped its "Wasp white-glove firm" and hired Flom for its takeover work.[25] At the end of the century, Skadden, Arps was a Wall Street giant, with something on the order of 1,500 lawyers.

Most lawyers in big firms who lived through the period felt that competition between firms became more intense in the last part of the twentieth century. The firms became "more openly commercial and profit-oriented"; they hired "professional managers and consultants." They were more ruthless in pruning out deadwood, even when the deadwood held a partnership interest. A partner's income depended on how much business he brought in: as the phrase went, you "eat what you kill." Costs, too, rose rapidly; the firms paid their associates more money—new associates in big-city firms started at well over $100,000 a year—and the firms had to earn more to cover these costs. Huge, one-shot megadeals and megacases gained in prominence. There was also more lateral hiring than in the 1950s, more splitting and dissolution of firms.[26]

Big law firms now began to hunt business more actively, prowling about the business world like leopards on the plains. They made presentations to clients like advertising agencies, they concerned themselves with public relations. Important partners became legal "stars," celebrities of the legal world. This was a style once reserved for personal-injury lawyers, divorce lawyers, criminal lawyers. Such lawyers (the high Wall Street bar despised them) were lawyers with "one-shot" clients; they needed a constant flow of new business, and thus had to advertise, one way or another. Because advertising as such had not been allowed, notoriety—getting your name in the paper—was the only substitute. But in a world of one-shot megadeals, even the partners at Skadden, Arps need publicity.

The ban on advertising, in fact, had come to an inglorious end in 1977. It was the United States Supreme Court that did the bloody deed, in *Bates v. State Bar of Arizona.*[27] Under the lawyers' code of ethics, advertising was a dirty word. Two junior lawyers, John Bates and Van O'Steen, launched an attack on this canon of ethics. They put an ad in the *Arizona Republic,* a newspaper, advertising their "legal clinic." "Do You Need a Lawyer? Legal Services at Very Reasonable Fees." For this grave offense, the Board of Governors of the Arizona bar recommended suspension. But Bates and O'Steen fought back—all the way to the Supreme Court. And the Court took their side: the public had a right to hear their message, and they had a First Amendment right to send it. The bar argued that advertising might "tarnish the dignified public image of the profession." Bankers, said the Court, are dignified; yet they advertise. Everybody knows that lawyers, like everybody else, are trying to make a living: why not let them tell their clients what they charge? The threat to "professionalism" was (in the Court's judgment) a red herring.

Bates and O'Steen's ad, significantly, mentioned "very reasonable fees." Price-cutting was anathema to the legal elite. The Canon of Ethics had specifically referred to schedules of minimum fees—lawyers were not supposed to "undervalue" their services, according to canon 12. Bar associations often drew up tables of minimum fees. The Illinois Bar Association, for example, as of the early 1960s, had an elaborate schedule of fees; it was "unethical" to charge less than the amounts set out in the schedule. After all, "All a lawyer has to sell is his time"; fees are "the life blood of any law practice"; and a lawyer was not supposed to "give his time away." The minimum charge was $25 an hour; and minimum fees were fixed for all sorts of business—$150 for an uncontested adoption, $250 for organizing a corporation, $25 for a simple will (but $150 for a "marital deduction will" with a "marital trust and family trust").[28] The Fort Worth Bar Association Fee Schedule, as described in December 1943, was a list of "recommended fees for legal services." The suggested fee for legal advice, if it was an easy question, answered by phone or in the office, was $5; if the lawyer

had to leave his office to go find the answer, the fee was $10. A plain, uncompli-
cated will was $25, an uncontested divorce, $50, a simple civil suit in district
court $150.[29] The Supreme Court struck down minimum fee schedules in 1975
in *Goldfarb v. Virginia State Bar*.[30] The practice, said the Court, was anti-
competitive—a violation of the Sherman Act.

Of course, the old, established Wall Street firms had never wanted or
needed to advertise, nor were they particularly interested in minimum fee
schedules. They got business through networks of business and personal relationships. They were also not interested in cutting prices to attract a volume of
business. Nor did they run after the grubby business that Bates and O'Steen
made a living from. Even after the Supreme Court said they could, they declined to advertise. The lawyers who advertised on TV or who bought full-page
ads in the yellow pages were lawyers looking for one-shot clients—often clients
who were poor and underserved; the ads were directed at people who had
accidents at work or on the street, or were arrested for drunk driving and the
like, with a scattering of bankruptcy, family law, and immigration problems. One
firm advertised in 1998 (in the yellow pages of the Seattle, Washington, phone
book), "If you've got money coming, I'll get it for you. The big insurance
companies can't wear me down and they can't wait me out." One lawyer who
placed an ad in this same phone book had also been trained as a registered
nurse. "Severe Injury? What most lawyers *don't* know . . . a nurse/attorney
does." Lawyers shouted out (in these pages) that they were "aggressive," and
could get "results." One firm promised "immediate response . . . 24-hour
message service." "Accused of a crime? Obtaining aggressive and effective legal
defense should be your *first* priority." In San Francisco a law firm put a small ad
on the back page of the *SF Weekly* in 1998, with the headline "Strange Law. We
handle all sorts of strange legal cases, often involving disputes with all levels of
government, or from romances." Just below this was an ad for "Safe Sex—Get
paid $1,000/wk"; and just above it was an advertisement for free pregnancy
testing.[31] Strange law makes for strange bedfellows. You can imagine what an
elegant San Francisco lawyer, high above the crowd on Montgomery Street,
would think of the lawyer who practiced "strange law."

But in fact, as we have seen, the big firms began to advertise too, though not
so blatantly. They lost their aversion to publicity. One sign of the times was the
rise of legal journalism. Steven Brill, a New York lawyer, founded *American
Lawyer* in the early 1980s. Later came the *National Law Journal*, a "weekly

newspaper for the profession." There was nothing new in the idea of magazines for lawyers—one magazine, *Case and Comment,* dated back to 1894. But these ..ew magazines were different; they were breezy, gossipy, full of inside dope and human interest. The classical Wall Street lawyer, like Boston Brahmins, believed that a gentleman's name never appeared in the newspapers except when he married or died. The new breed of big-firm lawyers, celebrity lawyers, women and men, felt otherwise. In a volatile, one-shot world, a world of "transactional" law, loyalty to a single firm was less important than before; and publicity was good, not bad. The people who did huge mergers and vast acquisitions seemed to need to spread the word, just as much as Melvin Belli ever did.

Changing times (and a push or two, as we have seen, from the Supreme Court) brought about changes in the codes of lawyers' ethics. The American Bar Association replaced the Canon of Ethics in 1970 with a Model Code of Professional Responsibility. Every state soon adopted this code, though sometimes with changes and variations. In 1977 the Bar Association appointed a commission, headed by Robert J. Kutak of Omaha, to draw up a new set of rules. The ABA approved of the Model Rules of Professional Conduct—the work of the Kutak Commission—in 1983. Most states have adopted these model rules. But whether these rules really work—or whether they work in the public interest—remains an open question. After all, it is the bar itself that disciplines the bar; and most citizen complaints end up going nowhere.

The organized bar, though it seems to lack zeal for self-policing, has more enthusiasm for the somewhat dubious battle against "unauthorized practice." This war is waged with very mixed motives. On the one hand, the bar has pursued crooks and scam artists who posed as lawyers or who promised legal advice they were simply not qualified to give. On the other hand, the bar fought to protect its own monopoly against other enemies. Who were these professionals? They were patent experts, tax experts, trust companies that did estate planning, accountants who gave tax and securities advice, among others. In forcing these professionals to stop giving "legal" advice, bar associations were engaging in a genteel form of featherbedding, not much different from the unions that insisted on extra crews for trains. No doubt many lawyers who denounced what the unions did approved of the bar's actions wholeheartedly. The danger seemed great. The Committee on Unauthorized Practice of the Tennessee Bar Association warned its members in 1958 that unless they mobilized and struck back, "the practice of law will soon consist of nothing more than what goes on inside the court rooms."[32]

Local bar associations brought dozens of lawsuits against "unauthorized practitioners." In addition to the usual suspects (banks, trust companies, and real estate agents), for example, an Ohio court in 1958 shut down the "unauthorized practice" of one Austin Shields, doing business as the National Inventors Institute. Shields was forbidden to claim that he could advise clients on "the preparation, the filing and prosecuting of patent applications." A West Virginia court stopped the business agent of Local 10–89, Chemical and Atomic Workers of America, CIO, from "representing members of said local . . . in their personal injuries claims for Workmen's Compensation" in front of trial examiners of the state compensation board.[33] When a popular radio program, *Good Will Court,* gave advice on the air in 1935, mostly to very ordinary folks, the bar brought its heaviest artillery to bear. The Appellate Division of the New York Supreme Court issued a rule which, in effect, prevented local attorneys from having anything to do with *Good Will Court.* The network bowed to the inevitable and canceled the show.[34]

The Rise of the Billable Hour

Lawyers, in their Law Day speeches and the like, like to praise themselves as men and women devoted to justice, the rule of law, the public interest, and all good things. But they are, after all, trying to make a living as well. Most of them would prefer a rather good living. Some, of course, make more money than others. The lawyers of Wall Street or La Salle Street or the equivalents in other cities are usually rich; so are the big personal injury lawyers who win million-dollar cases and take a healthy cut. Thousands of other lawyers do less well. Of all the leading professions, the legal profession has "had the highest levels of income inequality"; there is some evidence this inequality is getting worse.[35] At the end of the twentieth century, top partners of big firms could make half a million dollars a year or more; their brightest new associates made more than one hundred thousand dollars; other lawyers were barely scraping by.

Personal injury lawyers use the contingent fee. Other lawyers tend to charge by the job: so much for a will, so much for putting together the papers for forming a corporation. Billing, in some ways, was at one time quite haphazard. According to Simon Rifkind, Wall Street billing in the 1930s was a "fine art."

The lawyers just asked themselves, "What have we accomplished for the client?" and charged accordingly.[36]

As we have seen, the bar-sponsored fee schedule was a more systematic way to figure out what to charge. These schedules were quite common before the Supreme Court struck them down. In the 1950s another system began to challenge this one. This was time-based billing—the infamous "billable hour." In the 1960s more and more lawyers adopted this system; in Allegheny County, Pennsylvania, for example, three-quarters of the lawyers were using this method by 1965. Hourly billing became the standard method for pricing a lawyer's service—and the standard method for calculating how much work had to be squeezed out of young associates. These now became gilded prisoners of the billable hour. The number of hours a young lawyer was supposed to bill slowly inflated; in the early 1960s studies put the annual average about 1,200; in 1965 a study found that associates were expected to bill 1,400 to 1,600 hours. This continued to go up, up, up, sometimes as high as 2,000.[37]

When the Supreme Court eliminated minimum fee schedules, in 1975, it probably gave the time-based system a boost; but the billable hour was already a standard in many firms. Herbert Kritzer ascribes the practice to "the accounting culture, produced by elite business schools." Corporate clients had begun to demand an itemized list of hours and rates from their law firms.[38] Another factor, no doubt, was the "salary war." The firms kept bidding up the starting salaries for young associates, hoping to snag the cream of the crop. The young sprouts were indeed well paid: but it was a Faustian bargain. They had to work killing hours. Eben Moglen, now a professor at the Columbia Law School (a job whose pace is much less murderous) claimed that he once billed a twenty-seven-hour day, at the Cravath firm, in 1984. This trick was accomplished by flying "from New York to California as he worked around the clock."[39] The pressure of billable hours in the end drove many young lawyers into house counsel jobs, or to smaller firms, or out of the profession altogether.

Lawyers and the Economy

Many people feel there are too many lawyers, and that lawyers are essentially parasites. If they are indeed parasites, they have found a lot of extremely juicy hosts to prey on. Between 1960 and 1985 the legal-services share of national income just about doubled—in other words, the country was spending twice as much on lawyers in 1985 as in 1960.[40] The trend has continued. In the 1990s it was estimated that the country was putting out about $100 billion a year for legal services, an enormous sum. In 1970 the legal bill was probably less than a third of that, in constant dollars.[41]

We have already noticed the panic over the liability explosion. Lots of people, and even some economists, think that lawyers are blood-suckers and vampires, bottom-feeders who hurt the economy—smothering growth, garroting enterprise. Lawyers are certainly not angels; but the general case against them is pretty much unproven.[42] Some lawyers do bring groundless suits, some cheat their clients, some make a living by stirring up trouble. How many do so is another question. It is also hard to say whether there is in fact a plague of lawsuits that hurts the economy. One can, of course, measure the cost of lawsuits in blunt dollar terms. The trouble is that the benefits that lawyers bring about are much harder to translate into dollars. If a big company loses a sex discrimination suit, we can tote up the fine, the lawyers' fees, and so on; but how do we assign a value to what was gained? The sheer number of lawyers, and the fact that they are hardly starving—that some of them make millions— suggests that they serve *some* function; no society would tolerate a million useless blood-suckers. The truth is that the legal system is so complex, and so ubiquitous, that lawyers have become indispensable. People in trouble obviously need a lawyer. Other people need lawyers to stay out of trouble. Businesses need lawyers to help them cope with government regulations. In fact, Ronald Gilson has argued, business lawyers add value, they "enlarge the entire pie" in their role as "transaction cost engineers"—that is, they find a way to structure transactions so as to make them most efficient, and least costly. This may benefit both parties to a deal.[43]

The growth of Silicon Valley in the late twentieth century was one of the wonders of American economic development. Silicon Valley, south of San Francisco, was once the Santa Clara Valley, famous for succulent prunes. The pruneyards are almost all gone, paved over for malls and housing developments—and high-tech start-ups. Everybody knows about the economic exuberance of Silicon Valley. Less well known is the mushroom growth of its legal profession. In 1950, in the small city of Palo Alto, in the heart of Silicon Valley, there were about 40 lawyers; in 1960, when the population had reached nearly 50,000, there were still fewer than 100 lawyers practicing in Palo Alto. But in 1999 the leading Palo Alto firm, Wilson, Soncini, founded in 1961, had well over 500 lawyers.[44] There were 2,400 lawyers registered with the state bar practicing in Palo Alto. The city's population was still around 50,000; this was, perhaps, the densest concentration of lawyers, outside of Washington, D.C., in any town or city; extraordinary for a city of this size.

What were all these lawyers up to? There were personal-injury lawyers and estate-planning lawyers and divorce lawyers in Palo Alto; but most of the soldiers in this army of attorneys were servicing the high-tech industry. If these lawyers were parasites, they were hardly lethal ones. More likely, they must have been doing something beneficial: in the world of start-ups, IPOs, trade secrets and trademarks, patents and copyrights, the lawyers were undoubtedly guiding their clients across dangerous legal minefields. In the process, they were also getting rich.

Not all of the thousands who pour out of law schools and take the bar actually practice law. Many members of the bar leave the practice. Some practice for a while, then go elsewhere. This is, of course, nothing new. Northwestern University surveyed almost one thousand law alums in the 1920s; 82 percent of the respondents were practicing law, but the rest had left the field.[45] Where had they gone? Some lawyers, of course, try politics, which almost seems like a natural progression (and does not necessarily mean leaving the profession at all). Lawyers are all over Congress and the state legislatures: 26 percent of all state legislators were lawyers in 1966; more than half of all the members of Congress, historically, have been lawyers. The percentages are going down, but are still substantial; 16 percent of the state legislators were lawyers in 1986, and 43 percent of the members of Congress in 1996. Franklin Delano Roosevelt, Richard Nixon, and William Jefferson Clinton were lawyers. In Clinton's first term, lawyers made up 75 percent of his cabinet, and more than a third of the key subcabinet posts.[46] Many other lawyers go into business; this too seems to be a fairly easy transition. (This was what most of the dropouts in the Northwestern survey were doing.)

From law to business or politics seems like an easy step. Other occupations are less obvious. But possibilities appear endless. This is one of the reasons why law is an attractive field of study. One Linda Sutherland ran a seminar in 1994 on "400-plus things" a person could do with a law degree "other than practice law." For a mere $145, Sutherland would help prospective dropouts find work in one of these four hundred jobs.[47] There are indeed many prominent ex-lawyers. The historian Daniel Boorstin and the sociologist David Riesman were both trained as lawyers. Among former Stanford law graduates are schoolteachers, a dress designer, and a writer of Hollywood scripts. Kathy Hensley, a graduate of McGeorge Law School, worked for big San Francisco firms for six years, then quit in 1993 to become a sculptor; one of her works, done in art school, consisted of a key on a pillow, "encased in a locked wood-and-Plexiglas box." The box "opens without the key, which in turn does not open the box." She says this means that people think up reasons to avoid doing what they really want to do; but they can eventually do these things by "a different avenue."[48] This "three-dimensional art form" may have autobiographical meaning for Hensley.

Public interest lawyers hardly register on the map, statistically speaking; but they make a rather big splash in the world. These are lawyers who work for the Sierra Club, or for the NAACP, or for gay rights groups, or for Mexican-American groups; or they may do general poverty law. Lawyers have always done some pro bono work, but usually on a part-time basis. The public interest lawyer is a relatively recent phenomenon. The NAACP was a pioneer; the NAACP Legal Defense Fund was founded in 1938. The ACLU hired a staff counsel in 1941.[49] A 1973 study counted some forty-five public interest firms. They had an average of ten lawyers each.[50] This small band of men and women fought bureaucracy and big business, fought for the underdog, the downtrodden, and for the wilderness. They won some notable legal victories. The impact of lawyers for, say, the ACLU or the NAACP is far out of proportion to the numbers of such lawyers. One sign of their success is the rise of conservative counterparts. For example, the Mountain States Legal Foundation in Denver, headed by James G. Watt, who later became Ronald Reagan's secretary of the interior, aimed to defend "free enterprise" against the attacks of environmentalists.[51] If criminals could have their spokesmen, why not rich ranchers? If black people could enlist lawyers in their cause, why not white "victims" of affirmative action?

One special group of public interest lawyers consisted of poverty lawyers. Up until the 1960s there were only a few hundred or so, working for legal aid societies. The War on Poverty, as we saw, contained a legal component. Lawyers for poor people rose in numbers to 2,500 by 1971. And these were not do-nothing lawyers: between 1965 and 1974 these lawyers appealed 164 cases to the United States Supreme Court. At the core were a small group of dedicated men and women. The poverty lawyers attacked, for example, the cruel and discriminatory practices of state and local welfare agencies—agencies quick to throw poor women off the rolls and slow to put them on again. But in the end, welfare rights litigation and the efforts of the poverty lawyers ended in a kind of failure. It was doomed by the "social isolation and stigmatization of the poor"—or, put another way, white, middle-class America's deep distaste for the urban poor was too great a barrier.[52] Public interest lawyers can huff and puff; but they can blow down only houses made out of straw.

On the whole, lawyers are a fairly cautious and conservative group. But liberals and downright rebels can be found in the ranks. Clarence Darrow (1857–1938) was famous for taking up unpopular causes. In the latter half of the twentieth century, radical lawyers like Charles Garry, Arthur Kinoy, and, above all, William M. Kunstler, "the most hated lawyer in America," gained notoriety.[53] Kunstler represented the Chicago Seven, he worked for prisoners in Attica prison during their uprising in 1971, he defended radical leaders of the American Indian movement, he took cases of black radicals, of blacks accused of killing policemen, and of Arabs accused of terrorism. He even took on some prominent gangsters as clients; he argued that the country had "a long tradition of bias against Italian-Americans." (He also confessed to "a slight romantic attraction to the folk-hero quality" of gangsters.)[54] Kunstler battled throughout his life against what he saw as a corrupt, racist society, governed by a corrupt, biased legal system. But he was also, on the whole, a skillful lawyer; he won the grudging respect even of some of the judges he vilified.

Lawyers and Judges in Popular Culture

Lawyers as a group have always had a reputation which is, well, not of the highest. A strong strain of hostility to lawyers runs through American history. Yet there were also lawyer-heroes—men like Abraham Lincoln. The 1950s and 1960s, by some accounts, were a kind of "historic high point of public regard for law and lawyers."[55] Atticus Finch, in Harper Lee's novel *To Kill a Mockingbird* (made into a movie in 1962), was a small-town southern lawyer who defended (unsuccessfully) a black man accused of crime; Finch was painted as the very soul of integrity, a man totally committed to fairness and justice. After Atticus Finch, apparently, lawyers went into a long literary and popular decline. Lawyer heroes can still be found in books; but they are probably outnumbered by villains. Indeed, in a 1997 movie, *The Devil's Advocate,* a rich Wall Street lawyer (played by Al Pacino) does not merely work for the devil: he *is* the devil.

The astonishing number (and virulence) of jokes about lawyers says something, too, about the place of lawyers in popular culture. There are literally thousands of these jokes—certainly more than for any other profession or occupation. The jokes probably tell more about the status of lawyers in the public mind than movies and TV shows (certainly more than bar association speeches). The jokes picture lawyers as conniving and parasitic; as chronic cheats, without ethical standards. The jokes imply that the world would be better off if somebody, anybody, got rid of the lot of them. In one joke, two law partners are at lunch: one jumps up and says, "I have to go back to the office—I forgot to lock the safe." The other calms him down: "What are you worried about? We're both here."[56]

This, in fact, is not a new joke. It was recorded in 1922—but in 1922 it was not a joke about lawyers; rather it was a joke about two business partners (in most versions, Jewish). In 1989 it resurfaced as a lawyer joke, along with other recycled jokes originally told about mothers-in-law, Jews, and other conventional butts of humor.[57]

The profession had done rather well, however, on television. Perry Mason, Erle Stanley Gardner's fictional lawyer, was the hero of a television series on CBS from 1957 to the mid-1960s. Every episode ended with a dramatic trial scene—Perry manages to save his client (his clients were always innocent), and unmask the actual killer. Later came an enormously successful series, *LA Law,* which ran from 1986 to 1994; reruns keep both of these shows alive. As of 2001 there were other lawyer shows on the air; and they seemed to be quite popular.

In political rhetoric, lawyers are in much worse odor. A lot of campaign invective is heaped on lawyers, particularly by prominent Republicans. The usual theme is too much litigation; lawyers are accused of stirring it up. President George Bush was quoted as saying, "Let's stop America's love affair with lawsuits"; and Vice President Dan Quayle never tired of hitting on the legal profession.[58] Bashing lawyers, especially trial lawyers, seemed to be good politics. In 1999, for example, Representative John Shadegg of Arizona, in debates about a plan to allow people to sue HMOs, talked about tort lawyers who "get rich and drive Cadillacs and Lexuses"; a thirty-second TV commercial of the American Association of Health Plans showed a shark swimming, then eating bloody bait: a voice announced that "America's richest trial lawyers are circling —and your health plan is the bait. . . . Protect your family's health care from the trial lawyers' feeding frenzy."[59] In these instances, lawyers were convenient scapegoats. The real enemy was the liability explosion. The real causes of this "explosion," as we have seen, lie deep in American legal and social culture; but no politician is going to blame the voter or the ordinary citizen. Better to lay the blame on legal blood-suckers.

There has been much less attention to the role of the judge in popular culture. There are very few jokes about judges. The judge does figure, of course, in trial movies; but usually in a passive and neutral role—judges in movies are rarely shown as human beings, with families, sex lives, and ordinary emotions. On fictional TV programs, the judge is "customarily the most one-dimensional of the characters, often amounting to little more than a caricature."[60]

In a way, this is paradoxical. In common-law culture, the judge is far less faceless than the judge in a civil-law culture. Supreme Court justices avoid the limelight; but they are celebrities despite themselves. Recently, too, TV has created another kind of celebrity judge. Judge Lance Ito, a Los Angeles trial judge, presided over the O. J. Simpson trial, which was televised; Judge Ito became for a while the most famous judge in this country—perhaps in the world. Millions who would have to admit in embarrassment that they could not name the chief justice of the United States Supreme Court were totally familiar with Judge Ito, who he was, what he looked like, the sound of his voice. Almost nobody in California could name the *state's* chief justice—two levels up from Judge Ito.

Court TV, a cable channel entirely devoted to trials, made its debut on July 1, 1991. It was a sign of how much justice had become part of the entertainment business. In one sense, this was nothing new. In the early nineteenth century, in rural counties, where people were starved for amusement, court days were one source of entertainment. Beginning in the late nineteenth century, "yellow journalism" dished out an enormous amount of coverage of sensational trials, for the benefit of the mass public. Now Court TV gave them the real thing. Even more remarkable was the proliferation in the 1990s of "judge" shows: Judge Wapner, Judge Judy, Judge Brown, and others. *Fortune* magazine reported in May 1999 that the "hottest show" on TV was *Judge Judy,* starring a former family court judge named Judith Sheindlin, "a diminutive, abrasive Jewish grandmother from Manhattan," the "little judge who kicked Oprah's butt" that is, got an audience even larger than Oprah Winfrey's.[61]

These TV judges are not real judges, and they work in studios, not real courtrooms. But they look like judges, they dress like judges, and they act (more or less) like the audience thinks judges act. The cases in front of them come out of real disputes. The litigants, who have the kinds of complaints usually destined for small-claims court, are either so foolish, or so greedy for their fifteen minutes of fame, that they willingly wash their dirty linen in public and let a virtual judge decide their cases. Naturally, in these TV courtrooms, soft words, decorum, measured and balanced decisions, would simply not do: the judges harangue, quip, shout, and posture, the better to pander to the millions who are watching the show. The audience, in the studio and out, is vastly amused by the parade of litigants: quarrelsome neighbors, pitiful shuffling losers, dim-witted ex-boyfriends and deadbeat dads; a whole menagerie of people who have lost sight of the line between entertainment and private life, between real life and the life on movies and TV. Perhaps the whole society has.[62]

Judges and Litigants

Since the middle of the nineteenth century, judges in most states have been elected, the same as governors and mayors—usually from the supreme court down to the lowliest traffic court. There have been a few exceptions (Massachusetts is one). The other big exception is the federal judiciary; under the constitutional scheme, federal judges are appointed, and for life. They sit on the bench until they die or resign.

Many foreigners find it weird that Americans elect their judges. In general, however, Americans have a kind of elective mania; voters choose prosecutors, university trustees, trustees of sewer districts, and the like. But electing judges is anomalous. Judges are not supposed to be politicians. They are supposed to be neutral, impartial professionals. A report of the Arkansas Judiciary Commission in 1965 put it this way: "No one would think of popular election of doctors, architects, airplane pilots, locomotive engineers, or other professional people." The commission added that political campaigns, which include "television shows, newspaper ads, 'glad-handing,' 'back slapping,' 'baby kissing,' shopping center openings," and so on, tend to "cheapen the judicial position . . . and destroy traditional respect for the bench." Electioneering discouraged honorable men from running for judicial office; in the Arkansas survey of 1965, about half the lawyers who responded admitted they had at least "considered" becoming a judge; but though only a third would be willing to run under the elective system, 61 percent could imagine becoming a judge under a different sort of scheme, one that avoided the worst elements of the election process.[63]

For all its irrationality, the American system did recognize a fundamental fact: judges have power, and exercise power; and they do it in ways that have political meaning. How else, then, could you control your judges, except by electing them? Hence the elective system swept the country in the nineteenth century. Not without dissenting voices: and these voices became louder toward the end of the century, especially as evidence emerged about corrupt city judges, creations of big-city machines.

This somewhat elite reaction against the elective judiciary became even stronger in the twentieth century. Concretely, a number of states adopted the so-called Missouri plan. Under this scheme, the governor appoints judges. He does not have a free hand in his selections, however. A commission made up of citizens and lawyers draws up a list of names. The governor must choose from this list. The judge then serves until the next election; at that point, the judge runs for reelection on his or her record. That is, the judge does not run against anybody; the public simply votes yes or no. Because you cannot fight somebody with nobody, sitting judges under the Missouri plan rarely lose. Only a strong and dedicated opposition can even try to topple a sitting judge. But it does sometimes happen—at least it did in the late twentieth century. The voters got rid of Rose Bird, chief justice of the California Supreme Court, in 1987; she dragged two other justices down with her.

In other states, judges run for election in the usual way, often with party labels attached to them. Ordinarily, judicial elections are dull, low-key affairs. In New York between 1916 and 1973 no real contest ever took place in elections for the chief judge of the Court of Appeals. Candidates were "anointed in amiable cross-endorsements by Republicans and Democrats."[64] But in 1973 Jacob Fuchsberg ran against Charles Breitel, a sitting judge. Fuchsberg lost; but he tried again in 1974, and won a seat on the court as an associate justice. These were bitter, tough campaigns; and they generated a fair amount of publicity. Some observers think they see signs that by the end of the century, judges in state courts had become somewhat more vulnerable politically than before. The process does seem somewhat more tart and more partisan. Yet figures show that most judges still sail through without much trouble. In 4,588 "retention" elections between 1964 and 1999, only fifty-two judges lost out. And in 1998 not a single judge lost a job because the voters said no.[65]

Federal judges are appointed, and they serve for life; yet the appointment process is intensely political—perhaps more so than in the states. Sheldon Goldman studied the appointment strategy of presidents from Franklin D. Roosevelt on. He sees three basic strategies—or, as he puts it, three "agendas"—at work: a policy agenda, a partisan agenda, and a personal agenda. Some judges, in other words, are appointed in order to advance policy (pro–New Deal, for example; or prolabor); others "to shore up political support for the president or for the party" (for example, elevating a chum of some powerful senator, or appointing an Asian-American to woo that constituency); still others simply as a matter of "personal patronage" (that is, rewarding a crony of the president).[66]

Roosevelt took great personal interest in appointments. His papers document how much he cared about the process, and how much he intervened in it. He made appointments to fit all three agendas. Harry Truman, his successor, treated the process mostly as a patronage matter. Under Truman the American Bar Association began to play a role in the selection game. In 1946 the ABA set up a Standing Committee on Federal Judiciary, which began vetting appointments to the courts. President Eisenhower was elected in 1952 after twenty years of Democratic dominance; naturally enough, he seized the opportunity to appoint Republicans to the bench. Under Eisenhower, the ABA role was strengthened; the ABA gave "ratings" to judges—that is, labeled them as qualified or unqualified—and this became accepted practice, and influential practice; it remained so for the rest of the century. Indeed, when John F. Kennedy became president, after Eisenhower, he expressly agreed to let the ABA continue its role.[67]

Appointments, over time, were recognized more and more as politically significant. After cases like *Brown* and *Roe v. Wade*, there was more awareness of how much difference a judge could make. The business of appointments moved up on the agenda of presidents. This had some concrete results. For example, presidents virtually stopped appointing older men and women. Such appointees would be likely to sit on the bench for a fairly short time; they were not much use to a president who wanted to button down his policies until the end of time.

The higher state courts heard a more varied mix of cases than the federal courts did. The mix changed over time. In the course of the twentieth century, these courts heard more criminal and constitutional cases. A study of the decisions of sixteen state supreme courts found that public-law cases, which accounted for 13 percent of all cases in 1905–1935, comprised 19 percent in 1940–1970; criminal cases rose from 11 percent to 18 percent; in some states, the increases were even more dramatic: almost a third of the cases in Illinois in the later period were criminal cases, more than a quarter in California. Tort cases were another growth area. The fields that lost ground were, generally speaking, real estate and general business law: debt and contract cases, 29 percent in 1905–1935, were 15 percent in 1940–1970.[68]

As the center of gravity shifted (relatively speaking) from the states to the federal system, the caseload of the federal courts increased drastically. In the year that ended June 30, 1940, 34,734 civil cases were filed in the federal district courts; in fiscal year 1961 the figure had risen to 58,293; in the 1970s it passed 100,000; and in 1992 the figure was 230,509. The criminal caseload grew much more slowly: from 33,401 in 1939–1940 to 47,123 in 1992—more slowly, indeed, than population growth.[69] At the end of the twentieth century it was still true that the vast majority of cases began and ended in state courts; but many of the biggest and most significant cases were to be found on the federal docket.

The United States Supreme Court sits alone at the top of the federal pyramid. If the twentieth-century revolution in communications created the celebrity president, and shrank (relatively speaking) the power of governors and local satraps, the same was true in the court system. What the Supreme Court of the United States does is news; what the Supreme Court of Wyoming does is small potatoes; it may not even make much of a splash in Wyoming; elsewhere it will pass without a ripple.

The Supreme Court itself was transformed in many ways in the twentieth century. The Judiciary Act of 1925 was an important landmark, as we have seen. It gave the Court almost total power over its docket. It allowed the Court to "deny cert" to all but a few, monumental cases (or at least cases the Court defined as monumental). But the supply of litigants who would like the Supreme Court to hear their cases keeps growing. Most of these supplicants are doomed to disappointment. Four hundred or so cases were filed with the court in 1900; in 1989 there were 4,895. The Court takes only a handful of these. In the 1968 term the Court issued 120 written opinions and 104 short *per curiam* opinions, and denied *certiorari* no fewer than 2,586 times.[70] In recent decades the Court has usually handed down between 100 and 150 cases with written opinions each year.[71] In the late 1990s, for somewhat mysterious reasons, the number slid downward, to an average of about seventy-five.

At the beginning of the century, the Court still decided a good many ordinary cases—tort and contract cases coming out of diversity lawsuits; or appeals from territorial courts; or simple maritime cases. As the Court became more and more engrossed with constitutional questions and heavy federal matters, these cases disappeared. A few survived the 1925 watershed. In the *Wilson* case (1928), an accident on the high seas was the issue. The accident took place twelve miles off the shore of California, "sky clear, sea smooth and uninterrupted." The *Newport,* an "iron passenger steamer" of immense size, had plowed into the little *Svea,* a "wooden lumber steam schooner." The Court found the *Newport* totally liable: "Big vessels may not insolently disregard smaller ones; super size gives no right to domineer."[72] Life does not actually work that way; but in law, in this case, it did.

But soon the Court had no time for these "ordinary" cases. The decision in *Erie Railroad v. Tompkins* told federal courts to follow state law in diversity cases. The Supreme Court no longer ever takes a diversity appeal. There was also a shift in the Court's understanding of its role—its concept of what mattered, what needed its attention. Federal tax cases, which were 18 percent of the docket in 1933–1937, had shrunk to 3 percent in 1983–1987. Cases on federal regulation rose during the New Deal period, then fell in the 1960s; civil liberties cases rose in the civil rights era, and in the 1980s had a major position in the workload of the court.[73] The Warren Court was eager to reform the criminal justice system; the Rehnquist Court was not.

The So-Called Litigation Explosion

Had Americans become, in the twentieth century, incurably litigious? Particularly in the period after the Second World War there was a lot of talk about a "litigation explosion." One article in the 1980s claimed that "everybody is suing everybody" and spoke of an "age of litigation."[74] But how real was this "explosion?" An "explosion" would mean that litigation rates were skyrocketing far faster than the population. Yet facts and figures from longitudinal court studies showed little solid evidence of any such trend, as late as the early 1980s.[75] There is some evidence, to be sure, of an increase in litigation rates in the last twenty years of the century. In any event, certain kinds of cases had indeed increased rapidly in the latter half of the century; others, however, were in decline. Changes in the law can affect litigation—this is obvious. Title insurance and other factors make cases about who owns land less common. Federal deposit insurance and other measures that stabilize money and banking have all but eliminated whole classes of cases that once clogged the courts.

Federal litigation rates, to be sure, have risen dramatically in the course of the century. Civil rights laws give people chances to litigate questions they could not have gone to court with before. In general, the question is not how many cases but what *kinds* of cases. Big tort cases can make big trouble. A few huge environmental cases can throw whole industries into a stew. At bottom, nobody really cares, or should care, about the sheer numbers: what people care about is which oxen are getting gored. The outcry about a "litigation explosion" drowns out the voices that express the opposite complaint: the system is too expensive, too formal, too biased to serve the interests of ordinary people. As Gerry Spence, a trial lawyer, put it, justice is "like caviar—rotten, fishy, and usually only the rich can afford it."[76] This idea spurred the creation of a legal services component in Lyndon Johnson's War on Poverty, as we have seen. Businesspeople had their own litany of complaints; and these fueled the movement for alternative dispute resolution, or ADR, which was widely discussed in the last quarter of the century, and which inspired a number of reforms and experiments in this or that court system.

Law Schools and Admission to the Bar

By midcentury, to all intents and purposes, apprenticeship was dead; law school was the only practical way to become a lawyer. In February 1948 Connecticut made it official: only law school graduates could be admitted to the bar. The decree was hardly necessary: in New Haven County, apparently, only eight people in a quarter-century had applied to take the bar after serving an apprenticeship. Six of them failed.[77] A few states still allowed this practice at the end of the century. One of these was California. If you studied "diligently and in good faith" for at least four years in a law office "under the personal supervision of a member of The State Bar of California," or in the "chambers and under the personal supervision of a judge of a court of record of this State," you were allowed to take the bar without other schooling in the law. Not many people take advantage of this option. In July 1997 the California bar exam was administered to 7,716 hopefuls; only nine had no law school training. Seven of the nine were repeaters. They had failed the bar at least once before. All seven of these failed again. One lonely person without law school passed the bar. Four bar applicants in February 1998 had an apprenticeship background; all four were repeaters, and all four flunked the exam.[78]

All American law schools, unlike those in most countries, were graduate schools. This had not always been the case. In the twentieth century, law schools steadily raised their standards. By 1932 seventeen states demanded two years of prelegal college training; by 1938 all but eight states had this requirement.[79] Some of the tonier and would-be-tonier law schools required a college degree before admission: in the 1920s, this included Harvard, Pennsylvania, Pittsburgh, and Stanford. The faculty at Stanford decided in 1924 that the "time had come to place the school upon a purely graduate basis." The "growing complexity of the law" demanded students who were "well grounded" in a general education. The Board of Trustees agreed, and approved the new requirement on June 27, 1924.[80] In 1935 George Washington University joined the ranks of schools requiring a B.A., explaining that the "action was taken to give the school a place among other law schools which the prestige of the University requires." Not that this was a wholly selfish act: "The bar of the future" required lawyers with an educated background. Under pressure from the ABA and the AALS, three years of college became the standard in the 1950s; and in the 1960s, four years of college.[81]

During the Second World War many law schools almost went out of business. Harvard, which had enrolled 1,250 men in September 1941, had a mere 58 in the summer of 1944. Many faculty members, too (including James Landis, the dean) had gone to serve in the armed forces, or in government.[82] When the war ended, there was a backlog of demand for legal education; and the government had sacks of money for veterans, which they could use to go to school. The GI Bill of Rights was as revolutionary for legal education as for higher education in general. The gates of an expensive school like Harvard were no longer closed to bright young men without money or connections (it was still closed to women). The GI Bill provided tuition, book money, and a stipend. It was a fantastic equalizer.

Before this, class, money, and background had acted as (informal) filters for the elite law schools. No more. Veterans made up 93 percent of the Harvard class of 1947. Their average age was twenty-six or twenty-seven; 40 percent of them were married. This was a radically different kind of student body. The elite law schools like Harvard and Yale now also faced an "overwhelming task of selection"; 931 people applied for about 150 spaces, in Yale's entering class of fall 1949.[83] Representatives of "several of the leading law schools" approached the Educational Testing Service and asked for help; the result was the Law School Admission Test (LSAT).[84] It later became standard at virtually all law schools. They used this test, together with undergraduate grades, as a way to pick the right people from the mass of applicants.

The LSAT has terrorized thousands and thousands of young people; it has fed the mouths of the companies that sell preparation courses. A low LSAT score is death to any hope of law school; and anything but a very high score keeps you out of the top-ranked schools. Disappointment on the LSAT has forced countless young people to settle for schools with less prestige and marketing power than they had hoped for. There have been endless debates about the LSAT: is it testing anything real? Of course, the LSAT tests *something*; people who do very poorly are not likely to succeed in law school. But is the test culturally biased? Does it favor people with good backgrounds, and who can afford the expensive cram courses?

Probably. But the LSAT is *less* biased than the system it replaced. It also helped get rid of another curse of the law schools: a high flunk-out rate. Thirty-seven percent of the Harvard Law School class failed their exams in June 1926. Professor Edward Warren of Harvard—the notorious "Bull" Warren—according to a famous and often-repeated story, used to tell the entering class, "Look to the right of you. Look to the left of you. One of the three of you will be gone within a year."[85]

This gloomy prediction was not confined to Harvard. Young Gerry Spence entered the University of Wyoming—"perhaps the most remote, smallest, least prestigious of all university law schools"—in 1949. On the first day of school in September, the dean addressed the "thirty-five gawking, grimacing . . . lip-chewing types" of the freshman class. "Look around you," he bellowed. "When the first quarter is over . . . half your fellow students [will] have mysteriously disappeared."[86] Evelyn Williams entered the night program of St. Johns University Law School in Brooklyn, at the age of twenty-nine, in the early 1950s. Her entering class of 500 "was prepared at orientation for failure, and the school delivered on its promise." Only 154 of her class graduated—and she was one of only two blacks.[87] But in 1964–1965, long into the LSAT period, exactly four people failed at Harvard, out of a class of 550.

The LSAT undoubtedly accounts for much of the difference.[88] The schools simply exclude students who are doomed to fail. Today, at the most selective law schools, it is almost impossible to flunk out. Nothing short of a nervous breakdown will do the trick. In a typical year at Harvard, the rate of attrition for academic reasons is zero. And at the University of Wyoming Law School, which has come a long way since Spence entered its halls—it has a new building, and a bright young faculty—the first-year attrition rate is about 10 percent. At most one or two of these students drop out for "academic" rather than personal or emotional reasons.[89]

The years after the Second World War broke the prestige monopoly of the great eastern law schools. Harvard and Yale still had awesome reputations, but they had to share some of their cachet with other Ivy League law schools, and with such upstarts as the University of Chicago, Stanford, and Boalt Hall (University of California, Berkeley). The demand for legal education led to the founding of new law schools; some old ones grew in size. And the demand for lawyers meant that hungry firms often had to settle for bright students from lesser brand-name schools.

Nonetheless, legal education remained extremely hierarchical. A student did not choose Yale or Chicago because he was eager to study under this or that professor.[90] He chose the "best" school he could get into because it was the best ticket to a high-class, high-paying job. Students thus were almost obsessed with reputation, position, ranking. In 1990 *U.S. News and World Report* began to list and rank law schools. That year, it did this for the top twenty-five. Later, the magazine began to rank all law schools. The top fifty are ranked in order; the rest are consigned to three tiers; within the tiers, schools are listed alphabetically. A low ranking is a terrible blow to a school.[91] It affects the school's ability to attract students—and faculty. It disheartens the alumni. And it might just possibly be unfair.

Harvard Law School has been, and still is, a fertile manufacturer of law professors. At one time, one out of every four law teachers had a Harvard degree in his pocket; in 1975–1976, however, Harvard's share was 14 percent, and 13 percent in 1990. Yale—a much smaller school—had become a strong competitor:

7 percent in 1975–1976, and 8 percent in 1990. No other school produced as many as 5 percent of the law professors; but the top twenty schools, taken together, produced 60 percent of all the law professors in the country.[92]

The professoriate, like the bar in general, had become much more diverse. Before the 1930s Jewish professors were rare in legal education; anti-Semitism was rampant. Felix Frankfurter at Harvard was one of the rare exceptions. He became a professor at the Harvard Law School in 1919; the letter asking him to join the faculty was a shock: "If I had received a letter from an Indian princess asking me to marry her, I wouldn't have been more surprised."[93] But when the law school tried to offer a job to another Jewish candidate, Nathan Margold, in 1928, the administration vetoed the idea.[94] Harry Shulman was hired at Yale in the early 1930s; but when he became a serious candidate for the deanship, Arthur Corbin, the grand old man of the faculty, wrote that it was "unwise to elect as dean any one of the Jewish race."[95] After Hitler came to power in 1933, German legal scholars who were Jewish or had some other blemish were forced into exile. Many of them came to the United States. They had an impact on legal education—in particular, they dominated the study of comparative law. In the law schools anti-Semitism seemed largely to have disappeared by 1960. The elite schools began to recruit many Jewish professors; in some of these schools, they came to represent one-third to one-half of the total faculty. And the taboo against Jewish deans has long since been discarded.

The legal academy was slower in welcoming women and minorities to the faculty. As late as 1975–1976 the makeup of the law professoriate was 93 percent male and 96 percent white.[96] Since then, the number of women teachers has grown steadily. In the 1970s nearly 19 percent of the new hires were women. In the 1980s this percentage rose to 35 percent.[97] Women began to appear as deans as well—Soia Mentschikoff, who became dean of the University of Miami Law School in 1974, may have been the first. Since then there have been quite a few others. Barbara Black became dean of the Columbia Law School in 1986 and served for five years. Herma Hill Kay became the dean of Berkeley's law school in 1992; Kathleen Sullivan became dean at Stanford in 1999.

Minorities, however, continued to be sparse in law schools, except in schools like Howard, which were historically black. Richard Chused, who studied the professoriate in the 1980s, found tokenism alive and well. In 1980–1981, black faculty made up 2.8 percent of the professoriate in "majority" law schools (that is, those that were not historically black); this rose to 3.7 percent in

1986–1987. But one-third of all law schools had no black faculty members; and another third had exactly one each. Hispanics were even rarer. There were only a dozen tenured Hispanics in these "white" institutions in 1986–1987.[98] The numbers improved somewhat afterward. There were eight hundred or so faculty members in 1999 who defined themselves as "minority," although this included Asians as well as blacks, Hispanics, and Native Americans.

The actual number of law students, as one might expect, dipped somewhat during the Depression; in 1929–1930, there were something over 46,000 students in law schools of all sorts; in 1937 there were only 39,255.[99] The numbers began to grow in the postwar years. In 1950–1951 there were 39,626 students (three-quarters of them day students) in accredited law schools and another 8,000 or so in unaccredited schools.[100] This was, in part, a bulge caused by returning veterans, with money from the G.I. Bill, as we have seen. Then the numbers fell again, only to begin rising dramatically in the 1960s. In 1965 there were 65,000 law students, in 1970, no fewer than 86,000; and all but some 4,000 of these were students in "A.B.A. approved schools."[101]

The number of law schools also increased in the postwar period. The University of California started a new law school in Los Angeles in 1949; U.C. Davis opened its doors in 1965. George Mason University Law School, in Virginia, went into business in 1979. In 1971 the legislature of Hawaii decreed that "there shall be a school of law in Hawaii," and so there was; it began operations in 1973. Vermont had been without the blessings of a law school until 1972, when the Vermont Law School came into existence. Nevada, one of the few state holdouts, finally acquired a law school of its own: the William S. Boyd School of Law, affiliated with the University of Nevada at Las Vegas; it was officially open for business at the end of the century. Existing law schools grew in size as well; and teaching law was a growth industry. A directory published in 1922, listing teachers who taught at schools affiliated with the Association of American Law Schools, ran to 45 pages or so and listed perhaps 500 teachers, more or less (many of them part-timers).[102] The listings in the directory for 1998–1999 ran to more than 800 pages of smaller type; it listed 8,719 full-time faculty members at 182 law schools.[103]

By 1999 there was at least one law school in every single state, with the exception of Alaska. Most states had more than one. California, the biggest state, was the champion, with about seventy law schools. It had nineteen ABA-accredited schools; twenty schools that were "California-accredited";

seventeen nonaccredited schools, and twelve correspondence schools, includ-ing the world's first and only online law school.[104]

After law school, the young would-be lawyer still had to take the bar. This usually meant a cram course; it was folly to rely on what you learned in law school. At the end of the century, Wisconsin was the only exception: it still had the so-called diploma privilege. Graduates of the University of Wisconsin, or of Marquette Law School in Milwaukee—these were the only two law schools in the state—were automatically members of the bar. Everyone else and every-where else there was a bar examination to conquer. Some were more of a barrier than others. In 1997–1998 law graduates in New Mexico and Utah taking the bar for the first time passed at a 93 percent rate; the lowest percentage was in Louisiana, with 61 percent.[105]

There is an almost numbing sameness about the law schools. Of course some schools, like Harvard, are very rich; some are poor. Some are extremely selective, like Yale; some schools take, well, almost everybody who applies. One big difference is cost. There are public law schools that are cheap, and private law schools that are expensive. A private legal education cost, on average, $2,500 a year in 1957; public (in-state) education cost $780; by 1994 the private schools cost $19,000, and even public education carried a $6,000 price tag.[106] And the costs continued to rise—at public law schools, too. Students typically began their legal careers with a big burden of debt.

There are differences in curricula among schools, to be sure; but the first-year course of training is suspiciously similar all over the country. It has changed very little over the years. Every law student in the country takes courses in contracts, torts, property, and civil procedure. Most take criminal law and constitutional law as well. And almost all have some kind of course or training in research and writing.

What do the students actually learn in these courses? Of course, they learn "law"—they learn about the rules, about doctrine, and how to manipulate it; and they also learn to "think like a lawyer" (whatever that means). In some schools, they can get clinical training—working either with real clients (usually poor people), or with virtual clients. Law students try to get summer intern-ships with law firms. This practice began in the 1970s, apparently, and has now become standard. Firms have "come to depend on their internship programs to fill their needs for new associates."[107] Almost from day one, many law students worry about getting a job. The lucky or talented ones at New York University or Columbia or Harvard have nothing much to worry about; 950 firms recruited at the Harvard Law School in the late 1980s. At the top schools, nobody goes without a job. These schools send their students to work for big law firms on Wall Street or in Washington, or for the top firms in other cities. Many of these students clerk for judges in their first year out—an astonishing 50 percent of the Yale graduating class in the late 1980s. This was, however, quite exceptional. The figure for Harvard was 22 percent, for Michigan 9 percent, for Cornell 7 percent.[108]

At the other schools there is more of a scramble—and a panic—over jobs. There have been good times and bad times. Few of the graduates who do not have connections, and who are not "stars" in the school (law review editors, students with top grades) can aspire to Wall Street. Not much is known, however, about the ultimate career paths of young lawyers. Twenty years out, the Stanford graduates of 1980 (or those for whom there were data) were still mostly in private practice (some 60 percent); another quarter worked for corporations as lawyers or managers; a small number (6 percent) were in government or public service. The class of 1990 had a somewhat different profile some nine years out—more government and public service (17 percent), more law teachers (12 percent); only half were in private practice with firms or on their own.[109]

Legal Thought, and Thoughts (and Research) About Law

Throughout most of the century, legal scholarship was dry and jejune, at least by modern standards. Careful analysis of legal doctrine was the heart of legal scholarship. In the legal academy, the professors who wrote the big treatises had big reputations to match. These treatises were huge, ponderous tomes, encyclopedic, comprehensive, presumably useful to the profession; but on the whole utterly devoid of anything that could be called literary merit. They were, however, masterpieces of synthesis. They tied together vast masses of cases, giving them some kind of coherence, real or imaginary.

Among the most famous were the elephantine works of Samuel Williston of Harvard, on the law of contracts, and his great rival, Arthur Corbin of Yale; or Austin Wakeman Scott of Harvard, on the law of trusts; or William Prosser on torts. John Henry Wigmore's huge treatise on the law of evidence stands out because, unlike almost all the others, it had a personal, individual, quirky, and distinctive style; it was peppered with Wigmore's views on every aspect of the subject.

Another project, dominated by the treatise writers, was the heroic (and probably foolish) attempt to "restate" the common law. This was the goal of the American Law Institute, founded in 1923. The common law was confusing, complex, uncertain. Just as the great treatises attempted to untangle the messy sprawl of common-law case law, spread across all those years and all those states, so the restatements aimed to clarify and enlighten, by reducing the jumbled chaos to clear, consistent, coherent statements of rules and doctrines and standards.[110] The *Restatement of the Law of Contracts* saw the light of day in 1932; the *Restatement of Agency* in 1933. Restatements of torts, conflict of laws, and trusts soon followed. The hope was that courts would cite the restatements, adopt its principles, and make the common law more workable and uniform. But the draftsmen ignored, for the most part, the social and economic meaning of the working common law. They made it more logical and orderly; but at the cost of ripping out the living, pulsing heart of the system. Yet the restatements (and they are still alive, still in the process of revision) engaged the energy of whole platoons of lawyers and law professors. And they are, indeed, frequently cited by the courts, though whether they influence the progress of the law is much harder to prove.

The treatise writers were active in the restatement business, and they were also editors of major casebooks: Williston, Corbin, Prosser, Scott. Many other professors were known mainly for casebooks. It says something about a field (and something not particularly complimentary) that a professor could earn prestige and fame by putting together teaching materials—and (often enough) doing very little else. In the 1980s and 1990s, the scope of legal scholarship broadened—there were law professors who actually wrote real books. But the reign of the casebook is by no means over. For one thing, leading casebooks make money, sometimes lots of it. And the casebooks are less narrow than in the past. Langdell's original casebook (in 1870) was exactly that: a casebook. It had absolutely nothing else within its covers. Already in the 1930s a few pioneer casebooks were more expansive. Albert C. Jacobs of Columbia published *Cases and Materials on Domestic Relations* in 1933. It was generously peppered with statutes, and spiced with history and sociology. The twelve-page introduction even included two pages on "The Contemporary Family of Soviet Russia."

Another iconoclastic casebook (immensely long) was *Property, Wealth, Land: Allocation, Planning, and Development* (1948), edited by Myres McDougal of Yale and David Haber.

Generally speaking, the casebooks of the 1990s included a lot more than cases. Typically, they bristled with notes and questions; they sometimes included excerpts from law review articles and, occasionally, historical, philosophical, economic, or sociological material. Thus the sixth edition of *Tort Law and Alternatives: Cases and Materials* (1996), edited by Marc A. Franklin and Robert L. Rabin, presented the students with short excerpts from the writings of Richard Posner, Guido Calabresi, Richard Epstein, and Oliver Wendell Holmes, Jr., among others. Other casebooks veered even farther from Langdell's austere norm. The fourth edition of *Employment Law* (1998), edited by Mark A. Rothstein and Lance Liebman, printed an excerpt from an encyclical of Pope John Paul II on human work, on page 4 of the casebook; on page 7 there was an excerpt from Studs Terkel's book *Working*. An outstanding exception to the usual run of casebooks was the two-volume set *Contracts: Law in Action*, which was first published in 1992 by a team led by Stewart Macaulay at the University of Wisconsin, rich in attention to the context and social meaning of its subject. Still, to be honest, the bulk of the material in almost all casebooks remained highly traditional; and the students probably do little more than skim the "other stuff." Why pay much attention to it, if it isn't really "law"? Why read it if there is no chance it will be on the exam?

American Legal Thought

Philosophy of law was never a strong point among American jurists. The twentieth century did produce its share of famous names; at the end of the century, Ronald Dworkin was perhaps the best known of the living philosophers, especially for his 1977 book, *Taking Rights Seriously*. Overall, Roscoe Pound (1870–1964) was probably the most prolific and celebrated figure in American jurisprudence; he was also an educator, dean of the Harvard Law School for many years, and a commanding figure in the academy. Pound was born in Kansas, tutored at home by his mother, then trained at the University of Nebraska, where he studied botany. His dissertation was on "The Phytogeography of Nebraska," an exhaustive study of fungus in his home state. For a while, Pound vacillated between fungus and law. In between botanical stints, Pound had gone to Harvard Law School for a year. Back in Nebraska, he worked with his father, and was admitted to the Nebraska bar. He became a commissioner of the Supreme Court of Nebraska—a kind of temporary judge—then dean of the University of Nebraska Law School (1903). Almost immediately, he began furiously writing. From Nebraska, he went to Northwestern (1907), then to the University of Chicago, then (1910) to Harvard, where he stayed put until he retired. In 1916 he became dean, and he was dean for twenty years.

Pound's early writings were openly reformist. He criticized, early in the twentieth century, the formalist decisions of the *Lochner* era. In a famous speech in 1906, "Causes of Popular Dissatisfaction with the Administration of Justice," Pound decried the "mechanical operation of legal rules."[111] Pound's remedy, in later writings, came to be called "sociological jurisprudence," though there was precious little in it that could be called sociology. At Harvard, Pound had a mixed record as dean: he defended academic freedom, and recruited a forward-looking faculty. But he became more conservative with the passing of the years. He was a reformer, but basically only on the technical side: for Pound, the defects in law were defects of craft and failures of imagination. That judges might be politically biased and the rules skewed never seemed to occur to him.

Pound is also famous as the antirealist—as a sharp critic of the legal realist movement, which burst on the scene in the 1920s.[112] It is not easy to say what legal realism consisted of; much easier to say what it was not. It was not formalist, and it rejected the cold, deductive style of C. C. Langdell. The "realists" were a variegated bunch. What they had in common was the idea that the law needed fixing; it was out of step with reality—limping behind society, in a changing world. Legal realism was of a piece, perhaps, with other strands of American social thought: skeptical, inclined to look for social explanations for social situations, critical of old orthodoxies.[113]

Beyond this, the realists fell into a number of categories. Some of them believed in empirical research—in trying to discover how law actually functioned—and a few actually did some of this research. Most of them were "rule-skeptics"—that is, they doubted that judges decided cases on the basis of formal legal reasoning. They sneered at Langdell's idea of "legal science." Legal logic explaincd very little, they thought. Far more subtle factors were at work: economic factors, prejudices and personalities of judges, political winds and storms, general culture.

In 1930 Jerome Frank (1889–1957), a New York lawyer with the firm of

Chadbourne, Stanchfield, and Levy, who specialized in the dreary business of corporate reorganization, published *Law and the Modern Mind*. Frank wrote the book, in part, on the commuter train between New York and his home in Croton-on-Hudson. The book made quite a splash; it "catapulted Frank from the obscurity of corporate law to the forefront of . . . legal realism."[114] Frank later became a New Deal lawyer, chairman of the Securities and Exchange Commission, and, from 1941 on, a judge on the U.S. Court of Appeals, Second Circuit.

Frank was an insomniac, a classic bookworm, and a prodigious writer. *Law and the Modern Mind* is still the most famous, or notorious, of his works. It was a strange book: orthodox legal realism under the hypnotic influence of Sigmund Freud. Frank attacked legal formalism—the myth that law consisted of known rules that can be mechanically implied, the "illusion or dogma," as he put it, "of legal certainty." The law, said Frank, "is not a machine and the judges are not machine-tenders. There never was and there never will be a body of fixed and predetermined rules alike for all." Rules do not decide cases; they are only "the formal clothes" in which the judge "dresses up his thoughts." Legal certainty, in other words, was a myth. But people want myths, Frank thought. They want to believe in a comfortable, controllable world, just as they wanted to believe their daddies when they were very young. The law "is a near substitute for that father, a belief in whose infallibility is essential to the very life of the child."[115]

Thurman Arnold (1891–1969) was another leading realist. Arnold, born in Wyoming, had a long and distinguished career—lawyer, law teacher, "trustbuster" in Washington during the New Deal; judge of the United States Court of Appeals for the District of Columbia (1943–1945); founder and partner of the Washington firm of Arnold, Fortas, and Porter. Arnold was a prolific writer, best known for *The Symbols of Government* (1935) and *The Folklore of Capitalism* (1937). In mordant, sarcastic prose, Arnold flailed away at the "myths," "creeds," "superstitions," and "folklore" that prevailed (he thought) in law, government, and economic life. These beliefs, however, were a "unifying force," as "mysterious as the law of gravitation." Arnold had little patience with formal legal doctrine; he described the members of the American Law Institute (busy "restating" the law) as "a group of men sitting around and doing responsive readings of the law." The "language of the Constitution," he said, "is immaterial since it represents current myths and folklore rather than rules."[116]

A third leading legal realist, and one of the most fascinating thinker-writers of the twentieth century legal academy, was Karl N. Llewellyn (1893–1962). A colleague described him as an "extraordinary piece of radio-active material abroad in the Law School world."[117] Llewellyn was born in Seattle and graduated from the Yale Law School. He studied in Germany, wrote a book in German, fought on the side of Germany in the First World War (and was awarded the Iron Cross); he was infected with a Teutonic virus that affected his writing style (for the worse) and which he never quite got rid of. He was a man of extraordinary breadth and intelligence, an amateur poet (and not half bad), a much-married man, a heavy drinker (perhaps an alcoholic), and a distinguished professor of law, mostly at Columbia, then in his later years at the University of Chicago.

Llewellyn wrote some of the key essays that helped to define legal realism. For Llewellyn, the realists (not a school, he insisted, but a "movement" of individuals), agreed on a few core ideas: among them, that law was a "means to social ends and not . . . an end in itself"; a "distrust" of "traditional legal rules and concepts," as a description of what the system actually does; and an "insistence on evaluation of any part of law in terms of its effects."[118] The key, perhaps, was the revolt against formalism: the notion that rules were autonomous, independent of their social meaning; and that they actually decided concrete cases. Llewellyn also wrote *The Bramble Bush* (1930), a perky, savvy introduction to law for law students. He collaborated with an anthropologist, E. Adamson Hoebel, on *The Cheyenne Way* (1941), a pioneering study of a non-Western legal system; and, as we have seen, he was one of the leading figures behind the Uniform Commercial Code.

The legal realist movement did not in and of itself have any overt political bias. But many of the realists were at least slightly left of center. Many of them became New Dealers. As Barbara Fried has pointed out, behind the "methodological critique of formalism," there was in fact a "substantive agenda." The realists were eager to "debunk" the myth of a "freestanding, self-regulating market." They wanted to show how the market was in fact "ineluctably constituted by the legal regime in which it operated."[119] Formalism, after all, served as a cover, a screen, a defense for decisions that were antiprogressive at the core, just as "strict constructionism" today is a code phrase for conservative aims. Those who worked to pierce the veil of formalism did so in the hope that courts could be enlisted in the cause of progressive reforms; or, at worst, neutralized and rendered harmless.

In an important sense, legal realism ended up defeating its enemy almost totally. If, today, you told a group of law professors (or lawyers, for that matter) that you thought politics had an important influence on the legal system; that rules were more malleable and less decisive than they appeared; that you believed law is not and can never be totally neutral, and other sentiments along these lines, they might very well yawn and agree. (Many shrewd lawyers and jurists of the nineteenth century would also have signed on to these bland general sentiments.) What they *do* with this banality is another question. As far as scholarship is concerned, most of what passes for legal "research," even after the realists swept through the academy, is as antediluvian as ever. There are, however, more (and more varied) exceptions.

Legal realism was a product of the 1920s and 1930s. The so-called legal process school rode high in the 1950s; its mother church was Harvard. In a way, this "school" tried to snake its way through a narrow defile between two great peaks: legal realism on the one side, formalism on the other. The legal process scholars were quite willing to admit that formalism was dead dry bones. But they shrank back in horror from the ultimate message of the realists (as they read it): that law was only politics or economics or personal whim or whatever. Men of the process school, like Lon Fuller, thought that they had found the elusive middle ground—a "morality of process" which would be "independent of results."[120] Judges did have power; that was conceded. But they also had a duty to restrain themselves. The question one ought to ask was this: what was the best institutional way to handle any particular issue? Was the legislature, the court, or an administrative body most appropriate? Or should the issue be left to "private ordering"? If you answered such questions correctly, you would have a legal order that was rational, if not always just. If an issue was not properly one for courts to decide, then courts had no business interfering in what was work for Congress, or the president, or city hall.

Most law professors of the postwar period were moderate to mildly left of center: New Deal Democrats, by and large. They found their world soon under attack, both from the Left and from the Right. The left attack, critical legal studies, burst on the scene like a rocket, most notably after the first conference devoted to it, in 1977.[121] Duncan Kennedy and Roberto Unger of Harvard Law School were major figures. The rather ragged and undisciplined army of "crits" frightened the establishment almost as much as if they had been bomb-throwing radicals. Their actual message was hard to pin down; they shared a kind of wild and anarchic irreverence; but there were never any sacred and agreed upon texts. They attacked the still-surviving high priests of formalism; but they were also equally at war with the wishy-washy liberals of the center, who dominated the law schools. To the crits, the talk about restraint and rationality and "reasoned elaboration" was hogwash. Law was inherently political; it was never impartial, never mere procedure or process; on the contrary, it was always on the side of the rich and the powerful; it always deserved to be trashed, exposed, deconstructed. Critical legal scholars "jeered at the idea" that law could be "neutral, objective, or apolitical."[122]

Of course, legal realism had peddled a milder version of this message; and social scientists who put law under the microscope had their own, more rigorous version of this message (without the normative spin). But the crits made noise; they were angry and verbally disruptive; they were also boisterous, clever, even playful at times. The arts of public relations were not unknown to them; and many younger scholars found them endlessly attractive, at least in comparison to the competition, which seemed dreary, smug, and hopelessly gray. A fair number of younger scholars began to march under this welcoming banner.

Critical legal studies was noisy, but its battles of words and concepts were not, in themselves, legal scholarship; the crits on the whole did not investigate anything; and many "crits" (though certainly not all of them) had little or no use for empirical study or, for that matter, for data. But the movement had an influence on scholarship, of one sort or another. In particular, it spawned subsidiary forms of "critical theory"—very notably, in the 1980s, "critical race theory," led by such scholars as Derrick Bell, then on the Harvard law faculty.[123] The critical race theorists agreed that law did the bidding of a social and economic and political elite. But they split off from CLS to emphasize the festering state (as they saw it) of race relations; race, rather than class, was at the heart of their analysis. Mari Matsuda and Patricia Williams were also prominent members of this school. Critical race theory in turn had its own subsidiaries, focusing on Latinos or Asians instead of blacks.[124] The fate of the "critical" movement was symptomatic of the fate of the American Left in general. What began as a broad attack on class ended up splintered into separate movements, each clinging to its own identity, its own sense of victimization, its own agenda.

The attack on the old order which came from the Right was the law and economics movement. It is an odd mixture of hard science and soft ideology.

It has achieved an almost astonishing success in the academy. A number of streams of thought came together to produce this movement. It brought forth, eventually, an enormous literature; and it had a real impact on scholarship, on the curriculum, and on attitudes toward law. In essence, the movement applied economic thought to legal questions. Which rules were efficient, which ones were inefficient? What was the economic impact of this or that field, doctrine, or legal institution? What made the law and economics movement controversial —but also gave it a much needed shot of adrenaline—was its political meaning. Law and economics was, on the whole, intensely conservative. Its "economics" was, in the main, the economics of the free market, of Milton Friedman—it was certainly not the economics of Keynes or liberal labor economists.

One reason for the success of law and economics was that it helped fill the vacuum left when orthodox legal scholarship—ingrown, unworldly, arid—lost much of its luster and its legitimacy. The old-fashioned law teacher thought legal questions had right and wrong answers. If you started with sound legal principles, and applied sound reasoning, you reached sound and right results. The legal realists made mincemeat of this faith. But the economists refused to go the whole distance: to admit there were no valid answers to legal questions. Indeed, said many economists of law: there *were* right answers—if you asked the right question. Not whether some rule or arrangement is "correct" in a logical sense—that was the bad old way—but rather, whether it made economic sense. And only economists were able to tell you whether it did.

As early as the late 1940s an economist served on the faculty of the University of Chicago Law School.[125] And Chicago has always provided a strong intellectual base for law and economics, as it flourished from the 1950s on. Moreover, pride of place within the movement has to go to a scholar closely associated with the University of Chicago, Richard Posner, whom President Reagan later appointed a federal judge (on the 7th Circuit). Posner published a general "economic analysis" of law (1972), and ran it through several editions. Posner began his book with the assertion that economics was a "powerful tool" for analyzing legal questions. And he based his analysis of the law on the "assumption that man is a rational maximizer of his ends in life"; and that people's behavior "can be altered by changing their incentives."[126] He also produced a vast, entertaining, protean body of scholarship, on everything from sex to primitive man to the impeachment trial of President Clinton.[127] Some of this work was facile, some of it was exasperating, some of it was boldly insightful, some of it was jagged and nervy; but on the whole, it was an amazing achievement—and Posner the judge continued to write books as well as opinions; at the end of the twentieth century he was still going strong—the most prolific legal scholar, perhaps, in the country; certainly (and there are figures to prove this) the most often cited.

Posner did not, in fact, have a Ph.D. in economics; he was, essentially, a brilliant amateur. But more and more, law schools in the 1980s and 1990s began to hire men (and the occasional woman) who had this degree, usually, though not always, coupled with a law degree. At some schools, the economists made the big leap past tokenism: there were elite schools with three, four, or five economists on their faculty. No other social science has even come close to this level of representation; no other social science has been able to crack the law school walls of insularity and indifference. In a few obvious fields—antitrust law—sensitivity to economic issues is now almost essential for those who teach. But economic thinking pervades all sorts of other fields: contracts, torts, and business associations, to name only the most salient. Because economic thought was, on the whole, conservative, law and economics attracted funding more readily than, say, the sociology of law.

And economics was a *science;* or claimed to be. Its most powerful claim was that it was, after all, value free. Witness Posner, discussing the Wagner Act—it was, he said, a "decisive step" toward "policy favorable toward labor monopolizing." Some readers, he says, might "take umbrage" at using the word *monopoly* in talking about unions. But the "term is exact, and no pejorative connotation is intended." Economics "is a positive rather than a normative science." Hence an economist "steps out of his professional role when he condemns monopoly, in any context, as evil."[128] But of course the public considers "monopoly" evil; and the word has a "pejorative connotation," even when it wears the Halloween costume of science.

Legal scholarship had, since Langdell, tended to be self-centered, solipsistic, unmindful and unaware of scholarship outside the discipline. Toward the end of the century, the schools became somewhat more permeable. They reflected more what went on in the rest of the university—and in society at large. One symptom was the rise of "feminist jurisprudence." Legal scholarship before the 1960s had almost nothing to say by or about women. But then women began to enter the profession in droves—as students, teachers, deans, lawyers, even judges. The women in the law schools wrote about the same subjects as men—but they also produced specifically feminist writing.

"Feminist jurisprudence" was a fairly broad term, covering all sorts of tendencies, in all shapes and sizes. One aim—the least controversial—was to uncover buried cities: to stress the legal life and legal interests of women, which men had ignored or glossed over. Other strands of thought were more radical. Catharine MacKinnon pushed sexual harassment onto center stage, campaigned against pornography, and advanced a stern and "unmodified" feminism, in prose that was always mordant, pungent, and bold, though some-times a bit impenetrable.[129]

Law Reviews

The actual literature of all these legal scholars—orthodox, conservative, and reform—appeared, by and large, primarily in those extremely peculiar journals, the "law reviews." These date from the late nineteenth century, when the *Harvard Law Review* first appeared. The oddest thing about these journals is that they are almost entirely run by students. The typical law review is divided into two parts: in the front, articles written by law professors; in the back "case notes" or (more recently) shorter pieces, written by students. The students in most schools also decide which articles to print in the front of the journal, without (for the most part) anything remotely resembling peer review. You have, in other words, students sitting in judgment of the work of professors, in the majority of law schools. (The *Illinois Law Review,* founded at Northwestern in 1906, was an exception; it was run by the faculty itself.[130]) Typically, the stu-dents also edit the work of faculty contributors, often with a vengeance, chop-ping and hacking away, demanding total accuracy of citation, and sometimes mangling and rearranging and rewriting and turning the whole thing upside down, until the poor helpless author would hardly recognize his own work.

One would think that law professors as a group would rise up and crush this system, which turns the academic hierarchy upside down. On the contrary, they mostly seem (or seemed) to cherish it. Partly, this is because of tradi-tion; more important, the professors themselves, by and large, were graduates of the system—they were law review editors when they were in school, and they learned the hard way how to eviscerate the work of their elders. Only the elites of the school "made law review"—the men (and later women) with the very highest grades; the best firms chose their new associates from the ranks of ₁ₐw review editors; and law schools in the market for new professors looked to the same group for their raw recruits. In this way, the system became encrusted with honor and antiquity and prestige. It became unassailable—all the more so because real scholarship about law, in the law schools, was so weak and precarious.

In 1900 there were only seven of these university reviews. By the middle of the twentieth century, no school with any claim to prestige lacked a law review, and the number had grown to seventy or so, crammed for the most part with long, boring, arid expositions of legal doctrine. Most of them had "very limited circulations" in a "glutted market"; and their "immediate influence" was "disappointing," because they were "read principally by law teachers."[131] Still, no school dared tamper with the system.

Seventy journals seemed like a lot in the 1950s; the real population explosion was yet to come. Eventually, nearly all schools found the money and the energy to publish a law review. In 1985 there were more than three hundred journals; and by the late 1990s, more than four hundred. There was no academic equivalent of a birth control pill for law reviews. Because virtually all law schools had at least one, the more ambitious and high-toned schools had to have more than one. Harvard apparently has nine or ten; Tulane has six, Notre Dame five, Temple four.[132] In most other fields of scholarship—economics, philosophy, and so on—there are only a few leading journals; and articles have to be short and sweet. Not in the law school world. Long articles are normal—and welcome; there are, by one estimate, some 150,000 pages to be filled every year—150,000 hungry mouths to be fed. In 1985 the mean length of law review articles, in a sample of reviews, was 41.83 pages.[133] But articles of 70 or 100 pages are nothing special. Volume 82 of the Virginia Law Review contains an article 229 pages long, with 769 footnotes. This is by no means record length.

The journals are not only distressingly many, and distressingly long-winded; as they sit on library shelves, they are also quite fat. The *Harvard Law Review* publishes eight issues per year. Each yearly volume runs to more than 2,000 pages. Volume 95 of the *Michigan Law Review,* for 1997, ran to 2,658 pages. Volume 50 of the *Rutgers Law Review* ran to 2,321 pages. These were among the more obese reviews. A mere 1,000 pages a year is perhaps just as common.

The first such publications were general law reviews, and the flagship law reviews are still generalists; they print articles on any legal subject. There is only one *Harvard Law Review,* no matter how many other reviews the school puts out. The rest of Harvard's journals are more specialized. The same is true of other schools. Specialized journals have their own history. The *Journal of the American Institute of Criminal Law and Criminology,* which came out of Northwestern Law School, first appeared in 1910.[134] A few others were born in the 1930s and 1940s, very notably *Law and Contemporary Problems* (Duke University Law School). After the Second World War, there was no holding these journals back: 10 new journals appeared in the 1950s, including the *Journal of Law and Economics* (1958); there were 26 in the 1960s, 60 in the 1970s, 90 in the 1980s, and more than 135 in the 1990s. International law is a particularly sexy topic: nearly half of all law schools publish some sort of globalized or globalizing journal. Many of the specialized journals, of course, have high standards and make a real contribution; quite a few do not. Some of them have escaped from the tyranny of law students; they use a peer-review system. Peers, of course, can be as trendy and biased as students; but at least they can be expected to know what they are talking about.

The contents of the standard law reviews have changed a great deal over the years. At the turn of the century, they were reviews about law (mainly case law), in a very traditional sense. At the end of the twentieth century, they were a bewildering kaleidoscope of every form and mutation of scholarship. One can find critical theory, economic analysis, law and literature, feminist jurisprudence, critical race theory, material about philosophy, social construction and deconstruction, even the orthodox social sciences; along with doctrine-chopping (or instead of it), one can find regression equations, "narrative," game theory, and everything in the current intellectual circus world from diamond-hard to mushy-soft. Indeed, in the 1990s, you are far more likely to see references to Foucault, Habermas, Richard Rorty, or Catharine MacKinnon than to Blackstone or even to the dead white males who wrote treatises.

The change has come gradually. In an issue of the *Columbia Law Review* for 1904, I found no references at all to sources that could be called nonlegal; the footnotes were almost entirely cases and statutes. In the typical middle-of-the-road law review of, say, 1950, most references would still be legal—cases, statutes, treatises—but there were also citations to law reviews, and a sprinkling of citations to outside material. The scene at the end of the century was quite different. In a 1999 issue of the *North Carolina Law Review,* which I literally plucked at random off the shelves of the Stanford Law Library, I found references in footnotes to Edmund Burke, F. A. Hayek, Ludwig von Mises, James M. Buchanan, both Michael and Karl Polanyi, Gordon Wood, Alexis de Tocqueville, Hegel, Claude Lévi-Strauss, Bronislaw Malinowsky, Marcel Mauss, Erving Goffman, Gary Becker, and Richard Titmuss—to mention only a few well-known names. Probably none of these worthies is a member of the bar.

The law reviews, then, have gotten trendy. For whom are their contributors writing? Mostly for themselves, and for the academy. Courts certainly cite law reviews more frequently than in the past. In October term 1900, the United States Supreme Court cited exactly one law review article (admittedly there were not many to cite); in October term 1940, it cited 31; in October term 1978, it cited 286 (the *Harvard Law Review,* with 40 citations, was by far the winner).[135] Occasionally, this or some other court will adopt an idea or doctrine which it credits to this or that article in a law review. Whether this reflects anything we could honestly call "influence" is another question. Do lawyers in the real world read law reviews? Doubtful. But why should they? There is precious little practical guidance to be gotten from the reviews (if there ever was). Articles peppered with references to Foucault, or for that matter Catharine MacKinnon—and this applies not just to journals at elite schools—are worse than useless to the average practicing lawyer. What lawyers consult are works that are written *for* them, and to help them: works written for the practice. There is a huge supply of these, often kept up to date with "pocket parts" or loose-leaf supplements. Lawyers in the 1990s also leaned more and more on computerized databases, like Lexis and Westlaw—services which provided whole texts, and which make the job of searching for authority much easier. Law libraries, too, sprouted forests of machines, threatening to crowd out the bookshelves; and the students were more and more hunched over these machines, going "online" to find material, or perhaps to send e-mail to their friends; or to play solitaire.

The law reviews, even if they were not useful to the outside world, are nonetheless an important window on the culture of law schools; and they may tell us something about the mind of the lawyer, too, because so many of them passed through this doorway to the law. In 1900 law reviews were much concerned with expounding the law. In 2000 they were most concerned with criticizing it—or suggesting changes. The authors of law review articles have, on the whole, not much respect for courts as such; they show no particular deference to legislatures and administrative bodies. They were all realists, or postrealists; they did not believe in "legal science" *(Rechtswissenschaft)* as it had been recognized in Europe (and in the Langdell era)—that is, a body of coherent, systematic principles, of almost mathematical beauty. Rather, law was a motley and manmade collection of tools, instruments, devices. Law was something you used, something you manipulated—for economic and social ends. Doing law was a kind of craft; and the authors' highest aim was to show a way to burnish an argument, polish it to a fine finish, and put it at the service of some cause they admired. What they wrote was largely normative; also clever, "learned," and remote.

The Rise of Legal History

Modern scholarship on American legal history was, to a remarkable degree, the creation of a single individual, J. Willard Hurst (1910–1997). Hurst was born in Rockford, Illinois; he studied at Harvard, but his entire academic life centered around the University of Wisconsin Law School. In 1950, Hurst published *The Growth of American Law: The Lawmakers;* and in 1956, *Law and the Conditions of Freedom,* a short but brilliant essay on the nature of American law, mostly in the nineteenth century. In some ways, his magnum opus was *Law and Economic Growth,* published in 1964. This work was subtitled *The Legal History of the Lumber Industry in Wisconsin, 1836–1915.* It was a meticulous exploration of the "mutual involvement" of the law and the lumber industry: how they interacted and affected one another.[136] In the dark ages before these books were written, American legal history was highly formalist; it treated law as a narrow, self-contained little island. Why it grew and changed was mysterious: perhaps at the command of some unknown inner program. Hurst threw open the doors and brought law back into society, as part of society, flesh of its flesh, bone of its bone. He broke down the barriers between legal history, and general social and economic history.

Hurst was also a teacher and mentor of great gifts; he founded the "Wisconsin school" of legal history, but his influence was far greater than this term implies. His methods influenced the next generation of legal historians, men like Harry Scheiber of Berkeley, and the author of this book; his influence can be sensed in scholars like Morton Horwitz, who had little personal contact with

Hurst. In fact, all legal history since Hurst has been necessarily Hurstian, even when it struggles to revise his messages. Indeed, the reactions against his influence, among the younger legal historians, are perhaps the greatest witness to the continuing power of his thought.

Law and Society

The Hurstian idea, of course, went far beyond legal history. And to be sure, Hurst was one of the seminal influences on the developing "law and society movement." There had been a flurry of activity on the social study of law in the 1920s, as an outgrowth of the legal realist movement.[137] Some realists were not just interested in talk (or in "trashing"); they wanted to study what was going on in the legal world. The Johns Hopkins Institute of Law, in Baltimore, a research institute in the 1930s, was dedicated primarily to the scientific study of legal institutions. The institute had a fairly brief life. It did publish a number of studies—for example, a two-volume work on the divorce laws of Maryland, full of facts and figures.[138] But the Depression killed off the institute. There was also some work by individual scholars: for example, Underhill Moore of Yale, who did a rather ponderous study of commercial transactions. And Karl Llewellyn, as we have seen, collaborated with the anthropologist E. Adamson Hoebel on the "law-ways" of the Cheyenne tribe.[139]

After the Second World War, there was a great surge of hope that the social sciences were on the brink of a breakthrough. Biology and physics were taking giant steps forward: why not the social sciences too? It seemed sensible for sociologists to discover (or rediscover) law; if there were sociologies of medicine, sport, and religion, why not sociology of law? There was also a bit of money available. The Ford Foundation funded empirical research in law at the University of Chicago Law School in the early 1950s; one product of this research was the classic study by Harry Kalven and Hans Zeisel, *The American Jury* (1964). The *Brown* decision acted as a kind of catalyst. Sociology had historically been skeptical about law; the "mores"—customs and norms not part of the official structure—seemed vastly more important. The law was formal, dead, a false front that concealed the real workings of society. Yet here was a living example of social change, a revolution in race relations, and the law seemed to be playing a significant role. A group of young sociologists, piqued by considerations of this sort, founded the Law and Society Association.[140] They gathered together informally at a breakfast meeting at a convention of the American Sociological Association, in Montreal in August 1964. They set up a loose committee to advance the social study of law. Among the early leaders were Harry Ball, then at the University of Wisconsin, and Robert Yegge of the University of Denver. The Law and Society Association was formally organized in November 1964, in Colorado, as a not-for-profit corporation. The early founders were soon joined by members of other disciplines; one group, of particular importance, radiated out of the University of Wisconsin, where Willard Hurst's influence was strong in the law school; the university also had a critical mass of social scientists in various disciplines, interested in the legal order. Other universities, including Denver, California (Berkeley), and Northwestern, also developed somewhat similar interests. The association issued a newsletter; and then in 1966 began to publish the *Law and Society Review*. The first editor in chief was Richard D. Schwartz, a sociologist by training. Schwartz talked about a "growing need" for "interdisciplinary dialogue" between lawyers and sociologists. Legal policy "affects the whole of society"; it is a "conduit through which all the diverse institutional elements of the society simultaneously flow." The *Review* aimed to help create a "professional cadre," people able to "move freely from their original disciplinary base into the related fields."[141]

As Schwartz's words suggested, most members of the Law and Society Association were not, in fact, lawyers or law professors. Most came out of political science, psychology, sociology, anthropology, and related disciplines. A small group of law professors, however, also got on the bandwagon. Law professors have been among the presidents and board members of the association; a few have made real contributions to the field.[142] Both lawyers and nonlawyers tried to build up a body of work that examined the way the legal system actually operated—work intended to get below the surface, beyond the appellate cases that dominated legal education and orthodox legal scholarship. There were probably no major breakthroughs; no discoveries worthy of a Nobel Prize. But data gathering, middle-range theory, and the patient excavation of buried cities are not to be sneered at. A few works stand out: Stewart Macaulay's classic article (1963) on the ways in which Wisconsin businessmen used, and did not use, contract law; and some essays of Marc Galanter's, notably his study of why the "haves" come out ahead in litigation—a much admired, much cited work.[143]

The Law and Society Association was an umbrella organization. It grew steadily larger over the years. The membership was more than one thousand in the 1990s; annual meetings attracted hundreds of scholars to read and critique papers, or to mill about gossiping, finding soul mates and collaborators. Smaller but similar organizations developed around the psychology of law and in other fields—anthropology of law, for example. Political scientists who study courts and law have organized a special section of the American Political Science Association; members get together at the APSA annual meeting to talk shop and exchange papers. There are some interesting subspecialties of the law and society movement: jury studies, for example, has attracted the attention of a fair number of psychologists.[144]

Only in the law schools does the old scholarly order hang on. It is a bit battered and frayed about the edges, but the core of it is still intact. Students still feel, as John Schlegel put it, "that law is about rules." The professors still give them "a pile of appellate cases to chew on." In the law schools, the "notion of law as rule is as overwhelming as the smell of limburger cheese."[145] Not everybody finds this the most attractive of smells.

16

American Legal Culture in the Twentieth Century

The previous chapter dealt primarily with what we might call the internal legal culture: the world of the legal profession: judges, lawyers, jurists.

The internal legal culture does not, of course, exist in a vacuum. It has its own inner dynamic; but it is linked in many different ways to the general legal culture: the attitudes, opinions, and points of view of the population as a whole—lay people, whether investment bankers, factory workers, nurses, bus drivers, or anybody else. The ways in which the two cultures are linked have been a central theme—maybe *the* central theme—of this book: themes like the rise of plural equality; the changes in attitude that led to the liability explosion; the so-called sexual revolution, which swept whole clusters of crimes out of the penal code; and the backlashes and reactions to these changes.

Any book on a topic as bulky and unwieldy as this one has to deal in broad generalizations. The United States is a very complicated country. It seems clear that the civil rights movement set off a chain reaction; by 2000 attitudes of white America toward black America, and vice versa, were not what they had been in 1950—and certainly not what they were in 1900. But how much change? how deep? how many people? There is, by now, a kind of consensus that American apartheid was wrong and must never be repeated. But this, and every other "consensus," is only relative. Major legal change always implies a kind of consensus, but it also implies, necessarily, some degree of conflict. Nobody needs law to force people to do something they were already doing or would do anyway, even without a law. Each point, each locus of change, is the site of some big or little conflict. No matter how smooth the surface, a lot is always going on underneath. The legal order often shows us a bland, flat fiat; sometimes only under the microscope can we see the jagged edges, the rough contours, the teeming world of microbic life.

Plural equality developed in the course of the twentieth century. American faces on the street looked different at the end of the century—the country was racially more diverse; there were fewer white enclaves. People dressed differently, thought differently, ate different food, and, technologically speaking, lived in a different world. But not everybody was happy about the changes in society. Plural equality could not get rid of the strong streak of nativism and paranoia in American life. Rapid and unsettling change brings out the worst in some people. They look for scapegoats: for enemies. The enemies they think they see are insidious, treacherous, they bore from within. The enemies list has included Wobblies, reds, atheists, radical homosexuals; or the CIA or the FBI, or the "government" in general; or even Satan and his agents. America is a country of strong emotions and deep convictions, not all of them benign.

Religion and the Law: A Case Study

America also was and is an intensely religious country. Polls show that Americans are, by and large, churchgoers and believers. Yet nothing so surprised urban liberals in the last two decades of the twentieth century than the sudden arrival of the Christian Right as a political force. By the end of the century, this influence seemed to have waned a bit; a backlash had set in against what was itself a backlash. The real question is not why fundamental Christians have political strength, but how and when and why this huge mass of people became vocal and organized. In many ways, the actions of the Christian Right can be compared to the actions of the civil rights movement. They seem like polar opposites. But underlying both of them is something deep in American culture: a refusal to defer to experts, to constituted authority.

This may seem, on the surface, either paradoxical or just plain wrong. Conservative Christians seem to cling to traditional authorities like limpets to rocks. They do and do not, at the same time. They take the Bible as the literal word of God, and insist that they are totally committed to it. But they categorically refuse to defer to scientific experts, to educated elites—another kind of established authority.

A case in point was the famous "monkey" trial, the 1925 Scopes trial in Tennessee.[1] Tennessee, like a number of other southern states, had passed a law against the teaching of Darwin's theory of evolution in public schools. John T. Scopes, twenty-four years old, a general science teacher and part-time football coach at the high school in Dayton, Tennessee, agreed to serve as a sacrificial lamb defendant in a test case. The trial, blown up into a dramatic confrontation between science and old-time religion, had (as so often in America) a distinct odor of hucksterism. The town fathers of Dayton saw the trial as a way to put their town on the map. It was worth millions of dollars in publicity; and would attract free-spending tourists. Dayton did attract attention (not all of it favorable), though the tourist money proved a bit disappointing. The trial itself was an absolute sensation. Reporters jammed into the city; millions of words about the trial were sent by telegraph to the national and foreign press. At the trial, two famous men squared off against each other. William Jennings Bryan defended old-time religion. Bryan, the "Great Commoner," had run for president on the Democratic ticket three times (and lost). Clarence Darrow, the spokesman for Darwin, modernity, and freethinking, was just about the most famous trial lawyer in the country.

The actual outcome of the trial was never in much doubt; Scopes was, after all, obviously guilty of breaking the law. Darrow's goal was to make the law, the prosecution, and Bryan all seem ridiculous. The high point, for him, came when he cross-examined Bryan on such burning issues as whether a whale really could swallow Jonah, or where Cain got his wife from, and similar biblical puzzles.[2] Nobody much cared what actually happened to Scopes; the schoolteacher hardly figured at the trial. Both sides claimed victory. Shortly after the trial ended, Bryan died in his sleep during an afternoon nap. In the mythology of the Scopes trial, he was a defeated man, and he had defended a losing cause. But this is sheer romance.

What was the Scopes trial really about? Many things: religious fundamentalism, of course. But it was also about the problem of democracy in an increasingly plural society: it was about the right of the state (and the public) to decide what was and what was not to be taught in the schools. All scientific experts believed in evolution. Many people—with absolutely no training in science—thought otherwise. Who would prevail?

In the legend of the Scopes trial, the case was a turning point; Scopes lost, but science won, modernity won, Darrow won. But the issues in Scopes never really died, neither the particular issue (evolution) nor two broader issues: first, the role of religion in American public life, and second (and related to the first), who gets to control, to decide, on that role. Arkansas, too, had an antievolution law, adopted by referendum in 1928 (*after* the Scopes trial). The statute prohibited any public school (or university!) from teaching "the theory or doctrine that mankind ascended or descended from a lower order of animals." The schools had pretty much ignored the statute; but in the 1960s, the state teachers' association of Arkansas decided to challenge it. A young biology instructor, Susan Epperson, acted as plaintiff.[3] The United States Supreme Court declared the statute void. Because the statute outlawed the teaching of evolution "for the sole reason that it is deemed to conflict" with one "particular interpretation of the Book of Genesis," the statute was an "establishment of religion," which was forbidden by the First Amendment.[4] And in 1987 the Court also struck down a Louisiana Creationism Act; the law made it wrong for a public school to teach evolution unless it taught "creation science" along with it and gave the two "balanced treatment." The Court thought this too was an "establishment of religion."[5]

Yet even this was not the end. As late as 1999 the issue cropped up again, this time in Kansas. The Kansas Board of Education voted to "delete virtually any mention of evolution from the state's science curriculum." Schools could, if they wanted to, teach evolution; but the board had, in effect, authorized local school boards to ignore evolution entirely. The voters of Kansas later threw the conservatives on the Board of Education out of office; still, the time and place of this minor eruption were surprising.[6]

In Europe, the idea of teaching "creationism" (or not teaching evolution) would be unthinkable. One reason for the contrast, of course, is America's intense religious fervor. Much of that fervor is for the old-time religion, literal-minded, biblical. This brand of religion seems much rarer in Europe. But this is only part of the story, and perhaps the less interesting part. Another part turns on decentralization. American government is a patchwork; school matters in particular are extremely local. A unitary, central system of education, run from Washington, would probably be a lot different from the present system, in which every tub sits on its own little bottom. A third point may be the most crucial of all. European countries would never tolerate creationism because the men and women of science—that is, the experts—reject it. Elites, intellectuals, experts have had far more to say about how the schools are run—how society is run—in Europe than in the United States.

American religion, intense though it is, has changed radically over the years. What Americans believed in the late twentieth century was influenced greatly by American pluralism. Beliefs also reflected the power of modern, expressive individualism. To Americans religion is an intensely personal matter. Many Americans no longer believe that there is one true faith (in the old-fashioned sense); they think, rather, that for everybody there is a personally true religion; and that we all get to choose it on our own. All religions are valid, in a way. Most Americans simply cannot accept the idea that, say, non-Catholics or non-Baptists are going straight to hell. How could an American Catholic family, for example, think so when the nice family next door is Protestant, when one daughter has married a Jew, another a Lutheran, and their young, bearded son has just turned Buddhist?

Of course, the official theology of many religions runs contrary to this sort of tolerance. But Americans in general pay little or no attention to theology as such. They are interested in personal redemption, in personal spirituality; these are feelings of the heart, not of theology. Religion is, in other words, an individual quest for salvation; each person travels the path her own way.

The changing social meaning of religion underlies many of the cases on religion and the state. One of the most noted of these was *Wisconsin v. Yoder* (1972).[7] The defendants were members of the Old Order Amish and the Conservative Amish Mennonite Church. They lived in Green County, Wisconsin. Their religions in essence turn their back on the modern world. Wisconsin law required children to be in school until age sixteen; the Amish wanted their children out of school as soon as they had finished grade school and knew the rudiments of reading, writing, and arithmetic. High school, the defendants argued, was "contrary to the Amish religion and way of life." In fact, sending their children to high school might "endanger their own salvation and that of their children." The values taught in these schools, the Amish argued, were at "variance" with Amish values: they were values of success, social life, competitiveness, self-distinction. The Amish rejected all of these values. High school would be a threat to the core values of Amish society.

The Supreme Court agreed. The rights of the Amish—their freedom of religion—was at risk; and the state of Wisconsin and its school law would have to give way. This was, of course, a case about an old-time religion, and one of the most conservative and fundamental. But paradoxically, the case itself reeks of modernity: in a pluralist society, the majority can tolerate—can even empower and admire—those who reject that society and its pluralism. The worldly Supreme Court bailed out the otherworldly people of the Old Order Amish.

Religion and the Law

The Bill of Rights deals with religion in the First Amendment: Congress "shall make no law respecting an establishment of religion, or prohibiting the free exercise thereof." The "establishment" clause and the "free exercise" clause have somewhat inconsistent aims, and there is some trouble dealing with both of them at once. The establishment clause embodies the famous "wall of separation" between church and state; the second, however, tells the state it can do nothing that will impede or discourage religion or religious worship.

The Supreme Court, as we have seen, originally restricted the Bill of Rights to the federal government (and the reference to Congress makes that interpretation especially plausible for the First Amendment). Later, the Supreme Court, using the "incorporation doctrine," held that most (not all) of the Bill of Rights now applied to the states, because the Fourteenth Amendment had mysteriously "incorporated" them. This was true for those parts of the Bill of Rights which were supposed to be truly basic and fundamental. The religion clauses easily made the grade.

Religious issues moved to center stage because of American religious pluralism and the voting power of minority religions. American Catholics, for example, were a quarter of the population by the end of the twentieth century. In 1925, in *Pierce v. Society of Sisters,* the Supreme Court struck down an Oregon law (adopted by initiative) which in effect outlawed private schools.[8] This was a pet project of the Ku Klux Klan and was blatantly anti-Catholic. By the late 1940s, parochial (Catholic) schools were a nonissue. Indeed, in states with big Catholic populations, and big systems of parochial schools, Catholic voters resented the fact that they paid twice for their children's schools: once as taxpayers, and then again as tuition-paying parents. They were, after all, saving the state money by sending their children to private schools. It seemed only fair to reap some of those economic benefits.

Everson v. Board of Education (1947) challenged a New Jersey law which allowed local school boards to reimburse parents for the cost of school buses—including buses taking children to parochial schools.[9] The Court announced, in ringing tones, that "neither a state nor the Federal Government can set up a church. Neither can pass laws which aid one religion, aid all religions, or prefer one religion over another." The wall of separation between church and state had to be strong, high, impregnable. Despite this stirring talk, a bare majority of the Court found the New Jersey law acceptable. It did not breach the wall, or "establish" a religion. It just helped children—all children—get safely to school. Four justices disagreed.

In *Engel v. Vitale* (1962) the Court had to decide how far public schools could go to promote religion.[10] Schools at one time had been not at all bashful about religion; they assigned Bible readings and conducted prayers in school. But by the 1960s, plural equality had made strong inroads on the culture. *Engel* concerned the so-called "Regents prayer." The Board of Regents of the State of New York had composed a prayer, which they thought was bland enough and nondenominational enough for classroom recitation: "Almighty God, we acknowledge our dependence upon Thee, and beg Thy blessings upon us, our parents, our teachers and our Country." This was not bland enough for the American Civil Liberties Union, the American Jewish Committee, or for the Supreme Court itself. It was "no part of the business of government," said the Court, "to compose official prayers." A year later, the Court struck down a Pennsylvania law which ordered public schools to read ten verses from the Bible aloud each day in class. This too was an "establishment of religion" and therefore unconstitutional.[11]

Hardly any decisions of the Court have been less popular than the school prayer decisions. Congressmen have fulminated and raged, they have called the ban communistic; and, if you can believe the polls, most ordinary Americans have agreed. Yet here is a case in which the Court clings stubbornly to its principles; it has never wavered, and, indeed, it has extended the doctrine. When Alabama authorized schools to set aside a minute at the beginning of each school day for "meditation or voluntary prayer," even this mild measure was struck down; the law had no "secular purpose," it was a prayer bill in disguise, and it had to go (1985).[12] Amendments to the Constitution to allow prayers in school have been proposed over and over again—President Ronald Reagan was one of the proposers—but none has gotten much past the starting post.

Why have these rulings proved so hardy? Perhaps because many members of Congress know how difficult, and disruptive, it would be to reverse them. Millions of deeply religious Americans simply cannot understand why school children should not be encouraged to pray. What was so wrong with the New York prayer? But the structural problems—how to deal with minority religions; how to deal with nonbelievers; how to avoid offending *somebody*—are so deep-seated, that in a society with dozens and dozens of religions, and growing numbers of Jews, Muslims, Buddhists—and nonbelievers—school prayers simply cannot work, except in very homogeneous communities, and perhaps not even there. Lawyers know this; judges know this; school officials know this.[13] But the lay public, which hasn't thought these structural problems through, has not yet been convinced.

There is, of course, a deeper meaning to the school prayer decisions. They are cases about plural equality. Religious tolerance has a long and rather noble history in the United States (with some egregious exceptions). Nobody was ever burned at the stake, although mobs in the nineteenth century did burn down a convent or two, and the Mormon religion was persecuted rather severely. The Ku Klux Klan of the 1920s was stridently anti-Catholic. A more or less genteel anti-Semitism was always simmering in the melting pot; through the 1950s Jews were unwelcome in many clubs, some suburbs, many law firms, and quite a few industries. On the other hand, mosques, churches, temples, and synagogues were open for business and did their work in peace. Still, there was never any question in the nineteenth century that these religions were tolerated, and nothing more. They had no claim to symbolic parity. Normatively speaking, Protestant America was in the saddle.

The whole school curriculum was drenched with a Protestant ethos. Catholics, as we saw, established their own school system, at great expense, in part as a reaction to the blatant Protestantism of the public schools. The Pennsylvania law, which the Supreme Court struck down, ordered teachers (on pain of getting fired) to read "At least ten verses from the Holy Bible . . . without comment, at the opening of each and every . . . school day." It was hardly unique.[14] A North Dakota law of 1911 solemnly declared that the Bible was "not . . . a sectarian book." Hence it was not to be "excluded from any public school." At least the North Dakota law made Bible reading optional; and added that no pupil was "required to read it or to be present in the school room during the reading thereof, contrary to the wishes of his parents."[15]

Other states, particularly in the Midwest, were more stridently secular, for one reason or another; and insisted on rigorous separation of church and state. The Nebraska Constitution, since the nineteenth century, had provided (Art. VII, §11) that "no sectarian instruction shall be allowed in any school or institution supported in whole or in part by public funds"; and no state land or money was to support any "sectarian or denominational school." In a 1902 case the Nebraska Supreme Court interpreted the state constitution to mean no prayers or Bible reading, no singing of hymns in school.[16] Two Roman Catholics, interestingly, filed an *amicus* brief in support of this position: "We do not intend," they said, to have a Protestant version of the Bible "forced down our throat without protest."

The Supreme Court decisions in the 1960s, important though they are, simply reinforced a tendency that was already under way. Prayers were chased out of the schools because pluralism made them less and less practical. It became harder and harder to find any religious common denominator. Ultimately, it became so difficult to package religion without offending someone that the schools (and courts) totally gave up. Religion was politely shown the door.

Indeed, many religious parents are disturbed because the schools are now so godless. The schools teach evolution. They ban prayers and Bible reading. They teach nothing about religion. This makes them enemies of religion. The parents, of course, have a point. Neutrality is, strictly speaking, a mirage. Even silence is an ideology. As of 2001, the public schools ignore religion, one of the most powerful social forces in the world. But the same parents who decry this silence would object, and perhaps quite properly, to a purely "objective" study of religion, or a course on religion that was only sociological or historical or comparative. In the end, silence seems the safest course.

The Supreme Court continued to wrestle with state aid to parochial schools. In 1969 Rhode Island passed a "salary supplement" law. The state could supplement the salaries of teachers who taught secular subjects in nonpublic schools, up to 15 percent of their current salary. Private schools found it hard to pay competitive salaries. In Rhode Island "private school" and "Catholic school" were virtually synonymous. At the time the case was decided, 250 teachers had applied for supplements; all of them worked for Roman Catholic schools.

In *Lemon v. Kurtzman* (1971) the Supreme Court voided the Rhode Island plan.[17] The chief justice, Warren Burger, set out three "tests" that a statute which posed an "establishment" issue would have to meet to be sustained. First, the statute must have a "secular legislative purpose." Second, its "principal or primary effect must be one that neither advances nor inhibits religion." Third, it must not "foster" an "excessive government entanglement with religion." In the Rhode Island case, the Court found far too much "entanglement."

The Court has not yet repudiated these *Lemon* tests; but many critics consider them to be, well, lemons. Mostly they are simply too vague to be much use. Rhode Island was the focus of another case (1984); this time the issue was the Christmas display in Pawtucket. The city, working with local retailers, put up the display on public property. It included a Santa Claus house, reindeer pulling Santa's sleigh, candy-striped poles, a Christmas tree, cut-out figures including a "clown, an elephant, and a teddy bear"; but also a crèche. The crèche was the controversial part: was this too overtly religious? A bare majority of the Court thought that the crèche passed the *Lemon* test; it was too "far-fetched" to claim that these "symbols" threatened to "establish" a state church.[18]

There is a lot to be said for this result (and a lot to be said against it); and both sides could comfortably quote *Lemon*—which is one of the problems with this "test." Justice Scalia, in particular, came to loathe the *Lemon* test. In a characteristically colorful passage, Scalia compared the test to a "ghoul in a late-night horror movie that repeatedly sits up in its grave and shuffles abroad, after being repeatedly killed and buried."[19] This may be so; but for want of anything better, the *Lemon* test survived into the new millennium, as one of the (barely) living dead.

The problem in *Bob Jones University v. U.S.* (1983) was, in a way, the reverse of the problem in cases about helping religion.[20] Bob Jones is a school in Greenville, South Carolina, whose teachers all had to be "devout Christians," and in which all courses were "taught according to the Bible." Under school rules, any students in an "interracial marriage" or who dated "outside of their race" would be immediately expelled. The Internal Revenue Service cut off the school's tax exemption. The race rules were against "national policy." The school claimed that these rules were based on "sincerely held religious beliefs." But the Supreme Court sided with the IRS. Plural equality here trumped religion. The case added to the sense of religious conservatives that they were victims of a godless, liberal establishment. It helped galvanize the Christian Right, which, in the 1980s and beyond, played a major role in politics, especially in the South.

Inclusiveness and Sensitivity

Late-twentieth-century issues of church and state are rather neatly encapsulated in *Lee v. Weisman* (1992)—yet another Rhode Island case.[21] Deborah Weisman, who was fourteen at the time, graduated from Nathan Bishop Middle School in Providence. It was the custom to have prayers at the graduation ceremony. In Deborah's year, the principal invited Rabbi Leslie Gutterman to deliver the prayer. The principal also handed Rabbi Gutterman a pamphlet, "Guidelines for Civil Occasions," prepared by the National Conference of Christians and Jews. This pamphlet gave helpful advice about what kinds of prayers to give on what occasions—basically, nonsectarian prayers, prayers of "inclusiveness and sensitivity."

Rabbi Gutterman did just that. In his invocation, he spoke about the "legacy of America where diversity is celebrated and the rights of minorities are protected." His benediction was bland and, as it were, prayerful: he expressed gratitude to God for "having endowed us with the capacity for learning," and for "keeping us alive, sustaining us, and allowing us to reach this special, happy occasion."[22]

Bland as this was, Deborah Weisman and her father found Rabbi Gutterman's prayer offensive. They objected to any prayers at all. They went to federal court and got an order, telling the school district to stop the practice in the future. The Supreme Court took the case, and affirmed the lower courts, but by the narrowest of margins (5–4). The majority labeled the practice an "establishment of religion." Nobody was actually forced to attend graduation; but of course most students wanted to go, and did go; hence an officially sanctioned ceremony of this kind exerted (said the Court) "subtle coercive pressure."

Justice Scalia, speaking for four dissenters, disagreed; and rather violently. The majority opinion, according to Scalia, a master of hyperbole, "lays waste a tradition that is as old as public-school graduation ceremonies themselves." He accused the majority of "social engineering," which is apparently something truly awful. The Constitution, according to Scalia, cannot rest on "changeable philosophical predilections of the Justices." The Constitution must be read in line with "the historic practices of our people." He closed his dissent with a little disquisition about the wondrous effects of people praying together, voluntarily. The "simple and inspiring prayers" of Rabbi Gutterman would in fact "inoculate" listeners against "religious bigotry and prejudice." For this reason, it was "senseless" to strike down the practice.

Scalia's argument has its merits. But he was dead wrong about "history" and "tradition." No nineteenth-century public school administrator would have dreamt of inviting a rabbi to lead prayers; and whoever they invited—a Protestant clergyman no doubt—would have been much more sectarian than Rabbi Gutterman. Nobody in the period when Scalia's "tradition" flourished would ever have referred to "diversity" or "rights of minorities" in a benediction. Public schools were in fact extremely sectarian, as we have seen: sectarian enough to drive the Catholics out.

The Providence schools, like Rabbi Gutterman, no doubt sincerely wanted to be inclusive and sensitive. Whether they were inclusive and sensitive enough in a society deeply committed to (religious) pluralism is another question—and a question that split the Court in two. Yet Scalia's angry dissent masks a broader area of agreement. Scalia, a Catholic, would have joined the majority, beyond a doubt, if the school had forced students to listen to prayers, or take part in the prayers; or if the prayers had been blatantly sectarian. The majority of the Court read the establishment clause as a charter for pluralist neutrality; and, in the end, the rest of the Court did not in principle disagree.

The Triumph of the Self

The discussion of religion brings out what might be the master change in the general culture in the twentieth century: the triumph of the individual, the exaltation of the self. This is the century of what Robert Bellah has called expressive individualism: the notion that a person's highest need, or goal, is to develop or realize the self; to fashion a unique, satisfying life and lifestyle, and to achieve personal success, salvation, achievement, and happiness.[23] One of the rights of the individual that this idea implies, is a right to his own culture, or counterculture—including the right to shift, change, and alter cultures. An age of expressive individualism is an age which tolerates all sorts of religions, including many that people in the past would have mostly dismissed as lunatic. It also allows the Amish—who reject individual values root and branch—to live on, cocooned in their tenuous niche. (Whether the Amish way of life can survive television and the internet is another question.)

On the surface, law and society in the late twentieth century seem to have exalted group rights—the rights of blacks, Chinese people, gays, women, the handicapped, and so on. But in an important sense group rights are individual rights. To empower women, to give rights to women, means (among other things) letting women choose what they want to be—a profoundly individual choice. Getting rid of prejudice and discrimination levels the playing field, as we said; but for whom? For individuals. It expands the menu of choices. A blind man can work in a factory. A lesbian can run for Congress. A black man can preside in a courtroom. A woman can cook, or sew, or play baseball, or fly a jet. "Group rights" is just another name for mainstreaming.

Culture and Context

The main theme of this book is that law is a product of society. Perhaps law has a life of its own; but if so it is a very limited life. Law certainly has its own language. It has its customs and rituals. Every case discussed in this book presented a legal issue; each one came wrapped in a cloak of technicality, the lawyer's own special ropes, strings, and bits of glue. But every case—and every statute, every administrative rule—also had a context, a background. And it is the background which made the problem seem like a problem in the first place—defined it, constructed it—and in the end, helped dictate, or influence, the way the system solved it (or failed to solve it).

We have already discussed the case of Jo Carol La Fleur (1974).[24] She was the teacher at Patrick Henry Junior High School, an inner-city public school in Cleveland, who lost her job because she was pregnant. La Fleur was a fighter. She went to her union for help, but the head of the union told her, "Just go home and have your baby." La Fleur then "got desperate" and called on the American Civil Liberties Union; they too refused to help. But a women's group took up the cause, and a law professor, Jane Picker, carried the main burden of the litigation.

At the trial—which La Fleur lost—the Cleveland school board defended its policies. It was "embarrassing" to have pregnant teachers in the classroom; students often "giggled about it." There was also testimony about the health problems of pregnant women; and the danger to these women from abusive students. The case ultimately reached the Supreme Court; and here La Fleur won a smashing victory. The Fourteenth Amendment protected "freedom of personal choice," which included the right to get pregnant. The policy of the

Cleveland school board put too heavy a burden on that right. La Fleur's case, as we have seen, was a step on the road to gender equality.

The legal issues were rather complex, including the question of whether and when a state can indulge in "irrebuttable presumptions." The Supreme Court later backed away from some aspects of the case. Legally speaking, it is only a footnote in Supreme Court history. But the case sums up rather neatly a whole series of trends in late-twentieth-century legal culture.

There is, to begin with, La Fleur herself. As she tells her story, an earlier fight over school rules had partly "radicalized" her. Women at her high school "were not allowed to wear pants. . . . I finally was part of a group that . . . said, This is ridiculous. It is wintertime, it is cold, we're all going to wear pants tomorrow."[25] They won this battle. La Fleur had become rights conscious; she had become a feminist; she had become an expressive individualist. She had become, in fact, an archetype of the late-twentieth-century litigant.

The case is also about the sexual revolution. What was the point of the rule in the first place? The health reasons smell of hypocrisy. As we saw, the rules really reflected leftover Victorian morality. A pregnant woman advertises, through her swelling body, the facts of human sexuality. For a similar reason, some high schools refused to let married students—lawfully married students— take part in extracurricular activities. They could go to school, but that was all. A married student who wanted to play baseball challenged this rule in 1972, and won his case.[26] In an Indiana case (1975) the panjandrums of high school education expressed the policy behind these rules: married students were "bad examples"; they might discuss "marital intimacies" with others students, and indulge in corrupting "locker room talk."[27]

Of course, this seems terribly naive. Married students were probably less likely to babble about their sex lives than unmarried studs and imitation studs. On the other hand, married students, like pregnant teachers, were walking advertisements of subjects supposed to be taboo. By the 1970s these ideas were in full retreat. A harsh new sexual reality had overtaken them. As La Fleur herself pointed out, pregnancy was nothing new in her inner-city high school: one of the girls in her class "had just turned twelve and was pregnant." La Fleur thought of herself not as an embarrassment but as "a good role model," a model of family life and prenatal care.

Finally, the case illustrates the role of institutions in struggles over the new culture, the new social norms. La Fleur turned to her union, then to the ACLU, then to a women's group. She needed institutional help to go all the way to the top. It costs money—lots of it—to speak to the United States Supreme Court. The ACLU, the NAACP, public-interest law firms (on both sides of some issues)— twentieth-century law would not be the same without these.

III

The Way We Live Now

The Reagan and Post-Reagan Years

17

Backward and Forward

Counterrevolution and Its Aftershocks

An account which (like this one) ends in very recent times runs special risks. Recent times are hard to sum up. History, like fine wine, seems to need time to age. Recent history is also too controversial. Not many people have an opinion about Byzantine Greece; only a minority have opinions about the Civil War; but everybody thinks she is an expert on the meaning of her own times.

The last twenty years of the twentieth century were years of conservatism. Ronald Reagan, elected in 1980, was in many ways a president of remarkable mediocrity: somewhat lazy, amazingly uninformed on most issues, at times even foolish or simple-minded. Yet he had a genuine political gift; and he succeeded, somehow, in putting his stamp on the era. In part, this is because his personality summed up so well many of the submerged wishes, prejudices, and tendencies of the average (white) American; and because, veteran actor that he was, he projected these on the national stage with uncanny skill. Not since Franklin D. Roosevelt was there a president with such talent for talking to the public. Reagan was indeed the "great communicator." And, in the late twentieth century, unlike prior times, communication was all. Was Thomas Jefferson a good communicator? Did anybody care?

Reagan was followed in office by George Bush; then by a Democrat, William Jefferson Clinton, who was elected twice to office. But Clinton was a "new Democrat"—that is, fairly conservative on quite a few issues; in any event, after 1994 he had to put up with a virulently conservative Congress; the

Republicans lost a few seats in the House in 1996 but retained control, and even gained a bit in the Senate. At the end of the century, they still controlled both houses of Congress.

The Reagan and Bush administrations, and the Republican Congress elected in 1994, were committed to rolling back the welfare state, curbing judicial activism, defusing the "liability explosion," cracking down on crime, and upholding traditional religion and family values. They disliked government regulation of business. They wanted less government, and a freer hand for entrepreneurs. All in all, then, they stood for a kind of counterrevolution.

But it was a limited counterrevolution. Reagan and his cohorts disliked the "excesses" of regulation, the antibusiness bias (as they saw it) of much of the legislation since 1965. They did not dare to touch Social Security, or Medicare, or the essence of the civil rights revolution. They were pruners, not cutters-down. Perhaps they aimed for more; but prudence dictated how far they could go.

In some ways, they were more successful than anybody had ever dared hope. Some matters were put on the agenda and seriously discussed that were completely unthinkable before—the flat tax, for example; or privatizing social security. Deep tax cuts during the Reagan administration (together with increases in defense spending) led to huge deficits. Among other things, this made new social initiatives unlikely or impossible. Clinton's attempt at health care reform ended up nowhere—or worse than nowhere, because his party lost control of both houses of Congress in 1994. Reagan was still alive in 2000, lost in the fog of Alzheimer's disease but still casting a dramatic shadow on American politics.

The Post-Warren Judiciary

Reagan and Bush tried mightily to put their stamp on the Supreme Court and on the federal judiciary (as indeed Nixon had done before them). They wanted to appoint conservative judges, not "activist" or "liberal" judges. They were, to a considerable degree, successful.

When Earl Warren resigned, President Nixon (1969) appointed Warren Burger to replace him. Burger had been a judge on the federal Court of Appeals. He was much more conservative than Earl Warren. But Burger was only one justice; and the Burger Court simply held the line. It did not innovate the way the Warren Court had done; but most of the Warren Court inheritance stayed more or less as it was. And the Burger Court was the court that handed down *Roe v. Wade*.[1] Indeed, Burger was part of the majority.

When Burger retired, President Reagan named the most conservative of the sitting justices, William H. Rehnquist, to replace him as chief justice (1986). The Rehnquist Court was even more conservative than the Burger Court, although President Clinton's two appointments (Ruth B. Ginsburg and Stephen Breyer) somewhat redressed the balance.

Some (not all) of the appointments in the last part of the century were headline news. President Reagan nominated Robert Bork in 1987, and an enormous campaign of protest followed. The Democrats controlled the Senate. Bork was extremely conservative; he openly opposed *Roe v. Wade*, and found no justification whatsoever in the text of the Constitution for the whole line of privacy cases. After a bitter struggle, his nomination went down in flames.

Bork was a brilliant jurist; his personal life was without blemish. His only sin was his views. For many people, that was fair game. His backers, however, felt the liberals had smeared him, defamed him, tarred and feathered him; he had been, in other words, "borked." The Clarence Thomas nomination in 1991 set off an even more rancid and acrimonious process; here, however, the focus was less on Thomas's archconservative views than on his character—did he or did he not tell dirty jokes to Anita Hill? Was he a secret fan of pornography? All of this, he cried, amounted to a "high-tech lynching"; and in the end he won his seat, though by a narrow margin.[2]

At the end of the twentieth century, the Rehnquist Court had a solid conservative core: Rehnquist himself, Justices Scalia and Thomas, and two other conservatives, Kennedy and O'Connor, who sometimes defected to the center. The other four justices formed the liberal bloc—including David Souter, the "stealth justice" appointed by President Bush. Souter had been a justice of the New Hampshire Supreme Court—hardly a celebrity. Nobody knew much about him. But this was precisely his virtue: he had almost "no paper trail to link him one way or another to key issues"; and in the aftermath of the Bork nomination, this seemed like a very good thing.[3] Whether the four "liberals" would have seemed quite so liberal in the 1950s or 1960s is open to debate. At the end of the century, however, they were the best the liberals had to offer.

The Court was thus, by common repute, a very conservative Court in the year 2000. Yet despite a lot of noise, and a few bites and nibbles around the edges, the core of the old system, on balance, has held up surprisingly well; much of what the Court did in the past seems, so far, fairly irreversible. The Court has, of course, handed down quite a few significant decisions with a conservative twist. It would be wrong to trivialize twenty years of Reagan and his legacy. But what was true of legislation under Reagan and Bush was also true of the work of their courts. From the standpoint of the broad sweep of history, the changes they made seem marginal, not fundamental; more like a person pausing to catch her breath than like somebody running as fast as her legs can carry her in the opposite direction.

Why has this been the case? For one thing, there were no landslides to compare with the New Deal days, when the Republicans were reduced to a small, twittering minority. Reagan was enormously popular with the voters; but he had to deal, for the most part, with a Democratic Congress. The Republican Congresses of 1994 and 1996 had razor-thin margins; and they had to face a popular and wily president, Clinton. More fundamentally, the texture of American life and American society made it extremely hard to reverse direction. People could long for the good old days, or what they thought were the good old days; but good or bad, those days were gone forever. The social structure had changed in fundamental ways. People's concepts, ideas, values and habits had also changed in fundamental ways. The past was gone. Nobody could put Humpty Dumpty together again. And very few people actually wanted to, whatever they might say.

Take, for example, the key area of race relations. Minority rights, from the 1950s on, seemed to be on a roll; official segregation was dismantled; key civil rights laws were passed. This process stopped, rather abruptly, in the Reagan years; and in some ways it went into reverse, legally speaking. Outright, overt, shameless race discrimination was now legally impossible. But race was still a crucial element in American social and political life. "Affirmative action" was an issue that aroused passions. Affirmative action had never been really popular; but there was a kind of understanding, in both political parties, that something of the sort was probably necessary. Indeed, President Richard Nixon hatched the so-called Philadelphia plan, under which contractors with federal contracts worth fifty thousand dollars or more had to commit themselves to hiring a certain quota of black workers.[4]

Nixon's motives have been questioned, and it is not clear how effective this plan had been.[5] Or any plan. Craft unions resisted affirmative action. Police departments and fire departments balked at hiring blacks, and any form of affirmative action met with great hostility. But the case for affirmative action was a powerful one. After all, the wounds and scars of slavery and segregation ran deep; if you simply got rid of the old obstacles, you left the status quo pretty much in place—and that meant a kind of white supremacy, more genteel to be sure, and without lynch mobs; but white supremacy nonetheless. For blacks and their liberal allies, the lesson was clear: more vigorous steps had to be taken.

The Reagan government—and the Supreme Court—began to retreat from the consensus position. The administration opposed affirmative action in cases of race and gender. The battles found their way into court. *Johnson v. Santa Clara County* (1987) was a struggle over the job of dispatcher in the highway department of Santa Clara County.[6] Paul Johnson wanted the job and thought he had the best crack at it. Diane Joyce also wanted the job. No woman had ever held the job. Both were qualified (Johnson perhaps a shade more so). Joyce got the job. Johnson was outraged. He fought—all the way to the top. The Supreme Court, 6–3, gingerly embraced affirmative action; and Diane Joyce kept her job.

In *Fullilove v. Klutznick* (1980) affirmative action also won an important victory.[7] Congress had passed a law to give an edge to businesses owned by minorities in bidding for government contracts. The Supreme Court upheld this law. Yet in 1995, in *Adarand Constructors, Inc., v. Pena,* the Court seemed to change its mind.[8] The Department of Transportation had let a contract for a highway job in Colorado. The prime contractor asked for bids on providing guardrails. Adarand was the low bidder. But Gonzales Construction Company won the subcontract. This was because the prime contract promised extra money if the contractor hired subs controlled by "socially and economically disadvantaged individuals" (Hispanics in this case). That was official policy, under the Small Business Act. The Supreme Court, by a bare majority (5–4) took Adarand's side. Any government action based on a "racial classification" would get the "the strictest judicial scrutiny."[9] Nothing ever survives this kind of scrutiny.

A year later, a federal court held that affirmative action in admissions to public law schools was illegal; the Constitution, said the court, repeating a modern mantra, is color-blind; and this means no racial preferences, not for whites, not for blacks.[10] The case came out of Texas; the Supreme Court, for whatever reason, deigned not to hear it; the law remained in force in Texas (and two neighboring states), but nowhere else. In California, antiaffirmative action forces put Proposition 209, an initiative measure, on the ballot; the voters approved of it, by a sizable majority, on November 5, 1996. "Prop 209" added a clause to the California Constitution: the state was not to "grant preferential treatment" to anyone "on the basis of race, sex, color, ethnicity or national origin" in public employment, in public education, or in public contracts.[11] The first results of Prop 209 seemed quite drastic. In fall 1997 the law school of the University of California at Berkeley admitted fourteen blacks (this was in itself a severe reduction in numbers); none of them came; and there was also a catastrophic drop, initially at least, at the law school of the University of California at Los Angeles.[12] In Texas only four black students were enrolled in the law school in fall 1997. There were much less dramatic results, on the other hand, at the undergraduate level.

All of this, especially in the 1990s, can be read as strong evidence of backlash. After all, the cases did not come out of nowhere. Interest groups and conservative think tanks played a role. The Board of Regents of the University of California backed Proposition 209; the board had acted against affirmative action as early as 1995.[13] The (white) public was in the main opposed to "special" privileges for black people or Hispanics. Whenever "affirmative action" is on the ballot, the public shows its distaste.

But it is important not to exaggerate. American apartheid is dead beyond recall. Only a few lunatics, in camps in Montana or sending poisoned messages on the web, still dream about a republic for the white man only. There is a growing black middle class. White Americans, even in the Deep South, accept the role of blacks in politics, in professional sports, on television; they accept the integration of restaurants, workplaces, and hotels. Old-timers might still grumble among themselves or harbor resentments in their hearts; but the younger people find a certain level of equality only natural. In the 1990s blacks served in the president's cabinet. Virginia elected a black governor, Douglas Wilder, in 1990—surprising for a southern state. Old Dixiecrats and segregationists were among the leaders in the battle to confirm Clarence Thomas to the Supreme Court in 1991—a black man, married to a white woman, at that. The world had decisively changed.

Moreover, even the enemies of affirmative action insisted that they did not want lily-white universities and government departments. They scrambled to think up schemes and tricks to get more minorities enrolled. Not that racism was dead—far from it. It was still alive; but it had radically changed its character.

White backlash mostly calls itself a war against "special privileges." "Equality" (whatever that means) is not in dispute. The demographics of the country were also changing, and that makes a difference. The millions of immigrants who arrived in the 1980s and 1990s were mainly Asians and Hispanics; America even looked different than it did before. You could see every race and every mixture of race on the streets of New York and San Francisco—and, more and more, on the streets of Wichita and Atlanta as well. All of this brought about changes. Prime-time TV, in ads and regular programs, showed black people, Chinese people, gay people, people in wheelchairs, Hispanics. These images penetrated even the most remote outposts of America. They probably had an impact, if only in the sense that they affected what people came to expect as natural and normal.

The way men related to women, and women to men, socially and legally, had also changed drastically; and probably irreversibly. No way could the gender genie go back in its bottle. Feminism as an ideology was bruised and embattled; and, in many circles, deeply resented. But as *fact* it was firmly established. Many men, no doubt, secretly longed for the good old days—a world of dominant men and attractive, submissive women. But they also lusted in their hearts for the paychecks their wives brought home, which they more and more relied on for extras or luxuries or just plain making ends meet. It was Reagan the reactionary who put the first woman, Sandra Day O'Connor, on the United States Supreme Court. Abortion rights seem here to stay, at least in the near future, although the battle of course is still raging. Even on such an explosive issue as gay rights the country has shifted position, probably for good: in a survey in the 1990s, almost two-thirds of the public felt that homosexual relations between consenting adults should not be against the law.[14] Gay marriage, however, is still deeply offensive to most people; and people who claim that they are perfectly comfortable with "rights" for gays nonetheless resent and reject what they call "special privileges."

The Supreme Court has been cautious on the issue of same-sex relations. In *Bowers v. Hardwick* (1986) Michael Hardwick was arrested and charged with violating the Georgia sodomy statute.[15] A police officer had barged into his bedroom and found him having sex with another man. Under Georgia "any sexual act involving the sex organs of one person and the mouth or anus of another" was a crime. The statute by its terms could apply to anybody, not just gays. Five justices of the Supreme Court seemed to ignore this aspect of the law.

The statute, they said, was perfectly valid. There was no "right of privacy" that extended to "homosexual sodomy." Four justices dissented.

This narrow defeat for gay rights called a halt to the line of cases that started in *Griswold* and continued in *Roe v. Wade*. In the outside world, there was plenty of evidence of backlash. In 1992 voters in Colorado adopted an anti-gay rights amendment to their constitution, by a small majority (54 percent to 46 percent). The state, its agencies, and cities, towns, or school districts were not to adopt laws, ordinances, or policies under which "homosexual, lesbian or bisexual orientation, conduct or practices or relationships shall constitute or otherwise be the basis of or entitle any person or class of persons to have or claim any minority status, quota preferences, protected status or claim of discrimination." Defenders of the measure, as usual, said it did nothing more than get rid of "special rights" for sexual minorities, which they were not entitled to anyway.

Somewhat surprisingly, the highest court of Colorado struck down the amendment as unconstitutional; and the Supreme Court, even more surprisingly, agreed, 6–3.[16] Colorado had no right to single out gays and lesbians and subject them to this special disability. Scalia wrote one of his typically harsh and callous dissents. He made clear his distaste for gay rights, and referred to gays and lesbians as a rich and powerful elite, with "disproportionate political power."[17] This idea (or fantasy) assumed that the social situation had turned upside down in one short generation. Once upon a time, there was racism, sexism, and homophobia; but now these "minorities" were pampered favorites of the law; they had "special privileges"; and it was the majority which now suffered the pangs of disadvantage. Thus the world as seen by Antonin Scalia.

On questions of criminal law and criminal justice, as we have seen, the Rehnquist Court has been particularly severe, and a solid majority seems avid, even bloodthirsty, when it comes to the death penalty. Rehnquist, Thomas, and Scalia would love to clean out death row quickly. They probably have a good deal of public support. On abortion and gay rights, on the other hand, the country is deeply divided; and so is the Court.

The Rehnquist Court is legally conservative; but legal conservatism is not always the same as the conservativism of the nonlegal public. This comes out clearly in cases in which the Court flies in the face of public opinion. A prime example was the flag-burning case (1989).[18] Under Texas law, it was a crime to deface or damage the flag, if your act was likely to seriously offend "one or more persons likely to observe or discover" your desecration. Thirty-one states passed laws of this sort between 1897 and 1905.[19] The southern states were the slowest to act; the Civil War, still fresh in some people's minds, dimmed their enthusiasm for the stars and stripes. They fell into line somewhat later.

The defendant in the flag-burning case was Gregory Lee Johnson. He came to court every day in a T-shirt saying "Revolutionary Communist Youth Brigade" and with a picture of a man holding a rifle. He was convicted; but a narrow 5–4 majority of the Supreme Court reversed, on free speech grounds. The news burst like a bomb in the national press. Congress was buried under a blizzard of letters, protests, and state legislative resolutions. An orgy of tub-thumping, posturing, and flag-waving swept over Congress. According to public opinion polls, as many as 85 percent of the public found the Court's decision offensive.[20] Congress quickly passed a Flag Protection Act. In 1990 the Supreme Court struck this statute down, again by a 5–4 margin.[21] Apparently, only an amendment to the Constitution could save the flag; but the proposed amendment died in the House of Representatives (it got a majority, but not two-thirds). And then the whole issue seemed to vanish from the radar screens. The public did, apparently, want an amendment; but their high support had fairly low voltage. The public lost interest fairly quickly. Perhaps they were simply bored; flag-burning had become "very much like a summer television rerun, a formula notorious for killing public interest."[22]

The Court had no way of knowing, to be sure, that the issue would die a natural death, any more than it could have guessed, realistically, that *Roe v. Wade* would *not* fade away into obscurity. The justices know that some, perhaps many, decisions roil the waters only temporarily. Flag-burning touched on momentary passions, but nobody's vital interests. After one eruption, flag-burning went back into its closet of obscurity.

Abortion Wars

Justice Harry Blackmun, who wrote the majority opinion in *Roe v. Wade*, surely thought that he had reached a sensible compromise. Perhaps he expected the rumpus to die down (as it later would in the flag-burning case). Even *Brown v. Board of Education* was in the end almost universally accepted. It took time, of course. *Roe v. Wade* may be different. The issue was still terrifically divisive, and extremely salient, in 2000, more than twenty-five years after the decision was first handed down. From the first moment on, there have been attempts to reverse it—by amending the Constitution, by violence, by *any* means. The campaign for an amendment went nowhere; but legislatures did cut the decision down as much as they could. The Hyde Amendment, as we have seen, shut the door on federal funding for poor women; and the Supreme Court narrowly upheld this restriction.

Meanwhile, the cases continued to come up; legislatures in many states were busily grinding out laws to limit abortion rights, as much as they could. The struggle reached a kind of climax in 1992. With the new, conservative appointments to the Supreme Court, were there now, finally, five votes to overrule *Roe v. Wade?* It seemed likely; but some members of the Court looked over the edge of this particular cliff and decided not to jump. In *Planned Parenthood of Southeastern Pennsylvania v. Casey,* in a highly unusual move, three justices of the Court—O'Connor, Kennedy, and Souter—wrote a joint opinion holding that *Roe v. Wade* should, in essence, "be retained and once again affirmed."[23] They declined to "overrule under fire"; if they did so, they might "subvert the Court's legitimacy." For these justices, the issue was the "institutional integrity" of the Court. Four justices dissented; Justice Scalia's dissent was especially biting and vituperative—he described the joint opinion with words like "outrageous," and he argued that *Roe v. Wade* was the *cause* of divisiveness; that it had "fanned into life an issue that has inflamed our national politics." At the end of his opinion, he invoked the image of the *Dred Scott* case—the most wrong-headed and ill-fated decision in the Court's history. Scalia described a portrait of the aged chief justice, Roger Brooke Taney, who wrote the *Dred Scott* opinion, sitting in a chair, "right hand hanging limply, almost lifelessly," his eyes sad, hollow, and disillusioned. Now the Court was repeating Taney's colossal blunder: "We should get out of this area [abortion], where we have no right to be, and where we do neither ourselves nor the country any good by remaining." But these words fell on deaf ears; and Clinton's two appointments to the Court gave *Roe v. Wade,* at the very least, some breathing space.

The Nine Scorpions

The Court is fractured politically; but it is also fractured in another, perhaps deeper sense. The Court as an institution has changed a lot in the twentieth century. It is less a collegial body than it is nine separate law offices. Oliver

Wendell Holmes, Jr., once described the Court as nine scorpions in a bottle. Today it is much more like nine scorpions in nine bottles. Each justice runs his or her own little show.

In part, this reflects changes in the way the Court is organized. Until well into the twentieth century, justices wrote their own opinions, with the help of a clerk. The clerks were mostly just that: clerks. Each opinion bore the personal stamp of the justice who wrote it. It would be hard to imagine a clerk imitating or creating the tense, nervous, elegant prose of Oliver Wendell Holmes, Jr. After the 1920s, some justices began to rely more heavily on their clerks; some clerks actually drafted opinions. The custom arose of hiring bright young men (and later, bright young women), recent law school graduates, to serve one year as a law clerk and then move on. Young William H. Rehnquist served as law clerk for Justice Robert Jackson in 1952–1953; at that time, the justices had two clerks each (the chief justice had three; Justice Douglas made do with one). The clerks helped winnow out petitions for certiorari. Did they actually write opinions? Rehnquist denied that the law clerk was a kind of "legal Rasputin"; but he did feel the clerks as a whole had a "liberal" bias: "extreme solicitude for the claims of Communists and other criminal defendants, expansion of federal power . . . great sympathy toward any government regulation of business"—in short, the "political philosophy now espoused by the Court under Chief Justice Earl Warren." Rehnquist felt the clerks could influence the Court by slanting material.[24]

Rehnquist's ruminations led to a brief flurry of interest in the subject, and one senator, Stennis of Mississippi, actually called for an investigation.[25] Nothing came of this; and the clerks became more and more important. Today, each justice can have four of these clerks. And they definitely do write opinions. When young Byron White clerked for Chief Justice Vinson, in 1946–1947, seven of the justices still wrote their own; Vinson and Murphy were the exceptions.[26] How much the justices left to their clerks then and now varies from justice to justice. Unquestionably, first drafts at least are written by the clerks, for the most part. This is true of the whole federal system. Since 1936 even district court judges in the federal system have clerks; and the judges today are more opinion editors than opinion writers. The pressure of business makes this almost inevitable. At least this is what the judges think.[27] Richard Posner is one of the few federal judges who actually writes his own opinions.

A justice who has four bright, diligent clerks at his fingertips—not to mention computers and electronic databases—is not a justice likely to produce terse, compact opinions. This combination—warm bodies and hot technology—stimulates the production of long opinions, concurrences, and dissents. The published opinions of the Supreme Court show this: a fractured court; sprawling, bloated opinions—sometimes every justice puts in her or own two cents; and often the "majority" represents a "plurality" at most. Not every case has this problem; but it is certainly exceedingly common.

Here is an example: the case, *Saudia Arabia v. Nelson* (1993), was not especially earthshaking in itself.[28] Scott Nelson worked at the King Faisal Specialist Hospital in Riyadh; he blew one whistle too many (he claimed), and the Saudis arrested him. He was tortured, beaten, shackled, and thrown into a rat-infested jail. When he got out and returned home, he sued Saudi Arabia for damages. The defense was sovereign immunity. Justice Souter wrote the Court's opinion; four justices joined him. White wrote a concurring opinion. Blackmun joined that concurrence; but then wrote an opinion "concurring in the judgment in part and dissenting in part." Justice Kennedy concurred in part and dissented in part—taking exception to the "last paragraph of Part II." Blackmun and Stevens joined Kennedy "as to Parts I-B and II." Stevens wrote a separate dissent. Nelson, by the way, lost the case.

This sort of thing is becoming almost the norm. The justices agree and disagree in bits and pieces and snatches. This, of course, makes it tough to decide what, if anything, the Court has actually decided. Justices defer less to each other, they care less about crafting opinions that can shovel together some sort of consensus. Each justice seems concerned with building up and maintaining a separate identity, ideology, and body of opinions. Each acts as a kind of separate sovereignty.

State Courts

Many of the changes in the United States Supreme Court had parallels in the state courts. Most states, as we have seen, had moved to a three-tier system; and the Supreme Court of, say, California had almost as much freedom to choose as the United States Supreme Court. The state supreme courts also began to use law clerks, some as early as the 1930s. Each justice of the Supreme Court of Washington State, for example, had his own law clerk by 1949; in the 1980s each justice had two.[29] No state supreme court was as fractured as the United

States Supreme Court; but dissents and concurrences were more common than in the early part of the century.

Presidents Ronald Reagan and George Bush had twelve years between them to fill vacancies on the federal bench. They tried to appoint conservative judges; and on the whole they succeeded. Liberals became painfully aware that there was less to be gotten out of the federal courts. In desperation, they turned more attention to state courts, and to state constitutional law. We have already mentioned the doctrine of independent state grounds. If a state decision rested on its own constitution, federal courts had no power to interfere.

Some state courts have shown a real streak of independence. The Supreme Court of Kentucky struck down the state's law against "deviate sexual intercourse with another person of the same sex" in 1993, despite *Bowers v. Hardwick*. The case was *Commonwealth v. Wasson*. The defendant, Jeffrey Wasson, made a bad mistake; in a parking lot, he propositioned a man who turned out to be an undercover officer. But the Supreme Court of Kentucky overturned his conviction. The court invoked Kentucky's "right of privacy," which was, according to the court, part of a "rich and compelling tradition" and was much broader than the federal right.[30] Whether Kentucky actually had this kind of "rich and compelling tradition" seems a bit dubious; but in any event, the statute was dead. Even more surprising, the Georgia Supreme Court in November 1998 struck down the very statute that the Supreme Court of the United States had upheld in *Bowers v. Hardwick*. Apparently, Georgia also had a rich and compelling tradition of toleration, and a broad-band right of privacy, much broader than the federal right.[31] The majority opinion in Georgia did not even bother to mention *Bowers v. Hardwick*.

The battles over *Roe v. Wade* on the federal level had their echo in the states as well. Some state supreme courts have discovered abortion rights in their own constitutions—these states include Florida, California, Connecticut, Michigan, Massachusetts, and New Jersey. In these states, therefore, whatever the United States Supreme Court does—and whatever their legislatures do—*Roe v. Wade* or its equivalent is beyond legal reach.[32]

On the Domestic Front

In his first administration, Ronald Reagan cut taxes, and rather dramatically. (Congress did not resist very hard.) The Reagan administration also jacked up the budget for defense. This produced a whopping deficit. Nobody, of course, thought a big deficit was a good idea. But what was to be done? Raising taxes was an obvious solution. Major increases, however, were politically dangerous. Cutting spending was the only other way. Some archconservatives seduced themselves with dreams of getting rid of the welfare state. But people *liked* the welfare state—at least the parts that helped *them*. Still, the deficit kept the welfare state from expanding; and it even could be trimmed around the edges.

The deficits lasted until the late 1990s; at this point, a boom economy produced big tax revenues; the deficit shrank, and then vanished altogether. At the end of the century, Congress and the administration were wrangling over mountains of surplus money. The money was not in hand—it was all in the future, and could vanish like a desert mirage. But even imaginary money seems to burn a hole in the pockets of members of Congress, just as it does for the ordinary citizen. Tax cuts, new spending for education, paying off the national debt: all of these were now on the agenda.

Medicare and Social Security were both supposed to be in trouble. Not political trouble—nobody running for office, certainly, dared to suggest getting rid of them. But the programs were victims, in a way, of their very success. People were living longer and retiring early; modern medicine was miraculous—and very expensive. Fewer workers were putting money in, compared with the number taking money out; vast sums were needed to support more and more old people who were living and living and living. Would the systems go bankrupt (whatever that might mean)? It seemed possible; it was definitely discussed. Dire warnings were sounded.[33] Many people became convinced that the systems were on the way to ruin; that by the time the young folks needed them, the programs would be crippled or impoverished or gone.

Some people defined the problem as a struggle of young against old. But as we have seen, both Medicare and Social Security were not just for the old; the real beneficiaries included millions of people under sixty-five, who no longer had to think about mortgaging their house to keep Granma alive or to pay for her hip replacement. Reform, not repeal, was what everybody wanted; and what every politician promised. But the promises clashed with and contradicted each other. The century ended with the problem still unresolved.

Other parts of the welfare state had less luck: Aid to Families with Dependent Children (AFDC), for one. President Clinton promised the public to "end welfare as we know it." This was an extremely popular promise. He meant—

and the public means—"welfare" in the sense of money for poor people. Social Security or Medicare, in other words, were not "welfare." They were social insurance: psychologically at least, people felt they had earned their money.

Aid to the poor was unearned. And unpopular. And ineffective. (So taxpayers thought.) People who wanted money ought to earn it; they ought to work. In a society in which status is precarious, it is easy for working people, two steps away from the wolf at the door themselves, to hate people lower down who seem to be getting a free ride. In this way, aid to families came full circle. AFDC, in the beginning, embraced the idea that mothers of small children should not have to work to stay alive; it might be better if they were home with the kids. The central image was a poor widow in an apron, struggling to put food on the table; her children were ragged but legitimate. The new image— whether it conformed to reality or not—was strikingly different. The welfare mother was lazy, shiftless. She slept with any man who knocked on her door, and some who didn't bother to knock; she was addicted to drugs; she was irresponsible, a drag on society; she popped out babies helter-skelter in secure knowledge that a check would come her way. She was also, for the most part, black. Welfare became the "lightning rod for Americans' anxieties over their work, incomes, families, and futures"; welfare parasites were part of the "rot eating its way through the American dream."[34]

The solution was to put the social parasite to work—force her to get off the rolls. This would save money and help society. Clinton made his promise to "end . . . welfare as we know it" in a speech in 1991; temporary welfare was acceptable; after that, you must earn your keep. Welfare payments, pitifully low in many states, plunged even lower. States were cutting budgets on the backs of the poor. The states also began to experiment with "workfare."[35] Wisconsin was one of the pioneers. Its experiments received a lot of admiring attention in the media.

In 1996 Congress passed a mammoth "welfare reform" bill—its official title was the Personal Responsibility and Work Opportunity Reconciliation Act of 1996 (double-think in legislative titles is very much in vogue), and the president signed it.[36] This was a massive, complex piece of legislation—the text is about 250 pages long. Among other things, it ended a federal program that was more than sixty years old. No longer did the federal government guarantee poor people some cash assistance, however meager. Block grants to the states replaced AFDC. Now the states could put together their own programs of welfare, or workfare. Under the law, one can have benefits for two years; then they end. During a lifetime, the limit is five years on welfare. The states may, however, make some hardship exemptions. The law also contained some harsh provisions aimed at cutting benefits to aliens.

It is certainly a good idea to try to get people off welfare. The vast majority of people on welfare want to get off, want to work, want to improve their lives. But they need help, and help costs money. The federal bill was not just a bill to "reform" welfare: it was also a bill to cut welfare costs.[37] But cutting welfare budgets is not the way. How can a single mother take care of her three children if she has to take on a tough, grinding, low-wage job? There are some partial answers to this question—day care centers, for example—but they are all quite expensive. And the money was not forthcoming. In any event, as of 2001 it was hard to generalize about the impact of the new law—especially hard, because it devolved so much power to the states; there are fifty different experiences to take into account.[38]

Counterrevolution in Torts

The liability explosion in torts was another subject of counterrevolution. Many people (in particular, many businesspeople) felt that the law had gone crazy. Plaintiffs were collecting wild amounts in crackpot lawsuits. They were killing the goose that laid the golden eggs. An active campaign began to cut back on the excesses of the law of torts. The American Tort Reform Association (ATRA), established in 1986, lobbied for this cause. The members were big corporations, including insurance companies. They spread horror stories about weird cases in which whining, neurotic, careless or lying plaintiffs, abetted by runaway juries, extorted millions of dollars from honest companies. Newspapers gleefully reported on these follies: imagine, one woman won a million dollars because a CAT scan took away her psychic powers; a burglar sued the owner of a house because he fell through a skylight on the roof; an old woman won millions of dollars when she scalded herself with hot coffee at McDonald's.[39] The Republican Party regularly denounced greedy lawyers. Tort suits were killing the economy, driving doctors crazy, bankrupting businesses.

Of course, the stories were urban legends; or were slanted in the press to make something sensible look ridiculous.[40] The CAT scan woman never collected; the judge set the verdict aside. She lost completely at the second trial.[41]

The indignant burglar was a figment of the imagination: in the actual case, the plaintiff was a high school student, not a burglar. The student went on the roof of the high school to get a floodlight; he fell through a skylight that was covered with tar and hence not visible.[42] But these stories made the public gasp—a public which was willing, if not eager, to believe that the system had gone crazy. In the first place, the unusual and the scandalous are interesting; dull, efficient everyday cases are not. Business interests and conservative think tanks helped fan the flames. They stood to gain, or thought they did, from limitations on liability. And wasn't it true that tort claims made Americans lose jobs? The stories also tapped into a kind of vague, smoldering discontent: a feeling that America had lost its soul, or part of its soul. In some ways, the greedy old woman who sucked millions of dollars from McDonald's, and whose trouble was caused by her own foolishness, was a sister under the skin to the welfare queen: both were immoral people, parasites, bilking the public and honest businesses. A burglar collecting in tort fed on the fantasy that American judges coddle criminals. Many old themes, many ambiguities and ambivalences in American culture and life, strengthened the movement to cut down on liability.

It was no surprise, then, that the movement had considerable success. Many states drastically limited punitive damages. In Georgia, if a jury awards punitive damages, 75 percent of the money goes to the state, not the plaintiff; and, except in products liability cases, punitive damages were not to exceed $250,000.[43] In fact, few plaintiffs actually recover punitive damages; and only rarely do they collect huge amounts.[44] The statute was a solution without a problem. But more than thirty states enacted laws in the last two decades of the twentieth century to curb "abuse" in tort cases. Many of these statutes seem to have had an effect: in Texas personal injury suits apparently declined; and some plaintiffs who in the past would have collected substantial damages now had to settle for little or nothing. Texas, perhaps, had gone too far.[45]

In the workers' compensation system, the courts, as we have seen, vastly expanded liability over the years. Employers were, naturally, unhappy; and they positively panicked when workers began to make claims for psychological damage. The proposition that the job had driven someone crazy got short shrift in most of the earlier cases. Later judges and juries were much less skeptical. In one case, from Massachusetts (1985), Helen J. Kelly worked for Raytheon for twenty-two years; then she was told she would be laid off. She immediately "began to cry" and "was unable to compose herself." A few days later, the company gave her a transfer to another department; but there she "became depressed, developed chest pains," was hospitalized, and was ultimately declared disabled. She asked for, and got, workers' compensation, over the objection of the insurance carrier.[46] In *Wade v. Anchorage School District,* an Alaska case of 1987, Gerald Wade, the worker, was what has been called an "eggshell" claimant—fragile in the extreme.[47] Not physically: Wade, a black man, had once been Mr. Alaska, and his body bristled with muscles. His psychic makeup was another question. Wade had a security job; he complained constantly of disturbing incidents, race discrimination, even sexual harassment (a coach patted him on the butt). Wade was a deeply troubled man, and was diagnosed, eventually, as having a "paranoid personality." The administrators denied his claim for compensation; but the Alaska court reversed this decision. Wade, the court said, was entitled to recover; the job was not the cause of his mental disease, but it clearly played a role in the flare-up.

Cases of this sort frightened employers to death, especially when the claims began to multiply. By 1987 mental stress accounted for about one-quarter of all occupational disease claims in California. Total awards ballooned. Then employers struck back. They lobbied for changes in the law. An amendment to the law in California in 1989 aimed to establish a "new and higher threshold for psychiatric injury." The governor, when he signed the bill, referred to the "fraud-ridden workers' compensation system"; it was costing the state (he said) sixty thousand jobs a year. Under the new rule, no compensation for "psychiatric injury" could be paid if the injury was "substantially caused by a lawful, nondiscriminatory, good faith personnel action."[48] The California reforms made a difference; the cost of workers' compensation, which had risen from about $2 billion in 1976 to about $11 billion in 1993, dropped to about $8 billion in 1995.[49] Nor was California the only state to make these "reforms." Idaho amended its statute to bar any claims arising out of conditions "generally inherent in every working situation or from a personnel related action," including "changes in duty, job evaluation or employment termination."[50] Helen Kelly would have had no chance at all in Idaho.

Strangers Among Us

All Americans, except the native tribes, are descended from people who came from somewhere else, voluntarily or not. Yet anti-immigrant feeling or nativism has often been a powerful political force. Why are so many Americans unsympathetic to more recent immigrants? Perhaps some people feel, now that we're here, it's time to pull up the drawbridge. There is worry about jobs. There is a large element of racism. The new immigrants come from places like China, Korea, and El Salvador, after all. And there is also a vague sense of threat: American culture is under attack; the newcomers are weirdly different, and they do not share the old-fashioned values.

Quite similar ideas, early in the twentieth century, led to immigration restrictions and the quota system; these ideas influenced the purity crusade, and the rise of Prohibition. Then came the red scare and the campaign against anarchists and other aliens. In the 1920s the new Ku Klux Klan demanded "America for the Americans." Nativism, it seems, is almost always with us.

In the past two decades, the language issue has been particularly salient. The main danger here is supposed to come from the millions who speak Spanish. An "English-only" movement has been thriving. During the First World War, German was the scapegoat language; some people even decided to rename sauerkraut "liberty cabbage." Speaking German (or teaching it in school) seemed almost an act of disloyalty; among some extremists, any foreign language was suspect; the schools should confine themselves to English.[51] Nebraska, way back in 1920, declared English its "official language." Illinois in 1923 made "American" (whatever that means) its official language. (Later, it amended this to "English.") In neither case did the statute seem to make much difference—in Illinois, the square dance was the official state folk dance, in California the official state mollusk is the banana slug. Why not an official language as well?[52]

The English-only movement nonetheless has political meaning, and has gained some political success. In California, for example, the voters in 1986 chose, by a big margin, to designate English as the state's official language. Millions of people in the state speak Spanish at home; but the notion that they are a threat to the English language, or to the American system, is simply ridiculous. It is of course not English but the minority languages—Native American languages in particular—which are under threat. In any event, even though English is the "official" language of California, and no other language enjoys this status, the state prints ballots in Spanish and English; and the Department of Motor Vehicles offers a written driver's exam in Spanish to anyone who asks for it (and many do).

The English-only movement was not confined to California. State after state decided to give English official status—including states like North Dakota, where Spanish-speakers are not exactly common.[53] As in California, most of this language posturing had no practical consequences. The laws are best seen as pompous symbolic gestures. In one state, moreover, there are in fact two official languages. That state is Hawaii, whose constitution makes English and Hawaiian "official languages" of the state. This too is largely symbolic, but it is a different kind of symbolism. It is the symbolism of plural equality. In fact, the mellifluous Hawaiian language, a handful of consonants in a gentle sea of vowels, trembles, like native flowers and the island's honeycreeper birds, on the brink of total extinction.

Where Do We Stand?

The counterrevolution did, as we have seen, achieve some results. These are, on the whole, rather modest. Of course, for a paraplegic dumped from the welfare rolls during the Reagan years, for an undocumented alien scrounging about for crumbs, for black students who see the doors of Berkeley shutting fast, for a man on death row who can't get a court to look at his writs and appeals—for all these people, the modest changes loom very large. We live our lives one by one, and one at a time. Life at the bottom tail of the bell curve can be an awfully grim life, even when life in the fat part of the curve is better than ever.

The counterrevolution, moreover, breeds *its* backlash; and so on, ad infinitum, like a bouncing ball that never comes to rest. As of 2001 it is not easy to take stock of the state of the nation. On race: more than forty years have passed since *Brown v. Board of Education*. Despite all the controversy and the backsliding, race relations have drastically changed. Blacks at the end of the twentieth century were no longer a caste of untouchables, politically powerless. They voted, they held office, they made their voices heard. The black middle class, freed from the barriers that had held it back, took off and achieved enormous gains. Perhaps black students at Harvard or the University of Virginia sat by themselves in the cafeterias; but at least they were there. Still, many blacks remained desperately poor. All blacks, up and down the income scale, were aware of a residue of sullen hostility, like a droning noise in the background; aware, too, at times, of something much worse. Black anger and frustration fed white backlash; and white backlash, in turn, led to even more anger and frustration.

Black separatism has something of a history in the United States. Marcus Garvey, a Jamaican immigrant, founded the Universal Negro Improvement Association in Jamaica in 1914, and transferred it to New York in 1916. Garvey preached black unity. He advocated migration to Africa; he thought blacks should run their own businesses, and he himself founded a number of businesses, including a steamship company.[54] Garveyism ran its course; but black separatism popped up again in the 1960s. Many black intellectuals and thinkers abandoned integration as an ideal. The *Brown* decision, in the 1950s, had talked the language of integration: the need to put black back into the mainstream. "Many Negroes," wrote Chief Justice Warren, "have achieved outstanding success in the arts and sciences as well as in the business and professional world." They were contributing, in other words, to mainstream culture and life. Warren did not think of blacks as a "nation," as a separate entity or culture or identity. Neither did the leaders of the civil rights movement. They could not afford to. They wanted rights, they wanted seats at the same lunch counters as white folks, they wanted to send their children to the same universities, they wanted to shop at the same stores, they wanted jobs in the same factories—they wanted, in short, an end to segregation in all of its manifestations. And they wanted to *count*. They wanted the vote, they wanted black judges and sheriffs; they wanted black mayors and members of the city council; they wanted an end to white supremacy, so that they could take their place at the table, along with the rest of the country.

Only later did we begin to hear that black is beautiful. Only later was there a prominent black Muslim movement (and a "Nation of Islam"). Many blacks began literally to think of themselves as another nation. Integration seemed to be only skin deep. Where there *was* integration. If integration meant genuine harmony, "color-blindness," people working and playing and living together without regard to race, this was almost nowhere to be found. Hispanics more and more felt the same way. Moreover, the gap between black and white income levels—and white and Hispanic income levels—proved to be more stubborn than expected. Perhaps there was no real future in a white society.

The feminist movement, and other movements of minorities—the so-called sexual minorities, for example—traveled along a similar trajectory. First came a call for rights, for integration in the mainstream. Then, it turned out, despite success in gaining rights, the mainstream was not as welcoming as the group had hoped. This encouraged forms of rejection and separatism. It led to "gay pride," and gay neighborhoods. Every movement, too, generated a kind of radical fringe—a submovement in open revolt against the majority, its ideas, its ideals, its conceptions of the normal and the right. And every movement generated its backlash. Witness all the noise about "radical feminists," women who burn brassieres and hate men.

The fate of the proposed Equal Rights Amendment (ERA) gave the backlashers at least a symbolic victory. The ERA simply announced that "equality of rights under the law" was not to be denied or abridged, by federal or state governments, "on account of sex." The ERA was first proposed in the 1920s, and gradually gained support. The Senate passed it in 1972, by a vote of 84–2. The ERA needed to be ratified by thirty-eight states. At first, states rushed to do so; but then the backlash set in. The amendment was stopped cold at thirty-five states, and died a natural death in 1982. Engineers of a smear campaign against it accused the ERA of everything under the sun: it would force men and women to go to the same toilets, allow women to go topless because men can go topless; it was a Communist plot, a lesbian plot, and so on. And millions of deeply religious women believed that "God made us different," and that the Bible said "women should submit to their husbands," and the ERA would somehow put an end to all that.[55] Still, the defeat of the ERA was a hollow victory: women's rights, and women's new social role, kept marching on.

By the late twentieth century, wherever you looked in the political landscape, you seemed to see identity politics. There was black politics, or Hispanic politics, or gay politics, or the Gray Panthers, or feminist politics. There was, it seemed, no longer any national identity. There was no national consensus. The mirror of state had shattered into a thousand pieces. There were no longer any "Americans" as such; there was nothing but hyphen-Americans— black Americans, and gay Americans, and feminist Americans, and Swedish-Americans, and dozens of other bits and pieces.

People wondered: what had happened to unity in American life and thought? Gone with the wind, it seemed. There was no longer American culture; instead, there was multiculture. Some people found this appalling. The tendency horrified conservatives; and even some not-so-conservatives. Others found diversity exhilarating. What some saw as fragmentation others saw as pluralism; as the very flowering of a meaningful democracy.

Curiously enough, the debate about difference, the exalting and decrying of difference, occurred at a time when the country was culturally more unified, perhaps, than ever before: bound together, tightly, within a single mass culture—a culture spread by radio, movies, TV, stimulated by the American habit of shuttling about the country, from job to job and from home to home. There were fewer and fewer enclaves, fewer pockets of isolates. The truly different minorities—the Amish, the Pennsylvania Dutch, French speakers in the swamps of Louisiana, native American peoples following native religions and speaking native languages—were under cultural siege. It was harder and harder to resist zippers and electricity—not to mention rock music and the internet. The celebration of "difference" takes place against a backdrop of enormous similarity.

We can also ask: was there ever a period of unity or consensus? Was there any such golden age? Probably not. What looked like consensus may have really been simply domination—a country in which there was a hierarchy of values and norms. White, male, Protestant virtues and ideas were the only or the chief game in town. Still, many people sincerely believed that something awful was happening in America: a loss of standards, a decline in moral values, a decline in civility, a decline in civilization itself. Rapid change is unsettling, and often seems harmful. People who were upset about the changes were the ones who put backlash on the political map. They went to the polls and voted for the English language. They voted to get rid of affirmative action. They voted to strip illegal immigrants of their rights. They voted against "special" privileges for gay men and lesbians.

As we have seen, these voters did not always get their way; and when they did prevail, the courts sometimes undid their work and frustrated their ambitions. It is important, too, to remember that these people never really wanted to turn the clock back all the way. Nobody (or almost nobody) wants segregation. Nobody wants to keep women from voting—or practicing law. Plural equality seems here to stay—and so too does identity politics.

Is Government the Problem?

Since the New Deal there have been many attempts to roll back government; yet on the whole, it never happens. In fact, regulation and government intervention increase all the time. In the Reagan era, the government raised its hand and said,

Stop. But even this administration could hardly do more than inflict a slight bruise on Leviathan.

The New Deal shifted attention away from the raw, rancorous emphasis on the "individual," on "liberty of contract," which was so prominent a feature of the *Lochner* era. The New Deal flirted with corporatism at first. The more mature New Deal passed statutes (the National Labor Relations Act) which tried to give workers collective power, through unions. Individuals were submerged—for their own good—in institutions.

Developments since the New Deal have broadened, or changed, the whole concept of the individual. The "individual" of the *Lochner* era was homo economicus. The individual today still has some of this feature; but is more well-rounded. Today's individual is unique, a single soul struggling to find his or her true vocation in life. For many individuals of this new sort, unions are absurd; and government is a problem, not a solution. This is not simply right-wing backlash. Nobody mistrusts the government as much as the Left, though for different reasons.

Survey data suggest that the level of trust in the government is low, and getting lower.[56] Probably this is part of a more general decline—a loss of faith in experts and authorities in general. Muckraking plays a part. And there is a lot of muck to rake. There is ample evidence that government lies—blatantly, frequently, and baldly. This is, of course, nothing new. Lying becomes more acute, and more necessary, in an information age. Jefferson had to worry about public opinion, but not so consistently; and he was blessed by an absence of public opinion polls. In a media-driven, poll-driven age, the temptation to lie becomes almost overwhelming. So is the media urge to expose the lie. The war in Vietnam may have been something of a turning point; millions of people who might have trusted the government found out that the government had lied, lied, and lied—about Tonkin Bay, perhaps about everything. Further scandals—Watergate, Iran-Contra, even Monica Lewinsky—did nothing to reassure the public. The truth, the whole truth, and nothing but the truth was not to be had from official sources.

A symptom of this new suspicion—and the demand to do something about it—was the Freedom of Information Act, passed in 1966.[57] Everybody should have the right to look at government records, especially records about themselves. The FOIA authorized citizens to poke around in once-secret files. The act contained, to be sure, a long list of exceptions and exemptions (national security was a big one). Agencies, at first, tended to drag their feet and hide behind the exemptions. But later amendments strengthened the act considerably. In the 1970s, the number of FOI requests skyrocketed, as thousands of people decided to peep at their FBI files. The exemptions are still important, and it is still next to impossible to squeeze information out of the CIA (for one); moreover, some businesses have tried to use the FOIA to worm business secrets out of competitors (by asking for reports and investigations of those competitors). "Confidential commercial or financial information" is one of the exemptions, but there are difficult questions of interpretation.[58] The FOIA is far from perfect; but it has had an impact—it has allowed people to turn over a lot of rocks and see what came crawling out. And the principle is significant: as government becomes more and more powerful and intrusive, open files and dossiers are something of a comfort. Many states passed their own versions of the FOIA—for example, Arkansas, in 1967, a year after the federal law.[59] All government records in Arkansas (excluding tax, school, and medical records) were to be "open to inspection and copying"; and all meetings of governing bodies, boards, agencies and the like were likewise to be open to the public.

The concern over privacy and government snooping has, of course, only increased over time; at times it verges on paranoia. But as the saying goes, even paranoids have enemies; in the age of spy satellites, listening devices that can hear a cricket chirp on another continent, massive databases that can store and tell every last detail of a person's life, paranoia may be justified. Of course, government is not the only entity that has these powers: big business has them too. Only the government has the CIA and a fleet of black helicopters; but the large corporations have huge computers with storage capacities which are, for all practical purposes, infinite. In the age of credit cards—and e-commerce—all the data about one person, or one family, can be aggregated into a single dossier. Businesses can sell their lists and their dossiers to other businesses. Government is thus at one and the same time the enemy; and the only force with power enough to keep other enemies at bay. How can society balance these two aspects of government? Nobody has yet been able to come up with a solution—at least not to the satisfaction of the public.

18

Getting Around and Spreading the Word

One theme of this book has been the way technology has changed the world we live in, and the way we live in that world. If you change the world, you change the world's law as well. Any major advance in science, medicine, or technology leaves its mark on the law. Consider, for example, "the pill," and how it changed sexual behavior, sexual attitudes, family life—and both family law and the penal code. Not that the pill did this all by itself; in some ways, the pill is an effect as well as a cause. For our purposes, it is not necessary to decipher the mysteries of cause and effect. It is enough to know that cause and effect are there.

The pill is only one example out of many. It is probably harder to trace the impact of antibiotics, air-conditioning, or frozen foods on law and society. But the connections are surely there, if you only know how to read the code. Impact can be indirect. Air-conditioning makes Phoenix, Arizona, possible; and Las Vegas. That affects demography and politics. Las Vegas, in connection with other developments, has an impact on laws of gambling, on laws of marriage and divorce—to take two obvious examples. Whatever makes a difference to society is bound to penetrate, sooner or later, into the legal order, in one way or another.

Two areas in which technology has truly, deeply, and surely revolutionized American life, and therefore the law, are transportation and communication—ways of moving people and freight, ways of migrating and commuting and traveling; ways of spreading the image and the word. These two therefore deserve special treatment in this book.

The Century of the Automobile

In the preface, I called the twentieth century the century of the automobile. The automobile was invented toward the very end of the nineteenth century, but before 1900 it was essentially a curiosity, a toy for the rich. Cars were expensive, novel—and dangerous. They added something new to traffic on streets and roads. It soon became obvious that this new tool had to be regulated. Anything that moved that fast, and could inflict such damage, needed restraints and controls.

A body of automobile law grew up quickly. By 1910 many states required cars to be registered, and required a driver's license. Speed limits followed soon after. In New York in 1910, drivers were required to drive "in a careful and prudent manner," and at a safe speed; anything over thirty miles per hour, for a quarter-mile or more, was "presumptive evidence" of carelessness. Hit-and-run driving entered the penal codes as a serious crime.[1] In Kentucky in 1918, the maximum speed was twenty-five miles per hour, but that was on the open road: in cities the maximum was ten.[2] In Washington, D.C., in 1925, the speed limit was fixed at twenty-two miles per hour.[3]

Meanwhile, the social role of the automobile changed drastically. It was no longer quite such a luxury; ownership of cars penetrated further and further down into ordinary society. In 1910, 181,000 cars were sold; ten years later, 1.9 million; in 1920 there were more than 8 million cars registered in the United States; at the end of that decade, more than half of all American families owned a car. Sales declined during the Depression, not surprisingly; and private cars were not manufactured during the Second World War. After the war, there was no stopping the automotive society. Forty million cars were registered in the United States by 1950; sales of new cars were in the millions. By 1970 there were 89 million registered cars.[4] The two-car family and the two-car garage had become commonplace. Three million families owned two or more cars in 1949; by 1970, it was 28 million.[5] By 1990 "two or more car" households outnumbered the mere one-car households 50 million to 31 million; and there were 123 million cars in use in the United States.[6]

Driving to Suburbia

Cars need fuel—and roads. America's roads, not surprisingly, were simply not up to the new machine. Roads cost a lot of money; but the growing masses of drivers demanded them. A federal Road Aid Act was passed in 1916, and another in 1921; these laws gave money to states for road building. The federal law required the states to create highway commissions if they wanted a share of the loot. Even Mississippi, the poorest of the states, responded—although as late as 1923 there were no north-south connections worthy of the name, and only the three biggest cities, Meridian, Vicksburg, and Jackson, were joined by paved highways.[7] Out of the federal laws, however, came U.S. 1, running north and south, and U.S. 40 and 60, running east and west. And in the 1930s new limited-access roads were built—the West Side Highway in New York, the Pennsylvania Turnpike.[8] Road building in the states steadily improved, too, as time went on.

At the end of the Second World War there was a huge pent-up demand for cars, and plenty of money to buy cars with. In the postwar period, the automobile literally reshaped America. Government helped speed the process. In 1956 the federal government embarked on its most ambitious road-building spree: a few cents out of every gallon of gas was to go into a Highway Trust Fund, and the money was to be used to build a network of interstate highways, criss-crossing the country, north and south, east and west.[9] State and local money also poured into highways; public transportation shriveled and died in some cities; in others, it was sharply cut back.

The automobile was the great American machine. Rich people had big, flashy cars; poor people clunkers, used cars, small, old, rusty cars: anything, as long as it would go. The automobile became in many ways the key to American culture. It was the very motor force of American individualism; if the average family was a slave to its automobile, and utterly dependent on it, it was at the same time independent of shackles of time and space that had tied their grandparents to a specific place. The road system built paths to the suburbs. During the postwar period, government also lent money to veterans to buy homes. Suburbs like Levittown sprang up almost overnight. Millions of (mostly white) families deserted the cities and headed out for the fringes, where people had backyards and barbecue pits. The breadwinner did not usually work in the suburbs (later on, the factories and headquarters buildings followed the crowd out past the city limits); but the families lived there, they mowed their lawns and planted flowers, and they did their shopping in the new malls and shopping centers—islands of stores afloat in an ocean of parked cars. The old central cities stopped growing. The future was in suburbia, exurbia, and shopping malls. The future rode to work, to the store, and back home again, in cars.

The automobile was now a lifeline—the only way people could connect themselves and the places they lived, shopped, and worked, the people they wanted to visit, their extended families, their leisure-time activities. It altered every aspect of life. It led the way to the new consumer society, the suburban society, the society of entertainment and leisure. It produced a drive-in and drive-by society. You could, for example, watch a movie without getting out of your car—the postwar period was the heyday of the drive-in movie. Fifteen percent of all theaters were drive-ins by 1951, and they earned 20 percent of total theater receipts.[10] Teenagers called these magnificent establishments "passion pits"; young families used them to avoid the baby-sitter problem. The drive-in movie is now almost extinct; but the drive-in bank and the drive-in burger joint—and even the drive-in espresso bar—are very much alive and kicking.

As the automobile took over, older forms of transport fell into decay. The first casualty, of course, was the horse, and the wagons, carts, and buggies that horses dragged along. This was, on the whole, a good thing. By the end of the twentieth century, people were used to the idea that the automobile is choking the cities to death. In the 1930s the matter looked quite different. Edith Abbott, in her study of the slums of Chicago, considered the automobile a godsend. It drove out the horse, and along with it "the filthy stables and the dreadful manure heaps that accumulated." The alleys had once been "unspeakably filthy and disgusting." No more. And the auto also led to the "opening-up, widening, and repaving of many formerly little-used streets through dreary sections" of town.[11] The same was true in other cities as well. According to one estimate, in New York City horses deposited 2.5 million pounds of manure and sixty thousand gallons of urine on the streets every day; the city had to haul away fifteen thousand dead horses a year.[12] The automobile, of course, soon outlived its role of urban savior. Ultimately traffic got worse and worse, and the polluting fumes of millions of cars replaced the pollution of the horse. Clean air legislation was, in part at least, a response to the challenge of the car.

The horse was no match for the auto; and neither was the passenger train. The little engine that could no longer did; passenger rail travel limped gradually into obsolescence. Most younger Americans at the end of the twentieth century had never taken a serious railroad trip—at least not in America. The closest they had come was a ride in Disneyland; or perhaps a ride to town on a commuter train. The Interstate Commerce Commission, created in 1887, that great federal regulatory agency designed to tame the mighty railroad industry, died with a whimper in 1995.[13] Trains still carry a lot of freight; and the Surface Transportation Board still regulates them, to a degree. But intercity passenger travel survives, really, only in a few dense corridors, like the one between Boston and Washington.

The automobile even influenced crime and the war against crime. The famous bandits and gangs of the 1920s and 1930s, people like Bonnie and Clyde, depended on fast cars for their fast crimes and fast living. One writer in 1924 blamed autos and good roads for the increase in "banditry."[14] Crime had gone interstate, along with the automobile. And interstate crime, in turn, strengthened the case for interstate crime fighting—for institutions like the FBI. The automobile helped erode the borders that had been so prominent a feature of American criminal justice.

Crashing into History

The railroad accident had produced a huge body of law, and in the twentieth century, the automobile was no different: automobiles did so much damage, and killed or injured so many people, that a big corpus of law grew up around the auto accident. We have seen the impact on tort law. Traffic law in general is all about accidents: how to prevent them, and how to handle them. Traffic offenses are the dandelions of criminality. In California, in the first six months of 1950, motor vehicle violations generated 6,407 jail sentences; 2,377 combinations of fines and jail; 232,079 fines; and 299,214 cases of "forfeiture" (basically, a minor fine).[15] In North Carolina, in one twelve-month period in 1989–1990, there were 1.2 million motor vehicle crimes and infractions in the district courts.[16] Municipal courts, police courts, justice courts handled tens of thousands of minor traffic offenses; in the bigger cities there were specialized traffic courts. Most people did not take small traffic offenses seriously; neither did at least some of the judges. The traffic courts were fairly undignified; George Warren, who studied traffic courts around 1940, found judges who bantered with defendants, or even exchanged some "good-natured profanity."[17]

Drivers did not come away from traffic court with any sense of the majesty of the law.

But why should they? Traffic fines and tickets carry very little moral stigma. They are a kind of cost of driving, like the driver's license fee. Everybody who drives breaks the law—sometimes, or often. Nobody feels ashamed of himself for overtime parking; or even for making an illegal U-turn. There are, of course, much more serious traffic offenses: reckless driving, for example, or drunk driving. "Vehicular homicide" or "vehicular manslaughter" are separate, and very serious, crimes.[18]

It is particularly interesting to trace the history of laws against driving "under the influence." For a long time this has been a crime; but the campaign against drunken driving heated up considerably in the 1970s and 1980s. Doris Aiken founded RID (Remove Intoxicated Drivers) in Schenectady, New York, in the late 1970s, after a drunk driver killed a teenager. Another drunk driver killed Cari Lightner, a thirteen-year-old girl; her mother, Candy Lightner, founded an organization called MADD (Mothers Against Drunk Driving) in 1980. By the end of 1982 there were 93 chapters of MADD; by 1985 there were 320 chapters in forty-seven states, with thousands of members.[19]

These grassroots movements "brought drunk driving to the top of the social problems agenda"; and they prompted action at the state and federal levels. There followed a "deluge of new anti–drunk driving laws," all designed to toughen the law.[20] Historically, courts and juries were loath to punish drunk drivers severely; the average Joe cannot picture himself as a burglar or a stickup man but can easily imagine himself driving with one too many drinks under his belt. This attitude—"There but for the grace of God go I"—influenced juries to be lenient.[21] This attitude no doubt lingers; but the crusade has definitely made its mark on law and on law enforcement.

Regulating Cars

As millions of people bought automobiles, the automobile industry became one of the biggest, richest, most powerful in the country. It was also highly concentrated. As of 1950 three giant companies controlled almost the whole domestic market; and they had important investments overseas as well. This huge industry was essentially unregulated. In 1965 a lawyer named Ralph Nader published *Unsafe at Any Speed,* a savage attack on the auto industry. Nader accused the industry of ignoring safety, of designing dangerous cars, of blaming drivers for accidents, of elevating style over safety. He documented this with story after story of men and women killed, crushed, or maimed by cars that had been badly designed. The companies, he insisted, knew about these flaws, but chose to ignore them. The "sporty" Corvair, for example, could go out of control suddenly and unexpectedly. Nader called the Corvair "one of the greatest acts of industrial irresponsibility in the present century."[22]

General Motors, maker of the Corvair, was naturally quite perturbed. It decided to fight back; and it fought dirty. The company hired Vince Gillen, a private detective, to shadow Nader and dig up dirt on him. They found none, but not for lack of trying; there was perhaps even a crude attempt at "setting him up." The strong-arm tactics backfired: the story broke, and James Roche, president of General Motors, had to eat crow publicly; Nader sued GM, successfully; and with his winnings, founded a Public Interest Research Group.[23]

Meanwhile, in 1966 Congress enacted a National Traffic and Motor Vehicle Safety Act; a National Highway Traffic Safety Administration, in the Department of Transportation, had authority to make rules and regulations on auto safety, to cut down the slaughter on the highways. Soon came a rule that all new cars had to be equipped with seat belts. Later, the agency required cars either to have airbags, or an "ignition interlock" that prevented the driver from starting the car unless the seat belts were fastened.

This smacked too much of Big Brother for many motorists. Apparently, real men did not want to wear seat belts (or motorcycle helmets). The interlock, in the first place, often malfunctioned. And the air was full of "horror stories"; one senator claimed that he spent a half-hour trying to get his car started because he put a pound of cheese and a loaf of bread on the seat next to the driver. The interlock, said a congressman, was "un-American."[24] Congress got rid of the interlock in 1974. But in 1984, the Department of Transportation came out with a new regulation: automobile makers had to install either airbags or automatic seat belts by 1989. The regulation would lapse if states with two-thirds of the country's population passed seat-belt laws before April 1 of that year. The laws had to meet certain criteria, including a fine of at least twenty-five dollars for violators. In the event, the states did not meet the deadline; and the regulation went into effect. Time worked its magic as well; even real men got used to seat belts; and as the century ended, all new cars had both seat belts and air bags.

This account suggests that the ground had to be laid carefully with respect to any rule, regulation, or law which threatened the American love affair with automobiles, or their love affair with what they defined as freedom. Everybody had a car (well, almost everybody); drivers were voters, and driving was important to these voters. Money for roads was popular. Gas taxes were not; subsidies for public transportation also were not. Americans accepted certain restrictions (driver's licenses), perhaps out of habit; but there was a limit beyond which they hated to go—changes had to be slow, gradual, little by little. Most people also accepted traffic rules, including the speed limit. Of course, everybody broke this particular law from time to time; and some people did it persistently.

In 1974 Congress imposed a national maximum speed limit of fifty-five miles per hour, at first only as an emergency measure.[25] Under the law, if states did not go along with this speed limit, they stood to lose federal highway money. The point was to conserve oil—this was a year after the Arab oil embargo, which sent prices up, up, and up, and led to shortages and long lines at gas stations. The speed limit, however, outlasted the emergency; Congress made it permanent in 1975.[26] Lower speeds on highways, it turned out, saved lives as well as gas. But the national speed limit rankled millions of motorists, especially motorists in big, empty states like Montana. The limit was raised to sixty-five miles per hour on rural roads and interstate highways. And in 1995 Congress repealed the national speed limit altogether, along with motorcycle helmet laws.[27] Not all states took advantage of the chance to raise their speed limits. Montana was one that did. In fact, in 1995 Montana swept its speed limits entirely away—it adopted a "basic rule": drivers had to drive at a "reasonable and prudent" daytime speed.[28] What a driver in the country of the big sky considered "reasonable and prudent" was probably quite different from what would pass for "reasonable and prudent" in Providence, Rhode Island.

Gas conservation is a good idea, in theory. In practice, it carries very little heft. The auto industry misread American tastes and was buffeted by Japanese and German competition. American industry missed the boat on small cars. Carmakers stonewalled at first; then tried to meet the competition. But then consumer tastes veered once again. At the end of the twentieth century, pickup trucks and huge, lumbering cars—the infamous sport utility vehicles (suvs)—rescued the auto companies financially but guzzled whole oceans of imported oil. Environmental slogans were genuinely popular; environment action pretty much not.

In the Air and Everywhere

What the automobile began, the jet airplane continued: in the 1990s, only a handful of people traveled a serious distance by train, but millions took to the air. The jet airplane sealed the doom, for that matter, of the trans-Atlantic liner. An iceberg sank the *Titanic;* the Boeing 747 and its competitors sank its descendants. Boats survived only as cruise ships, as floating hotels and casinos; for actual travel to far-off places, the modern airplane had things all to itself.

The twentieth century was thus the century of the airplane as well as the century of the car. Wilbur and Orville Wright made their historic flight in Kitty Hawk, North Carolina, in December 1903. Until the First World War, flying was a novelty, a game for daredevils, a staple of shows at county fairs, stunts that fascinated wide-eyed audiences. There was little or no regulation. Connecticut in 1911 was apparently the first state to require pilots to get a license and register their aircraft.[29] Another early statute came out of Massachusetts in 1913. It called for a pilot's license, and registration and inspection of airplanes. The statute also tried to establish rules of the road: for example, "When two aeroplanes threaten to meet at an angle, that aeroplane which has the other on its left shall have the right of way." No airplane was to fly lower than five hundred feet when over a village, or three thousand feet when over a city; no aviator "shall intentionally throw or drop any missile or other article from an aeroplane . . . except over grounds devoted to flying or over open water." And a pilot was liable for any "injuries resulting from his flying," unless he had "taken every reasonable precaution to prevent such injury."[30]

The First World War was a huge shot in the arm for the aircraft industry; in 1916 the United States produced about four hundred airplanes, in 1918, fourteen thousand—for military purposes. All this stimulated design work and produced a crop of skillful pilots. After the war, airplanes got their first big commercial boost, transporting letters and packages. Airmail service began in 1918, between New York, Philadelphia, and Washington; then Chicago was added, and finally, San Francisco. A statute of 1925 authorized the postmaster general to enter into contracts with companies to transport air mail. An air mail stamp cost ten cents for a letter weighing an ounce or less.[31]

The Air Commerce Act of 1926 was a landmark.[32] It empowered the secretary of commerce to establish criteria for "airworthiness," a new term (on the analogy of *seaworthiness* from the law of admiralty). He was also given the authority to establish "air traffic rules for the navigation, protection, and identi-fication of aircraft"; and to establish civil airways and airports. A wave of state laws followed, on the licensing of pilots and aircraft, and on the building of airports. Airline companies now regularly carried passengers from city to city. Charles Lindbergh flew nonstop across the Atlantic in 1927 and became a hero; in 1931 Wiley Post flew around the world in a week and two days. In 1935 Pan American began its service from San Francisco to Manila (stopping at Hono-lulu, Midway, Wake, and Guam); its "flying Clippers" could carry forty-eight passengers across the Pacific; this was enormously expensive travel, definitely first-class, with lounge chairs, fine linens, silver, and porcelain service.[33] From the 1930s on there was no stopping the progress of air travel. Fewer than half a million passengers traveled by air in 1932; by 1941 the number had reached 4 million.[34]

The Civil Aeronautics Act of 1938 was another important law.[35] It estab-lished a Civil Aeronautics Authority, with five members, to be appointed by the president with the usual advice and consent of the Senate. The authority had extensive powers. A subsection of three members constituted an Air Safety Board. The CAA also had rate-setting and rate-reviewing power. Airlines were not to charge "unjust and unreasonable" fares. An airline that flew a certain route, say from Des Moines to Denver, could not just walk away from the route if it proved unprofitable; there had to be a hearing, and a finding that the abandonment was "in the public interest."

The nonscheduled carriers (or "nonskeds") had their heyday in the 1950s. They offered cheaper, leaner air travel; many of them were nonscheduled only in theory. The Civil Aeronautics Board put them out of business; they were too much of a threat to the regular carriers. But the nonskeds made their mark on the industry; they forced the regulars to offer economy-class tickets, and helped make air travel popular with a wider band of people.[36] The Boeing 707, the first jet airplane, made its debut in 1958. Up to this point, the vast majority of Americans had never flown in a plane. Now flying became cheap; and more common even than riding the Greyhound bus. As a result, plane service, as we have seen, killed off the passenger train almost completely. In 2001 this was a nation of "frequent fliers."

The airplane has been less influential than the automobile, but is nonethe-less enormously significant. It shrinks distances even more than the auto. It makes family reunions easier—after first making it easier for families to fly apart.

It is the meat and bones of the tourist industry. Where would Hawaii be, economically speaking, without the jet? The overseas tourist trade, without jets, would be limited to cruise ships. The same is true, to a lesser degree, of Las Vegas; without the jet, its customers would be mainly California gamblers. Easy, fast travel reduces the significance of borders; it is another powerful engine making for social, geographical, and cultural mobility.

The Airline Deregulation Act (1978) abolished the Civil Aeronautics Board. It left the airlines free to charge more or less what they wanted, and to juggle routes and destinations as they pleased. The result was lower prices for tickets—but within an overall pricing system so complicated that only a high-speed computer could cope with it. It is entirely possible that no two people on a flight from New York to Seattle have paid the same fare; and that one passenger paid four times as much for her ticket as her neighbor to the left, while her neighbor to the right rode free. All three sat in the same narrow, backbreaking seats, scarfed down the same rubber chicken or mystery meat, munched on the same small bag of pretzels. "Deregulation" allowed airlines to drop service to any city, big or small, that did not pay its way. It was a triumph of free-market economics. But safety, of course, was never deregulated; and government controls continue to play a crucial role in the way airlines operate and maintain their aircraft.

Sending Messages

There were tremendous advances in communication in the nineteenth century. At the beginning of the century, words traveled at a snail's pace. It took months for a message to get across the ocean, or from one end of the country to the other. The telegraph and the telephone entirely changed the situation. In this regard, as in so many others, the twentieth century outdid its predecessor. This was the century of radio and television; and then, later, of e-mail and the internet. Giuseppe Marconi invented the "wireless" in the late nineteenth century. His wireless was used mostly to send telegraph messages. In the twentieth century, ways were found to transmit voices, and over greater distances. Early regulation, such as it was, mainly concerned distress signals from ships at sea, one of the major uses of radio broadcasting. There was no control over signals and the broadcasting band, and the result, according to contemporary critics, was "pandemonium" (and static) in airspace, a "twentieth century Tower of Babel," with "jumbled and sporadic" reception.[37] Like the highways, the invisible roads in the air cried out for traffic rules.

The Wireless Ship Act of 1910 required all oceangoing passenger ships to have "an efficient apparatus for radio-communication."[38] In 1912, when the *Titanic* sank in the North Atlantic, wireless distress signals brought help from a nearby ship, and also spread the word of the disaster to American newspapers. Amateur radio operators jammed the airwaves with their messages. Chaos evoked demands for regulation; the navy added its own litany of complaints.[39] The result was the Radio Act of 1912.[40] Under this law, broadcasters had to be licensed; the secretary of commerce and labor had authority to give out the licenses. Drafters of the statute tried to ration or allocate the radio spectrum. Under the act, every station had to "designate a certain definite wave length as the normal sending and receiving wave length of the station."

Commercially speaking, radio came into its own in the 1920s. In 1920 there were only three radio stations broadcasting regularly in the United States; in 1925, there were almost six hundred.[41] A statute of 1927 created a five-member Federal Radio Commission.[42] Like its predecessors, the act had a lot to do with distress signals at sea. But it also attended to the business of licensing commercial stations. An applicant was entitled to a license if "public interest, convenience or necessity would be served by the granting thereof." It would be hard to think of vaguer language. In effect, then, Congress gave the administrators almost total discretion to make their own rules. Nothing was said about selling the licenses.

Not every aspect of the law was completely vague and boneless. Under section 18 of the act, whenever a candidate for public office made a political broadcast, the station had to "afford equal opportunities to all other such candidates for that office."[43] This language was carried over into the 1934 Communications Act, which replaced the Radio Commission with a seven-member board, the Federal Communications Commission.[44] The FCC (which later got jurisdiction over television as well) had the same unbridled discretion as its predecessor; and the same implicit right to give the airwaves away to private interests.

By this time radio was an important part of American culture; radio shows were entertaining the whole country. Most families had a radio, or two; and people sat around listening to comedians, news, soap operas, dramatic shows. Radio had a key political role as well. Franklin Delano Roosevelt, with his smooth, mellifluous voice, was a master communicator. His "fireside chats" helped to create the imperial presidency; he reached almost every home in the nation through radio. In the first ten months of the New Deal, the country heard the president twenty times, delivering his message; Eleanor Roosevelt was on no fewer than seventeen times, and members of the cabinet broadcast 107 times.[45] Radio was everywhere at once.

Roosevelt was not the only political figure to seize on this medium. Father Charles E. Coughlin, the "radio priest," at first a fan of the New Deal, then an implacable enemy, enjoyed an audience of millions. Coughlin's message got darker and more sinister as time went on, and the Catholic Church eventually silenced him; but, as one author put it, he was the "first public figure to obliterate the distinction between politics, religion, and mass media entertainment."[46] If the new medium rewarded smooth talkers, it punished those who were not. Herbert Hoover, unlike Roosevelt, was a poor speaker; and his shyness came across as a kind of coldness. H. L. Mencken put it this way: "If he had to recite the Twenty-third Psalm," he would "make it sound like a search warrant under the Volstead Act."[47] Radio—and then, exponentially more, television—made image and presentation all-important in political life.

On what basis did the FCC award operating licenses? There were a few concrete requirements—no aliens, for example, need apply. Under the "test" of "public convenience, interest, or necessity," the FCC could have exercised a good deal of control—could have laid down all sorts of rules about content and style; about educational broadcasting, culture, and so on. In practice, the commission exerted almost no control. You could argue that radio frequencies were public property, a resource that should have been treated like national parks, or navigable waters. But the airwaves were in fact treated like much of the public domain: given away to private businesses.

The FCC thus abdicated any responsibility. It never prevented the radio stations or television channels from becoming, in the words of Federal Communications Commission Chairman Newton Minow, a "vast wasteland."[48] But this could have been predicted. The United States is not a country of intellectuals. There was no commitment to high culture or education. European countries might have tried to spread these things through the media; in the United States, it was almost unthinkable.

The FCC did regulate, eventually: on issues like dirty words. At first, the broadcast industry tried to police itself. In 1935, for example, CBS made public a set of "program policies" to govern advertising: no "unpleasant discussion of bodily functions," no advertising of "laxatives, depilatories and . . . deodorants," nothing "slanderous, obscene, or profane." The National Association of Broadcasters had a code of ethical broadcasting from 1929 on. It was frequently revised.[49] In 1946 the broadcasters' code included these older restrictions, and many others: no advertisements for liquor, or for "fortune-telling" and astrology; no advertisements for matrimonial agencies, or from "professional people" (doctors, dentists, lawyers).[50] In 1948 Congress in its wisdom made it a crime to utter "any obscene, indecent, or profane language by means of radio communication."[51] The terms were not defined.

The standards of the FCC have been fairly Victorian. A disc jockey, Charlie Walker, who worked on station WDKD in Kingstree, South Carolina, ran afoul of the authorities for his bawdy rustic humor, and for using expressions like "let it all hang out." The FCC refused to renew his station's license in 1961. Radio, in the commission's opinion, was not like books or pictures: it is "available at the flick of a switch to young and old alike, to the sensitive and the indifferent, to the sophisticated and the credulous."[52] This, presumably, meant that it had to be squeaky clean. Congress obviously agreed. In the 1990s Howard Stern, the "shock jock" of morning radio, got into serious trouble with the FCC—trouble that resulted in hefty fines. When Stern described on the air how a guest at a party played the piano with his penis, the FCC uttered dark threats about loss of license.[53] The permissive society, apparently, stops short at the gates of the airwaves.

The commission intervened on this subject for a simple reason: it was one issue likely to send some part of the public into a lather. The commission could suspend licenses of stations that broadcast "communications containing profane or obscene words or language"; and these communications, as we have seen, were also a crime. Regulations, statutes, and court cases vacillated considerably on this delicate subject.[54] There was, after all, a free-speech issue. At one time, the FCC promulgated "safe harbor" regulations: dirty words were permissible so long as they were spoken in the middle of the night, when presumably no children were awake. In 1988 Congress ordered the FCC to extend the ban to a "24 hour per day basis," though this was later repealed.[55] The issue, on the whole, remains a live one.

The Silver Screen

Movies were an invention of the late nineteenth century; but their history really belongs to the twentieth. *The Great Train Robbery* (1903) was the first movie that could be described as a "connected narrative."[56] Within a few years, the medium became enormously popular; nickelodeons sprouted like mushrooms in the big cities.

From the start, this was a mass medium; it attracted huge audiences; it was cheap and vivid and exciting. Those who fancied themselves protectors of national morality found this situation disquieting. Soon cities and states began to experiment with censorship. They realized the power of the medium. Dime novels and lurid newspapers were bad enough; this was visual, and a quantum leap in sheer dramatic impact, in the power of its images.

A Chicago ordinance of 1907 made it illegal to show a movie without a permit from the chief of police; the chief was supposed to withhold permits from any "obscene or immoral picture." The chief disapproved of two such movies, one called *James Boys,* and another called *Night Riders.* In *Block v. City of Chicago* (1909) the Illinois Supreme Court upheld the ordinance.[57] The company that attacked the ordinance operated "five and ten-cent theatres, where moving pictures are displayed by means of moving picture machines." Because the theaters were so cheap, they attracted children, and people of "limited means who do not attend the production of plays and dramas given in the regular theatres." These audiences included "those classes whose age, education and situation in life specially entitle them to protection against the evil influence of obscene and immoral representations." (Whether these "classes" had asked for such protection, or thought they needed it, was never mentioned by the court.)

The court rejected all the arguments raised against the ordinance. Was the ordinance too vague? Not at all. The "average person of healthy and wholesome mind" can tell what is immoral or obscene, and "intelligently apply the test to any picture presented to him." What about these particular films? They portrayed "exhibitions of crime"; *Night Riders* showed "malicious mischief, arson and murder." Both films were "immoral and their exhibition would necessarily be attended with evil effects upon youthful spectators."

Chicago was not alone in its desire to protect the lower orders. Pennsylvania (1911) created a State Board of Censors and declared it illegal to show any "moving-picture film . . . or stereopticon view" unless approved in advance by the board. It was a two-person board, appointed by the governor—a male "chief censor" and a female "assistant censor." They had to view all movies and "withhold approval from such as shall tend to debase or corrupt the morals."[58] Similar laws were soon passed in Ohio, Kansas, and Maryland; New York State set up a licensing system in 1921. The Ohio Board of Censors was to approve only "such films as are in the judgment and discretion of the board of censors of a moral, educational or amusing and harmless character."[59] In addition, cities such as Detroit, Memphis, Atlanta, and Boston followed the lead of Chicago.[60]

The *Block* case assumed a single, dominant standard of morality; it assumed that respectable people know the difference between the moral and immoral—as if this was a fact of the natural world; and that the masses are like children, easily corruptible, and not to be trusted. It was the same mentality that allowed, say, a publisher to publish the works of the Marquis de Sade, so long as the salacious bits appeared only in French; the Satyricon of Petronius Arbiter, a late Roman sizzler, was acceptable so long as its juicy passages were left in the original Latin. In the present era of triple-X movies, the *Block* philosophy seems positively quaint; and undemocratic to boot.

But widespread censorship continued. Chicago censors in 1925 refused a license to a movie called *Deadwood Coach*—too much "gun-play" made this movie "immoral." Some movies were banned locally because they were racist or, more commonly, especially in the South, because they were not. Atlanta refused to allow the showing of *Lost Boundaries,* a movie in which a black family passes for white; the movie was "likely to have an adverse effect on the peace, morals, and good order" of the city.[61]

The Supreme Court weighed in on the subject, in 1915, when it had to decide whether the Ohio censorship law was valid.[62] The Court saw the world through the same lenses as the Illinois court: films were dangerous, seductive; they could be "used for evil"; they were, after all, shown widely, and men, women, and children made up the audience. And they might be all the more "insidious in corruption" if they pretended to have a "worthy purpose" and excited and appealed to "a prurient interest." Many subjects and issues should not have "pictorial representation in public places and to all audiences." So saying, the Court emphatically upheld the statute.

The courts and the local censorship boards were convinced that movies were dangerous—too powerful, emotional, and vivid for the public at large.

The movie industry defended itself by capitulating. The industry hired Will Hays, a former postmaster general (under President Harding), and made him head of an organization called the Motion Picture Producers and Distributors of America (almost always called the Hays office). The Hays office began cautiously, with voluntary guidelines; these had little effect. Private organizations—very notably the Catholic Church—took a more active role; in 1934 the American Catholic bishops organized the Legion of Decency to pass on the moral content of movies, and to assess them for the lay public. In response (and in fear of a boycott), the Hays office formed a Production Code Administration to make sure the industry's code was actually enforced.[63]

Basically, the code embodied the philosophy of the *Block* case and local censorship boards. Anything "dirty" or overtly sexual was taboo—in the original code, this included "lustful and open-mouth kissing . . . suggestive posture and gestures." There were to be no "indecent movements" in dancing. The "sanctity" of marriage was to be "upheld." Four-letter words were, of course, outlawed. Perhaps most important, "evil, sin, crime and wrong-doing" were never to be "justified." Crime had to be punished. In general, no movie should "lower the moral standards of those who see it"; movies were rather to present "correct standards of life." No film could heap "ridicule on any religious faith"; no minister of religion was ever to be used as a "comic character" or a villain. Certain subjects were not even to be mentioned: "sex perversion," illegal drug traffic, and "white slavery."[64]

Movies were silent in the 1920s, except for the mighty Wurlitzer organ, playing background music in the new "movie palaces" of the 1920s—great, opulent buildings, with gingerbread decoration, sweeping circular staircases and grand pianos. Then movies began to talk; or rather, at first, they began to sing. The first feature-length "talkie," *The Jazz Singer,* opened in New York in 1927; it was "essentially a silent movie with several songs interpolated," along with "a few lines of stage patter."[65] Soon talk began in earnest. But of course, it had to be genteel talk, censored talk, talk that did not "offend."

This cozy system began to break down in the 1950s. In the postwar period, as we have seen, the Supreme Court faced the issue of obscenity head on. Old taboos were under attack. The leading cases concerned obscene books; but the same principles applied to movies as well. It was, after all, a different era—the age of the Kinsey report, an age of heightened awareness of civil rights and civil liberties, an age of greater permissiveness. The crucial case (1952) concerned an

Italian movie, *The Miracle*. It told the story of a girl who imagined that her bastard son was the infant Jesus. Catholic groups picketed the theater where it was shown in New York. There were bomb threats. The state board of regents revoked the movie's license, on the grounds that it was "sacrilegious." The New York courts upheld this decision. But the Supreme Court reversed. It is not the "business of government," said the Court, "to suppress real or imagined attacks upon a particular religious doctrine." The case effectively destroyed the legal basis for censorship on any grounds other than obscenity.[66]

It took a while, but all censorship eventually broke down. Nudity, violence, crime that definitely did pay, adultery—not only did all of these become acceptable; one or more of these could be found in almost any movie shown to grown-ups. In most parts of the country, in fact, there was absolutely nothing that was taboo in the movies. The four-letter words were no longer banned; they were ubiquitous, and mainstream movies were peppered with the "f-word" and worse. The code no longer had any meaning. It was eliminated in 1967. What replaced it was a new, voluntary rating system—a labeling system for movies. Anybody could safely watch a G-rated movie: no sex, no nudity, no violence, drugs, or nasty language. From here, movies descended, through PG (parental guidance suggested), PG-13 (unsuitable for younger children), to R (nobody under seventeen admitted without an accompanying adult), and even X (since replaced, for regular Hollywood products, by NC-17, restricted to adults). A board sitting in Los Angeles decides on the ratings. The board works for the industry, and is funded by industry fees. It is hardly a board of experts: as of 1997 it included a microbiologist, a hairdresser, and a restaurant manager, among others. A moviemaker dissatisfied with his rating had the right to appeal. This private, unofficial system has neutralized the demand for censorship; its blend of warnings and information seems to work fairly well.[67] Complaints about sex in the movie were muted by the end of the twentieth century; and "dirty" words were so common there was no point even talking about the subject. The regular movies avoided hard-core pornography; but that was available in special theaters and video shops. Violence in the movies (and television) is positively epidemic, and has been much criticized. Congress has debated this issue over and over again, and considered this or that piece of legislation; in the end nothing has come of it.[68] The subject pops up, like a jack-in-the-box, after each egregious outburst of violence—some mass killing or shootout at a high school, for example. But so far without concrete result.

From the early days of the medium, movies have been, above all, a business; often a highly profitable one. A handful of big studios, however, came to dominate the business. They controlled the stars, they controlled the production of movies, and they controlled distribution. The big studios owned chains of movie palaces; they were able to crowd out independent producers and small, independent theaters; or squeeze them into tiny market niches.[69] One technique they used was "block booking." To get the rich, desirable "A" movies, a theater had to agree to buy and show a slew of "B" movies. These runts of the litter might otherwise have died at birth. The antitrust division of the Justice Department fought this practice, as well as the tight connection between the studios and their movie palaces. After many skirmishes, the government won a decisive victory, in the *Paramount* case (1948).[70] The studios had to spin off their theaters and dissolve their oligopoly of glamour and dreams.

The end, perhaps, was already in sight, although the studios perhaps did not know it. Moviegoing had peaked in 1946; in that year, estimated attendance at the movies, every week, was more than 79 million; in 1957, only eleven years later, attendance was down by more than half.[71] The problem, of course, was television. Hollywood did not die, however, and even made something of a comeback. It found its niche, flourished, and held its own in competition with the rest of the world of entertainment. In recent years, movies have become one of America's prime items of export. In the 1990s especially, American schlock essentially conquered the world. In 1991 the top-grossing film in Argentina was *Terminator 2;* in Egypt it was *Dances with Wolves;* in Sweden it was *Pretty Woman.*[72] Even in France, where elites passionately resisted American cultural imperialism, American movies proved more popular with the ordinary Frenchman than anything France itself could produce.

The Great Blue Box

The greatest crisis in the history of the movies was the rise of its great rival: television. Television brought pictures, images, stories—all the tricks of the movies—into everybody's living room. No need to buy a ticket. You could watch in the privacy of your own home, sitting on your own couch, eating a pizza, relaxing in your underwear, mesmerized by the magic of the tube.

Television was invented, practically speaking, in the 1930s.[73] The FCC licensed experiments in TV broadcasting after 1934; by 1939 a number of experimental stations were in operation. There was competition and infighting over the allocation of broadcast frequencies, and over the technical standards for television sets. Actual broadcasting started in 1941; at the end of the year there were some thirty-two stations in operation. But World War II arrested the growth of television as a medium for entertainment, enlightenment, and profit.

When the war ended, in 1945, the dam burst; television took off like a rocket. The public showed an insatiable lust for the magic box. FCC regulation operated, as it had with radio, on the basis of a simple principle: the airwaves were public property, but the government gave them away (in the form of licenses) for nothing. Theoretically, this was done on a competitive basis, and with the public interest at heart. In practice, the big networks monopolized the available frequencies. They muscled out all their rivals.

At first television was a flickering black-and-white presence; in the 1950s color TV appeared, and the public was even more entranced by the bright, splashy colors in their homes. Color TV became the standard quite quickly. Ninety-five percent of all households had a TV set by 1970; in 1996 there were 223 million sets in operation; almost everybody had one, and in fact, the average household had 2.3 sets.[74]

During the presidency of Lyndon Johnson—a period rich in government initiatives—Congress passed a Public Broadcasting Act.[75] The act created a Corporation for Public Broadcasting to run noncommercial programs; the corporation was, by law, supposed to be independent and free from pressures, and in no way an "agency or establishment of the United States Government." Yet from the start, conservatives bitterly attacked public broadcasting; they called it elitist, highbrow, indecent, and (worst of all) excessively liberal.[76] They also thought that it was unnecessary: the free market, and the zillions of stations (especially after the advent of cable and satellite TV), made public television redundant. The Reagan administration in 1981 proposed cutting back drastically on public broadcasting; Reagan actually vetoed a funding bill in 1984.[77] Nonetheless, despite the passion for privatizing everything, public television managed to cling to life through the end of the century.

Public television had a smallish audience; commercial television had an enormous one. In many homes, the set seemed to go on early in the morning and was never turned off until members of the family dropped into bed at night; even then, many continued to watch it, up to the point when, their eyelids drooping, they shut off the set by remote control. Television came to have a pervasive influence over every aspect of American life (and world life, for that matter). Its power dwarfed the power of radio, in its vividness, its immediacy, its seductiveness. Young people cannot imagine a world before television. To them, such a world must seem bleak, empty, colorless—and, worst of all, profoundly boring.

Television has, in a way, an interactive power, even though the audience sits passively and watches. Television invites and stimulates reaction. It has a unique ability to influence, to manipulate its audience. It has vast political power. It has made an enormous difference; it has shaped the course of American law in many ways—from the images of organized crime in the Kefauver hearings to those of the civil rights movement and the dogs and firehoses used by southern sheriffs, through the pictures of Vietnam, Watergate, O. J. Simpson, and the Clinton impeachment trial. Television also conveys to its viewers a host of hidden and implicit messages. These are, essentially, messages of individualism, consumerism, choice. Television shows us a world of leisure, glamour, excitement; it is a window on the world, and a potential educator of unique power; but mostly it abdicates this role, in favor of raw, naked fun. But fun, too, is a form of ideology.

Television has the world in its grip; but at the same time, in an open society, television's very power, its obvious presence, makes it unusually vulnerable to public opinion. Programs rise and fall on the basis of "ratings." The networks and the stations control content; but the public votes, and a program that loses its audience loses its life. Television is also nakedly exposed to public outrage. Everybody watches, and everybody has an opinion. Since television began, there have been calls for action against its excesses—sex, violence, mindlessness, or anything that offends the audience (or, perhaps even more powerfully, anything that offends the advertisers). The industry is exceedingly sensitive to these various forms of pressure.

The industry is naturally also leery of government regulation. To ward off control of style, language, and content, the industry opts for "self-regulation." In 1952 in the very infancy of the medium, the National Association of Broadcasters adopted a voluntary code of standards for television. Two-thirds of the country's stations soon subscribed to the code. In 1956, according to a study, one network took action 125 times either to comment (adversely) on the content of some program, or to change it or delete some offensive item. Sexual references were unacceptable, along with vulgarity, bad language, and ethnic slurs (for example, a reference to "dumb Polacks"). Other actions showed the depths of national timidity: "Use of leather jacket for hoodlum protested by tanners and jacket manufacturers"; or the objection to the "implication that dentists have no feelings."[78]

Censorship and self-censorship were continuing problems for both radio and television. It was understood that a station could not pollute the atmosphere with "dirty words." Particularly taboo were what came to be known as the "seven dirty words": *shit* was the mildest of these. On October 3, 1973, at 2 P.M.—a great day for freedom, or a day in the life of the decline of the West, as you prefer—station WBAI in New York City broadcast a program on which comedian George Carlin delivered a monologue in which he repeatedly made use of the words, "the ones that will curve your spine" and "grow hair on your hands." A man driving in his car with his young son heard this dreadful monologue and filed a complaint. The FCC gave the station a slap on the wrist and threatened to revoke the license if there were "subsequent complaints" along the same lines. The case was appealed all the way to the Supreme Court, which upheld the FCC.[79]

What is interesting, and somewhat odd, about this decision is that censoring the print media for using dirty words would be absolutely out of the question. In fact, the seven dirty words, and worse, are positively epidemic in printed literature. Why are broadcast media different? Because, as Justice Stevens put it, they are "uniquely pervasive"; and "uniquely accessible to children."[80] Of course, a houseful of pornography would be just as accessible to children, and print media are in a way just as pervasive. But Stevens's intuition told him something that was real, deep, and true: the power of broadcast media, especially television—the drama, the vividness, the seductiveness—these are social facts. Television is not only in every home; it is in almost every room, and children control it much more than they control the print media. It is easier to keep dirty books out of the home than it is to exclude offensive TV. At any rate, rightly or wrongly, it is still the case that networks cannot say or do what publishers can say and do every minute of the day.

For a long time, television was dominated by three great networks. Their stranglehold on the audience was broken after the 1970s; cable television and other new technologies gave the public a huge number of new choices. The Reagan administration was a fan of deregulation. The FCC gave up even its feeble attempts to insist on a certain minimum of educational programming.

Most cable stations vied with the networks in providing junk food for the mind. But with so many channels, there was room for news channels, weather channels, and arts channels, for religious and educational broadcasting. The future of television seemed almost limitless. But it too now had a growing rival—perhaps as much of a threat, in the long run, as TV had been to the world of films.

The World Wide Web

This was the internet. In the 1990s the internet, e-mail, and the World Wide Web—the creation of the strange new world of "cyberspace"—had a meteoric rise. In a few short years, "the Web" developed from almost nothing to an instrument of amazing, interactive power. Millions of people talk to each other through e-mail. Millions buy and sell, do research, trade on the stock market, check the weather in Tuscaloosa or Beijing, or auction off a Civil War sword, all on or through the Web. Other people shut the doors of their rooms, and in the privacy of cyberspace watch dirty pictures to their heart's desire. What will become of all this internetting was hard to say. But it was already clear by 2001 that the net has the capacity to change the way people live, work, buy, sell—almost everything they do except eating and making love; and even here there is bound to be an impact.

Indeed, in 1999 the world's "first internet law school" made its appearance. This was a school "tucked away" in obscure office space, a school without ivy on the walls—indeed, without walls—whose 180 students lived everywhere from Alaska to Switzerland; in fact, the dean of students lived in Boston, and the dean of faculty had his home in Denver. The school, according to a newspaper reporter, was "threatening to drag the future of legal education kicking and screaming into cyberspace."[81] Many people were convinced that all of this webbing and surfing *was* the future; and not only in legal education.

The Web is a tremendous storehouse of information. Every institution, school, business, club of any size or scope, at the end of the twentieth century, had its Web page. The Web makes it possible for people who have something—anything—in common to talk to each other, to get information (or misinformation), to exchange ideas. Women who give birth to two-pound babies, men who collect German porcelain, people who are fans of Jane Austen or Elvis Presley, or who suffer from cancer of the colon—all of these can find kindred souls, and learn a lot, from the Web. Much of this is free (once you pay for the connection); but how long can this situation continue? Who will buy newspapers if they become freely available on the Web? Who will go to a bookstore if you can buy books cheaper through the Web? What will the future bring to the Web? Will it always be a giant commons? Or will it be "commodified," turned into money-making property? And who will control it? What role will the long arm of the law play in all this? At century's end, these questions were as yet unanswered.

But this much is clear: in sum, the social impact of new technologies of transport and communication has been incalculable. More than anything else, they have shaped the world we live in. They have done this in many different ways. They are also essentially responsible for the rise of what I have elsewhere called the "horizontal society": a society of loose affiliations, a society of mass communication; a society tied together by the mass media.[82] A society of communicators is a society which is able to form, and does form, groups, tribes, clans, and pressure points, made up of people who share an interest or a cause, but who are not in physical contact with each other. Plural equality, the civil rights movement, interest-group politics, even nationalism itself become possible in, and are enabled by, the horizontal society.

The horizontal society profoundly affects the nature of authority itself. At one time, people in face-to-face contact with a child were almost the only powerful influences on his young life: parents, grandparents, other relatives, then later schoolteachers, priests, neighbors, and other local figures. All forms of authority were rooted in the neighborhood. Today, all this has changed. Almost literally from day one, the child is bombarded with images from the big outside world. The television screen is the most potent source of these images. Family and local notables once acted as filters and censors of the outside world. This is no longer the case. The dazzling, glittering world of TV and the movies is a powerful rival: and now the internet as well.

Movies, TV, and leisure: all these have served to put entertainment at the very core of life.[83] They have created the celebrity society. A celebrity is not just a famous person: a celebrity is a famous and familiar person, a person we see, hear, watch, and (apparently) know, from TV and other mass media. What this means for the presidency, for the legal system, and for the structure of authority will be explored in the final chapter.

19

Law: An American Export

t the beginning of the twentieth century, the United States was
already a rich and powerful country, stretching its muscles, reaching out toward an overseas empire. By the end of the century, it
was much richer, and much more powerful; *the* superpower in
the world. It had come out on top in two world wars (there were
more ambiguous outcomes in some smaller, less glorious
wars). Most of its rivals had faded away. When Queen Victoria died, in 1901, the
sun never set on the British empire; it controlled a quarter of the world. By 2000
the British empire had been reduced to a pitiful handful of islands; China
swallowed Hong Kong in 1997, the last significant outpost of empire; the
population of the bits and fragments left over from imperial days (Bermuda,
Gibraltar, the Falkland Islands, and others) would hardly fill a football stadium.

All the other empires, too, had crumbled into dust. Two world wars and the
winds of change stripped France of her *gloire;* her African and Asian colonies
were long since gone. She too still had an island here and there, and tattered
remnants of neocolonialism in French-speaking parts of Africa. Germany lost its
empire after the First World War, and had to disgorge its conquests after the
Second. The First World War put an end to the Austro-Hungarian empire, and
the Second World War put paid to the empire the Japanese had cobbled
together. Dutch and Portuguese possessions became independent after World
War II; the last Portuguese outpost, Macao, passed to China at the end of 1999.
The most recent empire to go was the Soviet Union, which never admitted it was

an empire; it collapsed like a house of cards in 1989. At the end of the century, the Russian bear was a sick, limping, lumbering mess. China loomed on the horizon; still something of an empire (certainly, the Tibetans thought so), vast, overpopulated; but so far not a serious rival to American rule in the world.

Economically, the United States was *the* world power, too. Some countries were almost as rich, or even richer, in terms of dollars per capita; but most of these were small, lucky places, awash in oil, like Brunei or Kuwait, or shrewd little statelets, like Singapore. Even the countries that were both big and rich, like Germany and Japan, were far behind the U.S. in total gross national product—the United States, with its GNP in the trillions of dollars, was more than twice as mighty in terms of sheer wealth as its nearest rival; and in military and cultural terms, other countries were absolutely nowhere.

That left the United States on top of the heap, pretty much alone; it spent more, consumed more, mattered more than any other country; and its movies, its television programs, its popular culture—even its language—resonated all over the world. From North Pole to South, everybody seemed to know America—its blue jeans, its movie stars, its rock-and-roll music, its hamburgers and Coca-Cola. American speech was the language of mass culture; it was despised, resented, admired, imitated, feared, and adored, sometimes all at once, and sometimes by the same people. Its politicians strutted and congratulated themselves on American achievements; whether America's preeminence was the result of God, virtue, or economic policies, or as accidental as winning the lottery or discovering oil, its place in the world was undeniable. Will the American hegemony last until 2100? Probably not. Will it shrivel like the British empire, or in some other way? Only time can tell; and time has nothing to say at the moment.

At any rate, American ideas, images, and objects are everywhere at once: high culture (American science, American art), and low culture (gangster movies, fast-food shops, rock-and-roll). In London it is hard to find a British film; in Germany, hard to find a German one. There is panic over cultural imperialism in France, and in Canada, whose population centers are dangerously close to the American border, and which is nakedly exposed to American media. The one thing both English-speaking Toronto and francophone Quebec City might agree on is that the United States is a threat to cultural integrity. The ordinary Canadian, on the other hand, like people all over the world, seems to lap up American garbage with glee.

But of course not every aspect of American society has traveled well, or spread its net over the globe. Everybody drinks Coca-Cola; nobody but Americans drink root beer, which most foreigners find painful and disgusting. Is American law Coca-Cola or root beer? As American culture, American products, American ways of behavior have spread over the world, how much of American legal culture—of American law itself—has gone along with it?

In some ways the expected answer is: not much. Law is the most parochial of disciplines. Chemical engineering is the same in Honduras or Laos or Greece as in the United States. Even the social sciences are somewhat cosmopolitan, or claim to be. Science is science. Art, high and low, has become more and more international. The same is true of architecture. Tall buildings look much the same all over the world. *Jurassic Park* and *Titanic* (assuming that these are art) draw crowds in every country. But law as a discipline is trussed up with jurisdictional ropes. Its mandate stops at its border.

Of course, it stops at state borders too, in a federal system. Or used to. One of the most striking aspects of American law in the twentieth century, as we have seen, was the growth of the federal, national sector of the legal order. Now, at the dawn of the twenty-first century, we are moving (perhaps) more and more to something vaguely similar, internationally. The borders between countries are dissolving: this is becoming, in some ways, one economic world, one cultural world. Are *legal* borders weakening as well? Is some sort of implicit world federalism developing? Yes and no. Sovereignty is still a powerful force, especially for big countries. Legal practice remains in many ways stubbornly parochial. Most lawyers are as local as barnacles. Yet, on the other hand, there *is* a kind of globalization of law. Something *is* happening. If culture and trade globalize, law will almost inevitably follow. And the emerging global law speaks, more and more, with an American accent.

Lenders and Borrowers

For much of our history, the United States was not a lender but a borrower of law. The United States is a common-law system; and the common law was, in its origins, essentially English. In the first part of the nineteenth century, American courts looked to English law for inspiration, to English jurists and treatise writers. Case law was peppered with citations of English cases. Notable scholar-judges, like James Kent and Joseph Story, also read, absorbed, and tried to import into American law key aspects and insights of European legal thought.

The British influence declined throughout the nineteenth century; and in the twentieth century it was all but dead. American cases rarely cite foreign materials. Courts occasionally cite a British classic or two, a famous old case, or a nod to Blackstone; but current British law almost never gets any mention. In the twentieth century, German philosophy had some residual influence; and Karl Llewellyn, for one, absorbed a good deal of German legal culture. It is fair to say, however, that American lawyers and jurists have been, on the whole, extremely parochial.

At some crucial points, scholars and statespeople did look abroad. English law influenced the shape of the workers' compensation statutes; key phrases were lifted almost verbatim from the English act. The English act, in turn owed something to legislation adopted earlier in Bismarck's Germany. The English Companies Law of 1929 and a Securities Act of 1933 were real influences on the text of the Securities and Exchange Act. Commercial statutes—the first, early-twentieth-century "uniform" statutes—similarly were indebted to British models.

In the 1930s, Hitler's madness in Germany sent hundreds of scholars, many of them Jewish, into exile. Some of the luckier ones made their way to the United States. For many of these scholars, the transition was lonely and difficult: torn from their roots, forced to learn a new language and a new legal culture. A surprising number of them, however, ultimately found a place in the United States, or were able to start over. They enriched the academy immensely. Europe's most famous legal philosopher, Hans Kelsen, ended his career at Berkeley. German and Austrian refugees breathed new life into the study of comparative law, which they dominated for decades. Some scholars, like Friedrich Kessler of Yale, helped to import European concepts into American legal thought. Some returned to Germany and Austria after the end of the Second World War; but many remained. Their influence is hard to measure, except in academic life; there it was definitely a factor.[1]

Because America was obviously a world power by 1900, it is no surprise that the flow of influence in the twentieth century more or less reversed itself. In Latin America, France and Spain were and remained the main influences on the intellectual life of the law; but there was no denying the colossus to the north. Common-law institutions made their way south of the border. Panama, for example, passed a law incorporating the Anglo-American trust into its body of law in 1924. Panama and Colombia both adopted the negotiable instruments law before 1950. The Cuban law on railroad corporations was said to be "substantially a translation of the New York law"; Panama and Mexico also borrowed ideas about corporation law from the United States.[2] Between 1923 and 1931 Dr. Edwin Kemmerer, an economics professor at Princeton, traveled to various Latin American countries, preaching economic reform—and introducing American banking laws and institutions.[3] How deeply these penetrated living law is an open question.

Constitutional Arrangements

American constitutional ideas were a major export commodity. The United States Constitution was a model for some aspects of Latin American constitutions. A model for texts, that is: the working constitutional system did not travel as well, in a part of the world that believed in oligarchy. American law also spread, of course, through conquest: it replaced the laws of the native peoples on the American continent (though not entirely), and continues to be an enormous influence on the surviving legal systems. It replaced the indigenous law of the Hawaiian Islands as well.

In the twentieth century, American law was also, in part, imposed on the Philippines and Puerto Rico, which fell into the American sphere after the Spanish-American War. This early expansion of American law was the result of conquest. The Philippine Constitution of 1935, which was supposed to guide the country into independence, drew on the texts of the Bill of Rights and the post–Civil War amendments. In other regards, too, this constitution closely followed its American model. And this continues to be true of the text of the most recent Philippine Constitution (1987).[4]

The United States invaded Haiti in 1915 and forced that country to sign a treaty which essentially made it an American protectorate. The Haitians had to swallow a new constitution. The Americans did not leave until 1934. This was not, of course, the only small country in the Western Hemisphere which felt the power of the big northern neighbor.

At the end of the Second World War, American troops occupied Japan, the southern half of Korea, and part of Germany, including a section of divided Berlin. The legal impact of American occupation was immense. The German Basic Law *(Grundgesetz)* is not explicitly based on American models, but it set up a federal system with a bill of rights; these owed a lot to American example. Federalism was not entirely new to German history, to be sure. The form of government of the United States had influenced German government even in the nineteenth century, and during the period of the Weimar Republic.[5] But the postwar influences were deeper and longer-lasting.

After Japan surrendered in 1945, General Douglas MacArthur became a kind of de facto emperor. On October 11, 1945, he ordered the Japanese to draw up a democratic constitution. After much rewriting and discussing and cajoling—and pressure from the occupiers—the Japanese did in fact adopt such a constitution. It contained provisions for judicial review—a very American institution. Parts of the constitution had even been drafted by Americans, then translated into Japanese.[6] In both Germany and Japan, the new constitutional regime has been in many ways an astonishing success. To be sure, the German constitutional court is much more active than its Japanese counterpart; the Germans took to judicial review like a duck to water. Japan had even less of a heritage of popular government than Germany; but it soon became a working democratic state, with full freedom of speech, press, and religion. Italy, too, another loser in the Second World War, adopted a new constitution in 1948, and that document, too, included judicial review. Neither Italy nor Germany, however, accepted the American system of giving constitutional matters to ordinary courts; they set up separate, special constitutional courts.[7]

American influence was powerful in South Korea. Japan had occupied Korea and made it a colony; the law had been strongly Japanized; there was certainly no tradition of judicial review. The military government in 1948 issued an "ordinance" of fundamental rights, which was essentially modeled on the United States Bill of Rights. Korean courts, from the 1960s on, looked more and more to American constitutional law and constitutional principles for guidance. On the other hand, South Korea suffered under authoritarian governments until the 1980s, and much of the discussion of civil rights and liberties was purely academic. In 1988 South Korea gave itself a Constitutional Court as a gift to its rapidly evolving democratic system. After this, many

"American" habits appeared in the judiciary: dissenting opinions, for example. The younger judges, many with American experience, have eagerly drunk the heady wine of activism. In one dramatic decision, in 1997, the Constitutional Court struck down a section of the Korean Civil Code which "banned the marriage between men and women possessing a common family name of the same 'roots.'" Women's groups had been unable to get the legislature to alter this "symbol of the Korean version of ancient Confucian ethics"; but the Constitutional Court swept it out of existence.[8]

In general, in the second half of the twentieth century there has been a positive epidemic of constitution writing. Country after country has reframed its system of government, and in the process adopted judicial review. Democracy, in one form or another, has been on the march. The United States is an old, strong, and obvious example to copy from. But in a deeper sense, the European constitutions are not American hand-me-downs. They are, rather, parallel developments. They drink from the same deep wells as American constitutionalism.

Borrowed or not, words and forms and texts are nothing; living practice is everything. Judicial review did not, after all, come naturally to European judges. whatever their constitutions said. European judges, as Mauro Cappelletti put it, writing in 1971, were often "psychologically incapable of the value-oriented, quasi-political functions involved in judicial review."[9] To some extent, this is still true. In Denmark, for example, judicial review is theoretically available, but the Danish Supreme Court, as of 1990, had yet to declare even one statute unconstitutional.[10] But in many other countries—Germany, as we have seen, but also Spain—the new constitutional courts have been surprisingly activist. And the European Union courts have, in effect, created, in the words of Alec Stone Sweet, a kind of "supranational constitution," whose influence has even penetrated the cold climate of England, traditionally hostile to anything remotely resembling a constitution or judicial review.[11]

Despite variations, and mixed results, the basic scheme—bill of rights, constitutional court, judicial review—is more and more popular in the world. Anthony Lester has spoken of the "overseas trade" in the American Bill of Rights.[12] He sees American influence, too, in the work of international conventions on human rights. These conventions have proliferated since the end of the Second World War. In Israel, a country without a written constitution, an influential chief justice, Simon Agranat, boldly transplanted into Israeli law American doctrines of constitutional law. Agranat was an American himself, born in Louisville, Kentucky, in 1906, and a graduate of the University of Chicago Law School. His admiration of American law came naturally.[13]

Deliberate Export

Particularly in the 1950s and the 1960s, during the cold war, United States policymakers made a conscious effort to spread the word. They were fighting communism in every way they could. Some of this fight was fairly dirty. The United States trained whole generations of sinister men in dark glasses, who got rid of communists (and lots of other people, too) in various Latin American countries; often enough they got rid of democracy in the process. More innocuous was the so-called law and development movement. The Agency for International Development provided the funds. American lawyers fanned out into the newly independent third-world countries; Latin America was again a popular site. The idea was to fight communism with American legality.

The scholars who took part in the movement were not consciously trying to export American common law. They were not that naive. They did feel that America had a lot to offer. Its form of legal education, for example (casebooks, the Socratic method), seemed to encourage open, free discussion, and was better than a system of dry-bones lectures. The American model of the lawyer as a kind of social engineer was also available for export.[14] The movement came to a rather inglorious end—there were scandals over financing, and accusations of espionage. Some of the scholars who took part later recanted and confessed to sins of legal imperialism.[15] The money dried up—government money, foundation money. The movement seemed completely dead.

But not for long. In the 1990s, after the collapse of the Soviet Union, American advisers (along with Europeans) helped write new constitutions and new codes of law.[16] All of the states of the former Soviet Union, including Russia itself, and the former members of the Soviet bloc embarked on a process of drafting fundamental laws.[17] They quite naturally looked to the West for models, and the work went on with expert help (such as it is) from the United States and other Western countries. An American political scientist from Berkeley, Martin Shapiro, spent time in Ulan Bator, advising the Mongolian republic on constitutional issues. The new constitutions have a lot in common with the American constitution—checks and balances, judicial review (for the most part), and bills of rights. Probably, on the whole, European influence is stronger than American: most of these constitutions (like Germany's and Italy's) provide for a special constitutional court or tribunal. This is true, for example, of Hungary.[18]

Bills of rights in the new constitutions tend to be broader and more detailed than the United States model, and often contain so-called "social rights," like the right to an education, to social security and social assistance, the right to form trade unions, and the "right to work"— examples taken from the Bulgarian Constitution of 1991.[19] None of this can be found in the text of the United States Constitution.

It is official United States policy to encourage the "rule of law" in the likes of Russia and China. In American eyes (at least as of the late twentieth century), the rule of law demands a free-market system as well. The American Bar Association and other organizations have sponsored programs to train Russian lawyers in American ways. As of the end of the century, the net results seemed fairly meager. The Russians eagerly embraced a freewheeling sort of capitalism; the new elites took what they wanted from the United States, and found ways to get rich; but the more admirable aspects of American legalism did not survive the long, tiring trip to Moscow.[20]

How much has American law actually influenced the laws and practices of other countries, aside from such obvious cases as South Korea? *Influence* is a tricky word. It is not the same as brainwashing. It is not the same as imperialism. On the one hand, it would be inaccurate to speak about American "influence" on Puerto Rico; American legal institutions were in fact stuffed down Puerto Rican throats. An influence in the more usual sense is like a television broadcast: it has no effect unless somebody turns the set on, and listens; and there is no influence on someone who does not want to be influenced. Much of what looks like American influence is actually convergence—that is, the global forces that shaped American law in a particular direction do the same to other countries too. So, for example, country after country in Latin America has reformed its system of criminal justice (on paper at least), in directions that looked more American—they made the trial look more like an American trial; they brought in oral testimony and cross-examination, or even experimented with a jury. But much of this "influence" came by way of the more recent

European codes—and it was the spirit of the age, rather than America, that made these laws what they were.[21]

In countries that were willing and able to receive the advice, whose leaders knew what they wanted, and had institutions that could support the innovations, Western law, including American law, was able to find a home. This was particularly true of the more technical laws: laws about stock exchanges, or intellectual property. The Securities and Exchange Commission has extended an eager hand to Bulgaria, Hungary, and Poland, among other countries— giving advice on securities laws and regulations. These were sophisticated countries, on the whole, with educated populations. In other places, the export of law came close to utter futility. An anecdote from the Mongolian republic illustrates this extreme. A young Mongolian official "gratefully accepts a stack of documents detailing United States securities laws from American experts" visiting his country. In fact he asks for more such documents, to be sent from the United States. He explains to another American adviser that "the texts are, of course, of little use" in his country "but that the blank side of the pages will help to alleviate his office's chronic shortage of quality paper."[22] American law thus has some unexpected ways of going global.

The Long Arm of the Law

Great powers can afford to bully little powers; and to ignore their complaints. America was the greatest power in the late twentieth century, and often acted accordingly. If a country like Nicaragua thinks it can drag the United States before an international court, and bring it to the bar of justice, it has another think coming. The United States feels free to invade a Grenada or a Panama with impunity. It has made many ham-handed efforts to carry the war on drugs into other countries, chiefly in Latin America. Congress too finds it hard to resist throwing its weight around. Laws telling foreign countries what to do are irresistible, if they have juicy political payoff domestically. The so-called Jackson-Vanik Amendment to the Trade Act of 1974 linked "most favored nation" status to emigration policy; the point was to get the Soviet Union to let Russian Jews leave for other countries.[23] The Helms-Burton Act of 1996 was intended to force other countries to stop trading with Cuba; those that dared violate the American embargo faced sanctions.[24] This law, of course, was aimed less at Cuba than at the rabidly anti-Castro voters of southern Florida.

International Treaties

America, like all other countries, is part of the bigger world, and that world has been shrinking. Like other countries, the United States has entered into hundreds of treaties, compacts, and agreements. This is a bulky body of law that might rival in size the federal code of laws. We have not examined it in this book, but it is a subject of enormous and growing importance.

Treaty law covers every imaginable subject. It concerns diplomats and diplomatic immunity; but this is only the beginning. Suppose an American author (like this one) gets royalties from an Italian translation of one of his books; or an Italian author—say, Umberto Eco—gets royalties from America. Who pays what taxes, to which countries, and how much? Tax treaties with various countries cover this subject—for example, there is a Convention Between the Government of the United States of America and the Government of the United Mexican States for the Avoidance of Double Taxation and the Prevention of Fiscal Evasion with Respect to Taxes on Income.[25] A treaty with Canada of 1916 was designed to protect migratory birds, which were "in danger of extermination" from "indiscriminate slaughter."[26] Trade treaties, agreements on tariffs, and the like are of overwhelming importance in the world today. Free-trade dogmas depend on these treaties—bilateral, multilateral. National sovereignty—even for a megapower like the United States—is eroded by a forest of treaties that tie the economy to the economies of other countries. There seems to be no alternative.

Tariffs are taxes, sometimes quite heavy, imposed on imported goods. Tariff schedules were, in the past, quite elaborate. The famous tariff act of 1930 ran to 173 printed pages and covered almost every commodity and product under the sun—including acetic acid, chemicals of all sorts, ink and ink products, manganese and other metals, manufactured goods, clothing, food products, automobiles and bicycles, umbrellas, fountain pens, truffles, and turtles.[27] Today, tariffs are in bad odor; free-market ideology is riding high, and tariffs are odious to this ideology. They still exist, however, in a weakened and limited form. So do "antidumping" laws, to protect American businesses from cut-throat foreign competition. The first of these laws was passed in 1916; another, in 1921, aimed at sales in the United States "at less than . . . fair value"; but these laws were overshadowed by tariff laws and were of little moment until the 1970s.[28]

More and more, the United States is part of the world economy. That economy helps make the United States rich, but also exposes it to danger. Capital and goods are supposed to flow freely across our borders; but labor is another question entirely. The whole point of immigration law is to keep this factor of production out, except to the degree we need it and want it. The United States has other vital interests to protect, which need full global protection. Intellectual property law—copyright, patent, and trademark law—need worldwide safeguards. There are many, many modern pirates, who steal rock-and-roll CDs and software programs, instead of boarding ships at sea. The problem is real. According to one estimate, 82 percent of the software used in Mexico in the early 1990s was pirated—copied, stolen, or however you want to put it.[29] The United States has battled hard to get other countries to respect at least the core concepts of its laws. An act of 1988, for example, aimed to provide "more effective remedies" (including sanctions) against foreign companies who violated the intellectual property rights of Americans.[30]

Lawyering Goes Global

In Europe and elsewhere, lawyers until recently operated as solo practitioners, or in smallish firms. In recent years, however, the American system—the big-firm system—has spread to other countries. Indeed, the largest law firm in the world in 1999 was not an American firm but a firm of British solicitors, Fresh-fields. In country after country, big law firms have been organized on the American pattern. Moreover, American firms now often have overseas branches. In 1952, among New York firms, certainly the most cosmopolitan in the country, there were only a handful of foreign branches: three each in London and Paris, one in Mexico City; one sole practitioner maintained an office in Zurich.[31] By 1999 the major firms had gone global, as we have seen. Skadden, Arps, Slate, Meagher and Flom had branches in Tokyo, London, Hong Kong, Sydney, Toronto, Brussels, Frankfurt, Paris, Beijing, Moscow, and Singapore.[32] This was exceptional, but other firms have at least one branch abroad. The Chicago firm of Mayer, Brown and Platt had offices in Berlin, Cologne, and London, and "representative offices" in Turkmenistan, the Kyrgyz Republic, Uzbekistan, and Russia, as well as the less exotic locales of Mexico City and Paris. It is less common for foreign firms to have branches in the United States, but many of the leading firms maintain some presence in New York and Washington. No doubt there are all sorts of formal and informal arrangements between firms, across borders. The practice of law, at least at this lofty level, is becoming truly transnational. But often transnational with an American flavor—American lawyers, posted abroad, carry their culture and their habits with them, no matter how cosmopolitan they may become. Along with the transnational practice of law, there is also the transnational practice of alternatives to law—commercial arbitration, for example.[33] Here the Americans have important rivals, in London and elsewhere, but they are more than holding their own.

The result of all this globalizing is what some scholars have called the Americanization of law; we even hear of a "reception" of American law, particularly in Europe.[34] In legal affairs, Anglo-American law, like the English language, has become the most available candidate; and in the phrase *Anglo-American* the American more and more tends to outweigh the Anglo. This influence is (naturally enough) especially marked in commercial law. The German bankruptcy code of 1994 was "strongly influenced by American ideas and conceptions"; it introduced, for example, the "totally new concept of reorganization," with an eye to chapter 11 of the United States bankruptcy code of 1978.[35] Nor is this kind of influence confined to Europe; American law and American models are felt as well in Asia and Latin America.

What was spreading the gospel of American law? Obviously, American power and wealth were important factors. Another factor was the ubiquity of American lawyers themselves—doing a stint in Paris or Beijing. But a global economy, and a global mass culture, require a kind of common language—a way for buyers, sellers, traders, dealmakers to communicate with each other. Air traffic controllers, similarly, have to be able to talk to pilots; if a Brazilian jet is about to land in Istanbul, it would be too much to expect the Portuguese or Turkish languages to be used. In any event, the next jet to land might be from Japan or France or Indonesia. The solution is that everybody uses English—all over the world.

Dealmaking, of course, is not like landing an airplane; it can be done through interpreters. But this is clumsy and inexact. And sometimes not even possible. How many people are available to translate Estonian into Tagalog? So in dealmaking, too, English has become the new lingua franca; there is no serious rival. The process builds on itself. As English becomes indispensable, lawyers and accountants and businesspeople in general feel that they have to know English to be "players." At a prominent law firm in Warsaw, Poland, at the end of the twentieth century, twenty-six of twenty-nine lawyers claimed fluency in English. Virtually all the 150 lawyers in Korea's largest firm made a similar claim.[36] Many of these lawyers learned English in school, or by traveling, or simply by living for a while in the United States (or, to a lesser extent, in England). Bright and ambitious young jurists from foreign countries often chose to spend a year or so in the United States, finishing their legal education. Most elite law schools had some sort of graduate program, geared mostly to the needs and wants of foreign students. Harvard, for example, processes gaggles of such students each year. The programs are attractive to Asians, Europeans, Latin Americans—in short, to almost everybody. At Stanford in 1997–1998, the law school directory listed fifty-seven candidates for advanced degrees. Eleven were American; the rest were from everywhere else—Germany, Spain, Italy, Israel, Korea, Taiwan, Indonesia, Mexico, Kenya, and Nigeria were among the countries represented.[37] In the early 1990s, Harvard Law School claimed that among its 150 or so candidates for an Ll.M. degree were students from fifty-seven countries; Columbia's graduate students in law came from forty-one.[38] These foreign students inevitably pick up a good deal of American law; and they also imbibe some of the flavor of American legal culture. They certainly learn to speak English, more or less fluently. (Most knew English before they came, though probably not as well.) And the degree itself no doubt carries a certain cachet in their native land. There is probably some traffic, too, in the opposite direction—Americans studying law abroad—but if so it is relatively slight.[39]

In some ways, it is less accurate to say that law is becoming more American on a global scale than to say that law is simply becoming more global, and American law gets global along with the rest of the legal systems of the world. What is often overlooked is that economic development itself is inherently global, at least in these times. To "develop" means to produce, to manufacture, to trade. A country does not develop by increasing haircuts or plastic surgery; or by creating national parks. Nor can you become a "developed country" if all you make and sell are native handicrafts. Development, in practice, means making and selling consumer products—for your country, or for somebody else. A few countries, sitting on top of pools of oil, get rich from raw materials, which they sell abroad, in exchange for consumer products. The consumer products themselves are much the same all over the world. A developed country is a country that makes cars, television sets, computers, air conditioners, and all the other toys of modernity; or that makes something that it sells in order to buy cars, television sets, computers, and air conditioners. Countries that produce also consume. A country that wants to consume has to produce. Thus economic development means entering the global game of consumer culture. And this, in practice, means entering also into transnational legal ordering—and, more likely than not, the world of the English language, and American law.

Trade flows across borders. So do problems. The world of 2000 was the world of what Ulrich Beck has called a "risk society."[40] Global warming does not respect national borders. Neither do holes in the ozone layer. Huge forest fires in Indonesia poison the air in neighboring countries. No man (or woman) is an island; no state, not even an island state, is an island. One might think that killing elephants in Africa for their ivory is nobody's business but the Africans'; but the rest of the world thinks otherwise. Environmental concerns also cross borders. Sovereignty seems a poor excuse for actions that despoil the earth. Americans can save the black-footed ferret and the California condor (or try to); but Americans are also concerned with pandas, elephants, and the Siberian tiger—none of them natives of the United States. Congress—in many regards a narrow, provincial, chauvinistic bunch—passed an elaborate African Elephant Conservation Act in 1988.[41] A congressional finding declared that the African elephant (animals "of the species loxodonta africana") had "declined at an alarming rate since the mid-1970s." The act provided money for conservation efforts, and banned the importation of ivory.

More and more, nations have to deal not only with problems that spill over borders but with conflicts between their laws and the laws of other countries. As people travel more and more, as they migrate from country to country, these conflicts multiply. Family law is supposed to be the least global of all fields of law, the most conservative, the most culture-bound. In some ways it is. But global trends put it, too, under enormous pressure. Changes in family structure brought about by modernization undermine the cultural assumptions of family law, even in "traditional" countries. And "traditional" people no longer stay home and marry the daughter of the family next door. An American goes to Italy and marries an Italian woman. A Nigerian man comes to the United States and takes an American bride. Suppose these marriages hit the rocks; suppose there are children, and one spouse decides to go "home." Who gets the children? In what country shall they live? Who decides? There are treaties and conventions that try to straighten out the tangle, with limited success.[42]

The United States has not, in fact, signed the International Custody Treaty.

In many regards, the United States is a classic nonsigner. A superpower does not pay much attention to world opinion. A treaty banning land mines? No thanks. An international tribunal with power to try war criminals? A dangerous threat to U.S. sovereignty. There are people in the United States who fly into a rage at the very mention of the words *United Nations.*

But the United States cannot secede from the world. It tries to—selectively; but isolation is no longer an option. Even some of America's cherished sovereignty is gone. The days of gunboat diplomacy are over. Economically speaking, the United States is part of a global system. The General Agreement on Tariffs and Trade (GATT) went into effect in 1948. GATT led to a series of "rounds," or trade negotiations. The goal was to cut tariffs and liberate trade. By 1967 GATT had 75 members; by 1994 it had 128. In 1995 the World Trade Organization came into being. Its main document, the so-called Final Act, ran to twenty-six thousand pages. As a member of the WTO, the United States has made promises that are presumably binding and enforceable. The United States cannot discriminate between countries A and B, if both are members of the WTO; and it cannot discriminate between imported goods and domestic goods—cannot discriminate, that is, between Italian shoes and American shoes.[43] Of course, there are many ifs and buts (twenty-six thousand pages of them); but the general thrust is clear. In October 1992 the United States also signed the text of the North American Free Trade Agreement (NAFTA), an agreement with Mexico and Canada. This too carried with it a certain loss of freedom to maneuver—and certain risks. Presidential candidate Ross Perot predicted a "giant sucking sound" of jobs moving south.[44] He was not the only one who was afraid of the consequences of NAFTA.

But the worst nightmares of Perot and the others have not been realized. The world cannot ignore the wishes of the superpower. The United States has a lot to say about the policies of the World Bank and the World Trade Organization, and even more to say about NAFTA. The flag still flies high. Still, more and more, over time, power slides quietly into the hands of big organizations that have no real national home. They are global citizens and global institutions. Thus even the king, the power of powers, finds itself tied down by dozens of large and small ropes, strings, and bonds: a Gulliver pinned to the earth by Lilliputians.

20

Taking Stock

A final chapter is a place for summing up. Where did we stand, at the end of the twentieth century—in federal and state law; in the position of law in American society; in the growth or decline of this or that field of law; in the status and role of the legal profession? These are, of course, not easy questions. The chapters up to this point have, I hope, at least suggested some general principles and answers.

One dominant theme of this book has been the relation between law and society; and between law and culture. Society changed drastically in the course of the century. We have seen this on almost every page. Technology turned the world upside down; social structure changed along with it. These drastic alterations, in a fluid, open society, get translated almost automatically into changes in law and the legal order.

People sometimes think that law is slow, torpid, hidebound, difficult to change—full of archaic hangovers; that its past clings to it like barnacles. But this is largely an illusion. The law of 2000 is every bit as different from the law of 1900 as society of 2000 is different from its ancestor in 1900. Is there no such thing as legal inertia? In one sense, no. Whenever the law is accused of inertia, it is not some abstraction called "the law" which holds back progress: real forces, real interest groups, real passions oppose change for concrete reasons. When people say some law or aspect of law is "archaic," they mean they disapprove of it (perhaps correctly); but archaic laws do not survive unless some living, nonarchaic people insist on keeping these arrangements alive.

That law is a creature of society is almost banal; nobody would disagree.

All legal scholars—and judges and lawyers—are in some sense legal realists. (Most legal scholarship, however, at least implicitly ignores the lessons of legal realism, and the lessons of social science.) The real question is what aspects of society make the legal system run, and how; at what pace, and for what reasons. Social change leads to legal change; but never automatically. Take technology: the automobile has changed society drastically; in the process, it created mountains of law. But the steps along the way were subtle and incremental. The immediate source of law is not social change but what we can call legal culture.[1] By this I mean people's ideas, attitudes, values, and expectations with regard to law. If we have traffic laws it is, yes, because of the automobile (ultimately); but the laws that emerged were responses to demands from people and organizations and interests, who are led to want certain things, or expect certain things, precisely because their life had been changed by the automobile; or because they thought it had been changed.

And what makes legal culture? What makes people respond in some specific way to a change in technology; or to any change in social conditions? Obviously, there is no quick and dirty answer. What happens can best be described as a kind of complicated chemical reaction. Something in the situation alters—new technology, or a change in some feature of the world at large. This has an impact on the way people feel, think, behave; how they go about their daily lives. Of course, how minds change depends in part on how people felt, thought, behaved and went about their daily lives before these changes took place. It depends, too, on the structures that are already there: they are the bony architecture of a system that comes to seem usual, and therefore normal and natural. Not changeless, of course. But what is new—jet airplanes, antibiotics, the Second World War—does not write on a blank mental slate. It does not enter a structural vacuum. It makes its mark on a complicated, existing system, a system of crosscurrents and interrelations, a web of values and norms.

I mentioned—stressed, in fact—changes in technology. As we know, the twentieth century has been a period of enormous technological advance—*revolution* is not too strong a word. It was the century of the automobile, the radio, television, heart transplants, gene splicing, computers. There have been social revolutions, too, to match these changes—in social relations; in sexual behavior and in family life; in identity and rights consciousness; in economic ordering. These have led to legal revolutions—civil rights, the liability explosion, no-fault divorce, to mention only a few.

Of the technological changes, probably the most significant for our purposes have been the changes in communication and transportation. At the dawn of the twenty-first century, the influence of the media on society seems almost unimaginably great. Television exposes at least some aspects of law to the full glare of publicity. It expresses powerful ideologies that ultimately have an impact on the law. And it accentuates the tendency for scandals and incidents to flare up, create a big bang, and influence the lawmaking process.

This is not, of course, a new phenomenon. To a certain extent, much of what became salient in the later part of the century was true, in embryo, earlier on. Scandal and incident, for example, had always been significant. The first food and drug regulations sailed into law partly because of the hullaballoo over Upton Sinclair's novel *The Jungle*. In the 1930s the elixir of sulfa scandal led to a strengthened food and drug law. "Sex crime" panics in the 1930s led to the passage of sexual psychopath laws.[2] Ralph Nader and *Unsafe at Any Speed* raised the consciousness of the public about auto safety and design flaws, and made its mark on consumer safety law. Rachel Carson and *The Silent Spring* had a similar role with regard to pesticides and toxic substances. The media helped drive the backlash against the liability explosion in tort law. Eruptions of scandal, incident, public outbursts have become common, almost routine. This was because of the immense, boundless power and immediacy of television, because of instant communication and instant feedback. "Investigative reporting" and its evil twin, yellow journalism, fed the appetite for scandal. The atmosphere became even more intense after the Watergate affair of the 1970s— a scandal in which much of the credit for exposing bad deeds went to crusading reporters.

The power of scandal and incident has thus become immense. Would Watergate have been such a huge affair—driving a president from office—without the white heat of media attention? Would President Clinton have suffered so much from his "bimbo eruptions"? The media do not invent scandals; but TV has a magic eye, a charismatic power; it can transform whatever it sees and transmit that transformed image to an audience of millions. Or billions. Publicity even feeds on itself. The mystery writer Erle Stanley Gardner, talking about the Loeb-Leopold case, said that "some cases suddenly reach a point where they generate their own heat as a brush fire generates its own wind."[3] The same could be said about many more recent scandals, trials, lawsuits, incidents, and general uproar, the stuff of newspaper headlines and dramatic "updates" on television. We live in an age of self-generated wind.

There is always a premium on the sensational. What the yellow press began, radio, the movies, and, especially, TV have immeasurably strengthened. Scandal is gripping, exciting; it interests people inordinately; consequently, it sells. To the media, obsessed with advertising revenues and ratings, this is not just the bottom line; it is virtually the only line.

More than ever, perhaps, criminal justice too responds to screeching headlines and TV news about violent crimes, rapes, horrendous murders, savage and unspeakable acts. "Megan's law" is a recent innovation that stems from a shocking crime. Little Megan Kanka was raped and strangled in New Jersey by a man who lived across the street from her. He had two prior convictions for sex offenses. The neighbors, including the Kankas, knew nothing about his dark past. A great cry of horror rose up when the killer was arrested. The man was sentenced to death; and New Jersey in 1994 quickly passed a statute to make sure that this situation would never recur. Under Megan's law, sex offenders, after they get out of prison, must register with the authorities; and from then on they are marked men. The law follows them wherever they go, and wherever they live: for the most dangerous sex offenders, the authorities have a duty to notify everybody "likely to encounter the person registered," including the neighbors.[4] They are hardly likely to greet their new neighbor, the convicted sex offender, with a welcome wagon. "Megan's laws" spread rapidly from state to state after 1994. By the end of the century some twenty-one states had put their registries on the internet, too, so that it is possible now to surf for pedophiles.[5]

Young Polly Klaas in California in the early 1990s was the victim of another shocking crime: snatched from her bedroom, in her own home, and brutally murdered. This crime was a powerful stimulus to some truly draconian pieces of legislation. California adopted its so-called "three-strikes" law by referendum in 1994. The law has layers and layers of complexity. The public, however, heard only a beguiling slogan—"three strikes and you're out"—catchy and easy to understand. It was a variation on traditional "habitual offender" laws. But the devil was in the details. If a defendant with two or more prior convictions for "serious" felonies (not necessarily violent ones) was convicted of yet another felony, he was to receive a life sentence—and had to serve a minimum of twenty-five years in prison.[6] In theory—and often in practice—there was no flexibility whatsoever in the new system, no room for judicial discretion, no room for plea bargaining; and no locus for mercy. California's statute was the most severe— and perhaps, in operation, the most disastrous—but other states chimed in with their own versions of this kind of law.

Again: a young gay man, Matthew Shepard, was murdered in 1998 in Wyoming—beaten and tied to a fence and left to die in the cold, like an animal in a trap. This horrendous crime stimulated demands for new hate-crime laws.[7] In Littleton, Colorado, in 1999, two disturbed high schools boys shot up their school; they killed twelve students and a teacher, and then killed themselves.[8] A shocked public (or part of it) demanded more gun laws and better means of gun control. Of course, clamor does not always get results; the furor often dies back in time. Many of these crises blow out quickly, like a Roman candle; others leave a mark behind, but perhaps a small one. The bulk of the "three-strikes" laws (California's is probably an exception) have had little or no impact on the way the criminal justice system operates. But the influence of Gothic horror and hair-raising scandal seems destined to increase, simply because the empire of the media grows and grows and grows. Scandal and incident are thus potent sources of law. The media do more than report; they also modify, exaggerate, and reflect. The medium may not be the message, but the medium makes the message; or helps make it, at any rate.

The media, too, are at least partly responsible for the so-called imperial presidency. There are other factors; but the media deserve pride of place. The president of the United States is a true celebrity. How many people, before radio and TV, ever actually saw the American president? A handful, at most. Now we see him constantly, day in and day out. In 1998, in the movie *The Truman Show,* a man named Truman Burbank lived his whole life on TV. His life was a television show. The other people in his life were actors and actresses; and everybody knew it but Truman himself. The president of the United States lives this kind of life, but with this crucial difference: he knows his life is a TV show; he knows he is a celebrity, he knows that his face, his voice, his family, his dogs and cats are familiar to millions of people; millions of people see him every day; they notice his hair, his clothes, the inflections of his voice. The media mold and shape and encompass his life. The president's zone of true privacy has shrunk to a tiny fraction of what it was. The infamous Monica Lewinsky crisis of 1998 made this abundantly clear. Could anybody imagine, in Jefferson's time, or even Roosevelt's or Kennedy's, national discussion on the subject of the president's penis?

The whole world watches its governments on television. And the governments know it. The result is what we might call the public opinion state. The government tries to manipulate public opinion; but it is also a slave to public opinion. It does nothing, or almost nothing, without consulting its modern witch doctors: pollsters, people who run focus groups, and everybody who claims to be good at feeling the public pulse. On the other hand, government deploys witch doctors for its own purposes: spin experts, specialists in deniability, practitioners of the dark arts of public relations. Thus the rulers and the ruled are locked into a weird kind of symbiosis. Rulers cannot rule without the approval of the subjects; yet the subjects depend on the rulers for at least some of the raw material out of which they form their approval.

Law and Popular Culture

Law and legal institutions are not merely affected by the media; they are also prime subjects of media attention. It is impossible to turn on TV today without bumping into the criminal justice system; prime time is awash with police, trials, courts, judges, prisons, and other trappings of the legal system. All this, of course, produces a distorted view of how the criminal justice system actually works. The public never sees the grimy, boring routine; it never sees plea bargaining, for example. TV and the movies are about good guys and bad guys. There is no room on the screen for ambiguity. In mystery stories, we always find out in the end "who did it"; that the perpetrator would (or should) escape punishment, because a law enforcement officer slipped up procedurally—this we never see or read; or, if we do, we violently disapprove.

The portrayal of lawyers in literature (if you can call it that), on TV, and in the movies has grown darker, more cynical. The same is true of law enforcement officers. At one time, police, detectives, and others of this breed were usually portrayed sympathetically. Once in a while, the police were shown as bumbling fools, as in the old silent movies about the Keystone Kops. In most "private eye" novels and movies the private eye, not the police, solves the case. This tradition is at least as old as Sherlock Holmes, whose instincts were always sounder than those of poor Inspector Lestrade. But in the Sherlock Holmes stories, and in most novels about private eyes, the police were merely incompetent, or less acute than Miss Marple or Hercule Poirot or Miss Silver or the ,her amateurs; they were rarely if ever brutal and malevolent.

Until roughly the 1960s, the FBI and the CIA were also invariably good guys—heroic crime fighters, as shown on such programs as the *FBI in Peace and War.* But this is emphatically no longer the case. Portrayals of the police, the CIA, the FBI in the late decades of the century were negative, if not downright paranoid. This is true, too, of portrayals of government in general: movies, in particular, peddle the most extreme conspiracy theories: about the Kennedy assassination, or the machinations of the CIA. In *The Manchurian Candidate,* the Communists brainwash a man and train him to carry out an assassination that would turn the government over to evil conspirators. (The plot fails in the end.) The president is not immune from these images of darkness. True, in *Air Force One* the president (a handsome dog played by Harrison Ford) is as heroic as one can possibly get. In other movies of the 1990s, however, the president has been a villain; or even a deep-dyed criminal. Earlier, in *Dr. Strangelove,* the president was sensible enough, but he was surrounded by dangerous fools, and a lunatic in the air force set off a nuclear holocaust: this was a black comedy indeed. Popular culture is also quite ambiguous in the way it portrays the outlaw, the gunman, the Mafia—the people on the other side of the law. Hays office rules insisted that crime must not pay; criminals had to be brought to justice. But the gangsters of the 1930s and 1940s, played by men like Jimmy Cagney and Edward G. Robinson, had brio, stature, and a snakelike fascination for the audience. Then came *Bonnie and Clyde,* and the three *Godfather* movies—all of them tremendous box-office hits. They were by no means the last. People who make a living in organized and disorganized crime seem to both attract and repel the audience. Official and unofficial censorship has completely broken down; a moviemaker, or a television director can, if she wishes, make a hero out of a criminal, depict the president as a liar and a thief, and turn conventional morality upside down in any way that attracts an audience. High criminals are, after all, celebrities. Most people live humdrum lives; lives of danger and glamour give them a vicarious, almost sexual thrill. Decline in trust in government (much of it richly deserved) and a general suspicion of authority blur the line between good guys and bad guys. Moreover, in American society, entertainment is king—witness how justice and entertainment merge in television judge shows, on *Court TV,* and through the presence of cameras in the courtroom.

The legal order has penetrated deep into the bowels of the culture. Law, legal issues, legal behavior are not just on TV but everywhere—often unnoticed, like the air we breathe. America is supposed to be a litigious society, a society obsessed with law, a uniquely "adversarial" society; a society that sues at the drop of a hat. This is almost certainly exaggerated. But it is true that Americans are not as shy about using legal tools as are people in certain other countries. And it is certainly true that the legal system is large, in dollars, in personnel, in importance; and it is also true that, as of 2000, it seemed to be getting larger all the time. No aspect of American life remained untouched.

The Federal System

One theme of this book has been the drift, or stampede, of law and legal order toward the center, toward Washington, D.C. This trend was surely inevitable. The country is a unit, economically and culturally; TV and jet airplanes, if nothing else, make it so. America in 2000 was still, to be sure, a country of fifty sovereignties, with a federal elephant sitting on top of the heap. State governments and state legal systems were in fact almost certainly more important in 2000 than in 1900, in absolute (though not relative) terms. Government at all levels is just so much bigger, and does so many more things, and taxes and spends so much more than it did in 1900. Even though the states play second fiddle to the federal government, they do so in an orchestra a hundred times the size of the orchestra a century ago.

Even in the age of the imperial presidency, and the massive, gigantic engine of federal power, the mixture of state and national authority survives. The governor is a more powerful figure than he or she was in 1900 (and yes, there are women governors at last). State supreme courts have flexed their muscles in ways parallel to the workings of the United States Supreme Court. Local government produces tons of rules, regulations, and ordinances—about schools, land use, traffic, safety, and so on. The legislatures are powerful bodies that produce enormous quantities of legislation. They are also far more professional than at the beginning of the twentieth century. They have researchers, legislative analysts, staffs. In 1979 the Alabama legislature had 200 permanent staff attached to it; in 1996 it had 316. In 1996 California had 2,506 permanent staff, Michigan 1,357, New York 3,461. Of course, smaller states had small staffs, and some were not growing: Wyoming had 18 in 1979, and 18 in 1996. In general, legislatures met more often and passed more bills—3,422 in California in 1994, enacted by legislators who were full-time lawmakers and who were paid $72,000 a year. (By way of contrast, the 1905 session—at that time the legislature met every other year—enacted some 600 laws.) Of course, there were big differences among the states: Idaho's part-time legislators got $12,360 for their service in 1994, and passed 456 bills; Louisiana's part-time lawmakers earned $16,800, and for this churned out a measly 152 new statutes.[9] Numbers alone, of course, do not tell the story; but they do suggest a more vibrant, active, and serious lawmaking effort in the big, important states.

Separation of powers is still a reality as well. Congress, like the states, has lost power relatively speaking—to the imperial presidency, and the huge armada of civil servants. If we ask, who governs? the right answer might be: the civil service. It certainly has more impact on daily life than either the courts or the president himself (short of war). But Congress is by no means impotent. It shares in the general explosion of sheer government. For one thing, it has more resources at its command. Congress until the 1920s had basically no professional staff—nothing but clerks. A 1946 law authorized each congressional committee to hire four professional staff members. In 1947 there were 399 aides on House and Senate committees; in 1982 there were 3,278. The personal staffs of members of the House of Representatives swelled from 2,441 in 1957 to 7,278 in 1991; in the Senate the increase was from 1,115 to 4,294. Since 1919 Congress has had a legislative drafting service (the Office of the Legislative Counsel) to help write laws. Congress is obviously an institution with much more muscle, bone, and fiber than it had at the beginning of the twentieth century.[10]

Federalism is still a reality. The states are little sovereignties, in their spheres. This makes for a kind of competitive market for law. Delaware became the motherland of corporations because a corporation could get itself chartered wherever it pleased, and Delaware had nice, easy laws. The migratory divorce was another example of the legal free market at work. Here, in the long-running battle between tight states and loose states, the loosest of all—Nevada—won.

Nevada is an instructive (or horrible) example of federalism at work in other ways, too. One historian called the state the "great rotten borough."[11] Nevada is in essence a barren desert, hostile to most forms of life, including humans. No crops to speak of grow there. In 1900 its population was tiny—the skimpiest of all the states, and shrinking, not growing. Then Nevada, in a burst of ingenuity, built an economy by exploiting its sovereignty. Its strategy was to legalize all sorts of things that were illegal in California—its neighbor, a state with plenty of people, and eventually lots of cars. After easy divorce came easy marriage and casino gambling. Even prostitution is legal in Nevada, in any county that decides to allow it. Quite a few of them do.

Nevada, as we have seen, required schools to teach "thrift." This seemed ironic by the end of the century, when billions of dollars flowed through the slot machines and roulette tables. Gambling, however, did not take off in Nevada until after the Second World War; everybody seemed to have a car, and the travel and entertainment bug bit hard. At the end of the century, Nevada had to scramble to keep ahead of the competition: the country had caught up with Nevada, in permissiveness, and in the worship of fun.

Federalism is thus in many ways alive and well; state law also still controls most of the law of torts, contracts and commercial law, domestic relations, and criminal law. The states and their subdivisions run the schools, collect the garbage, issue building permits, administer zoning laws, hire the police, arrest speeders, and handle burglary cases. You apply to local government for a license to get married; you turn to local courts to get a divorce. The states grant dog licenses and hunting licenses; they also license lawyers and doctors and nurses and pharmacists and architects and accountants. They definitely matter in the American legal world.

Still, federalism 2000 is not what it was in 1900; and certainly not what it was in 1800. The federal government can intervene whenever and wherever it chooses—or almost. The federal courts all but gave up their role in limiting federal power, and policing the boundaries of federalism. There were a few twitches of doctrine toward the very end of the century; the Supreme Court in 1995, in *United States v. Lopez,* struck down the Gun-Free School Zones Act, which made it a federal offense to bring a gun into a school zone; in so doing, it overturned the conviction of Alfonso Lopez, Jr., a senior who carried a .38 caliber handgun and five bullets into Edison High School in San Antonio, Texas.[12] A bare majority of the court, speaking through Chief Justice Rehnquist, felt the law was beyond the power of Congress. If Congress could regulate guns in the schoolyard, and use the commerce power as an excuse, then there were really no limits to what Congress could do.

The *Lopez* case caused a stir in the law reviews. They reacted as if a corpse had come to life, as if a biologist had discovered an actual dinosaur in the depths of the Amazon jungle. It is too early to tell if the case is an actual turning point. Some of the justices, unquestionably, would like to go farther down this road; they would like to rebuild something out of the rubble of states' rights. On the whole, it seems unlikely that *Lopez,* and later cases that went a bit further, will make much of a difference. Most of the talk about giving power back to the states is just talk. The Court can throw a monkey wrench or two into the mechanism; but its role is bound to be peripheral. There is, to be honest, no way to turn back the clock.

True, America is still quite decentralized—compared with, say, England or France. Nobody wants Washington to micromanage the whole society. Local rule, in many fields and situations, is a good idea. But the decision to go local or go national is now a policy decision. It is a pragmatic choice, not a command from the dead men who wrote the Constitution. There probably was such a command; but more than two centuries have gone by since it was issued. Today, few people really think it has to be obeyed. If Congress so desires, it can regulate almost anything it wants. I doubt very much whether the Supreme Court has the will or the guts to say no—at least in any major way. The early twenty-first century might bring a change, of course. This would be a big surprise; but life, after all, is full of surprises.

For years, there has been talk about a new kind of federalism—a new relationship between the states and the federal government; and much discussion about turning tasks back to the states, where they belong. In some areas of law, changes have indeed occurred. Certainly, the federal government goes in more for block grants than in the immediate past: in welfare law, for example. But the stark reality is still the same: power has gravitated toward the center. Washington in the twentieth century became a great capital, a true capital. The process seems irreversible. Moreover, the same people who talk about devolving government to the states are quite eager for federal intervention when it suits them; they forget all about states' right and local rule when the the question is about, say, cyberporn or tort reform, or stopping states from validating marriages of same-sex couples.

Leviathan

I have used the phrase "federal government"; but these two bland words, of course, mask enormous complexity. Part of the story of law in the twentieth century is the story of the way the administrative state—the bureaucracy—has expanded. The federal government is a huge, shapeless beast. The federal government is Congress and the Supreme Court; but more and more the executive branch is the federal government.

But even the phrase "executive branch" is much too bland. Dozens and dozens of separate agencies constitute the executive branch, many of them almost a law unto themselves. There are too many of them to count. Congress rarely puts any of them to sleep. (The late, unmourned Interstate Commerce Commission is a rare exception.) There is also the presidency itself. This has been, in many ways, *the* growth element of twentieth-century government. The president is not only the celebrity of celebrities, he is a man of enormous and growing power. (So far, of course, all presidents have been men.) One of the most significant developments of the twentieth century—one easily overlooked or forgotten—was the establishment of the Executive Office of the President in the 1930s; and the vast power it attracted to itself.[13] The president's staff—not the cabinet, not the agencies, but the people who work in and for the White House—now number in the thousands. The president runs, in effect, a parallel government. Who gives the president advice on foreign policy? Not just the secretary of state; and sometimes not even primarily the secretary of state. There are foreign policy advisers "in the White House"; and they often have more real say than the cabinet department which, in theory, runs foreign policy and advises the president. The president's economic advisers, his social advisers, his staff in general—these are, in many senses, the heart of the government.

How much power does the president actually have? Enormous power. In foreign affairs, he is basically an elected four-year dictator. Especially since the beginnings of the cold war, at the end of the Second World War, the president and his minions have presided over a vast, secret, shadow government—a kind of state within a state. Partly because of the foul seeds sown in the struggle against communism, a monstrous, bloated structure arose, deep in the bowels of a democratic society: a national security and intelligence apparatus, including the CIA and its covert operations, all of this virtually unchecked and unbalanced, with vast sums of money at its disposal. The public never saw it, never wanted to see it; Congress dished out the money (hidden in various nooks and crannies of the budget) and either blinded itself or was co-opted or approved or did not care. All of this underground government answers, in theory, to the president. The practice is no doubt more complex.

Congress, under the Constitution, has the power to declare war—the president does not. But this is now only theory. The president, in fact, now always fires the first shot. In the second half of the twentieth century, he was the one who declared the wars; he decided on war or peace. In 1950 the North Koreans crossed the 38th parallel into South Korea. This was a major crisis, and the president, Harry S. Truman, responded to it—vigorously and immediately. What followed was a real war, and a bloody one; real people died; real armies clashed; but Congress never "declared" it a war. Since then, the United States has deployed armies many times—in Vietnam, in Grenada, in the Persian Gulf, in Yugoslavia. Never once has Congress made the first move; never has it voted to declare a war. President Kennedy backed an ill-fated invasion of Cuba, which came to grief at the Bay of Pigs. This was only the most notorious of many actions which a whole series of presidents planned, connived at, or arranged during the cold war—a whole series of dirty, covert, warlike moves, many of which amounted (legally) to acts of war. Congress did enact a War Powers Resolution in 1973, insisting that the president had to "consult with Congress," if at all possible, before sending troops "into hostilities."[14] But this is mostly sound and fury, signifying nothing. For the most part, in foreign affairs both Congress and the public accept the imperial presidency.

Of course, even dictators take public opinion into account; and presidents certainly do. In this country what people think and feel and want can be a powerful restraint on the president's power. It matters what people say on the street, in barber shops, in town meetings, and in letters to the editor. Sit-ins, riots, demonstrations, and other acts of civil disobedience also matter. It was public opinion, not law, that brought down President Lyndon Johnson and ended the war in Vietnam. The formal law was toothless and unavailing.

The president, in domestic affairs, is extraordinarily powerful, too; but he is definitely not above the law. An instructive instance was the famous steel seizure case.[15] The president was the same Harry Truman who took the country into the Korean War—a move few people really questioned. In 1951, in the midst of this war, steel companies and their unions locked horns over a work contract. Attempts to mediate the controversy failed. In April 1952 the United Steelworkers announced an intention to strike. The president ordered the secretary of commerce to seize the steel mills. Management was told to keep the mills going, under presidential rule. Truman told Congress what he had done. Congress did nothing one way or another.

The steel industry now went to court. No statute authorized the president to seize steel mills. But a war was going on—an undeclared one, to be sure. Truman insisted that his authority to carry on the war gave him inherent power to act as he had. Six justices of the Supreme Court disagreed. Truman had overstepped the bounds. Only Congress could have ordered or authorized the seizure; and Congress had specifically refused. A generation later, in *United States v. Nixon* (1974), in the midst of the Watergate scandal, the Supreme Court again solemnly (and this time unanimously) declared that the president was not above the law.[16] The president had to answer a subpoena demanding that he release certain tape-recordings of conversations in his office. And in the case of Paula Jones, the Supreme Court (again unanimously) allowed a lawsuit against President Clinton (for sexual harassment) to proceed. The incident had happened (if at all) long before Clinton became president. A sitting president, said the Court, has to answer for claims, so long as they do not arise out of his official conduct.[17]

America can be proud of these cases, of course. Nobody is above the law, not even the man in the White House, the man with his finger on the atomic button, the man with the red telephone, the leader of the free world. These cases were a ringing endorsement of the rule of law. But they were atypical and extraordinary—even for domestic affairs. The power of the presidency, under law, and through law, is of awesome, stark dimensions. Many of the major statutes of the twentieth century simply handed over power, almost without restrictions or limits, to the president (which means, in essence, to the executive branch). It is the president, for example, and nobody else, who declares an emergency when a disaster occurs; it is the president who mobilizes resources of the government to do something about this disaster.[18]

The media helped create the imperial and celebrity president. But much of his power is the product of sheer necessity. Congress does not have time or knowledge or desire to handle every little matter; does not want to be responsible for deciding each item of detail: how much of this or that grant goes to Tulsa, Oklahoma, and how much to Bangor, Maine; which chemical dyes are not to be used to make cucumbers green. Of course, the president does not and cannot do this either. It gets done by the executive branch, in his name—by the bureaucracy, in short. Right now, no other way seems practical.

The number of federal civilian employees gives some idea of the way Leviathan has grown. To be sure, this includes everybody from mail carriers and file clerks up to the heads of great departments. But the figures tell a story:

239,476 in 1901; about 400,000 in 1916; more than 1.1 million in 1940; nearly 2.9 million in 1970. Since then the number has more or less leveled off. Meanwhile, state and local governments have gained personnel just as dramatically. In 1940 they had about 3.3 million employees, in 1970 more than 10 million; in 1997 it was 16.7 million or so. About half of this vast horde consisted of teachers and other educational workers.[19]

This huge army of civil servants were the foot soldiers of bureaucracy, the corps of a giant administrative state. How that state grew and flourished has been one of the major themes of this book. It was a story repeated all over the Western world. Every developed country went through the same process, more or less. They all regulated and controlled; they all provided benefits; they all expanded both these functions tremendously between 1900 and 2000.

Each country, of course, had its own peculiar style. The administrative style of the United States has been, in many ways, rather distinctive. In some ways, it has been more legalistic, bureaucratic—slower, less efficient—than some of its competitors. David Vogel pointed out that FDA procedures for approving new drugs in the United States were "far more burdensome" than the English procedures; the British approved Tagamet, an antiulcer drug, in two months; the FDA took thirteen months. During the 1970s many new drugs were available in England years before they were available in the United States.[20] Steven Kelman compared OSHA with its Swedish equivalent around 1980. American inspectors swooped down on factories and businesses without warning; they were tough and formal, and their main job was looking for violations (which they usually found). Their Swedish counterparts were more informal, were announced in advance, and stressed advice, cooperation, working things out.[21] The American system, not surprisingly, led to a lot of grumbling, resentment, and letters to Congress.

This difference in administrative styles seems, in a way, topsy-turvy. Americans are supposed to be wild individualists; they distrust government; they have an inveterate libertarian streak. They are also, supposedly, rights conscious to a fault. Why then is the administrative state so intrusive? Perhaps *because* of American culture. Kelman, speculating on differences between Sweden and the United States, mentions different "dominant values." Swedish values encourage people to "accept government wishes." The American tradition is more "self-assertive."[22] The American tradition creates its own style of bureaucracy: a bureaucracy which is rule-bound and formal, because it is afraid of lawsuits, because it cannot expect or does not expect cooperation, deference, respect. Hatred of government regulation thus may breed the kind of government regulation people love to hate.

American legal culture cannot, of course, be summed up in a single slogan, or captured in a few lapidary sentences. It is full of contradictions. It reflects, as it must, a very big, very diverse country. Like all modern countries, it shares in the particular culture of modernism; but at the same time, it has its own unique features. Robert Kagan talks about "adversarial legalism," which he defines as "policy making, policy implementation, and dispute resolution by means of lawyer-dominated litigation."[23] Adversarial legalism has its good points and its bad points. It produces a lot of justice; but at a very heavy cost.

Kagan argues that adversarial legalism has both a cultural and a structural side. The structural side consists of federalism, the jury system, and other American institutions that fragment, decentralize, and privatize. He also feels that adversarial legalism has grown much stronger in the latter half of the twentieth century. This is the period of plural equality—the period of civil rights and civil liberties; the period of total justice. If you pour a culture of total justice into the vessels of fragmented government, what you get is a system of rights and litigation of the very kind that flourished in the latter half of the century.

Peeking into the Future

Prediction is, of course, a dangerous activity. What will the next century bring? No one can know. There is no crystal ball. Suppose we asked someone in 1900 to look ahead to the year 2000 and make predictions. Most of the guesses, almost certainly, would have been dead wrong; most of the predictions would have gone fatally astray.

To take one example: a decent, upstanding member of the middle class in 1900 might have felt optimistic about the battle against vice. Progress was being made. Perhaps the trend would continue. The temperance movement was a good example of the trend. The days of the saloon might be numbered. In fact, the movement would, indeed, achieve a smashing victory in national Prohibition. Barbarism and degeneracy were bound to diminish. Eugenics promised a better future; it might be possible to breed a race of bourgeois moralists. History was the story of a steady evolution, away from everything crude and animal, toward higher civilization. Vice and rampant sexuality were signs of degeneracy, atavism, and worse. Virtue was bound to triumph, in the end, over prostitution, gambling, and drunkenness; the law would play a part in bringing this about.

These good people would be surprised, and surely horrified, to see how the story actually turned out. By 2000 not only was "vice" triumphant; it was not even defined (for the most part) as vice. Gambling was a huge national industry, and in the main completely legal. It had spread from Nevada to . . . well, everywhere. Pornography leered at the public from all sides. The second edition of the *Oxford English Dictionary* finally admitted the existence of a four-letter word beginning with f—a word everybody knew and most people used. The first edition, in the late nineteenth century, had simply left it out. In 2000 it barely shocked anybody anymore. The laws against sodomy had been repealed in many states; and the "infamous crime against nature" was no longer a crime against nature or against anyone, legally speaking, except in the Bible Belt (and hardly enforced even there). People who openly admitted to the "love that dares not speak its name" went on parades, celebrated gay pride, and even held high office. None of this was easily predictable, certainly not in 1900.

The American world in 1900 was a white man's world; this was the high-water mark of Jim Crow; blacks were a "problem," but the white South had a solution: white supremacy and rigid segregation. Not many white people, north or south, really believed in racial equality. Who could have predicted the civil rights revolution? People talked about the "melting pot" in 1900; but realistically, who foresaw the end of empires, or the end of the white monopoly on legitimacy, or the multicultural society, with its (apparent) rejection of assimilation? Who looked into the tea leaves and saw the feminist revolution; or the age-discrimination law; or rights for the handicapped, or the American Indian movement? For that matter, who could have predicted television, or the jet airplane, or antibiotics, or the invention of the computer, with all their consequences? Who would have predicted a million lawyers—a quarter of them women? Who would have predicted two million people in prison or jail? And so it goes. A hundred years is nothing to geologists or astrophysicists; but for social life, for the stuff of modern history, a hundred years is an eternity—way beyond the power to predict. Even twenty years may be too long for even the most rough and ready prediction. There was tremendous change in the twentieth century, in every regard; and the rate of change seems to be accelerating.

Samuel Walker, whom I mentioned at the beginning of this book, begins his book on the "rights revolution" of the late twentieth century by asking us to imagine a certain Reitz van Winkle, a "ne-er-do-well son of an old Atlanta family," who fell into a deep drunken sleep in 1956 and did not wake up for forty years.[24] When poor Van Winkle fell asleep whites and blacks were still segregated in Georgia, the civil rights movement was in its infancy, gay rights were not even mentioned in polite society, abortion was mostly illegal, and women's rights were rudimentary. Van Winkle awoke to a world that had changed, root and branch, in almost unimaginable ways.

Walker's book is about the rights revolution. His Van Winkle had also slept through the war in Vietnam and the Reagan years. He had fallen asleep in a world in which few people had heard about computers, and even scientists could hardly imagine what computers would do in society. He had fallen asleep at the very beginning of the age of TV. When he drifted off into slumberland, the word *cyberspace* was not yet in the dictionary; and nobody talked about derivatives, hedge funds, and the like. If Van Winkle had been a lawyer, he would have awakened to a strange world in this regard as well. Lawyers did not advertise when he had fallen asleep. Almost all lawyers were white, and men. No woman sat on the Supreme Court; or for the most part on any court. The largest law firms of his day were pygmies compared to the largest firms of 1996.

What would a new Van Winkle find if he fell asleep on January 1, 2000, and woke up forty, sixty, one hundred years later? What will people think and do in, say, 2100 (if there are still people around)? Nobody knows. Our expectations, like those of our great-great-grandparents in 1900, will surely turn out to be wrong.

Take, for example, the future of federalism. State sovereignty has been shrinking for a hundred years. But now we are in the age of cyberspace. The internet is everywhere and nowhere. It is just a baby now, but who knows what it will grow into? The whole idea of jurisdiction, of the dependence of law on boundaries, borders, definite spaces: is this headed for the junkheap? Will a global network centralize authority—or will it, in fact, do the opposite?

A sheep has been cloned; this was big news in 1997. Will we clone people by the time 2100 rolls around? Will scientists find a way to extend life to 160 years? Will we have test-tube babies, colonies on Mars, communications with aliens from other galaxies? Nobody knows. Most likely what will occur is something we cannot even imagine right now. But what *is* probable (I dare not say certain) is this: whatever is in store for us will affect the legal order; indeed, it will operate somehow *through* the legal order, and affect the legal order (and us) in a deep and profound way.

December 31, 1999. In most of the country, a cold, wintry day; coldest, of course, in Alaska; warmest in Hawaii and southern Florida, where winter has no meaning, as far as weather is concerned. In California, the weather was clear, warm, and unusually dry. Cold or warm, there was excitement in the air. The end of the century: and the end of the millennium. There was a certain amount of fear, and a sense of drama. The world was on the brink of a new era (at least, a new calendar era). In New York crowds began to gather in Times Square in the afternoon. The millennium actually began long before it reached the United States—almost a day before, at the international date line. It crept slowly westward, hour after hour.

This was different from 1900—in many ways. There was no television then. Now the New Yorker or Californian could watch the fireworks in Beijing, and the celebration in Sydney; by the time the fateful hour reached the United States, it was almost an anticlimax. As the invisible shadow of time passed over the world, people celebrated, quietly or raucously; in the squares of big cities, millions of people (mostly young) shouted and screamed and counted and danced and partied through the night. A few people expected some sort of apocalypse, a colossal cosmic event, or some new or old Messiah; others were worried about a gigantic computer breakdown, causing plane crashes, blackouts and power failures. Most people expected neither the rapture at the end of the world nor the cataclysm of technological collapse. In the rich countries, including the United States, most people were simply looking for a grand old time.

It was a busy night for law enforcement people, among others. Emergency services, disaster agencies worked around the clock, guarding against tragedies which were fortunately uncommon. The police patrolled the streets for drunk drivers, for parties that got out of control, for minor riots. In other ways the law took a holiday. Shops and offices stayed shuttered on January 1, 2000. The courts were not in session. People slept in if they could. But the processes of law were not asleep. They are never asleep. They patrol our social space, just as the police patrol the streets; but more silently and subtly. In our times, and in our society, law is pervasive. The end of a year, a century, a millennium does not interrupt the law at its work. Its story continues.

A century from now, someone—not me—might write a book (if books still exist) about American law in the twenty-first century. Right now, I feel reasonably sure it would be a story about growth, transformation, adaptation—a story about change. More than that is impossible to say. The future is truly unknown country—a great void, a black hole, a vacuum. We can peek a little way forward, a few steps into it, as if we were walking in dark woods on a moonless night—a few steps, but nothing more. Beyond that is an utter blank; the ultimate darkness. The future is a country in another galaxy, mysterious, remote, inaccessible to the mortals here on earth.

Notes

Introduction

1 The account of New Year's Day 1900 is taken from Judy Crichton, *America 1900: The Turning Point* (1998), pp. 3–19.

2 For an overview, see Lawrence M. Friedman, *A History of American Law* (2d ed., 1985).

3 Samuel Walker, *The Rights Revolution: Rights and Community in Modern America* (1998), introduction, viii–x.

4 See William J. Novak, *The People's Welfare: Law and Regulation in Nineteenth-Century America* (1996).

5 Lawrence M. Friedman, *Total Justice* (1985).

6 First Biennial Report, Cal. State Division of Motor Vehicles (period ending Feb. 1, 1925), pp. 1–2.

7 Marc Galanter, "Reading the Landscape of Disputes: What We Know and Don't Know (and Think We Know) About our Allegedly Contentious and Litigious Society," *UCLA Law Review* 31:4 (1983).

8 163 U.S. 537 (1896).

1.
Structure, Power, and Form

1 198 U.S. 45 (1905). See Howard Gillman, *The Constitution Besieged: The Rise and Demise of Lochner Era Police Powers Jurisprudence* (1993).

2 Laws N.Y. 1897, ch. 415, §§110 ff.

3 208 U.S. 1 (1908).

4 The so-called Erdman Act, 30 Stat. 424 (1898).

5 In *Coppage v. Kansas,* 236 U.S. 1 (1915), the Supreme Court followed Adair, and struck down a Kansas statute which outlawed yellow dog contracts, as repugnant to the due process clause of the Fourteenth Amendment.

6 236 U.S. 1 (1914). Two justices dissented.

7 Ibid., at 17.

8 In general, on the child-labor reform movement, see Stephen B. Wood, *Constitutional Politics in the Progressive Era: Child Labor and the Law* (1968).

9 39 Stat. 675 (act of Sept. 1, 1916).

10 William F. Swindler, *Court and Constitution in the Twentieth Century: The Old Legality, 1889–1932* (1969), pp. 206–208. A court "enjoins" an action (issues an injunction) when it issues an order directly commanding somebody, or some group, to do a certain act, or refrain from doing something else.

11 *Hammer v. Dagenhart,* 247 U.S. 259, 62 L. Ed. 1101 (1918). Hammer was the United States attorney for the area where Dagenhart lived.

12 40 Stat. 1057, at 1138 (Title XII of the general revenue act) (act of Feb. 24, 1919).

13 Child Labor Tax Case *(Bailey v. Drexel Furniture Co.),* 259 U.S. 20 (1922).

14 *Hoke v. United States,* 227 U.S. 308 (1913).

15 Lottery Case *(Champion v. Ames),* 188 U.S. 321 (1903) (interstate or mail transport of lottery tickets). In *Hoke* the Court referred to the power of Congress over the "demoralization of lotteries, the debasement of obscene literature . . . debauchery of women, and . . . girls," at 322.

16 This was the famous doctrine enunciated in *Munn v. Illinois,* 94 U.S. 113 (1877).

17 On this general subject, see Barry Cushman, *Rethinking the New Deal Court: The Structure of a Constitutional Revolution* (1998).

18 208 U.S. 412 (1908).

19 *Sturges & Burn Mfg. Co v. Beauchamp,* 231 U.S. 320 (1913). This was actually a personal-injury case. Arthur Beauchamp, who was under sixteen, worked for a company that made tinware and other metal products. He operated a "punch press used in stamping sheet metal," and was injured. Illinois law prohibited the employment of children under sixteen in such jobs. The Supreme Court ruled that the statute was constitutional.

20 243 U.S. 426 (1917).

21 279 U.S. 392, 49 S. Ct. 372 (1929).

22 208 U.S. at 421, 422.

23 214 U.S. 91 (1909).

24 239 U.S. 394 (1915).

25 Similarly, *Laurel Hill Cemetery v. San Francisco,* 216 U.S. 358 (1910): here too the expanding city engulfed the cemetery, which then became illegal. No recovery.

26 For a more moderate assessment of the work of the Court in the first decade of the century, see James W. Ely, Jr., *The Chief Justiceship of Melville W. Fuller, 1888–1910* (1995).

27 264 U.S. 504 (1924).

28 238 U.S. 491 (1915).

29 Ernst Freund, *The Police Power: Public Policy and Constitutional Rights* (1904), p. 109.

30 See, in general, Lawrence M. Friedman, "Freedom of Contract and Occupational Licensing, 1890–1910: A Legal and Social Study," *Cal. L. Rev.* 53:487.

31 Laws N.H. 1917, ch. 118, p. 603.

32 Laws Texas 1907, pp. 273, 275.

33 *State v. Walker,* 48 Wash. 8, 92 Pac. 775 (1907).

34 *Commonwealth v. Boston Advertising Co.,* 188 Mass. 348, 74 N.E. 601 (1905). The precise holding was that the commissions' rules were so gross an interference with the property that they amounted to a "taking," forbidden under the Fifth Amendment.

35 Maine Laws 1913, ch. 129, sec. 10.

36 Edward C. Bailly, "The Legal Basis of Rate Regulation: Fair Return on the Value Employed for the Public Service," *Columbia L. Rev.* 11:532 (1911).

37 *Bluefield Waterworks & Improvement Co. v. Public Service Commission of West Virginia,* 262 U.S. 679 (1923); in this case, the company successfully attacked the rates which the West Virginia Public Service Commission had set.

38 *Spring Valley Water Co. v. City and County of San Francisco,* 165 Fed. R. 667, 711 (C.C. N.D. Cal., 1908).

39 *Wenham v. State,* 65 Neb. 394 (1902).

40 244 Ill. 509, 520, 91 N.E. 695 (1910).

41 Ibid., at 520.

42 *Ritchie v. People,* 155 Ill. 98, 40 N.E. 454 (1895). Freund felt this decision was not "justified either in the light of reason or authority." Freund, *Police Power,* at 520.

2.
The Legal Profession in the Early Twentieth Century

1 *Historical Statistics of the United States,* part I, p. 140 (1975).

2 Ken Dornstein, *Accidentally on Purpose: The Making of a Personal Injury Underworld in America* (1996), p. 87.

3 Robert R. Bell, *The Philadelphia Lawyer: A History, 1735–1945* (1992), p. 206.

4 *Martindale's American Law Directory* (1930), p. 1316.

5 Harold M. Hyman, *Craftsmanship and Character: A History of the Vinson & Elkins Law Firm of Houston, 1917–1997* (1998), p. 93.

6 *Martindale's American Law Directory* (1931), p. 716.

7 Robert T. Swaine, *The Cravath Firm and Its Predecessors, 1819–1948* (vol. 2, 1948), pp. 1–13.

8 Ellen D. Langill, *Foley & Lardner, Attorneys at Law, 1842–1992* (1992), p. 126.

9 *Hubbell's Legal Directory* (1919), appendix, pp. 140–141, 152, 153, 270.

10 William G. Thomas, *Lawyering for the Railroad: Business, Law, and Power in the New South* (1999), pp. 138–139.

11 Richard O. Boyer, *Max Steuer, Magician of the Law* (1932), p. 16.

12 On Darrow's life see Kevin Tierney, *Darrow: A Biography* (1979).

13 Patrick T. Conley, *Liberty and Justice: A History of Law and Lawyers in Rhode Island, 1636–1998* (1999), p. 465.

14 Theron G. Strong, *Landmarks of a Lawyer's Lifetime* (1914), p. 414.

15 Bell, *Philadelphia Lawyer,* pp. 226–227.

16 Michael E. Parrish, *Felix Frankfurter and His Times: The Reform Years* (1982), p. 157.

17 *Martindale's American Law Directory,* 1924, pp. 1147–1148, 1208–1209.

18 Richard L. Abel, *American Lawyers* (1989), p. 86.

19 Arthur L. Liman, *Lawyer: A Life of Counsel and Controversy* (1998), pp. 17–18.

20 Bell, *Philadelphia Lawyer,* p. 237.

21 The standard treatment of the history of legal education is Robert Stevens, *Law School: Legal Education in America from the 1850s to the 1980s* (1983).

22 William P. LaPiana, *Logic and Experience: The Origin of Modern American Legal Education* (1994), p. 145.

23 Stevens, *Law School*, p. 116.

24 Frank L. Ellsworth, *Law on the Midway: The Founding of the University of Chicago Law School* (1977), pp. 68–69. Beale clashed at first with Ernst Freund of the university—a German-born and law-trained political scientist. Freund's plans to enrich the curriculum with courses in political science and the like were vetoed by Beale, but the two men eventually reached an accommodation.

25 Alfred Z. Reed, *Present-Day Law Schools in the United States* (1928), p. 25.

26 Quotation: *Proceedings, 12th Ann. Meeting, Association of American Law Schools* (1912), p. 45.

27 *Harvard Law School Bulletin*, no. 2, July 1948, p. 7.

28 "Ten Largest Law Schools, 1901–1902," *American Law School Review* 1:21 (1903).

29 Jerold S. Auerbach, *Unequal Justice: Lawyers and Social Change in Modern America* (1976), p. 94.

30 Abel, *American Lawyers*, p. 42.

31 Robert W. Gordon, "Legal Thought and Legal Practice in the Age of American Enterprise, 1870–1920," in Gerald L. Geison, ed., *Professions and Professional Ideologies in America* (1983). For "legal science," see the fine discussion on p. 70.

32 Auerbach, *Unequal Justice*, p. 95.

33 Alfred Zantzinger Reed, *Present-Day Law Schools in the United States and Canada* (1928), p. 310.

34 John H. Wigmore, "Should the Standard of Admission to the Bar Be Based on Two Years or More of College-Grade Education? It Should," *American Law School Review* 4:30 (1915).

35 These remarks were made in 1931, at a meeting of the Section on Legal Education and Admissions to the Bar of the American Bar Association, reprinted in *American Law School Review* 7:320, 323 (1931).

36 Lee's remarks too were at a meeting of the Section on Legal Education and Admissions to the Bar of the American Bar Association, this time in 1932, reprinted in *American Law School Review* 7:609, 616 (1932).

37 Edward T. Lee, "The Evening Law School," *American Law School Review* 1:290, 292–293 (1905).

38 Yet more comments of Lee at the meeting of the Section on Legal Education and Admission to the Bar of the American Bar Association, this time in 1933, reprinted in *American Law School Review* 7:938, 947 (1933).

39 Alfred Z. Reed, *Training for the Public Profession of the Law* (1921), p. 393.

40 Robert Schaus and James Arnone, *University at Buffalo Law School: 100 Years, 1887–1987* (1992), pp. 42–43.

41 Herbert Harley, "Organization of the Bar," in *Reform in Administration of Justice,* annals, vol. 52 (March 1914), pp. 77–79.

42 Reed, *Training,* p. 103.

43 Abel, *American Lawyers,* pp. 62–65.

44 Herbert F. Goodrich, "Bar Examinations and Legal Education," *American Law School Review* 7:307 (1931).

45 Stevens, *Law School,* pp. 98–99; Abel, *American Lawyers,* p. 62.

46 Quoted in Auerbach, *Unequal Justice,* p. 41.

47 But the Committee on Professional Ethics of the American Bar Association voiced the opinion in May 1930 that a *mandatory* fee schedule was a violation of canon 12, because lawyers were supposed to consider all the circumstances in setting a fee. An obligatory fee schedule, said the committee, would "necessarily conflict with that independence of thought and action which is necessary to professional existence," and put lawyers' pay on a kind of "labor union" basis, an idea which no doubt filled the committee with horror. American Bar Association, *Opinions of the Committee on Professional Ethics and Grievances* (n.d., circa 1936), pp. 92–93. Needless to say, even if minimum fee schedules were not formally mandatory, they were widespread in practice.

48 In 1933 the canon was amended; such fees were to be "reasonable" under all the circumstances, and were still subject on this score to the "supervision" of the court.

49 Abel, *American Lawyers,* pp. 45, 46.

50 Auerbach, *Unequal Justice,* p. 120.

51 Ibid., p. 66.

52 Abel, *American Lawyers,* p. 90.

53 Michael J. Powell, *From Patrician to Professional Elite: The Transformation of the New York City Bar Association* (1988), pp. 48, 72.

54 *Atchison, Topeka & Santa Fe Rr. Co. v. Calhoun,* 213 U.S. 1 (1909); *Equitable Life Assurance Society v. Brown,* 213 U.S. 25 (1909); *Sand Filtration Corp. v. Cowardin,* 213 U.S. 360 (1909).

55 On the early jurisdiction of the Court, through the 1925 reforms, the classic work of Felix Frankfurter and James M. Landis, *The Business of the Supreme Court: A Study in the Federal Judicial System* (1927), is still crucial.

56 39 Stat. 726 (act of Sept. 6, 1916).

57 43 Stat. 936 (act of Feb. 13, 1925).

58 Frankfurter and Landis, *Business of the Supreme Court,* p. 295.

59 Frankfurter and Landis, "The Business of the Supreme Court at October Term, 1929," *Harvard L. Rev.* 44:1, 7 (1930).

60 Walter W. Manley II, *The Supreme Court of Florida and Its Predecessor Courts, 1821–1917* (1997), p. 331. The court could also sit "en banc" (that is, all the judges together) in some cases.

61 Laws Calif. 1903, p. 737.

3.
The Law of Business and Commerce

1 *Historical Statistics of the United States,* vol. 1 (1975), pp. 140–145.

2 Alfred D. Chandler, Jr., *The Visible Hand: The Managerial Revolution in American Business* (1977), p. 368.

3 Samuel Williston, *Life and Law* (1940), pp. 217–219.

4 Samuel Williston, *The Law Governing the Sale of Goods* (rev. ed., 1948, vol. 1) p. 2.

5 39 Stat. 538 (act of Aug. 29, 1916).

6 This account is taken largely from Grant Gilmore, *Security Interests in Personal Property,* vol. 1 (1965), chap. 4, pp. 86–119.

7 *Annual Report of the Attorney-General of the United States for the Year, 1904* (1904), p. 155.

8 47 Stat. 1474 (act of Mar. 3, 1933).

9 Warner Fuller, "The Background and Techniques of Equity and Bankruptcy Railroad Reorganizations: A Survey," *Law and Contemporary Problems* 7:377 (1940).

10 See Lawrence M. Friedman, *A History of American Law* (2d ed., 1985), pp. 188–201, 511–525.

11 Morton Keller, *Regulating a New Economy: Public Policy and Economic Change in America, 1900–1933* (1990), p. 86.

12 See, in general, Christopher Grandy, *New Jersey and the Fiscal Origins of Modern American Corporation Law* (1993).

13 Russell C. Larcom, *The Delaware Corporation* (1937), p. 167.

14 Joel Seligman, *The Transformation of Wall Street* (rev. ed., 1995), p. 43; Laws N.Y. 1912, ch. 351, p. 687 (on issuance of stock without any nominal or par value).

15 Laws Del. 1917, ch. 113, sec. 3; Larcom, *The Delaware Corporation,* pp. 95–113.

16 Grandy, *New Jersey and the Fiscal Origins,* pp. 61–68; Keller, *Regulating a New Economy,* p. 89.

17 Larcom, *The Delaware Corporation,* p. 177.

18 James Willard Hurst, *The Legitimacy of the Business Corporation* (1970), p. 152.

19 Laws Ill. 1919, p. 316.

20 23 Del. Ch. 255, 5 Atl. 2d 503 (1939).

21 24 Stat. 379 (act of Feb. 4, 1887).

22 See, on this point, Stephen Skowronek, *Building a New American State: The Expansion of National Administrative Capacity* (1982).

23 32 Stat. 847 (act of Feb. 19, 1903).

24 Neil Fligstein, *The Transformation of Corporate Control* (1990), p. 87.

25 34 Stat. 584 (act of June 29, 1906).

26 Richard D. Stone, *The Interstate Commerce Commission and the Railroad Industry: A History of Regulatory Policy* (1991), p. 13; I. L. Sharfman, *The Interstate Commerce Commission: A Study in Administrative Law and Procedure* (part 1, 1931), pp. 40–52.

27 Joseph H. Beale and Bruce Wyman, *Railroad Rate Regulation* (2d ed., 1915), p. 31.

28 36 Stat. 539, 547–549 (act of June 8, 1910).

29 The Sherman Act is 26 Stat. 209 (act of July 2, 1890); see William Letwin, *Law and Economic Policy in America: The Evolution of the Sherman Antitrust Act* (1965).

30 Herbert Hovenkamp, *Enterprise and American Law, 1836–1937* (1991), p. 351.

31 See, on the early period, Hans B. Thorelli, *The Federal Antitrust Policy: Origination of an American Tradition* (1955).

32 193 U.S. 197 (1904). On this case, see Hovemkamp, *Enterprise and American Law,* pp. 264–266; Martin J. Sklar, *The Corporate Reconstruction of American Capitalism, 1890–1916: The Market, the Law, and Politics* (1988), pp. 138–141.

33 193 U.S. 197, at 327–328.

34 C. C. Langdell, "The Northern Securities Case and the Sherman Anti-Trust Act," *Harv. L. Rev.* 16:539, 545 (1903). Langdell was actually commenting on the lower-court decision in this case.

35 193 U.S., at 407, 409.

36 Thorelli, *Federal Antitrust Policy,* p. 427.

37 *United States v. Swift & Co.,* 193 U.S. 391 (1905).

38 *Standard Oil v. United States,* 221 U.S. 1 (1911).

39 See, in general, Sklar, *Corporate Reconstruction;* Tony Freyer, *Regulating Big Business: Antitrust in Great Britain and America, 1880–1990* (1992), pp. 116–117; Rudolph J. R. Peritz, *Competition Policy in America, 1888–1992: History, Rhetoric, Law* (1996), pp. 50–52.

40 *American Tobacco Co. v. U.S.,* 221 U.S. 106 (1911).

41 251 U.S. 417 (1920). The case was a close one: only seven justices took part in the decision, and they divided 4–3. See Freyer, *Regulating Big Business,* p. 189.

42 See, in general, Sklar, *Corporate Reconstruction.*

43 Herbert R. Dorau, "The Rise and Decline of Municipal Ownership in the Electric Light and Power Industry of Wisconsin," *J. Land and Public Utility Economics* 3:172 (1927).

44 32 Stat. 827 (act of Feb. 14, 1903), §6.

45 38 Stat. 718 (act of Sept. 16, 1914).

46 Sklar, *Corporate Reconstruction,* p. 330.

47 38 Stat. 730 (act of Oct. 15, 1914).

48 *Annual Report of the Attorney-General of the United States for the Year 1905* (1905), p. 19.

49 *Standard Oil,* 221 U.S. 1, at 30–31.

50 See Stewart Macaulay, Lawrence M. Friedman, and John Stookey, *Law and Society: Readings on the Social Study of Law* (1995), pp. 233–235.

51 Mo. Stats. 1906, §§2266, 2269, pp. 1427–1428.

52 Quoted in Macaulay, Friedman, and Stookey, *Law and Society,* p. 235.

53 Upton Sinclair, *American Outpost: A Book of Reminiscences* (1932), p. 175.

54 Mark Aldrich, *Safety First: Technology, Labor, and Business in the Building of American Work Safety, 1870–1939* (1997), preface.

55 Roosevelt quoted in W. L. Hsieh, *Railroad Safety Problems: Federal Safety Legislation and Administration* (1930), p. 92. 34 Stat. 1415 (act of Mar. 4, 1907).

56 27 Stat. 531 (act of Mar. 2, 1893).

57 35 Stat. 476 (act of May 30, 1908).

58 36 Stat. 350 (act of May 6, 1910). But ICC reports were not to be "admitted as evidence" or used in any way in personal injury cases.

59 36 Stat. 913 (act of Feb. 17, 1911).

60 Aldrich, *Safety First,* p. 41.

61 36 Stat. 369 (act of May 16, 1910).

62 24 Stat. 379 (act of Feb. 4, 1887).

63 Gen. Stats. Minn. 1913, §4171.

64 Ky. Rev. Stats. 1915, ch. 32 §830.

65 Mass. Rev. Stats. 1921, ch. 160, §§163, 166, p. 1736.

66 Laws Neb. 1909, chs. 1, 4, 5, 6; pp. 53, 55–62.

67 Laws Neb. 1909, ch. 89, p. 359.

68 Laws Neb. 308, ch. 67, pp. 308–309.

69 Laws Neb. 1909, ch. 68, pp. 311, 313, 314–315.

70 Laws Vt. 1915, no. 165, p. 292.

71 Laws Ariz. 1929, ch. 95, §24, pp. 306, 319–321; there were also special provisions for head lettuce, ibid., §25, p. 321.

72 Rev. Civil Stats. Texas, vol. 1 (1925), pp. 20–45.

73 Rev. Civil Stats. Texas, vol. 1 (1925), art. 4477, pp. 1198–1216.

74 Laws Ill. 1919, p. 570.

75 Pa. Stats. 1920, §§13591, 13592.

76 E.g., Ohio Stats. 1926, §926.

77 Laws Texas 1907, ch. 178, p. 331.

78 City of Fresno, ord. no. 607, in effect Feb. 11, 1911, in *Charter and Ordinances of the City of Fresno, California* (1911), p. 148.

79 William Graebner, *Coal-Mining Safety in the Progressive Period: The Political Economy of Reform* (1976), pp. 87–88.

80 See Compiled Okla. Stats. Ann., 1921, ch. 24, art. III, §4162, p. 1727.

81 Keller, *Regulating a New Economy,* pp. 201–204.

82 38 Stat. 251 (act of Dec. 23, 1913).

83 Keller, *Regulating a New Economy,* p. 203.

84 Ga. Code 1926, §3436.

85 See, in general, David J. Gallert, Walter S. Hilborn, Geoffrey May, *Small Loan Legislation* (1932).

86 For a description, see Victor K. Meador, *Loan Sharks in Georgia* (1948) (a report published by the Junior Bar Conference of the American Bar Association).

87 Thomas Plate, *Crime Pays* (1975), pp. 145–146.

88 This information, and much of the surrounding material in the text, is drawn from Mark J. Roe, "Foundations of Corporate Finance: The 1906 Pacification of the Insurance Industry," *Columbia L. Rev.* 93:639 (1993).

89 Spencer L. Kimball, *Insurance and Public Policy* (1960); this is a study of insurance regulation in Wisconsin between 1835 and 1959.

90 Edwin W. Patterson, *The Insurance Commissioners in the United States: A Study in Administrative Law and Practice* (1927), p. 29.

91 Laws N.Y. 1906, ch. 3267, p. 763.

92 See Morton Keller, *The Life Insurance Enterprise, 1885–1910: A Study in the Limits of Corporate Power* (1963), pp. 254–259.

93 H. Roger Grant, *Insurance Reform: Consumer Action in the Progressive Era* (1979), pp. 61–63.

94 *Historical Statistics of the United States,* part 2 (1975), p. 1122.

95 157 U.S. 429; 158 U.S. 601 (1895).

96 See Robert Stanley, *Dimensions of Law in the Service of Order: Origins of the Federal Income Tax, 1861–1913* (1993), p. 211.

97 38 Stat. 166 (act of Oct. 3, 1913).

98 John F. Witte, *The Politics and Development of the Federal Income Tax* (1985), pp. 78–79.

99 39 Stat. 756 (act of Sept. 8, 1916).

100 Witte, *Politics and Development,* p. 79.

101 Elliott Brownlee, *Federal Taxation in America: A Short History* (1996), pp. 60, 61.

102 39 Stat. 756, Title II, at 777 (act of Sept. 8, 1916); upheld in *New York Trust Co. v. Eisner,* 256 U.S. 345 (1921).

103 Stanley, *Dimensions of Law,* p. 205.

104 Carroll's Ky. Stats. (6th ed., 1922), chap. 108, §§4019, 4020, pp. 1897, 1904. Of the forty cents, fifteen was to go for ordinary expenses of the state, eighteen to support the schools, three for the state road fund, and the rest to support higher education and contribute to the "sinking fund."

105 Iowa Rev. Stats. 1919, Title XIV, §4482, p. 1345.

106 Glenn W. Fisher, *The Worst Tax? A History of the Property Tax in America* (1996), p. 142.

107 Fla. Stats. 1920, §§803, 819, 829, 830, 858, 942, 956. Florida mellowed on the subject of clairvoyants and the like over the years. Thirty years later, the license fee for "every fortune teller, clairvoyant, palmist, spirit medium, absent treatment healer or mental healer" was only one hundred dollars.

108 A professor, Louis Levine, was fired from the state university in 1919 for writing a scholarly monograph on the taxation of mining properties—though he was later reinstated. Arnon Gutfeld, *Montana's Agony: Years of War and Hysteria, 1917–1921* (1979), chap. 10.

109 California State Government, Financial Statement, 1915–1917, p. 2.

110 John H. Sears, *Minimizing Taxes* (1922), preface, iii–v.

111 Melvyn Dubofsky, *The State and Labor in Modern America* (1994), pp. 40–43.

112 Ernst Freund, *The Police Power: Public Policy and Constitutional Rights* (1904), p. 322.

113 On the origins and early use of the injunction, see the classic work of Felix Frankfurter and Nathan Greene, *The Labor Injunction* (1930), and William E. Forbath, *Law and the Shaping of the American Labor Movement* (1989).

114 Forbath, *Law and the Shaping*, p. 193.

115 38 Stat. 730 (act of Oct. 15, 1914), §§6, 20.

116 Forbath, *Law and the Shaping*, pp. 106–107.

117 *Duplex Printing Press Co. v. Deering*, 254 U.S. 443 (1921); see Hovenkamp, *Enterprise and American Law*, pp. 237–238.

118 Frankfurter and Greene, *Labor Injunction*, p. 176.

119 257 U.S. 312 (1921).

120 Forbath, *Law and the Shaping*, p. 152.

121 Irving Bernstein, *The Lean Years: A History of the American Worker, 1920–1933* (1960), chap. 11, "The Anti-Injunction Movement."

122 On this thesis, see Forbath, *Law and the Shaping*, especially p. 7.

123 Colin Gordon, *New Deals: Business, Labor, and Politics in America, 1920–1935* (1994), p. 90.

124 Gen. Stats. Minn. 1913, §8890.

125 Wis. Laws 1907, ch. 402.

126 40 Stat. 506 (act of Apr. 5, 1918).

127 40 Stat. 276 (act of Aug. 10, 1917).

128 40 Stat. 451 (act of Mar. 21, 1918); Christopher N. May, *In the Name of War: Judicial Review and the War Powers Since 1918* (1989), p. 27.

129 May, *In the Name of War*, pp. 37–54.

130 See 40 Stat. 440 (act of Mar. 8, 1918).

131 40 Stat. 593 (act of May 31, 1918).

132 Dubofsky, *State and Labor*, p. 62.

133 Ibid., p. 74.

4.
Crime and Punishment in the New Century

1 *U.S. Compiled Statutes* (1901), §§5473, 5369, 5368.

2 *Annual Report, Att'y General of the United States for the Year 1905* (1905), p. 121.

3 See, in general, Lawrence M. Friedman, *Crime and Punishment in American History* (1993), chap. 12.

4 Pure Food Act: 34 Stat. 768 (act of June 30, 1906); Alaska Game Act: 43 Stat. 739 (act of Jan. 13, 1925).

5 Lawrence M. Friedman and Robert V. Percival, *The Roots of Justice: Crime and Punishment in Alameda County, California, 1870–1910* (1981), p. 300.

6 Friedman, *Crime and Punishment,*, p. 269.

7 Paul W. Keve, *Prisons and the American Conscience: A History of U.S. Federal Corrections* (1991), p. 53.

8 Friedman, *Crime and Punishment,* p. 270.

9 41 Stat. 324 (act of Oct. 29, 1919).

10 John A. Noakes, "A 'New Breed of Detective': The Rise of the FBI Special Agent," in Susan S. Silbey and Austin Sarat, eds., *Studies in Law, Politics, and Society* 14:25 (1994).

11 Samuel Walker, *Popular Justice: A History of American Criminal Justice* (1980), pp. 183–189.

12 See Claire Bond Potter, *War on Crime: Bandits, G-Men, and the Politics of Mass Culture* (1998).

13 The right to trial by jury is guaranteed by the Sixth Amendment to the United States Constitution; see also, for example, Del. Const. 1897, art. 1, §7.

14 Quoted in Friedman, *Crime and Punishment,* p. 384.

15 Sam Bass Warner and Henry B. Cabot, *Judges and Law Reform* (1936), pp. 33–34.

16 Roscoe Pound and Felix Frankfurter, eds., *Criminal Justice in Cleveland* (1922), pp. v, vii.

17 *Annual Report, Director of Administrative Office of the U.S. Courts, 1940* (1940), p. 15.

18 Note, "R.I. Statistics," *J. American Inst. of Criminal Law and Criminology* 31:475 (1941).

19 Charles E. Clark and Harry Shulman, *A Study of Law Administration in Connecticut* (1937), table 112, p. 188.

20 Laws Mich. 1927, act no. 175, pp. 281, 284.

21 Eli Frank, "Trying Criminal Cases Without Juries in Maryland," *Virginia Law Review* 17:253, 258, 259, 263 (1930).

22 William J. Blackburn, *The Administration of Criminal Justice in Franklin County, Ohio* (1935), p. 62.

23 *Patten v. U.S.,* 281 U.S. 276 (1930).

24 Sean Doran Joan et al., "Rethinking Adversariness in Nonjury Criminal Trials," *American J. of Criminal Law* 23:1 (1995).

25 On the history of plea bargaining, see Lawrence M. Friedman, "Plea Bargaining in Historical Perspective," *Law and Society Review* 13:247 (1949); George Fisher, "Plea Bargaining's Triumph," *Yale L.J.* 109:855 (2000).

26 Friedman and Percival, *Roots of Justice,* pp. 177–178.

27 Sam Bass Warner and Henry B. Cabot, *Judges and Law Reform* (1936), p. 127.

28 *Illinois Crime Survey* (1929), p. 241.

29 On this famous trial, see Friedman, *Crime and Punishment,* pp. 397–8.

30 Irvin S. Cobb, *Exit Laughing* (1942), p. 198.

31 Leon Green, *Judge and Jury* (1930), p. 403.

32 Some jurors today, in rare cases that hold the public's attention, will kiss and tell; or even write a book about their experiences. Before the TV era, this was almost unknown. And nobody can *require* a juror to explain what she did.

33 Thomas J. Kernan, "The Jurisprudence of Lawlessness," *Green Bag* 18:588 (1906).

34 Marvin J. Wolf and Katherine Mader, *Fallen Angels: Chronicles of L.A. Crime and Mystery* (1986), pp. 143–147.

35 Jerry Giesler, as told to Pete Martin, *The Jerry Giesler Story* (1960), p. 174.

36 Nathan F. Leopold, Jr., *Life Plus 99 Years* (1958), p. 78.

37 Hal Higdon, *The Crime of the Century: The Leopold and Loeb Case* (1975); Paula S. Fass, "Making and Remaking an Event: The Leopold and Loeb Case in American Culture," *J. American History* 80:919 (1993).

38 "The Indeterminate Sentence," by "A Prisoner," *Atlantic Monthly* 108:330 (1911).

39 Laws N.Y. 1901, vol. 2, chap. 428, pp. 115–116; Laws Cal. 1903, chap. 34, pp. 34–35.

40 Keve, *Prisons and the American Conscience,* pp. 65–66.

41 Friedman and Percival, *Roots of Justice,* pp. 232–233.

42 Hans von Hentig, "Degrees of Parole Violation and Graded Remedial Measures," *Journal of Criminal Law and Criminology* 33:363 (1943).

43 Jonathan Simon, *Poor Discipline: Parole and the Social Control of the Underclass, 1890–1990* (1993), p. 49.

44 Herbert H. Lou, *Juvenile Courts in the United States* (1927), p. 24.

45 *Commonwealth v. Fisher,* 213 Pa. 48 (1905).

46 Ala. Code 1907, vol. 2, chap. 185, sec. 6450, 6453.

47 Emory S. Bogardus, "A Study of Juvenile Delinquency and Dependency in Los Angeles County for the Year 1912," *J. of the American Institute of Criminal Law and Criminology* 5:327 (1914).

48 Anthony Platt, *The Child Savers: The Invention of Delinquency* (1969).

49 Friedman, *Crime and Punishment,* p. 214.

50 David Rothman, *Conscience and Convenience: The Asylum and Its Alternatives in Progressive America* (1980), p. 230.

51 Friedman and Percival, *Roots of Justice,* pp. 224.

52 Martha Sonntag Bradley, "Reclamation of Young Citizens: Reform of Utah's Juvenile Legal System, 1888–1910," *Utah Historical Q.* 51:328, 342 (1983).

53 On Van Waters's career, see Estelle B. Freedman, *Maternal Justice: Miriam Van Waters and the Female Reform Tradition* (1996).

54 Scott Christianson, *With Liberty for Some: 500 Years of Imprisonment in America* (1998), pp. 239–240.

55 Quoted in Frank Tannenbaum, *Osborne of Sing Sing* (1933), pp. 6–7.

56 Joseph F. Fishman, *Crucibles of Crime: The Shocking Story of the American Jail* (1923), pp. 15, 21, 101.

57 Thomas Mott Osborne, *Society and Prisons* (1916), pp. 134–135.

58 Lewis E. Lawes, *Twenty Thousand Years in Sing Sing* (1932), p. 107.

59 Oscar Dowling, "The Hygiene of Jails, Lock-Ups, and Police Stations," *Journal of the American Institute of Criminal Law* 5:695, 697, 698 (1915).

60 Robert E. Burns, *I Am a Fugitive from a Georgia Chain Gang* (1932), p. 5.

61 Ibid., p. 48.

62 Friedman, *Crime and Punishment,* p. 311.

63 Friedman, *Crime and Punishment,* pp. 311, 313.

64 Keve, *Prisons and the American Conscience,* pp. 68–69.

65 Leopold, *Life Plus 99 Years,* p. 135.

66 Laws Texas 1907, pp. 246, 248; see Barbara Meil Hobson, *Uneasy Virtue: The Politics of Prostitution and the American Reform Tradition* (1987), pp. 148–149.

67 Friedman, *Crime and Punishment,* pp. 328–332.

68 Reprinted in Vice Commission of Chicago, *The Social Evil in Chicago* (1911), pp. 329–330.

69 Ibid., p. 25.

70 Report, *Vice Commission of Philadelphia* (1913), pp. 9, 10.

71 *Report of the Minneapolis Vice Commission* (1911), pp. 64–65.

72 *San Francisco Examiner,* Mar. 17, 1937, p. A1. I am indebted to Paul Schrecongost for this reference.

73 David J. Langum, *Crossing over the Line: Legislating Morality and the Mann Act* (1994), pp. 27–28. This fascinating book is the source of much of the material in this chapter on the Mann Act and its enforcement. See also Hobson, *Uneasy Virtue,* pp. 141–147.

74 Laws Ill. 1908, ch. 47.

75 I am indebted for this reference to a paper by David H. Orozco, Stanford Law School, 1999.

76 36 Stat. 263 (act of Mar. 26, 1910).

77 Langum, *Crossing over the Line,* chapter 5, deals with the Caminetti case.

78 Ibid., pp. 142, 148.

79 Marlene D. Beckman, "The White Slave Traffic Act: The Historical Impact of a Criminal Law Policy on Women," *Georgetown L. Rev.* 72:1111 (1984).

80 Langum, *Crossing Over the Line,* pp. 180–194.

81 "Blackmail Rich Men by White Slave Act," *New York Times,* Jan. 13, 1916, p. 1. See also John C. Knox, *Order in the Court* (1943), p. 191.

82 Gen. Stats. Conn. 1918, §6399, p. 1750.

83 Gen. Stats. Conn. 1918, §6398, p. 1750.

84 Ky. Rev. Stats. 1946, §436.130, p. 3057.

85 The source of these data is Mary E. Odem, *Delinquent Daughters: Protecting and Policing Adolescent Female Sexuality in the United States, 1885–1920* (1995).

86 Ibid., pp. 49, 53, 76–77.

87 Philip Jenkins, *Moral Panic: Changing Concepts of the Child Molester in Modern America* (1998), p. 67.

88 I am indebted for this reference to Andrea Tone, *Devices and Desires: A History of Contraceptives in America* (2001).

89 Philip Jenkins, *Moral Panic,* pp. 67–69.

90 The Jane Addams quotation, and the discussion of it, is from Barbara Meil Hobson, *Uneasy Virtue: The Politics of Prostitution and the American Reform Tradition* (1987), pp. 154–155.

91 See, in general, Richard F. Hamm, *Shaping the 18th Amendment: Temperance Reform, Legal Culture, and the Polity, 1880–1920* (1995).

92 Ibid., p. 211. The discussion of the Webb-Kenyon bill is drawn from Hamm as well.

93 Ibid., pp. 218–19.

94 Laws Miss. 1918, ch. 189, p. 210 ff.

95 Laws Kans. 1917, ch. 215, p. 283.

96 Ark. Stats. 1916, §6035, p. 1437.

97 Hamm, *Shaping the 18th Amendment*, p. 240.

98 National Prohibition Act, 41 Stat. 305 (act of Oct. 28, 1919).

99 The statute was Laws Cal. 1921, ch. 80, p. 77; but it did not go into effect until the referendum of 1922.

100 Herbert Asbury, *The Great Illusion: An Informal History of Prohibition* (1950), pp. 280–286.

101 Joseph Gusfield, *Symbolic Crusade: Status Politics and the American Temperance Movement* (1963), p. 122.

102 Charles L. Zelden, *Justice Lies in the District: The U.S. District Court, Southern District of Texas, 1902–1960* (1993), pp. 68–70.

103 Asbury, *Great Illusion*, p. 167.

104 For much of the history of drug laws, see David F. Musto, *The American Disease: Origins of Narcotics Control* (1973).

105 35 Stat. 614 (act of Feb. 9, 1909).

106 38 Stat. 785 (act of Dec. 17, 1914).

107 249 U.S. 96 (1919).

108 Musto, *American Disease*, p. 140.

109 Troy Duster, *The Legislation of Morality: Law, Drugs, and Moral Judgment* (1970), p. 19.

110 Rufus G. King, "The Narcotics Bureau and the Harrison Act: Jailing the Healers and the Sick," *Yale L.J.* 62:736 (1953).

111 Musto, *American Disease*, pp. 210–229.

112 Okla. Laws 1919, ch. 60, p. 95.

113 Laws Ore. 1923, ch. 27, p. 35, §2.

114 Code So. Car. 1942, §§5129–1, 5128–2, 5128–3, 5128–6, 5129–12, 5128–19. The act was passed in 1934.

115 See, in general, Ysabel Rennie, *The Search for Criminal Man: A Conceptual History of the Dangerous Offender* (1978).

116 Henry Herbert Goddard, *The Kallikak Family: A Study in the Heredity of Feeble-Mindedness* (1925); see Lawrence M. Friedman, *Crime and Punishment*, pp. 335–339.

117 15th Ann. Rpt., Municipal Court of Chicago (1921), pp. 182–183, 187.

118 Earnest Albert Hooton, *Crime and the Man* (1939), pp. 239–240.

119 Thomas Mott Osborne, *Society and Prisons*, p. 25.

120 Friedman, *Crime and Punishment*, p. 338.

121 George T. Skinner, "A Sterilization Statute for Kentucky?" *Kentucky Law Journal* 33:168, 174 (1934).

122 Laws Ind. 1907, ch. 215; see Philip R. Reilly, *The Surgical Solution: A History of Involuntary Sterilization in the United States* (1991).

123 Laws Cal. 1913, ch. 720, p. 109. An amendment to the penal code in 1923 authorized a judge to order an "operation . . . for the prevention of procreation" to be performed on men found guilty of "carnal abuse of a female person under the age of ten years."

124 Friedman, *Crime and Punishment,* p. 336.

125 Laws Wash. 1921, p. 162.

126 J. H. Landman, "The History of Human Sterilization in the United States: Theory, Statutes, Adjudication," *Illinois L. Rev.* 23:463, 473 (1929).

127 *Smith v. Board of Examiners,* 85 N.J. L. 46, 88 Atl. 963 (1913). The court rested its case on the equal-protection clause; it was an irrational classification to single out epileptics who, because they were poor, were in state institutions. But the opinion makes clear that the court found the statute distasteful as a whole.

128 274 U.S. 200 (1927).

129 Robert Reinhold, "Virginia Hospital's Chief Traces 50 Years of Sterilizing the 'Retarded,'" *New York Times,* Feb. 23, 1980; "Sterilization of Teen-Age Woman Haunting Virginia Decades Later," *New York Times,* Mar. 7, 1980.

5.
Race Relations and Civil Liberties

1 Laws Va. 1924, ch. 371 (an act to preserve "racial integrity"); Va. Code 1924, §5099(a)(5). Under this statute, a white was allowed to marry someone whose bad blood was American Indian, provided that the blood was "one-sixteenth or less"; see, in general, Peggy Pascoe, "Miscegenation Law, Court Cases, and Ideologies of 'Race' in Twentieth-Century America," *J. of American History* 83:44 (1996).

2 *Moreau v. Grandich,* 114 Miss. 560, 75 So. 434 (1917). The Grandich family pointed out that under the marriage laws of Mississippi, whites could not marry blacks, but black was defined in terms of one-eighth or more of "negro blood," which their children, under any theory, did not have. The court brushed this argument aside. The marriage statute dealt with marriages only, and had no bearing on this school case.

3 Pascoe, "Miscegenation Law" at 55, 56; *Estate of Monks,* 48 Calif. App. 2d 603, 120 P. 2d 167 (1941).

4 The rule did not apply to other races—neither legally nor socially. But see *Gong Lum v. Rice,* 275 U.S. 78 (1927), in which the Supreme Court upheld a decision that a Chinese child living in Mississippi (not a numerous class) had to go to the colored school.

5 Ga. Code 1911, §§1484, 2718, 2724, pp. 382–383, 721–722.

6 Laws. Ark. 1903, p. 160.

7 Laws No. Car. 1913, ch. 831, pp. 127–128.

8   Laws No. Car. 1935, ch. 422, pp. 716–717.

9   Cited in *Strauss v. State,* 173 S.W. 663 (Tex., 1915). The ordinance called for a fine of up to two hundred dollars. Each act of intercourse was a separate offense.

10 Laws Texas 1933, ch. 241, §11 (f), p. 843.

11 John R. Howard, *The Shifting Wind: The Supreme Court and Civil Rights from Reconstruction to Brown* (1999), p. 178.

12 211 U.S. 45 (1908).

13 218 U.S. 71 (1910).

14 So. Car. Const. 1895, art. II, §4, as amended; see *Franklin v. South Carolina,* 218 U.S. 162 (1910).

15 Quoted in Leon F. Litwack, *Trouble in Mind: Black Southerners in the Age of Jim Crow* (1998), p. 227.

16 Ibid., pp. 225–226.

17 See *Giles v. Harris,* 189 U.S. 475 (1903).

18 *Guinn v. U.S.,* 238 U.S. 347 (1915). A companion case, *Myers v. Anderson,* 238 U.S. 368 (1915), struck down a similar arrangement from Annapolis, Maryland.

19 David M. Oshinsky, *"Worse Than Slavery": Parchman Farm and the Ordeal of Jim Crow Justice* (1996), p. 116.

20 219 U.S. 231 (1911).

21 3 Code Ala. 1907, §6845.

22 14 Stat. 546 (act of Mar. 2, 1867). The statute was chiefly aimed at the labor system of the Territory of New Mexico, but applied also to "any other Territory or State" in which there were in fact "peons."

23 See William Cohen, "Negro Involuntary Servitude in the South, 1865–1940: A Preliminary Analysis," *J. Southern History* 42:31 (1976).

24 3 Ala. Code 1907, §§6849, 6850.

25 3 Code Ala. 1907, §7843 (13).

26 John M. Barry, *Rising Tide: The Great Mississippi Flood of 1927 and How It Changed America* (1997), pp. 314–320.

27 George C. Wright, *Racial Violence in Kentucky, 1865–1940: Lynchings, Mob Rule, and "Legal Lynchings"* (1990), pp. 112–113, 123–124.

28 Lawrence M. Friedman, *Crime and Punishment in American History* (1993) pp. 190–191.

29 Arthur F. Raper, *The Tragedy of Lynching* (1933), pp. 1, 3, 7.

30 Litwack, *Trouble in Mind,* p. 289.

31 Oshinsky, *"Worse Than Slavery,"* p. 105.

32 Ala. Code, 1928, §§4939, 4940.

33 James H. Chadbourn, *Lynching and the Law* (1933), p. 118.

34 Quoted in Litwack, *Trouble in Mind,* p. 265.

35 Oshinsky, *"Worse Than Slavery,"* chapter 3, p. 149.

36 See, in general, Dan T. Carter, *Scottsboro: A Tragedy of the American South* (1969).

37 *Powell v. Alabama*, 287 U.S. 45 (1932).

38 Joel Williamson, *The Crucible of Race: Black-White Relations in the American South Since Emancipation* (1984).

39 David Delaney, *Race, Place, and the Law* (1998), p. 105.

40 245 U.S. 60 (1917).

41 On the early years, see Charles Flint Kellogg, *NAACP* (vol. 1, 1909–1920) (1967).

42 For an account of the administration of the laws, see Lucy E. Salyer, *Laws Harsh as Tigers: Chinese Immigrants and the Shaping of Modern Immigration Law* (1995). To be fair, it seems pretty clear that many of the claims of citizenship *were* fraudulent. Chinese immigrants, in other words, were cheating: but of course this does not excuse the laws themselves, which were frankly and openly racist.

43 Charles Wollenberg, *All Deliberate Speed: Segregation and Exclusion in California Schools, 1855–1975* (1976), pp. 44–45.

44 Angelo N. Ancheta, *Race, Rights, and the Asian-American Experience* (1998), p. 26.

45 Quoted in Wollenberg, *All Deliberate Speed*, p. 73.

46 Ronald T. Takaki, *Strangers from a Different Shore: A History of Asian Americans* (1998), p. 204.

47 Ore. Code Ann. 1930, §33–102.

48 Laws Cal. 1913, ch. 113, p. 206. A casual reader of the text would probably not guess that this was the aim of the law. The statute began by saying that aliens "eligible to citizenship" (which Asians were not) had the same land rights as citizens; but all the others (that is, the ineligible ones) had only whatever land rights they were guaranteed by treaty, which was basically nothing.

49 Wash. Const. Art. 2, §33; Wash. Rev. Stats. 1922, §10582. The constitution forbade ownership of land by aliens other than those who "in good faith have declared their intention to become citizens," which of course excluded Asians. The Arizona law is Laws Ariz. 1921, ch. 29, p. 26.

50 Quoted in Milton M. Gordon, *Assimilation in American Life: The Role of Race, Religion, and National Origins* (1964), p. 120.

51 Huntington Wilson, "Our National Fences," *North American Review* 199:383, 387 (1914).

52 260 U.S. 178 (1922). On this case and the *Thind* case, discussed below, see Donald Braman, "Of Race and Immutability," *UCLA Law Review* 46:1375 (1999), quotations at 185.

53 *In re Najour*, 174 Fed. 735 (1909).

54 *In re Shahid*, 205 Fed. 812 (E.D. So. Car. 1913).

55 *United States v. Thind*, 261 U.S. 204 (1922).

56 The quotation is from Justice Sutherland's opinion in *Thind*, at p. 13.

57 Laws Utah 1917, ch. 93, p. 285.

58 For a description of how the laws were administered around 1930, see William C. Van Vleck, *The Administrative Control of Aliens* (1932).

59 198 U.S. 253 (1905).

60 See *Ng Fung Ho v. White,* 259 U.S. 276 (1921).
    Compagnie Française de Navigation à Vapeur v. Louisiana State Board of Health, 186
    U.S. 380 (1902). Federal immigration laws "do not purport to abrogate the quarantine
    laws of the several States," the Court said.

62 32 Stat. 1213 (act of Mar. 3, 1903).

63 34 Stat. 898 (act of Feb. 20, 1907).

64 39 Stat. 874 (act of Feb. 5, 1917).

65 42 Stat. 5 (act of May 19, 1921).

66 Elliott Robert Barkan, *And Still They Come: Immigrants and American Society, 1920 to
    the 1990s* (1996), pp. 11, 14.

67 43 Stat. 153 (act of May 26, 1924).

68 Abraham Hoffman, *Unwanted Mexican Americans in the Great Depression: Repatria-
    tion Pressures, 1929–1939* (1974), p. 7.

69 Ibid., p. 10.

70 Ibid., pp. 31, 32.

71 "St. Paul's Bureau of Welfare paid the way of one hundred Mexicans on 4 November
    1932, and in 1934 over three hundred more left. . . . Ohio paid an average of $15 to
    repatriate 300 Mexicans from Lucas County." Ibid., p. 120. On the tapering off of
    repatriation, ibid., p. 164.

72 The defendants, after spending nearly two years in San Quentin, were released when
    the court of appeals reversed the trial court. See Robin F. Scott, "The Sleepy Lagoon
    Case and the Grand Jury Investigation," in Manuel P. Servín, *The Mexican-Americans:
    An Awakening Minority* (1970), pp. 105–115.

73 See Janis Appier, "Juvenile Crime Control: Los Angeles Law Enforcement and
    the Zoot-Suit Riots," in *Criminal Justice History: An International Annual* 11:147
    (1990).

74 Michael C. LeMay, *From Open Door to Dutch Door: An Analysis of United States
    Immigration Policy Since 1820* (1987), pp. 109–114.

75 24 Stat. 388 (act of Feb. 8, 1887).

76 *Lone Wolf v. Hitchcock,* 187 U.S. 553 (1903); discussed in Blue Clark, *Lone Wolf v.
    Hitchcock: Treaty Rights and Indian Law at the End of the Nineteenth Century* (1994).

77 John R. Wunder, *"Retained by the People": A History of American Indians and the Bill of
    Rights* (1994), pp. 40–41.

78 231 U.S. 28 (1913).

79 Wunder, *"Retained by the People,"* pp. 44–47.

80 34 Stat. 182 (act of May 8, 1906).

81 198 U.S. 371 (1905). I am indebted to a paper by Melissa Schatzberg (Stanford Law
    School, 2000) for this reference and the material on the Yakama Indians and their
    salmon rights.

82 The United States acquired more islands: it acquired, from the native chiefs, American

Samoa from 1900 on; and in 1916 it picked up the Virgin Islands, formerly owned by Denmark.

83 On these cases, see James E. Kerr, *The Insular Cases: The Role of the Judiciary in American Expansionism* (1982).

84 182 U.S. 244 (1901).

85 *Downes v. Bidwell,* at 287.

86 Harlan, J., dissenting in *Downes v. Bidwell,* 182 U.S. 244 (1901), at 380, 384.

87 32 Stat. 691 (act of July 1, 1902).

88 Winfred Lee Thompson, *The Introduction of American Law in the Philippines and Puerto Rico, 1898–1905* (1989), p. 95.

89 39 Stat. 545 (act of Aug. 29, 1916).

90 39 Stat. 351 (act of Mar. 2, 1917).

91 *Balzac v. People of Porto Rico,* 258 U.S. 298 (1922).

92 *Fornaris v. Ridge Tool Co.,* 400 U.S. 41, 42–43 (1970). The question in the case was whether a law of 1964, passed by the legislature of Puerto Rico, was constitutional. The Supreme Court of Puerto Rico had never construed the statute. The United States Supreme Court sent the case back to the district court, and instructed the court to "stay its hand" until the Supreme Court of Puerto Rico had "authoritatively ruled on the local law question."

93 Lizabeth A. McKibben, "The Political Relationship Between the United States and Pacific Islands Entities: The Path to Self-Government in the Northern Mariana Islands, Palau, and Guam," *Harvard International Law Journal* 31:257, 287–289 (1990).

94 The Comstock law was 17 Stat. 598 (act of Mar. 3, 1873).

95 See, in general, David M. Rabban, *Free Speech in Its Forgotten Years* (1997).

96 Dennis Baron, *The English-Only Question* (1990), p. 109. *New York Times* quotation, p. 110.

97 Chris Richardson, "With Liberty and Justice for All? The Suppression of German-American Culture During World War I," *Missouri Historical Review* 90:79, 85, 87 (1995).

98 40 Stat. 217 (act of June 15, 1917).

99 40 Stat. 411, 425 (act of Oct. 6, 1917).

100 Rabban, *Free Speech,* pp. 254–269.

101 40 Stat. 553 (act of May 16, 1918).

102 La Vern J. Rippley, "Conrad Kornmann, German-Language Editor: A Case-Study of Anti-German Enthusiasm During World War I," *So. Dak. History* 27:107 (1997).

103 For details, see Arnon Gutfeld, *Montana's Agony: Years of War and Hysteria, 1917–1921* (1979).

104 Shirley K. Burton, "The Espionage and Sedition Acts of 1917 and 1918: Sectional Interpretation in the United States District Courts of Illinois," *Ill. Hist. J.* 87:48 (1994).

105 These accounts are drawn from *American State Trials* (vol. 12, 1919), pp. 897–961, 943, and 960–961, respectively.

106 The account of this incident, and the trial of Harry E. Wootton, come from *American State Trials* (vol. 17, 1936), pp. 1–175.

107 Ibid., pp. 153, 155.

108 See William Preston, Jr., *Aliens and Dissenters: Federal Suppression of Radicals, 1903–1933* (1963); Robert K. Murray, *Red Scare: A Study in National Hysteria, 1919–1920* (1955).

109 Rabban, *Free Speech,* p. 175.

110 On this see Michael Kent Curtis, *Free Speech, "The People's Darling Privilege": Struggles for Freedom of Expression in American History* (2000).

111 249 U.S. 47 (1919).

112 250 U.S. 616 (1919). The case, its people, and its background are discussed in Richard Polenberg, *Fighting Faiths: The Abrams Case, the Supreme Court, and Free Speech* (1987).

113 Polenberg, *Fighting Faiths,* p. 142.

114 Felix Frankfurter, *The Case of Sacco and Vanzetti* (1927), p. 59.

115 See Francis Russell, *Sacco and Vanzetti: The Case Resolved* (1986).

116 See Wyn Craig Wade, *The Fiery Cross: The Ku Klux Klan in America* (1987), chap. 5.

117 Ibid., pp. 180, 227.

118 41 Stat. 1008 (act of June 5, 1920).

119 Friedman, *Crime and Punishment,* p. 367.

120 *Gitlow v. New York,* 268 U.S. 652 (1925).

121 *Whitney v. California,* 274 U.S. 357 (1927).

122 Brandeis wrote a stirring and eloquent concurrence, protesting against the repression of free speech. It was a concurrence, not a dissent, because Brandeis felt that Whitney had not raised the issue at the right time and in the right forum. Holmes joined in Brandeis's opinion. Charlotte Whitney never went to prison, however; she was released on bail during the long period of her appeal. She received a pardon in 1927. Kevin Starr, *Endangered Dreams: The Great Depression in California* (1996), pp. 54–57.

123 William G. Ross, *Forging New Freedoms: Nativism, Education, and the Constitution, 1917–1927* (1994), p. 61.

124 262 U.S. 390 (1923). On the background of the case, see Ross, *Forging New Freedoms,* chap. 4.

125 *Meyer v. Nebraska,* at 395 (argument for the state).

126 Ross, *Forging New Freedoms,* p. 87.

127 In *Bartels v. Iowa,* 262 U.S. 404 (1923), decided the same day, the Court, on the strength of *Meyer v. Nebraska,* consigned the restrictive statutes of Iowa and Ohio to the ash heap. Holmes dissented, in his usual stance of weary resignation: let the legislatures do what they please.

128 *Farrington v. Tokushige,* 273 U.S. 284 (1927); for a discussion of the case and its background, see Ross, *Forging New Freedoms,* chap. 9.

6.
The Roosevelt Revolution

1 47 Stat. 709 (act of July 21, 1932).

2 Maxwell Bloomfield, *Peaceful Revolution: Constitutional Change and American Culture from Progressivism to the New Deal* (2000), p. 104.

3 *Historical Statistics of the United States,* pp. 1102–1103.

4 See, in general, Peter H. Irons, *The New Deal Lawyers* (1982).

5 48 Stat. 128 (act of June 13, 1933).

6 48 Stat. 162, 168 (act of June 16, 1933).

7 See, in general, Donald S. Howard, *The WPA and Federal Relief Policy* (1943), a comprehensive study under the auspices of the Russell Sage Foundation.

8 Ibid., pp. 139, 229.

9 David M. Kennedy, *Freedom from Fear* (1999), p. 364.

10 Franklin D. Roosevelt, quoted in Howard, *WPA and Federal Relief Policy,* p. 228.

11 Howard, *WPA and Federal Relief Policy,* p. 229.

12 Lawrence M. Friedman, *Government and Slum Housing: A Century of Frustration* (1968), pp. 94–115.

13 See Marguerite Owen, *The Tennessee Valley Authority* (1973), p. 19 and passim.

14 48 Stat. 195 (act of June 16, 1933); see Ellis W. Hawley, *The New Deal and the Problem of Monopoly* (1966).

15 Melvyn Dubofsky, *The State and Labor in Modern America* (1994), p. 112.

16 *Federal Trade and Industry Service,* vol. 1, paragraphs 10,052, 10,089, 10,189.

17 Hawley, *New Deal,* p. 27.

18 48 Stat. 31 (act of May 12, 1933).

19 Thomas W. Ross, "Winners and Losers Under the Robinson-Patman Act," *J. Law and Economics* 27:243, 246 (1984).

20 Thomas W. Ross, "Store Wars: The Chain Tax Movement," *J. Law & Economics* 29:125 (1986).

21 *State Board v. Jackson,* 283 U.S. 527 (1931).

22 Laws Texas 1935, p. 1589.

23 49 Stat. 1526 (act of June 19, 1936).

24 Frederick M. Rowe, *Price Discrimination Under the Robinson-Patman Act* (1962), p. 5.

25 *Dr. Miles Medical Co. v. John D. Park & Sons,* 220 U.S. 373 (1911).

26 50 Stat. 693 (act of Aug. 17, 1937).

27 Robert H. Bork, *The Antitrust Paradox: A Policy at War with Itself* (1993), p. 382.

28 William E. Leuchtenburg, *The Supreme Court Reborn: The Constitutional Revolution in the Age of Roosevelt* (1995), p. 89.

29 295 U.S. 495 (1935).

30 297 U.S. 1 (1936).

31 Leuchtenburg, *The Supreme Court Reborn,* chapter 5.

32 301 U.S. 1 (1937).

33 The doctrinal story is told in detail, and argued forcefully, by Barry Cushman in *Rethinking the New Deal: The Structure of a Constitutional Revolution* (1998); Cushman places great emphasis on the *Nebbia* case as a more significant turning point.

34 291 U.S. 502 (1934).

35 317 U.S. 111 (1942).

36 348 U.S. 483 (1955).

37 304 U.S. 144 (1938).

38 Jonathan R. Macey and Geoffrey P. Miller, "Origin of the Blue Sky Laws," *Texas L. Rev.* 70:348 (1991).

39 Ibid., p. 369.

40 Joel Seligman, *The Transformation of Wall Street: A History of the Securities and Exchange Commission and Modern Corporate Finance* (rev. ed., 1995), p. 46.

41 48 Stat. 74 (act of May 27, 1933). For an account of the history and scope of the law, see Seligman, *Transformation of Wall Street.*

42 73d Cong., 1st sess., H.R. report no. 85, "Federal Supervision of Traffic in Investment Securities in Interstate Commerce," May 4, 1933, pp. 2–3.

43 Quoted in Seligman, *Transformation of Wall Street,* p. 100.

44 Ibid., pp. 101–112.

45 48 Stat. 163 (act of June 16, 1933).

46 49 Stat. 803 (act of Aug. 26, 1935).

47 Neil Fligstein, *The Transformation of Corporate Control* (1990), pp. 164–167.

48 Quoted ibid., p. 165.

49 49 Stat. 449 (act of July 5, 1935).

50 *National Labor Relations Board v. Jones & Laughlin Steel Corp.,* 301 U.S. 1 (1937).

51 Sidney Fine, "The General Motors Sit-Down Strike: A Re-Examination," *American Historical Review* 70:691 (1965).

52 Dubofsky, *State and Labor,* pp. 137–142.

53 52 Stat. 1060 (act of June 25, 1938).

54 312 U.S. 100 (1941).

55 *Hammer v. Dagenhart:* 247 U.S. 251 (1918).

56 *Historical Statistics of the United States* (1975), part 1, pp. 176–177.

57 *National Labor Relations Board v. Jones & Laughlin Steel Corp.,* at 26–27.

58 Stephen Skowronek, *Building a New American State: The Expansion of National Administrative Capacities, 1877–1920* (1982), p. 290.

59 For this, and much of the following discussion, see George B. Shepherd, "Fierce Compromise: The Administrative Procedure Act Emerges from New Deal Politics," *Northwestern U. L. Rev* 90:1557 (1996).

60 See Robert M. Cooper, "The Proposed Administrative Court," *Mich. L. Rev.* 35:193 (1936).

61 49 Stat. 500 (act of July 26, 1935).

62 60 Stat. 237 (act of July 11, 1946).

63 On the legislative history, see John Dickinson, "Administrative Procedure Act: Scope and Grounds of Broadened Judicial Review," *American Bar Association Journal* 33:434, 513 (1947).

64 12 Fed. Reg. 8207 (Dec. 3, 1947).

65 13 Fed. Reg. 8313 (Dec. 24, 1948).

66 *Leach v. Carlile*, 258 U.S. 138 (1922).

67 James M. Landis, *The Administrative Process* (1938), pp. 1, 155.

68 See, in general, James T. Patterson, *The New Deal and the States: Federalism in Transition* (1969).

69 Laws Md. 1935, ch. 574.

70 Patterson, *New Deal and the States,* pp. 102–103.

71 Edith Abbott, *The Tenements of Chicago, 1908–1935* (1936), pp. 441, 449.

72 Laws Minn. ch. 339, p. 514.

73 Laws Texas, 1933, ch. 92, p. 198.

74 *Langever v. Miller*, 79 S.W. 2d 634 (Ct. Civ. App. Texas, 1934).

75 290 U.S. 398 (1934).

76 *Grandin Farmers' Co-op. Elevator Co. v. Langer*, 5 F. Supp. 425 (D.C. D. No. Dak., 1934); the Supreme Court affirmed this case, summarily, in one paragraph, *Langer v. Grandin Farmers' Co-op. Elevator Co.*, 292 U.S. 605 (1934). See Catherine McNicol Stock, *The Great Depression and the Old Middle Class on the Northern Plains* (1992), pp. 139–141; on Langer and the moratorium, see Walter C. Anhalt and Glenn H. Smith, "He Saved the Farm? Governor Langer and the Mortgage Moratoria," *North Dakota Quarterly* 44, no. 4, p. 5 (1976).

77 See Irons, *New Deal Lawyers* (1982); for a discussion of the ideology of the lawyers on the conservative side as well, see Ronen Shamir, *Managing Legal Uncertainty: Elite Lawyers in the New Deal* (1995).

78 49 Stat. 620 (act of Aug. 14, 1935).

79 R.I. Rev. Stats. 1923, ch. 106; So. Dak. Rev. Stats. 1929, §10065.

80 Ohio Code 1930, §§2526 ff.

81 Michael B. Katz, *In the Shadow of the Poorhouse: A Social History of Welfare in America* (rev. ed., 1996), p. 207.

82 Laws So. Car. 1921, No. 147, p. 204.

83 Code Ohio 1930, §§2930 ff, 2950.

84 Code Ohio 1930, §2965.

85 Molly Ladd-Taylor, *Mother-Work: Women, Child Welfare, and the State, 1890–1930* (1994), p. 76.

86 Ibid., p. 78.

87 Viviana A. Zelizer, *Pricing the Priceless Child: The Changing Social Value of Children* (1985), p. 210.

88 Theda Skocpol, *Protecting Soldiers and Mothers: The Political Origins of Social Policy in the United States* (1992), p. 424.

89 Laws Ill. 1913, p. 127.

90 Laws Ill. 1913, p. 128.

91 Skocpol, *Protecting Soldiers and Mothers,* p. 476.

92 Ladd-Taylor, *Mother-Work,* p. 149.

93 42 Stat. 224 (act of Nov. 23, 1921).

94 Skocpol, *Protecting Soldiers and Mothers,* p. 500.

95 Ladd-Taylor, *Mother-Work,* p. 167.

96 Kriste Lindenmeyer, "Saving Mothers and Babies: The Sheppard-Towner Act in Ohio, 1921–1929," *Ohio History* 99:105 (1990).

97 On the rise and fall of Sheppard-Towner, see Ladd-Taylor, *Mother-Work,* chap. 6.

98 Roy Lubove, *The Struggle for Social Security, 1900–1935* (1986), p. 136.

99 Laws Del. 1931, ch. 85, p. 331.

100 Blanche D. Coll, *Safety Net: Welfare and Social Security, 1929–1979* (1995), p. 42.

101 Jackson K. Putnam, *Old-Age Politics in California* (1970), chap. 4.

102 Robert Harrison, *State and Society in Twentieth-Century America* (1997), p. 262.

103 Ibid., p. 263.

104 49 Stat. 620, Title X, at 645 (act of Aug. 14, 1935).

105 William Haber and Merrill G. Murray, *Unemployment Insurance in the American Economy: An Historical Review and Analysis* (1966), pp. 63–65.

7.
War and Postwar

1 55 Stat. 838 (act of Dec. 18, 1941).

2 George Q. Flynn, *The Draft, 1940–1973* (1993), p. 22.

3 See the study (for a somewhat later period) by James W. Davis, Jr., and Kenneth M. Dolbeare, *Little Groups of Neighbors: The Selective Service System* (1968).

4 54 Stat. 1178 (act of Oct. 17, 1940).

5 56 Stat. 23 (act of Jan. 30, 1942); it was amended, 56 Stat. 765 (Oct. 2, 1942), to authorize the president "to issue a general order stabilizing prices, wages, and salaries, affecting the cost of living." The president was to do this, as far as practicable, on the basis of levels of prices as of September 15, 1942.

6 John W. Willis, "A Short History of Rent Control Laws," *Cornell L. Q.* 36:54 (1950).

7 Marshall B. Clinard, *The Black Market: A Study of White Collar Crime* (1952), pp. 10, 27, 33, 35.

8 Melvyn Dubofsky, *The State and Labor in Modern America* (1994), pp. 182–191.

9 Quoted by Rep. Robert F. Rich of Pennsylvania, in the House of Representatives; *Congressional Record* 95:A1469 (Mar. 13, 1949).

10 60 Stat. 23 (act of Feb. 20, 1946).

11 Alan Brinkley, *The End of Reform: New Deal Liberalism in Recession and War* (1995), pp. 260–264.

12 This was the Servicemen's Readjustment Act of 1944, 58 Stat. 284 (act of June 22, 1944).

13 This was a new suburb on Long Island, built by William Levitt, who sold tract houses for $7,500.

14 Milton Greenberg, *The GI Bill: The Law That Changed America* (1997), pp. 36–37.

15 Brinkley, *End of Reform,* p. 269.

16 61 Stat. 136 (act of June 23, 1947).

17 The Labor-Management Reporting and Disclosure Act, 73 Stat. 519 (act of Sept. 14, 1959).

18 Lawrence M. Friedman, *Government and Slum Housing: A Century of Frustration* (1968), pp. 116–118.

19 Ibid., p. 122.

20 "St. Louis Is Revising Housing Complex," *New York Times,* March 19, 1972.

21 Paul Starr, *The Social Transformation of American Medicine* (1982), pp. 280–289.

22 78 Stat. 508 (act of Aug. 20, 1964).

23 On this program, see Earl Johnson, Jr., *Justice and Reform: The Formative Years of the Legal Services Program* (1974). Johnson was at one time the director of the program.

24 *Ann. Rpt., American Bar Association,* vol. 90 (1966), p. 111 (resolution of Feb. 8, 1965).

25 79 Stat. 286 (act of July 30, 1965).

26 Benjamin Werne, "Medicaid: Has National Health Insurance Entered by the Back Door?" *Syracuse L. Rev.* 19:49 (1966).

27 78 Stat. 703 (act of Aug. 31, 1964).

28 See National Science Foundation, *An Analysis of Federal R & D Funding by Budget Function* (1971), for figures.

29 79 Stat. 845 (act of Sept. 29, 1965).

30 On these developments, see Gary C. Bryner, *Blue Skies, Green Politics: The Clean Air Act of 1990 and Its Implementation* (2d ed., 1995), p. 98.

31 "A Darkness in Donora," *New York Times,* Nov. 1, 1999.

32 69 Stat. 322 (act of July 14, 1955).

33 77 Stat. 392 (act of Dec. 17, 1963).

34 79 Stat. 992 (act of Oct. 20, 1965).

35 81 Stat. 485 (act of Nov. 21, 1967).

36 Bryner, *Blue Skies, Green Politics.*

37 Laws New York 1957, ch. 931.

38 Richard N. L. Andrews, *Managing the Environment, Managing Ourselves: A History of American Environmental Policy* (1999), p. 287.

39 Robert L. Rabin, "Federal Regulation in Historical Perspective," *Stanford L. Rev.* 38:1189, 1287 (1986).

40 Andrews, *Managing the Environment.*

41 Ibid., p. 243.

42 90 Stat. 2003 (act of Oct. 11, 1976).

43 86 Stat. 1207 (act of Oct. 27, 1972).

44 On this scandal, see Charles O. Jackson, *Food and Drug Legislation in the New Deal*

(1970), chap. 8; Paul M. Wax, "Elixirs, Diluents, and the Passage of the 1938 Federal Food, Drug and Cosmetic Act," *Annals of Internal Medicine* 122:456 (1995).

45 52 Stat. 1040, 1052 (act of June 25, 1938). To market a new drug, a company had to file an application with the agency for approval; and the agency had the power to deny or withhold this approval.

46 The statute is 83 Stat. 743 (act of Dec. 30, 1969); it was amended by the Federal Coal Mine Health and Safety Act of 1977, 91 Stat. 1290 (act of Nov. 9, 1977).

47 91 Stat. 447 (act of Aug. 3, 1977).

48 The report is *Smoking and Health: Report of the Advisory Committee to the Surgeon General of the Public Health Service* (U.S. Department of HEW, 1964). The quotation is from p. 29.

49 79 Stat. 282 (act of July 27, 1965).

50 Murray L. Weidenbaum, *Business and Government in the Global Marketplace* (6th ed., 1999), p. 33.

51 D. Harper Simms, *The Soil Conservation Service* (1970), pp. 55, 68.

52 Susan Wagner, *The Federal Trade Commission* (1971), chap. 4.

53 Ronald Brickman, Sheila Jasanoff, Thomas Ilgen, *Controlling Chemicals: The Politics of Regulation in Europe and the United States* (1985), pp. 158–159.

54 Laws Mich. 1974, pp. 7, 16.

55 Laws Mich. 1974, p. 49.

56 Laws Mich. 1974, p. 893.

8.
Crime and Criminal Justice in the Postwar World

1 These figures are taken from Roger Lane, *Murder in America: A History* (1997), pp. 306–309.

2 Lawrence M. Friedman, *Crime and Punishment in American History* (1993), pp. 274.

3 79 Stat. 828 (act of Sept. 22, 1965).

4 82 Stat. 197 (act of June 19, 1968).

5 *Barron v. Baltimore,* 7 Pet. (32 U.S) 243 (1833).

6 302 U.S. 319 (1937).

7 367 U.S. 643 (1961).

8 The case was *Benton v. Maryland,* 395 U.S. 784 (1969).

9 *Miranda:* 384 U.S. 436 (1966). See Liva Baker, *Miranda: Crime, Law and Politics* (1983). *Gideon:* 372 U.S. 335 (1963). See Anthony Lewis, *Gideon's Trumpet* (1964), which tells the story of this famous case.

10 Baker, *Miranda,* pp. 408–409.

11 316 U.S. 455 (1942).

12 Richard A. Leo, "Police Interrogation and Social Control," *Social and Legal Studies* 3:93 (1994).

13 See "Texas Lawyer's Death Row Record a Concern," *New York Times,* June 11, 2000.

14 Ernest Jerome Hopkins, *Our Lawless Police* (1931), p. 208.

15 Kagan et al., "The Business of State Supreme Courts, 1870–1970," *Stanford L. Rev.* 30:121, 148 (1977).

16 Angela B. Bartel, "Wisconsin Post Conviction Remedies—Habeas Corpus: Past, Present, and Future," *Wisc. L. Rev.* 1970:1145, 1151.

17 *People v. Jackson,* 391 Mich. 323, 217 N.W. 2d 22 (1974).

18 Marvin E. Frankel, *Criminal Sentences: Law Without Order* (1973), pp. 5, 89, 97.

19 Laws Maine 1975, ch. 499, pp. 1275, 1359; Criminal Code, ch. 51, §1251(2).

20 Laws Minn. 1978, ch. 723, p. 761; Lynne Goodstein and John Hepburn, *Determinate Sentencing and Imprisonment: A Failure of Reform* (1985), pp. 76–80.

21 Friedman, *Crime and Punishment,* p. 412.

22 108 Stat. 1796 (act of 1994).

23 See Richard S. Frase, "Sentencing Guidelines in Minnesota, Other States, and the Federal Courts: A Twenty-Year Retrospective," *Fed. Sent. R.* 12:69 (1999).

24 Simon L. Singer, *Recriminalizing Delinquency: Violent Juvenile Crime and Juvenile Justice Reform* (1996), pp. 38–39.

25 387 U.S. 1 (1967).

26 Frederick M. Thrasher, *The Gang: A Study of 1,313 Gangs in Chicago* (2d ed., 1936).

27 Quoted in Singer, *Recriminalizing Delinquency,* p. 47.

28 Ore. Rev. Stats. ch. 419, ch. 349, 352, ch. 422, sec. 58.

29 Nancy Mitford, *Kind and Usual Punishment* (1973), pp. 244–245.

30 309 F. Supp. 362 (E.D. Ark., 1970).

31 On this case and the prisoners' rights movement in general, see Malcolm M. Feeley and Edward L. Rubin, *Judicial Policy Making and the Modern State: How the Courts Reformed America's Prisons* (1998). The *Holt* cases are discussed at pp. 59–73.

32 Bureau of Justice Statistics, *Challenging the Conditions of Prisons and Jails: A Report on Section 1983 Litigation* (1995).

33 Feeley and Rubin, *Judicial Policy Making,* p. 363.

34 On this point, see ibid., pp. 369–375.

35 Donald Clemmer, *The Prison Community* (1940).

36 See Paige Heather Ralph, "Texas Prison Gangs," Ph.D. diss., Sam Houston State University, 1992.

37 David M. Oshinsky, *"Worse Than Slavery": Parchman Farm and the Ordeal of Jim Crow Justice* (1996), p. 153.

38 In Massachusetts's Framingham reformatory for women, accusations of same-sex practices, supposedly condoned by Miriam Van Waters, who ran the institution, led to a sensational attempt to remove Van Waters in the late 1940s—an attempt that ultimately failed. See Estelle B. Freedman, *Maternal Justice,* pp. 274–312.

39 Joseph F. Fishman, *Sex in Prison: Revealing Sex Conditions in American Prisons* (1934), pp. 156–157.

40 James Gilligan, *Violence: Our Deadly Epidemic and Its Causes* (1992), pp. 169, 174.

41 James B. Jacobs, "Prison Violence and Formal Organization," in Albert K. Cohen et al., *Prison Violence* (1976), p. 79.

42 Gilligan, *Violence,* pp. 163–185.

43 Bert Useem and Peter Kimball, *States of Siege: U.S. Prison Riots, 1971–1986* (1989), p. 10.

44 On the history of the death penalty, see Stuart Banner, *Dangling Between Heaven and Earth: A History of Capital Punishment in the United States* (forthcoming).

45 "Capitalizing Capital Punishment in Mississippi," *Literary Digest* 51:338 (1915). I am indebted to Stuart Banner for this reference.

46 The event is described in detail in Perry T. Ryan, *The Last Public Execution in America* (1992).

47 For these figures, and much of the material on methods of execution, see Deborah W. Denno, "Getting to Death: Are Executions Constitutional?" *Iowa L. Rev.* 82:321, 365, and appendixes (1997).

48 Laws Nev. 1921, ch. 246, p. 387.

49 Laws Colo. 1933, ch. 61, p. 420; in Arizona, the legislature proposed the matter as a constitutional amendment and put the question to a referendum, Laws Ariz. 1933, p. 588; the amendment, Ariz. Const. Art. 22, §22, went into effect Oct. 28, 1933.

50 Denno, "Getting to Death," pp. 401, 412–438.

51 Banner, *Dangling Between Heaven and Earth,* chap. 8.

52 Robert M. Bohm, "American Death Penalty Opinion, 1936–1986: A Critical Examination of the Gallup Polls," in Robert M. Bohm, ed., *The Death Penalty in America: Current Research* (1991), pp. 113, 116.

53 408 U.S. 238 (1972). On *Furman* and what followed, see Robert Weisberg, "Deregulating Death," *Supreme Court Review* (1983), p. 305.

54 428 U.S. 153 (1976).

55 For these figures, I have relied on information supplied by the Death Penalty Information Center Home Page, http://www.essential.org/dpic/dpicreg.html (visited Aug. 9, 1999).

56 Friedman, *Crime and Punishment,* p. 320.

57 See William M. Kunstler, *Beyond a Reasonable Doubt? The Original Trial of Caryl Chessman* (1961).

58 Weisberg, "Deregulating Death," pp. 305, 386.

59 U.S. Department of Justice, *Sourcebook of Criminal Justice Statistics,* table 6.76, http://www.albany.edu/sourcebook/1995/pdf/t676.pdf (visited Aug. 6, 1999).

60 The law is 110 Stat. 1214 (act of Apr. 24, 1996).

61 See *American Bar Association Journal* 83:26 (Apr. 1997).

62 See *Albany Times Union,* Aug. 15, 1999; *St. Louis Post-Dispatch,* Aug. 26, 1999.

63 102 Stat. 926 (act of Aug. 11, 1988).

64 Donald Cressey, *Other People's Money* (1953), p. 90.

65 For an assessment, see Stanton Wheeler, David Weisburd, and Nancy Bode, "Sentencing the White-Collar Offender: Rhetoric and Reality," *Am. Sociolog. Rev.* 47:641 (1982).

66 See Kitty Calavita, Henry N. Pontell, and Robert H. Tillman, *Big Money Crime: Fraud and Politics in the Savings and Loan Crisis* (1997).

67 Milken served twenty-two months, and then was released to a halfway house. *New York Times,* Jan. 5, 1993.

68 *New York Times,* July 4, 1988.

69 *New York Times,* Dec. 3, 1998.

70 Calavita, Pontell, and Tillman, *Big Money Crime,* p. 11.

71 Ga. Code 1933, §§26-901, 26-902, 26-904.

72 For an account of this case, see Charles H. Martin, *The Angelo Herndon Case and Southern Justice* (1976); a shorter account is Charles H. Martin, "The Angelo Herndon Case and Southern Justice," in Michal R. Belknap, ed., *American Political Trials* (1981), p. 177.

73 301 U.S. 242 (1937).

74 On this trial, see Leo P. Ribuffo, "*United States v. McWilliams:* The Roosevelt Administration and the Far Right," in Belknap, *American Political Trials,* p. 201.

75 For an account of the trial, see David J. Langum, *William M. Kunstler: The Most Hated Lawyer in America* (1999), pp. 100–128.

76 82 Stat. 73, 75 (act of Apr. 11, 1968).

77 Langum, *Kunstler,* p. 114.

78 David Dellinger, *From Yale to Jail: The Life Story of a Moral Dissenter* (1993), p. 361.

79 Tom Hayden, *Trial* (1970), pp. 34–35.

80 Laws W. Va. 1931, ch. 3, p. 10.

81 Laws N. Mex. 1981, ch. 259.

82 Genl. Laws Vt., 1917, §§7097, 7099, pp. 1209–1210. To be sure, the punishment for these offenses was mild: a fine, and only up to two dollars.

83 Miss. Code, 1927, §1159, p. 898.

84 Page's Ohio Gen. Code 1938, §§13048, 13049.

85 The referendum was held Nov. 7, 1916; see Laws Ore. 1917, ch. 1, p. 13.

86 Genl. Laws Vt., §8568, p. 1607.

87 Code Ala. 1975, §13A-12-1.

88 *State v. K-Mart Corporation,* 482 So. 2d 1270 (Ct. of Crim. Appeals of Ala., 1985).

89 Alfred C. Kinsey et al., *Sexual Behavior in the Human Male* (1948), pp. 230–231. There is a growing literature on Kinsey and his report; see Julia A. Ericksen, *Kiss and Tell: Surveying Sex in the Twentieth Century* (1999), especially pp. 48–61.

90 Kinsey et al., *Sexual Behavior in the Human Male,* p. 392; Alfred C. Kinsey et al., *Sexual Behavior in the Human Female* (1953).

91 Friedman, *Crime and Punishment,* pp. 346–347.

92 Langum, *Kunstler,* pp. 190–194.

93 Friedman, *Crime and Punishment,* p. 343; 92 Stat. 7 (act of Feb. 6, 1978); 100 Stat. 3511 (act of Nov. 7, 1986).

94 Friedman, *Crime and Punishment,* p. 350.

95 *United States v. One Book Called "Ulysses,"* 5 F. Supp. 182 (S.D.N.Y., 1933); this decision was upheld in *United States v. One Book Entitled Ulysses by James Joyce,* 72 Fed. 2d 705 (C.A. 2, 1934).

96 Friedman, *Crime and Punishment,* p. 351.

97 The statute is Pa. Stats. Ann. 1963, tit. 18 §3831.

98 354 U.S. 476 (1957).

99 *A Book Named "John Cleland's Memoirs of a Woman of Pleasure" et al. v. Attorney General of Massachusetts,* 383 U.S. 413, 419, 425–6 (1966).

100 Miss. Code 1972, §97–29–1.

101 *American Booksellers Ass'n v. Hudnut,* 771 Fed. 2d 323 (C.A. 7, 1985).

102 *Central Ave. News, Inc. v. City of Minot,* 631 F. 2d 565 (1981).

103 Posner, J., in *Miller v. Civil City of South Bend,* 904 Fed. 2d 1081, 1091 (7th Cir., 1990). The original case was *Barnes v. Glen Theatre,* 501 U.S. 560 (1991).

104 On the trial of Lenny Bruce, see Martin Garbus, with Stanley Cohen, *Tough Talk* (1998), chap. 2.

105 William N. Eskridge, Jr., "Privacy Jurisprudence and the Apartheid of the Closet, 1946–1961," *Florida St. University L. Rev.* 24:703, 814 (1997).

106 62 Stat. 346, 347 (act of June 9, 1948).

107 Leslie J. Reagan, *When Abortion Was a Crime: Women, Medicine, and Law in the United States, 1867–1973* (1997), pp. 197–199.

108 Ibid., p. 192.

109 651 F. 2d, at 571–2.

110 65 Stat. 767 (act of Nov. 2, 1951).

111 70 Stat. 567 (act of July 18, 1956).

112 79 Stat. 226 (act of July 15, 1965).

113 Quoted in United States Sentencing Commission, *Special Report to the Congress: Cocaine and Federal Sentencing Policy* (Feb. 1995), p. 114.

114 86 Stat. 67, 85 (act of Mar. 21, 1972).

115 100 Stat. 3207 (act of Oct. 27, 1986).

116 Drug Law Enforcement Statistics, http://www.usdoj.gov/dea/lawstats.htm (visited Dec. 15, 1999).

117 For the story of this drug law, see Malcolm M. Feeley, *Court Reform on Trial: Why Simple Solutions Fail* (1983), pp. 118–128.

118 Laws Mich. 1978, p. 975. The same punishment applied to anyone who even possessed that quantity of drugs, if the possession was with the intent to make or deliver and so on.

119 See for example, Col. Rev. Stats. §18–18–426.

120 *State v. Munson* 714 S.W. 2d 585 (Mo., 1986).

121 Eva Bertram et al., *Drug War Politics: The Price of Denial* (1996), p. 98.

122 *Cocaine and Federal Sentencing Policy.* p. 122 and table 12. Crack cocaine is a solid substance, derived from powder cocaine. The powder "is simply dissolved in a solution of sodium bicarbonate and water"; the solution is boiled and what comes out is a

solid, which is cut into "rocks." Ibid., p. 14. See Michael Tonry, *Malign Neglect: Race, Crime, and Punishment in America* (1995), pp. 188–190.

123 Friedman, *Crime and Punishment,* p. 357.

124 Bureau of Justice Statistics Bulletin, *Felony Sentences in the United States, 1996,* pp. 2, 5.

125 *Statistical Abstract of the United States* (1999), p. 323.

126 Laws Tex. 1907, pp. 479, 485; Laws Ore. 1913, ch. 256, p. 497. I am indebted for these references, and for much of the information in the text, to Michael A. Bellesiles and his paper "The Regulation of Firearms, 1865–1939," presented at the annual meeting of the American Society for Legal History, Toronto, Oct. 23, 1999.

127 Laws N.Y. 1905, ch. 92, pp. 129, 130.

128 Laws N.Y. 1911, ch. 195.

129 Laws Mich. 1925, no. 313, p. 473.

130 48 Stat. 1236 (act of June 26, 1934).

131 *U.S. v. Miller,* 307 U.S. 174 (1938).

132 See Michael Bellesiles, *Arming America: The Origins of a National Gun Culture* (2000).

133 107 Stat. 1539 (act of Nov. 30, 1993). Certain temporary aspects of the law were ruled unconstitutional by the Supreme Court in *Printz v. U.S.,* 521 U.S. 898 (1997).

134 See, in general, Thomas Meader, *Crime and Madness: The Origins and Evolution of the Insanity Defense* (1985).

135 *M'Naghten's Case,* 10 Cl. & F. 200, 8 Eng. Rep 718 (1843).

136 214 Fed. 2d 863 (D.C. Cir. 1954).

137 *United States v. Brawner,* 471 F. 2d 969 (D.C. Cir., 1972).

138 Cal. Pen. Code §25(b).

139 On the trial itself, see Richard J. Bonnie, John C. Jeffries, Jr., and Peter W. Low, *A Case Study in the Insanity Defense: The Trial of John W. Hinckley, Jr.* (2d ed., 2000).

140 Idaho: Laws Idaho 1982, ch. 368; Montana: Laws Mont. 1979, ch. 173, p. 1979.

141 Laws Idaho 1972, ch. 336.

142 Utah Crim. Code, §76-2-305. "It is a defense to a prosecution . . . that the defendant, as a result of mental illness, lacked the mental state required as an element of the offense charged." Mental illness is "not otherwise a defense," but might be evidence in mitigation of certain charges.

143 *San Francisco Examiner,* Oct. 22, 1985.

144 James B. Jacobs, *Gotham Unbound: How New York City Was Liberated from the Grip of Organized Crime* (1999), p. 8.

145 Victor S. Navasky, *Kennedy Justice* (1971), p. 49.

146 Jacobs, *Gotham Unbound,* pp. 130–131, 132.

147 See, in general, Ethan A. Nadelmann, *Cops Across Borders: The Internationalization of U.S. Criminal Law Enforcement* (1993).

148 Bulletin, Bureau of Justice Statistics, *Prison and Jail Inmates at Midyear 1998* (Mar. 1999), p. 4.

149 Friedman, *Crime and Punishment,* p. 422.

150 Deborah L. Rhode, *Justice and Gender* (1989), p. 239.

151 Angela Browne, *When Battered Women Kill* (1987), p. 10.

152 89 N.C. App. 384, 366 S.E. 2d 586 (1988).

153 Rhode, *Justice and Gender,* p. 246

154 Harry Kalven, Jr., and Hans Zeisel, *The American Jury* (1966), pp. 250–252.

155 See Mary E. Odem, "Cultural Representations and Social Contexts of Rape in the Early Twentieth Century," in Michael A. Bellesiles, *Lethal Imagination: Violence and Brutality in American History* (1999), p. 353.

156 So, for example, Arkansas: Ark. Rev. Stats. (1984), §16–42–101. The judge can admit this evidence if it is "relevant," and if its "probative value outweighs its inflammatory or prejudicial nature."

157 *People v. McIlwain,* 55 Cal. App. 2d 322, 130 P. 2d 131, 133 (1942).

158 Cal. Penal Code, §261.

159 Cal. Penal Code, §261.6.

160 *State ex rel. M.T.S.,* 129 N.J. 422, 609 A. 2d 1266 (1992).

161 California, for example, basically abolished the exemption by the beginning of the 1980s; see Cal. Penal Code §262.

162 Jeanne C. Marsh. Alison Geist, and Nathan Caplan, *Rape and the Limits of Law Reform* (1982).

163 Quoted ibid., p. 93.

9.
Courts, Trials, and Procedures in the Twentieth Century

1 Roscoe Pound, "The Causes of Popular Dissatisfaction with the Administration of Justice," *Rpts of American Bar Ass'n* 29:395 (1906).

2 William E. Nelson, "Civil Procedure in Twentieth-Century New York," *St. Louis University Law Journal* 41:1157, 1169 (1997).

3 Armistead M. Dobie, *Handbook of Federal Jurisdiction and Procedure* (1928), §148, p. 585.

4 Thomas W. Shelton, quoted in Stephen N. Subrin, "How Equity Conquered Common Law: The Federal Rules of Civil Procedure in Historical Perspective," *U. Penn. Law Rev.* 135:909, 959 (1987). I have drawn on the Subrin article for much of this account of the rise of the Federal Rules.

5 48 Stat. 1064 (act of June 19, 1934).

6 Subrin, "How Equity Conquered Common Law," p. 974.

7 On the history of the class action suit, see Stephen C. Yeazell, *From Medieval Group Litigation to the Modern Class Action* (1987), especially chaps. 8 and 9.

8 Ibid., p. 248.

9 Ibid., p. 249.

10 See Deborah R. Hensler et al., *Class Action Dilemmas: Pursuing Public Goals for Private Gains* (2000), p. 18.

11 See, in general, Robert A. Kagan, Bliss Cartwright, Lawrence M. Friedman, and Stanton Wheeler, "The Business of State Supreme Courts, 1870–1970," *Stanford L. Rev.* 30:121 (1977).

12 Roger D. Groot, "The Effects of an Intermediate Appellate Court on the Supreme Court Work Product: The North Carolina Experience," *Wake Forest L. Rev.* 7:548 (1971).

13 Arthur T. Vanderbilt II, *Changing Law: A Biography of Arthur T. Vanderbilt* (1976), p. 78.

14 On Vanderbilt's career, there is the biography by his son, ibid., and Eugene C. Gerhart, *Arthur T. Vanderbilt: The Compleat Counsellor* (1980).

15 Robert A. Kagan, *Adversarial Legalism: The American Way of Law* (forthcoming 2001).

16 28 U.S.C.A. §1332.

17 On this point, and generally on federal jurisdiction, see Edward Purcell, *Litigation and Inequality: Federal Diversity Jurisdiction in Industrial America, 1870–1958* (1992), especially chaps. 4, 5, and 6, on the "battle for forum control."

18 16 Pet. 1 (1842).

19 On this doctrine, and its demise, see Tony Freyer, *Harmony and Dissonance: The Swift and Erie Cases in American Federalism* (1981).

20 276 U.S. 518 (1928).

21 304 U.S. 64 (1938); the account of the case in Freyer, *Harmony and Dissonance,* is the source for the description of the facts of the case.

22 Edward A. Purcell, Jr., *Brandeis and the Progressive Constitution: Erie, the Judicial Power, and the Politics of the Federal Courts in Twentieth-Century America* (2000).

23 Administrative Office of the United States Courts, *Federal Judicial Workload Statistics* (1980), p. 29.

24 Administrative Office of the United States Courts, *Federal Judicial Caseload Statistics* (1999), p. 48.

25 Donald R. Songer, Reginald S. Sheehan, and Susan B. Haire, *Continuity and Change on the United States Courts of Appeals* (2000), p. 54.

26 Edson R. Sunderland, "The Inefficiency of the Jury," *Mich. L. Rev.* 13:302, 311 (1915).

27 See Randolph Bergstrom, *Courting Danger: Injury and Law in New York City, 1870–1910* (1992), p. 131.

28 Charles E. Clark and Harry Shulman, *A Study of Law Administration in Connecticut* (1937), p. 213.

29 Ibid., p. 28.

30 Ann. Rpt., Adm've Office of the Courts, No. Car., 1994–1995, p. 66; 1993 Ann. Rpt, Judicial Council of California, vol. 2 (Judicial Statistics), p. 56.

31 Ky. Stats. 1903, §2253.

32 Maine Stats. 1903, p. 860, ch. 180.

33 Conn. Stats. 1918, §5681.

34 Parker's *New York Code of Civil Procedure* (1904), §1079, p. 297. The juror had to be

under seventy years of age as well, and neither infirm nor "decrepit." And he had to know the English language.

35 *People v. M'Laughlin,* 2 App. Div. 419, 39 N.Y. Supp. 1005 (1896).

36 Ala. Code, 1923, §§8600, 8603.

37 *Fay v. New York,* 332 U.S. 261 (1947).

38 Ill. Rev. Stats. 1921, ch. 78 §4; Code No. Car. 1939 §2329, p. 1005; Va. Rev. Stats. 1919 §5985.

39 Iowa Code Ann. 607A5.

40 John Henry Wigmore, *A Treatise on the Anglo-American System of Evidence in Trials at Common Law* (vol. 1, 2d ed., 1923), p. 125.

41 Ibid., pp. 151–152.

42 John Henry Merryman, *The Civil Law Tradition* (2d ed., 1985), p. 114.

43 *Funk v. U.S.,* 290 U.S. 371 (1933).

44 *In re Contempt of Emil Swenson,* 183 Minn. 602, 237 N.W. 589 (1931). The precise legal question turned on the meaning of a statute which gave the privilege to a religious "confession"; the claim was that this referred only to the Catholic confessional. The court read the statute more broadly. Meanwhile, Minnesota broadened the statute to apply to clergymen of "any religion" and to "any communication . . . by any person seeking religious or spiritual advice, aid or comfort." Laws Minn. 1931, ch. 206, p. 343.

45 *Frye v. United States,* 293 Fed. 1013 (C.A. D.C., 1923).

46 Sheila Jasanoff, *Science at the Bar: Law, Science, and Technology in America* (1995), pp. 52–53.

47 509 U.S. 579 (1993).

48 Karl Llewellyn, *The Common Law Tradition: Deciding Appeals* (1960), pp. 36, 51, 140–141.

49 Saul Brenner and Harold J. Spaeth, *Stare Indecisis: The Alteration of Precedent on the Supreme Court, 1946–1992* (1995), p. 23.

50 Lawrence M. Friedman et al., "State Supreme Courts: A Century of Style and Citation," *Stanford L. Rev.* 33:773, 787, 790, 811–812 (1981).

51 John Henry Merryman, "Toward a Theory of Citations: An Empirical Study of the Citation Practice of the California Supreme Court in 1950, 1960, and 1970," *So. Cal. L. Rev.* 50:381, 405–407 (1977).

52 Henry R. Glick, *Supreme Courts in State Politics: An Investigation of the Judicial Role* (1971).

53 See, for example, J. Gillis Wetter, *The Styles of Appellate Judicial Opinions: A Case Study in Comparative Law* (1960).

54 I am indebted for these figures to the research of Iddo Porat.

55 There is a huge literature on Cardozo. See, in particular, Richard Polenberg, *The World of Benjamin Cardozo: Personal Values and the Judicial Process* (1997).

56 Gerald Gunther, *Learned Hand: The Man and the Judge* (1994).

57 On the work of Posner as a judge, see William Domnarski, *In the Opinion of the Court* (1996), chap. 6.

58 Gunther, *Learned Hand,* pp. 502–513; *United States v. Manton,* 107 Fed. 2d 834 (C.A. 2, 1938).

59 There is a huge literature on Warren; see especially G. Edward White, *Earl Warren: A Public Life* (1982).

60 There are many collections of Holmes's writings, and of his voluminous correspondence. On his life and career, see, in particular, G. Edward White, *Justice Oliver Wendell Holmes: Law and the Inner Self* (1993).

61 On this study, see Herbert M. Kritzer, "Studying Disputes: Learning from the CLRP Experience," *Law and Society Review* 15:503 (1980–1981); Richard E. Miller and Austin Sarat, "Grievances, Claims, and Disputes: Assessing the Adversary Culture," ibid. at 525; William L. F. Felstiner, Richard L. Abel, and Austin Sarat, "The Emergence and Transformation of Disputes: Naming, Blaming, Claiming . . .," ibid. at 631.

62 Curtis J. Berger and Patrick J. Rohan, "The Nassau County Study: An Empirical Look into the Practices of Condemnation," *Col. L. Rev.* 67:430, 440 (1967).

63 H. Laurence Ross, *Settled Out of Court: The Social Process of Insurance Claims Adjustments* (1970).

64 On the role of the conference, see Jerold Auerbach, *Justice Without Law? Resolving Disputes Without Lawyers* (1983), p. 123.

65 104 Stat. 5090 (act of Dec. 1, 1990).

66 104 Stat. 2736 (act of Nov. 15, 1990).

67 See, for example, Utah Laws 1994, ch. 228.

68 On this procedure, see Linda R. Singer, *Settling Disputes: Conflict Resolution in Business, Families, and the Legal System* (2d ed., 1994), pp. 57–58. The Singer book is a source of information, in general, on ADR.

10.
Race Relations and Civil Rights

1 Ed Cray, *Chief Justice: A Biography of Earl Warren* (1997), p. 121.

2 *Korematsu v. United States,* 323 U.S. 214 (1944); on the Japanese internment cases, see Peter Irons, *Justice at War* (1983).

3 Civil Rights Act of 1988, 102 Stat. 903 (act of Aug. 10, 1988). If the internee was dead, the spouse or children could claim the money.

4 Harry N. Scheiber and Jane L. Scheiber, "Bayonets in Paradise: A Half-Century Retrospect on Martial Law in Hawai'i, 1941–1946," *U. Hawai'i Law Review* 19:477, 483–484, 515 (1997).

5 327 U.S. 303 (1946).

6 310 U.S. 586 (1940). This case, and the whole issue of the persecution of the Witnesses, is treated in David R. Manwaring, *Render unto Caesar: The Flag-Salute Controversy* (1962), and in Shawn Francis Peters, *Judging Jehovah's Witnesses: Religious Persecution and the Dawn of the Rights Revolution* (2000).

7 Peters, *Judging Jehovah's Witnesses,* p. 95.

8 Ibid., p. 277.

9 391 U.S. 624 (1943).

10 Gunnar Myrdal, with the Assistance of Richard Sterner and Arnold Rose, *An American Dilemma: The Negro Problem and Modern Democracy* (1942).

11 Myrdal, *American Dilemma* (1962 ed.), p. 1021.

12 Ibid., pp. 483, 485, 540–541.

13 On this theme, see Mary L. Dudziak, *Cold War Civil Rights: Race and the Image of American Democracy* (2000), quotations from pp. 99, 100.

14 334 U.S. 1 (1948).

15 David Delaney, *Race, Place, and the Law, 1836–1948* (1998), p. 151.

16 On the Sipuel affair, see Melvin I. Urofsky, *Division and Discord: The Supreme Court Under Stone and Vinson, 1941–1953* (1997), pp. 250–253. Ultimately, Sipuel was admitted to the University of Oklahoma Law School, graduated from it, and in 1992 became a regent of the University of Oklahoma; ibid., p. 250n.

17 339 U.S. 637 (1950).

18 Urofsky, *Division and Discord*, pp. 253–254.

19 339 U.S. 629 (1950).

20 Urofsky, *Division and Discord*, p. 254.

21 345 U.S. 483 (1954). There is, of course, an enormous literature on this case. See Richard Kluger, *Simple Justice* (1975); Austin Sarat, ed., *Race, Law, and Culture: Reflections on Brown v. Board of Education* (1997).

22 William H. Harbaugh, *Lawyer's Lawyer: The Life of John W. Davis* (1973), p. 515.

23 He had also been instrumental in ensuring that Eisenhower won the nomination. Warren was the "favorite son" candidate of California's delegation. He had no hope of winning the nomination, but the California vote did prevent Robert A. Taft from becoming the choice of the Republican Party. See Ed Cray, *Chief Justice: A Biography of Earl Warren* (1997), pp. 241–245.

24 Kluger, *Simple Justice*, p. 702.

25 In an important companion case, *Bolling v. Sharpe,* 347 U.S. 497 (1954), decided the same day as *Brown,* the court struck down school segregation in the District of Columbia. The Fourteenth Amendment applied only to the states, not to the federal government; but it was "unthinkable" that the federal government should legally be able to continue to segregate its schools. The Court then pumped enough fresh meaning into the Fifth Amendment (the original due-process clause), which of course did apply to the federal government, to justify outlawing segregation.

26 *Brown v. Board of Education of Topeka,* 349 U.S. 294 (1955).

27 Michal R. Belknap, *Federal Law and Southern Order: Racial Violence and Constitutional Conflict in the Post-Brown South* (1987), p. 29.

28 Jack Bass, *Unlikely Heroes* (1981).

29 Steven J. Whitfield, *Death in the Delta: The Story of Emmett Till* (1988), p. 14.

30 Wyn Craig Wade, *The Fiery Cross: The Ku Klux Klan in America* (1987), p. 303.

31 Ibid., pp. 299, 300.

32 Kevin Sack, "Mississippi Reveals Dark Secrets of a Racist Time," *New York Times,* March 18, 1998; Kevin Sack, "The Nation: Pride and Prejudice; the South's History Rises, Again and Again," *New York Times,* March 22, 1998.

33 For an account of these judges, see Bass, *Unlikely Heroes.*

34 Belknap, *Federal Law and Southern Order,* pp. 44–52.

35 *Cooper v. Aaron,* 358 U.S. 1 (1958).

36 Gerald N. Rosenberg, *The Hollow Hope: Can Courts Bring About Social Change?* (1991), p. 52.

37 See the discussion in Michael J. Klarman, "How *Brown* Changed Race Relations: The Backlash Thesis," *J. American History* 81:81 (1994).

38 See Bruce Nelson, "Organized Labor and the Struggle for Black Equality in Mobile During World War II," *J. American History* 80:952 (1993).

39 Klarman, "How *Brown* Changed Race Relations," pp. 116, 118.

40 *Dawson v. Mayor and City Council of Baltimore City,* 220 Fed. 2d 386 (C.A. 4, 1955); *Mayor and City Council of Baltimore City v. Dawson,* 350 U.S. 877 (1955).

41 Herbert Wechsler, "Toward Neutral Principles of Constitutional Law," *Harv. L. Rev.* 73:1, 22–23 (1959).

42 388 U.S. 1 (1967). See Peggy Pascoe, "Miscegenation Law, Court Cases, and Ideologies of 'Race' in Twentieth-Century America," *J. Am. Hist.* 83:44 (1996).

43 377 U.S. 218 (1964).

44 Benjamin Muse, *Virginia's Massive Resistance* (1961).

45 402 U.S. 1 (1970).

46 See J. Anthony Lukas, *Common Ground: A Turbulent Decade in the Lives of Three American Families* (1985).

47 *Keyes v. School District No. 1, Denver, Colorado,* 413 U.S. 189 (1973).

48 *Milliken v. Bradley,* 418 U.S. 717 (1974); see the discussion in J. Harvie Wilkinson III, *From Brown to Bakke: The Supreme Court and School Integration, 1954–1978* (1979), pp. 216–249.

49 See the material in Robert D. Loevy, ed., *The Civil Rights Act of 1964* (1997).

50 78 Stat. 241 (act of July 2, 1964).

51 109 U.S. 3 (1883).

52 The cases: *Heart of Atlanta Motel v. United States,* 379 U.S. 241 (1964) (motel which served many interstate travelers); *Katzenbach v. McClung,* 379 U.S. 294 (1964) (Ollie's Barbecue).

53 *First Annual Report, Equal Employment Opportunity Commission* (1966), pp. 5, 58–59.

54 U.S. Equal Employment Opportunity Commission, http://www.eeoc.gov/stats/race .html (visited July 11, 2000).

55 401 U.S. 424 (1971).

56 71 Stat. 634, 637 (act of Sept. 9, 1957).

57 79 Stat. 437 (act of Aug. 6, 1965).

58 *United States Code and Administrative News,* 94th Cong., 1st Sess. (vol. 2, 1975), pp. 774, 778.

59 Kathryn Healy Hester, "Mississippi and the Voting Rights Act, 1965–1982," *Mississippi Law Journal* 52:803 (1982).

60 The Voting Rights Act had a time limit, but it was extended in 1982, 96 Stat. 131 (act of June 29, 1982).

61 392 U.S. 409 (1968).

62 42 U.S.C. §1982.

63 *Jones v. Mayer Co.*, at 443. Two justices dissented.

64 82 Stat. 73, 81 (act of Apr. 11, 1968).

65 For these figures, see *Historical Statistics of the United States*, vol. 1, pp. 129, 131.

66 Laws N.Y. 1912, p. 660, ch. 331.

67 Pa. Stats. 1920, §§13542–13551, pp. 1331–1332; §13580, p. 1334.

68 Pa. Stats. 1920, §11925, p. 1166.

69 Conn. Stats. 1949, §§4243, 4244, 4246, pp. 1580–1581.

70 Mich. Comp. Laws. 1929, §8340.

71 Pa. Stats. 1920, §21432, p. 2081.

72 77 Stat. 56 (act of June 10, 1963).

73 *Hoyt v. Florida*, 368 U.S. 57 (1961).

74 404 U.S. 71 (1971).

75 421 U.S. 7 (1975).

76 411 U.S. 677 (1973).

77 *Craig v. Boren*, 429 U.S. 190 (1976).

78 414 U.S. 632 (1974).

79 In *La Fleur*, the Court cited a line of cases which cast constitutional doubt on the use of "irrebuttable presumptions." But the Supreme Court, in *Weinberger v. Salfi*, 422 U.S. 749 (1975), rejected this particular doctrine of *La Fleur*.

80 417 U.S. 484 (1974).

81 92 Stat. 2076 (act of Oct. 31, 1978).

82 450 U.S. 464 (1981).

83 Cal. Pen. Code §261.5.

84 453 U.S. 57 (1981).

85 433 U.S. 321 (1977). The Court did find, however, that the male prisons were "jungles," full of sex offenders and the like, and the Court bought the argument that using women as guards would "pose a substantial security problem."

86 Information from website: eeoc.gov/stats/enforcement.html (visited July 12, 2000).

87 *Diaz v. Pan American World Airways, Inc.*, 311 F. Supp. 559 (D.C. S.D. Fla, 1970).

88 *Diaz v. Pan American World Airways*, 442 Fed. 2d 385 (C.A. 5, 1971).

89 Deborah L. Rhode, *Justice and Gender: Sex Discrimination and the Law* (1989), p. 94; the case is *Wilson v. Southwest Airlines*, 517 Fed. Supp. 292 (D.C. N.D. Texas, 1989).

90 *Mississippi University for Women v. Hogan*, 458 U.S. 718 (1982).

91 Rhode, *Justice and Gender*, p. 231.

92 Catharine MacKinnon, *Sexual Harassment of Working Women* (1979).

93 *Meritor Savings Bank v. Vinson*, 477 U.S. 57 (1986).

94 See Deborah L. Rhode, *Speaking of Sex: The Denial of Gender Equality* (1997), pp. 96–107.

95 EEOC website: eeoc.gov/stats/harass.html (visited July 12, 2000).

96 *Suttles v. Hollywood Turf Club,* 114 P. 2d 27 (1941).

97 Paul D. Moreno, *From Direct Action to Affirmative Action: Fair Employment Law and Policy in America, 1933–1972* (1997), p. 107.

98 Alfred W. Blumrosen, "Antidiscrimination Laws in Action in New Jersey: A Law-Sociology Study," *Rutgers Law Review* 19: 189, 216 (1965).

99 Laws No. Car. 1977, ch. 726.

100 Laws So. Car. 1989, ch. 72.

101 369 U.S. 186 (1962).

102 328 U.S. 549 (1946).

103 *Reynolds v. Sims,* 377 U.S. 533 (1964).

104 Lucas A. Powe, Jr., *The Warren Court and American Politics* (2000), pp. 239–255.

105 Pa. Laws 1920 (1928 Cum. Supp.), §§11563c-902, 11568a-240, pp. 490, 504.

106 432 U.S. 1 (1977).

107 *Sugarman v. Dougall,* 413 U.S. 634 (1973); *In re Griffiths,* 413 U.S. 717 (1973), respectively.

108 *Bernal v. Fainter,* 467 U.S. 216 (1984).

109 Rehnquist, dissenting in *Sugarman v. Dougall,* at 654.

110 *Cabell v. Chavez-Salido,* 435 U.S. 291 (1978).

111 393 U.S. 503 (1969). See John W. Johnson, *The Struggle for Student Rights: Tinker v. Des Moines and the 1960s* (1997).

112 *Valentine v. Independent School District of Casey,* 183 N.W. 434 (Iowa, 1921).

113 This portion of the text relies on Lawrence M. Friedman, "Limited Monarchy: The Rise and Fall of Student Rights," in David L. Kirp and Donald N. Jensen, eds., *School Days, Rule Days: The Legalization and Regulation of Education* (1986), p. 238.

114 *Stephenson v. Wheeler County Board of Education,* 306 F. Supp. 97 (DCSD Ga., 1969); aff'd, 426 F. 2d 1154, cert. den. 400 U.S. 957 (1970).

115 The Oklahoma case is *Eaton v. City of Tulsa,* 415 U.S. 697 (1974); the seat of the pants case is *Smith v. Goguen,* 415 U.S. 566 (1974). The jacket case is *Cohen v. California,* 403 U.S. 15 (1971). Paul Robert Cohen, the defendant, was charged with violating a section of the California Penal Code which prohibited disturbing the peace or quiet "of any neighborhood . . . by . . . offensive conduct," if done "maliciously and willfully." The canned music case is *Public Utilities Commission v. Pollak,* 343 U.S. 451 (1952).

116 430 U.S. 705 (1977).

117 304 U.S. 144 (1938).

118 It had always been standard practice to give a hobo (for example) a choice: pay a small fine, or work it off in jail at so many dollars a day. The Court has not stopped this practice. But it has set limits. In *Williams v. Illinois,* 399 U.S. 235 (1970), Williams was convicted of petty theft. He got the maximum penalty: a year in jail, and $500 fine. If he failed to pay up, he would get extra time in jail. This, the Court said, went too far,

because it meant that Williams would spend more than the statutory maximum in jail simply because he was too poor to pay off his fine.

119 401 U.S. 371 (1971).

120 *United States v. Kras*, 409 U.S. 434 (1973).

121 *Ortwein v. Schwab*, 410 U.S. 656 (1973).

122 The definitive work on the evolution of military justice is Jonathan Lurie, *Arming Military Justice*, vol. 1, *The Origins of the United States Court of Military Appeals, 1775–1950* (1992).

123 The story is told in Jonathan Lurie, *Pursuing Military Justice*, vol. 2, *The History of the United States Court of Appeals for the Armed Forces, 1951–1980* (1998).

124 John R. Wunder, *"Retained by the People": A History of American Indians and the Bill of Rights* (1994), pp. 62–63.

125 Quoted ibid., p. 65.

126 48 Stat. 984 (act of June 18, 1934).

127 25 CFR (1937), §§161.38 ff.

128 Felix Cohen, *Handbook of American Indian Law* (1942), p. 149.

129 Quoted in Robert J. McCarthy, "Civil Rights in Tribal Courts: The Indian Bill of Rights at Thirty Years," *Idaho Law Review* 34:466, 485 (1998).

130 67 Stat. 588 (act of Aug. 15, 1953).

131 Cohen, *Handbook* (1982 ed.), pp. 170–180.

132 Sharon O'Brien, *American Indian Tribal Governments* (1989), p. 242.

133 For an account of the trial, see John William Sayer, *Ghost Dancing the Law: The Wounded Knee Trials* (1997), from which much of the material in the text is taken.

134 88 Stat. 2203 (act of Jan. 4, 1975).

135 92 Stat. 469 (act of Aug. 11, 1978).

136 See, for example, *In the Matter of the Estate of Boyd Apachee, Navajo Reports* 4:178 (1983).

137 McCarthy, "Civil Rights"; the statute is 82 Stat. 73, 77 (act of Apr. 11, 1968).

138 Charles Wollenberg, *All Deliberate Speed: Segregation and Exclusion in California Schools, 1855–1975* (1976), p. 111.

139 *Lopez v. Seccombe*, 71 F. Supp. 769 (D.C. S.D., Cal., 1944).

140 See, on the Orange County case and its background, Christopher Arriola, "Knocking on the Schoolhouse Door: *Mendez v. Westminster:* Equal Protection, Public Education and Mexican Americans in the 1940's," *La Raza Law Journal* 8:166 (1995).

141 *Westminister School District of Orange County v. Mendez*, 161 Fed. 2d. 774 (C.A. 9, 1947).

142 *Mendez v. Westminister School District of Orange County*, 65 F. Supp. 544 (D.C. S.D. Cal., 1946).

143 Wollenberg, *All Deliberate Speed*, p. 132.

144 Joyce Kuo, "Excluded, Segregated, and Forgotten: A Historical View of the Discrimination of Chinese Americans in Public Schools," *Asian Law Journal* 5:181, 210 (1998).

145 *San Francisco Chronicle*, October 2, 1989; Apr. 9, 1993.

146 481 U.S. 604 (1987). The precise question was whether the plaintiff could invoke 42 U.S. C. §1981, an old post–Civil War statute, which gave all citizens a bundle of the same rights as are "enjoyed by white persons." The argument of the college was that the statute outlawed race discrimination; and what Al-Khazraji complained about, whatever it was, was not race discrimination.

147 *Shaare Tefila Congregation v. Cobb*, 481 U.S. 615 (1987).

148 On the background of the age discrimination laws, see Lawrence M. Friedman, *Your Time Will Come: The Law of Age Discrimination and Mandatory Retirement* (1984).

149 79 Stat. 218 (act of July 14, 1965).

150 81 Stat. 602 (act of Dec. 15, 1967).

151 College and university teachers had to wait seven more years, but they too are now covered—including the author of this book.

152 U.S. Equal Employment Opportunity Commission, eeoc.gov/stats/adea/html (site visited July 17, 2000).

153 104 Stat. 327 (act of July 26, 1990).

154 Robert E. Rains, "A Pre-History of the Americans with Disabilities Act and Some Initial Thoughts as to Its Constitutional Implications," *St. Louis U. Pub. L. Rev.* 11:85 (1992).

155 29 Code of Federal Regulations, §1630.2(i) (1998).

156 104 Stat. 327, at 376.

157 U.S. Equal Employment Opportunity Commission, ccoc.gov/stats/ada-charges.html (site visited July 17, 2000).

158 316 U.S. 535 (1942).

159 Stone wrote a concurrence; the idea that criminality is inherited, he said, had a weak basis in science, and it was a denial of due process to sterilize Skinner without any attempt to find out whether his form of criminality passed on through the genes.

160 381 U.S. 479 (1965). On the background of this case, see Mary L. Dudziak, "Just Say No: Birth Control in the Connecticut Supreme Court Before *Griswold v. Connecticut*," *Iowa L. Rev.* 75:915 (1990).

161 David J. Garrow, *Liberty and Sexuality: The Right to Privacy and the Making of Roe v. Wade* (1994), pp. 42–43.

162 Ibid., p. 128.

163 *Poe v. Ullman*, 367 U.S. 497 (1961).

164 410 U.S. 113 (1973).

165 See David J. Garrow, *Liberty and Sexuality*, for a general account of the background of this case; also Leslie J. Reagan, *When Abortion Was a Crime: Women, Medicine, and Law in the United States, 1867–1973* (1997).

166 Garrow, *Liberty and Sexuality*, pp. 285–289.

167 *Harris v. McRae*, 448 U.S. 297 (1980).

168 Reprinted in Ellen Schrecker, *The Age of McCarthyism: A Brief History with Documents* (1994), p. 213.

169 David Caute, *The Great Fear: the Anti-Communism Purge under Truman and Eisenhower* (1978), pp. 70, 75–76, 81.

170 See Samuel Walker, *In Defense of American Liberties: A History of the ACLU* (1990), pp. 173–214.

171 On the trial and the *Dennis* case, see Ellen Schrecker, *Many Are the Crimes: McCarthyism in America* (1998), pp. 190–200.

172 Ibid., p. 198.

173 341 U.S. 494 (1951).

174 *Garner v. Board of Public Works of Los Angeles,* 341 U.S. 716 (1951).

175 Caute, *The Great Fear,* p. 445.

176 *Rosenberg v. U.S.,* 344 U.S. 838 (1952); Justice Black dissented.

177 The New York case is *United States v. Coplon,* 185 Fed. 2d 629 (C.A. 2, 1950); the Washington case is *Coplon v. United States,* 191 Fed. 2d 749 (D.C. Circuit, 1951); cert. den. 342 U.S. 926 (1952).

178 See Sam Tanenhaus, *Whittaker Chambers: A Biography* (1997).

179 For an overview, see Lucas Powe, *Warren Court and American Politics,* pp. 75–103, 135–156.

180 On the events of this day, see Arthur J. Sabin, *In Calmer Times: The Supreme Court and Red Monday* (1999).

181 354 U.S. 298 (1957).

182 367 U.S. 1 (1961), at 96.

183 382 U.S. 70 (1965).

184 384 U.S. 11 (1966).

185 Quoted in Schrecker, *Age of McCarthyism,* pp. 211, 214.

186 376 U.S. 254 (1964).

187 283 U.S. 697 (1931).

188 *Brewer v. Memphis Publishing Co.,* 626 Fed. 2d 1238 (C.A. 5, 1980).

189 62 Stat. 1009 (act of June 25, 1948).

190 64 Stat. 987 (act of Sept. 23, 1950).

191 66 Stat. 163 (act of June 27, 1952).

192 79 Stat. 911 (act of Oct. 3, 1965).

193 94 Stat. 102 (act of Mar. 17, 1980).

194 Elliott Robert Barkan, *And Still They Come: Immigrants and American Society, 1920 to the 1990s* (1996), p. 179.

195 On this theme, see Lawrence M. Friedman, *The Horizontal Society* (1999).

196 G. Alan Tarr, *Understanding State Constitutions* (1998), p. 21.

197 Ibid., p. 136–137.

198 See Elmer E. Cornwell, Jr., Jay S. Goodman, and Wayne R. Swanson, *State Constitutional Conventions: The Politics of the Revision Process in Seven States* (1975).

199 Ibid., p. 5.

200 Tarr, *Understanding State Constitutions,* pp. 151–152.

201 William E. Nelson, "The Changing Meaning of Equality in Twentieth-Century Constitutional Law," *Washington & Lee Law Rev.* 52:3 (1995).

202 *People v. Wise,* 281 N.Y.S. 2d 539 (Crim. Ct. N.Y. County, 1967); see Nelson, "The
Changing Meaning," pp. 82–83.

203 Cynthia L. Fountaine, "Article III and the Adequate and Independent State Grounds
Doctrine," *Am. U. L. Rev.* 48:1053 (1999).

204 Tarr, *Understanding State Constitutions,* p. 168.

205 447 U.S. 74 (1980).

11.
The Liability Explosion

1 On this, see Lawrence M. Friedman, *A History of American Law* (2d ed., 1985), part 3,
chap. 6.

2 77 N.H. 33 (1913).

3 Randolph E. Bergstrom, *Courting Danger: Injury and Law in New York City, 1870–
1910* (1992), pp. 159, 163.

4 Lawrence M. Friedman and Thomas D. Russell, "More Civil Wrongs: Personal Injury
Litigation, 1901–1910," *American J. of Legal History* 34:295, 308 (1990).

5 Arthur F. McEvoy, "The Triangle Shirtwaist Factory Fire of 1911: Social Change,
Industrial Accidents, and the Evolution of Common-Sense Causality," *Law and Social
Inquiry* 20:621 (1995); Marc Galanter, "The Transnational Traffic in Legal Remedies,"
in Sheila Jasanoff, ed., *Learning from Disaster: Risk Management After Bhopal* (1994),
pp. 133, 140.

6 Galanter, "The Transnational Traffic," p. 141.

7 William Graebner, *Coal-Mining Safety in the Progressive Period: The Politics of Reform*
(1976), p. 113.

8 Laws N.Y. 1902, vol. 2, ch. 600, p. 1748.

9 35 Stat. ch. 149, p. 65 (act of Apr. 22, 1908). Under the common-law rule, any
"contributory negligence," however slight, cost a plaintiff his rights. FELA also provided that the employer could not wriggle out of the act by making employees sign a
waiver. Any such contract was "void." Ibid., §21, p. 66.

10 Second Employers' Liability Cases, 223 U.S. 1 (1912).

11 41 Stat. 988, ch. 33, at 1007 (act of June 5, 1920).

12 On the rise of workers' compensation, see Lawrence M. Friedman and Jack Ladinsky,
"Social Change and the Law of Industrial Accidents," *Columbia L. Rev.* 67:50 (1967).

13 *Ives v. South Buffalo Railway Co.,* 201 N.Y. 271, 94 N.E. 431 (1911).

14 *New York Central Rr. Co. v. White,* 243 U.S. 188 (1917).

15 Laws Miss. 1948, ch. 354, p. 507.

16 *Report to the Legislature of the State of Ohio of the Commission Appointed under Senate
Bill No. 250 of the Laws of 1910,* part 1 (1911), p. lvi.

17 Crystal Eastman, *Work-Accidents and the Law* (1910), pp. 121–122.

18 Ibid., pp. 12, 13.

19 Price V. Fishback and Shawn Everett Kanton, "The Adoption of Workers' Compensation in the United States, 1900–1930," *J. of Law and Economics* 41:305, 316–317 (1998).

20 Ibid., pp. 337, 317. For the attitude about jury behavior see the letter to the Employees' Liability Commission of Ohio, in 1910, from the treasurer of the La Belle Iron Works. Quoted ibid., p. 339.

21 Laws Conn. 1913, ch. 138 is the general law; the sections quoted are from part B, §1.

22 Ibid., part B, §§9, 12. There were separate death-benefit provisions if the worker was survived only by family members who were "partially dependent"; and if someone died without any dependents, $750 was to go to the state treasury as a fund to help pay for the "lawful expenses of the commissioners."

23 So. Dak. Rev. Stats. 1929, §9443; Gen. Stats. Minn. 1913, §8202; "domestic servants" were excluded as well in both states.

24 Galanter, "The Transnational Traffic," p. 135.

25 217 N.Y. 382, 111 N.E. 1050 (1916).

26 Andrew L. Kaufman, *Cardozo* (1998), pp. 269–275; William L. Prosser, *Handbook of the Law of Torts* (1941), p. 678.

27 24 Cal. 2d 453, 105 P. 2d 436 (1944).

28 65 F. Supp. 138 (D.D.C. 1946).

29 *Leal v. C. C. Pitts Sand and Gravel, Inc.,* 419 S.W. 2d 820, 822 (Tex. S. Ct., 1967).

30 32 N.J. 358, 161 Atl. 2d 69 (1960).

31 *Christy Bros. Circus v. Turnage,* 38 Ga. App. 381, 144 S.E. 680 (1928).

32 128 Conn. 231, 21 A. 2d 402 (1941).

33 *Gable v. Salvation Army,* 186 Okla. 687, 100 P. 2d 244 (1940).

34 *Bing v. Thunig,* 2 N.Y. 2d 656, 143 N.E. 2d 3 (1957).

35 William Prosser, *The Law of Torts* (3d ed. 1964), pp. 1023–1024.

36 35 Stat. 65, 66 (act of Apr. 22, 1908).

37 41 Stat. 1007 (act of June 5, 1920).

38 248 N.Y. 339, 162 N.E. 99 (1928). On the background of the case, see John Noonan, *Persons and Masks in the Law* (1976), chap. 4.

39 Samuel B. Horovitz, "Assaults and Horseplay Under Workmen's Compensation Laws," 41 *Ill. L. Rev.* 311 (1946).

40 *Karlslyst v. Industrial Commission,* 243 Wis. 612, 11 N.W. 2d 179 (1943).

41 *Young v. Melrose Granite Company,* 152 Minn. 512, 189 N.W. 426 (1922).

42 *Beaver v. Morrison-Knudsen Co.,* 55 Ida. 275, 41 P. 2d 275 (1934).

43 Laws Ill. 1911, p. 330. The statute covered occupational diseases in general, and it also had specific provisions for employees who use lead, paris green, and similar substances—which were "especially dangerous to the health" of the workers. The law gave a private cause of action for damages, and was struck down in 1935, in *Boshuizen v.*

Thompson & Taylor Co., 360 Ill. 160, 195 N.E. 625 (1935). Gertrude Boshuizen was a worker in a spice, coffee, and tea import and packing company, and the complaint was about pepper and other "irritating and injurious dusts."

44 Okla. Comp. Stats. 1926, §§7283, 7284, pp. 662–663.

45 Laws N.Y. 1920, ch. 538, at 1366–1371.

46 See, for their story, Claudia Clark, *Radium Girls: Women and Industrial Health Reform, 1910–1935* (1997).

47 Laws N.J. 1949, ch. 29, p. 102.

48 La. Laws 1975, act. no. 583, pp. 1226, 1228.

49 The cases are *Ellis v. American Hawaiian S.S. Co.,* 165 Fed. 2d 999 (C.A. 9, 1948); and *Koistinen v. American Export Lines,* 83 N.Y. Supp. 2d 297 (City Ct. of N.Y., 1948); see also *Aguilar v. Standard Oil Co. of New York,* 318 U.S. 724 (1943).

50 Federal Security Agency, Vital Statistics—Special Reports, vol. 36, no. 19, *Accident Fatalities in the United States, 1949* (1952), pp. 366, 370.

51 Jonathan Simon, "Driving Governmentality: Automobile Accidents, Insurance, and the Challenge to the Social Order in the Inter-War Years, 1919 to 1941," *Connecticut Insurance L. J.* 4:521, 541 (1998).

52 *Report by the Committee to Study Compensation for Automobile Accidents to the Columbia University Council for Research in the Social Sciences* (1932), pp. 20, 56.

53 Laws Mass. 1925, ch. 346, p. 426.

54 Laws Conn. 1925, ch. 183.

55 Contrast Emma Corstvet, "The Uncompensated Accident and its Consequences," *Law and Contemporary Problems* 3:466 (1936), and Robert Monaghan, "The Liability Claim Racket," ibid., 491.

56 Richard M. Nixon, "Changing Rules of Liability in Automobile Accident Litigation," ibid., at 476, 490.

57 H. Laurence Ross, *Settled Out of Court: The Social Process of Insurance Claims Adjustment* (1970), p. 255.

58 The case is *Salgo v. Leland Stanford Jr. University Bd. of Trustees,* 317 P. 2d 170 (Cal. App., 1957).

59 Bergstrom, *Courting Danger,* p. 20.

60 Michael G. Shanley and Mark A. Peterson, *Comparative Justice: Civil Jury Verdicts in San Francisco and Cook Counties, 1959–1980* (1983), pp. 7, 11, 31.

61 Ibid., table, p. 31; *Salgo,* at 578.

62 *Borel v. Fibreboard Paper Products Corp.,* 493 Fed. 2d 1076 (C.A. 5, 1973).

63 Deborah R. Hensler, "Fashioning a National Resolution of Asbestos Personal Injury Litigation: A Reply to Professor Brickman," *Cardozo Law Review* 13:1967, 1970 (1992).

64 See, in general, Deborah R. Hensler et al., *Asbestos in the Courts: The Challenge of Mass Toxic Torts* (1985).

65 U.S. District Court, E.D. N.Y, *In re "Agent Orange" Product Liability Litigation,* Preliminary Memorandum and Order on Settlement, Sept. 25, 1984 (Weinstein, J.), p. 7.

66 See Georgene M. Vairo, "*Georgine*, the Dalkon Shield Claimants Trust, and the Rhetoric of Mass Tort Claims Resolution," *Loyola of Los Angeles Law Review* 31:79 (1997).

67 "Lilly in a DES Settlement," *New York Times*, May 19, 1992.

68 Samuel D. Warren and Louis D. Brandeis, "The Right of Privacy," *Harv. L. Rev.* 4:193 (1890).

69 Robert E. Mensel, "'Kodakers Lying in Wait': Amateur Photography and the Right of Privacy in New York, 1885–1915," *American Quarterly* 43:24 (1991).

70 *Roberson v. Rochester Folding Box Co.*, 171 N.Y. 538, 64 N.E. 442 (1902); Mensel, "'Kodakers Lying in Wait,'" pp. 36–39.

71 Laws N.Y. 1903, ch. 132.

72 *Pavesich v. New England Life Insurance Co.*, 122 Ga. 190, 50 S.E. 68 (1905).

73 *Melvin v. Reid*, 121 Cal. App. 285, 297 Pac. 91 (1931).

74 See Joshua Gamson, *Freaks Talk Back* (1998).

75 *Virgil v. Time Inc.*, 527 Fed. 2d 1122 (C.A. 9, 1975).

76 Mark A. Peterson, *Compensation of Injuries: Civil Jury Verdicts in Cook County* (1984), p. 4.

77 On this development, see Viviana A. R. Zelizer, *Morals and Markets: The Development of Life Insurance in the United States* (1979).

78 H. Roger Grant, *Insurance Reform: Consumer Action in the Progressive Era* (1979), p. 6.

79 This generalization has, however, been disputed; see Peter Karsten, *Heart versus Head: Judge-Made Law in Nineteenth-Century America* (1997).

80 Prosser, *Handbook*, p. 21.

81 These examples are from Melvin Belli, *My Life on Trial* (1976), pp. 108, 114.

82 See Stuart M. Speiser, *Lawsuit* (1980).

83 See Lawrence M. Friedman, *Total Justice* (1985).

84 For a discussion, see Robert A. Kagan, "How Much Do National Styles of Law Matter?" in Robert A. Kagan and Lee Axelrad, eds., *Regulatory Encounters: Multinational Corporations and American Adversarial Legalism* (2000), p. 1.

85 27 Stat. 531 (act of Mar. 2, 1893).

86 Eugene Bardach and Robert A. Kagan, *Going by the Book* (1982), p. 11.

87 83 Stat. 742 (act of Dec. 30, 1969).

88 Child Protection and Toy Safety Act of 1969, 83 Stat. 187 (act of Nov. 6, 1969), amending the Federal Hazardous Substances Labeling Act, 74 Stat. 372 (act of July 12, 1960). This law repealed the Federal Caustic Poison Act (44 Stat. 1406, act of Mar. 4, 1927), a labeling law for certain specific substances, such as sulphuric and hydrochloric acid.

89 84 Stat. 1590 (act of Dec. 29, 1970).

90 84 Stat. 1620 (act of Dec. 29, 1970).

91 86 Stat. 1207 (act of Oct. 27, 1972).

92 Laws Tex. 1945, ch. 339, p. 554.

93 Tenn. Laws 1972, ch. 561.

12.
Business Law in an Age of Change

1 *Dean Milk Co. v. Madison,* 340 U.S. 349 (1951).

2 *Philadelphia v. New Jersey,* 437 U.S. 617 (1978).

3 *Chemical Waste Management v. Hunt,* 504 U.S. 334 (1992).

4 These cases are *South Carolina Highway Department v. Barnwell Bros.,* 303 U.S. 177 (1938); *Southern Pacific Rr. Co. v. Arizona,* 325 U.S. 761 (1945); *Bib v. Navajo Freight Lines,* 359 U.S. 529 (1959).

5 Allen R. Kamp, "Uptown Act: A History of the Uniform Commercial Code, 1940–49," *Southern Methodist L. Rev.* 51:275, 283, 292 (1998).

6 Allen R. Kamp, "Downtown Act: A History of the Uniform Commercial Code, 1949–54," *Buffalo L. Rev.* 49:359 (2001).

7 A tenth article dealt with such technical details as the effective date of the law, and a list of the existing state laws which the code repealed.

8 Title I of the Consumer Credit Protection Act, 82 Stat. 146 (act of May 29, 1968).

9 88 Stat. 2183 (act of Jan. 4, 1975).

10 Laws Cal. 1970, ch. 1333, p. 2481.

11 Laws Cal. 1995, ch. 503.

12 For an important corrective, see William J. Novak, *The People's Welfare: Law and Regulation in Nineteenth-Century America* (1996).

13 Stewart Macaulay et al., eds., *Contracts in Action* (1995), p. 24.

14 See Lawrence M. Friedman, *Contract Law in America* (1965).

15 Grant Gilmore, *The Death of Contract* (1974).

16 Friedrich Kessler, "Contracts of Adhesion: Some Thoughts About Freedom of Contract," *Columbia L. Rev.* 43:629 (1943).

17 172 Fed. 2d 80 (C.A. 2, 1948).

18 212 So. 2d 906 (Fla., 1968).

19 Laws Cal. 1971, ch. 375; Civil Code §1689.6.

20 See Clarence Morris, "Waiver and Estoppel in Insurance Policy Litigation," *U. Pa. L. Rev.* 105:925 (1957).

21 Spencer L. Kimball, *Insurance and Public Policy* (1960), p. 301.

22 Stewart Macaulay, "Non-Contractual Relations in Business: A Preliminary Study," *American Sociological Review* 28:55 (1963).

23 Russell J. Weintraub, "A Survey of Contract Practice and Policy," *Wisc. L. Rev.* 1 (1992).

24 52 Stat. 840 (act of June 22, 1938).

25 Herbert Jacob, *Debtors in Court: The Consumption of Government Services* (1969), pp. 65–71. Quotation from p. 36.

26 L. H. Grinstead, *The Operation of the Ohio Wage Garnishment Law* (1933).

27 Neumeyer Foundation, *Wage Garnishment: Impact and Extent in Los Angeles County* (n.d.), p. 34.

28 "Wage Garnishment in Washington: An Empirical Study," *Washington Law Review* 43:743, 752 (1968).

29 Ill. Stats. 1947, ch. 62, §14, p. 1888.

30 82 Stat. 146, 163 (act of May 29, 1968).

31 On the law and its background, see Bruce G. Carruthers and Terence C. Halliday, *Rescuing Business: The Making of Corporate Bankruptcy Law in England and the United States* (1998), pp. 78–106.

32 92 Stat. 2549 (act of Nov. 6, 1978); on the creation of the new courts, ibid., at 2657.

33 Administrative Office of the United States Courts, *Tables of Bankruptcy Statistics,* fiscal year ended June 30, 1942, p. 13; ibid., fiscal year ended June 30, 1945, p. 7; ibid., fiscal year ended June 30, 1954, p. 1.

34 Carruthers and Halliday, *Rescuing Business,* p. 264.

35 *Monthly Labor Review,* no. 11 (1983), p. 73.

36 Mark S. Bever, "Manville Corporation and the 'Good Faith' Standard for Reorganization Under the Bankruptcy Code," *U. Toledo L. Rev.* 14:1467 (1983).

37 Adolph A. Berle and Gardiner C. Means, *The Modern Corporation and Private Property* (1933).

38 48 Stat. 162 (act of June 16, 1933).

39 70 Stat. 133 (act of May 9, 1956).

40 David A. Skeel, Jr., "An Evolutionary Theory of Corporate Law and Corporate Bankruptcy," *Vanderbilt L. Rev.* 51:1325, 1337 (1998).

41 On this case, see John Herling, *The Great Price Conspiracy: The Story of the Antitrust Violations in the Electrical Industry* (1962).

42 William G. Shepherd, "Antitrust Repelled, Inefficiency Endured: Lessons of IBM and General Motors for Future Antitrust Policies," *Antitrust Bulletin* 34:203 (1994).

43 Richard Hofstadter, "What Happened to the Antitrust Movement?" in *The Paranoid Style in American Politics and Other Essays* (1965), pp. 188, 213.

44 These examples are from CCH, *The Federal Antitrust Laws with Summary of Cases Instituted by the United States, 1890–1951* (1952), pp. 394, 400, 402, 404.

45 For this point, and the material in the rest of this paragraph, see Rudolph J. R. Peritz, *Competition Policy in America, 1888–1992* (rev. ed., 2000), pp. 278–282.

46 Elliott Brownlee, *Federal Taxation in America: A Short History* (1996), chap. 2.

47 Ibid., pp. 91, 94.

48 57 Stat. 126 (act of June 9, 1943).

49 Brownlee, *Federal Taxation in America,* pp. 94–96; Randolph Paul, *Taxation in the United States* (1954), p. 348.

50 Carolyn C. Jones, "Class Tax to Mass Tax: The Role of Propaganda in the Expansion of the Income Tax During World War II," *Buffalo L. Rev.* 37: 685 (1989).

51 Nancy F. Cott, *Public Vows: A History of Marriage and the Nation* (2000), pp. 191–193.

52 This gem is 26 U.S.C.A. §170 (d) (1) (A).

53 *Statistical Abstract of the United States* (1998), pp. 307–308.

54 Ibid.

55 95 Stat. 172 (act of Aug. 13, 1981).

56 100 Stat. 2085 (act of Oct. 22, 1986).

57 Art. 13A, Cal. Const., approved June 6, 1978. Prop 13 did not apply to new houses or commercial buildings; and to new buyers of old houses. A young couple that buys a house today in California may pay five times as much in property taxes as the family in an identical house across the street, which has been owned by the same people since the 1970s.

13.
The Law of Property

1 Patricia Burgess, *Planning for the Private Interest: Land Use Controls and Residential Patterns in Columbus, Ohio, 1900–1970* (1994), p. 61.

2 Seymour I. Toll, *Zoned American* (1969), p. 124.

3 Quoted in John Delafons, *Land-Use Controls in the United States* (1962), p. 21.

4 Edward M. Bassett, *Zoning* (1936), pp. 20–21.

5 Delafons, *Land-Use Controls,* p. 23.

6 Burgess, *Planning for the Private Interest,* pp. 80–83.

7 *State ex rel. Carter v. Harper, Wis.* 196 N.W. 451 (1923). I am indebted to Lesley Barnhorn for this citation.

8 272 U.S. 388 (1926).

9 E. C. Yokley, *Zoning Law and Practice* (1948), p. 33.

10 Va. Code 1942, §3091 (13).

11 Laws N.J. 1930, ch. 235, p. 1039.

12 *Mansfield & Swett, Inc. v. West Orange,* 120 N.J.L. 145, 198 Atl. 225 (1938).

13 *South Burlington County NAACP v. Township of Mount Laurel,* 67 N.J. 141, 336 Atl. 2d 713 (1975).

14 *South Burlington County NAACP v. Township of Mount Laurel,* 92 N.J. 158, 456 Atl. 2d 390 (1983).

15 See Douglas S. Massey and Nancy A. Denton, *American Apartheid: Segregation and the Making of the Underclass* (1993), pp. 190–191.

16 63 Stat. 413 (act of July 15, 1949).

17 Massey and Denton, *American Apartheid,* p. 56.

18 Charles Abrams, *The City Is the Frontier* (1965), pp. 168–169.

19 Ibid., p. 169.

20 Michael F. Wiedl III, "Historic District Ordinances," *Conn. L. Rev.* 8:209 (1975).

21 Opinion of the Justices, Mass., 128 N.E. 2d 557 (1955). The justices also gave their stamp of approval to a Beacon Hill historic district in Boston, 333 Mass. 783, 128 N.E. 2d 563 (1955).

22 63 Stat. 927 (act of Oct. 29, 1949);

23 80 Stat. 915 (act of Oct. 15, 1966).

24 Edward H. Rabin, "The Revolution in Residential Landlord-Tenant Law: Causes and Consequences," *Cornell L. Rev.* 69:517 (1984).

25 128 Fed. 2d 1071 (D.C., 1970).

26 Quoted in Edward H. Rabin, "The Revolution in Residential Landlord-Tenant Law: Causes and Consequences," *Cornell L. Rev.* 69:517, 549 (1984).

27 397 Fed 2d 698 (C.A. D.C., 1968).

28 The statutes are Laws N.J. 1970, ch. 210; Laws N.J. 1974, ch. 49.

29 See Richard W. Hemingway, "Selected Problems in Leases of Community and Regional Shopping Centers," *Baylor Law Review* 16:1 (1964).

30 75 Stat. 149, 160 (act of June 30, 1961).

31 Evan McKenzie, *Privatopia: Homeowner Associations and the Rise of Residential Private Government* (1994).

32 *Nahrstedt v. Lakeside Village Condominium Association,* 8 Cal. 4th 361, 878 P. 2d 1275 (1994).

33 John Dillon, *Commentaries on the Law of Municipal Corporations* (4th ed., vol. 1, 1890), §21, p. 40.

34 These figures are from Robert G. Dixon and John R. Kerstetter, *Adjusting Municipal Boundaries: The Law and Practice in 48 States* (1959).

35 *Statistical Abstract of the United States* (1999), p. 334.

36 Carole Shammas, Marylynn Salmon, and Michel Dahlin, *Inheritance in America: From Colonial Times to the Present* (1987), pp. 184–185. In the larger estates, in both periods, the spouse fared less well.

37 John H. Langbein, "The Twentieth-Century Revolution in Family Wealth Transmission," *Michigan L. Rev.* 86: 722 (1988).

38 *Matter of Totten,* 179 N.Y. 122, 71 N.E. 748 (1904).

39 Norman Dacey, *How to Avoid Probate* (1965).

40 *Chapter House Circle of the King's Daughters v. Hartford National Bank & Trust Co.,* 121 Conn. 558, 186 Atl. 543 (1936).

41 W. Barton Leach, "Perpetuities in a Nutshell," *Harv. L. Rev.* 51:638 (1938).

42 *Shenandoah Valley National Bank v. Taylor,* 192 Va. 135, 63 S.E. 2d 786 (1951).

43 See *Howard Savings Inst. v. Peep,* 34 N.J. 494, 170 A. 2d 39 (1961).

44 F. Emerson Andrews, *Philanthropic Foundations* (1956), p. 59.

45 B. Carroll Reece, preface to Rene A. Wormser, *Foundations: Their Power and Influence* (1958), pp. v–vi, 304–305. I am indebted to Margarete E. McGuinness for this reference.

46 Andrews, *Philanthropic Foundations,* p. 17; Evelyn Brody, "Charitable Endowments and the Democratization of Dynasty," *Arizona Law Review* 39:873, 927 (1997); *Statistical Abstract of the United States* (1997), p. 392, table 617.

47 *Statistical Abstract of the United States* (1999), p. 405.

48 Lawrence M. Friedman and Mark Savage, "Taking Care: The Law of Conservatorship

in California," *Southern Cal. L. Rev.* 61:273 (1988); Lawrence M. Friedman and June O. Starr, "Losing It in California: Conservatorship and the Social Organization of Aging," *Washington U.L.Q.* 73:1501 (1995).

49 Dean Starkman, "Guardians May Need Someone to Watch Over Them," *Wall Street Journal,* May 8, 1998. I am indebted to Anne M. Schneiderman for this reference.

50 Much of the material on pensions and ERISA is from John H. Langbein and Bruce A. Wolk, *Pension and Employee Benefit Law* (2d ed., 1995).

51 *Statistical Abstract of the United States* (1998), p. 236.

52 32 Stat. 388 (act of June 17, 1902).

53 33 Stat. 547 (act of Apr. 28, 1904).

54 35 Stat. 639 (act of Feb. 19, 1909).

55 John Opie, *The Law of the Land: Two Hundred Years of American Farmland Policy* (1987), p. 106.

56 61 Stat. 1315, 1335 (act of Mar. 3, 1921).

57 Laws Pa. 1923, ch. 228, art. X.

58 Laws Minn. 1931, ch. 309, p. 399.

59 35 Stat. 251, 267 (act of May 23, 1908).

60 39 Stat. 1702 (treaty signed Aug. 16, 1916; promulgated in December). The treaty was in fact with the United Kingdom, but with reference to Canada. It was upheld by the Supreme Court in *Missouri v. Holland,* 252 U.S. 416 (1920), against the claim that it interfered with the rights of the states.

61 40 Stat. 755 (act of July 3, 1918); 45 Stat. 1222 (act of Fcb. 18, 1929).

62 80 Stat. 926 (act of Oct. 15, 1966).

63 78 Stat. 890 (act of Sept. 3, 1964). I am indebted to a student paper by Paul Logan (1999) for information on the origins and nature of the Wilderness Act.

64 85 Stat. 649 (act of Dec. 15, 1971).

65 86 Stat. 1027 (act of Oct. 21, 1972).

66 87 Stat. 884 (act of Dec. 28, 1973), sec. 3 (14), p. 886.

67 Shannon Peterson, "Congress and Charismatic Megafauna: A Legislative History of the Endangered Species Act," *Environmental Law* 29:463 (1999); Shannon Peterson, "Bison to Blue Whales: Protecting Endangered Species Before the Endangered Species Act of 1973," *Environs: Environmental Law and Policy Journal* 29:71 (1999).

68 *TVA v. Hill,* 437 U.S. 153 (1978); the justice in question, Justice Powell, is quoted in Zygmunt J. B. Plater, "In the Wake of the Snail Darter: An Environmental Law Paradigm and its Consequences," *U. Mich. J. Law Reform* 19:805, 848 (1986).

69 I am indebted to Shannon Peterson for these references.

70 Plater, "In the Wake of the Snail Darter," p. 814.

71 Christopher McGrory Klyza, *Who Controls Public Lands? Mining, Forestry, and Grazing Policies, 1870–1990* (1996), pp. 115–116.

72 Note, "Farmland and Open Space Preservation in Michigan: An Empirical Analysis," *U. Mich. J. Law Reform* 19:1107 (1986).

73 I am much indebted to Paul Goldstein's lucid exploration of copyright law, *Copyright's Highway: The Law and Lore of Copyright from Gutenberg to the Celestial Jukebox* (1994).

74 *Bleistein et al. v. Donaldson Lithographing Co.,* 188 U.S. 239 (1903).

75 Goldstein, *Copyright's Highway,* pp. 68–77.

76 66 Stat. 792 (act of July 15, 1952).

77 96 Stat. 25, 38 (act of Apr. 2, 1982).

78 46 Stat. 376 (act of May 23, 1930).

79 *Diamond v. Chakrabarty,* 447 U.S. 303 (1980).

80 33 Stat. 724 (act of Feb. 20, 1905).

81 Under the Lanham Act of 1946, 60 Stat. 431 (act of July 5, 1946), §8, trademark registration had a ten-year term, renewable forever.

82 60 Stat. 427 (act of July 5, 1946).

83 *Aunt Jemima Mills Co. v. Rigney & Co.,* 247 Fed. 407 (C.A. 2, 1917).

14.
Family Law and Family Life

1 47 Stat. 406 (act of June 30, 1932).

2 James B. Atleson, *Labor and the Wartime State: Labor Relations and Law During World War II* (1998), pp. 164–169.

3 Matthew J. Lindsay, "Reproducing a Fit Citizenry: Dependency, Eugenics, and the Law of Marriage in the United States, 1860–1920," *Law & Social Inquiry* 23:541, 578 (1998). Quotations at p. 572.

4 On the origin of this device, see Lawrence M. Friedman, *A History of American Law,* pp. 202–204.

5 *McChesney v. Johnson,* 79 S.W. 2d 658, 659 (Ct. Civ. Appeals, Texas, 1935). I am indebted to Cliff Z. Liu for this reference.

6 Laws Neb. 1923, ch. 40, p. 154.

7 Morris Ploscowe, *Sex and the Law* (1951), p. 23; I am indebted to Cliff Z. Liu for this reference.

8 *Luther v. Shaw,* 157 Wis. 231, 147 N.W. 17 (1914). Elsie's father also sued the hapless Shaw, to recover damages "for loss of services of a daughter, caused by her seduction and consequent sickness"; and he too was successful. An award of $1,500 was upheld. *Luther v. Shaw,* 157 Wis. 231, 234, 147 N.W. 17, 20 (1914).

9 Theodore W. Cousens, "The Law of Damages as Applied to Breach of Promise of Marriage," *Cornell L. Rev.* 17:367, 372 (1932).

10 Nathan P. Feinsinger, "Legislative Attack on 'Heart Balm,'" *Michigan Law Review* 33:979 (1935).

11 Laws Indiana 1935, ch. 208.

12 *Kreyling v. Kreyling,* 20 N.J. Misc. 52, 23 Atl. 2d 800 (1942).

13 Chester G. Vernier, *American Family Laws* (vol. 2, 1932), pp. 67, 69.

14 Paul H. Jacobson, *American Marriage and Divorce* (1959), p. 122.

15 These cases are San Diego Superior Court no. 17650, filed Jan. 13, 1912; and no. 28198, filed Nov. 9, 1917.

16 Sam B. Warner, "San Francisco Divorce Suits," *Cal. L. Rev.* 9:175 (1921).

17 Jacobson, *American Marriage and Divorce,* p. 123.

18 Ibid., p. 113.

19 Cited in Note, "Collusive and Consensual Divorce and the New York Anomaly," *Columbia L. Rev.* 36:1121, 1131n (1936).

20 Frank W. Ingram and G. A. Ballard, "The Business of Migratory Divorce in Nevada," *Law and Contemporary Problems* 2:302 (1935).

21 317 U.S. 287 (1942); 325 U.S. 226 (1944).

22 J. Herbie DiFonzo, *Beneath the Fault Line: The Popular and Legal Culture of Divorce in Twentieth-Century America* (1997), p. 61.

23 William O'Neill, *Divorce in the Progressive Era* (1967).

24 See Paul W. Alexander, foreword to Maxine B. Virtue, *Family Cases in Court* (1956), p. xxxi.

25 See DiFonzo, *Beneath the Fault Line,* pp. 114–120.

26 Louis H. Burke, "Conciliation: A New Approach to the Divorce Problem," *Journal of the State Bar of California* 30:199 (1955).

27 These typical agreements are found ibid., p. 207; Louis H. Burke, *With This Ring* (1958), pp. 270–280. For a discussion, see Di Fonzo, *Beneath the Fault Line,* p. 164.

28 Laws N.Y. 1966, ch. 254, p. 833.

29 On the background and spread of no-fault, see Herbert Jacob, *Silent Revolution: The Transformation of Divorce Law in the United States* (1988)

30 On these statutes, see DiFonzo, *Beneath the Fault Line,* pp. 69–70, 75–80.

31 Jacob, *Silent Revolution,* p. 80.

32 DiFonzo, *Beneath the Fault Line,* p. 172.

33 Allen M. Parkman, *No-Fault Divorce: What Went Wrong?* (1992), pp. 79–88.

34 *In the Matter of Baby M,* 109 N.J. 396, 537 A. 2d 1227 (1988).

35 Ky. Rev. Stat., §199.590 (1988); Ariz. Rev. Stat. Ann., §25–218 (1989); Neb. Rev. Stat., §25–21 (1988).

36 E.g., Mich. Comp. Laws, §§722.851 ff. (1988).

37 Fla. Stat. §63.212 (1) (1988).

38 Laws Mass. 1851, ch. 324, p. 815.

39 See, for example, Robert D. McFadden, "Girl, 4, Is Dead in Manhattan and Her Mother Is Charged," *New York Times,* Sept. 2, 1966.

40 Laws Minn. 1917, ch. 222, p. 335.

41 The case is described in William E. Nelson, "Patriarchy or Equality: Family Values or Individuality," *St. John's Law Review* 70:435, 473–475 (1996).

42 Laws Ill. 1931, p. 734; Laws Ill. 1937, p. 1006; Ill. Rev. Stat. 1939, ch. 111 1/2 §§48a, 57.6, pp. 2486, 2489.

43 Stuart W. Thayer, "Moppets on the Market: The Problem of Unregulated Adoption," *Yale L.J.* 50: 715 (1950).

44 *National Committee for Adoption, Adoption Factbook* (1985).

45 "3 Accused Here in Adoption Ring," *New York Times,* Dec. 6, 1949.

46 Thayer, "Moppets on the Market," pp. 734, 736.

47 Linda Gordon, *The Great Arizona Orphan Abduction* (2000).

48 See Ruth-Arlene W. Howe, "Adoption Practice, Issues, and Laws, 1958–1983," *Family Law Quarterly* 17:273 (1983).

49 92 Stat. 3069 (act of Nov. 8, 1978).

50 Laws Ariz. 1921, ch. 114, p. 248.

51 Laws No. Dak. 1969, ch. 466, p. 1002.

52 391 U.S. 68 (1968).

53 *Glona v. American Guarantee and Liability Insurance Company,* 369 U.S. 73 (1968), at 80. *Glona* struck down a statute which did not allow the mother of an illegitimate child to collect for its wrongful death. Harlan's dissent was to both *Glona* and *Levy.*

54 *Statistical Abstract of the United States* (1999), p. 79.

55 *People v. C. H. Hamilton,* San Diego Superior Court no. 17701 (January 1912).

56 18 Cal. 3d 660, 557 P. 2d 106, 134 Cal. R. 815 (1976).

57 *Hewitt v. Hewitt,* 394 N.E. 2d 1209 (Ill., 1979).

58 *Davis v. Davis,* 643 So. 2d 931 (Mississippi, 1994).

59 Laws Minn. 1980, ch. 553.

60 Fla. Rev. Stat. 1920, ch. 8, §668, p. 510.

61 Laws Nev. 1921, ch. 168, p. 255.

62 Miss. Code 1930, §6843, p. 2765.

63 Laws Ill. 1909, p. 415.

64 La. Rev. Stat. 17:274.

65 La. Rev. Stat. 17:281.

66 On this point, see Warren I. Susman, *Culture as History: The Transformation of American Society in the Twentieth Century* (1985), ch. 14.

67 487 P. 2d 1241 (Cal., 1971), at 1247.

68 411 U.S. 1 (1973).

69 *Thompson v. Engelking,* 96 Idaho 793, 537 P. 2d 635 (1975).

70 *Rose v. Council for Better Education,* 790 S.W. 2d 186 (1989).

71 Stephen K. Bailey and Edith Mosher, *ESEA: The Office of Education Administers a Law* (1968), pp. 17–18.

72 39 Stat. 929 (act of Feb. 23, 1917).

73 60 Stat. 230 (act of June 4, 1946).

74 58 Stat. 284 (act of June 22, 1944).

75 68 Stat. 897, 900 (act of Aug. 28, 1954).

76 72 Stat. 1580 (act of Sept. 2, 1958).

77 Quoted in *Congressional Quarterly, Congress, and the Nation, 1945–1964: A Review of*

Government and Politics in the Postwar Years (1965), p. 1203. I am indebted to Chris Glaros for this reference.

78 79 Stat. 27 (act of Apr. 11, 1965).

79 See 81 Stat. 804 (act of Jan. 2, 1968).

80 Laws Terr. Hawaii 1949, Act. 29, p. 98.

81 *State ex rel. Beattie v. Board of Education of Antigo,* 169 Wis. 231, 172 N.W. 153 (1919).

82 334 F. Supp. 1257 (D.C.E.D. Pa., 1971). Another important case was *Mills v. Board of Education of the District of Columbia,* 348 F. Supp. 866 (D.C.D.C., 1972).

83 89 Stat. 773 (act of Nov. 29, 1975).

84 Philip Jenkins, *Moral Panic: Changing Concepts of the Child Molester in Modern America* (1998), p. 225.

85 Ibid., p. 129.

15
Internal Legal Culture

1 Barbara A. Curran and Clara N. Carson, *The Lawyer Statistical Report: The U.S. Legal Profession in the 1990s* (1994), p. 1.

2 *Chronicle of Higher Education,* almanac issue, 44, no. 1, p. 26 (1998).

3 U.S. Department of Labor, *Employment Opportunities for Women in Legal Work,* Women's Bureau Bulletin, no. 265, p. 10 (1958).

4 Arthur E. Sutherland, *The Law at Harvard: A History of Ideas and Men, 1817–1967* (1967), pp. 319–320.

5 Paul Anderson, *Janet Reno: Doing the Right Thing* (1994), pp. 37–39.

6 *Chronicle of Higher Education,* 1998 almanac issue.

7 Sheldon Goldman, *Picking Federal Judges: Lower Court Selection from Roosevelt Through Reagan* (1997), p. 350.

8 *Lawyer's Almanac* (1999), pp. J-27–32.

9 Allan P. Sindler, *Bakke, DeFunis, and Minority Admissions: The Quest for Equal Opportunity* (1978), p. 141.

10 Goldman, *Picking Federal Judges,* p. 101.

11 On Garza's life and career, see Louise Ann Fisch, *All Rise: Reynaldo G. Garza, the First Mexican American Federal Judge* (1996).

12 Paul Marcotte, "Few Asian-American Judges," *American Bar Association Journal* 76:16 (1990).

13 Michael J. Powell, *From Patrician to Professional Elite: The Transformation of the New York City Bar Association* (1988), p. 49.

14 Ann. Rpt., American Bar Ass'n 76:224 (1951).

15 Michael D. Goldhaber, "Minorities Surge at Big Law Firms," *National Law Journal* 21, no. 14, p. A1 (1998).

16 Darryl Van Duch, "Minority GCs Are Few, Far Between: Only 10 Fortune 500 Firms Have Minority General Counsel," *National Law Journal* 22, no. 8, p. A1 (Oct. 18, 1999).

17 John P. Heinz and Edward O. Laumann, *Chicago Lawyers: The Social Structure of the Bar* (1982), p. 40. Eight percent of the legal effort was put in the category of "general, unspecified legal work."

18 Survey of the Legal Profession *The Second Statistical Report on the Lawyers of the United States* (1952), p. 2; Barbara Curran et al., *The Lawyer Statistical Report: A Statistical Profile of the U.S. Legal Profession in the 1980s* (1985), pp. 17, 19; Curran and Carson, *The Lawyer Statistical Report* (1994), p. 7; Clara N. Carson, *The Lawyer Statistical Report: The United States Legal Profession in 1995* (1999), p. 10.

19 Joseph A. Ranney, *Trusting Nothing to Providence: A History of Wisconsin's Legal System* (1999), p. 603.

20 Marc Galanter and Thomas Palay, *Tournament of Lawyers: The Transformation of the Big Law Firm* (1991), p. 46.

21 Carson, *The Lawyer Statistical Report* (1999), p. 17.

22 Ranney, *Trusting Nothing to Providence,* p. 603.

23 Lawrence M. Friedman, *American Law: An Introduction* (2d ed., 1998), p. 271.

24 Galanter and Palay, *Tournament of Lawyers,* p. 36.

25 Ron Chernow, *The House of Morgan* (1990), pp. 599–600.

26 Galanter and Palay, *Tournament of Lawyers,* chap. 4.

27 433 U.S. 350 (1977).

28 These are taken from Illinois State Bar Association, *Manual on Fees and Charges Including Suggested Minimum Fee Schedule of the Illinois State Bar Association* (1962).

29 Robert M. Rowland, "Lawyers' Fees," *Texas Bar Journal* 6:538 (1943).

30 421 U.S. 773 (1975).

31 *SF Weekly* vol. 17, no. 12, p. 112 (1998).

32 This report is reprinted in *Unauthorized Practice News* 34, no. 4, pp. 1, 17 (1958).

33 Ibid., pp. 22, 35 (1958).

34 The incident is related in Catherine J. Lanctot, "Attorney-Client Relationships in Cyberspace: The Peril and the Promise," *Duke L. Journal* 49:147, 198–218 (1999).

35 Robert L. Nelson, "The Futures of American Lawyers: A Demographic Profile of a Changing Profession in a Changing Society," *Case Western Reserve Law Review* 44:345, 373 (1994).

36 Quoted in Stephanie B. Goldberg, "Then and Now: 75 Years of Change," *ABA Journal* 76:56, 58 (1990).

37 William G. Ross, *The Honest Hour: The Ethics of Time-Based Billing by Attorneys* (1996), pp. 18, 20.

38 Herbert M. Kritzer, "Lawyers' Fees and the Holy Grail: Where Should Clients Search for Value?" *Judicature* 77:187 (1994).

39 Goldberg, "Then and Now," p. 60.

40 Galanter and Palay, *Tournament of Lawyers,* p. 40.

41 Marc Galanter, "Law Abounding: Legalization Around the North Atlantic," *Modern L. Rev.* 55:1 (1992); Richard H. Sander, "Elevating the Debate on Lawyers and Economic Growth," *Law and Social Inquiry* 17:659 (1992).

42 Charles P. Epp, "Do Lawyers Impair Economic Growth?" *Law & Social Inquiry* 17:585 (1992).

43 Ronald J. Gilson, "Value Creation by Business Lawyers: Legal Skills and Asset Pricing," *Yale L.J.* 94:239 (1984).

44 *San Francisco Recorder,* Dec. 20, 1999, p. 1.

45 Northwestern University School of Law, *Report of the Dean of the Faculty of Law* [John H. Wigmore] *on an Educational Survey, 1925* (1925), p. 258.

46 Friedman, *American Law,* pp. 285–286.

47 James Barron, "400 Jobs for Lawyers Who Don't Want to Be Lawyers," *New York Times,* Jan. 28, 1994.

48 L. Christina Valdes, "Former Big-Firm Lawyer Finds Happiness as an Artist," *San Jose Post-Record,* April 25, 1995.

49 Samuel Walker, *In Defense of American Liberties* (1990), p. 111.

50 Joel F. Handler, Ellen J. Hollingsworth, and Howard S. Erlanger, *Lawyers and the Pursuit of Legal Rights* (1978), p. 70.

51 Tamar Lewin, "Talking Business with Roger J. Marzulla of Mountain States Legal Foundation: Free Market Philosophy," *New York Times,* July 20, 1982; see Roger K. Newman, "Public-Interest Firms Crop Up on the Right," *National Law Journal* 18, no. 52, p. A1 (1996).

52 Martha F. Davis, *Brutal Need: Lawyers and the Welfare Rights Movement, 1960–1973* (1993), pp. 10, 144.

53 The quotation is the subtitle of David J. Langum's biography, *William M. Kunstler* (1999).

54 William M. Kunstler, with Sheila Isenberg, *My Life as a Radical Lawyer* (1994), pp. 340–341.

55 Marc Galanter, "The Faces of Mistrust: The Image of Lawyers in Public Opinion, Jokes, and Political Discourse," *U. of Cincinnati L. Rev.* 66:805, 811 (1998).

56 Ibid., p. 820.

57 Ibid.

58 "Bashing Lawyers. Also Justice," *New York Times,* Feb. 15, 1992.

59 David Rosenbaum, "House Hears Grim Tales About Managed Care," *New York Times,* October 8, 1999; Robin Toner, "The Ad Campaign: Health Plans Depict Lawyers as Threat," ibid.

60 David Ray Papke, "Conventional Wisdom: The Courtroom Trial in American Popular Culture," *Marquette L. Rev.* 82:471, 478 (1999).

61 Marc Gunther, "The Little Judge Who Kicked Oprah's Butt: Daytime Television's Hottest Property," *Fortune,* May 10, 1999, p. 32.

62 See Neal Gabler, *Life, the Movie: How Entertainment Conquered Reality* (1998).

63 Arkansas Judiciary Commission, *Report to 1965 General Assembly,* p. 124, appendix, n.p.

64 Cynthia O. Philip, Paul Nejelski, and Aric Press, *Where Do Judges Come From?* (1976), introduction, pp. i, ii.

65 Larry Aspin, "Trends in Judicial Retention Elections, 1964–1998," *Judicature* 83:79 (1999).

66 Sheldon Goldman, *Picking Federal Court Judges: Lower Court Selection from Roosevelt Through Reagan* (1997), p. 3; I have relied heavily on the Goldman book in this section.

67 Ibid., pp. 86–88, 177.

68 Robert A. Kagan et al., "The Business of State Supreme Courts, 1870–1970," *Stanford L. Rev.* 30:121 (1977).

69 These figures come from the Annual Reports of the Administrative Office of the United States Courts: 1940, pp. 68, 86; 1961, pp. 222–223; 1992, p. 31.

70 These figures are from table III, "The Supreme Court, 1968 Term," *Harvard Law Review* 83:282 (1969).

71 Jeffrey A. Segal and Harold J. Spaeth, *The Supreme Court and the Attitudinal Model* (1993), p. 186.

72 *Wilson v. Pacific Mail Steamship Co.,* 276 U.S. 454 (1928).

73 Richard L. Pacelle, Jr., *The Transformation of the Supreme Court's Agenda: From the New Deal to the Reagan Administration* (1991), pp. 56–57 and graph, p. 194.

74 Quoted in Lawrence M. Friedman, *Total Justice* (1985), p. 16.

75 See the account in Marc Galanter, "Reading the Landscape of Disputes: What We Know and Don't Know (and Think We Know) about our Allegedly Contentious and Litigious Society," *UCLA Law Review* 31:4 (1983).

76 Gerry Spence, *The Making of a Country Lawyer* (1996), p. 320.

77 Charles M. Lyman, "A Tradition Dies in Connecticut: Law Office Preparation for the Bar is Abolished," *American Bar Association Journal* 36:21 (1950). Lyman, a practicing lawyer in New Haven, regretted the passing of this "tradition."

78 State Bar of California, www.calbar.org/shared/2admst/797.htm; calbar.org/shared/2admst/298.htm (visited Aug. 19, 1999).

79 Robert Stevens, *Law School: Legal Education in America from the 1850s to the 1980s* (1983), pp. 177, 180.

80 Marion Rice Kirkwood and William Bowers, *A Brief History of the Stanford Law School, 1893–1946* (1961) (typescript, Stanford Law Library, pp. 40–41).

81 Stevens, *Law School,* pp. 197, 209.

82 Arthur E. Sutherland, *The Law at Harvard: A History of Ideas and Men, 1816–1967* (1967), pp. 308–309.

83 George D. Braden, "Use of the Law School Admission Test at the Yale Law School," *J. Legal Education* 3:202 (1950).

84 A. Pemberton Johnson, "The Development and Use of Law Aptitude Tests," *J. Legal Education* 3:192, 193 (1950).

85 Sutherland, *The Law at Harvard,* pp. 221, 322.

86 Spence, *The Making of a Country Lawyer,* pp. 222–223.

87 Evelyn Williams, *Inadmissible Evidence* (1993), p. 31.

88 Sutherland, *The Law at Harvard,* p. 320.

89 Attrition figures for 1991–1995 are from the annual reports of the American Bar Association, Section of Legal Education and Admissions to the Bar, *A Review of Legal Education in the United States.* Figures for 1998 are from American Bar Association, Section

of Legal Education and Admissions to the Bar, *ABA Approved Law Schools: Statistical Information on American Bar Association Approved Law Schools* (1998).

90 This was, in any event, not really possible; at least the first-year curriculum was fixed, and students did not choose their professors—they were assigned to them.

91 See David C. Yamada, "Same Old, Same Old: Law School Rankings and the Affirmation of Hierarchy," *Suffolk U. L. Rev.* 31:249 (1997).

92 Donna Fossum, "Law Professors: A Profile of the Teaching Branch of the Legal Profession," *American Bar Foundation Research Journal* 1980:501, 507; Robert J. Borthwick and Jordan R. Schau, "Gatekeepers of the Profession: An Empirical Profile of the Nation's Law Professors," *University of Mich. J. of Law Reform,* 25:191, 227 (1991).

93 Harlan B. Phillips, ed., *Felix Frankfurter Reminisces* (1960), p. 78.

94 Michael E. Parrish, *Felix Frankfurter and His Times: The Reform Years* (1982), p. 157.

95 Laura Kalman, *Legal Realism at Yale,* p. 143.

96 Fossum, "Law Professors," p. 506.

97 Borthwick and Schau, "Gatekeepers of the Profession," p. 199.

98 Richard H. Chused, "The Hiring and Retention of Minorities and Women on American Law School Faculties," *U. Pa. L. Rev.* 137:537, 539, 556 (1988).

99 American Bar Association, *Annual Review of Legal Education for 1937,* p. 63.

100 *Law Schools and Bar Admission Requirements in the United States,* 1951 Review of Legal Education, Section of Legal Education and Admissions to the Bar of the American Bar Association, p. 18.

101 American Bar Association, *Review of Legal Education: Law Schools and Bar Admission Requirements in the United States,* fall 1970, p. 46.

102 Association of American Law Schools, *Directory of Teachers in Member Schools,* 1922.

103 Figures from Richard A. White, *Association of American Law Schools Statistical Report on Law School Faculty,* www.aals.org/statistics/rpt9899w.html (visited in July 2000).

104 The figures are from the California State Bar Association, quoted in Howard Mintz, "Law School Online," *San Jose Mercury,* Nov. 15, 1999.

105 *Official ABA Guide to Approved Law Schools,* 1999, pp. 36–37.

106 Michael A. Olivas, "Paying for a Law Degree: Trends in Student Borrowing and the Ability to Repay Debt," *J. Legal Education* 49:335 (1999).

107 Mark Hansen, "The Party's Over for Summer Interns," *ABA Journal* 80:22 (1994).

108 Cynthia L. Cooper, *The Insider's Guide to the Top Fifteen Law Schools* (1990), pp. 396–397.

109 Information supplied by the Alumni Relations Office of Stanford Law School.

110 On the jurisprudence of the Restatements, see G. Edward White, "The American Law Institute and the Triumph of Modernist Jurisprudence," *Law and History Review* 15:1 (1997).

111 *American Bar Ass'n Rpts* 29:395 (1906).

112 On Pound and the realists, see N. E. H. Hull, *Roscoe Pound and Karl Llewellyn: Searching for an American Jurisprudence* (1997).

113 Morton J. Horwitz, *The Transformation of American Law, 1870–1960: The Crisis of Legal Orthodoxy* (1992), pp. 187–188.

114 Robert Jerome Glennon, *The Iconoclast as Reformer: Jerome Frank's Impact on American Law* (1985), p. 22.

115 Jerome Frank, *Law and the Modern Mind* (1930), pp. 118, 120, 131, 248.

116 Thurman Arnold, *Folklore of Capitalism* (1937), pp. 25, 29, 348.

117 Quoted in William Twining, *Karl Llewellyn and the Realist Movement* (1973), p. 126. The Twining book is an excellent study of Llewellyn's work and thought. On Llewellyn's relationship with Pound, and the polemics on the realist movement in the 1930s, see Hull, *Roscoe Pound and Karl Llewellyn.*

118 Karl N. Llewellyn, "Some Realism About Realism: Responding to Dean Pound," *Harv. L. Rev.* 44:1222, 1236–1237 (1930).

119 Barbara Fried, *The Progressive Assault on Laissez Faire: Robert Hale and the First Law and Economics Movement* (1998), p. 13.

120 Horwitz, *Transformation of American Law,* p. 253.

121 See, for a general account of the thought of this movement, Mark Kelman, *A Guide to Critical Legal Studies* (1987).

122 Laura Kalman, *The Strange Career of Legal Liberalism* (1996), p. 84.

123 One of Bell's major works was *And We Are Not Saved: The Elusive Quest for Racial Justice* (1987).

124 See, for example, Francisco Valdes, Foreword, "Under Construction: LatCrit Consciousness, Community, and Theory," *Cal. L. Rev.* 85:1089 (1997); Robert S. Chang, "Toward an Asian American Legal Scholarship: Critical Race Theory, Post-Structuralism, and Narrative Space," *Cal. L. Rev.* 81:1241 (1993).

125 Robert Hale, who had both a law degree and an economics degree, had been on the faculty of Columbia Law School from around 1920.

126 Richard A. Posner, *Economic Analysis of Law* (1952), p. 1.

127 Richard Posner, *Sex and Reason* (1992); *An Affair of State: The Investigation, Impeachment, and Trial of President Clinton* (1999).

128 Posner, *Economic Analysis,* pp. 134–135.

129 Catharine MacKinnon, *Feminism Unmodified: Discourses on Life and Law* (1987).

130 Northwestern University School of Law, *Report of the Dean of the Faculty of Law* [John H. Wigmore] *on an Educational Survey, 1925* (1925), p. 75.

131 Albert J. Harno, *Legal Education in the United States* (1953), pp. 193–194.

132 Bernard J. Hibbitts, "Last Writes? Reassessing the Law Review in the Age of Cyberspace," *New York U. L. Rev.* 71: 615, 638–639 (1996).

133 Michael L. Closen and Robert J. Dzielak, "The History and Influence of the Law Review Institution," *Akron L. Rev.* 30: 15, 38 (1996).

134 This journal, since 1931, has been called the *Journal of Criminal Law and Criminology.* For this and other information about the specialized law reviews, I have relied on Tracey E. George and Chris Guthrie, "An Empirical Evaluation of Specialized Law

Reviews," *Fla. St. U. L. Rev.* 26: 813 (1999).

135 Wes Daniels, " 'Far Beyond the Law Reports': Secondary Source Citations in United States Supreme Court Opinions; October Terms 1900, 1940, and 1978," *Law Library Journal* 76:1, 30 (1983).

136 J. Willard Hurst, *Law and Economic Growth* (1964), p. 4; a special issue of *Law and History Review,* vol. 18, no. 1 (spring 2000), was devoted to the life and work of Hurst.

137 John Henry Schlegel, *American Legal Realism and Empirical Social Science* (1995).

138 Leon C. Marshall and Geoffrey May, *The Divorce Court* (2 vols., 1932).

139 Karl N. Llewellyn and E. Adamson Hoebel, *The Cheyenne Way: Conflict and Caselaw in Primitive Jurisprudence* (1941).

140 On the history of the movement, see Bryant Garth and Joyce Sterling, "From Legal Realism to Law and Society: Reshaping Law for the Last Stages of the Social Activist State," *Law & Society Review* 32:409 (1998).

141 *Law and Society Review,* 1:3, 6–7 (1966).

142 I myself served a stint as president of the Law and Society Association, and have also been a member of its Board of Trustees. Other law-professor presidents have included Stewart Macaulay, Marc Galanter, and Joel Handler.

143 Stewart Macaulay, "Non-Contractual Relations in Business: A Preliminary Study," *American Sociological Review* 28:55 (1963); in 1985, the Wisconsin Law Review published a symposium on the occasion of the twentieth anniversary of this famous study, under the title "Symposium: Law, Private Governance, and Continuing Relationships." Marc Galanter, "Why the Haves Come Out Ahead: Speculation on the Limits of Legal Change," *Law & Society Review* 9:95 (1974).

144 See, for example, Valerie P. Hans and Neil Vidmar, *Judging the Jury* (1986).

145 Schlegel, *American Legal Realism,* p. 256.

16.
American Legal Culture in the Twentieth Century

1 The best account of this case is Edward J. Larson, *Summer for the Gods: The Scopes Trial and America's Continuing Debate over Science and Religion* (1997).

2 Ibid, pp. 188–189.

3 Ibid., p. 250.

4 *Epperson v. Arkansas,* 393 U.S. 97 (1968).

5 *Edwards v. Aguillard,* 482 U.S. 578 (1987). Scalia and Rehnquist dissented.

6 Pam Belluck, "Board for Kansas Deletes Evolution from Curriculum," *New York Times,* Aug. 12, 1999; the board of education also "deleted from its standards a description of the Big Bang theory of cosmic origins." *New York Times,* Oct. 10, 1999. The election in 2000, in which the conservative candidates for the Kansas Board of Education were defeated, turned largely on the controversy over evolution.

7 406 U.S. 205 (1972).

8 268 U.S. 510 (1925); on the background of this law, see William G. Ross, *Forging New Freedoms: Nativism, Education, and the Constitution, 1917–1927* (1994), chap. 8, "The Oregon School Law."

9 330 U.S. 1 (1947).

10 370 U.S. 421 (1962).

11 *Abington School District v. Schempp,* 374 U.S. 203 (1963).

12 *Wallace v. Jaffree,* 472 U.S. 38 (1985).

13 On this point, see Herbert McClosky and Alida Brill, *Dimensions of Tolerance: What Americans Believe About Civil Liberties* (1983); on school officials, see William K. Muir, Jr., *Prayer in the Public Schools: Law and Attitude Change* (1967).

14 Pa. Stats. 1920, §§5093, 5094.

15 Laws No. Dak. 1911, ch. 266, §276, p. 474.

16 *State ex rel. Freeman v. Scheve,* 65 Neb. 853, 91 N.W. 846 (1902).

17 403 U.S. 602 (1971). A Pennsylvania program of state aid to church-related schools for teachers' salaries, similar to the Rhode Island plan, was also struck down.

18 *Lynch v. Donnelly,* 465 U.S. 668 (1984). The dissent pointed out that the crèche had a "distinctively religious element," and was not just part of holiday and commercial cheer.

19 Scalia, J., concurring in *Lamb's Chapel v. Center Moriches School District,* 508 U.S. 384 (1993), at 398.

20 461 U.S. 574 (1983).

21 505 U.S. 577 (1992).

22 These last phrases are translations into English, with some changes, of a standard Hebrew prayer.

23 Robert Bellah et al., *Habits of the Heart: Individualism and Commitment in American Life* (1985); Lawrence M. Friedman, *The Republic of Choice: Law, Authority, and Culture* (1990).

24 414 U.S. 632 (1974); the account of the case is taken from Peter Irons, *The Courage of Their Convictions* (1988), chap. 13, pp. 307–329.

25 Irons, *Courage of Their Convictions,* p. 321.

26 *Davis v. Meek,* 462 Fed. 2d 960 (C.A. 5, 1972).

27 *Indiana High School Athletic Association v. Raike,* 329 N.E. 2d 66 (Ind. App. 1975).

17.
Backward and Forward

1 410 U.S. 113 (1973).

2 R. W. Apple, Jr., "The Thomas Confirmation," *New York Times,* Oct. 16, 1991.

3 George L. Watson and John A. Stookey, *Shaping America: The Politics of Supreme Court Appointments* (1995), p. 63.

4 See J. Larry Hood, "The Nixon Administration and the Revised Philadelphia Plan for Affirmative Action: A Study in Expanding Presidential Power and Divided Government," *Presidential Studies Quarterly* 23:145 (1993).

5 Bayard Rustin, "The Blacks and the Unions," *Harper's Magazine,* May 1971, p. 73.

6 480 U.S. 616 (1987); for an account of the case and its significance, see Melvin I. Urofsky, *Affirmative Action on Trial: Sex Discrimination in Johnson v. Santa Clara* (1997).

7 448 U.S. 448 (1980).

8 515 U.S. 200 (1995).

9 In *Richmond v. J. A. Croson Co.,* 488 U.S. 469 (1989), the city of Richmond, Virginia, decided that 30 percent of its contracting had to go to minority-owned businesses. The Supreme Court struck this arrangement down.

10 *Hopwood v. Texas,* 84 Fed. 3d 96 (C.A. 5, 1996); the denial of certiorari is *Texas v. Hopwood,* 518 U.S. 1033 (1996).

11 Cal. Const. Art. 1, §31.

12 "Minority Admissions Fall with Preferences Ban," *Washington Post,* May 19, 1997.

13 See, for example, "Tien's Alternative to Affirmative Action," *San Francisco Chronicle,* Jan. 2, 1996.

14 *The State of Disunion: 1996 Survey of American Political Culture* (vol. 2, summary tables, 1996), table 42F. A bare majority thought that homosexuals should be allowed to serve in the armed forces; but sizable majorities opposed gay marriage and adoption of children by gays. Ibid., tables 42B, 42C, 42D.

15 478 U.S. 186 (1986).

16 The Colorado decision was *Evans v. Romer,* 882 P. 2d 1335 (Colo., 1994); the Supreme Court decision was *Romer v. Evans,* 517 U.S. 620 (1996). The case, as one can imagine, evoked a great deal of comment. See, for example, Jane S. Schacter, "*Romer v. Evans* and Democracy's Domain," *Vanderbilt Law Review* 50:362 (1997).

17 *Romer v. Evans,* at 647.

18 *Texas v. Johnson,* 491 U.S. 397 (1989).

19 Robert Justin Goldstein, *Burning the Flag: The Great 1989–1990 American Flag Desecration Controversy* (1996), p. 5.

20 Ibid., pp. 40, 113–122.

21 *United States v. Eichman,* 486 U.S. 310 (1990).

22 Goldstein, *Burning the Flag,* p. 334.

23 505 U.S. 833 (1992).

24 William H. Rehnquist, "Who Writes Decisions of the Supreme Court?" *U.S. News and World Report,* Dec. 13, 1957, p. 74.

25 William Domnarski, *In the Opinion of the Court* (1996), p. 41.

26 Dennis J. Hutchinson, *The Man Who Once Was Whizzer White: A Portrait of Justice Byron R. White* (1998), p. 206.

27 Domnarski, *In the Opinion of the Court,* pp. 42–43.

28 507 U.S. 349 (1993).

29 Charles H. Sheldon, "The Evolution of Law Clerking with the Washington Supreme Court: From 'Elbow Clerks' to 'Puisne Judges,'" *Gonzaga Law Rev.* 25:45, 47 (1988).

30 *Commonwealth v. Wasson,* 842 S.W. 2d 487 (Ky. S. Ct., 1993). The Court also empha-

sized an equal-protection point: unlike the Georgia statute, the Kentucky statute was aimed only at same-sex behavior. Three justices dissented.

31 *Powell v. State,* 270 Ga. 327, 510 S.E. 2d 18 (1998).

32 Barbara H. Craig and David M. O'Brien, *Abortion and American Politics* (1993), pp. 348–349.

33 See Robert Pear, "Benefit Funds May Run Out of Cash Soon, Reports Warn," *New York Times,* Apr. 12, 1994.

34 Michael B. Katz, *In the Shadow of the Poorhouse: A Social History of Welfare in America* (rev. ed., 1996), p. 327.

35 Clinton quoted in Joel F. Handler, *The Poverty of Welfare Reform* (1995), p. 110; for a critique of workfare plans, ibid., pp. 113–124.

36 110 Stat. 2105 (act of Aug. 22, 1996).

37 Katz, *In the Shadow of the Poorhouse,* p. 330.

38 See, for example, Carol S. Weissert, ed., *Learning from Leaders: Welfare Reform Politics and Policy in Five Midwestern States* (2000). The states are Ohio, Kansas, Wisconsin, Minnesota, and Michigan.

39 See, in general, Robert M. Hayden, "The Cultural Logic of a Political Crisis: Common Sense, Hegemony, and the Great American Liability Insurance Famine of 1986," in *Studies in Law, Politics, and Society,* vol. 11, p. 95 (1991). On the McDonald's coffee incident and its coverage, see Mark B. Greenlee, "Kramer v. Java World: Images, Issues, and Idols in the Debate over Tort Reform," *Cap. U. L. Rev.* 26:701 (1997).

40 See, in general, Stephen Daniels and Joanne Martin, *Civil Juries and the Politics of Reform* (1995).

41 See Marc Galanter, "An Oil Strike in Hell: Contemporary Legends about the Civil Justice System," *Ariz. L. Rev.* 40:717, 726–727 (1998).

42 Carl T. Bogus, "Pistols, Politics, and Products Liability," *Univ. Cin. L. Rev.* 59:1103, 1158–1161 (1991).

43 Punitive damages are those that are in excess of actual losses—extra damages piled on as punishment or deterrence against defendants who were reckless or malicious.

44 See Stephen Daniels and Joanne Martin, "Myth and Reality in Punitive Damages," *Minn. L. Rev.* 75:1 (1990).

45 See William Glaberson, "Damage Control, a Special Report: Some Plaintiffs Losing Out in Texas' War on Lawsuits," *New York Times,* June 7, 1999.

46 *Helen J. Kelly's Case,* 394 Mass. 684, 477 N.E. 2d 582 (1985).

47 741 Pac. 2d 634 (Alaska, 1987).

48 Cal. Labor Code, §3208.3; Laws Cal. 1989, ch. 892, §25.

49 *California Department of Industrial Relations, 1996–1997 Biennial Report,* p. 14.

50 Idaho Code, Tit. 72, §72–451 (2). There were also to be no claims for psychological injuries without "accompanying physical injury."

51 See, in general, Dennis Baron, *The English-Only Question* (1990).

52 Lawrence M. Friedman, *The Horizontal Society* (1999), p. 186.

53 A map showing these laws, as of mid-1990, is in Baron, *The English-Only Question,* p. 201.

54 See E. Cronon, *Black Moses: The Story of Marcus Garvey and the Universal Negro Improvement Association* (1955); Gary Peller, "Race Consciousness," 1990 *Duke L.J.* 758, 785.

55 Jane J. Mansbridge, *Why We Lost the ERA* (1986), pp. 1, 175. The Mansbridge book is the source for most of this account of ERA.

56 William A. Galston, "Rethinking Progressive Politics," *New Democrat,* Sept.–Oct., 1996, p. 48: "As late as the mid-1960s, three-quarters of the American people trusted the federal government to do the right thing all or most of the time; today, that figure is below 25 percent." See also, Ronald Brownstein, "Clinton's Job One: Reversing the Anti-Government Tide," *The Public Perspective* 5, no. 4, p. 3.

57 80 Stat. 383 (act of Sept. 6, 1966).

58 See Charles J. Wichmann III, "Ridding FOIA of Those 'Unanticipated Consequences': Repaving a Necessary Road to Freedom," *Duke L. Journal* 47:1213 (1998).

59 Laws Ark. 1967, No. 93, p. 209.

18.
Getting Around and Spreading the Word

1 Laws N.Y. 1910, vol. 1, ch. 374, §§287, 290(3), pp. 681, 685.

2 Ky. Stats. 1915 (vol. 3, 1918 supp.), p. 610, §§2739g-9, 2739g-9a.

3 43 Stat. 1119 (act of Mar. 3, 1925).

4 *Historical Statistics of the United States,* vol. 2, p. 716 (1975); Jonathan Simon, "Driving Governmentality: Automobile Accidents, Insurance, and the Challenge to Social Order in the Inter-war Years, 1919–1941," *Conn. Ins. L. Journal* 4:521, 531–532 (1998).

5 *Historical Statistics of the United States,* vol. 2, p. 717.

6 *Statistical Abstract of the United States, 1998,* pp. 633, 635.

7 Corey T. Lesseig, " 'Out of the Mud': The Good Roads Crusade and Social Change in Twentieth-Century Mississippi," *J. Mississippi History* 60:51, 59 (1998).

8 Ruth Schwartz Cowan, *A Social History of Technology* (1997), pp. 233–234.

9 The law was 20 Stat. 374, 378 (act of June 29, 1956). Earlier acts had supported road building with federal money: an act of 1916 aimed at helping states build "rural post roads," 39 Stat. 355 (act of July 11, 1916); see also 58 Stat. 838 (act of Dec. 20, 1944).

10 On this point, I am indebted to James Sweet and his unpublished paper (Stanford Law School, 1999), "Monopoly in the Motion Picture Industry: 1900–1950."

11 Edith Abbott, *The Tenements of Chicago* (1936), pp. 477–478.

12 Cowan, *Social History,* p. 234.

13 109 Stat. 803 (act of Dec. 29, 1995).

14 Quoted in Claire Bond Potter, *War on Crime: Bandits, G-Men, and the Politics of Mass Culture* (1998), p. 62.

15 Supplemental Report, Senate Interim Committee on Traffic and Motor Vehicle Violations, State of California (1950), p. 24.

16 Lawrence M. Friedman, *Crime and Punishment in American History* (1993), p. 279.

17 George Warren, *Traffic Courts* (1942) p. 114.

18 See, for example, Cal. Penal Code, §192 (c) (vehicular manslaughter); §191.5, on gross vehicular manslaughter while intoxicated.

19 Frank J. Weed, "Grass-Roots Activism and the Drunk Driving Issue: A Survey of MADD Chapters," *Law & Policy* 9:259 (1987); James B. Jacobs, *Drunk Driving: An American Dilemma* (1989).

20 Jacobs, *Drunk Driving*, p. xvii.

21 See, on this point, Harry Kalven, Jr., and Hans Zeisel, *The American Jury* (1966), pp. 294–296.

22 Ralph Nader, *Unsafe at Any Speed* (1965), pp. 4–5.

23 Giles Whittel, "The Outsider," *New York Times*, November 2, 1996.

24 Jerry L. Mashaw and David L. Harfst, *The Struggle for Auto Safety* (1990), pp. 137–138.

25 87 Stat. 1046 (act of Jan. 2, 1974).

26 88 Stat. 2286 (act of Jan. 4, 1975).

27 109 Stat. 568 (law of Nov. 28, 1995).

28 This had been the law in Montana since 1955—but the national speed limit, of course, did away with it. See Robert E. King and Cass R. Sunstein, "Doing Without Speed Limits," *Boston University L. Rev.* 79:155 (1999).

29 Laws Conn. 191, ch. 86, p. 1348.

30 Laws Mass. 1913, ch. 663, p. 609.

31 43 Stat. 805 (act of Feb. 2, 1925).

32 44 Stat. 568 (act of May 20, 1926).

33 Kevin Starr, *Endangered Dreams: The Great Depression in California* (1996), p. 353.

34 Cowan, *Social History*, p. 256.

35 52 Stat. 973 (act of June 23, 1938).

36 Michael E. Levine, "Airline Competition in Deregulated Markets: Theory, Firm Strategy, and Public Policy," *Yale J. on Reg.* 4:393, 402 (1987).

37 Francis S. Chase, *Sound and Fury* (1942), p. 21, quoted in Steven J. Simmons, *The Fairness Doctrine and the Media,* (1978), p. 18.

38 36 Stat. 629 (act of June 24, 1910).

39 Cowan, *Social History*, p. 279.

40 37 Stat. 302 (act of Aug. 13, 1912).

41 Simmons, *Fairness Doctrine*, p. 16.

42 44 Stat. 1162 (act of Feb. 23, 1927).

43 Ibid., §18, at 1170.

44 48 Stat. 1064 (act of June 19, 1934).

45 Richard W. Steele, *Propaganda in an Open Society: The Roosevelt Administration and the Media, 1933–1941* (1985), pp. 22–23.

46 Donald I. Warren, *Radio Priest: Charles Coughlin, the Father of Hate Radio* (1996), p. 6.

47 Quoted in Maxwell Bloomfield, *Peaceful Revolution: Constitutional Change and American Culture from Progressivism to the New Deal* (2000), p. 104.

48 Quotation is from an address before the National Association of Broadcasters, May 9, 1961, rpt. in Newton N. Minow and Craig L. LaMay, *Abandoned in the Wasteland: Children, Television, and the First Amendment* (1995), pp. 185, 188.

49 Douglas B. Craig, *Fireside Politics: Radio and Political Culture in the United States, 1920–1940* (2000), p. 264.

50 Quoted in Harry P. Warner, *Radio and Television Law* (1948), pp. 420–421.

51 62 Stat. 769 (act of June 25, 1948).

52 In re Applications of E. G. Robinson, Jr., for Renewal of Licence, *FCC Reports* 33: 265, 298 (1961).

53 See Seth T. Goldsamt, " 'Crucified by the FCC'? Howard Stern, the FCC, and Selective Prosecution," *Colum. J. L. & Soc. Probs.* 28:203 (1995).

54 See F. Leslie Smith, Milan Meeske, and John W. Wright II, *Electronic Media and Government* (1995), pp. 356–369.

55 102 Stat. 2186, 2228 (act of Oct. 1, 1988)

56 Richard S. Randall, *Censorship of the Movies: The Social and Political Control of a Mass Medium* (1968), p. 10.

57 239 Ill. 251, 87 N.E. 1011 (1909).

58 Laws Pa. 1911, p. 1067.

59 Ohio Stats. 1926, §871–49.

60 Randall, *Censorship of the Movies*, p. 17.

61 Ibid., p. 24.

62 Laws Ohio 1913, p. 399; *Mutual Film Corporation v. Ohio Industrial Commission*, 236 U.S. 230 (1915).

63 Randall, *Censorship of the Movies*, pp. 16, 200.

64 Quoted ibid., pp. 201–202.

65 Andrew Sarris, *"You Ain't Heard Nothin' Yet"* (1998), pp. 31–32.

66 Randall, *Censorship of the Movies*, pp. 27–32; *Joseph Burstyn, Inc., v. Wilson*, 343 U.S. 495 (1952).

67 Richard M. Mosk, "Motion Picture Rating in the United States," *Cardozo Arts & Ent. L.J.* 15:135 (1997).

68 See, for example, the statement of Senator Kent Conrad in *Hearings on Television Violence Before the Senate Committee on Commerce, Science, and Transportation*, July 12, 1995, pp. 66–70.

69 See, in general, Michael Conant, *Antitrust in the Motion Picture Industry: Economic and Legal Analysis* (1960).

70 *U.S. v. Paramount Pictures*, 334 U.S. 131 (1948).

71 Conant, *Antitrust*, p. 4.

72 Benjamin R. Barber, *Jihad vs. McWorld* (1995), pp. 299–300.

73 I am indebted to Vladimir Jevremovic, a student at Stanford Law School for information about the early history of television broadcast regulation.

74 *Statistical Abstract of the United States, 1998,* table 915, p. 573.

75 81 Stat. 365, 367 (act of Nov. 7, 1967).

76 Meredith C. Hightower, "Beyond Lights and Wires in a Box: Ensuring the Existence of Public Television," *Journal of Law and Policy* 3:133 (1994).

77 Jeremy Tunstall, *Communications Deregulation: The Unleashing of America's Communication Industry* (1986), p. 157.

78 Charles Winick, "Censor and Sensibility: A Content Analysis of the Television Censor's Comments," *J. of Broadcasting* 5:117, 125 (1960).

79 *FCC v. Pacific Foundation,* 438 U.S. 726 (1978); see Jeff Deman, "Seven Dirty Words: Did They Help Define Indecency?" *Communications and the Law* 20:39 (1998); Matthew L. Spitzer, *Seven Dirty Words and Six Other Stories* (1986), chap. 7.

80 Spitzer, *Seven Dirty Words,* pp. 119–125.

81 Howard Mintz, "Law School Online," *San Jose Mercury,* Nov. 15, 1999. The school is the Concord University School of Law.

82 Lawrence M. Friedman, *The Horizontal Society* (1999).

83 See on this point, Neil Gabler, *Life the Movie: How Entertainment Conquered Reality* (1998).

19.
Law: An American Export

1 See the essays collected in Marcus Lutter, Ernst C. Stiefel, and Michael H. Hoeflich, *Der Einfluss deutcher Emigranten auf die Rechstentwicklung in den USA und in Deutschland* (1993).

2 Phanor J. Eder, "The Impact of the Common Law on Latin America," *Miami Law Quarterly* 4:435 (1950).

3 Paul W. Drake, *The Money Doctor in the Andes: The Kemmerer Missions, 1923–1933* (1989).

4 A. Caesar Espiritu, "Constitutional Development in the Philippines," in Louis Henkin and Albert J. Rosenthal, eds., *Constitutionalism and Rights: The Influence of the United States Constitution Abroad* (1990), p. 260.

5 See Helmut Steinberg, "Historic Influences of American Constitutionalism upon German Constitutional Development: Federalism and Judicial Review," *Columbia J. Transnational Law* 36:189 (1997).

6 Hiroshi Itoh, *The Japanese Supreme Court: Constitutional Policies* (1989), pp. 12–19; Lawrence W. Beer, "Constitutionalism and Rights in Japan and Korea," in Henkin and Rosenthal, *Constitutionalism and Rights.*

7 Mauro Cappelletti, John Henry Merryman, and Joseph M. Perillo, *The Italian Legal System: An Introduction* (1967), pp. 75–79.

8 Kyong Whan Ahn, "The Influence of American Constitutionalism on South Korea," *Southern Ill. U. L.J.* 22:71, 105 (1997).

9 Mauro Cappelletti, *Judicial Review in the Contemporary World* (1971), p. 45.

10 Louis Favoreu, "Constitutional Review in Europe," in Henkin and Rosenthal, *Constitutionalism and Rights,* pp. 38, 47.

11 For later developments, see Jaako Husa, "Guarding the Constitutionality of Laws in the Nordic Countries: A Comparative Perspective," *American J. Comparative Law* 48:345, 372 (2000). See, in general, Alec Stone Sweet, *Governing with Judges: Constitutional Politics in Europe* (2000).

12 Anthony Lester, "The Overseas Trade in the American Bill of Rights," *Columbia L. Rev.* 88:537 (1988).

13 See Pnina Lahav, *Judgment in Jerusalem: Chief Justice Simon Agranat and the Zionist Century* (1997).

14 On the law and development movement, see James A. Gardner, *Legal Imperialism: American Lawyers and Foreign Aid in Latin America* (1980); Lawrence M. Friedman, "On Legal Development," *Rutgers L. Rev.* 24:11 (1969); John H. Merryman, "Comparative Law and Social Change: On the Origins, Style, Decline and Revival of the Law and Development Movement," *American J. Comparative Law* 25:457 (1977).

15 See David M. Trubek and Marc Galanter, "Scholars in Self-Estrangement: Some Reflections on the Crisis in Law and Development Studies in the United States," *Wisconsin L. Rev.* 1974: 1062.

16 See, in general, Jacques DeLisle, "Lex Americana?: United States Legal Assistance, American Legal Models and Legal Change in the Post-Communist World and Beyond," *U. Pa. J. of International Economic Law* 20:179 (1999).

17 See, in general, Rett R. Ludwikowski, *Constitution-Making in the Region of Former Soviet Dominance* (1996).

18 Constitution of the Republic of Hungary, chapter IV, article 32/A, reprinted ibid., p. 424.

19 Reprinted ibid., pp. 356–357.

20 See David Lempert, "Pepsi-Stroika: American Cultural Influence on the Russian Political and Legal System," *Legal Studies Forum* 20:345 (1996).

21 I am indebted for information about Latin America to Mauricio Duce.

22 DeLisle, "Lex Americana?" pp. 180, 233.

23 88 Stat. 2056 (act of Jan. 3, 1975).

24 110 Stat. 785 (act of Mar. 12, 1996).

25 Reprinted in *Tax Notes International* 93:211–228 (1993).

26 Convention for the Protection of Migratory Birds, 39 Stat. 1702 (Aug. 16, 1916).

27 46 Stat. 590 (act of June 17, 1930).

28 42 Stat. 9, 11 (act of May 27, 1921).

29 Amy R. Edge, "Preventing Software Piracy Through Regional Trade Agreements: The Mexican Example," *No. Car. J. Int'l Law and Commercial Regulation* 20:175, 198 (1994).

30 102 Stat. 1107, 1212 (act of Aug. 23, 1988). See Edge, "Preventing Software Piracy," p. 187.

31 *Martindale-Hubbell Law Directory,* vol. 2, pp. 3630–3633, 3639–3643, 3650 (1952).

32 *Martindale-Hubbell Law Directory,* vol. 13, p. NYC411P (1999).

33 See, in general, Yves Dezalay and Bryant G. Garth, *Dealing in Virtue: International Commercial Arbitration and the Construction of a Transnational Legal Order* (1996).

34 Wolfgang Wiegand, "Reception of American Law in Europe," *Am. J. Comp. Law* 39:229 (1991).

35 Wolfgang Wiegand, "Americanization of Law: Reception or Convergence?" in Lawrence M. Friedman and Harry N. Scheiber, eds., *Legal Culture and the Legal Profession* (1996), pp. 137, 140.

36 *Martindale-Hubbell International Law Directory,* vol. 1, EU1445B–EU 1447B, AS271B–AS281B (1998).

37 *Stanford Law School Photo Directory,* 1997–1998, pp. 18–20.

38 *Official Guide to U.S. Law Schools* (1994).

39 There are, however, many American law schools which operate overseas campuses, often in summer. The students are mostly Americans studying American law, and enjoying some tourism; but a few such programs enroll foreign students, and a few schools run overseas programs to teach American law to foreign students. DeLisle, "Lex Americana?" p. 206. But American students rarely study laws in non-English-speaking countries. On the insignificant number of Americans studying for an advanced law degree in Germany, see Otto Sandrock, "Über das Ansehen des deutschen Zivilrecht in der Welt," *Zeitschrift für Vergleichenden Rechtswissenschaft* 100:3, 27 (2001).

40 Ulrich Beck, *Risikogesellschaft: Auf dem Weg in eine andere Moderne* (1986).

41 102 Stat. 2318 (act of Oct. 7, 1988).

42 For example, the Hague Convention on the Civil Aspects of International Child Abduction. See June Starr, "The Global Battlefield: Culture and International Child Custody Disputes at Century's End," *Arizona J. of Int'l and Comparative Law* 15:791 (1998).

43 Jeffrey S. Thomas and Michael A. Meyer, *The New Rules of Global Trade: A Guide to the World Trade Organization* (1997), p. 56.

44 William A. Lovett, Alfred E. Eckes, Jr., and Richard L. Brinkman, *U.S. Trade Policy: History, Theory, and the WTO* (1999), p. 98.

20.
Taking Stock

1 On legal culture see Lawrence M. Friedman, *The Legal System: A Social Science Perspective* (1975), pp. 193–194.

2 Deborah W. Denno, "Life Before the Modern Sex Offender Statutes," *Northwestern U. L. Rev.* 92:1317 (1998).

3 Erle Stanley Gardner, introduction to Nathan F. Leopold, Jr., *Life Plus 99 Years* (1958), p. 14.

4 Laws N.J. 1994, cc. 128, 133. Even for those with a small likelihood of repeat performances, law enforcement agencies have to be notified; for "moderate" risks, schools,
religious and youth organizations have to be told.

5 Paul Zielbauer, "Posting of Sex Offender Registries on Web Sets Off Both Praise and
Criticism," *New York Times,* May 22, 2000.

6 Cal. Penal Code, §667 (adopted by initiative of June 8, 1982). For a careful and devastating critique of this law in action, see Franklin E. Zimring, Gordon Hawkins, and Sam
Kamin, *Punishment and Democracy: Three Strikes and You're Out in California* (2000).

7 See "Reno Urges Expansion of Hate-Crime Laws," *New York Times,* Oct. 19, 1998;
James Brooke, "Witnesses Trace Brutal Killing of Gay Student," Nov. 21, 1998.

8 "Terror in Littleton," *New York Times,* Apr. 24, 1999.

9 National Conference of State Legislatures, http://www.ncsl.org/programs/legman/
about/stf1.htm (visited Jan. 2001).

10 Congressional Quarterly, *How Congress Works* (1983), p. 106; William J. Keefe and
Morris S. Ogul, *The American Legislative Process* (9th ed., 1997), p. 204.

11 Gilman M. Ostrander, *Nevada: The Great Rotten Borough, 1859–1964* (1966).

12 514 U.S. 549 (1995).

13 See for example, Reorganization Plan no. 1, 53 Stat. 1423 (effective July 1, 1939),
transferring the Bureau of the Budget to the Executive Office of the President.

14 87 Stat. 555 (act of Nov. 7, 1973). Within forty-eight hours of any warlike action of the
president, he has to report to Congress; unless Congress agreed to declare war within a
certain period, or extended the deadline, the president has to withdraw the troops.

15 *Youngstown Sheet & Tube Co. v. Sawyer,* 343 U.S. 579 (1952); for a discussion of the
case, see Maeva Marcus, *Truman and the Steel Seizure Case: The Limits of Presidential
Power* (1977).

16 418 U.S. 683 (1974).

17 *Clinton v. Jones,* 520 U.S. 681 (1997).

18 See 42 U.S.C.A. §§5122, 5170.

19 These figures are from *Historical Statistics of the United States,* vol. 2, pp. 1100, 1102;
Statistical Abstract of the United States, 1999, p. 338.

20 David Vogel, *National Styles of Regulation: Environmental Policy in Britain and the
United States* (1986), p. 213.

21 Steven Kelman, *Regulating America, Regulating Sweden: A Comparative Study of Occupational Safety* and Health Policy (1981), p. 203.

22 Ibid., p. 221.

23 Robert A. Kagan, *Adversarial Legalism: The American Way of Life* (forthcoming, 2001).

24 Samuel Walker, *The Rights Revolution: Rights and Community in Modern America*
(1998), p. viii.

A Bibliographical Note

I
n one sense, there is so much written about American law in the twentieth century that nobody could possibly absorb it all, not in a hundred lifetimes. There are more than a million volumes in the Harvard Law Library, most of them about American law, most of them published in the twentieth century; almost all of these are, in a way, sources that could potentially be used by somebody writing this kind of book. There are hundreds of law reviews, and most of the material in their millions of pages concerns American law in the twentieth century; archives are chock full of court records, lawyers' papers, and the like; tons of this stuff lie around in county courthouses and historical societies; in recent years, you can add to what is in these books and articles and archives the almost limitless contents of legal cyberspace, a mysterious science-fiction world of electronic data, which grows and grows and is nowhere and everywhere at once.

Moreover, the line between secondary literature and primary sources, for a period this recent, is naturally rather indistinct. Older studies—crime surveys of the 1920s, like the *Illinois Crime Survey* (1929); classics like Kalven and Zeisel's *The American Jury* (1966)—are works of scholarship, and at the same time, by now, genuine historical documents. I will, for the most part, ignore these in this survey of the literature, and concentrate on books of the more recent past.

Despite the fact that there is way too much literature for any one human being to absorb, general narrative accounts of the history of law in this century are actually so scarce as to be almost nonexistent. My own book, *A History of American Law* (2d ed., 1985), despite its promising title, essentially peters out in 1900; there is a forty-page epilogue which deals with the twentieth century, but I cannot honestly call this more than a sketch of a few major themes. Kermit Hall's book *The Magic Mirror: Law in American History* (1989) does, in fact, include the twentieth century. Hall's book is 336 pages long; and the twentieth century gets about a third of this. There are many good qualities to Hall's treatment of the twentieth century, but it is, after all, quite short; it cannot honestly be considered definitive. Gerald L. Fetner, *Ordered Liberty: Legal Reform in the Twentieth Century* (1983), has only 96 pages of text, along with some documents; and it leaves out criminal law and most private law topics. There are some efforts to sum up or describe American legal culture in the twentieth century. I made modest attempts in *Total Justice* (1985) and *The Republic of Choice: Law, Authority, and Culture* (1990). An important interpretation of the latter half of the century is Robert A. Kagan, *Adversarial Legalism: The American Way of Law* (forthcoming, 2001).

There are also some annotated collections of documents (casebooks, in a way), such as Stephen B. Presser and Jamil S. Zainaldin, *Law and Jurisprudence in American History: Cases and Materials* (3d edition, 1995); this devotes some 200 pages to the twentieth century, but most of this deals with schools of legal thought, and constitutional doctrine, with some bits about contract and tort law. Another collection is Kermit L. Hall, William M. Wiecek, and Paul Finkelman, *American Legal History: Cases and Materials* (2d edition, 1996). It puts somewhat less weight on the twentieth century; the general themes of this collection, and the points of emphasis, are much the same as in Presser and Zainaldin. In other words, there is a crying need for some kind of synthesis. Whether *this* book fills the gap—or at least some part of the gap—I leave to the reader to judge.

I should also point out that law is so important a part of the American story in the twentieth century that almost every significant account of American history, politics, or culture is bound to have material about the law. You cannot write the history of the New Deal, for example, without talking about its massive legislative program. And indeed, there is a tremendous amount of legal history in David M. Kennedy, *Freedom from Fear: The American People in Depression and War, 1929–1945* (1999). A similar point could be made about any major twentieth-century study.

So far I have been talking about the general literature of legal history. Few books recount the legal history of any particular state. An exception is Joseph A. Ranney, *Trusting Nothing to Providence: A History of Wisconsin's Legal System* (1999). Histories of the bench and bar are, unfortunately, rarely of any real value—the authors would never get tenure at any respectable university—but they sometimes provide bits of useful information.

The situation, of course, is quite different in some more specific areas. There is, for example, an enormous literature on constitutional history and the work of the Supreme Court in the twentieth century; indeed, this is a bottomless pit. I can mention only a few of these multitudes—those which I found especially useful or compelling for one reason or another. Melvin I. Urofsky, *A March of Liberty: A Constitutional History of the United States* (1988), devotes several hundred pages to the twentieth century, and often goes far beyond constitutional history; this is a valuable book. William F. Swindler wrote a three-volume history, covering the first two-thirds of the century, under the general title *Court and Constitution in the 20th Century*. The three volumes are: *The Old Legality, 1889–1932* (1969); *The New Legality, 1932–1968* (1970); and *The Modern Interpretation* (1974). On the Fuller Court, see James W. Ely, Jr., *The Chief Justiceship of Melville W. Fuller, 1888–1910* (1995); see also, on the Fuller and White Courts, John E. Semonche, *Charting the Future: The Supreme Court Responds to a Changing Society, 1890–1910* (1978); a recent and innovative addition to the literature is Maxwell Bloomfield, *Peaceful Revolution: Constitutional Change and American Culture from Progressivism to the New Deal* (2000). On the Stone and Vinson Courts, see Melvin I. Urofsky, *Division and Discord: The Supreme Court Under Stone and Vinson, 1941–1953* (1997); on the Warren Court, there is a large literature, including Lucas A. Powe, Jr., *The Warren Court and American Politics* (2000), and Morton J. Horwitz, *The Warren Court and the Pursuit of Justice* (1998). On more specific topics: Howard Gillman, *The Constitution Besieged: The Rise and Demise of Lochner Era Police Powers Jurisprudence* (1993); on Roosevelt's court-packing plan, William E. Leuchtenburg, *The Supreme Court Reborn: The Constitutional Revolution in the Age of Roosevelt* (1995); and on the New Deal developments on the Court, and what led up to them, Barry Cushman, *Rethinking the New Deal Court: The Structure of a Constitutional Revolution* (1998). On the Burger Court, there is a useful, if uneven, collection of essays: Bernard Schwartz, ed., *The Burger Court: Counter-Revolution or Confirmation?* (1998). A vivid picture of the Court at work, from the worm's-eye view of a Court clerk, is Edward Lazarus, *Closed Chambers* (1998), which he subtitles *The First Eyewitness Account of the Epic Struggles Inside the Supreme Court*. On the selection of federal judges, there is a fine and exhaustive monograph, Sheldon Goldman, *Picking Federal Judges: Lower Court Selection from Roosevelt Through Reagan* (1997). On the work of the Courts of Appeals, see Donald R. Songer, Reginald S. Sheehan, and Susan B. Haire, *Continuity and Change on the United States Courts of Appeals* (2000). Alexander Keyssar, *The Right to Vote: The Contested*

History of Democracy in the United States (2000), sheds new light on the history of suffrage.

There are also innumerable biographies of Supreme Court justices. The literature on Oliver Wendell Holmes, Jr., is especially voluminous; a well-written overview is G. Edward White, *Justice Oliver Wendell Holmes: Law and the Inner Self* (1993). Richard Polenberg, *The World of Benjamin Cardozo: Personal Values and the Judicial Process* (1997) is a fine study of this judge; another recent biography of Cardozo is Andrew L. Kaufman, *Cardozo* (1998). Alpheus Thomas Mason's classic biography, *Brandeis: A Free Man's Life* (1946) is still worth reading. On Felix Frankfurter's career before the Court, see Michael E. Parrish, *Felix Frankfurter and His Times: The Reform Years* (1982). Not surprisingly, there are many biographies of Earl Warren; one noteworthy example is G. Edward White, *Earl Warren: A Public Life* (1982). The biography of Thurgood Marshall by Howard Ball, *A Defiant Life: Thurgood Marshall and the Persistence of Racism in America* (1998), is also rich in details about the civil rights movement, and Marshall's part in the movement before he was appointed to the Supreme Court. Other good biographies of Supreme Court justices include Dennis J. Hutchinson, *The Man Who Once Was Whizzer White: A Portrait of Justice Byron R. White* (1998), and Laura Kalman, *Abe Fortas: A Biography* (1990). Lower federal judges, naturally enough, get much less play. Here one must mention Gerald Gunther, *Learned Hand: The Man and the Judge* (1994), and Robert Jerome Glennon, *The Iconoclast as Reformer: Jerome Frank's Impact on American Law* (1985). State-court judges are even more neglected; but biographies of Cardozo, for example, are a partial exception, because his most notable work was done in New York, not in Washington.

Jerome Frank was more famous as a legal thinker than as a judge. Legal thought and legal thinkers have had their share of literature. On Karl Llewellyn, see William Twining, *Karl Llewellyn and the Realist Movement* (1973); since Twining wrote, the Llewellyn literature has grown substantially; see, for example, N. E. H. Hull, *Roscoe Pound and Karl Llewellyn: Searching for an American Jurisprudence* (1997). On the legal realist movement, see Laura Kalman, *Legal Realism at Yale, 1927–1960* (1986); Kalman deals with later developments in *The Strange Career of Legal Liberalism* (1996); see also John Henry Schlegel, *American Legal Realism and Empirical Social Science* (1995). Morton Horwitz, *The Transformation of American Law, 1870–1960: The Crisis of Legal Ortho-*

doxy (1992), is a general treatment of the intellectual history of the American legal system.

On individual decisions of the Supreme Court, and individual areas of decision, there is also an inexhaustible literature. The books and articles about *Brown v. Board of Education,* and what came before and after, could fill a sizable room. One has to mention, however, Richard Kluger, *Simple Justice* (1976), a richly detailed account of the background of this case. Also useful is Mary L. Dudziak, *Cold War Civil Rights: Race and the Image of American Democracy* (2000). On the reaction to *Brown,* and the impact of the case, there are many studies. Jack Bass, *Unlikely Heroes* (1981), deals with the southern federal judges who bore the brunt of the legal struggle to integrate; see also Michal Belknap, *Federal Law and Southern Order: Racial Violence and Constitutional Conflict in the Post-Brown South* (1995). Peter Irons, *Justice at War* (1983), tells the story of the Japanese internment cases in World War II; and in *The Courage of Their Convictions* (1988), Irons provides first-person accounts by the men and women who figured in sixteen notable Supreme Court cases—a most interesting and enlightening book. The *Oxford Guide to United States Supreme Court Decisions* (1999), edited by Kermit Hall, has brief sketches of the most prominent Supreme Court cases. It is an exceedingly useful reference book.

A wonderful account of the early freedom of speech cases is Richard Polenberg, *Fighting Faiths: The Abrams Case, the Supreme Court, and Free Speech* (1987); indeed, this book goes far beyond the case itself, dealing with the whole period of the red scare. David J. Garrow has written a rich and interesting study of the abortion cases and their precursors in *Liberty and Sexuality: The Right to Privacy and the Making of Roe v. Wade* (1994); there is a fairly big literature on this subject, including Barbara Hinkson Craig and David M. O'Brien, *Abortion and American Politics* (1993). Among other noteworthy accounts of individual cases are Melvin I. Urofsky, *Affirmative Action on Trial: Sex Discrimination in Johnson v. Santa Clara* (1997); Christopher P. Manfredi, *The Supreme Court and Juvenile Justice* (1998); Maeva Marcus, *Truman and the Steel Seizure Case: The Limits of Presidential Power* (1994). A lucid and useful summary of many of the changes in constitutional law (and in society) can be found in Samuel Walker's book, *The Rights Revolution: Rights and Community in Modern America* (1998).

There is considerable material on the legal profession. Richard L. Abel's book, *American Lawyers* (1989), contains a great deal of historical material. See also Jerold S. Auerbach, *Unequal Justice: Lawyers and Social Change in Modern America* (1976); Peter H. Irons, *The New Deal Lawyers* (1982), looks at New Deal legislation from the standpoint of the government lawyers who worked on the statutes and the cases; see also Ronen Shamir, *Managing Legal Uncertainty: Elite Lawyers in the New Deal* (1995). On public-interest lawyers, see Martha F. Davis, *Brutal Need: Lawyers and the Welfare Rights Movement, 1960–1973* (1993). On legal education in general, the standard work is Robert B. Stevens, *Law School: Legal Education in America from the 1850s to the 1980s* (1983); but this is a growing literature. There are quite a few histories of particular law schools, of variable quality. Histories of law firms also exist, but most of them are bland and self-congratulatory. One of the few written by a professional historian is Harold Hyman, *Craftsmanship and Character: A History of the Vinson and Elkins Law Firm of Houston, 1917–1997* (1998). There are also dozens and dozens of biographies of lawyers, and many autobiographies, most dedicated to the proposition that the author was a heroic figure; few of these are any good. But a handful have been written by real, honest-to-goodness historians; one of the best of these is William H. Harbaugh, *Lawyer's Lawyer: The Life of John W. Davis* (1973). Clarence Darrow was flamboyant enough to attract his share of biographers; see, especially, Kevin Tierney, *Darrow: A Biography* (1979). There is also David J. Langum's fascinating biography, *William M. Kunstler: The Most Hated Lawyer in America* (1999).

Rights and violations of rights have generated quite a literature. On free speech, see Polenberg, *Fighting Faiths;* and, for the earlier period, David Rabban, *Free Speech in Its Forgotten Years* (1997). There is also Samuel Walker, *In Defense of American Liberties: A History of the ACLU* (1990). Shawn Francis Peters, *Judging Jehovah's Witnesses: Religious Persecution and the Dawn of the Rights Revolution* (2000), deals with this important chapter in the history of civil liberties. On the civil rights cases of the 1920s, see William G. Ross, *Forging New Freedoms: Nativism, Education, and the Constitution, 1917–1927* (1994). On the travails of the McCarthy period, there are many books, and the controversy seems to be getting steamier. See David Caute, *The Great Fear: The Anti-Communist Purge Under Truman and Eisenhower* (1978); Arthur L. Sabin, *Red Scare in Court: New York Versus the International Workers Order* (1993), and *In Calmer Times: The Supreme Court and Red Monday* (1999); Ellen Schrecker, *Many Are the Crimes: McCarthyism in America* (1998). On immigration, see Elliott Robert Barkan, *And Still They Come: Immigrants and American Society, 1920 to the 1990s* (1996), a clear, well-written summary.

Americans are fascinated with trials (mostly criminal trials), and there are almost too many books to mention. I single out two that are particularly interesting and incisive: Edward J. Larson, *Summer for the Gods: The Scopes Trial and America's Continuing Debate over Science and Religion* (1997), and Dan Carter, *Scottsboro: A Tragedy of the American South* (1971).

The literature on specific fields varies from sparse to vast. On criminal justice, I will take the liberty of citing my own book, *Crime and Punishment in American History* (1993); also, Roger Lane, *Murder in America: A History* (1997). Both of these devote a good deal of space to the twentieth century; the same is true of Samuel Walker, *Popular Justice: A History of American Criminal Justice* (2d ed., 1998). There is a rather rich literature on prisons and prison life—for example, James B. Jacobs, *Stateville: The Penitentiary in Mass Society* (1977), and David M. Oshinsky, *"Worse Than Slavery": Parchman Farm and the Ordeal of Jim Crow Justice* (1996), about a mostly black penal institution in Mississippi. Some subareas have produced fine monographs—for example, Leslie J. Reagan's prize-winning study, *When Abortion Was a Crime: Women, Medicine and Law in the United States, 1867–1973* (1997), and David J. Langum's excellent study of the Mann Act, *Crossing Over the Line: Legislating Morality and the Mann Act* (1994); also, Mary Odem, *Delinquent Daughters: Protecting and Policing Adolescent Female Sexuality in the United States, 1885–1920* (1995); and Jonathan Simon, *Poor Discipline* (1993), which deals with the parole system in the century between 1890 and 1990. Philip Jenkins, *Moral Panic: Changing Concepts of the Child Molester in Modern America* (1998), is broader than its title suggests; it gives a good overview of laws against sexual psychopaths, child abuse, and child pornography in the twentieth century.

There is a real shortage of books on the history of family law in the twentieth century; see, however, Herbert Jacob, *Silent Revolution: The Transformation of Divorce Law in the United States* (1988); J. Herbie DiFonzo, *Beneath the Fault Line: The Popular and Legal Culture of Divorce in Twentieth-Century America* (1997); and E. Wayne Carp, *Family Matters: Secrecy and Disclosure in the History of Adoption* (1998). On the regulatory state, there are two important books by Morton Keller, *Regulating a New Economy: Public Policy and Economic Change in America, 1900–1933* (1990), and *Regulating a New Society: Public Policy and Social Change in America, 1900–1933* (1994). A useful overview is Robert Harrison, *State and Society in Twentieth Century America* (1997). There is also a literature on particular government agencies—for example, Joel Seligman's *The Transformation of Wall Street: A History of the Securities and Exchange Commission and Modern Corporate Finance* (rev. ed., 1995). Legal histories of agriculture and the like are in short supply, but there are honorable exceptions, for example, Victoria Saker Woeste, *The Farmer's Benevolent Trust: Law and Agricultural Cooperation in Industrial America, 1865–1945* (1998), and Arthur McEvoy, *The Fisherman's Problem: Ecology and Law in the California Fisheries, 1850–1980* (1986).

There is quite a bit on welfare policy and its history—for example, Molly Ladd-Taylor, *Mother-Work: Women, Child Welfare, and the State, 1890–1930* (1994); Michael B. Katz, *In the Shadow of the Poorhouse: A Social History of Welfare in America* (revised ed., 1996), which has a great deal of material on the twentieth century; and James T. Patterson, *America's Struggle Against Poverty in the Twentieth Century* (2000), a good overview. Labor law has also produced an impressive number of thoughtful studies; see in particular William E. Forbath, *Law and the Shaping of the American Labor Movement* (1989); Melvyn Dubofsky, *The State and Labor in Modern America* (1994); and Daniel R. Ernst, *Lawyers Against Labor: From Individual Rights to Corporate Liberalism* (1995).

On an often neglected corner of legal history, military justice, there is now a substantial study, Jonathan Lurie, *Arming Military Justice*, vol. 1, *The Origins of the United States Court of Military Appeals, 1775–1950* (1992), and *Pursuing Military Justice*, vol. 2, *The History of the United States Court of Appeals for the Armed Forces, 1951–1980* (1998). Administrative law is another important but neglected field. A good overview is Robert L. Rabin's book-length article "Federal Regulation in Historical Perspective," *Stanford Law Review* 38:1189 (1986).

It should come as no surprise that there is a shortage of rigorous historical studies of such things as procedure, appellate process, federal jurisdiction and the like. One honorable exception is Edward A. Purcell, Jr., *Litigation and Inequality: Federal Diversity Jurisdiction in Industrial America, 1870–1958* (1992). Even more impressive is Purcell's more recent book, *Brandeis and the Progressive Constitution: Erie, the Judicial Power, and the Politics of the Federal Courts in Twentieth-Century America* (2000), which gives political and social meaning to shifts in the jurisprudence of federal jurisdiction. Stephen C.

Yeazell, *From Medieval Group Litigation to the Modern Class Action* (1987), deals mostly with the period before the twentieth century, but the sections on the past century are well worth consulting.

Fields like business law, property law, commercial law, antitrust law, land law, intellectual property, and the like produce mountains of practical and scholarly writing, but not much of it is overtly historical, and most of what is is both dull and formalistic. One exception is Paul Goldstein's sparkling book on copyright, *Copyright's Highway: The Law and Lore of Copyright from Gutenberg to the Celestial Jukebox* (1994); see also Joel Seligman's book on the SEC mentioned above, and Herbert Hovenkamp, *Enterprise and American Law, 1836–1937* (1991). Here there really is a lot more to be accomplished. But that is true of the whole business of interpreting the past. It is never signed, sealed, and delivered; it is always incomplete, always inchoate, always a work in progress, a work that is never done.

Index

Abbott, Edith, 551

Abortion, 236–237, 329–330, 531–532, 605, 685; rights, 529, 535

Abrams, Charles, 405

Abrams v. United States, 142–143

Accidents, 61–62, 278, 349–355, 363, 372; concept of, 351–352

Acheson, Dean, 285, 339

Activism, judicial. *See* Judicial activism

Adair v. United States, 18, 19, 609

Adarand Constructors, Inc., v. Pena, 527

Addams, Jane, 102

Administrative Dispute Resolution Act, 279

Administrative law, 172, 688

Administrative Procedure Act, 171–172

Administrative reform, 171

Administrative state, x, 602

Adoption, 443–448

Advertising, 428, 464

Affirmative action, 12, 323, 526–527, 545

Africa, 572, 586

African Elephant Conservation Act, 586

Age discrimination, 324–325, 604

Age Discrimination in Employment Act, 324

Agency for International Development, 579

Agent Orange, 368

Age of consent, 100

Agranat, Simon, 579

Agricultural Act, 452

Agricultural Adjustment Act, 156, 159, 161

A. H. Robins Company, 368

Aid to Dependent Children, 182

Aid to Families with Dependent Children, 536–537

Aiken, Doris, 553

Air Commerce Act, 556

Air Force One (film), 594

Airline Deregulation Act, 558

Airlines, 308, 556

Air Quality Act, 197

Air Safety Board, 557

Alabama: anti-lynching law, 119; black

workers, 116; blue laws, 230; convict miners, 119; death row, 221; delinquency law, 91; hazardous waste law, 378; juries, 265; legislature, 595; prison rapes, 216; school prayer, 511; Scottsboro case, 120; state association, 41; voting, 114; voting rights, 301, 311

Alameda County, Calif., 350

Alaska, 420; constitution, 344, 346; divorce, 441; Inuit, 452; law school, 485; pension law, 180; voting rights, 301; workers' compensation, 540

Alaska Game Act, 81

Albertson v. Subversive Activities Control Board, 337

Alcatraz Island, 319

Alexander, Sadie Tabbler Massell, 33

Alien Land Law, 123

Aliens, 313, 538; illegal, 130

Aliquippa and Southern Railroad Company, 169

Alternative dispute resolution, 480

Ambulance chaser, 29–30

American Association for Retired People, 324

American Association of Health Plans, 473

American Bar Association, 34, 37, 39, 41, 49, 193, 223, 258, 459–460, 466, 481, 580, 611, 612, 616; judicial selection, 477

American Civil Liberties Union, 283, 284, 333, 471, 511, 517, 519

American Dilemma, An (Myrdal), 284–285

American Federation of Labor, 76, 78, 79

American Indian Movement, 319, 472, 604

American Indians. *See* Native Americans

American Jewish Committee, 511

American Judicature Society, 38, 41

American Jury, The (Kalven and Zeisel), 502, 681

American Law Institute, 358, 379, 488, 491

American Lawyer (periodical), 465

American Legion, 283

American Medical Association, 180, 193

691